The Introductory Reader in Human Geography

The Introductory Reader in Human Geography:
Contemporary Debates and Classic Writings

Edited by

William G. Moseley,
David A. Lanegran,
and
Kavita Pandit

Blackwell Publishing

© 2007 by Blackwell Publishing Ltd
except for editorial material and organization © 2007 by William G. Moseley, David A. Lanegran, and Kavita Pandit

BLACKWELL PUBLISHING
350 Main Street, Malden, MA 02148-5020, USA
9600 Garsington Road, Oxford OX4 2DQ, UK
550 Swanston Street, Carlton, Victoria 3053, Australia

First published 2007 by Blackwell Publishing Ltd

1   2007

Library of Congress Cataloging-in-Publication Data
The introductory reader in human geography: contemporary debates and classic writings/edited by William G. Moseley, David A. Lanegran, and Kavita Pandit.
    p. cm.
    Includes bibliographical references and index.
    ISBN 978-1-4051-4921-1 (hardback : alk. paper) – ISBN 978-1-4051-4922-8 (pbk. : alk. paper)
1. Human geography. I. Moseley, William G. II. Lanegran, David A. III. Pandit, Kavita, 1956-

    GF41.I576   2007
    304.2–dc22

2007001173

A catalogue record for this title is available from the British Library.

Set in 10/12.5 Sabon
by SNP Best-set Typesetter Ltd, Hong Kong
Printed and bound by Courier Digital Solutions

The publisher's policy is to use permanent paper from mills that operate a sustainable forestry policy, and which has been manufactured from pulp processed using acid-free and elementary chlorine-free practices. Furthermore, the publisher ensures that the text paper and cover board used have met acceptable environmental accreditation standards.

For further information on
Blackwell Publishing, visit our website:
www.blackwellpublishing.com

For my parents, Harry and Ellie (W. M.)
For my granddaughters, Claire and Charlotte (D. L.)
For my students (K. P.)

Contents

List of Figures   xi
Notes on the Editors   xiii
Preface and Acknowledgments   xiv
Introduction: Situating Human Geography   1
William G. Moseley, David A. Lanegran, and Karita Pandit

Part I: Introductory Readings   **11**
  Introduction   13
  William G. Moseley and David A. Lanegran

1   The Four Traditions of Geography   16
   William D. Pattison

2   Geography's Perspectives   22
   National Research Council

3   Geography and Foreign Policy   37
   H. J. de Blij

4   Reflections of an American Geographer on the Anniversary of
   September 11th   39
   William G. Moseley

5   How to Lie with Maps   42
   Mark Monmonier

6   Every Step You Take, Every Move You Make   46
   Jerome E. Dobson

Part II: Population and Migration   49
   Introduction   51
   William G. Moseley and Kavita Pandit

7 An Essay on the Principle of Population   54
   Thomas Robert Malthus

8 Population Growth and a Sustainable Environment   65
   Michael Mortimore and Mary Tiffen

9 Population Geography and HIV/AIDS: The Challenge of a "Wholly
   Exceptional Disease"   81
   W. T. S. Gould and R. I. Woods

10 Interprovincial Migration, Population Redistribution, and Regional
   Development in China: 1990 and 2000 Census Comparisons   96
   C. Cindy Fan

Part III: Environment, Agriculture, and Society   111
   Introduction   113
   William G. Moseley

11 The Worst Mistake in the History of the Human Race   116
   Jared Diamond

12 The Future of Traditional Agriculture   122
   Donald Q. Innis

13 Geography and the Global Environment   132
   Diana M. Liverman

14 Water Resource Conflicts in the Middle East   142
   Christine Drake

15 Americans and Their Weather   156
   William B. Meyer

16 The Trouble with Wilderness; or, Getting Back to the Wrong Nature   167
   William Cronon

Part IV: Cultural Geography and Place   179
   Introduction   181
   David A. Lanegran

17 Minnesota: Nature's Playground   184
   David A. Lanegran

18 American Microbreweries and Neolocalism: "Ale-ing" for a Sense
    of Place   198
    Wes Flack

19 Transplanting Pilgrimage Traditions in the Americas   206
    Carolyn V. Prorok

20 Kitchenspace, Fiestas, and Cultural Reproduction in Mexican
    House-Lot Gardens   221
    Maria Elisa Christie

Part V: Urban Geography   **233**
    Introduction   235
    David A. Lanegran

21 Greenville: From Back Country to Forefront   238
    Eugene A. Kennedy

22 Ethnic Residential Concentrations in United States
    Metropolitan Areas   247
    James P. Allen and Eugene Turner

23 South Africa's National Housing Subsidy Program and Apartheid's
    Urban Legacy   264
    Kimberly Lanegran and David Lanegran

24 World-City Network: A New Metageography?   279
    Jonathan V. Beaverstock, Richard G. Smith, and Peter J. Taylor

Part VI: Economic Geography   **291**
    Introduction   293
    William G. Moseley

25 Geographies of Knowledge, Practices of Globalization: Learning
    from the Oil Exploration and Production Industry   296
    Gavin Bridge and Andrew Wood

26 The Impact of Containerization on Work on the New York–
    New Jersey Waterfront   306
    Andrew Herod

27 Wine, Spirits, and Beer: World Patterns of Consumption   310
    David Grigg

28   Producing and Consuming Chemicals: The Moral Economy of the
     American Lawn   323
     Paul Robbins and Julie T. Sharp

29   Women at Work   337
     Mona Domosh and Joni Seager

Part VII: The Geography of Development and Underdevelopment   **349**
     Introduction   351
     William G. Moseley and Kavita Pandit

30   The Re-scaling of Uneven Development in Ghana and India   354
     Richard Grant and Jan Nijman

31   Development Alternatives: Practice, Dilemmas, and Theory   369
     A. J. Bebbington and D. H. Bebbington

32   Rural Development in El Hatillo, Nicaragua: Gender, Neoliberalism,
     and Environmental Risk   381
     Julie Cupples

33   The Sahel of West Africa: A Place for Geographers?   395
     Simon Batterbury

34   Geography, Culture, and Prosperity   400
     Andres Oppenheimer

Part VIII: Political Geography   **403**
     Introduction   405
     David A. Lanegran

35   Revisiting the "Pivot": The Influence of Halford Mackinder on
     Analysis of Uzbekistan's International Relations   408
     Nick Megoran

36   Euroregions in Comparative Perspective: Differential Implications
     for Europe's Borderlands   422
     Joanna M. M. Kepka and Alexander B. Murphy

37   The End of Public Space? People's Park, Definitions of the Public,
     and Democracy   437
     Don Mitchell

Index   449

Figures

0.1	Distribution of maize production in the world	6
2.1	The matrix of geographic perspectives	23
8.1	Population distribution in the Machakos District of Kenya in 1932 and 1979	66
8.2	The recorded output of four market crops in the Machakos District from 1963 to 1988	72
8.3	The farm output of the Machakos District from 1930 to 1987 in constant 1957 maize prices	77
9.1	Estimated proportion of adults HIV+, Africa, 2002	85
9.2	Projected age and sex structure and AIDS deaths, South Africa, 2009	88
10.1	Provincial-level units and the three regions (China)	103
10.2	Regional distribution and inequality of GDP per capita, 1985–2001	103
10.3	Prominent interprovincial net migration flows, 1985–1990	106
10.4	Prominent interprovincial net migration flows, 1995–2000	107
14.1	The Tigris-Euphrates basin	147
14.2	The Nile basin	149
14.3	The Jordan-Yarmuk basin	150
21.1	Greenville County, South Carolina	241
23.1	Map of built-up districts of George (South Africa)	271
23.2	Street pattern of Pacaltsdorp and Thembalethu	276
24.1	Shared presences, primary vectors, and secondary vectors among Alpha world cities	285
24.2	World city links to London	286
27.1	The leading alcoholic beverage, 1997–9	313
27.2	The consumption of wine, litres per adult of absolute alcohol per year, 1997–9	314

27.3	The consumption of beer, litres per adult of absolute alcohol per year, 1997–9	316
27.4	The consumption of spirits, litres per adult of absolute alcohol per year, 1997–9	319
30.1	Mumbai's regional push and scales of uneven development in India	362
30.2	Accra's regional push and scales of uneven development in Ghana	364
32.1	Location of El Hatillo, Department of Matagalpa, Nicaragua	382
33.1	The West African Sahel	396
35.1	The Republic of Uzbekistan	412
36.1	Euregio Meuse-Rhin	427
36.2	Members of the Euregio Meuse-Rhin Council by province	428
36.3	Transnational political parties in the Euregio Meuse-Rhin Council	429
36.4	Euroregion Neisse-Nisa-Nysa	430

Notes on the Editors

William G. Moseley is Associate Professor of Geography at Macalester College. He is a human-environment and development geographer who has lived and worked in Africa for several years. His books include: two editions of *Taking Sides: Clashing Views on African Issues* (McGraw-Hill/Dushkin, 2004, 2007) and (with B. Ikubolajeh Logan) *African Environment and Development: Rhetoric, Programs, Realities* (Ashgate, 2004). He has authored and co-authored over 25 peer-reviewed articles and book chapters and is associate editor of the *African Geographical Review*.

David A. Lanegran is Professor and Chair of Geography at Macalester College. He is an urban geographer with a keen interest in K-12 geography education. His books include: (with Billione Young) *Grand Avenue: Renaissance of an Urban Street* (North Star Press, 1996) and (with Risa Palm) two editions of *An Invitation to Geography* (McGraw-Hill, 1973, 1978). He has authored and co-authored over 40 peer-reviewed articles and book chapters. He is an advisor to the Advanced Placement (AP) geography program, Director of the Minnesota Alliance for Geographic Education, and an editorial board member for the *Journal of Geography*. He served as vice-president and then president of the National Council for Geographic Education from 1996 to 1998.

Kavita Pandit is Professor of Geography and Associate Dean of the Franklin College of Liberal Arts at the University of Georgia. She is a population and development geographer. Her books include (with Suzanne Withers) *Migration and Restructuring in the United States: A Geographic Perspective* (Rowman & Littlefield, 1999). She has authored and co-authored over 30 peer-reviewed articles and book chapters. She is serving as president of the Association of American Geographers from 2006 to 2007, and is an editorial board member for the *Professional Geographer*, the *Southeastern Geographer*, and *Geographical Analysis*.

Preface and Acknowledgments

All three of us teach introductory human geography. In an age when tenure track professors increasingly seek to offer courses on specialized research themes, we genuinely enjoy shepherding students through their first encounter with human geography. Given that geography is a relatively small, and often poorly understood, discipline in the United States, nothing beats the thrill of sharing this dynamic and burgeoning field with the uninitiated. We all can indicate turning points in our academic careers, those moments when we suddenly saw the world in a new way, those times when we were intellectually turned on. A good introductory human geography class is fertile ground for such occurrences, and that is why we keep coming back for more.

While most human geography courses likely include a certain amount of lecture, there comes a point when students need to engage with written material and discuss it with their peers and instructor. Such a process challenges the student in a different way, often leading to the most lasting memories of course material and the development of critical thinking skills. We hope this reader can facilitate such a process.

This book has been a long time in coming. While there are other human geography readers on the market, we felt none contained all the elements we were looking for when catering to introductory students. Some of the readers were clearly too advanced. Others, while replete with accessible articles from the popular press, did not contain enough material that was actually penned by geographers. This reader features previously published articles and book chapters (either as excerpts or in their entirety) by *geographers* that are accessible to introductory students, yet enduring in their insights or relevant to contemporary policy debates. Readings have been chosen that reflect a balance of several selection criteria, including: ability to provoke discussion; contemporary relevance; a nuanced yet accessible style; influence in the development of the discipline; and a generally positive stance about the contributions of geography to understanding a particular subject. Concerning the last point, our experience is that a more critical perspective on geographic contributions should await upper-level courses. The readings have been organized thematically (as opposed to regionally) as this is how the majority of introductory courses are taught today. Space limitations meant that we had to curtail the number of readings per theme. This reader is a start, and we can only hope that you will come to see it as a useful tool for igniting many a provocative discussion.

This book would not have been possible without the understanding and support of our families. We also wish to thank Erika Jermé, a former Macalester College student, who spent a considerable amount of time doing research for this project, and Justin Vaughan, Kelvin Matthews, and Brigitte Lee at Blackwell Publishing, for being open to the idea of such a reader and for seeing it through to publication. Finally, we are grateful to the numerous anonymous reviewers, not to mention our wonderful students, who provided feedback on the various articles we considered for inclusion in this volume.

William G. Moseley	David A. Lanegran	Kavita Pandit
Macalester College	Macalester College	University of Georgia
Saint Paul, MN	Saint Paul, MN	Athens, GA

Acknowledgments

The editor and publisher gratefully acknowledge the permission granted to reproduce the copyright material in this book:

Chapter 1. Pattison, William D., "The Four Traditions of Geography," pp. 203–6 from *Journal of Geography*, September/October (1990) (reprint of 1964 article with new foreword). © 1990. Reprinted with permission from the National Council for Geographic Education.

Chapter 2. National Research Council, "Geography's Perspectives," pp. 28–46 from *Rediscovering Geography: New Relevance for Science and Society* (Washington, DC: National Academy Press, 1997). © 1997 by the National Academy of Sciences. Reprinted with permission from the National Academies Press, Washington, DC.

Chapter 3. de Blij, H. J., "Geography and Foreign Policy," from the *Washington Examiner*, July 22, 2005. © 2005. Reprinted with permission from the author.

Chapter 4. Moseley, William G., "Reflections of an American Geographer on the Anniversary of September 11th," pp. 11–12 from *Association of American Geographer's Newsletter*, 37.11 (2002). © 2002. Reprinted with permission from the Association of American Geographers.

Chapter 5. Monmonier, Mark, "Introduction" and "Epilogue," pp. 1–4, 184–6 from *How to Lie with Maps*, 2nd edition (London and Chicago: University of Chicago Press, 1991). © 1991 by Mark Monmonier. Reprinted with permission from the author and The University of Chicago Press.

Chapter 6. Dobson, Jerome E., "Every Step You Take, Every Move You Make," from *Chicago Tribune*, February 25, 2005. © 2005 by Jerome E. Dobson. Reprinted with permission from the author.

Chapter 7. Malthus, Thomas Robert, "An Essay on the Principle of Population," pp. 97–103 from Scott W. Menard and Elizabeth W. Moen (eds.), *Perspectives on Population* (New York: Oxford University Press, 1987). © 1987. Reprinted with permission from Oxford University Press, Inc.

Chapter 8. Mortimore, Michael and Tiffen, Mary, "Population Growth and a Sustainable Environment," pp. 10–20, 28–30 from *Environment*, 36.8 (1994). © 1994. Reprinted with permission from Heldref Publications.

Figure 8.1. Tiffen, M., Mortimore, M., and Gichuki, F., *More People, Less Erosion: Environmental Recovery in Kenya* (Chichester: John Wiley, 1994), p. 49. © 1994. Reprinted with permission from John Wiley & Sons, Ltd.

Table 8.1. Tiffen, M., Mortimore, M., and Gichuki, F., *More People, Less Erosion: Environmental Recovery in Kenya* (Chichester: John Wiley, 1994). © 1994. Reprinted with permission from John Wiley & Sons, Ltd.

Figure 8.2. Mbogoh, S. G., "Crop Production," in M. Tiffen (ed.), *Environmental Change and Dryland Management in Machakos District, Kenya, 1930–90: Production Profile*, ODI Working Paper no. 55 (London: Overseas Development Institute, 1991). © 1991. Reprinted with permission from Overseas Development Institute.

Chapter 9. Gould, W. T. S. and Woods, R. I., "Population Geography and HIV/AIDS: The Challenge of a 'Wholly Exceptional Disease,'" pp. 265–81 from *Scottish Geographical Journal*, 119.3 (2003). © 2003. Reprinted with permission from Edinburgh University Press, www.eup.ed.ac.uk

Table 9.1. UNAIDS, *AIDS Epidemic Update, 2002* (UNAIDS: Geneva, 2002), p. 6.

Figure 9.1. UNAIDS, *AIDS Epidemic Update, 2002* (UNAIDS: Geneva, 2002).

Figure 9.2. Shell, R. C. H., "Halfway to the Holocaust: The Rapidity of the HIV/AIDS Pandemic in South Africa and its Social, Economic and Demographic Consequences." In *The African Population in the 21st Century*. Proceedings of the Third African Population Conference. Dakar: IUSSP/Union for African Population Studies, 1999, Volume 1, pp. 145–66; p. 164. © 1999 by R. C. H. Shell. Reprinted with permission from the author.

Chapter 10. Fan, C. Cindy, "Interprovincial Migration, Population Redistribution, and Regional Development in China: 1990 and 2000 Census Comparisons," pp. 295–309 from *Professional Geographer*, 57.2 (2005). © Copyright 2005 by Association of American Geographers. Reprinted with permission from Blackwell Publishing Ltd.

Tables 10.1 and 10.2. State Statistical Bureau, *Zhongguo renkou tongji nianjian 1992* [China Population Statistical Yearbook 1992] (Beijing: China Statistical Publishing House, 1992); National Bureau of Statistics, *Zhongguo 2000 nian renkou pucha ziliao*, Vol. 1 and 2 [Tabulation on the 2000 Population Census of the People's Republic of China] (Beijing: China Statistics Press, 2002).

Figure 10.2. China Statistical Yearbooks and Provincial Statistical Yearbooks, various years; Hsueh, T., Li, Q., and Liu, S. (eds.), *China's Provincial Statistics, 1949–1989* (Boulder, CO: Westview Press, 1993).

Figure 10.3. State Statistical Bureau, *Zhongguo renkou tongji nianjian 1992* [China Population Statistical Yearbook 1992] (Beijing: China Statistical Publishing House, 1992).

Figure 10.4. National Bureau of Statistics, *Zhongguo 2000 nian renkou pucha ziliao*, Vol. 1 and 2 [Tabulation on the 2000 Population Census of the People's Republic of China] (Beijing: China Statistics Press, 2002).

Chapter 11. Diamond, Jared, "The Worst Mistake in the History of the Human Race," pp. 64–6 from *Discover*, May (1987). © 1987 by Jared Diamond. Reprinted with permission from the author.

Chapter 12. Innis, Donald Q. "The Future of Traditional Agriculture," pp. 1–8 from *Focus*, 30.3 (January/February, 1980). © 1980 by American Geographical Society. Reprinted with permission from American Geographical Society.

Chapter 13. Liverman, Diana M., "Geography and the Global Environment," pp. 107–10, 113–16 from *Annals of the Association of American Geographers*, 89.1 (1999). © 1999 by Association of American Geographers. Reprinted with permission from Blackwell Publishing Ltd.

Chapter 14. Drake, Christine, "Water Resource Conflicts in the Middle East," pp. 4–12 from *Journal of Geography*, 96.1 (1997). © 1997. Reprinted with permission of National Council for Geographic Education.

Figure 14.2. Adapted from Kliot, N., *Water Resources and Conflict in the Middle East* (New York: Routledge, 1994).

Chapter 15. Meyer, William B., "Introduction," pp. 3–15 from *Americans and Their Weather* (New York: Oxford University Press, 2000). © 2000 by William B. Meyer. Reprinted with permission from Oxford University Press, Inc.

Chapter 16. Cronon, William, "The Trouble with Wilderness; or, Getting Back to the Wrong Nature," pp. 7–9, 15–24 from William Cronon (ed.), *Uncommon Ground: Toward Reinventing Nature* (New York: W. W. Norton, 1995). Copyright © 1995 by William Cronon. Reprinted with permission from W. W. Norton & Company, Inc.

Chapter 17. Lanegran, David A., "Minnesota: Nature's Playground," pp. 81–100 from *Daedalus*, 129.3 (2000). © 2000 by the American Academy of Arts and Sciences. Reprinted with permission from MIT Press Journals.

Chapter 18. Flack, Wes, "American Microbreweries and Neolocalism: 'Ale-ing' for a Sense of Place," pp. 37–54 from *Journal of Cultural Geography*, 16.2 (Spring/Summer, 1997). © 1997 by JCG Press. Reprinted with permission from the *Journal of Cultural Geography*/Oklahoma State University, 2006.

Chapter 19. Prorok, Carolyn V., "Transplanting Pilgrimage Traditions in the Americas," pp. 283–303 from *Geographical Review*, 93.3 (July, 2003). © 2003 by American Geographical Society. Reprinted with permission from American Geographical Society.

Chapter 20. Christie, Maria Elisa, "Kitchenspace, Fiestas, and Cultural Reproduction in Mexican House-Lot Gardens," pp. 370–83, 385–8 from *Geographical*

Review, 94.3 (2004). © 2004 by American Geographical Society. Reprinted with permission from American Geographical Society.

Chapter 21. Kennedy, Eugene A., "Greenville: From Back Country to Forefront," pp. 1–6 from *Focus*, 45.1 (Spring, 1998). © 1998 by American Geographical Society. Reprinted with permission from American Geographical Society.

Figure 21.1. Karen Severud Cook, University of Kansas Map Associates. © 1998 by Karen Severud Cook. Reprinted with permission from the author.

Chapter 22. Allen, James P. and Turner, Eugene, "Ethnic Residential Concentrations in United States Metropolitan Areas," pp. 267–73, 275–84 from *Geographical Review*, 95.2 (2005). © 2005 by American Geographical Society. Reprinted with permission from American Geographical Society.

Tables 22.1, 22.4, 22.5. US Census Bureau, 2001, Census of Population and Housing, 2000. Summary File 1 (factfinder.census.gov).

Tables 22.2, 22.3. US Census Bureau, 2001, Census of Population and Housing, 2000. Summary File 1; US Census Bureau, 2003, Census of Population and Housing, 2000. Summary File 4 (factfinder.census.gov).

Chapter 23. Lanegran, Kimberly and Lanegran, David, "South Africa's National Housing Subsidy Program and Apartheid's Urban Legacy," pp. 671–86 from *Urban Geography*, 22.7 (2001). © 2001 by V. H. Winston & Son, Inc., 360 South Ocean Boulevard, Palm Beach, FL 33480. All rights reserved. Reprinted with permission from *Urban Geography* and V. H. Winston & Son, Inc.

Table 23.1. George Development Consortium, 2000, Greater George: Development Profile, Table 20.

Table 23.2. George Development Consortium, 2000, Greater George: Development Profile, Table 24.

Chapter 24. Beaverstock, Jonathan V., Smith, Richard G., and Taylor, Peter J., "World-City Network: A New Metageography?" pp. 123–32 from *Annals of the Association of American Geographers*, 90.1 (2000). © Copyright 2000 by Association of American Geographers. Reprinted with permission from Blackwell Publishing Ltd.

Chapter 25. Bridge, Gavin and Wood, Andrew, "Geographies of Knowledge, Practices of Globalization: Learning from the Oil Exploration and Production Industry," pp. 199–207 from *Area*, 37.2 (2005). © 2005 by Royal Geographical Society (with The Institute of British Geographers). Reprinted with permission from Blackwell Publishing Ltd.

Chapter 26. Herod, Andrew, "The Impact of Containerization on Work on the New York–New Jersey Waterfront," pp. 5–7 from *Social Science Docket*, 4.1 (Winter/Spring, 2004). © 2004 by Andrew Herod. Reprinted with permission from the author.

Chapter 27. Grigg, David, "Wine, Spirits, and Beer: World Patterns of Consumption," pp. 99–110 from *Geography*, 89.2 (2004). © 2004 by Geography. Reprinted with permission from The Geographical Association.

Figures 27.1, 27.2, 27.3, 27.4. Food and Agriculture Organization (FAO), "Food Balance Sheets," www.fao.org (accessed December 2002). © 2002. Reprinted with permission from the Food and Agriculture Organization of the United Nations.

Chapter 28. Robbins, Paul and Sharp, Julie T., "Producing and Consuming Chemicals The Moral Economy of the American Lawn," pp. 425–45 from *Economic Geography*, 79.4 (2003). © 2003 by Clark University. Reprinted with permission from Clark University.

Chapter 29. Domosh, Mona and Seager, Joni, "Women at Work," pp. 35–41, 47–50, 52, 60–3 from *Putting Women in Place: Feminist Geographers Make Sense of the World* (New York: Guilford Press, 2001). © 2001 by Mona Domosh and Joni Seager. Reprinted with permission from the authors and Guilford Publications, Inc.

Chapter 30. Grant, Richard and Nijman, Jan, "The Re-scaling of Uneven Development in Ghana and India," pp. 467–78 from *Tijdschrift voor Economische en Sociale Geografie*, 95.5 (2004). © 2004 by the Royal Dutch Geographical Society KNAG. Reprinted with permission from Blackwell Publishing Ltd.

Chapter 31. Bebbington, A. J. and Bebbington, D. H., "Development Alternatives: Practice, Dilemmas, and Theory," pp. 7–16 from *Area*, 33.1 (2001). © 2001 by Royal Geographical Society (with The Institute of British Geographers). Reprinted with permission from Blackwell Publishing Ltd.

Chapter 32. Cupples, Julie, "Rural Development in El Hatillo, Nicaragua: Gender, Neoliberalism, and Environmental Risk," pp. 343–57 from *Singapore Journal of Tropical Geography*, 25.3 (2004). © Copyright 2004 Department of Geography, National University of Singapore, and Blackwell Publishers Ltd. Reprinted with permission from Blackwell Publishing Ltd.

Chapter 33. Batterbury, Simon, "The Sahel of West Africa: A Place for Geographers?" pp. 391–4 from *Geography*, 81.353 (1996). Geography © 1996. Reprinted with permission from The Geographical Association.

Chapter 34. Oppenheimer, Andres, "Geography, Culture, and Prosperity," pp. B–9 from the *Miami Herald*, August 1, 2000. © 2000. Reprinted with permission from Copyright Clearance Center on behalf of *Miami Herald*.

Chapter 35. Megoran, Nick, "Revisiting the 'Pivot': The Influence of Halford Mackinder on Analysis of Uzbekistan's International Relations," pp. 347–56 from *Geographical Journal*, 170.4 (2004). © 2004 by Royal Geographical Society (with The Institute of British Geographers). Reprinted with permission from Blackwell Publishing Ltd.

Chapter 36. Kepka, Joanna M. M. and Murphy, Alexander B., "Euroregions in Comparative Perspective: Differential Implications for Europe's Borderlands," pp. 50–67 from David H. Kaplan & Jouni Häkli (eds.), *Boundaries and Place: European Borderlands in Geographical Context* (Boulder, CO: Rowman & Littlefield, 2002). © 2002. Reprinted with permission from Rowman & Littlefield Publishing Group.

Figures 36.1, *Euroregio Meuse-Rhin* 1997. Brochure produced by SEGEFA (Service d'Etude en Géographie Economique Fondamentale et Appliquée de l'Université de Liège). Liège: SEGEFA. © 1997. Reprinted with permission from SEGEFA.

Figures 36.2, 36.3 *Euroregio Meuse-Rhin* 1997. Brochure produced by SEGEFA (Service d'Etude en Géographie Economique Fondamentale et Appliquée de l'Université de Liège). Liège: SEGEFA.

Figure 36.4. *Euroregion Nysa* 1994. Jelenia Góra and Warsaw, Poland: Regionalny Urzad Statystyczny i Centralny Urzad Statystyczny.

Chapter 37. Mitchell, Don, "The End of Public Space? People's Park, Definitions of the Public, and Democracy," pp. 108, 116–22, 123–5, 127 from *Annals of the Association of American Geographers*, 85.1 (1995). © Copyright 1995 by Association of American Geographers. Reprinted with permission from Blackwell Publishing Ltd.

Every effort has been made to trace copyright holders and to obtain their permission for the use of copyright material. The publisher apologizes for any errors or omissions in the above list and would be grateful if notified of any corrections that should be incorporated in future reprints or editions of this book.

Introduction: Situating Human Geography

William G. Moseley, David A. Lanegran, and Kavita Pandit

Without geography you're nowhere.
Jimmy Buffett (Singer/Songwriter)

There is an old fable about three blind villagers who encounter an elephant. The first, feeling a stout leg and believing it to be a tree trunk, declares that what they have encountered must be a tree. The second, grasping the coarse tail, announces that this must be a rope. Finally, the third, feeling the elephant's undulating trunk, suggests that this is a snake. In an age when many disciplines increasingly focus on understanding one aspect of human systems or the natural world, geography has distinguished itself by seeking to comprehend the connections between different elements of the human and biophysical realms. In other words, geographers seek to recognize the proverbial elephant by trying to understand the location of its various parts and how these relate to one another. While once considered unfashionable, interest in geography has surged in recent years. Geographers have been at the forefront of studying complex worldwide phenomena such as economic globalization, global climate change, and international migration. They have long contributed to our understanding of the social dimensions of natural disasters, such as hurricanes, tsunamis, earthquakes, and droughts, as well as to our comprehension of urban systems. Geographic techniques for presenting and analyzing spatial information, including geographic information systems, remote sensing, and basic mapping, are increasingly considered essential components of the modern scientific tool kit. Geographers are also engaged in the everyday workings of the world as urban planners, non-profit workers, international development workers, policy analysts, and environmental managers.

What Is Human Geography?

Geography is so basic that we all seem to have some idea of what it is, yet curiously, many would have trouble describing the subject to another person at a cocktail party. Geography comes from the Greek words meaning earth writing or earth describing. Even though the emphasis in geography has changed over the years, this is still a fairly accurate statement. While the Greeks were the first to organize geography as a coherent body of knowledge, the need for geographic knowledge is as old as humankind. For as long as people have been traveling, exploring, and migrating, they have been encountering different environments and other human societies. As such, the survival and success of human populations meant that they needed to understand other groups, faraway lands, where these were located spatially (if for no other reason than to know how to get there again), the processes that connect one human group to others, and ways in which each group is unique. In the process, such travelers, explorers, and migrants learned a lot about where they had come from, that is, it helped them to understand what was special about their own homes. Geography is a broad discipline that essentially seeks to understand and study the spatial organization of human activity and of people's relationships with their environment. It is also about recognizing the interdependence among places and regions, without losing sight of the individuality and uniqueness of specific places.

Although the definition of the academic discipline of geography may not be on the tip of your tongue, any time you make a location decision, or try to understand a place, you are using the principles of geography to solve a problem. Your location questions might range from where to get the best cup of coffee in the morning, to how to get to school, to where to attend college or look for the first job in your career. As you are a member of various social groups (including your race or ethnicity, gender, socioeconomic status, nationality, sexual orientation, and age), your location questions and decisions are often filtered through a number of personal and social filters (and thereby made more complex), and then amplified or muted when combined with the decisions of others. In response, other actors, such as city planners, private businesses, or neighbors, may create landscapes based on your (and others') decisions. At the same time, your location decisions, and those of others, may be conditioned by the preexisting built and natural environments. As such, people's socially conditioned choices, and reactions to existing environments, often interact synergistically to produce new landscapes. For example, when your travel plans (which may be shaped by existing options) are combined with those of others in your community, a demand for roads and transit systems is created. In response to your search for recreational facilities, a pattern of landscapes ranging from protected wilderness areas to skateboard pipes may be developed. Your quest for a place to live creates demands for the construction of housing in particular types of places and not in others. Your preference for shopping in certain types of stores, when aggregated with others, influences how developers create and locate a wide range of shops, malls, and boutiques. In other instances, a combination of racism, ethnic affinity, and socioeconomic status may lead certain groups to develop ethnic enclaves in large urban areas.

Your activities and those of others in your community have stimulated the development of a formalized body of geography, known as location analysis, designed to understand your behavior and plan for your needs. Other geographers seek to understand how people's mental or cognitive maps of a neighborhood, city, or the world may influence their movement through such spaces. Still others examine how one's gender or race leads to differences in the way they interact with, and are impacted by, the surrounding urban or rural landscape.

As the title suggests, this volume is focused on a subset of the broader field of geography known as human geography. The general tenets of a geographic approach (i.e., attention to spatial patterns, human–environment dynamics, the uniqueness of place, connections between regions and across scales) apply to all areas of geography. Over time, however, geography has grown to recognize sub-specialties within the discipline based on the subject matter addressed. At the broadest level, there is a commonly recognized divide between the study of biophysical phenomena (physical geography) and the examination of human or social phenomena (human geography). Physical geographers seek to understand long-term climate patterns and change (climatology), patterns of plant and animal distribution (biogeography), and the origin and evolution of landforms (geomorphology).

Human geographers study the patterns and dynamics of human activity on the landscape. Broadly conceived, human geography includes both those areas of geographic study that are more narrowly focused on human activity, and those that are particularly concerned with human–environment dynamics (or the nature–society tradition). As Table 0.1 depicts, human geography and the nature–society geography are sometimes viewed as distinct enough to be separate realms within the discipline. For this volume, we have adopted the broad view of human geography as most introductory courses deal with themes in the nature–society tradition. Furthermore, at a conceptual level, it is often difficult to categorize research as either nature–society or human geography as nearly all forms of human geography deal with the environment broadly construed. For example, in terms of generic interactions with the environment, what makes a peasant farmer any different than a suburban homeowner? Both live in environments modified by human activity, both manipulate the landscape (the farmer tilling her field, and the suburbanite tending his lawn), and both are influenced by environmental conditions (the farmer planting six different varieties of millet in her field because rainfall varies from year to year, and the suburbanite driving to the grocery store because his neighborhood has no sidewalks, is removed from shopping areas, and lacks access to public transportation).

Table 0.1 shows the many themes studied by human geographers. While human geographers have taught and do teach the discipline in terms of world regions (e.g., Africa, Latin America, Asia), introductory human geography courses increasingly are organized thematically. This reflects the dominant tendency in academia toward a systematic or thematic organization of knowledge. While many geographers are regional experts (for which they must have a broad understanding of the forces at play in a particular region), most have well-developed thematic expertise. Human geographers working in various subfields often interact with other academics or professionals working on similar themes (e.g., urban geographers with urban sociologists and urban planners, population geographers with demographers and public health officials).

Table 0.1 Human geography within the discipline of geography

Human geography broadly defined		Physical geography (e.g., biogeography, climatology, geomorphology)
Human geography narrowly defined (e.g., urban geography, economic geography, population geography, cultural geography, development geography, political geography)	Nature–society (e.g., cultural ecology, political ecology, agricultural geography, water resources, human dimensions of global change, hazards geography)	
Techniques (e.g., geographic information systems (GIS), remote sensing, cartography, statistics)		

Geography has long been known for its techniques for presenting and manipulating spatial data, particularly cartography or mapping. What is important to remember is that most geographers (human geographers and physical geographers) use these techniques as a means to an end. For example, population geographers may use dot maps to present and understand population distributions, geographic information systems (GIS) to analyze the potential relationship between population density and soil fertility, or remote sensing (aerial photography and satellite imagery) to count the number of housing structures in a district. Some geographers specialize in a particular technique rather than a thematic area of geography. These geographers often focus on further developing such technologies, devising methods for interpreting the data produced by them, or reflecting on the social implications of their use. A few selections in the volume will focus on the use of these technologies by human geographers.

The Geographic Perspective and How It Is Different

Like any discipline, the way geographers look at the world is somewhat unique. As discussed above, the geographic perspective is often characterized by its attention to: spatial patterns; a synthetic understanding of various factors in a particular place or region; human interactions with the landscape; and connections between different points on the landscape and across geographic scales. But let us consider a tangible example to illustrate how the geographer's view of the world differs from that in other disciplines. While rather mundane, consider the humble plant known as maize, corn, or *Zea mays*. Chances are that you may have consumed some maize today, most likely in the form of corn syrup that is a base ingredient in many food products. After wheat and rice, this is the most important cereal worldwide. It is also one of the most widely distributed crops (being grown in the tropics, subtropics, and temperate areas of the world). Given this crop as our subject of study, we can compare how different disciplines might approach this task. To keep things simple, let us briefly consider: a crop scientist (or agronomist), an economist, a soil scientist, and a geographer. An agronomist might want to know how the productivity of this plant can be maximized. He or she would seek to determine the optimal conditions under which the crop is grown and then make recommendations on where the plant should be cultivated and how (e.g., tillage methods, fertilizers, insecticides). An economist might study the micro and macro economics of the crop. In other words, what are the costs of producing maize, how much should one produce and earn given a certain market price, how much maize is traded between different countries, and what is the relative economic importance of this crop in different contexts? A soil scientist would likely focus on the impacts of maize farming on soil chemistry and structure.

When approaching the study of maize, a geographer might begin with the spatial pattern of the crop and ask why its production is distributed in such a manner (see Figure 0.1). A geographer might also explore how maize is grown in different contexts, its impact on local people and landscapes, and where the maize is actually going after it is produced. A geographer's analysis would reveal that maize, like any crop, is not just a lowly plant in the ground. For starters, maize is grown both as a food crop by subsistence producers and as a cash crop by commercial farmers. There is a history as to why maize is grown where, by whom, in what quantity, and with which techniques that involves international politics, local traditions, colonial power, environmental factors, and coercion in some instances. Maize is grown by people and families who take risks to grow this crop (in terms of money borrowed, impacts that the crop may have on the land, and pesticide exposure in the fields) and who depend on the income this plant generates. Maize often links farmers to the international economy. Farmers sell their maize to private and state-owned companies whose stakeholders depend on the sale of the crop and who may have instituted a number of policies and programs to guarantee the continued production of this crop and flow of money into their coffers. Multilateral banks (such as the World Bank or Asian Development Bank) may have an interest in the crop if it means that their loans to governments are repaid on schedule. Maize is sold on international markets at a price largely related to: the actions of the global powers (e.g., whether China will be exporting or importing maize in a given year and the level of American subsidies to its maize farmers); and the world's growing appetite for grain-fed livestock. As such, geography helps us understand that maize is not just a crop, it is a commodity rooted in the soil, with local livelihood consequences, and that the pattern of where it is grown is situated in an international web of economic transfers reflecting historical and contemporary power structures.

To make the geographic perspective even more tangible, we will use the rest of this section to examine the contributions of three geographers who made a difference in the way we understand the world. These are: John Borchert, an urban geographer working in North America; Judith Carney, a human-environment geographer producing scholarship on Africa and the Americas; and Piers Blaikie, a development geographer largely working in Asia.

In a series of scholarly articles, policy reports, and books written for the non-academic reader, John Borchert (1918–2001) applied the abstract concepts of how cities were connected to their trade areas, and to other cities around the world

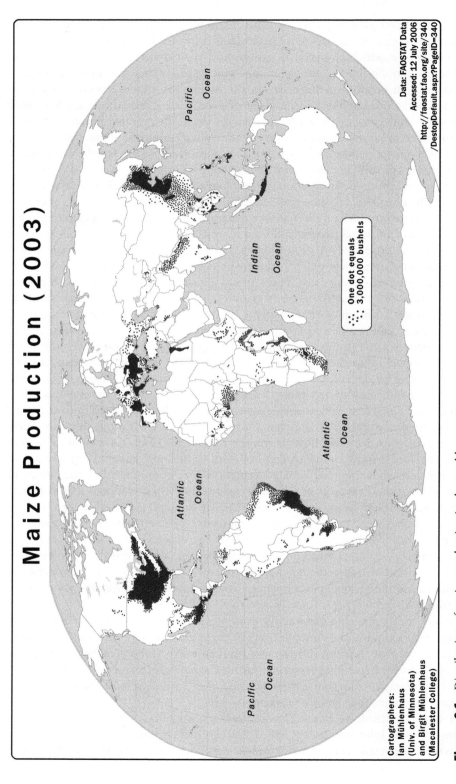

Maize Production (2003)

Pacific
Ocean

Atlantic
Ocean

Atlantic
Ocean

Indian
Ocean

Pacific
Ocean

One dot equals
3,000,000 bushels

Data: FAOSTAT Data
Accessed: 12 July 2006
http://faostat.fao.org/site/340
/DestopDefault.aspx?PageID=340

Cartographers:
Ian Mühlenhaus
(Univ. of Minnesota)
and Birgit Mühlenhaus
(Macalester College)

Figure 0.1   Distribution of maize production in the world.
Source: FAOSTAT data, accessed July 12, 2006.

(known as central place theory), to explain and predict changes in the size and wealth of cities in a large region of the United States. In his final book, *America's Northern Heartland* (University of Minnesota Press, 1987), he blended work on the physical environment, demographic change, and the development of transportation and communications technology to explain the evolution of the system of cities in the Upper Midwest. His integrated view of how cities are connected with each other and to the landscape has enabled generations of planners and leaders to guide the development of metropolitan areas in the United States.

In *Black Gold: The African Origins of Rice Cultivation in the Americas* (Harvard University Press, 2001), University of California at Los Angeles geographer Judith Carney uniquely merged her understanding of rice production and history on two different continents. Carney's earlier work on rice production in the Gambia (West Africa) led her to recognize the remnants of similar systems in the Americas. This, combined with exhaustive historical research, allowed Carney to convincingly argue that African slaves must have been the source of know-how behind the initial development, and then expansion, of rice production in the southeastern United States in the seventeenth and eighteenth centuries. Her work has been the catalyst for a new body of literature focused on the Atlantic basin, and for renewed appreciation of the contributions of African Americans in the development of the United States.

The British geographer Piers Blaikie published an influential book in 1985 entitled *The Political Economy of Soil Erosion*. Up until this point, many environmental problems (soil erosion in this instance) had been studied as a biophysical process in relation to local management practices. What Blaikie expertly combined was an understanding of soil erosion with an analysis of broader-scale political and economic processes. He showed, for example, that erosion produced by farming on steep slopes often had as much, or more, to do with poor farmers being pushed off of good land into marginal areas by powerful actors than it did with the actual farming practices of the poor farmers in question. His book, and the approach he described, eventually led to development of an empirically and theoretically rich interdisciplinary field known as political ecology.

Geography and the Academy

Geography became recognized as a discrete discipline and part of the typical university curriculum in Europe (especially Paris and Berlin) by the nineteenth century, although not in the United Kingdom (UK), where geography was generally taught as a subdiscipline of other subjects. While Halford Mackinder was appointed to the faculty of Oxford as Reader in Geography in 1887, the UK did not get its first full Chair of Geography until 1917. As a discipline, geography is quite strong in most nations with highly developed systems of education. Several years of secondary school geography are required in France, Germany, Russia, and Switzerland, while many other European countries require at least one year for graduation. Similarly, secondary school students in Japan, Korea, Taiwan, Singapore, and Malaysia are required to take several years of geography. Geography is also growing in China as that culture becomes more engaged in the global economy and world affairs. Geography ranks among the most popular fields of study throughout the English-speaking world, particularly in the UK, Australia, Canada, India, New Zealand, and South Africa. Geographers based at research universities in all these countries continue to advance the research frontiers of geography and collaborate on many critical issues through the International Geographical Union.

An exception to the global trend is the United States (US), where geography is a relatively small discipline. In the US, the first university-based geographers were at Harvard in the 1870s and 1880s, the first stand-alone department of geography was created at the University of California at Berkeley in 1898, and the first department of geography offering a doctoral degree was established at the University of Chicago in 1903. Interestingly, geography as a field of study has grown dramatically in popularity in the US over the past 15 years. University of Oregon geography professor Alec Murphy has explained much of this growth in terms of five general factors: (1) a heightened sense of the importance of geography among the general public (brought on by global political events, globalization, and devastating natural disasters); (2) greater awareness and appreciation of geography by scholars in other disciplines; (3) an explosion of interest in Geographic Information Science; (4) an expanding job market for those with geography training; and (5) the emergence of more sophisticated geography in some primary and secondary schools.[1] All the evidence suggests that geography will only continue to grow as a discipline in the US. Given its emphasis on synthesis, geography historically has had strong links with the sciences of geology and botany, as well as with economics, anthropology, sociology, and demography. Geographers also often work closely with interdisciplinary programs, including urban studies, environmental studies, international studies, development studies, and area studies programs.

Why a Human Geography Reader?

Introductory textbooks are important for sketching out the major themes and perspectives of a discipline, but they almost always summarize and interpret the work of others when doing this. A reader is different in that it contains a selection of previously published articles and book chapters from other sources. Many of these articles have been published in peer-reviewed[2] academic journals, the major forums via which geographers communicate with one another.

There are a number of on-going conversations in any academic discipline. Scholars read the work of others, often use this to inform the type of research they undertake, and then frequently challenge, confirm, modify, or extend the findings of others when they report their own results. Academic journals and books then become the written record of these conversations. These publications also allow one to see how understanding of a particular topic or phenomenon has changed over time. This reader allows you to explore the research publications of geographers directly, rather than having such findings interpreted and summarized by others. Given that this is an introductory reader, we have selected articles written in fairly straightforward language and covering a broad range of topics. Were you to read through geography journals (in order to write a class paper, for example), you would notice that there are many articles on the same topic which speak in varying degrees to one another. The more you did this, the more you would become familiar with the specialized vocabulary that is often used by scientists as short-hand to communicate with one another. As your studies advance, some of you may even end up participating in such conversations by writing articles, chapters, and books.

The important thing to remember is that these academic conversations (repre-sented in journal articles, chapters, and books) are not the exclusive domain of scholars. Nearly all of these discussions, even the most rarified, have real-world implications. The way we understand the world often provides the backdrop for policy formulation, city planning, and even decisions to go to war, choices that affect all of us. By reading and discussing these articles, you allow on-going aca-demic conversations to enter your classroom. Do not hesitate to share your analysis of an author's argument (and nearly every article in this volume is articulating some form of an argument) with your classmates. The process of reading and discussion will not only sharpen your critical thinking skills, but it may also lead to new insights by you and your classmates.

Structure of the Book

The rest of this book is devoted to introducing and presenting selections of research and reflection from human geography's various subdisciplines. We start with a set of introductory readings, then move on to the major thematic areas covered in most introductory human geography courses: population and migration; environment, agriculture, and society; cultural geography and place; urban geography; economic geography; development geography; and political geography. Each section starts with a brief opener that is meant not only to introduce the various selections but also to narrate how they relate to one another. In other words, the section intro-ductions generally articulate the broader conversations in each subfield, and the relationship of the readings to those evolving debates and discussions. The articles have had references removed, and been trimmed in some instances, because of space considerations.

NOTES

1. A. B. Murphy, "Geography's Place in Higher Education in the United States," *Journal of Geography in Higher Education* (forthcoming).
2. Peer-reviewed means that an article or book has been vetted by other specialists (usually three) in the field before it is published.

Part I

Introductory Readings

Introduction

William G. Moseley and David A. Lanegran

Ideally we learn to view the world from several different angles while we are secondary, college, or university students. These different lenses on the world are often codified as academic disciplines. For example, economists study the production, distribution, and consumption of wealth; political scientists analyze the principles, organization, and methods of government; and biologists study the origins, history, and life processes of plants and animals. All of these academic perspectives are valuable and they will serve you well in your chosen profession, as well as in your potential roles as citizens, parents, friends, spouses, activists, scholars, leaders, travelers, consumers, and custodians. The task at hand in this course is to come to grips with geography as an academic discipline and as a way of looking at the world. By the end, we want you to be able to look at the world as a geographer would. Some of you will go on to specialize in geography, while this may be the only course on the subject for others. We want both groups to have a solid introduction to this longstanding yet increasingly important discipline.

As discussed in the general introduction, people have been practicing geography for as long as they have been encountering different environments and peoples when traveling, exploring, or migrating. The long-term success of a group meant that it needed to comprehend where they were located in relation to other groups and resources, as well as to have an understanding of distant peoples and lands. History shows us that those who fail to understand basic geography often pay dearly for this ignorance. Consider Napoleon's failure to grasp the severity of continental winters, and the distances involved, when he fatefully attacked Russia; or the myopia of those who build luxury homes on hurricane-prone coastlines. While often identified with the tools it employs to understand the world (such as maps, geographic information systems (GIS), or basic place-name literacy), the modern field of geography is much more. Geography is a broad discipline that essentially seeks to understand and study the spatial organization of human activity and of people's relationships with their environment. It is also about recognizing the interdependence among places and regions, without losing sight of the individuality and uniqueness of specific places.

We believe the best way to learn geography is to just do it. Dive right in, observe the landscape, think about your own location decisions, read the articles, and discuss what you see, read, and think with your peers. In this introductory section, we hope to accomplish three tasks with the readings we have selected. First, we expose you to some different ways in which geographers have conceived of their discipline. Second, we explore the contemporary relevance of geography. Third, we problematize the use of some geographic technologies.

Being a broad discipline is both a blessing and a curse. It is a blessing because we can do things that other disciplines cannot do. For example, we are not inhibited by the social science/natural science divide, and as such we have been at the forefront of studying both the social and biophysical dimensions of human–environment interactions. We also are not wedded to studying one particular category of human activity (e.g., economics), but rather have developed a spatial perspective (and associated tools such as maps, GIS, remote sensing) that is highly attuned to local, regional, and global causality. This has allowed geographers to be on the cutting edge of understanding broad-scale phenomena such as globalization and global environmental change. But being a broad discipline has meant that there is a need to pause from time to time and reflect on our approach. The first reading by William Pattison, "The Four Traditions of Geography," was originally written in 1964. In it, Pattison discusses four traditions within geography: (1) the spatial tradition, (2) the area studies tradition, (3) the man–land tradition, and (4) the earth science tradition. The second selection by the National Research Council, entitled "Geography's Perspectives," defines geography along three dimensions, the way geographers look at the world, geography's domains of synthesis, and the different forms of spatial representation.

The next two readings make a case for the contemporary relevance of geography. The editorial by de Blij, "Geography and Foreign Policy," discusses the implications of a world power that is limited by geographic illiteracy. This is a problem not only for the leaders of the United States, but also for its citizenry at large. Citizens may blindly accept a policy if they do not have a sound understanding of the location of the area affected, its cultural and physical geography, and its connections to other parts of the world. Fortunately, many elite educational institutions are reinstating geography programs in the US, not to mention a raft of new programs at the secondary school level and in public universities. The article by Moseley, "Reflections of an American Geographer on the Anniversary of September 11th," emphasizes the insights gained by geographers' attention to the links between places and regions. The character of these connections can vary tremendously, from the links between the spatial arrangement of US cities, energy consumption, and geopolitics, to the dovetailing of religion and popular reactions to globalization, to the imagined nature of national boundaries.

The final two readings help us reflect on common tools used by geographers, maps and global positioning systems. The title of the first selection by Monmonier, "How to Lie with Maps," gets at his essential point, that all maps are in some sense a "lie," that is, a distortion of the reality they seek to present. More troubling (or intriguing, depending on your perspective) is his point that mapmakers (cartographers) may knowingly or unknowingly exaggerate these distortions. Since computer-generated maps are often unquestionably accepted as fact, understanding how maps may deviate from reality is a critical skill for any student, citizen, or leader. In "Every Step You Take, Every Move You Make," Dobson writes about the increasing use of global positioning system (GPS) units as human tracking devices. While GPS units, which use satellites to determine a location's geographic coordinates, have allowed for tremendous gains in mapping accuracy, Dobson raises a number of ethical issues related to their use in tracking human movements. How would you like someone else to know your location at all times? Are there situations in which such tracking is acceptable?

DISCUSSION READINGS

Pattison, W. (1990). "The Four Traditions of Geography." *Journal of Geography*, September/October. (Reprint of 1964 article with new Foreword.)

National Research Council. (1997). "Geography's Perspectives." In *Rediscovering Geography: New Relevance for Science and Society*. Washington, DC: National Academy Press. Pp. 28–46.

de Blij, H. J. (2005). "Geography and Foreign Policy." *Washington Examiner*. Op-ed from July 22.

Moseley, W. G. (2002). "Reflections of an American Geographer on the Anniversary of September 11th." *Association of American Geographer's Newsletter*, 37(11): 11–12.

Monmonier, M. (1991). "Introduction" and "Epilogue." In *How to Lie with Maps*, 2nd edition. London and Chicago: University of Chicago Press. Pp. 1–4, 184–6.

Dobson, J. (2005). "Every Step You Take, Every Move You Make." *Chicago Tribune*. Op-ed from February 25.

Chapter 1

The Four Traditions of Geography

William D. Pattison

In 1905, one year after professional geography in this country achieved full social identity through the founding of the Association of American Geographers, William Morris Davis responded to a familiar suspicion that geography is simply an undisciplined "omnium-gatherum" by describing an approach that as he saw it imparts a "geographical quality" to some knowledge and accounts for the absence of the quality elsewhere. Davis spoke as president of the AAG. He set an example that was followed by more than one president of that organization. An enduring official concern led the AAG to publish, in 1939 and in 1959, monographs exclusively devoted to a critical review of definitions and their implications.

Every one of the well-known definitions of geography advanced since the founding of the AAG has had its measure of success. Tending to displace one another by turns, each definition has said something true of geography. But from the vantage point of 1964, one can see that each one has also failed. All of them adopted in one way or another a monistic view, a singleness of preference, certain to omit if not to alienate numerous professionals who were in good conscience continuing to participate creatively in the broad geographic enterprise.

The thesis of the present paper is that the work of American geographers, although not conforming to the restrictions implied by any one of these definitions, has exhibited a broad consistency, and that this essential unity has been attributable to a small number of distinct but affiliated traditions, operant as binders in the minds of members of the profession. These traditions are all of great age and have passed into American geography as parts of a general legacy of Western thought. They are shared today by geographers of other nations.

There are four traditions whose identification provides an alternative to the competing monistic definitions that have been the geographer's lot. The resulting

Pattison, William D., "The Four Traditions of Geography," pp. 203–6 from *Journal of Geography*, September/October (1990) (reprint of 1964 article with new foreword).

pluralistic basis for judgment promises, by full accommodation of what geographers do and by plain-spoken representation thereof, to greatly expedite the task of maintaining an alliance between professional geography and pedagogical geography and at the same time to promote communication with laymen. The following discussion treats the traditions in this order: (1) a spatial tradition, (2) an area studies tradition, (3) a man-land tradition and (4) an earth science tradition.

Spatial Tradition

Entrenched in Western thought is a belief in the importance of spatial analysis, of the act of separating from the happenings of experience such aspects as distance, form, direction and position. It was not until the 17th century that philosophers concentrated attention on these aspects by asking whether or not they were properties of things-in-themselves. Later, when the 18th-century writings of Immanuel Kant had become generally circulated, the notion of space as a category including all of these aspects came into widespread use. However, it is evident that particular spatial questions were the subject of highly organized answering attempts long before the time of any of these cogitations. To confirm this point, one need only be reminded of the compilation of elaborate records concerning the location of things in ancient Greece. These were records of sailing distances, of coastlines and of landmarks that grew until they formed the raw material for the great *Geographia* of Claudius Ptolemy in the 2nd century AD.

A review of American professional geography from the time of its formal organization shows that the spatial tradition of thought had made a deep penetration from the very beginning. For Davis, for Henry Gannett and for most if not all of the 44 other men of the original AAG, the determination and display of spatial aspects of reality through mapping were of undoubted importance, whether contemporary definitions of geography happened to acknowledge this fact or not. One can go further and, by probing beneath the art of mapping, recognize in the behavior of geographers of that time an active interest in the true essentials of the spatial tradition – *geometry* and *movement*. One can trace a basic favoring of movement as a subject of study from the turn-of-the-century work of Emory R. Johnson, writing as professor of transportation at the University of Pennsylvania, through the highly influential theoretical and substantive work of Edward L. Ullman during the past 20 years and thence to an article by a younger geographer on railroad freight traffic in the US and Canada in the *Annals* of the AAG for September 1963.

One can trace a deep attachment to geometry, or positioning-and-layout, from articles on boundaries and population densities in early 20th century volumes of the *Bulletin of the American Geographical Society*, through a controversial pronouncement by Joseph Schaefer in 1953 that granted geographical legitimacy only to studies of spatial patterns and so onward to a recent *Annals* report on electronic scanning of cropland patterns in Pennsylvania.

One might inquire, is discussion of the spatial tradition, after the manner of the remarks just made, likely to bring people within geography closer to an

understanding of one another and people outside geography closer to an understanding of geographers? There seem to be at least two reasons for being hopeful.
First, an appreciation of this tradition allows one to see a bond of fellowship uniting
the elementary school teacher, who attempts the most rudimentary instruction in
directions and mapping, with the contemporary research geographer, who dedi-
cates himself to an exploration of central-place theory. One cannot only open the
eyes of many teachers to the potentialities of their own instruction, through proper
exposition of the spatial tradition, but one can also "hang a bell" on research
quantifiers in geography, who are often thought to have wandered so far in their
intellectual adventures as to have become lost from the rest. Looking outside geography, one may anticipate benefits from the readiness of countless persons to associate the name "geography" with maps. Latent within this readiness is a willingness
to recognize as geography, too, what maps are about – and that is the geometry of
and the movement of what is mapped.

Area Studies Tradition

The area studies tradition, like the spatial tradition, is quite strikingly represented
in classical antiquity by a practitioner to whose surviving work we can point.
He is Strabo, celebrated for his *Geography* which is a massive production
addressed to the statesmen of Augustan Rome and intended to sum up and
regularize knowledge not of the location of places and associated cartographic
facts, as in the somewhat later case of Ptolemy, but of the nature of places, their
character and their differentiation. Strabo exhibits interesting attributes of the
area-studies tradition that can hardly be overemphasized. They are a pronounced
tendency toward subscription primarily to literary standards, an almost
omnivorous appetite for information and a self-conscious companionship with
history.

It is an extreme good fortune to have in the ranks of modern American geography the scholar Richard Hartshorne, who has pondered the meaning of the area-
studies tradition with a legal acuteness that few persons would challenge. In his
Nature of Geography, his 1939 monograph [. . .], he scrutinizes exhaustively the
implications of the "interesting attributes" identified in connection with Strabo,
even though his concern is with quite other and much later authors, largely German.
The major literary problem of unities or wholes he considers from every angle. The
Gargantuan appetite for miscellaneous information he accepts and rationalizes.
The companionship between area studies and history he clarifies by appraising the
so-called idiographic content of both and by affirming the tie of both to what he
and Sauer have called "naively given reality."

The area-studies tradition (otherwise known as the chorographic tradition)
tended to be excluded from early American professional geography. Today it is
beset by certain champions of the spatial tradition who would have one believe
that somehow the area-studies way of organizing knowledge is only a subdepart-
ment of spatialism. Still, area-studies as a method of presentation lives and prospers
in its own right. One can turn today for reassurance on this score to practically

any issue of the *Geographical Review,* just as earlier readers could turn at the opening of the century to that magazine's forerunner.

What is gained by singling out this tradition? It helps toward restoring the faith of many teachers who, being accustomed to administering learning in the area-studies style, have begun to wonder if by doing so they really were keeping in touch with professional geography. (Their doubts are owed all too much to the obscuring effect of technical words attributable to the very professionals who have been intent, ironically, upon protecting that tradition.) Among persons outside the classroom the geographer stands to gain greatly in intelligibility. The title "area-studies" itself carries an understood message in the United States today wherever there is contact with the usages of the academic community. The purpose of characterizing a place, be it neighborhood or nation-state, is readily grasped. Furthermore, recognition of the right of a geographer to be unspecialized may be expected to be forthcoming from people generally, if application for such recognition is made on the merits of this tradition, explicitly.

Man-Land Tradition

That geographers are much given to exploring man-land questions is especially evident to anyone who examines geographic output, not only in this country but also abroad. O. H. K. Spate, taking an international view, has felt justified by his observations in nominating as the most significant ancient precursor of today's geography neither Ptolemy nor Strabo nor writers typified in their outlook by the geographies of either of these two men, but rather Hippocrates, Greek physician of the 5th century BC who left to posterity an extended essay, *On Airs, Waters and Places.* In this work, made up of reflections on human health and conditions of external nature, the questions asked are such as to confine thought almost altogether to presumed influence passing from the latter to the former, questions largely about the effects of winds, drinking water and seasonal changes upon man. Understandable though this uni-directional concern may have been for Hippocrates as medical commentator, and defensible as may be the attraction that this same approach held for students of the condition of man for many, many centuries thereafter, one can only regret that this narrowed version of the man-land tradition, combining all too easily with social Darwinism of the late 19th century, practically overpowered American professional geography in the first generation of its history. The premises of this version governed scores of studies by American geographers in interpreting the rise and fall of nations, the strategy of battles and the construction of public improvements. Eventually this special bias, known as environmentalism, came to be confused with the whole of the man-land tradition in the minds of many people. One can see now, looking back to the years after the ascendancy of environmentalism, that although the spatial tradition was asserting itself with varying degrees of forwardness, and that although the area-studies tradition was also making itself felt, perhaps the most interesting chapters in the story of American professional geography were being written by academicians who were reacting against environmentalism while deliberately remaining within the broad man-land tradition. The rise of culture historians during the last 30 years has meant the dropping of a curtain of culture between land and man, through which it is asserted all influence must pass. Furthermore work of both culture historians and other geographers has exhibited a reversal of the direction of the effects in Hippocrates, man appearing as an independent agent, and the land as a sufferer from action. This trend as presented in published research has reached a high point in the collection of papers titled *Man's Role in Changing the Face of the Earth*. Finally, books and articles can be called to mind that have addressed themselves to the most difficult task of all, a balanced tracing out of interaction between man and environment. Some chapters in the book mentioned above undertake just this. In fact the separateness of this approach is discerned only with difficulty in many places; however, its significance as a general research design that rises above environmentalism, while refusing to abandon the man-land tradition, cannot be mistaken.

The NCGE seems to have associated itself with the man-land tradition, from the time of founding to the present day, more than with any other tradition, although all four of the traditions are amply represented in its official magazine, *The Journal of Geography*, and in the proceedings of its annual meetings. This apparent preference on the part of the NCGE members *for defining geography in terms of the man-land tradition* is strong evidence of the appeal that man-land ideas, separately stated, have for persons whose main job is teaching. It should be noted, too, that this inclination reflects a proven acceptance by the general public of learning that centers on resource use and conservation.

Earth Science Tradition

The earth science tradition, embracing study of the earth, the waters of the earth, the atmosphere surrounding the earth and the association between earth and sun, confronts one with a paradox. On the one hand one is assured by professional geographers that their participation in this tradition has declined precipitously in the course of the past few decades, while on the other one knows that college departments of geography across the nation rely substantially, for justification of their role in general education, upon curricular content springing directly from this tradition. From all the reasons that combine to account for this state of affairs, one may, by selecting only two, go far toward achieving an understanding of this tradition. First, there is the fact that American college geography, growing out of departments of geology in many crucial instances, was at one time greatly overweighted in favor of earth science, thus rendering the field unusually liable to a sense of loss as better balance came into being. (This one-time disproportion found reciprocate support for many years in the narrowed, environmentalistic interpretation of the man-land tradition.) Second, here alone in earth science does one encounter subject matter in the normal sense of the term as one reviews geographic traditions. The spatial tradition abstracts certain aspects of reality; area studies is distinguished by a point of view; the man-land tradition dwells upon relationships; but earth science is identifiable through concrete objects. Historians, sociologists and other academicians tend not only to accept but also to ask for help from this part of geography. They readily appreciate earth science as something physically associated with their subjects of study, yet generally beyond their competence to treat. From this appreciation comes strength for geography-as-earth-science in the curriculum.

Only by granting full stature to the earth science tradition can one make sense out of the oft-repeated addage, "Geography is the mother of sciences." This is the tradition that emerged in ancient Greece, most clearly in the work of Aristotle, as a wide-ranging study of natural processes in and near the surface of the earth. This is the tradition that was rejuvenated by Varenius in the 17th century as "Geograph a Generalis." This is the tradition that has been subjected to subdivision as the development of science has approached the present day, yielding mineralogy, paleontology, glaciology, meterology and other specialized fields of learning.

Readers who are acquainted with American junior high schools may want to make a challenge at this point, being aware that a current revival of earth sciences is being sponsored in those schools by the field of geology. Belatedly, geography has joined in support of this revival. It may be said that in this connection and in others, American professional geography may have faltered in its adherence to the earth science tradition but not given it up.

In describing geography, there would appear to be some advantages attached to isolating this final tradition. Separation improves the geographer's chances of successfully explaining to educators why geography has extreme difficulty in accommodating itself to social studies programs. Again, separate attention allows one to make understanding contact with members of the American public for whom surrounding nature is known as the geographic environment. And finally, specific reference to the geographer's earth science tradition brings into the open the basis of what is, almost without a doubt, morally the most significant concept in the entire geographic heritage, that of the earth as a unity, the single common habitat of man.

An Overview

The four traditions though distinct in logic are joined in action. One can say of geography that it pursues concurrently all four of them. Taking the traditions in varying combinations, the geographer can explain the conventional divisions of the field. Human or cultural geography turns out to consist of the first three traditions applied to human societies; physical geography, it becomes evident, is the fourth tradition prosecuted under constraints from the first and second traditions. Going further, one can uncover the meanings of "systematic geography," "regional geography," "urban geography," "industrial geography," etc.

It is to be hoped that through a widened willingness to conceive of and discuss the field in terms of these traditions, geography will be better able to secure the inner unity and outer intelligibility to which reference was made at the opening of this paper, and that thereby the effectiveness of geography's contribution to American education and to the general American welfare will be appreciably increased.

Chapter 2

Geography's Perspectives

National Research Council

Geography's relevance to science and society arises from a distinctive and integrating set of perspectives through which geographers view the world around them. This chapter conveys a sense of what is meant by a geographic perspective, whether it be applied in research, teaching, or practice. Due to space limitations, it does not attempt to cite the many excellent examples of research illustrating geography's perspectives; the citations refer mainly to broad-ranging summaries of geographic research that are intended as resources for further reading.

Taking time to understand geography's perspectives is important because geography can be difficult to place within the family of academic disciplines. Just as all phenomena exist in time and thus have a history, they also exist in space and have a geography. Geography and history are therefore central to understanding our world and have been identified as core subjects in American education. Clearly, this kind of focus tends to cut across the boundaries of other natural and social science disciplines. Consequently, geography is sometimes viewed by those unfamiliar with the discipline as a collection of disparate specialties with no central core or coherence.

What holds most disciplines together, however, is a distinctive and coherent set of perspectives through which the world is analyzed. Like other academic disciplines, geography has a well-developed set of perspectives:

1. *geography's way of looking at the world* through the lenses of place, space, and scale;
2. *geography's domains of synthesis:* environmental-societal dynamics relating human action to the physical environment, environmental dynamics linking

National Research Council, "Geography's Perspectives," pp. 28–46 from *Rediscovering Geography: New Relevance for Science and Society* (Washington, DC: National Academy Press, 1997).

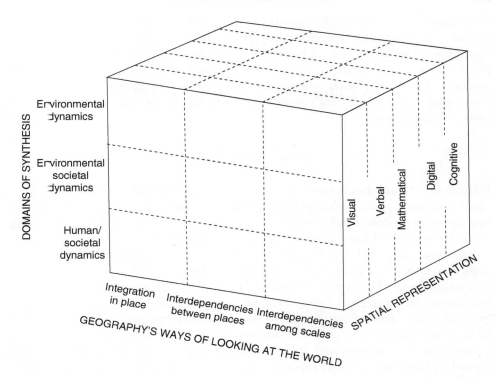

Figure 2.1 The matrix of geographic perspectives. Geography's ways of looking at the world – through its focus on place and scale (horizontal axis) – cuts across its three domains of synthesis: human-societal dynamics, environmental dynamics, and environmental-societal dynamics (vertical axis). Spatial representation, the third dimension of the matrix, underpins and sometimes drives research in other branches of geography.

    physical systems, and human-societal dynamics linking economic, social, and political systems; and
3. *spatial representation* using visual, verbal, mathematical, digital, and cognitive approaches.

These three perspectives can be represented as dimensions of a matrix of geographic inquiry as shown in Figure 2.1.

Geography's Ways of Looking at the World

A central tenet of geography is that "location matters" for understanding a wide variety of processes and phenomena. Indeed, geography's focus on location provides a cross-cutting way of looking at processes and phenomena that other disciplines tend to treat in isolation. Geographers focus on "real-world" relationships and dependencies among the phenomena and processes that give character to any location or *place*. Geographers also seek to understand relationships among places:

for example, flows of peoples, goods, and ideas that reinforce differentiation or enhance similarities. Geographers study the "vertical" integration of characteristics that define place as well as the "horizontal" connections between places. Geographers also focus on the importance of scale (in both space and time) in these relationships. The study of these relationships has enabled geographers to pay attention to complexities of places and processes that are frequently treated in the abstract by other disciplines.

Integration in place

Places are natural laboratories for the study of complex relationships among processes and phenomena. Geography has a long tradition of attempting to understand how different processes and phenomena interact in regions and localities, including an understanding of how these interactions give places their distinctive character.

The systematic analysis of social, economic, political, and environmental processes operating in a place provides an integrated understanding of its distinctiveness or character. The pioneering work of Hägerstrand, for example, showed how the daily activity patterns of people can be understood as the outcome of a process in which individuals are constrained by the availability and geographic accessibility of locations with which they can interact. Research in this tradition since has shown that the temporal and spatial sequences of actions of individuals follow typical patterns in particular types of environments and that many of the distinctive characteristics of places result from an intersection of behavioral sequences constrained by spatial accessibility to the opportunities for interaction. Such systematic analysis is particularly central to regional and human geography, and it is a theme to which much geographic research continually returns. When such systematic analysis is applied to many different places, an understanding of *geographic variability* emerges. Of course, a full analysis of geographic variability must take account of processes that cross the boundaries of places, linking them to one another, and also of scale.

Interdependencies between places

Geographers recognize that a "place" is defined not only by its internal characteristics but also by the flows of people, materials (e.g., manufactured goods, pollutants), and ideas from other places. These flows introduce interdependencies between places that can either reinforce or reduce differences. For example, very different agricultural land-use practices have evolved under identical local environmental conditions as a result of the distance to market affecting the profitability of crops. At a macroscale, the widespread and global flow of Western cultural values and economic systems has served to reduce differences among many peoples of the world. An important focus of geography is on understanding these flows and how they affect place.

The challenge of analyzing the flows and their impacts on place is considerable. Such relationships have all the characteristics of complex nonlinear systems whose behavior is hard to represent or predict. These relationships are becoming increasingly important for science and decision making [. . .].

Interdependencies among scales

Geographers recognize that the scale of observation also matters for understanding geographic processes and phenomena at a place. Although geography is concerned with both spatial and temporal scales, the enduring dimension of the geographic perspective is the significance of *spatial* scales, from the global to the highly local.

Geographers have noted, for example, that changing the spatial scale of analysis can provide important insights into geographic processes and phenomena and into understanding how processes and phenomena at different scales are related. A long-standing concern of geographers has been the "regionalization problem," that is the problem of demarcating contiguous regions with common geographic characteristics. Geographers recognize that the internal complexity and differentiation of geographic regions is scale dependent and, thus, that a particular set of regions is always an incomplete and possibly misleading representation of geographic variation.

Identifying the scales at which particular phenomena exhibit maximum variation provides important clues about the geographic, as well as the temporal, scope of the controlling mechanisms. For example, spectral analyses of temperature data, revealing the geographic scales at which there is maximum similarity in temperature, can provide important clues about the relative influence of microclimates, air masses, and global circulation on temperature patterns. A global rise in average temperature could have highly differentiated local impacts and may even produce cooling in certain localities because of the way in which global, regional, and local processes interact. By the same token, national and international economic and political developments can have highly differentiated impacts on the economic competitiveness of cities and states. The focus on scale enables geographers to analyze the impact of global changes on local events – and the impact of local events on global changes.

Domains of Synthesis

Geography's most radical departure from conventional disciplinary specializations can be seen in its fundamental concern for how humans use and modify the biological and physical environment (the *biophysical environment*) that sustains life, or *environmental-societal dynamics*. There are two other important domains of synthesis within geography as well: work examining interrelationships among different biophysical processes, or *environmental dynamics*, and work synthesizing economic, political, social, and cultural mechanisms, or *human-societal dynamics*. These domains cut across and draw from the concerns about place embedded in geography's way of looking at the world.

Environmental-societal dynamics

This branch of the discipline reflects, perhaps, geography's longest-standing concern and is thus heir to a rich intellectual tradition. The relationships that it studies – the dynamics relating society and its biophysical environment – today are not only a core element of geography but are also of increasingly urgent concern to other disciplines, decision makers, and the public. Although the work of geographers in this domain is too varied for easy classification, it includes three broad but overlapping fields of research: human use of and impacts on the environment, impacts on humankind of environmental change, and human perceptions of and responses to environmental change.

Human use of and impacts on the environment

Human actions unavoidably modify or transform nature; in fact, they are often intended specifically to do so. These impacts of human action have been so extensive and profound that it is now difficult to speak of a "natural" environment. Geographers have contributed to at least three major global inventories of human impacts on the environment and have contributed to the literature of assessment, prescription, and argument regarding their significance. Studies at local and regional levels have clarified specific instances of human-induced landscape transformation: for example, environmental degradation in the Himalayas, patterns and processes of deforestation in the Philippines and the Amazon, desiccation of the Aral Sea, degradation of landscapes in China, and the magnitude and character of pre-Hispanic environmental change in the Americas.

Geographers study the ways in which society exploits and, in doing so, degrades, maintains, improves, or redefines its natural resource base. Geographers ask why individuals and groups manipulate the environment and natural resources in the ways they do. They have examined arguments about the roles of carrying capacity and population pressures in environmental degradation, and they have paid close attention to the ways in which different cultures perceive and use their environments. They have devoted considerable attention to the role of political-economic institutions, structures, and inequities in environmental use and alteration, while taking care to resist portraying the environment as an empty stage on which social conflicts are acted out.

Environmental impacts on humankind

Consequences for humankind of change in the biophysical environment – whether endogenous or human induced – are also a traditional concern for geographers. For instance, geographers were instrumental in extending the approaches of environmental impact analysis to climate. They have produced important studies of the impact of natural climate variation and projected human-induced global warming on vulnerable regions, global food supply, and hunger. They have studied the impacts of a variety of other natural and environmental phenomena, from floods and droughts to disease and nuclear radiation releases. These works have generally focused on the differing vulnerabilities of individuals, groups, and geographic

areas, demonstrating that environmental change alone is insufficient to understand human impacts. Rather, these impacts are articulated through societal
structures that give meaning and value to change and determine in large part the
responses taken.

Human perceptions of and responses to environmental change

Geographers have long-recognized that human-environment relations are greatly
influenced not just by particular activities or technologies but also by the very ideas
and attitudes that different societies hold about the environment. Some of geography's most influential contributions have documented the roots and character of
particular environmental views. Geographers have also recognized that the impacts
of environmental change on human populations can be strongly mitigated or even
prevented by human action. Accurate perception of change and its consequences
is a key component in successful mitigation strategies. Geographers studying
hazards have made important contributions to understanding how perceptions of
risk vary from reality and how communication of risk can amplify or dampen risk
signals.

Accurate perceptions of available mitigation strategies is an important aspect
of this domain, captured by Gilbert F. White's geographic concept of the "range
of choice," which has been applied to inform policy by illuminating the options
available to different actors at different levels. In the case of floodplain occupancy,
for instance, such options include building flood control works, controlling development in flood-prone areas, and allowing affected individuals to absorb the costs
of disaster. In the case of global climate change, options range from curtailing
greenhouse gas (e.g., carbon dioxide) emissions to pursuing business as usual and
adapting to change if and when it occurs. Geographers have assembled case studies
of societal responses to a wide variety of environmental challenges as analogs for
those posed by climate and other environmental change and have examined the
ways in which various societies and communities interpret the environments in
questions.

Environmental dynamics

Geographers often approach the study of environmental dynamics from the vantage
point of natural science. Society and its roles in the environment remain a major
theme, but human activity is analyzed as one of many interrelated mechanisms of
environmental variability or change. Efforts to understand the feedbacks among
environmental processes, including human activities, also are central to the geographic study of environmental dynamics. As in the other natural sciences, advancing theory remains an overarching theme, and empirical verification continues to
be a major criterion on which efficacy is judged.

Physical geography has evolved into a number of overlapping subfields, although
the three major subdivisions are biogeography, climatology, and geomorphology.
Those who identify more with one subfield than with the others, however, typically
use the findings and perspectives from the others to inform their research and

teaching. This can be attributed to physical geographers' integrative and cross-cutting traditions of investigation, as well as to their shared natural science perspective. Boundaries between the subfields, in turn, are somewhat blurred. Biogeographers, for example, often consider the spatial dynamics of climate, soils, and topography when they investigate the changing distributions of plants and animals, whereas climatologists frequently take into account the influences that landscape heterogeneity and change exert on climate. Geomorphologists also account for climatic forcing and vegetation dynamics on erosional and depositional processes. The three major subfields of physical geography, in other words, not only share a natural science perspective but differ simply with respect to emphasis. Each subfield, however, will be summarized separately here in deference to tradition.

Biogeography

Biogeography is the study of the distributions of organisms at various spatial and temporal scales, as well as the processes that produce these distribution patterns. Biogeography lies at the intersection of several different fields and is practiced by both geographers and biologists. In American and British geography departments, biogeography is closely allied with ecology.

Geographers specializing in biogeography investigate spatial patterns and dynamics of individual plant and animal taxa and the communities and ecosystems in which they occur, in relation to both natural and anthropogenic processes. This research is carried out at local to regional spatial scales. It focuses on the spatial characteristics of taxa or communities as revealed by fieldwork and/or the analysis of remotely sensed images. This research also focuses on historic changes in the spatial characteristics of taxa or communities as reconstructed, for example, from land survey records, photographs, age structures of populations, and other archival or field evidence. Biogeographers also reconstruct prehistoric and prehuman plant and animal communities using paleoecological techniques such as pollen analysis of lake sediments or faunal analysis of midden or cave deposits. This research has made important contributions to understanding the spatial and temporal dynamics of biotic communities as influenced by historic and prehistoric human activity as well as by natural variability and change.

Climatology

Geographic climatologists are interested primarily in describing and explaining the spatial and temporal variability of the heat and moisture states of the Earth's surface, especially its land surfaces. Their approaches are quite varied, including (1) numerical modeling of energy and mass fluxes from the land surface to the atmosphere; (2) in situ measurements of mass and energy fluxes, especially in human-modified environments; (3) description and evaluation of climatically relevant characteristics of the land surface, often through the use of satellite observations; and (4) the statistical decomposition and categorization of weather data. Geographic climatologists have made numerous contributions to our understanding of urban and regional climatic systems, and they are beginning to examine macroscale climatic change as well. They have also examined the statistical relationships among weather, climate, and sociological data. Such analyses have suggested some intriguing associations, for example, between urban growth and warming and the seasonal heating cycle and crime frequency.

Geomorphology

Geomorphological research in geography emphasizes the analysis and prediction of Earth surface processes and forms. The Earth's surface is constantly being altered under the combined influences of human and natural factors. The work of moving ice, blowing wind, breaking waves, collapse and movement from the force of gravity, and especially flowing water sculptures a surface that is constantly being renewed through volcanic and tectonic activity.

Throughout most of the twentieth century, geomorphological research has focused on examing stability in the landscape and the equilibrium between the forces of erosion and construction. In the past two decades, however, emphasis has shifted toward efforts to characterize change and the dynamic behavior of surface systems. Whatever the emphasis, the method of analysis invariably involves the definition of flows of mass and energy through the surface system, and an evaluation or measurement of forces and resistance at work. This analysis is significant because if geomorphologists are to predict short-term, rapid changes (such as landslides, floods, or coastal erosion in storms) or long-term changes (such as erosion caused by land management or strip mining), the natural rates of change must first be understood.

Human-societal dynamics: From location theory to social theory

The third domain focuses on the geographic study of interrelated economic, social, political, and cultural processes. Geographers have sought a synthetic understanding of such processes though attention to two types of questions: (1) the ways in which those processes affect the evolution of particular places and (2) the influence of spatial arrangements and our understanding on those processes. Much of the early geographical work in this area emphasized locational decision making; spatial patterns and their evolution were explained largely in terms of the rational spatial choices of individual actors.

Beginning with Harvey, a new cohort of scholars began raising questions about the ways in which social structures condition individual behavior and, more recently, about the importance of political and cultural factors in social change. This has matured as an influential body of work founded in social theory, which has devoted considerable effort to understanding how space and place mediate the interrelations between individual actions and evolving economic, political, social, and cultural patterns and arrangements and how spatial configurations are themselves constructed through such processes.

This research has gained wide recognition both inside and outside the discipline of geography; as a result, issues of space and place are now increasingly seen as central to social research. Indeed, one of the principal journals for interdisciplinary research in social theory, *Environment and Planning D: Society and Space*, was founded by geographers. The nature and impact of research that has sought to bridge the gap between social theory and conceptualizations of space and place are evident in recent studies of both the evolution of places and the interconnections among places.

Societal synthesis in place

Geographers who study societal processes in place have tended to focus on micro- or mesoscales. Research on cities has been a particularly influential area of research, showing how the internal spatial structure of urban areas depends on the operation of land markets, industrial and residential location decisions, population composition, forms of urban governace, cultural norms, and the various influences of social groups differentiated along lines of race, class, and gender. The impoverishment of central cities has been traced to economic, social, political, and cultural forces accelerating suburbanization and intraurban social polarization. Studies of urban and rural landscapes examine how the material environment reflects, and shapes, cultural and social developments, in work ranging from interpretations of the social meanings embedded in urban architecture to analyses of the impacts of highway systems on land uses and neighborhoods.

Researchers have also focused on the living conditions and economic prospects of different social and ethnic groups in particular cities, towns, and neighborhoods, with particular attention recently to how patterns of discrimination and employment access have influenced the activity patterns and residential choices of urban women. Researchers have also attempted to understand the economic, social, and political forces reinforcing the segregation of poor communities, as well as the persistence of segregation between certain racial and ethnic groups, irrespective of their socioeconomic status. A geographical perspective on such issues ensures that groups are not treated as undifferentiated wholes. By focusing attention on disadvantaged communities in inner cities, for example, geographers have offered significant evidence of what happens when jobs and wealthier members of a community leave to take advantage of better opportunities elsewhere.

Geographical work on place is not limited to studies of contemporary phenomena. Geographers long have been concerned with the evolving character of places and regions, and geographers concerned with historical developments and processes have made important contributions to our understanding of places past and present. These contributions range from sweeping interpretations of the historical evolution of major regions to analyses of the changing ethnic character of cities to the role of capitalism in urban change. Studies along these lines go beyond traditional historical analysis to show how the geographical situation and character of places influence not only how those places develop but larger social and ideological formations as well.

Space, scale, and human-societal dynamics

Studies of the social consequences of linkages between places focus on a variety of scales. One body of research addresses spatial cognition and individual decision making and the impact of individual action on aggregate patterns. Geographers who study migration and residential choice behavior seek to account for the individual actions underlying the changing social structure of cities or shifting inter-urban populations. Research along these lines has provided a framework for modeling the geographical structure of interaction among places, resulting inter alia in the development of operational models of movement and settlement that are now widely used by urban and regional planners throughout Europe.

Geographers also have contributed to the refinement of location theories that reflect actual private and public decision making. Initially, much of this research looked at locational issues at particular moments in time. Work by Morrill on political redistricting, for example, provided insights into the many ways in which administrative boundary drawing reflects and shapes political ideas and practices. More recent work has focused on the evolution of industrial complexes and settlement systems. This work has combined the insights of location theory with studies of individual and institutional behavior in space. At the interurban and regional scales, geographers have studied nationwide shifts in the location and agglomeration of industries and interurban migration patterns. These studies have revealed important factors shaping the growth prospects of cities and regions.

An interest in the relationship between individual behavior and broader-scale societal structures prompted geographers to consider how individual decisions are influenced by, and affect, societal structures and institutions. Studies have tackled issues ranging from human reproduction and migration decisions to recreation and political protest. Researchers have shown how movement decisions depend on social and political barriers, the distribution of economic and political resources and broader-scale processes of societal restructuring. They have examined how the increased mobility of jobs and investment opportunities have affected local development strategies and the distribution of public resources between firms and households.

Indeed, there is new interest in theorizing the geographical scales at which different processes are constituted and the relationship between societal processes operating at different scales. Geographers recognize that social differences from place to place reflect not only differences in the characteristics of individual localities but also differences in how they are affected by societal processes operating at larger scales. Research has shown, for example, that the changing growth prospects of American cities and regions cannot adequately be understood without taking into account the changing position of the United States in the global system and the impact of this change on national political and economic trends.

Geographic research also has focused explicitly on the spatial manifestations of institutional behavior, notably that of large multilocational firms; national, state, and local governments; and labor unions. Research on multilocational firms has examined their spatial organization, their use of geographical strategies of branch-plant location and marketing in order to expand into or maintain geographically defined markets, and the way their actions affect the development possibilities of different places. Research into state institutions has focused on such issues as territorial integration and fragmentation; evolving differences in the responsibilities and powers exercised by state institutions at different geographical scales; and political and economic rivalries between territories, including their impact on political boundaries and on geopolitical spheres of influence. Observed shifts in the location of political influence and responsibility away from traditional national territories to body local states and supranational institutions demonstrate the importance of studying political institutions across a range of geographical scales.

Spatial Representation

The importance of spatial representation as a third dimension of geography's perspectives (see Figure 2.1) is perhaps best exemplified by the long and close association of cartography with geography. Research emphasizing spatial representation complements, underpins, and sometimes drives research in other branches of geography and follows directly from the thesis that location matters. Geographers involved in spatial representation research use concepts and methods from many other disciplines and interact with colleagues in those fields, including computer science, statistics, mathematics, geodesy, civil engineering, cognitive science, formal logic, cognitive psychology, semiotics, and linguistics. The goals of this research are to produce a unified approach to spatial representation and to devise practical tools for representing the complexities of the world and for facilitating the synthesis of diverse kinds of information and diverse perspectives.

How geographers represent geographic space, what spatial information is represented, and what space means in an age of advanced computer and telecommunications technology are critical to geography and to society. Research linking cartographic theory with philosophies of science and social theory has demonstrated that the way problems are framed, and the tools that are used to structure and manipulate data, can facilitate investigation of particular categories of problems and, at the same time, prevent other categories of problems from even being recognized as such. By dictating what matters, representations help shape what scientists think and how they interpret their data.

Geographic approaches to spatial representation are closely linked to a set of core spatial concepts (including location, region, distribution, spatial interaction, scale, and change) that implicitly constrain and shape how geographers represent what they observe. In effect, these concepts become a priori assumptions underlying geographic perspectives and shaping decisions by geographers about how to represent their data and what they choose to represent.

Geographers approach spatial representation in a number of ways to study space and place at a variety of scales. Tangible representations of geographic space may be visual, verbal, mathematical, digital, cognitive, or some combination of these. Reliance on representation is of particular importance when geographic research addresses intangible phenomena (e.g., atmospheric temperature or average income) at scales beyond the experiential (national to global) and for times in the past or future. Tangible representations (and links among them) also provide a framework within which synthesis can take place. Geographers also study cognitive spatial representations – for example, mental models of geographic environments – in an effort to understand how knowledge of the environment influences peoples' behavior in that environment and make use of this knowledge of cognitive representation in developing approaches to other forms of representation.

Visual representation of geographic space through maps was a cornerstone of geographic inquiry long before its formal recognition as an academic area of research, yet conventional maps are not the only visual form used in geographic research.

Due to the centrality of geographic maps as a means for spatial representation, however, concepts developed for mapping have had an impact on all forms of spatial representation. This role as a model and catalyst for visual representation throughout the sciences is clear in Hall's recent popular account of mapping as a research tool used throughout science, as well as the recognition by computer scientists that maps are a fundamental source of many concepts used in scientific visualization.

An active field of geographic research on spatial representation involves formalizing the "language" for visual geographic representation. Another important field of research involves improved depiction of the Earth's surface. A notable example is the recent advance in matching computational techniques for terrain shading with digital elevation databases covering the conterminous United States.

Verbal representation refers to attempts to evoke landscapes through a carefully constructed description in words. Some of the geographers who have become best known outside the discipline rely almost exclusively on this form of representation. Geographers have drawn new attention to the power of both verbal and visual representations, exploring the premise that every representation has multiple, potentially hidden, and perhaps duplicitous, meanings.

A current field of research linking verbal and visual forms of spatial representation concerns hypermedia documents designed for both research and instructional applications. The concept of a geographic script (analogous to a movie script) has been proposed as a strategy for leading people through a complex wed of maps, graphics, pictures, and descriptions developed to provide information about a particular issue.

Mathematical representations include models of space, which emphasize location, regions, and distributions; models of functional association; and models of process, which emphasize spatial interaction and change in place. Visual maps, of course, are grounded in mathematical models of space, and it can be demonstrated that all map depictions of geographic position are, in essence, mathematical transformations from the Earth to the plane surface of the page or computer display screen. The combination of visual and mathematical representation draws on advantages inherent in each.

A good example of the link between mathematical and visual representation is provided by the Global Demography Project. In this project more than 19,000 digitized administrative polygons and associated population counts covering the entire world were extrapolated to 1994 and then converted to spherical cells. The data are available as a raster map, accessible on the World Wide Web from the National Aeronautics and Space Administration's Consortium for the International Earth Science Information Network, Socioeconomic and Economic Data Center, which supported the project.

Cognitive representation is the way individuals mentally represent information about their environment. Human cognitive representations of space have been studied in geography for more than 25 years. They range from attempts to derive "mental maps" of residential desirability to assessing ways in which knowledge of spatial position is mentally organized, the mechanisms through which this knowledge expands with behavior in environments, and the ways in which environmental knowledge can be used to support behavior in space. The resulting wealth of knowledge about spatial cognition is now being linked with visual and digital forms of spatial representation. This link is critical in such research fields as designing interfaces for geographic information systems (GISs) and developing structures for digital geographic databases. Recent efforts to apply the approaches of cognitive science to modeling human spatial decision making have opened promising research avenues related to way finding, spatial choice, and the development of GIS-based spatial decision support systems. In addition, research about how children at various stages of cognitive development cope with maps and other forms of spatial representation is a key component in efforts to improve geography education.

Digital representation is perhaps the most active and influential focus of representational research because of the widespread use of GISs and computer mapping. Geographers have played a central role in the development of the representational schemes underpinning GISs and computer mapping systems. Geographers working with mathematicians at the US Census Bureau in the 1960s were among the first to recognize the benefits of topological structures for vector-based digital representations of spatial data. This vector-based approach (the Dual Independent Map Encoding system, more recently replaced by the Topologically Integrated Geographical Encoding and Referencing system, or TIGER) has become the linchpin of the Census Bureau's address-matching system. It has been adapted to computer mapping through an innovative system for linking topological and metrical geographic representations. Related work by geographers and other scientists at the US Geological Survey's (USGS) National Mapping Division led to the development of a digital mapping system (the Digital Line Graph format) and has allowed the USGS to become a major provider of digital spatial data.

Geographers working in GIS research have investigated new approaches to raster (grid-based) data structures. Raster structures are compatible with the structure of data in remote sensing images, which continue to be a significant source of input data for GIS and other geographic applications. Raster structures are also useful for overlying spatial data. Developments in vector and raster data structures have been linked through an integrated conceptual model that, in effect, is eliminating the raster-vector dichotomy.

US geographers have also played a leading role in international collaboration directed at the generalization of digital representations. This research is particularly important because solutions to key generalization problems are required before the rapidly increasing array of digital georeferenced data can be integrated (through GISs) to support multiscale geographic analysis. Generalization in the digital realm has proved to be a difficult problem because different scales of analysis demand not only more or less detailed information but also different kinds of information represented in fundamentally different ways.

Increasingly, the aspects of spatial representation discussed above are being linked through digital representations. Transformations from one representation to another (e.g., from mathematical to visual) are now routinely done using a digital representation as the intermediate step. This reliance on digital representation as a framework for other forms of representation brings with it new questions concerning the impact of digital representation on the construction of geographic knowledge.

One recent outgrowth of the spatial representation traditions of geography is a multidisciplinary effort in geographic information science. This field emphasizes coordination and collaboration among the many disciplines for which geographic information and the rapidly emerging technologies associated with it are of central importance. The University Consortium for Geographic Information Science (UCGIS), a nonprofit organization of universities and other research institutions, was formed to facilitate this interdisciplinary effort. UCGIS is dedicated to advancing the understanding of geographic processes and spatial relationships through improved theory, methods, technology, and data.

Geographic Epistemologies

This survey of geography's perspectives illustrates the variety of topics pursued by geography as a scientific discipline, broadly construed. The methods and approaches that geographers have used to generate knowledge and understanding of the world about them – that is, its epistemologies – are similarly broad. The post-World War II surge in theoretical and conceptual geography, work that helped the discipline take its place alongside other social, environmental, and natural sciences at that time, was triggered by adoption of what has been termed a "positivist" epistemology during the quantitative revolution of the 1960s. Extensive use is still made of this approach, especially in studying environmental dynamics but also in spatial analysis and representation. It is now recognized, however, that the practice of such research frequently diverges from the ideals of positivism. Many of these ideals – particularly those of value neutrality and of the objectivity of validating theories by hypothesis testing – are in fact unattainable.

Recognition of such limitations has opened up an intense debate among geographers about the relative merits of a range of epistemologies that continue to enliven the field. Of particular interest, at various points in this debate, have been the following:

1. Approaches stressing the role of political and economic structures in constraining the actions of human agents, drawing on structural, Marxist, and structurationist traditions of thought that emphasize the influence of frequently unobservable structures and mechanisms on individual actions and thereby on societal and human-environmental dynamics – carrying the implication that empirical tests cannot determine the validity of a theory.
2. Realist approaches, which recognize the importance of higher-level conceptual structures but insist that theories be able to account for the very different observed outcomes that a process may engender in different places.

3. Interpretive approaches, a traditional concern of cultural geography, which recognize that similar events can be given very different but equally valid interpretations, that these differences stem from the varying societal and geographical experiences and perspectives of analysts, and that it is necessary to take account of the values of the investigator rather than attempting to establish his or her objectivity.

4. Feminist approaches, which argue that much mainstream geography fails to acknowledge both a white masculine bias to its questions and perspectives and also a marginalization of womens' lives in its analysis.

5. Postmodernist or "countermodernist" approaches, which argue that all geographic phenomena are social constructions, that understandings of these are a consequence of societal values and norms and the particular experiences of individual investigators, and that any grand theory is suspect because it fails to recognize the contingent nature of all interpretation. It is argued that this has resulted in a "crisis of representation," that is, a situation in which the relative "accuracy" of any representation of the world becomes difficult to adjudicate. Feminist and postmodern scholars argue that it is necessary to incorporate a diverse group of subjects, researchers, and ways of knowing if the subject matter of geography is to embrace humankind.

Geographers debate the philosophical foundations of their research in ways similar to debates among other natural scientists, social scientists, and humanists, although with a particular emphasis on geographical views of the world and on representation. These debates have not been restricted to the philosophical realm but have had very practical consequences for substantive research, often resulting in contrasting theoretical interpretations of the same phenomenon. For example, neopositivist and structural accounts of the development of settlement systems have evolved through active engagement with one another, and debates about how to assess the environmental consequences of human action have ranged from quantitative cost-benefit calculations to attempts to compare and contrast instrumental with local and indigenous interpretations of the meaning and significance of nature. [. . .]

While we recognize that different perspectives frequently lead to intense debates engaging very different views of the same phenomenon, there is no space in this report to detail these debates. Such often vigorous interchanges and differences strengthen geography as both a subject and a discipline, however, reminding researchers that different approaches may be relevant for different kinds of questions and that the selection of any approach shapes both the kind of research questions asked and the form the answers take, as well as the answers themselves.

Chapter 3

Geography and Foreign Policy

H. J. de Blij

As a professional geographer living in Washington in the 1990s, I dreaded the intermittent appearance of media reports on international surveys that ranked American high-school students near the bottom of the geographic-literacy league. Dinner-party conversation would be spiked with sarcastic commentary ("they couldn't name the Pacific?") and enlivened by amusing stories of adults – some of them politicians and diplomats – embarrassing themselves and their nation in international settings. A repeat favorite concerned President Reagan, who had opened a conference in Brasilia by pronouncing himself pleased to be in Bolivia.

Worse, those reports and anecdotes tended to confirm the public's image of geographic knowledge as equivalent to skill in naming places. It is a useful skill, to be sure, but it has about as much relevance to geographic knowledge as a vocabulary table has to literature. No, geographers were troubled by the decline in geographic literacy in America because we knew it would have foreign-policy implications.

When Robert McNamara published his mea culpa on Vietnam, many of us wondered what the nation might have been spared if the author of America's Indochina policy had taken just one course in human or cultural geography at Harvard University. But Harvard closed its Department of Geography after World War II, and so did Yale – President Bush's alma mater. When we read of the President comparing democracy-building efforts in the Middle East to previous achievements in Japan and Germany, the echoes of those closures are not difficult to hear.

What is lost when geographic education – at all levels – withers? Take a comprehensive undergraduate curriculum in the "social" sciences and you will see three recurring perspectives: the temporal (historical), spatial (geographic) and structural (political, economic). Each informs the others, but the spatial perspective is

de Blij, H. J., "Geography and Foreign Policy," from the *Washington Examiner*, July 22, 2005.

indispensable because it alerts us to the significance of place and location in any analysis of issues ranging from the environmental to the political. That's why geographers tend to reach for their map when they first hear of a major development – such as the intervention in Iraq – and put their Geographic Information Systems to work. But as those dreaded surveys show, even well-educated Americans, on average, are not able to use maps to maximum effect.

A second, and crucial, loss involves environmental awareness and responsibility. Geography, alone among the "social" sciences, has a strong physical – that is, natural – dimension. Before geography's decline in American high schools, young students first heard of weather systems and climate change in their geography classes and learned how resource distribution relates to conservation and responsible use. My marvelous geography teacher, Eric de Wilde, raised a question in class in 1948 that kept me thinking forever after: Given the seesaw of ice-age temperature changes, how has history been influenced by climate? From him I learned that we live in an ice age and that we are lucky to experience a brief warm spell between glaciations. Ask the average citizen today what the difference is between an ice age and a glaciation and you are not likely to get a satisfactory answer. Small wonder that politicians can capitalize on public confusion.

So long as we have national leaders who do not adequately know the environmental and cultural geographies of the places they seek to change through American intervention and whose decisions in environmental arenas are insufficiently informed by geographic perspectives, we need to enhance public education in geography. Whether the world likes it or not, the United States has emerged from the 20th century as the world's most powerful state, capable of influencing nations and peoples, lives and livelihoods from pole to pole. That power confers on Americans a responsibility to learn as much as they can about those nations and livelihoods, and for this there is no better vehicle than geography.

The United States and the world will face numerous challenges in the years ahead, among which three will stand out: rapid environmental change, a rising tide of terrorism empowered by weapons of mass destruction and the emergence of China as a superpower on the global stage. To confront these challenges, the American public needs to be the world's best informed about the factors and forces underlying them and the linkages among them. Geography is the key to understanding these interconnections.

Chapter 4

Reflections of an American Geographer on the Anniversary of September 11th

William G. Moseley

While nearly every discipline has some insight to share regarding the events of September 11, 2001, I believe geography is particularly well equipped to put these occurrences in context and give us some understanding as to why they transpired. At the simplest level, knowledge of other places and peoples aids us in putting the actions of a few individuals in perspective. Geographic understanding helps us avoid errant conjecture, stereotypes, and xenophobia. It enables us to realize that most Muslims are peace-loving people and that violence-prone Islamic extremists are not the norm. Geography is also about recognizing the connections between different places and regions. To this end, I share an observation and two stories about interconnectedness in the world that relate to September 11th.

First, there are interesting connections between oil use in the United States, politics in Saudi Arabia, and the global promotion of a conservative brand of Islam. Americans consume more energy per capita than any other people on earth. With only 5% of the world's population, we consume 25% of the world's energy. US car culture is largely responsible for our energy addiction as motor vehicles consume two-thirds of the oil used in America. Exacerbating our auto dependence is cheap fuel and an urban infrastructure that encourages us to use cars (cities with large roads, limited sidewalks, and little to no public transportation). The problem is that we must import oil to satisfy our energy addiction, and this addiction increasingly drives our foreign policy. With tacit US support, the Saudi royal family has cut a Faustian bargain in which the Saudi Arabian government has given free reign to conservative Muslim clerics in exchange for uncritical support of the ruling family. The well financed Saudi religious establishment has promoted conservative Koranic schools around the Muslim world (including Pakistan and Afghanistan), produced the likes of Osama bin Laden, and served to focus popular outrage at

Moseley, William G., "Reflections of an American Geographer on the Anniversary of September 11th," pp. 11–12 from *Association of American Geographer's Newsletter*, 37.111 (2002).

Israel (and away from any critique of undemocratic leadership in Saudi Arabia). Yet, the United States implicitly fosters this situation because of its oil addiction.

Second, the promotion of a conservative brand of Islam dovetails with a rapidly globalizing world that many find troubling. I served in the Peace Corps in the West African nation of Mali in the late 1980s. In Mali, there has been a great deal of intermingling between Islam and traditional religions, with most Malians practicing a very tolerant brand of Islam. The rural community where I was based numbered about 200 people, and I continue to return to this area every 2–3 years for the purposes of research. These return visits have allowed me to witness change over time. One such change involves a good friend in the village who has become an increasingly devout and fundamentalist Muslim over the years. During my return visits, this friend and I inevitably get into heated debates about his increasingly conservative religious and political views. What he appreciates about Islam is that it makes a disorderly world neat. It gives him a clear framework to classify things as good or evil (ironically in a way that our president likes to classify things as good or evil). Mali, like much of the developing world, is a messy place. While Mali has experienced democratic rule since 1992, corruption continues to be a problem. Westernization has meant that traditional values are under assault: the young no longer seem to respect the old; crime is a growing problem in many areas; and young adults have children out of wedlock. To make matters worse, the marketing of Americana overseas is often of the worst variety – cheap films and TV programs, Coca Cola, and Marlboro. While I am a liberal thinker, I can understand how the rigidity of some versions of Islam may appeal to those who see their world falling apart.

Finally, the edges of the developing world are unruly in a way unknown to Westerners. Furthermore, we have played a role in the oppression that occurs in these areas. When I finished my Peace Corps service I traveled over land for several months across the Sahara desert. With two friends, I went north on the Niger River to Gao, where we found a truck that was heading to Algeria and willing to take passengers. Other passengers in the truck included several sheep, a group of Tuareg nomads trying to sneak into Algeria, a one-legged Senegalese man looking for work in Libya, the former chauffeur of Sekou Toure (the first leader of independent Guinea) and an explosives expert who used to be in the Algerian underground army.

There are two interesting observations related to this trip. First, about five miles before we got to the Algerian border from Mali, half of our fellow passengers disappeared into the desert, only to reappear on the other side. Although governments may try to enforce borders in developing countries, this is a bit like building a dam in the ocean. American imposition of order in these areas, if attempted, will be illusory. My second observation relates to the explosives expert who had served in the Algerian underground army. As you may know, Algeria was a former French colony that went through a bloody independence war in the 1950s. As the Algerians could not beat the French on the battlefield, they formed the Algerian underground army that undertook missions of sabotage in French territory. These soldiers were labeled as terrorists, but they also were fighting for the independence of their country.

This raises the tricky question of when saboteurs are terrorists and when they are revolutionaries? I am not suggesting that those who blew up the twin towers were freedom fighters, but since September 11th, our government has been looking around the world and labeling a lot of people as terrorists (and ignoring the fact that this can be a somewhat subjective decision). Nor do I mean to condone violence as a form of resistance, but I can understand how people react violently when they feel oppressed. Perhaps the best way to end armed struggle and terrorism is not through violence, but through ending our support for undemocratic regimes. While there have been calls for Americans to be patriotic by shopping, possibly the best thing we could do is limit our energy consumption and, by extension, our unsavory connections with dictators.

Geography helps us understand connections like the ones just described, but sadly, most Americans are very poor geographers.

Chapter 5

How to Lie with Maps

Mark Monmonier

Introduction

Not only is it easy to lie with maps, it's essential. To portray meaningful relationships for a complex, three-dimensional world on a flat sheet of paper or a video screen, a map must distort reality. As a scale model, the map must use symbols that almost always are proportionally much bigger or thicker than the features they represent. To avoid hiding critical information in a fog of detail, the map must offer a selective, incomplete view of reality. There's no escape from the cartographic paradox: to present a useful and truthful picture, an accurate map must tell white lies.

Because most map users willingly tolerate white lies on maps, it's not difficult for maps also to tell more serious lies. Map users generally are a trusting lot: they understand the need to distort geometry and suppress features, and they believe the cartographer really does know where to draw the line, figuratively as well as literally. As with many things beyond their full understanding, they readily entrust mapmaking to a priesthood of technically competent designers and drafters working for government agencies and commercial firms. Yet cartographers are not licensed, and many mapmakers competent in commercial art or the use of computer workstations have never studied cartography. Map users seldom, if ever, question these authorities, and they often fail to appreciate the map's power as a tool of deliberate falsification or subtle propaganda.

Because of personal computers and electronic publishing, map users can now easily lie to themselves – and be unaware of it. Before the personal computer, folk cartography consisted largely of hand-drawn maps giving directions. The direction giver had full control over pencil and paper and usually had no difficulty

Monmonier, Mark, "Introduction" and "Epilogue," pp. 1–4, 184–6 from *How to Lie with Maps*, 2nd edition (London and Chicago: University of Chicago Press, 1991).

transferring routes, landmarks, and other relevant recollections from mind to map. The computer allows programmers, marketing experts, and other anonymous middlemen without cartographic savvy to strongly influence the look of the map and gives modern-day folk maps the crisp type, uniform symbols, and verisimilitude of maps from the cartographic priesthood. Yet software developers commonly have made it easy for the lay cartographer to select an inappropriate projection or a misleading set of symbols. Because of advances in low-cost computer graphics, inadvertent yet serious cartographic lies can appear respectable and accurate.

The potential for cartographic mischief extends well beyond the deliberate suppression used by some cartographer-politicians and the electronic blunders made by the cartographically ignorant. If any single caveat can alert map users to their unhealthy but widespread naïveté, it is that *a single map is but one of an indefinitely large number of maps that might be produced for the same situation or from the same data.* The italics reflect an academic lifetime of browbeating undergraduates with this obvious but readily ignored warning. How easy it is to forget, and how revealing to recall, that map authors can experiment freely with features, measurements, area of coverage, and symbols and can pick the map that best presents their case or supports their unconscious bias. Map users must be aware that cartographic license is enormously broad.

The purpose of this book is to promote a healthy skepticism about maps, not to foster either cynicism or deliberate dishonesty. In showing how to lie with maps, I want to make readers aware that maps, like speeches and paintings, are authored collections of information and also are subject to distortions arising from ignorance, greed, ideological blindness, or malice.

[. .]

A book about how to lie with maps can be more useful than a book about how to lie with words. After all, everyone is familiar with verbal lies, nefarious as well as white, and is wary about how words can be manipulated. Our schools teach their pupils to be cautious consumers who read the fine print and between the lines, and the public has a guarded respect for advertising, law, marketing, politics, public relations, writing, and other occupations requiring skill in verbal manipulation. Yet education in the use of maps and diagrams is spotty and limited, and many otherwise educated people are graphically and cartographically illiterate. Maps, like numbers, are often arcane images accorded undue respect and credibility. This book's principal goal is to dispel this cartographic mystique and promote a more informed use of maps based upon an understanding and appreciation of their flexibility as a medium of communication.

The book's insights can be especially useful for those who might more effectively use maps in their work or as citizens fighting environmental deterioration or social ills. The informed skeptic becomes a perceptive map author, better able to describe locational characters and explain geographic relationships as well as better equipped to recognize and counter the self-serving arguments of biased or dishonest mapmakers.

Where a deep mistrust of maps reflects either ignorance of how maps work or a bad personal experience with maps, this book can help overcome an unhealthy skepticism called *cartophobia.* Maps need be no more threatening or less reliable than words, and rejecting or avoiding or ignoring maps is akin to the mindless fears of illiterates who regard books as evil or dangerous. This book's revelations about how maps *must* be white lies but may *sometimes* become real lies should provide the same sort of reassuring knowledge that allows humans to control and exploit fire and electricity.

[. . .]

Epilogue

The preceding chapters have explored the wide variety of ways maps can lie: why maps usually must tell some white lies, how maps can be exploited to tell manipulative lies, and why maps often distort the truth when a well-intentioned map author fails to understand cartographic generalization and graphic principles. The wise map user is thus a skeptic, ever wary of confusing or misleading distortions conceived by ignorant or diabolical map authors.

Let me conclude with a cautionary note about the increased likelihood of cartographic distortion when a map must play the dual role of both informing and impressing its audience. Savvy map viewers must recognize that not all maps are intended solely to inform the viewer about location or geographic relationships. As visual stimuli, maps can look pretty, intriguing, or important. As graphic fashion statements, maps not only decorate but send subtle or subliminal messages about their authors, sponsors, or publishers. Some advertising maps, for instance, announce that a power company or chain restaurant is concerned about the city or region, whereas free street guides attest to the helpfulness of a real estate firm or bank. A flashy map, in color with an unconventional projection, touts its author's sense of innovation, and cartographic window dressing in a doctoral dissertation or academic journal suggests the work is scholarly or scientific. An ornate print of an eighteenth-century map of Sweden not only decorates a living room wall but proclaims the household's pride in its Scandinavian heritage. A world map behind a television newscaster reinforces the network's image of excellence in global news coverage, and a state highway map is a convenient vehicle for a political message from the governor, image-building photos of the state's tourist attractions, and a cartographic statement about tax dollars well spent on roads, recreation sites, and forest preserves. A local map titled "Risk of Rape" can shock and can advocate more diligent police patrols and stricter sentencing. A cartogram comparing wealth or life expectancy among the world's nations can foster complacent pride or evoke compassionate guilt.

Maps with dual roles are not inherently bad. Indeed, some perfectly correct maps exist primarily to lend an aura of truth, and others exist largely as visual decoration. The impetus for an increased use of news maps was the perception among publishers that a better "packaged," more graphic newspaper could compete effectively with television as well as with rival papers. Their motivation might not have been better reporting, but the conscious decision to use more maps has improved their coverage of many news stories in which location is important. Similarly, competition for audience attention has led to more news maps in the electronic media; local television stations offer highly informative sequences of weather maps, and network news programs usefully complement the newscaster's "talking head" with simple yet instructive maps of relative location for major news events. Maps intended to decorate or impress can educate a public appallingly ignorant about basic place-name geographic. Were it not for the map's power as a symbol of geographic knowledge, we would know a great deal less about our neighborhoods, our nation, and the world.

Dual motives are risky, of course. Map authors pursuing aesthetic goals might violate cartographic principles or suppress important but artistically inconvenient information. Maps, like buildings, suffer when the designer puts form ahead of function. Map authors with propagandist motives might suppress ideologically inconvenient information as well as knowingly adopt an inappropriate projection or dysfunctional symbols. And expedient map authors distracted by a need to decorate can deliver sloppy, misleading maps. The skeptical map viewer will assess the map author's motives and ask how the need to impress might have subverted the need to inform.

Although recognizing this versatility for dual roles should enhance the informed map viewer's healthy skepticism about the map author's expertise or motives, neither this recognition nor the map's demonstrated ability to distort and mislead should detract from an appreciation of the map's power to explore and explain geographic facts. White lies are an essential element of cartographic language, an abstraction with enormous benefits for analysis and communication. Like verbal language and mathematics, though, cartographic abstraction has costs as well as benefits. If not harnessed by knowledge and honest intent, the power of maps can get out of control.

Chapter 6

Every Step You Take, Every Move You Make

Jerome E. Dobson

When public school students in Sutter, Calif., were ordered to wear radio frequency identification tags around their necks, the children's parents objected and the principal backed down. Already, schoolchildren in Osaka, Japan, are required to carry similar tags tucked into their belongings. The government of Mexico tracks court officials with RFID tags implanted in their shoulders. Finland changed its national laws to allow cell-phone tracking of children. A woman in Kenosha discovered her estranged husband had hidden a Global Positioning System tracker in her car. All are current news items.

Once viewed as a futuristic nightmare, human-tracking is now affordable and available without restriction. For $200, plus a monthly service fee of $20, anyone can purchase an electronic device that puts George Orwell's 1984 surveillance technology to shame. They're marketed as "kid-tracking" devices, though some ads also mention pets and senior citizens. In vivid shades of doublespeak, one company offers service plans named "Liberty, Independence and Freedom," but surveillance and control are their purpose.

At the very least, human-tracking devices will alter relationships between some parents and children, husbands and wives, employers and employees more dramatically than any other product emerging from the information revolution. Ultimately, they offer a new form of human slavery based on location control. They pose the greatest threat to personal freedom ever faced in human history. Whatever legitimate uses there may be – to safeguard a child or incapacitated adult, for example– abuses will occur. Even full-blown geo-slavery is inevitable: The uncertainty is how many people will suffer from it – hundreds, thousands or millions.

People welcome GPS receivers for personal navigation, especially for travel and outdoor recreation. There's much good and certainly no harm as long as the

Dobson, Jerome E., "Every Step You Take, Every Move You Make," from *Chicago Tribune*, February 25, 2005.

coordinates go directly to the user and no one else. Current devices display maps produced by geographic information systems containing detailed information about businesses, residences and individuals. Human-tracking devices add radio communication that reports location data to a service center with its own powerful GIS. Subscribers pay for the privilege of peeking in at will to check on the individual being tracked.

After decades of fretting over Orwell's vision, hardly a whimper has been heard since the devices went on sale. Media attention has focused entirely on the advertised case: parents of good intention watching over their own children. Far from critical review, news and talk show coverage amounts to little more than blind acceptance of manufacturers' claims.

Will the practice really protect children? Or will it introduce new risks? How will children react, emotionally and behaviorally, to constant surveillance and control? Will tracking be confined to children and incapacitated adults? Or will it become a ubiquitous tool of control throughout society? Peter F. Fisher, professor of geographic information science at the University of Leicester and editor of the *International Journal of Geographic Information Science*, and I have raised these and other crucial questions in scholarly journals and trade magazines, but questioning of any sort is strangely absent elsewhere.

It's time for an explicit national debate on human-tracking that goes for beyond privacy, per se. Which applications are acceptable and which are not? Which will require informed consent, legal proceedings or medical hearings? Which existing laws must be amended to place electronic means on a par with traditional means of branding, stalking, incarceration and enslavement? Should human-tracking companies be licensed? Should their employees undergo background checks? What other safeguards are needed?

Initially, the front line will be in the workplace. How will union leaders value workers' right with human-tracking as a bargaining chip in contract negotiations?

None of this debate will happen until citizens become alarmed enough to educate themselves and demand answers, and it's not clear they will resist.

At church one recent morning, a fellow member told me how a friend, the owner of a construction firm, uses GPS-based cell phones to track "his 20 Mexicans." He envied his friend's constant control and hoped to adopt the technology himself though he has only "three Mexicans of his own."

That conversation occurred in the oldest church in Kansas, established by abolitionists who came to make Kansas a free state and thereby sparked the Civil War. The irony was overwhelming.

The American debate begins in Sutter, Calif.

Part II

Population and Migration

Introduction

William G. Moseley and Kavita Pandit

The geographic study of human population dynamics has a long and distinguished history. One of the earliest concerns was the relationship between population growth and food/resource production. Thomas Malthus's classic 1798 treatise, entitled "An Essay on the Principle of Population," is the lead discussion article in this section. Malthus was concerned that the exponential growth of the human population numbers would outstrip society's ability to produce food. Because of his religious views, he regarded contraception as inherently immoral and felt the only other option to reduce birth rates – abstention – was unworkable. Consequently, Malthus saw a bleak future for humankind – one characterized by hunger, famine, and wars over increasingly scarce natural resources. According to Malthus, overpopulation was the single greatest contributor to poverty and he therefore cautioned against providing aid to the poor, for fear that this would only encourage them to produce more children and thereby worsen the problem.

Although most scholars have moved away from Malthus's doomsday view of the future, the spirit of his ideas continues to strongly influence contemporary approaches to population and environment. The neo-Malthusian perspective fully accepts Malthus's assertion that population growth is outstripping resource production. However, neo-Malthusians do not agree with Malthus's dismissal of contraception. Instead, they place a strong emphasis on fertility control as a mechanism for restoring the balance between population and resources (or, to use their term, the "carrying capacity"). Neo-Malthusians support socioeconomic investments that will accelerate fertility declines and bring about a demographic transition, namely, the transition of society from a condition of high birth and death rates to one of low birth and death rates with rising levels of economic development.

A more fundamental critique of Malthus's ideas came from Karl Marx and Friedrich Engels. In his 1844 tract, "Outlines of a Critique of Political Economy," Engels argued that since labor was the basis of all wealth, growing populations (read labor) actually generated new wealth. According to him it was capitalism, not overpopulation, that caused poverty because those who owned farms and factories exploited their workers for profit. This critique is echoed in the work of more recent neo-Marxist scholars who contend that our overall production of food and resources is more than adequate to support the world's population, but that the real source of the problem is the unequal distribution of resources. Neo-Marxists challenge policy prescriptions that focus on lowering fertility rates in Third World countries by pointing out that one child born in a highly industrialized country consumes far more resources (and, by extension, inflicts much greater harm on the environment) than a child born in a poor country.

Yet another critique of Malthus comes from the technocrats or cornucopians who challenge his assumption that the earth's resources are fixed or grow very slowly. They point to spectacular rises in agricultural productivity in the twentieth century due to widespread mechanization and fertilizer use. According to the technocratic view, human ingenuity (spurred by a free market system) brings about technological innovation that allows our resource production to remain ahead of population growth. Indeed, some technocrats go further, arguing that large populations are an asset because they increase the pool of smart and innovative people.

Did Malthus conceptualize the population–resource link backwards? In 1965, the political economist Ester Boserup published a highly influential study entitled *The Conditions of Agricultural Growth: The Economics of Agrarian Change Under Population Pressure* in which she contended just this. Instead of agricultural production (or resources) controlling the size of a human population (as Malthus thought), Boserup argued that it was the population (or the size of the labor force) that determined how much food could be produced. She noted that periods of rapid population growth in human history were associated with dramatic rises in productivity through agricultural intensification, allowing more food to be produced on the same amount of land. The second discussion reading in this section by Mortimore and Tiffen, entitled "Population Growth and a Sustainable Environment," describes, in the manner noted by Boserup, how growing population numbers in a region of Kenya actually led to improved environmental management and food production.

The study of population dynamics also includes topics beyond those concerned with population–resource relationships. One topic that has engaged population geographers is the spatial patterning of disease and mortality, and the manner of spread of infectious diseases such as smallpox, cholera, malaria, and HIV/AIDS. In the article by Gould and Woods, titled "Population Geography and HIV/AIDS: The Challenge of a 'Wholly Exceptional Disease,'" the authors point out that HIV/AIDS is distinctively different from other infectious diseases because it is contracted and transmitted primarily by sexually active adults, rather than children. This has important implications for the geography of its transmission and its impacts on the population structure. The article also illustrates how cultural and political factors (in addition to purely physical factors) can facilitate or inhibit the spatial spread of a disease.

The study of population movement or migration also has been a major theme in population geography. The final reading addresses the important theme of internal migration (migration within national boundaries). This may be contrasted with external or international migration (migration across national boundaries). In "Interprovincial Migration, Population Redistribution, and Regional Development in China," Cindy Fan discusses how Chinese migration patterns have changed over the past couple of decades as the country moved from a socialist to a free market economy. Her work highlights the powerful influence of regional economic conditions on migration.

DISCUSSION READINGS

Malthus, Thomas. (1987/1798). "An Essay on the Principle of Population." In Scott W. Menard & Elizabeth W. Moen (eds.), *Perspectives on Population*. New York: Oxford University Press.

Mortimore, Michael & Tiffen, Mary. (1994). "Population Growth and a Sustainable Environment." *Environment*, 36(8): 10–20, 28–30.

Gould, W. T. S. & Woods, R. I. (2003). "Population Geography and HIV/AIDS: The Challenge of a 'Wholly Exceptional Disease.'" *Scottish Geographical Journal*, 119(3): 265–81.

Fan, C. Cindy. (2005). "Interprovincial Migration, Population Redistribution, and Regional Development in China: 1990 and 2000 Census Comparisons." *Professional Geographer*, 57(2): 295–311.

Chapter 7

An Essay on the Principle of Population

Thomas Robert Malthus

The Basic Argument

I think I may fairly make two postulata.

First, That food is necessary to the existence of man.

Secondly, That the passion between the sexes is necessary and will remain nearly in its present state.

These two laws, ever since we have had any knowledge of mankind, appear to have been fixed laws of our nature, and, as we have not hitherto seen any alteration in them, we have no right to conclude that they will ever cease to be what they now are, without an immediate act of power in that Being who first arranged the system of the universe, and for the advantage of his creatures, still executes, according to fixed laws, all its various operations.

Assuming my postulata as granted, I say, that the power of population is indefinitely greater than the power in the earth to produce subsistence for man.

Population, when unchecked, increases in a geometrical ratio. Subsistence increases only in an arithmetical ratio. A slight acquaintance with numbers will shew the immensity of the first power in comparison of the second.

By that law of our nature which makes food necessary to the life of man, the effects of these two unequal powers must be kept equal.

This implies a strong and constantly operating check on population from the difficulty of subsistence. This difficulty must fall some where and must necessarily be severely felt by a large portion of mankind.

Through the animal and vegetable kingdoms, nature has scattered the seeds of life abroad with the most profuse and liberal hand. She has been comparatively

Malthus, Thomas Robert, "An Essay on the Principle of Population," pp. 97–103 from Scott W. Menard and Elizabeth W. Moen (eds.), *Perspectives on Population* (New York: Oxford University Press, 1987).

sparing in the room and the nourishment necessary to rear them. The germs of existence contained in this spot of earth, with ample food, and ample room to expand in, would fill millions of worlds in the course of a few thousand years. Necessity, that imperious all pervading law of nature, restrains them within the prescribed bounds. The race of plants, and the race of animals shrink under this great restrictive law. And the race of man cannot, by any efforts of reason, escape from it. Among plants and animals its effects are waste of seed, sickness, and premature death. Among mankind, misery and vice. The former, misery, is an absolutely necessary consequence of it. Vice is a highly probable consequence, and we therefore see it abundantly prevail, but it ought not, perhaps, to be called an absolutely necessary consequence. The ordeal of virtue is to resist all temptation to evil.

This natural inequality of the two powers of population and of production in the earth and that great law of our nature which must constantly keep their effects equal form the great difficulty that to me appears insurmountable in the way to the perfectibility of society. All other arguments are of slight and subordinate consideration in comparison of this. I see no way by which man can escape from the weight of this law which pervades all animated nature. No fancied equality, no agrarian regulations in their utmost extent, could remove the pressure of it even for a single century. And it appears, therefore, to be decisive against the possible existence of a society, all the members of which should live in ease, happiness, and comparative leisure; and feel no anxiety about providing the means of subsistence for themselves and families.

Consequently, if the premises are just, the argument is conclusive against the perfectibility of the mass of mankind.

I have thus sketched the general outline of the argument, but I will examine it more particularly, and I think it will be found that experience, the true source and foundation of all knowledge, invariably confirms its truth.

Population and the Early Stages of Civilization

In the rudest state of mankind, in which hunting is the principal occupation, and the only mode of acquiring food, the means of subsistence being scattered over a large extent of territory, the comparative population must necessarily be thin. It is said that the passion between the sexes is less ardent among the North American Indians than among any other race of men. Yet notwithstanding this apathy, the effort towards population, even in this people, seems to be always greater than the means to support it. This appears from the comparatively rapid population growth that takes place whenever any of the tribes happen to settle in some fertile spot and to draw nourishment from more fruitful sources than that of hunting, and it has been frequently remarked that when an Indian family has taken up its abode near any European settlement and adopted a more easy and civilized mode of life, that one woman has reared five or six, or more children, though in the savage state it rarely happens, that above one or two in a family grow up to maturity. The same observation has been made with regard to the Hottentots near the Cape. These facts prove the superior power of population to the means of subsistence in nations of hunters, and that this power always shews itself the moment it is left to act with freedom.

It remains to inquire whether this power can be checked, and its effects kept equal to the means of subsistence, without vice or misery.

The North American Indians, considered as a people, cannot justly be called free and equal. In all the accounts we have of them, and, indeed, of most other savage nations, the women are represented as much more completely in a state of slavery to the men than the poor are to the rich in civilized countries. One half the nation appears to act as Helots to the other half, and the misery that checks population falls chiefly, as it always must do, upon that part whose condition is lowest in the scale of society. The infancy of man in the simplest state requires considerable attention, but this necessary attention the women cannot give, condemned as they are to the inconveniences and hardships of frequent change of place and to the constant and unremitting drudgery of preparing every thing for the reception of their tyrannic lords. These exertions, sometimes during pregnancy or with children at their backs, must occasion frequent miscarriages, and prevent any but the most robust infants from growing to maturity. Add to these hardships of the women, the constant war that prevails among savages, and the necessity which they frequently labour under of exposing their aged and helpless parents, and of thus violating the first feelings of nature, and the picture will not appear very free from the blot of misery.

Of the manners and habits that prevail among nations of shepherds, the next state of mankind, we are even more ignorant than of the savage state. But that these nations could not escape the general lot of misery arising from the want of subsistence, Europe, and all the fairest countries in the world, bear ample testimony. Want was the goad that drove the Scythian shepherds from their native haunts, like so many famished wolves in search of prey. Set in motion by this all powerful cause, clouds of Barbarians seemed to collect from all points of the northern hemisphere. Gathering fresh darkness and terror as they rolled on, the congregated bodies at length obscured the sun of Italy and sunk the whole world in universal night. These tremendous effects, so long and so deeply felt throughout the fairest portions of the earth, may be traced to the simple cause of the superior power of population, to the means of subsistence.

In these savage contests many tribes must have been utterly exterminated. Some, probably, perished by hardship and famine. Others, whose leading star had given them a happier direction, became great and powerful tribes, and, in their turns, sent off fresh adventurers in search of still more fertile seats. The prodigious waste of human life occasioned by this perpetual struggle for room and food was more than supplied by the mighty power of population, acting, in some degree, unshackled from the constant habit of emigration. The tribes that migrated towards the South, though they won these more fruitful regions by continual battles, rapidly increased in number and power, from the increased means of subsistence. Till at length, the whole territory, from the confines of China to the shores of the Baltic was peopled by a various race of Barbarians, brave, robust, and enterprising, inured to hardship, and delighting in war. Some tribes maintained their independence. Others ranged themselves under the standard of some barbaric chieftain who led them to victory after victory, and what was of more importance, to regions abounding in corn, wine, and oil, the long wished for consummation, and great reward of their labours. An Alaric, an Attila, or a Zingis Khan, and the chiefs around them, might fight for glory, for the fame of extensive conquests, but the true cause that set in motion the great tide of northern emigration, and that continued to propel it till it rolled at different periods, against China, Persia, Italy, and even Egypt, was a scarcity of food, a population extended beyond the means of supporting it.

The Power of Population

I think it will be allowed, that no state has hitherto existed (at least that we have any account of) where the manners were so pure and simple, and the means of subsistence so abundant, that no check whatever has existed to early marriages, among the lower classes, from a fear of not providing well for their families, or among the higher classes, from a fear of lowering their condition in life. Consequently in no state that we have yet known has the power of population been left to exert itself with perfect freedom.

Whether the law of marriage be instituted or not, the dictate of nature and virtue seems to be an early attachment to one woman. Supposing a liberty of changing in the case of an unfortunate choice, this liberty would not affect population till it arose to a height greatly vicious; and we are now supposing the existence of a society where vice is scarcely known.

In a state therefore of great equality and virtue, where pure and simple manners prevailed, and where the means of subsistence were so abundant that no part of the society could have any fears about providing amply for a family, the power of population being left to exert itself unchecked, the increase of the human species would evidently be much greater than any increase that has been hitherto known.

In the United States of America, where the means of subsistence have been more ample, the manners of the people more pure, and consequently the checks to early marriages fewer than in any of the modern states of Europe, the population has been found to double itself in twenty-five years.

This ratio of increase, though short of the utmost power of population, yet as the result of actual experience, we will take as our rule, and say, that population, when unchecked, goes on doubling itself every twenty-five years or increases in a geometrical ratio.

Let us now take any spot of earth, this Island for instance, and see in what ratio the subsistence it affords can be supposed to increase. We will begin with it under its present state of cultivation.

If I allow that by the best possible policy, by breaking up more land and by great encouragements to agriculture, the produce of this Island may be doubled in the first twenty-five years, I think it will be allowing as much as any person can well demand.

In the next twenty-five years, it is impossible to suppose that the produce could be quadrupled. It would be contrary to all our knowledge of the qualities of land. The very utmost that we can conceive, is, that the increase in the second twenty-five years might equal the present produce. Let us then take this for our rule, though certainly far beyond the truth, and allow that by great exertion, the whole produce of the Island might be increased every twenty-five years, by a quantity of subsistence equal to what it at present produces. The most enthusiastic speculator cannot suppose a greater increase than this. In a few centuries it would make every acre of land in the Island like a garden.

Yet this ratio of increase is evidently arithmetical.

It may be fairly said, therefore, that the means of subsistence increase in an arithmetical ratio. Let us now bring the effects of these two ratios together.

The population of the Island is computed to be about seven millions, and we will suppose the present produce equal to the support of such a number. In the first twenty-five years the population would be fourteen millions, and the food being also doubled, the means of subsistence would be equal to this increase. In the next twenty-five years the population would be twenty-eight millions, and the means of subsistence only equal to the support of twenty-one millions. In the next period, the population would be fifty-six millions, and the means of subsistence just sufficient for half that number. And at the conclusion of the first century the population would be one hundred and twelve millions and the means of subsistence only equal to the support of thirty-five millions, which would leave a population of seventy-seven millions totally unprovided for.

A great emigration necessarily implies unhappiness of some kind or other in the country that is deserted. For few persons will leave their families, connections, friends, and native land, to seek a settlement in untried foreign climes, without some strong subsisting causes of uneasiness where they are, or the hope of some great advantages in the place to which they are going.

But to make the argument more general and less interrupted by the partial views of emigration, let us take the whole earth, instead of one spot, and suppose that the restraints to population were universally removed. If the subsistence for man that the earth affords was to be increased every twenty-five years by a quantity equal to what the whole world at present produces, this would allow the power of production in the earth to be absolutely unlimited, and its ratio of increase much greater than we can conceive that any possible exertions of mankind could make it.

Taking the population of the would at any number, a thousand millions, for instance, the human species would increase in the ratio of – 1, 2, 4, 8, 16, 32, 64, 128, 256, 512, &c. and subsistence as – 1, 2, 3, 4, 5, 6, 7, 8, 9, 10, &c. In two centuries and a quarter, the population would be to the means of subsistence as 512 to 10: in three centuries as 4096 to 13, and in two thousand years the difference would be almost incalculable, though the produce in that time would have increased to an immense extent.

No limits whatever are placed to the productions of the earth; they may increase for ever and be greater than any assignable quantity; yet still the power of population being a power of a superior order, the increase of the human species can only be kept commensurate to the increase of the means of subsistence, by the constant operation of the strong law of necessity acting as a check upon the greater power.

The effects of this check remain now to be considered.

Among plants and animals the view of the subject is simple. They are all impelled by a powerful instinct to the increase of their species, and this instinct is interrupted by no reasoning or doubts about providing for their offspring. Wherever therefore there is liberty, the power of increase is exerted, and the superabundant effects are repressed afterwards by want of room and nourishment, which is common to animals and plants, and among animals, by becoming the prey of others.

The effects of this check on man are more complicated. Impelled to the increase of his species by an equally powerful instinct, reason interrupts his career and asks him whether he may not bring beings into the world, for whom he cannot provide the means of subsistence. In a state of equality, this would be the simple question. In the present state of society, other considerations occur. Will he not lower his rank in life? Will he not subject himself to greater difficulties than he at present feels? Will he not be obliged to labour harder? and if he has a large family, will his utmost exertions enable him to support them? May he not see his offspring in rags and misery, and clamouring for bread that he cannot give them? And may he not be reduced to the grating necessity of forfeiting his independence, and of being obliged to the sparing hand of charity for support?

These considerations are calculated to prevent, and certainly do prevent, a very great number in all civilized nations from pursuing the dictate of nature in early attachment to one woman. And this restraint almost necessarily, though not absolutely so, produces vice. Yet in all societies, even those that are most vicious, the tendency to a virtuous attachment is so strong that there is a constant effort towards an increase of population. This constant effect as constantly tends to subject the lower classes of the society to distress and to prevent any great permanent amelioration of their condition.

The way in which these effects are produced seems to be this.

We will suppose the means of subsistence in any country just equal to the easy support of its inhabitants. The constant effort towards population, which is found to act even in the most vicious societies, increases the number of people before the means of subsistence are increased. The food therefore which before supported seven millions must not be divided among seven millions and a half or eight millions. The poor consequently must live much worse, and many of them be reduced to severe distress. The number of labourers also being above the proportion of the work in the market, the price of labour must tend toward a decrease, while the price of provisions would at the same time tend to rise. The labourer therefore must work harder to earn the same as he did before. During his season of distress, the discouragements to marriage, and the difficulty of rearing a family are so great that population is at a stand. In the mean time the cheapness of labour, the plenty of labourers, and the necessity of an increased industry amongst them, encourage cultivators to employ more labour upon their land, to turn up fresh soil, and to manure and improve more completely what is already in tillage, till ultimately the means of subsistence become in the same proportion to the population as at the period from which we set out. The situation of the labourer being then again tolerably comfortable, the restraints to population are in some degree loosened and the same retrograde and progressive movements with respect to happiness are repeated.

This sort of oscillation will not be remarked by superficial observers, and it may be difficult even for the most penetrating mind to calculate its periods. Yet that in all old states some such vibration does exist, though from various transverse causes, in a much less marked, and in a much more irregular manner than I have described it, no reflecting man who considers the subject deeply can well doubt.

Population, Poverty, and Welfare

The positive check to population by which I mean the check that represses an increase which is already begun, is confined chiefly, though not perhaps solely, to the lowest orders of society. This check is not so obvious to common view as the other I have mentioned, and, to prove distinctly the force and extent of its operations would require, perhaps, more data than we are in possession of. But I believe it has been very generally remarked by those who have attended to bills of mortality that of the number of children who die annually, much too great a proportion belongs to those who may be supposed unable to give their offspring proper food and attention, exposed as they are occasionally to severe distress and confined, perhaps, to unwholesome habitations and hard labour. This mortality among the children of the poor has been constantly taken notice of in all towns. It certainly does not prevail in an equal degree in the country, but the subject has not hitherto received sufficient attention to enable any one to say that there are not more deaths in proportion among the children of the poor, even in the country, than among those of the middling and higher classes. Indeed, it seems difficult to suppose that a labourer's wife who has six children, and who is sometimes in absolute want of bread, should be able always to give them the food and attention necessary to support life. The sons and daughters of peasants will not be found such rosy cherubs in real life as they are described to be in romances. It cannot fail to be remarked by those who live much in the country that the sons of labourers are very apt to be stunted in their growth, and are a long while arriving at maturity. Boys that you would guess to be fourteen or fifteen, are upon inquiry, frequently found to be eighteen or nineteen. And the lads who drive plough, which must certainly be a healthy exercise, are very rarely seen with any appearance of calves to their legs; a circumstance, which can only be attributed to a want either of proper or of sufficient nourishment.

To remedy the frequent distresses of the common people, the poor laws of England have been instituted; but it is to be feared, that though they may have alleviated a little the intensity of individual misfortune, they have spread the general evil over a much larger surface. It is a subject often started in conversation and mentioned always as a matter of great suprise that notwithstanding the immense sum that is annually collected for the poor in England, there is still so much distress among them. Some think that the money must be embezzled, others that the church-wardens and overseers consume the greater part of it in dinners. All agree that some how or other it must be very ill-managed. In short the fact that nearly three millions are collected annually for the poor and yet that their distresses are not removed is the subject of continual astonishment. But a man who sees a little below the surface of things would be very much more astonished if the fact were otherwise than it is observed to be, or even if a collection universally of eighteen shillings in the pound instead of four, were materially to alter it.

The poor-laws of England tend to depress the general condition of the poor in two ways. Their first obvious tendency is to increase population without increasing the food for its support. A poor man may marry with little or no prospect of being able to support a family in independence. They may be said therefore in some measure to create the poor which they maintain, and as the provisions of the country must, in consequence of the increased population, be distributed to every man in smaller proportions, it is evident that the labour of those who are not supported by parish assistance will purchase a smaller quantity of provisions than before and consequently more of them must be driven to ask for support.

Secondly, the quantity of provisions consumed in workhouses upon a part of the society that cannot in general be considered as the most valuable part diminishes the shares that would otherwise belong to more industrious and more worthy members, and thus in the same manner forces more to become dependent. If the poor in the workhouses were to live better than they now do, this new distribution of the money of the society would tend more conspicuously to depress the condition of those out of the workhouses by occasioning a rise in the price of provisions.

I fell no doubt whatever that the parish laws of England have contributed to raise the price of provisions and to lower the real price of labour. They have therefore contributed to impoverish that class of people whose only possession is their labour. It is also difficult to suppose that they have not powerfully contributed to generate that carelessness and want of frugality observable among the poor, so contrary to the disposition frequently to be remarked among petty tradesmen and small farmers. The labouring poor, to use a vulgar expression, seem always to live from hand to mouth. Their present wants employ their whole attention, and they seldom think of the future. Even when they have an opportunity of saving they seldom exercise it, but all that is beyond their present necessities goes, generally speaking, to the ale-house. The poor-laws of England may therefore be said to diminish both the power and the will to save among the common people, and thus to weaken one of the strongest incentives to sobriety and industry, and consequently to happiness.

The mass of happiness among the common people cannot but be diminished, when one of the strongest checks to idleness and dissipation is thus removed, and when men are thus allured to marry with little or no prospect of being able to maintain a family in independence. Every obstacle in the way of marriage must undoubtedly be considered as a species of unhappiness. But as from the laws of our nature some check to population must exist, it is better that it should be checked from a foresight of the difficulties attending a family and fear of dependent poverty than it should be encouraged, only to be repressed afterwards by want and sickness.

The evils attendant on the poor-laws are in some degree irremediable. If assistance be to be distributed to a certain class of people, a power must be given somewhere of discriminating the proper objects and of managing the concerns of the institutions that are necessary, but any great interference with the affairs of other people, is a species of tyranny, and in the common course of things the exercise of this power may be expected to become grating to those who are driven to ask for support. The tyranny of Justices, Churchwardens, and Overseers, is a common complaint among the poor, but the fault does not lie so much in these persons, who probably before they were in power, were not worse than other people, but in the nature of all such institutions.

The evil is perhaps gone too far to be remedied, but I feel little doubt in my own mind that if the poor-laws had never existed, though there might have been a few more instances of very severe distress, yet that the aggregate mass of happiness among the common people would have been much greater than it is at present.

Proposed Remedies

By encouraging the industry of the towns more than the industry of the country, Europe may be said, perhaps, to have brought on a premature old age. A different policy in this respect, would infuse fresh life and vigour into every state. While from the law of primogeniture, and other European customs, land bears a monopoly price, a capital can never be employed in it with much advantage to the individual; and, therefore, it is not probable that the soil should be properly cultivated. And, though in every civilized state, a class of proprietors and a class of labourers must exist; yet one permanent advantage would always result from a nearer equalization of property. The greater the number of proprietors, the smaller must be the number of labourers: a greater part of society would be in the happy state of possessing property; and a smaller part in the unhappy state of possessing no other property than their labour.

To remove the wants of the lower classes of society is indeed an arduous task. The truth is that the pressure of distress on this part of a community is an evil so deeply seated that no human ingenuity can reach it. Were I to propose a palliative, and palliatives are all that the nature of the case will admit, it should be, in the first place, the total abolition of all the present parish-laws. This would at any rate give liberty and freedom of action to the peasantry of England, which they can hardly be said to possess at present. They would then be able to settle without interruption, wherever there was a prospect of a greater plenty of work and a higher price for labour. The market of labour would then be free, and those obstacles removed, which as things are now, often for a considerable time prevent the price from rising according to the demand.

Secondly, Premiums might be given for turning up fresh land, and all possible encouragements held out to agriculture above manufactures, and to tillage above grazing. Every endeavour should be used to weaken and destroy all those institutions relating to corporations, apprenticeships, &c, which cause the labours of agriculture to be worse paid than the labours of trade and manufactures. For a country can never produce its proper quantity of food while these distinctions remain in favour of artizans. Such encouragements to agriculture would tend to furnish the market with an increasing quantity of healthy work, and at the same time, by augmenting the produce of the country, would raise the comparative price of labour and ameliorate the condition of the labourer. Being now in better circumstances, and seeing no prospect of parish assistance, he would be more able, as well as more inclined, to enter into associations for providing against the sickness of himself or family.

Lastly, for cases of extreme distress, county workhouses might be established, supported by rates upon the whole kingdom, and free for persons of all counties, and indeed of all nations. The fare should be hard, and those that were able obliged to work. It would be desirable that they should not be considered as comfortable asylums in all difficulties, but merely as places where severe distress might find some alleviation. A part of these houses might be separated, or others built for a most beneficial purpose, that of providing a place where any person, whether native or foreigner, might do a day's work at all times and receive the market price for it. Many cases would undoubtedly be left for the exertion of individual benevolence.

A plan of this kind, the preliminary of which should be an abolition of all the present parish laws, seems to be the best calculated to increase the mass of happiness among the common people of England. To prevent the recurrence of misery, is alas! beyond the power of man. In the vain endeavour to attain what in the nature of things is impossible, we now sacrifice not only possible but certain benefits. We tell the common people that if they will submit to a code of tyrannical regulations, they shall never be in want. They do submit to these regulations. They perform their part of the contract, but we do not, nay cannot, perform ours, and thus the poor sacrifice the valuable blessing of liberty and receive nothing that can be called an equivalent in return.

It is undoubtedly a most disheartening reflection that the great obstacle in the way to any extraordinary improvement in society is of a nature that we can never hope to overcome. The perpetual tendency in the race of man to increase beyond the means of subsistence is one of the general laws of animated nature which we can have no reason to expect will change. Yet, discouraging as the contemplation of this difficulty must be to those whose exertions are laudably directed to the improvement of the human species, it is evident that no possible good can arise from any endeavours to slur it over to keep it in the back ground. On the contrary, the most baleful mischiefs may be expected from the unmanly conduct of not daring to face truth because it is unpleasing. Independently of what relates to this great obstacle, sufficient yet remains to be done for mankind to animate us to the most unremitted exertion. But if we proceed without a thorough knowledge and accurate comprehension of the nature, extent, and magnitude of the difficulties we have to encounter, or if we unwisely direct our efforts towards an object, in which we cannot hope for success, we shall not only exhaust our strength in fruitless exertions and remain at as great a distance as ever from the summit of our wishes, but we shall be perpetually crushed by the recoil of this rock of Sisyphus.

Chapter 8

Population Growth and a Sustainable Environment

Michael Mortimore and Mary Tiffen

Many people believe that rapid population growth is incompatible with sustainable management of the environment. Because such concerns frequently focus on Africa, where the population growth is the highest in the world, a careful look at how population growth, the environment, and human welfare have fared over time in a densely populated area of Kenya is most instructive. It illuminates the fact that the technological achievements in the Machakos District were neither a miracle nor an accident; rather, they resulted from an endogenous process whereby the Akamba farmers selected and adapted new ideas from multiple sources.

A recent study of the resource management practices of African smallholders in the Machakos District of Kenya from 1930 to 1990 showed positive, not negative, influences of increasing population density on both environmental conservation and productivity. Machakos is in southeast Kenya. Its northernmost point is about 50 kilometers from the capital, Nairobi; from there, it stretches some 300 kilometers southward. Since at least the 18th century, Machakos has been inhabited by agro-pastoralists known as the Akamba, who also populate the neighboring Kitui District. Historically, the Akamba men have looked after the livestock and cleared the land, while the women have cultivated small plots for food crops.

A Setup for Ecological Disaster?

In the first decade of the 20th century, the British colonial regime that had been established in 1890 became strong enough to impose boundaries on the indigenous peoples, which it did to make room for white settlement in designated Scheduled Areas. This confinement was known as the White Highlands policy. A map of the

Mortimore, Michael and Tiffen, Mary, "Population Growth and a Sustainable Environment," pp. 10–20, 28–30 from *Environment*, 36.8 (1994).

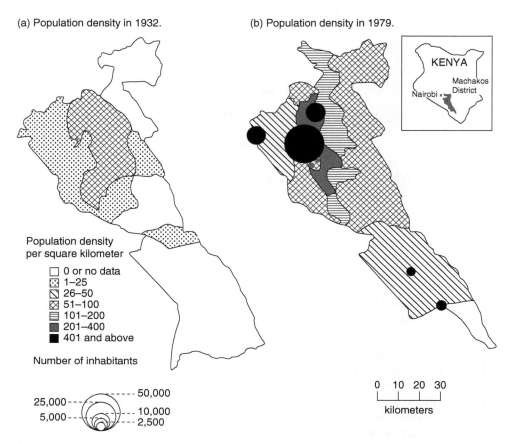

Figure 8.1 Population distribution in the Machakos District of Kenya in 1932 and 1979.
Source: M. Tiffen, M. Mortimore, and F. Gichuki, *More People, Less Erosion: Environmental Recovery in Kenya* (Chichester: John Wiley, 1994), p. 49.

population distribution in 1932 (see Figure 8.1(a)) shows clearly the boundaries of the reserve where the Akamba were then confined. Farms and ranches of European settlers bordered the reserve on two sides; the other two sides abutted uninhabited Crown Lands, whose use the government controlled. Thus encircled, the Akamba, and their livestock, grew in number.

Although they constantly protested against the boundaries, the Akamba actually lost little cultivated land. This was because their confinement prevented them from responding as they normally would to population growth, falling fertility, or drought conditions. Traditionally, they would move to a new site or extend their grazing range. It was only with independence in 1962 that the district was increased, from less than 7,000 square kilometers to 13,600 square kilometers. Between 1932 and 1989, the population of the district grew from 240,000 to 1,393,000, and from the 1950s until after 1985, it grew at an annual rate of more than 3 percent (see Table 8.1).

Table 8.1 Growth in the population of the Machakos District of Kenya from 1932 to 1989

Year	Total population (thousands)	Annual growth rate (percent)	Average population density (hectare/person)
1932	240	*	2.66
1948	366	2.68	1.93
1962	566	3.17	1.38
1969	707	3.22	1.92[a]
1979	1,023	3.76	1.33
1989	1,393	3.09	0.97

* Not available.
[a] In 1962, the district roughly doubled in size with the incorporation of Scheduled Areas and Crown Lands, but with only a small addition to the population.
Source: Calculated from relevant Kenyan census data M. Tiffen, M. Mortimore, and F. Gichuki. More People, Less Erosion: Environmental Recovery in Kenya (Chichester, UK: John Wiley & Sons, 1994).

Most of the Machakos District is semi-arid and often subject to moisture stress. The mean annual rainfall ranges from 500 to 1,000 millimeters. In each of its two short growing seasons, less than one-half of the district has more than a 60 percent chance of receiving enough rain to grow a crop of maize. The hilly central and northern area receives the more reliable rainfall, which combines with lower temperatures to create the most favorable climatic conditions for agriculture in the district. In the surrounding plains, higher temperatures and variable rainfall greatly increase the agricultural risk. Ninety seasonal droughts (70 of them in runs of two or more consecutive seasons) have occurred during the past 100 years.

The areas highest in elevation are agroecological zones (AEZs) II and III. AEZ III is classified as subhumid, marginally suited to growing coffee, and constitutes the greater part of the nine percent of the district, which, for Kenya, is considered of high potential for agriculture. The moist semi-arid AEZ IV constitutes about 40 percent of the district, and the dry, semi-arid AEZs V and VI together make up 50 percent. AEZs V and VI have been classified as mainly suited to raising livestock and growing millet, although even in these areas the Akamba now grow maize and beans.

The soils of the district, except on the wettest hills, tend not to be very fertile. They especially lack carbon, nitrogen, and phosphorus. The soils are also susceptible to erosion at rates of 5 to 15 tons of soil per hectare per year. These characteristics are the result of long, continued cultivation and grazing and the removal of protective vegetation.

This combination of rapid population growth, unreliable rainfall, frequent moisture stress, low soil fertility, and high erodibility seems to suggest the likelihood of population-induced degradation occurring on a large scale, and this indeed was the assessment of the reserve in the 1930s. A series of disastrous droughts (in 1929, 1933, 1934, 1935, and 1939) caused major crop failures, losses of livestock, invasions of pests, the deterioration of plant cover, and accelerated erosion. In 1937,

Colin Maher, the government's chief soil conservation officer, wrote despairingly:

> *The Machakos Reserve is an appalling example of a large area of land which has been subjected to uncoordinated and practically uncontrolled development by natives whose multiplication and the increase of whose stock has been permitted, free from the checks of war and largely from those of disease, under benevolent British rule. Every phase of misuse of land is vividly and poignantly displayed in this Reserve, the inhabitants of which are rapidly drifting to a state of hopeless and miserable poverty and their land to a parching desert of rocks, stones and sand.*

The government's recommendations after commissioning eight visits and reports on Machakos between 1929 and 1939 strongly reflected an official consensus that overstocking, inappropriate cultivation, and deforestation were occurring in the reserve, which was already overpopulated in relation to its carrying capacity.

Saving Soil or Water?

The 1930s saw worldwide concern about soil erosion. As the axioms of soil conservation were being hammered out in the dust bowl of the United States, the severity of the problem in African territories, such as Kenya, Lesotho, South Africa, and Nigeria, was being studied. The cause of the problem there was generally perceived to be inappropriate use of the land by the indigenous people.

In 1931, an agricultural officer was appointed to the Machakos District and he began performing soil conservation experiments in cooperation with local elders. But the slow progress of this program of experimentation and persuasion became increasingly unacceptable as concern over soil erosion mounted worldwide. In 1937, the government established a Soil Conservation Service within the Agricultural Department under the direction of Maher, with R. O. Barnes responsible for work in Machakos. Maher was convinced that a large-scale program, involving the removal of people from the most severely eroded areas and their resettlement elsewhere, was essential. The government also made a disastrous attempt to partially destock the reserve of cattle in 1938.

Fears spread among the Akamba that their existing land rights, which by custom were established by clearing and cultivation, would be threatened by work done by government tractors or government-paid labor gangs. To the mystification of officials, the Akamba adamantly refused both kinds of assistance but reluctantly accepted compulsory labor on terracing and grass-planting two mornings a week, which was enforced by the government-appointed chiefs of each location (an administrative subunit). One person per household had to be sent; it was often a woman because many of the men were working out of the district. In 1937, Barnes photographed an experiment using trash lines of crop residues to slow down water flow. This technique was later discouraged because it was thought to heighten the prevalence of pests and diseases. Experimental bench terraces, which were made by throwing soil uphill from a ditch (a technique the Akamba call *fanya juu*), were established near a school in Matungulu Location in 1937.

Bench terraces fell out of favor after Maher visited the United States in 1940 and brought back the "narrow-based" technique. Attracted by its simplicity and economy of labor, Maher made the method the basis of the government's promotion of terrace construction for the next 14 years.

During World War II, the soil conservation program suffered because of the decline in technical staff and resources. But after the war, the promotion of terrace construction gathered strength as the urgency of dealing with erosion in the reserve became apparent and more famines occurred. Agricultural officers again supported bench terraces, particularly after Maher's retirement in 1951. In fact, benches were compulsory for coffee, which African farmers were allowed to grow for the first time in 1954, under strict supervision. Some farmers had already found bench terracing to be well suited to horticulture (the growing of fruits and vegetables), and a 1949 annual report tells of an ex-soldier bringing the technique back with him from India for this purpose.

Between 1946 and 1962, the African Land Development Board (ALDEV) committed about £1.5 million to land improvement schemes in the Machakos District through an expanded Department of Agriculture. Of this, about 30 percent went to "betterment," a government program that included soil conservation and agricultural extension. The Akamba's initial hostility to this government-directed program was gradually overcome as terracing proved its worth. Providing free hand tools was part of ALDEV's land improvement plan and a popular tactic among farmers too poor to buy the tools.

A real breakthrough in making the labor involved in soil conservation more socially acceptable to the Akamba happened about 1956 when an Akamba officer in the Community Development Department secured the replacement of compulsory work directed by officials with a variant of the traditional work party, or *mwethya*. A *mwethya* would be involved in a special project, such as building a hut, where the person responsible would call on neighbors to help and would provide them with food in return for their labor. The terracing *mwethyas* met regularly and operated on the farms under the direction of their own chosen leaders. The groups also chose the technology they used, and the *fanya juu* was usually selected as the first stage to constructing a bench terrace. Because these groups were composed mostly of women, women came to hold leadership positions in society almost for the first time.

In the 1950s, more than 40,000 hectares of land were terraced, a situation described by one contemporary observer as a "Machakos miracle." But despite this progress, a hiatus in terracing occurred as independence approached in 1962. The Soil Conservation Program had been corrupted, in the eyes of the Akamba, by its association with the colonial authority, which was soon to be removed. Many terraces fell into disrepair, and few new ones were built. After Kenya became independent, the special funding Machakos had been receiving through the ALDEV was not renewed, and agricultural staff and resources were switched from the district to areas of higher potential in other districts, especially areas in which former European land of good quality was being divided among African smallholders.

From about 1965, farmers, on their own initiative, began to terrace again and to renew the conservation efforts they had come to neglect. Over the years, the Akamba had seen that crops grew better on terraces. This was not the result of soil conservation per se but rather an upshot of the superior soil moisture on bench terraces, which improves yields in the dry plains and, in bad years, even in the wetter hills. Air photographs show a relatively small increase in terracing between 1948 and 1961, partly because many narrow-based terraces deteriorated. But a remarkable amount of terracing occurred between 1961 and 1978, despite the lack of any large-scale government assistance. This was achieved by the better-off farmers hiring labor or participating in *mwethya*.

The drought of 1975 prompted new externally supported programs for soil conservation. These programs did not get under way until 1978, when the Swedish International Development Agency began providing tools, food aid, and supervision of soil conservation in parts of northern Machakos. The local Catholic diocese, supported by some nongovernmental organizations (NGOs), also began a food aid program. The Machakos Integrated Development Program was established in 1978 and operated until 1988. Its soil conservation component organized terracing by farmers on a catchment basis, particularly in the areas of newer settlement where farmers had not yet been able to gather their own resources for the task. Now, almost all terraces in Machakos are of the *fanya juu* or bench terrace type.

In the 1980s, more than 4,500 kilometers of terraces were constructed annually with donor or agency support, compared with a peak of about 5,000 kilometers annually in the 1950s that were also constructed solely through voluntary efforts. Air surveys show, however, that the actual total area terraced during the 1980s was much larger: 8,500 kilometers were constructed each year between 1981 and 1985. About half of this construction, then, was due to the unassisted efforts of the farmers during a time when agency and donor contributions for this effort peaked. The same air surveys show that by 1985, 54 percent of the district's arable land was adequately conserved, and in hilly areas, no less than 83 percent.

Farmers still construct terraces in Machakos today, with some technical assistance from the Agriculture Department, and they accept conservation as a good farming practice. In the district, with its low-level and variable rainfall, saving moisture is at least as important as saving soil.

The Machakos story shows the importance of a substantial improvement in profits to farmers. The bench terrace, despite its higher labor demand, was adopted initially because its water conservation made possible sales of profitable crops, such as vegetables and coffee. By conserving water, which is the main cause of soil erosion, bench terracing also conserved the soil and the nutrients in the manure the farmer placed on it. After seeing the better yields that can be obtained through the use of bench terracing, farmers now use benches for the crops they grow for their own families with such good results that many farmers in AEZs IV, V, and VI are in most years able to sell grain to more specialized farmers in AEZs II and III and to local urban communities.

The farmers have rejected the narrow-based terrace because it is so easily damaged. This shows the importance of offering farmers a choice of technologies. They are the best judges of the payoff in terms of cost (in work and money) and the variety of benefits they seek. Even so, outside assistance can be of real value in introducing new technologies that farmers can add to the results of their own observations and experiments. Although the farmers found the *fanya juu* to be appropriate to conditions in Machakos, it does not mean that it is the right technology for soil conservation everywhere. The adoption of technology by poorer farmers can be speeded up by providing judicious assistance in terms of tools and advice but the Swedish International Development Agency soon found it advisable to reduce the food-for-work component, which can lead to construction for the sake of food in places where it is useless for conservation.

A Farming Revolution

The technical innovations in the Machakos District were not restricted to soil and water conservation. Seventy-six production technologies have been identified that were either introduced from outside the district or whose use was greatly extended between 1930 and 1990. They include 35 field and horticultural crops, 5 tillage technologies, and 6 methods of soil fertility management. These technical options have added flexibility to the farming system in Machakos – a great advantage in a risky environment.

Making money from farming

In the 1930s, most of the Akamba's capital was locked up in livestock, and occasional sales provided needed cash. Farmers who then cultivated maize, beans, and pigeon peas for subsistence have since moved into cultivating market crops. Coffee, which some Akamba had learned to grow while employed on European coffee farms, was their most successful market crop from 1954 until its price fell in the 1980s. After the government's ban on "native" coffee growing – which was established in 1938 to protect European producers' interests – was removed in 1954, strict rules were enforced on the growing, processing, and marketing of coffee. The African producers quickly achieved high grades as a result of the strict rules. The production of coffee, which was an attractive component of the ALDEV programs because coffee was profitable and had to be grown on terraces, increased spectacularly in the "boom" of the later 1970s (see Figure 8.2). Coffee production generated investment funds and supported improved living standards in the subhumid zone where it could be grown. Although coffee is grown in only a small proportion of the district (just a few assiduous farmers can get it to grow in AEZ IV), it has helped spread prosperity into neighboring drier areas through the demands of coffee growers for labor, food crops, and livestock products, as well as for nonfarm products and services. In the district as a whole, 41 percent of rural incomes in a 1981/1982 survey were generated by nonfarm businesses and wages.

Unlike coffee, cotton, which is recommended for the drier areas, was not a long-term success in Machakos. Its price was rarely high enough to compensate for its tendency to compete with the food crops for labor and capital, and the profit

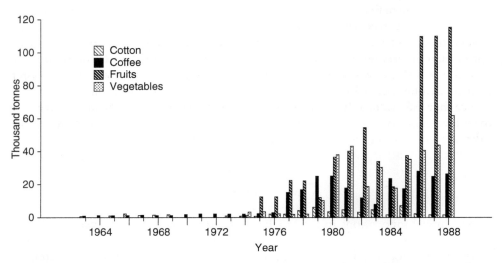

Figure 8.2 The recorded output of four market crops in the Machakos District from 1963 to 1988. This figure shows the production of the four most important market crops according to government figures. These data are reliable for coffee and cotton, which are sold to marketing boards, but are probably underestimated for fruits and vegetables. The performance of cotton compared unfavorably with the performances of coffee, fruits, and vegetables. Coffee is confined to the subhumid zone, and vegetables are most important there. But fruit production has been successfully extended to drier areas, since mango and citrus trees can use subsurface water, and bananas are grown in pits, ditches, and natural hollows. Sales of livestock products, grain, and pulses, which are not shown, were also substantial.
Source: S. G. Mbogoh, "Crop Production," in M. Tiffen (ed.), *Environmental Change and Dryland Management in Machakos District, Kenya, 1930–90: Production Profile*, ODI Working Paper no. 55 (London: Overseas Development Institute, 1991).

margins were reduced by marketing inefficiencies. Three attempts to promote cotton – in the 1930s, 1960s, and 1970s – were unsuccessful.

Under a program of the Machakos Integrated Development Program, which ran from 1978 to 1988, to provide assistance to the Co-operative Union in buying trucks, building stores, and improving roads, growing cotton became temporarily attractive. But in the second half of the 1980s, the late payments of the Cotton Marketing Board, combined with lower prices and deteriorating roads, led many farmers to seek higher value products. In Makueni and other dry areas, many farmers have switched from growing cotton to growing citrus, pawpaws, and mangoes.

Both coffee and cotton received governmental assistance in terms of extension advice, assisted provision of seeds and fertilizer, supervision, grading, marketing, and pricing. By contrast, the promotion and adoption of horticulture were closely linked with the growth of Kenya's canning industry and Nairobi's retail markets, which were often supported by itinerant Asian buyers. The same channels are now reaching export markets via the Nairobi airport. A generally high value of fruit crops per hectare facilitated the skillful exploitation of wet microenvironments even in the driest areas, as well as the development of certain technologies, such as microirrigation and the cultivation of bananas in pits. Women farmers found fruit production attractive because trees do not compete with the food crops (for which the women are often responsible) in terms of land or labor. Figure 8.2 shows the remarkable success of fruits and vegetables (especially if compared with cotton) since the 1970s.

The Akamba farmers have adapted rather well to the opportunities provided by the market, and, given the incentives available to them, they are innovative in both their production and marketing practices. Meanwhile, livestock sales, on which they depended for income in the late 1930s, have steadily declined, although they remain important in semi-arid areas in drought years.

Experimenting with staple food options

White maize is the staple food of the Akamba. Having two short growing seasons and a high probability of drought calls for varieties that either resist drought or escape it by maturing quickly. In 1968, the government's local research station released a drought-escaping variety known as Katumani Composite B (KCB) maize.

The new maize was promoted by the extension service, and some surveys suggest that from two-thirds to three-quarters of the farmers grow it. It is not known, however, how much of the maize area is planted with KCB or what proportion of KCB makes up the total maize output. Of 40 farmers interviewed in five locations in 1990, only one-third said they grew it exclusively and one-third said they grew it along with local and hybrid varieties.

Although this new maize has caused no "green revolution," given the unpredictable rainfall, it has provided farmers with another option. The local varieties, though slower to mature, are more resistant to drought, and hybrids do better in wetter sites. In combination with other varieties, the KCB strengthens rather than undermines this flexibility. Some farmers crosspollinate KCB with the local varieties to achieve desirable traits, only buying new KCB seed every two or three years.

With and without KCB, food crop production per person kept up with population growth from 1930 to 1987. The district's dependence on imported food from 1974 to 1985 was less than it was between 1942 and 1962 (8 kilograms per person annually compared with 17 kilograms), despite major droughts in both periods. Food output in 1984 (after two severe and one moderate seasonal droughts) was slightly higher, per person, than it was in 1960/1961 (when one severe and one moderate drought were followed by a season of very excessive rain).

Introducing faster tillage

The ox plow, introduced to the Machakos District as early as 1910, was being used by about 600, or 3 percent, of the district's households by the 1930s. Farmers trained their cattle to plow, and plows were cheap (about equivalent to the price of a cow in 1940). Furthermore, the technology was being tested and developed on nearby European farms where some Akamba worked. By owning plows, farmers could greatly increase the area they could cultivate, and this enabled them to sell maize or pulses. It also made shifting cultivation inefficient and row planting, which facilitates weeding, necessary.

After World War II, the use of plows increased as ex-soldiers returned from India with the money needed to buy them. Also, farmers used their earnings from employment outside the district to buy plows. The government, which had imposed a plow-based farming system in the newly settled area at Makueni after 1946, provided some credit for their purchase, as did some Asian traders. Coffee (after 1954), horticulture, and cotton (in some years) generated investment funds to be used to buy plows. By the 1980s, surveys found that 62 percent or more of the farmers owned a plow, with the rest being too poor to buy one or having fields too small and steep for plowing with oxen.

The plow proved to be both a durable and a flexible technology. Initially, plows with teams of six or eight oxen were used to open new land. Lighter, two-oxen plows were later developed for work on small, terraced, permanent fields. The Victory mouldboard plow is now used everywhere and for several operations – primary plowing, seedbed preparation, and interrow weeding. It saves labor, and its use by women frees more men for off-farm employment. Though much criticized on technical grounds, attempts to improve it have failed to gain wide acceptance. The "oxenization" of Akamba agriculture was, to some extent, a triumph of capitalization in a capital-poor, risk-prone, and low productive farming system.

Fertilizing the soil

Akamba farmers once relied on long fallows to replenish the soil. In the 1930s, there was very little systematic manuring, and the fertility of arable land, as measured by yields, was low. The Agricultural Department favored farmyard manure over inorganic fertilizers and promoted composting. But it was not until the 1950s that manuring became widespread in the northern subhumid areas, where most arable fields were fixed and cultivated twice a year. The widespread adoption of manuring can be judged from the fact that by the 1980s, 9 out of 10 farmers were doing it, in both wetter and drier areas. Now, most of the arable land of the district is cultivated twice a year – in both rainy seasons.

Manure is made in the *boma* (stall or pen) and supplemented with burned trash and waste. The amount applied depends on the number of livestock and on how much labor and transport are available when needed. The Akamba farmers know that, under present technical and economic conditions, sustaining output depends on using *boma* manure. Few of the farmers can afford large quantities of inorganic fertilizers, which are used very little and then mostly on coffee.

Feeding the livestock

In the 1930s, the Akamba women cultivated food crops at home, while the Akamba men took the livestock to common grazing lands in the southern part of the reserve or, by permit, on Crown Lands for several months of the year. After about 1960, settlement on Crown Lands could no longer be restrained, and, as thousands of families moved into them, common access to grazing was extinguished by private enclosures. Each household must now maintain its animals on the family farm or obtain permission to use another family's land, often in return for some rent or service. More than 60 percent of the cattle, sheep, and goats are stall-fed or tethered for part or all of the year. Cutting fodder and bringing residues to the animals when they are in the *boma* require additional labor. Fodder grass is grown on terrace banks, residues lie in cultivated fields, and feed is cut from hedges and wayside verges. The change from pasture grazing to stall feeding is most noticeable in the subhumid zone. There, only one-third of the livestock are grazed on pastures all the time, mostly in the dry semi-arid zone. The effort required to maintain livestock is making grade and crossbred cattle popular (estimated to be about 12 percent of the total in 1983). Their milk yields and value are superior to those of the native zebu, though their increased health risks call for frequent dipping and they require more food and water.

Farming the trees

In the 1920s, the Forest Department believed that afforestation was necessary to arrest environmental desiccation and to fulfill the growing need for domestic fuel and construction timber. For the next several decades, the department struggled, with insufficient resources, to reserve and replant hilltop forests. In 1984, when estimates of household fuel requirements put the need for new plantations at 226,000 hectares (15 times the area of the government's forest reserves), the destruction of surviving natural woodland seemed imminent.

But pictures of sites photographed in both 1937 and 1991 show little sign of woodland degradation. A fuel shortage on the scale predicted has not developed, and the district does not import wood or charcoal in large quantities. The miscalculation can be partly explained by the fact that the calculations upon which the predictions were based ignored the use the Akamba make of dead wood, farm trash, branch wood from farm trees, and hedge cuttings for domestic fires. A failure to appreciate a major area of innovative practice – the planting, protection, and systematic harvesting of trees – also contributed to the miscalculation. Meanwhile, forest reservation was unpopular with the Akamba (who suspected the government of alienating them from their land), and its increasing costs and technical difficulty forced a shift to on-farm forestry in the 1970s. While forest policy was shifting to farm forestry promotion, however, a revolution was already occurring, as the following example shows.

Tree densities on Mbiuni's farmlands, according to a survey published in 1982, averaged more than 34 per hectare (14 when bananas are excluded). Furthermore, the smaller the farm, the greater the density. The range of trees planted included both exotic and indigenous fruit and timber species. In general, the Akamba women manage fruit trees, while the Akamba men look after timber trees. [. . .] Owners of grazing land have given details of how they manage the regeneration of woody vegetation, which is used for timber, fuel, fodder, honey production, and edible and medicinal products.

Producing More with Less

These factors – making money from farming, experimenting with staple food options, introducing faster tillage, fertilizing the soil, and changing practices relating to livestock and tree cultivation – contributed to a revolution in farming that was wrought in unpromising circumstances. What were the driving forces behind the changes? Three important developments accompanied population growth in the Machakos District: Landholdings were subdivided among sons; land became increasingly scarce; and grazing land was privately appropriated. These developments have profoundly changed how the land is used in the district. In general, the percentage under cultivation now declines from the wetter to the drier and from the older to the newly settled areas. [. . .]

Over time, as the size of holdings shrank owing to division on inheritance, the cultivated proportion of the district rose, leaving less land for grazing, at the same time the cultivated area per person stagnated. These changes made agricultural intensification and the integration of crop and livestock enterprises within the bounds of family farms imperative.

Two trends – one toward intensive livestock feeding systems and the other toward permanent manured fields, often under plow cultivation – were pivotal in this transformation. The result of these trends is an increasingly efficient system of nutrient cycling through plants, animals, and soil. But the changes could not have occurred without the Akamba custom that the first man to clear and cultivate the land owned it. He was then free to sell it or to pass it on to the sons of the wife who helped to cultivate it. Older sons often established a new farm after their marriage, but, as land became scarce, they insisted on their right to share their mother's land, which earlier they might have relinquished to their youngest brother. Some of those who inherited small farms in the 1960s and 1970s sold them and moved to the new part of the district, but others stayed and invested in improving productivity. Although formal registration of title did not begin in Machakos until 1968, and is not yet complete, the strong customary ownership rights have ensured that the investors and their children reap the rewards of foresight.

Equally important in this transformation were sources of investment capital. To clear and cultivate new land, build hedges, or plant trees often requires hiring labor, tools, and expertise. The off-farm incomes earned outside the district by the Akamba men have contributed for decades to agricultural investment. Such incomes are often high in households with small farms, and there is no evidence that investment per hectare is lower where farmers have little or poor land – quite the contrary.

This process of intensification resulted in an overall increase in the value of output per square kilometer (at constant prices) from 1930 to 1987 (see Figure 8.3).

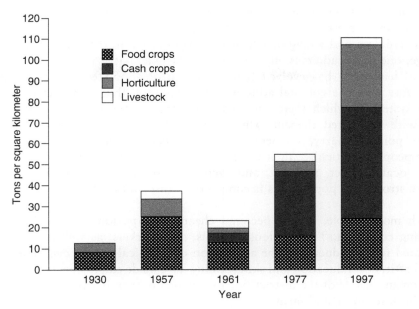

Figure 8.3 The farm output of the Machakos District from 1930 to 1987 in constant 1957 maize prices.

This conclusion was reached by taking output data for the only three years for which data were available before 1974 (1930, 1957, and 1961), selecting two later years (1977 and 1987), and converting all the values into a maize equivalent at 1957 prices. Because 1957 was a good year and 1961 was a severe drought year, the upward trend appears interrupted. The area used in the calculations is that of the district, which includes both arable and grazing land. This area roughly doubled in size after independence, the addition being poorer quality land, yet the upward trend continued. Output per capita closely reflected this curve.

Contrary to the expectations expressed in the 1930s, the Akamba of Machakos have reversed land degradation, conserved and enhanced their free stocks, invested in their farms, and improved their overall productivity.

Facilitating Change

Many social and institutional factors facilitated the agricultural changes in the Machakos District. Between 1930 and 1990, the often polygynous patriarchal family, in which wives and cattle were highly valued, evolved into a smaller unit characterized by greater partnership between a man and (one) wife. With men often away, women were left in charge of the farms. A flexible division of labor and longer working hours are called for in intensive farming, and families may pool their resources for collective effort through membership in *mwethyas*. Women's leadership and participation have been crucial to many of these groups. Although farms are smaller now than they were in the 1930s, labor is still in short supply because children and young people are at school (often to the age of 20), and, on average, one of the adults is engaged in a nonfarm activity.

Local leadership has evolved from a system of appointed chiefs, obliged to collaborate with the colonial administration and not always respected for that, into a system in which there are competing organizations and interest groups, often with an elected element. These include the strong local churches as well as the political party, cooperatives, and other associations. These groups enable people to articulate their needs and to obtain access to resources available at the local, district, national, and even international levels. Such institutions become stronger as populations become more dense and people can interact more easily.

With more people, it also becomes cheaper per person to provide services, including education. The missions, schools, and markets, as well as travel have facilitated formal education, the acquisition of technical knowledge, and experimental attitudes. Education and skill training have made employment for both men and women outside of the district possible, which in turn has brought investment funds back to house and farm.

Government attempts to influence the course of change relied too much, especially before the late 1950s, on coercive or directive methods. Yet from the many techniques tried, with varying success, the Akamba seemed to gain experience that stood them in good stead when, after independence, they came to feel more in control of their resources and destiny.

Were the achievements in Machakos due to disproportionate investments of public funds? From 1947 to 1962, 32 percent of the expenditures of the African Land Development Board in Kenya were committed to the district. Yet much of this was lost (for example, in subsidizing terraces that were not maintained). The most lasting effects of the ALDEV program included 300 small dams, the Makueni resettlement scheme, better farming promotion, and tsetse fly control. More recently, the considerable expenditures of the Machakos Integrated Development Program (MIDP) in the early 1980s did not exceed the average expenditures (on a per-capita basis) for Kenya's semi-arid lands as a whole. The greatest proportion of MIDP's expenditures was on water development because a domestic water supply for expanding settlements has always been a local priority, and its smaller soil conservation program was useful in supplementing local efforts. MIDP's improvements to roads often had only a temporary effect because of a lack of funding for maintenance. While the Akamba have always willingly contributed communal work to roads, the main roads to which feeder roads connect require national resources. Innovation, roads, and population centers are all closely connected.

Particularly since independence, the government's main role in the Machakos transformation was to pursue an open-market path to economic development, provide national economic infrastructure, support individual title to land, and promote channels for learning and communicating new or adapted knowledge.

No Miracle in Machakos?

What happened in Machakos resulted from a combination of factors: increasing population density, market growth, and a generally supportive economic environment. The technological changes in conservation and production cannot be adequately understood as exogenous, as mere accidents that gave breathing space in a remorseless progression toward irreversible environmental degradation and poverty. Instead, as Ester Boserup argued long ago and Julian Simon has argued more recently, they were mothered by necessity. Technological change in Machakos was an endogenous process, which occurred as the Akamba selected and adapted new ideas form multiple sources.

Increasing population density has had positive effects in Machakos. The increasing scarcity (and value) of land promoted investment, both in conservation and in yield-enhancing improvements. Integrating crop and livestock production improved the efficiency of nutrient cycling and, thereby, the sustainability of the farming system. A positive link between productivity and improved resource management is demonstrated. While many changes were small and incremental, larger changes, if evidently profitable, were financed by hard effort and savings (for example, the introduction of the plow) and the planting of coffee and fruit trees.

The Machakos experience offers an alternative to the Malthusian models, which are based on the theory that population tends to increase faster than the resources to provide for it. In addition to Machakos, documented cases of positive associations between increasing population density and environmental conservation and productivity elsewhere in Africa also exist, although it would be foolish to ignore the differences among them and between them and the Machakos experience. Although rapidly degrading farming systems under high densities are rare, under Boserup's hypothesis, degradation is predictable where, at low and rising densities, the preconditions for intensification have not been met. These preconditions are, in addition to an increasing density of population, peace and security for trade and investment and a marketing and tenure system in which the benefits of these are widely shared. Degradation may occur, as it did in Machakos, when the necessity for a change from a long fallowing system is felt, but population density and certain other conditions are not conducive to labor investments, the spread of knowledge, and commercialization. Commercialization adds to the stick of necessity the carrot of incentive for investment in new technologies. Normally, however, as population grows, so do the opportunities for specialization and trade. In Machakos, the expansion of trade and investments, both public and private, that occurred after the restrictions of World War II, provided the conditions in which the adaptation to a more productive farming system was accelerated (although the rising trend in incomes was checked from time to time by climatic or commercial hazards).

Development planners in the past tried to transform farming systems that were seen as inefficient and technically conservative. In fact, the farmers have been changing them themselves, and, as studying them over time shows, there is room to support positive change with appropriate policies. The Machakos study has shown that a high-density population in an area that is steep and dry can be sustained through – and perhaps be driven by – a combination of exogenous and endogenous practices and much local initiative.

Chapter 9

Population Geography and HIV/AIDS: The Challenge of a "Wholly Exceptional Disease"

W. T. S. Gould and R. I. Woods

Introduction

In 1981 when Huw Jones' *Population Geography* was first published, HIV/AIDS was unknown to science; by the time of the Second Edition in 1990 it was certainly known and widely recognised as a major global phenomenon. The condition was specifically mentioned, albeit briefly, in that Second Edition, both in the context of fertility, where it was identified with other sexually transmitted diseases as one of the range of biological proximate determinants of fertility (p. 138), and also and more extensively in the context of mortality, where Huw Jones identified HIV/AIDS as 'a wholly exceptional infectious disease' (p. 58). This paper considers some aspects of how and why the disease is exceptional, and the nature of the challenges this offers to geographers for the study of the disease and its impacts.

The scale and pattern of the global HIV/AIDS pandemic are now well known and readily available to analysts, notably through the web site of the Joint United Nations Programme on AIDS, UNAIDS (www.unaids.org). Table 9.1 summarises the global position by major world region for 2002. An estimated 42 million people, adults and children, are HIV+ (i.e. are clinically affected by the HIV virus), and there were 5 million new infections in 2002, but 3.1 million AIDS deaths in that year. However, Table 9.1 also shows that there is no single epidemic, in the sense of having a uniform causation or means of transmission. In Sub-Saharan Africa, with 70% of the global cases and 70% of new infections in 2002 but 77% of AIDS deaths in that year, the main transmission is through heterosexual sex, with more women affected than men. In Western Europe, North and South America, by contrast, the main agent of transmission is in male homosexual transmission,

Gould, W. T. S. and Woods, R. I., "Population Geography and HIV/AIDS: The Challenge of a 'Wholly Exceptional Disease,'" pp. 265–81 from *Scottish Geographical Journal*, 119.3 (2003).

Table 9.1   Regional HIV/AIDS statistics and features, end of 2002[a]

Region	Adults and children who are HIV+	New infections in 2003	Adult prevalence rate	% HIV+ who are women	main mode(s) of transmission[b]
Sub-Sabaran Africa	29.4 million	3.5 million	8.8%	58%	Hetero
North Africa and Middle East	550,000	83,000	0.3%	55%	Hetero, IDU
South and South-East Asia	6.0 million	700,000	0.6%	36%	Hetero, IDU
East Asia and Pacific	1.2 million	270,000	0.1%	24%	IDU, hetero, MSM
Latin America	1.5 million	150,000	0.6%	30%	MSM, IDU, hetero
Caribbean	440,000	60,000	2.4%	50%	Hetero, MSM
Eastern Europe and Central Asia	1.2 million	250,000	0.6%	27%	IDU
Western Europe	570,000	30,000	0.3%	25%	MSM, IDU
North America	980,000	45,000	0.6%	20%	MSM, IDU, hetero
Australia and New Zealand	15,000	500	0.1%	7%	MSM
Total	42 million	5 million	1.2%	50%	

[a] The proportion of adults (15 to 49 years of age) living with HIV/AIDS in 2002, using 2002 population numbers.
[b] Hetero (heterosexual transmission); IDU (transmission through injecting drug use); MSM (sexual transmission among men who have sex with men).
Source: UNAIDS, *AIDS Epidemic Update, 2002* (UNAIDS: Geneva, 2002), p. 6.

male cases greatly out-numbering females, and in Eastern Europe the main agent of transmission is intravenous drug use. There are also different variants of the virus, further differentiating the regional experience. Such variation within a single pandemic is in itself wholly exceptional.

Geographer' analyses of the causes, patterns and impacts of HIV/AIDS are by now very familiar in the literature. Some of that literature has been very general, especially early work from the mid-1980s on the patterns and diffusion of the disease, driven by assumptions rather than evidence-based work, these assumptions being derived primarily from the study of other diseases, as if HIV/AIDS were not particularly exceptional. By the 1990s, however, there was the appearance of more detailed empirical work, globally as in Smallman-Raynor. Cliff and Haggett's *International Atlas of ALDS* (1992), and particularly in Africa where the syndrome was more apparent and by then making a major impact on economic and social life. Most notable in the early African work was Tony Barnett and Piers Blaikie's still much quoted analysis of the development and impacts of the disease in Uganda (1991), with, for the first time, details of the demography and geography of the disease in Uganda, and in Africa generally, and identify HIV/AIDS as a development problem and not merely a medical one. This was followed by other work on Africa explicitly by geographers, e.g. Douglas Webb's PhD study and subsequent book (1997) on the spatial parameters of the disease in Southern Africa. Recent empirical work by geographers has been on the local impacts in Zambia and Malawi, on sexual behaviour and migration in Ghana and on schooling in Tanzania and Uganda. Much of the most influential work in the social science of HIV/AIDS in Africa has inevitably been inter- and multi-disciplinary, led by medical sciences on the biology, etiology and spread of the disease, and by sociologists, demographers and economists, and in multi-disciplinary teams on the socio-economic impacts of the disease.

In developed countries, where the basic causation has been until recently rather different (primarily through male homosexual sex and intravenous drug use with infected needles rather than heterosexual sex), the study of the geography of the disease has developed in rather different directions. There has been more concern for modelling the spread, using increasingly sophisticated methods, well beyond the naïve and simplistic crude diffusionism of earlier work, epitomised by the late Peter Gould's *The Slow Plague* (1993). This early and highly influential work, rooted in patterns of the disease in the USA, took an essentially apocalyptic diffusion model that was applied globally (including Africa) to predict a very gloomy future of a disease without cure spreading spatially and socially through whole populations. More recent work, such as Craddock's study of AIDS, social identity and risk in Malawi, has integrated AIDS studies into the 'cultural turn', stressing how behaviour dictated by culture and tradition is impacting on the spread and control of the disease.

It is not the intention of this paper to systematically review geographers' work on HIV/AIDS. Nor is it the intention to contribute to the mountain of largely (but not exclusively) pessimistic studies identifying the extent and intractability of the global, regional and local problems associated with HIV/AIDS. A brief encounter with the UNAIDS web site would suffice to introduce that. It is the intention, however, to examine some of the constraints that the nature of the disease imposes on geographical work, and how geographers have dealt with them: why it is 'wholly exceptional', and what this means for integrating discussion of the disease into the mainstream of Population Geography. It is argued in this paper that the disease is wholly exceptional not only in an empirical sense, i.e. because of its new, particular and severe impacts on affected populations, but also in a methodological sense, i.e. because its essential features will have an effect on the ways in which population geographers can approach the analysis of those individuals and societies that are affected by HIV/AIDS.

Why and How is HIV/AIDS Exceptional?

HIV/AIDS is a wholly exceptional infectious disease in three major dimensions: medical, demographic, and behavioural.

Medical

HIV/AIDS is a syndrome (Acquired Immuno-Deficiency Syndrome) rather than a specific condition. The human immuno-deficiency virus (HIV) attacks the body's immune system to make individuals much more susceptible to any infections, many of which are not normally serious or even noticed, but are transmitted into the immune system through bodily fluids and the blood stream through sex or injections, and it is these infections that cause illness and death. The virus can lie dormant for many years – a mean of eight years in developed countries, less in Africa – before the natural immune system begins to collapse. HIV+ individuals then succumb to tuberculosis, pneumonia or other infections, especially where they are ill-nourished. After a period from several months to a few years of being ill, typically associated with severe weight loss, diarrhoea and sickness, they die – often of these infections, commonly of multiple infections. Thus, even where the death is documented by a qualified medical practitioner, as in developed societies, the cause of death is seldom recorded as 'AIDS', but as one of the more familiar direct causes of infectious disease. In Africa, even where there is evidence of two or more infections from a list and the patient is HIV+, with a clear medical diagnosis of AIDS, relatives are typically reluctant to attribute a death to AIDS due to social stigma. Data on AIDS deaths are thus very hard to separately identify and measure, and are certainly not directly available as unambiguous sources for analysts.

Short of performing sero-positivity tests on all dead people as part of a post-mortem (or on dying patients), there will always be a problem of identifying the patterns and prevalence of HIV/AIDS. Given the social and political sensitivity surrounding the disease in all cultures, there have been few national surveys of HIV-prevalence. Even where voluntary tests are encouraged by governments and civil agencies as part of control and monitoring, there is usually a strong resistance to being tested, especially among those who may be at high risk: how will it help them individually to know whether or not they are HIV positive? However, in a recent national survey in the Demographic and Health Survey programme, in Mali in 2003, for the first time there were sero-positivity tests on the national sample. Up till now most data on HIV prevalence rates come from blood tests on women in ante-natal clinics, or from men in hospital visits, both of which have problems of representativeness associated with them. In Africa there are a growing number of HIV/AIDS surveillance sites in most countries, but still too few to produce comprehensive and secure national estimates of prevalence or infection rates. These serious data difficulties, over quality as well as quantity, certainly separate HIV/AIDS from most other infectious diseases in a purely statistical and analytical sense: it is not 'notifiable' in the technical sense in which that term is used in UK and by the World Health Organisation.

Despite the difficulties of quantity and quality of data, much to the fore in the presentation and discussion of data sources in each of the national *Edidemiological Fact Sheets On HIV/AIDS and sexually transmitted diseases* of UNAIDS/WHO/ UNICEF, it is possible to derive global and national estimates of HIV/AIDS prevalence rates. These show a very clearly variable geography at the national and

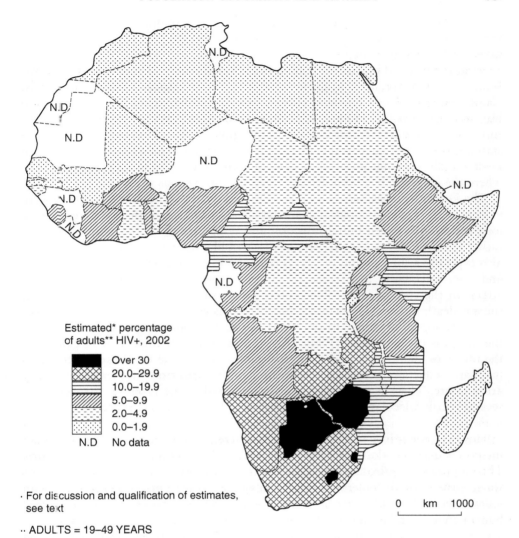

Estimated* percentage
of adults** HIV+, 2002

Over 30
20.0–29.9
10.0–19.9
5.0–9.9
2.0–4.9
0.0–1.9
N.D   No data

· For discussion and qualification of estimates,
  see text

·· ADULTS = 19–49 YEARS

Figure 9.1 Estimated proportion of adults HIV+, Africa, 2002.
Source: UNAIDS, *AIDS Epidemic Update, 2002* (UNAIDS: Geneva, 2002).

regional scale. As noted above and despite substantial under-reporting, 30 million
people in Sub-Saharan Africa were estimated to be HIV+ in 2002, disproportionately concentrated in Southern and Eastern Africa (Figure 9.1), with sero-
prevalence rates of over 30% in the adult population being HIV+ in four countries
(Botswana, Swaziland, Lesotho and Zimbabwe), and South Africa, with a prevalence rate of 20%, having the largest absolute number of infections (5 million adults
and children). Prevalence rates decline northwards and westwards (it is likely that
the Democratic Republic of Congo (formerly Zaire), with its very weak public
health service, is most affected by under-reporting), with all West African countries

having less than 10% sero-prevalence, and most less than 5%. In North Africa prevalence rates are less than 2%, low levels similar to the Middle Eastern countries taken as a whole.

Asia, the next most affected region, has approximately 11 million cases. Prevalence rates, however, are much lower than for most of Africa. These are highest in Cambodia (2.7%) and Thailand (1.8%), but with India having 3.8 million cases, but only 0.8% of the national adult population. The epidemic does not seem to threaten to grow to African levels in this region, though there are fears for substantial spread particularly in China in the next decade. The world region with the most rapidly growing problem is Eastern Europe and the former Soviet Union, where the epidemic has been driven largely by intravenous drug use.

The key differences between HIV/AIDS and most other infectious diseases are evident in their epidemiological characteristics. In particular, there is an extremely long gestation between initial infection and symptoms of illness – typically years rather than the days characteristic of diseases like influenza or measles. There is also typically a long period of illness once the infections begin to have an effect, and eventually build to become the multi-symptom phenomenon of full-blown AIDS. In the case of HIV/AIDS, unlike most other familiar infectious diseases, there is death rather than recovery, for there is as yet no cure for AIDS. Therapies so far developed, notably anti-retroviral drugs, have only been able to slow down the progress of the disease. While these ARVs been very important in extending the life span and greatly improving the quality of lifestyle for those affected and in greatly reducing the vertical transmission of the virus from mother to child, they are no cure. There is a search for a vaccine, with some promise of success but several recent false dawns, so that disease-specific mortality is expected to remain high.

However, the principal epidemiological difference between HIV/AIDS and other infectious diseases, thus affecting its geography, is in terms of risk and exposure. The virus is not environmental in that it is not airborne (as with tuberculosis) or waterborne (as with cholera); it is not contagious (as with measles); nor is there an animal vector (as with malaria or bubonic plague). It is caused by direct human/human contact and exchange of bodily fluids in heterosexual or male homosexual sex, or through contaminated blood, whether in 'normal' medically supervised blood transfusion or through contaminated needle use. It is an unexpected consequence of normative behaviour by adults in their everyday lives. Individual risk of infection has no simple spatial relationship with distance, as at the heart of standard diffusion models, but rather it is a function of these interpersonal 'interactions', mostly though sexual encounters. As will be more fully discussed below, sexual behaviour and frequency of and nature of the sexual encounter and number of sexual partners are the critical variables. They are behavioural rather than biological, culture bound and often based on tradition.

Demographic

Population geography typically interacts with health matters through demographic analysis. The mortality revolution of the last 100 years has been largely associated with the control of infectious diseases, with substantial falls in mortality, even in the poorest countries due to the improved treatments, or even, in the case of small-pox, its eradication. The greatest impacts have been on childhood survival with sharp falls in infant and childhood mortality rates, led in developing countries by improved sanitation and living conditions and by vaccination programmes. In direct contrast however, the main direct effects of AIDS mortality and morbidity are among adults, and particularly in the sexually active age groups, roughly 15–50. No other infectious disease affects young adults primarily, and therefore resulting in sharp rises in adult mortality rates for both sexes, and associated reductions in the standard life-table based indices of expectation of life, both in the standard measure of expectancy of life at birth (e_0), but more spectacularly in expectancy of life at 15 years (e_{15}). In extreme cases of high AIDS prevalence, as in the countries of southern Africa, life expectancy at birth had been improving substantially between about 1950 and 1980, in particular as a result of sharply falling infant and childhood mortality. As a result of HIV/AIDS, they have now regressed to levels they were at more than 50 years ago. In the early 1990s the life expectancy at birth in South Africa had risen to over 65 years, but by 2000 it was less than 57 and falling due to AIDS mortality. Both males and females are affected, but female prevalence rates are typically 10–20% higher than those of males in Africa. In developed countries, where the epidemic has in the past been dominated by male mortality and associated with homosexual transmission, the male:female ratio has been changing rapidly as a result of the growing relative importance of heterosexual transmission, often associated with immigrant popula-tions, especially from Africa. In the UK it is estimated that by 2002 there were more AIDS cases as a result of heterosexual transmission than of male homosexual transmission.

The demographic effects are most clearly demonstrated by the typical age/sex pyramid of affected populations. In Africa it is estimated that about 30% of children born to HIV+ mothers are themselves HIV+, and very few of these survive beyond five years. Fortunately this proportion is being reduced as a result of the increasing targetting of anti-retroviral drugs to pregnant HIV+ women. There is now also evidence of reduced fertility among HIV+ women, partly as a result of lower natural fecundity of infected and ill women, but also as a result of behavioural and relationship changes where one or both partners in a relationship is HIV+. Figure 9.2 shows a projection done in 1999 of the age/sex structure of the population of South Africa by 2009, including the age and sex distribution of the over 6 million people expected to die of AIDS by that date. The greatest demographic impact is clearly on the mortality of young adults, at rather older ages for males than for females, and on infants. The national impact of losing large numbers of people in the economically active age groups is sharply and adversely altering traditional 'age dependency' ratios in affected populations. This has immediate adverse economic effects, as in the likely effects of HIV/AIDS and associated rural labour force declines in exacerbating the current famine conditions in southern Africa through production shortfalls. The child-hood mortality indicated is associated directly with mother/child transfer of infantile AIDS.

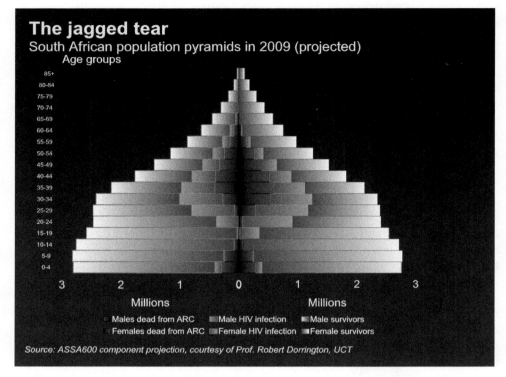

Figure 9.2   Projected age and sex structure and AIDS deaths, South Africa, 2009.
Source: R. C. H. Shell, "Halfway to the Holocaust: The Rapidity of the HIV/AIDS Pandemic in South Africa and its Social, Economic and Demographic Consequences." In *The African Population in the 21st Century*. Proceedings of the Third African Population Conference. Dakar: IUSSP/Union for African Population Studies, 1999, Volume 1, pp. 145–66; p. 164.

Behavioural

As noted above, HIV/AIDS is primarily a condition associated with behaviour and lifestyle choice. In Africa, where causation dominated by heterosexual transmission, this makes the factors responsible more akin to typical factors in fertility than in mortality. Whereas mortality is typically affected by large scale and impersonal structural factors, such as the economic condition of the population, the condition of health services and public health measures, all of which are beyond the direct control of individuals, fertility in modern contracepting societies is a matter of choice, and even in more traditional societies still with contraceptive prevalence rates of less than 50%, fertility levels have been shown to be associated with cultural values and individual or household economic relations, including intergenerational flows of wealth and gender relations, rather than impersonal macro-economic or social circumstances. In modern societies where the structural conditions are largely controlled, mortality fluctuates less over time and varies less between socio-economic groups than does fertility, affected as it is by cultural values and behaviour affecting individual decisions. HIV/AIDS, like conception, can be avoided, at least in Africa, if high risk unprotected heterosexual sex can be avoided. Behavioural change, notably having fewer sexual partners and having condom-protected sex, has been very important in reducing and controlling infection rates, more in developed countries than in Africa. However, even in Africa, and most notably in Uganda where, uniquely, prevalence rates have been falling since the mid-1990s, and in other developing areas, notably in Thailand, behavioural change has been a strong and sometimes successful target for public health programmes, especially for adolescents.

More broadly, it is clear that understanding the spatial social patterning of HIV/AIDS must involve a full appreciation of power relations in societies. The behaviours that are associated with infections and risks of infection, not only in the heterosexual epidemics in Africa, but also in the other transmission contexts of male homosexual and intravenous drug use, are conditioned by gender, generational and socio-economic status relationships that have brought so much insight to the recent work of social and cultural geographers. The behavioural characteristics of HIV/AIDS are exceptional, and thus require similar new insights.

HIV/AIDS clearly has unique characteristics that certainly justify the description of 'wholly exceptional'. The medical, demographic and behavioural aspects identified above all overlap to give the syndrome a distinctiveness that presents a very different set of patterns and relationships from other infectious diseases, and therefore presents very specific challenges to analysts, including population geographers, to integrate the disease and its effects into their discourses and methodologies. In the following sections of this paper, the relevance of two of the leading models used by population geographers – the Demographic Transition Model and the Disease Diffusion Model – are elaborated for AIDS-affected populations. The paper concludes by linking the approaches required by population geographers to discuss a primarily behavioural disease within the more behavioural dimensions of recent work in Demography and Geography.

HIV/AIDS and the Demographic Transition Model

The Demographic Transition Model (DTM) has been central to geographers' analysis of population change over time. The 'transition' describes the process of moving from a high equilibrium and low growth, with a balance of births and deaths at pre-industrial levels, to a low equilibrium and also low growth, but with the balance of births and deaths at post-industrial levels. In pre-industrial societies, with examples from all regions of the world, there needed to be high fertility (with a crude birth rate of 35–40/1000, i.e. a Total Fertility Rate (TFR) of about five children) to compensate for a high mortality. Life expectancy at birth was perhaps only 30–35 years, but mortality fluctuated substantially from year to year as a result of crisis mortality associated with epidemics or famines. The transition to a low equilibrium is associated with mortality falling from crude death rates of 35–40/1000 to 10–15/1000 as life expectancy at birth rose to over 70 in most developed societies. It was then followed, first in Europe but thereafter in most other global regions, by fertility decline from crude birth rates of 35–40/1000 to about 10–15/1000, and a near replacement TFR of two children per woman: from high level homeostasis towards low level homeostasis. Globally the transition is far from complete, but UN and most other estimates are that there is a high probability that it will be complete by about 2050, with a global population levelling out at about 9 billion compared with the estimated 6 billion for 2000.

While the conceptual validity of the DTM as a global model is not uncontested, it seems to have an empirical justification, at least for its early stages. Most analytical controversy is about the drivers and triggers of the transition. It would appear from the experience of the developed world and more recently in East Asia that population change has been driven by economic development in its various forms, more strongly associated with income growth in some countries, with urbanisation in others, with industrialisation in yet others, and with associated social and legislative changes (especially associated with abortion, as in Japan) in others. Overall, however, mortality decline has been associated with both livelihood improvements (better nutrition, better housing, better environmental conditions) and also improved medical knowledge and care; by contrast, fertility decline has been more directly associated with the social changes – in family structures and individual relationships, including the status of women – that have accompanied the economic development. The classic low equilibrium outcome of the DTM assumes technical and economic control over mortality, and that fertility levels have adjusted, often 'spontaneously', to these low mortality levels.

But what levels of mortality are the triggers for fertility decline to begin? Caldwell has argued that the experience of developed countries is that fertility transition began when infant mortality rates had fallen below 70/1000, and fertility in Asia did begin to fall in most countries in the 1970s when the infant mortality rate had indeed fallen below 70. However, it seems that fertility transition has begun in Africa (in that fertility seems to have fallen by over 10% in most countries over the last 10 years), but the infant mortality rate remains stubbornly well above 70/1000 in most countries. The triggers that others have identified do not seem to be universally applicable, but are variable from context to context.

However in HIV/AIDS-affected populations in Africa there currently seems to be little prospect in the medium term of mortality falling to these threshold levels. Even the substantial achievements in infant mortality declines, so noticeable in the 1970s and 1980s, seem to have stalled, and have even gone into reverse in some countries. In Kenya, for example, infant mortality rates rose from a low of nearly 60/1000 in the mid-1980s to 73/1000 in the 1998 DHS, and under-five mortality from 90/1000 to 111/1000 in the same period, in part attributable to declining health services, in part to vertical transmission of HIV from infected mothers to their infants. More powerfully, as AIDS drives sharp increases in adult mortality and as overall life expectancy at birth falls rapidly for so many African countries, with the possibility for other regions being affected as the disease spreads, mortality seems to be going into a medium- to long-term reverse that was not anticipated in the classic DTM formulations.

This provides a further justification of the notion of a 'crisis-led fertility transition': that the trends towards lower fertility in developing countries, and particularly in Africa, should be construed not in terms of economic improvement, as in the classic explanation of demographic transition, but rather in terms of economic and social crisis, clearly exacerbated by HIV/AIDS. Even though there have been nearly three decades of severe economic recession in Africa since the mid-1970s, mortality continued to fall till the 1990s, and fertility decline seemed to begin in the 1980s. These falls were certainly sharper in the richer countries (notably South Africa, Botswana, Zimbabwe, Kenya) than elsewhere. However, in each of these countries the fertility declines began at times of relative economic recession and were led by urban populations and those in relatively prosperous rural regions where the desire for smaller families, felt mostly by relatively well educated couples, was increasingly felt. Furthermore, the rather lower fertility of HIV+ women further contributed to fertility decline in HIV/AIDS-affected countries. Equally importantly, the desire for smaller families was increasingly realisable with the widespread availability of modern contraception, provided often as part of externally funded population programmes. Such changes would seem to suggest changes in a range of social institutions (e.g. marriage, households, inheritance) were associated with the economic downturns, and these contributed to continuing fertility declines.

So there seems to have been rising mortality but falling fertility in Africa. Nevertheless, though the overall rates of population growth are falling more sharply than hitherto, they remain high: over 2% per year in most African countries. With further rises in mortality predicted as a result of HIV/AIDS but continuing falls in fertility, there is every prospect of a new demographic equilibrium being reached in Africa. This might be struck at a crude death rate of about 20/1000, or a life expectancy at birth of about 45 years (lower than the expectancy of recent years), and a crude birth rate at about the same level of about 20/1000, corresponding to a TFR of about 3.5–4 children. In conditions of high mortality this TFR might represent replacement fertility, and with it the prospects for a new homeostasis, hopefully relatively short-lived given the medium-term prospects of affordable drugs and effective vaccines.

These demographic effects of HIV/AIDS, in the absence of any cure for or eradication of the disease, do not undermine the validity of the predictive presumption in the DTM of a transition from high to low equilibrium, but these exceptional features and effects may introduce a stage in that transition of homeostasis at a higher equilibrium level. Given the difference in the strength and nature of the epidemic between major world regions, they may also require some region-specific reassessment of any expected mortality threshold that may trigger fertility declines. Incorporating AIDS-driven mortality reversal into the DTM not only weakens the model's general applicability, but it casts even more doubt on the wisdom of drawing predictive lessons from Europe's demographic past.

HIV/AIDS and Diffusionism

The study of spatial diffusion has been enormously important to population and medical geographers, as it has to colleagues in other areas of the discipline. The concept has been most widely applied in population analysis at the global scale in the global diffusion of the fertility transition, with its most influential manifestation in the 1984 *World Development Report* of the World Bank, explicitly extending Coale and Watkins' (1986) study of the diffusion of European fertility decline to the global scale. While the excesses of seeing diffusion as a purely spatial process separated from any human agency have long been widely condemned and modified, this does not apply to the study of disease diffusion in a purely epidemiological sense. For many diseases there are purely spatial processes of contagion at work, but even these may also be affected by human agency.

HIV/AIDS at first sight lends itself to a diffusionist approach that would be applicable to any infectious disease, and operationalised through spatial modelling. Among the earliest studies of the disease by a geographer was Peter Gould's (1993), which adopted a strongly deterministic diffusionist perspective. He argued that since data on HIV/AIDS in any context are not only patchy in quantity and spatial coverage, but also intrinsically unreliable and subject to deliberate as well as technical misenumeration, geographers would find spatial diffusion models to be highly appropriate to any examination of the spread of the disease. This allowed him to come to the essentially pessimistic conclusions about the disease in general, identifying Africa in particular as a 'continent in catastrophe':

> Nowhere in the world can we see the tragic effects of hierarchical and spatially contagious diffusion so devastatingly at work as in the continent of Africa.

> But we know, as geographers, a great deal about how things spread in space and time over a map structured by human beings. The metaphor of a 'spot height' is not an idle one: our map is the crude estimated topography of the pandemic, with high peaks, the connecting ridges and the low valleys of infection extrapolated from what we know. . . . It is a devastating picture, and it will get worse over the next decade; the black on the map round the spot heights will enlarge to the medium grey tone; this will spread to the light grey, and this in turn will enclose the areas still relatively free.

This is very much 'a ripples in a pool' conceptualisation, based on purely spatial assumptions about the nature of spread and a fairly even and essentially predictable distribution of risk away from existing foci of infection, citing a range of evidence about the role of transportation networks and of migrants in the spread of the disease.

Jack and Pat Caldwell at about the same time were offering a radically different perspective that has proved to be much more insightful and a better prediction of what we now know a decade further into the epidemic. Their approach, as sociologists but explicitly using a series of large scale maps, focused on the human constraints on diffusion rather than spatial contagion:

> There are marked geographic differentials in the HIV/AIDS epidemic, especially rural/urban ones that look like a simple pattern of diffusion, eventually spreading the epidemic evenly across each country. There is probably some diffusion, and rural HIV/AIDS will likely rise. But marked rural/urban differences will probably continue.

They argue against a universal and inevitable diffusion of the disease in favour of differentiated patterns in which the early foci will experience increasing prevalence, since there is a large pool of infection. In low prevalence areas, by contrast, there may be strong behavioural (e.g. the nature of urban areas and social relationships in West Africa) and epidemiological (i.e. too small a pool of infectives) reasons for hypothesising a continuing low incidence in many areas:

> clearly the present Sub-Saharan AIDS epidemic will continue to spread, but it will not engulf the whole region in the kind of epidemic that Uganda, Zambia or Mali are experiencing. The greatest further spread, as measured by the number of new cases, may be within the uncircumcised belt itself . . . Elsewhere there will be some kind of stability, although national levels of 15–20% sero-positive are not impossible. Some countries may remain relatively unscathed.

Although the picture in 2003 is not quite as optimistic as the Caldwells had predicted, the current situation in Africa is much nearer their view than it is to Peter Gould's. As Figure 9.1 has shown, there are now seven countries with over 20% sero-positivity, four of them with over 30%, with the greatest growth and most serious problems in the male 'uncircumcised' belt of Southern and Central Africa. But West Africa remains generally much less affected, although the areas of much higher prevalence in the earlier period, notably Côte d'Ivoire, remain countries of higher prevalence, and with still relatively low rates in Nigeria (despite recent evidence of some growth), Ghana and Senegal, three major countries with substantial international exposure where rates might have been expected to have risen sharply.

There has certainly been a spread to rural areas from the original urban and transport routes focus, to some extent 'hierarchical and spatially contagious' diffusion in Peter Gould's terms. As infected urban migrants return to their rural homes, they will spread the infection to their wives and to other sexual partners. So too with the mobile 'high risk' carriers, truckers, traders and fishermen, as they travel along the transport routes. If distance and spatial networks and hierarchies were the only factors at work then indeed Gould's pessimism would be justified.

However, we now have evidence for substantial behavioural change in some countries and in some areas that are modifying the patterns of prevalence and the patterns of spread. Uganda is the leader in this respect. It was the first country to be seriously affected by the epidemic, and had the highest national rates till the mid-1990s. However, its recorded national sero-positive rate has fallen from a peak of 13% in 1996 to 5% for 2002 (the most recently available national figure), the only country to have recorded such a fall. Just as important as the decline in the national prevalence is the fact that the greatest decline has been in urban areas, and especially among the adolescent urban population. The UNAIDS *Epidemiological Fact Sheet* for Uganda identifies rural rates to be falling, though only slightly, and these remain below the urban rates. There is very strong evidence of a substantial behavioural change by the educated and urban groups in favour of safe sex (i.e. protected by condoms) and a reduction in the number of sexual partners. Uganda has seen major public education campaigns, led directly by President

Museveni himself, and these have clearly had a great effect in bringing behaviour change. This of course is in stark contrast to the situation in South Africa, where the political leadership of President Thabo Mbeki has been hostile to HIV/AIDS campaigns, perhaps a symptom of national denial, but in a context of an acutely deteriorating situation of high and rising HIV/AIDS prevalences in both urban and rural areas.

The key point here is that, since the patterns of spread of the infection can be controlled through behaviour change, human agency becomes the key factor. Passive contagion, a core assumption of classic disease diffusion models, is not appropriate for HIV/AIDS; by contrast, human intervention and human decision-making can alter both the level and the distribution of the disease. These structures also apply in developed countries, with their rather different causation and levels of infection, as well as in Africa. Diseases directly associated with aspects of human behaviour and with geographies that can be significantly altered by the behaviour of those 'at risk' are clearly not consistent with the assumptions and models of crude spatial diffusionism.

Population Geography and Human Behaviour

This discussion has emphasised the distinctiveness of HIV/AIDS as a lifestyle condition, a 'behavioural' infection, a syndrome associated in the most affected parts of the world with very basic human behaviour – sexual activity – as its primary proximate determinant. Since its patterns and rates are therefore a function of behavioural parameters, of culture and choice rather than structure and passivity, its analytical discourse must move towards the behavioural, to the study of human agency and individual choices in a range of cultural and economic contexts, including engaging with debates over such difficult but clearly central issues such as human sexuality, as in the classic exchange on the nature of African sexuality between Caldwell and Ahlberg.

In this respect Population Geography has a great deal in common with demographic analysis, where there has been a distinct effort in recent years to complement traditional statistical analysis and modelling with more qualitative and anthropological methodologies. The particular stimulus to such a change has been associated with Susan Greenhalgh's edited collection, *Situating Fertility* (1995), and an associated collection of papers on qualitative methods in Demography in *Population and Development Review* in 1997. As has been argued, the background and proximate determinants of HIV/AIDS have behavioural characteristics that make them more akin to the background and proximate determinants of fertility than to the essentially structural and biological determinants of mortality. Methodologies now associated with fertility analysis, including a range of in-depth qualitative investigation techniques at the individual, household and community scales, seems to be more appropriate for HIV/AIDS analysis than the narrowly statistical and broad survey methodologies that have traditionally been used, and are still being used, by geographers and others for mortality analysis more generally. Feelings and emotions play their part too in contemporary demographic perspectives on mortality, as in discussion of infant deaths. Clearly HIV/AIDS can also attract considerable emotional involvement. HIV/AIDS can also be analysed from the broader social science perspectives of human rights (associated, in particular, with economic denial of ARV treatments to the majority of those affected in Africa) or of poverty alleviation programmes.

In this respect Demography and Geography have been moving along similar methodological trajectories in seeking interpretations of human behaviour. In their search for further methodological rigour, population geographers have thoroughly debated the relationships between demographic and geographical epistemologies, and especially since Findlay and Graham argued the case for more Geography (on the presumption that it is more culturally sensitive to human agency) and less Demography (on the presumption that it is positivist and statistical) in Population Geography. With hindsight these debates now seem to have been based on a false dichotomy of essential difference between the disciplines. There are now stronger similarities between them than there seemed to be a decade ago, and nowhere are these more apposite than in the study of HIV/AIDS. Behavioural population analysis can be given a great boost by further work by geographers on HIV/AIDS, in developed and in developing countries, and the extent of severe economic and social disruption associated with high prevalences of HIV/AIDS strongly suggests that the challenges of this 'wholly exceptional disease' to population geographers are not only empirical and practical, but also methodological.

Chapter 10

Interprovincial Migration, Population Redistribution, and Regional Development in China: 1990 and 2000 Census Comparisons

C. Cindy Fan

Introduction

It is well known that migration is an important factor of population redistribution and that it is strongly related to regional economic development. A large body of literature has examined these relationships. Most migration studies, however, focus on capitalist economies where decisions at the individual and household levels constitute the primary determinants of migration. This assumption is less valid in socialist and transitional economies. During much of the socialist period in China, especially from the late 1950s to the early 1980s, rural–urban migration was strictly controlled. Since the mid-1980s, economic reforms and the relaxation of migration controls have brought about sharp increase in mobility. These changes hint at new roles and conceptualizations of migration in the Chinese economy, which can be summarized by two notions. First, migration has become a more effective factor of population redistribution, and, second, the relationship between migration and regional development is becoming stronger. In this article, I examine these themes by analyzing interprovincial migration data from China's 1990 and 2000 censuses.

Compared to most capitalist economies, China's population mobility is low. Intercounty migrants between the years 1985 and 1990 accounted for, respectively, 19 percent and 4 percent of the US and Chinese populations aged five and above in 1990. In the same period, the rate of interstate migration in the US was 9 percent, while its counterpart in China – rate of interprovincial migration – was only 1 percent. The interstate/interprovincial migration rate for the 1995–2000 period was 8 percent in the US and 3 percent in China, indicating a narrower, but still

Fan, C. Cindy, "Interprovincial Migration, Population Redistribution, and Regional Development in China: 1990 and 2000 Census Comparisons," pp. 295–309 from *Professional Geographer*, 57.2 (2005).

large, gap in mobility. The recent and substantial surge in mobility in China, however, signals that migration is playing an increasingly central role in shaping its demographic and economic landscape. What also makes China interesting are the ways in which economic reforms and uneven regional development have driven population movement.

In the next section, I briefly review established theoretical perspectives relating migration to regional development. This is followed by two background sections on China, focusing on changes between the socialist and transitional periods and on data issues. Then, the first part of the empirical analysis assesses the effect of interprovincial migration on population redistribution and the second part examines the relationship between migration and regional development in China.

Theories of Migration

Most macrolevel theories on migration deal with the relationships between mobility on one hand and regional development and population redistribution on the other. Ravenstein's (1889) laws of migration introduced the notion that people move in order to better themselves economically. In this view, migration is considered as the individual's response to regional differentials in economic development. Similarly, neoclassical theory views migration as an outcome of geographic differences in labor demand and supply and of individuals' rational calculation of costs and returns. At the same time, neoclassical theorists see migration as an equilibrating tool and predict that labor movement from low-wage to high-wage areas will eventually even out regional wage differentials. On the contrary, researchers subscribing to structural approaches emphasize the cumulative causation of regional growth and contend that flows of human resources from peripheral, less-developed regions, to core, more-developed regions, will accelerate polarization. Regardless of which view one adopts, it is quite clear that the relationship between migration and regional economic development is a "chicken or egg" one. One scenario, for example, is that economic and employment growth induces labor in-migration, which further boosts investment and economic growth. Such a relationship has been analyzed by methods that identify bidirectional causality, such as simultaneous equations.

Studies of both developed and developing countries have emphasized the role of migration in population redistribution and regional development. For example, research has identified the snowbelt–sunbelt shifts of jobs and population as key processes that accelerated the economic development of southern and western US since the 1960s. In Japan, increased and renewed concentration of population in the Tokyo metropolitan region has played an important role shaping its space economy. In these advanced industrialized economies, natural increase is low, and thus, migration is an especially important explanation of regional variation of population growth. But even in developing countries that have relatively high rates of natural increase, internal migration contributes to uneven population distribution and regional development. The continued growth of core regions in, for example, Ecuador, Philippines, and Egypt, is the outcome of net migration from their respective peripheral regions.

Most migration studies deal with contexts where "free-individual" migration is the norm. In socialist and transitional economies, however, mobility control limits the magnitude and impact of migration. In the former Soviet Union, migration was subject to official approval. Even after the late 1980s, mobility in Russia was still unduly affected by the legacy of the Soviet-period registration system and access to services and resources tied to that system. Likewise, migration control exists in China (covered in the next section).

Migration in Socialist and Transitional China

Central planning is a key factor in understanding migration during China's socialist period. Mao's radical ideology led to the sending of urban youths to the countryside and to remote regions in the 1960s and 1970s. The Third Front program between the mid-1960s and early 1970s involved the transfer of resources, including human resources, from more developed coastal provinces to relatively poor and remote provinces in central and western China. Contrary to neoclassical logic, therefore, migration took place down, rather than up, the gradient of development. This was mainly due to the socialist state's adoption of egalitarian ideology and its use of migration as a tool of political and economic planning.

The *hukou* (household registration) system curtailed self-initiated moves and limited migration from rural to urban areas. This system, implemented in the late 1950s and still being enforced today, assigns a hukou location (*hukou suozaidi*) to every Chinese citizen. For the most part, these placed-based statuses are inherited from one's parents. The details of the hukou system have been extensively reviewed elsewhere and are not repeated here. Suffice it to say that, until the mid-1980s, the system strictly controlled rural–urban migration because only persons with an urban hukou had access to jobs, housing, food, and other necessities in urban areas.

After the late 1970s, China began to transform itself into a "socialist market economy," whereby market mechanisms operated alongside central planning legacies. During this transitional period, the state undertook a developmental role and actively pursued economic reforms, including refocusing investment to coastal, more developed provinces, and opened the economy to foreign investors. Much of the new investment occurred in labor-intensive manufacturing such as garments and consumer electronics. It became increasingly clear over time that cheap labor from rural areas would facilitate the type of industrialization being pursued and that strict migration control was not compatible with such a strategy. Moreover, rapid development of sectors such as construction and services in urban areas accelerated the demand for cheap labor. Since the mid-1980s, therefore, the state has relaxed migration control, enabling the movement of rural labor to urban areas. Yet the state continued to withhold urban hukou from rural migrants, who could now survive in cities because markets for housing and daily necessities existed but who were still denied access to the full array of jobs and subsidized services available to urban residents. These migrants were channeled to low-paid, manual jobs, and the bottom rung of urban society. I have argued elsewhere that by relaxing migration controls and continuing to deny migrants urban hukou status, the state has fostered a migrant labor regime in order to accelerate industrialization at a low cost.

The peculiar institutional structure reviewed above has given rise to the coexistence of "permanent migrants" – migrants whose movements are state sponsored or officially recognized and are thus accompanied by hukou change – and "temporary migrants" whose movements are self-initiated and not associated with hukou change. The term "floating population" (*liudong renkou*) loosely describes temporary migrants. Not surprisingly, increased mobility since the 1980s is largely attributable to temporary migrants. Further relaxation of the hukou system in the 1990s, especially in towns and small cities, continued to boost migration.

The analysis in this article focuses on the relationships between migration on one hand and population redistribution and regional development on the other hand during the transitional period. First, as China's natural increase declines, in part due to a draconian birth control policy, migration is expected to be an increasingly effective factor of population redistribution. Second, economic reforms have widened the development gaps between regions. Economic growth, job opportunities, and higher wages in more developed regions exert a strong pull to migrants from poorer regions. Third, migrants from poor provinces are the major source of cheap labor to facilitate industrialization in more developed regions, further accelerating the latter's economic growth. Thus, the relationship between migration and regional development is expected to be strong and bidirectional. Indeed, the reciprocal relationships between migration and regional development are often implied, if not explicitly analyzed, in recent studies on China. In this article, the analysis seeks to document the similarities of the spatial patterns of interprovincial migration and uneven regional development. Compared with intraprovincial migration, interprovincial migration is a more prominent factor of population redistribution and economic development at the national and regional levels.

Chinese Migration Data

The first Chinese census that provided systematic information about migration occurred in 1990. The most recent census, taken in 2000, also recorded information about migration. Sample surveys between the two censuses provided estimates of population chage but offered much less detail.

China's National Bureau of Statistics, which conducts census surveys, uses two main criteria to define migration. The first criterion is spatial. The 1990 census defined a migrant as a person five years or older who on 1 July 1990 resided in a county-level unit (hereafter, counties) different from that on 1 July 1985. This criterion is similar to that used in the US population census, which requires that an individual must have moved across a county boundary during the five years prior to the census in order to be defined a migrant.

The second census criterion is temporal and is tied to the concept of hukou. In the 1990 census, in addition to satisfying the spatial criterion, an individual must (1) have moved his/her hukou to the place of enumeration or (2) have physically stayed in the place of enumeration or have left the hukou location for more than one year, in order to be defined as a migrant. The first condition defines permanent migrants and the second condition defines temporary migrants. These two terms refer to hukou status rather than the duration of stay. As described earlier, even though a migrant may have stayed in a destination for an extended period of time, he/she is still considered a temporary migrant so long as he/she has not managed to move the hukou to the destination. In this regard, urban hukou assumes the function of urban citizenship.

By definition, the 1990 census did not include migrants who died between 1985 and 1990, migrants under five years of age in 1990, migrants who returned to the place of origin by the time of the census, and migrants who moved within counties, nor did it document multiple moves. These are limitations similar to those in censuses conducted in other parts of the world. In addition, the one-year temporal criterion excluded short-term migrants, that is, those who stayed in the destination for less than one year or left the hukou location for less than one year. All of the above suggests that the census underestimated population movement and that caution must be taken when interpreting migration data.

The 2000 census used different spatial and temporal criteria for defining migration. The spatial criterion changed to the subcounty level, and the temporal criterion changed to six months. Thus, a migrant was defined as an individual who on 1 November 2000 resided in a subcounty-level unit different from that on 1 November 1995 and who (1) had moved his/her hukou to the place of enumeration or (2) had stayed in the place of enumeration for more than six months or had left the hukou location for more than six months. Both the spatial and temporal changes increased the number of migrants. In particular, persons who moved between subcounty-level units but within a county were not considered migrants in the 1990 census but were counted as migrants in the 2000 census. Thus, the total migration volumes from the two censuses are not comparable. Indeed, the censuses documented a substantial increase in the number of intraprovincial migrants – from 24 million or 2 percent of the age 5+ population in 1990 to 91 million or 7 percent of the age 5+ population in 2000. This surge in volume reflects not only actual mobility increases but also the changes in the census definition.

Clearly, definitional changes present a challenge to researchers wishing to compare data across census intervals. This article focuses on interprovincial migration, which is less problematic than intraprovincial migration for comparison purposes because data for the former are not affected by spatial criterion change. The 2000 census documented a total of 33 million interprovincial migrants, accounting for 3 percent of the age 5+ population in 2000, compared to the respective figures of 12 million and 1 percent in 1990. The effect of the temporal criterion change – from one year to six months – is difficult to determine. However, since the literature suggests that mobility did increase significantly in the 1990s, it is reasonable to assume that the surge in interprovincial migration between the 1990 and 2000

Table 10.1 Interprovincial migration

	1985–1990	1995–2000
Volume (million)	10.76	31.81
Rate (% of 5 + population)	1.06	2.72
In-migration rate (% of 5 + population)		
Highest	6.59 (Beijing)	14.43 (Guangdong)
Lowest	0.42 (Guangxi)	0.54 (Henan)
Standard deviation	1.44	4.13
Out-migration rate (% of 5 + population)		
Highest	2.48 (Qinghai)	7.12 (Jiangxi)
Lowest	0.45 (Guangdong)	0.55 (Guangdong)
Standard deviation	0.46	1.62
Net migration rate (% of 5 + population)		
Highest	5.37 (Beijing)	13.88 (Guangdong)
Lowest	−1.04 (Guangxi)	−6.49 (Jiangxi)
Standard deviation	1.43	5.09
Migration effectiveness		
System	28.28	63.31
Provincial		
Highest	68.62 (Beijing)	92.67 (Guangdong)
Lowest	−55.44 (Guangxi)	−83.85 (Jiangxi)
Standard deviation	32.34	56.18

Tibet is excluded and Chongqing is combined with Sichuan.
Source: State Statistical Bureau, *Zhongguo renkou tongji nianjian 1992* [China Population Statistical Yearbook 1992] (Beijing: China Statistical Publishing House, 1992); National Bureau of Statistics, *Zhongguo 2000 nian renkou pucha ziliao*, Vol. 1 and 2 [Tabulation on the 2000 Population Census of the People's Republic of China] (Beijing: China Statistics Press, 2002).

census was primarily due to a mobility increase. In their recent analysis of census and sample survey data from 1987 to 2000, Cai and Wang suggest that migration data based on different statistical criteria be used primarily to compare changes in migration directions. Along the same vein, this article's analysis focuses more on changes in spatial patterns than on changes in volume.

The empirical analysis in this article excludes Tibet because of data limitations. And, since Chongqing was not a separate province until 1996, it is combined with Sichuan. After these adjustments, the analysis includes twenty-nine provinces. In this data set, the volume of interprovincial migration is 11 million and 32 million in 1990 and 2000, respectively; and the migration rate is 1 percent in 1990 and 3 percent in 2000 (Table 10.1). Because, at the time of this article's writing, published data from the 2000 census do not report the hukou status of migrants, the empirical analysis includes all migrants and does not separately examine permanent migrants and temporary migrants.

Migration and Population Redistribution

I assess here the effect of interprovincial migration on population redistribution by examining migration rates, migration effectiveness, and the correlation between migration and population growth. First, Table 10.1 depicts that provincial migration rates diverged between the 1990 and 2000 censuses. The standard deviation of in-migration, out-migration, and net migration rates increased from 1 percent, 0.5 percent, and 1 percent to 4 percent, 2 percent, and 5 percent, respectively. Guangdong had the highest in-migration rate in 2000, more than twice the highest rate in 1990 (Beijing); Jiangxi, on the other hand, had the highest out-migration rate in 2000, almost triple the highest rate in 1990 (Qinghai). The range of net migration rates also increased, and Guangdong and Jiangxi had the highest and lowest rates in 2000, respectively. These changes indicate that gainers are adding more population from migration and sending areas are losing more through it.

[. . .]

Migration and Regional Development

The large regional disparity in economic development in China is well documented. The "three economic belts," a product of the seventh Five-Year Plan (1985–1990) that conceptualized the nation as comprising three regions, each having its own comparative advantage and economic specialization, provides a convenient regionalization scheme to describe the level and changes of regional inequality (Figure 10.1). Using GDP per capita as a proxy for the level of economic development, Figure 10.2 illustrates the gap between the three regions and the trend of interprovincial inequality since the mid-1980s. It is clear that the eastern region has had the most rapid economic growth and, as a result, differences between this region and the central and western regions widened over time. In 2001, GDP per capita for the eastern region as a whole stood at 12,071 yuan, nearly two times that of the central region and over two times that of the western region. The gap between the central and western regions has also widened, but to a smaller degree.

Taking provinces as units of observation, I assess interprovincial inequality by computing the coefficient of variation (CV) of GDP per capita (Figure 10.2). Though the decline in interprovincial inequality during the second half of the 1980s seems to depict regional convergence, more detailed analyses show that the trend toward more equality can be traced to the relatively slow growth of the traditional economic core in the northern coastal region and the northeast, including Beijing and Liaoning, which offset the rapid growth of previously less developed provinces in the southeastern coastal region such as Guangdong and Fujian. The increase in the CV during the 1990s shows that the regional convergence was shortlived and quickly replaced by increase of interprovincial inequality.

Comparing 1988 and 1998 GDP per capita trends over space reveals that the three centrally administered municipalities – Shanghai, Beijing and Tianjian – had the largest GDP per capita in 1988. Most other eastern-region provinces, the northeastern provinces of Heilongjiang and Jilin, and the northwestern provinces

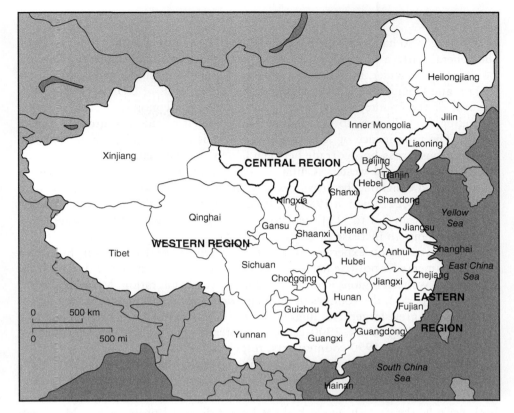

Figure 10.1 Provincial-level units and the three regions.

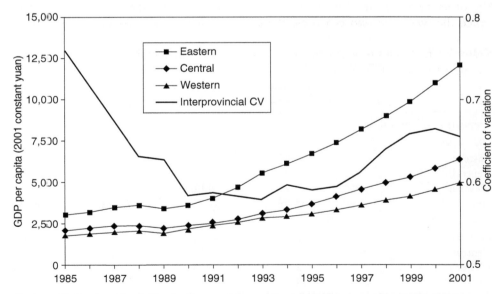

Figure 10.2 Regional distribution and inequality of GDP per capita, 1985–2001.
Note: Tibet is excluded, and Chongqing is combined with Sichuan. CV = coefficient of variation.
Sources: China Statistical Yearbooks and Provincial Statistical Yearbooks, various years; Hsueh, T., Li, Q., and Liu, S. (eds.), *China's Provincial Statistics, 1949–1989* (Boulder, CO: Westview Press, 1993).

of Xinjiang, also had relatively high levels of GDP per capita at that time. In 1998, the general pattern of regional disparity persisted, but the absolute gaps among provinces grew wider. In particular, Beijing, Tianjin, Jiangsu, Shanghai, Zhejiang, Fujian, and Guangdong enjoyed significantly higher levels of GDP per capita than the rest of the country. This pattern reveals that the contiguous coastal region extending from Jiangsu to Guangdong had emerged as the new growth core of China. The prominence of Xinjiang in the west is also notable, due in no small part to robust cross-border trade between China and the Central Asian Republics. Much of central and western China, however, remained poor. The gap between Shanghai and Guizhou, the provinces with the highest and lowest GDP per capita, widened from 9,211 yuan in 1988 to 21,142 yuan in 1998. The Shanghai–Guizhou ratio surged from 7:1 to 11:1, depicting not only an increase in the absolute level of disparity but an increase in relative disparity.

The eastern region experienced a gain in interprovincial migration. Both censuses documented a positive net migration for the eastern region and that both the central and western regions experienced a negative net migration. Moreover, in the 1995–2000 period, the volumes of net migration and the discrepancies among the three regions grew larger. Net migration rates in the eastern, central, and western regions, according to the 2000 census, registered approximately nine, fourteen, and five times their 1990 counterparts, respectively.

To more specifically identify the migration flows among the three regions, Table 10.2 shows the proportions of interprovincial migration attributable to intraregional and interregional flows, represented by diagonal and off-diagonal cells. In both periods, the eastern region had the largest diagonal proportion – 24 percent and 18 percent, indicating more active interprovincial migration three than within the other two regions. Intraregional flows, however, declined in relative importance. Between the two censuses, the sum of off-diagonal proportions increased

Table 10.2 Interprovincial migration within and among regions

| To | From | | | |
	Eastern	Central	Western	Sum
Proportion of total flows				
1985–1990				
Eastern	24.41	21.03	11.51	56.95
Central	10.67	9.20	6.28	26.15
Western	3.71	4.06	9.12	16.90
Sum	38.79	34.29	26.92	100.00
1995–2000				
Eastern	18.35	41.82	18.24	78.41
Central	3.83	4.00	2.37	10.20
Western	2.36	3.19	5.84	11.38
Sum	24.54	49.01	26.45	100.00

Tibet is excluded and Chongqing is combined with Sichuan.
Source: State Statistical Bureau (1992); *National Bureau of Statistics* (2002) [as for Table 10.1].

from 57 percent to 72 percent, depicting the increased prominence of interregional flows relative to intraregional flows. Of the six off-diagonal cells, only two – the central-to-eastern and the western-to-eastern – increased over time, indicating an acceleration of migration flows from the two noncoastal regions to the eastern region. The flow from the central region to the eastern region is especially noteworthy, as it increased in proportion from 21 percent to 42 percent. The 1985–1990 western-to-central flow (6 percent) was bigger than that of central-to-western flow (4 percent), but in the 1995–2000 period, the latter (3 percent) was bigger than the former (2 percent). This change reflects the increased prominence of western region provinces such as Xinjiang and Yunnan in attracting migrants.

[. . .] From the 1895–1990 to the 1995–2000 periods, all flows increased in volume, with the most pronounced increases within the eastern region and those from the central and western regions to the eastern region. The 1995–2000 central-to-eastern flow exceeded the 1985–1990 flow by six times, and the western-to-eastern flows stood five times greater.

[. .] In the 1985–1990 period, Beijing and Shanghai revealed the highest net migration rates of migrants. Other eastern-region provinces, including Liaoning, Tianjin, Shandong, Jiangsu, Fujian, Guangdong, and Hainan, the two central-region provinces of Shanxi and Hubei, and the three western-region provinces of Ningxia, Qinghai, and Xinjiang, also demonstrated positive migration rates. The rest of the country had negative rates. In the 1995–2000 period, variations in provincial rates increased. Guangdong, Beijing, and Shanghai led the nation with two-digit positive rates. Other eastern-region provinces, except Hebei and Guangxi, all registered positive net migration rates. As in the previous period, Shanxi, Ningxia, and Xinjiang continued to have positive rates, and they were further joined by Yunnan in the southwest. Xinjiang, in particular, produced a larger net migration rate than most other provinces, suggesting that its economic growth related to cross-border trade offered a significant attraction to migrants. Yunnan's case is less clear, but its attraction to migrants possibly reflects its recent success in tobacco production. Both Xinjiang and Yunnan are members of the western region, and their positive rates have likely contributed to the reversal of positions between the central and western regions in the 1995–2000 period, as observed earlier (Table 10.2).

Among provinces with negative net migration rates, the most prominent ones – with rates more negative than –3.0 – constitute a contiguous zone spanning south central and southwestern China and including Anhui, Jiangxi, Hunan, Guangxi, Guizhou, and Sichuan. Sichuan provided the largest source of interprovincial migration. As shown earlier, these provinces are among the least developed in China. Recent research has documented that Anhui, Jiangxi, Hunan, and Sichuan suffered from negative employment growth in the 1990s. And Anhui, Jiangxi, and Hunan – all in the central region – experienced the most negative net migration rates, respectively, –5 percent, –7 percent, and –5 percent. Clearly, these three provinces have contributed significantly to making the central region the largest donor of migrants among the three regions.

The pattern of increased divergence of net migration rates between the two censuses, observed above, apparently paralleled the increased divergence in the levels of economic development shown earlier. Specifically, the southern half of the eastern region, along with Beijing and Tjianjin, and Xinjiang in the northwest, received the largest shares of interprovincial migration. At the same time, they led all provinces in increases in development levels. The south central and southwestern provinces of Anhui, Jiangxi, Hunan, Guangxi, Guizhou, and Sichuan became the most prominent donors of migrants, and they also stood among the poorest provinces in China.

Figures 10.3 and 10.4 map the most prominent net migration flows between pairs of provinces [. . . .]

The nine migration flows in the 1985–1990 period, depicted by Figure 10.3, reflect two patterns, both with coastal and more developed provinces as destinations. The first pattern reflects substantial levels of economic disparity between origin and destination provinces. Flows from Xinjiang and Sichuan to Shanghai, Sichuan to Fujian and Guangdong, and Guizhou to Jiangsu, are of this type. The second pattern includes short-distance moves from neighboring provinces to coastal and more developed provinces, reflecting the well-known idea that migration is

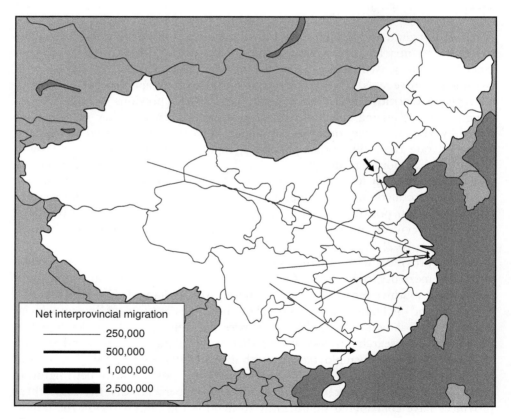

Figure 10.3   Prominent interprovincial net migration flows, 1985–1990.
Source: State Statistical Bureau, *Zhongguo renkou tongji nianjian 1992* [China Population Statistical Yearbook 1992] (Beijing: China Statistical Publishing House, 1992).

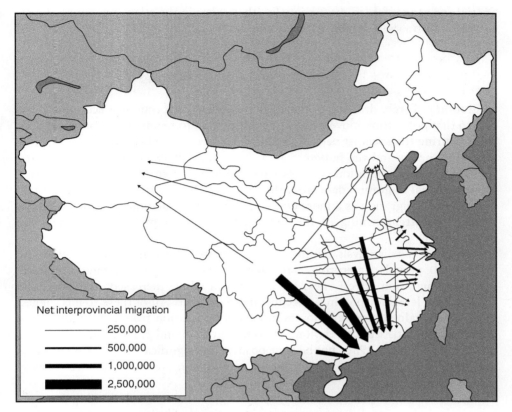

Figure 10.4 Prominent interprovincial net migration flows, 1995–2000.
Source National Bureau of Statistics, *Zhongguo 2000 nian renkou pucha ziliao*, Vol. 1 and 2 [Tabulation on the 2000 Population Census of the People's Republic of China] (Beijing: China Statistics Press, 2002).

negatively related to distance. Flows from Hebei to Beijing and Shandong to Tianjin are characterized by relatively short distances. In addition, flows from Anhui to Shanghai and Guangxi to Guangdong reveal both short-distance characteristics and significant economic disparities.

Net migration flows in the 1995–2000 period exhibit significantly bigger volumes (Figure 10.4). They also display a more concentrated pattern. The most striking destination is Guangdong, which experienced very large net migration flows from a number of central and western region provinces. In addition, Beijing, Jiangsu, Shanghai, Zhejiang, and Fujian also became prominent destinations. The only noncoastal province with significantly large net flows is Xinjiang. Donor provinces with prominent flows to several destinations include Anhui, Jiangxi, and Sichuan. Again, both economic disparity and adjacency appear to be important factors contributing to this concentrated pattern.

Increased heterogeneity of migration rates and the concentration of donor and destination provinces suggest that the degree of "spatial focusing" has increased.

Spatial focusing refers to the "inequality that exists in the relative volumes of a set of origin-destination-specific migration flows." [. . .]

Summary and Conclusion

Migration research, drawing primarily on experiences of capitalist economies, has shown that population movement is strongly related to regional economic development. During the socialist period of China, however, mobility was constrained by central planning and the hukou system. Since the 1980s, economic reforms and the relaxation of migration controls have resulted in a surge in migration. Using interprovincial migration data from the 1990 and 2000 censuses, I examined two themes: first, migration as a more effective factor in population redistribution, and second, the strengthening of the relationship between migration and regional development.

Results of data analysis reinforce both notions. Between the 1985–1990 and 1995–2000 periods, interprovincial migration volumes surged, migration rates diverged, migration effectiveness for China as a whole increased, and migration effectiveness levels for provinces became more extreme. All of these trends suggest that gainers gained more and losers lost more population from net migration. In addition, the statistical correlation between migration and population growth was not significant in the 1980s but became positive and significant in the 1990s. Thus, the role of migration in redistributing population among provinces clearly increased.

Studies in both China and elsewhere suggest that the relationship between migration and regional development is bidirectional. The analysis presented here also indicates that the relationship between migration and regional development has become stronger over time. Migration flows from the central and western regions to the eastern region increased exponentially in the 1995–2000 period. Beijing, Tianjin, and the southern half of the eastern region, which led the country in level of development, were the most prominent destinations. Guangdong, in particular, which has experienced remarkable economic growth since the economic reforms, further increased its attractiveness and become a nationwide magnet to migrants. Xinjiang in the west, which enjoyed relatively high rates of economic growth in the 1990s, also gained population from migration. By contrast, several south central and southwestern provinces, among the poorest regions in China, emerged as the most prominent donors of migrants. Furthermore, analyses of stream effectiveness (between pairs of provinces) and spatial focusing indicate that the pattern of interprovincial migration was more concentrated in the 1990s than in the 1980s. The concentrated migration pattern once again mirrors the increased heterogeneity in economic development among provinces.

More so than in the first decade of the transitional period, migration in the 1990s had a significant impact on regional population distribution and a strong relationship with regional development. This finding reflects an accelerated penetration of market mechanisms and hints at the increased relevance of existing migration theories and of the experiences of other countries for conceptualizing population movement in China. Though not examined in this article, the specific impacts of migration, such as labor market changes in the destination and remittances received by the origin, warrant special attention by researchers. A greater understanding of the interplay between migration and regional development in China will shed further light on how economic transition has shaped its space economy.

Part III

Environment, Agriculture, and Society

Introduction

William G. Moseley

The study of human–environment interactions, or the nature–society tradition in geography, is as old as the discipline itself. Even the early Greek geographers were very interested in describing different environments, and people's relationship to those landscapes. As geography took form as an academic discipline in the nineteenth century, geographers became particularly concerned with the influence of climate on the development of various human societies. Unfortunately, geographers, and practitioners in allied disciplines such as anthropology, began categorizing human societies by their level of development and attributing differences solely to climatic factors. At its extreme, Europeans were characterized as industrious and clever because of their brisk climate, whereas peoples of the tropics were slow-witted and complacent because of their warm, lush environments. Some have suggested that the colonial enterprise itself may have popularized such thinking because it helped rationalize the (often duplicitous) colonial goal of civilizing peoples of the Global South. The fallacy of this perspective, known as environmental determinism, soon became apparent as the theory could not account for the large number of well-developed, organized societies in the tropics (e.g., the Maya, Aztec, and Inca temples and towns in Central and South America; the Egyptian pyramids in North Africa; the Great Zimbabwe stone fortress in southern Africa).

Environmental determinism gave way to environmental possibilism, a perspective that acknowledged the ability of human groups to surmount environmental constraints and modify their landscapes, yet which asserted that natural environments often limit the range of choices available to a culture. Environmental possibilism heavily influenced the development of cultural ecology, an interdisciplinary approach that had bubbled to the forefront of the nature–society tradition by the 1960s. Cultural ecologists were interested in the study of the interactions between cultural groups and their natural surroundings, particularly the adaptive processes by which human societies adjust through subsistence patterns to local environments (giving much of the scholarship in this domain a distinctly developing world focus).

In revealing the ingenuity and sustainability of traditional agricultural practices in the tropics and elsewhere, this approach was important as a counter-balance to colonialism, neocolonialism, and modernization, which often portrayed peasant farmers as backward and environmentally destructive. The selections by Jared Diamond, "The Worst Mistake in the History of the Human Race," and Donald Innis, "The Future of Traditional Agriculture," reflect the cultural ecology perspective. In his provocative essay, Diamond argues that the transition from hunting and gathering to farming does not necessarily represent progress. In describing the strengths of traditional agriculture and the pitfalls of modern farming, Innis also questions conventional notions of progress. Many of the questions he raises about modern farming inspired by the "green revolution" of the 1960s and 1970s are also pertinent to debates today about the biotech revolution in agriculture. His concerns about energy use in modern agriculture, then inspired by the energy crisis of the 1970s, are also eerily relevant given recent rises in fuel costs.

The 1970s birthed environmentalism as a popular movement in many Western countries. In "Geography and the Global Environment," Diana Liverman describes her personal journey as geography student during this period. In the process, she touches on several other approaches in the nature–society tradition that existed or were beginning to emerge at this time. Of course, she spends the greatest amount of space discussing an approach that she has been a key player in, and one that did not really come to the fore until the 1990s, the "human dimensions of global change." Liverman also mentions many resource geography fields that were inspired by environmentalism, or the growing concern about human impacts on the environment. One of the most prominent areas of resource geography addresses water resources. The article by Christine Drake, entitled "Water Resource Conflicts in the Middle East," is a good example of this type of scholarship. While many are concerned with the politics of oil in the Middle East, Drake explains how tensions related to water may actually be more pronounced.

Another important tradition that Liverman touches on is hazards geography, an approach that is often closely associated with the work of Gilbert White and his students. In the 1940s, White argued that an over-reliance on dams and levees in the central US had led to increased, rather than decreased, damage from flooding. The problem, he suggested, was that public confidence in structural works increased occupation and building on floodplains. His students went on to study natural hazards in many other contexts. The selection by William Meyer, "Americans and Their Weather," articulates many of the traditional concerns of hazards geography. Meyer adroitly explains how the impacts of weather vary over time and amongst different groups of people. This perspective seems especially relevant today given the devastation, human suffering, and loss of life engendered by tsunamis in Southeast Asia and hurricanes along the American Gulf Coast.

Political ecology is arguably the dominant approach in geography's nature–society tradition today. It arose in the early 1980s (in works by Piers Blaikie, Michael Watts, and Suzanna Hecht) as a reaction to hazards geography and cultural ecology. The approach was heavily influenced by radical development geography. A key concern was that the cultural ecology and hazards geography of the time did not sufficiently consider the potential impact of broader-scale political economy on local human–environment interactions. Political ecologists have described how global commodity flows and powerful business and political interests often have as much or more to do with environmental degradation than local management practices. The final article by William Cronon, "The Trouble with Wilderness; or, Getting Back to the Wrong Nature," deals with another concern of political ecology, the idea that "nature" is socially constructed. In other words, what most North Americans have come to define as natural or wilderness areas are not really all that natural as humans have done a lot to create them (most notably by kicking out or eliminating the local people who formerly resided in these areas). Cronon's overriding concern is that the way we view nature, as separate from us and far away in a national park, will lead us to not recognize the nature around us and act irresponsibly.

DISCUSSION READINGS

Diamond, Jared. (1987). "The Worst Mistake in the History of the Human Race." *Discover*, May. Pp. 64–6.

Innis, Donald Q. (1980). "The Future of Traditional Agriculture." *Focus*, 30(3): 1–8.

Liverman, Diane M. (1999). "Geography and the Global Environment." *Annals of the Association of American Geographers*, 89(1): 107–10, 113–16.

Drake, Christine. (1997). "Water Resource Conflicts in the Middle East." *Journal of Geography*, 96(1): 4–12.

Meyer, William B. (2000). "Introduction." In *Americans and Their Weather*. New York: Oxford University Press. Pp. 3–15.

Cronon, William. (1995). "The Trouble with Wilderness; or, Getting Back to the Wrong Nature." In William Cronon (ed.), *Uncommon Ground: Toward Reinventing Nature*. New York: W. W. Norton. Pp. 7–25.

Chapter 11

The Worst Mistake in the History of the Human Race

Jared Diamond

To science we owe dramatic changes in our smug self image. Astronomy taught us that our earth isn't the center of the universe but merely one of billions of heavenly bodies. From biology we learned that we weren't specially created by God but evolved along with millions other species: Now archaeology is demolishing another sacred belief: that human history over the past million years has been a long tale of progress. In particular, recent discoveries suggest that the adoption of agriculture, supposedly our most decisive step toward a better life, was in many ways a catastrophe from which we have never recovered. With agriculture came the gross social and sexual inequality, the disease and despotism, that curse our existence.

At first, the evidence against this revisionist interpretation will strike twentieth century Americans as irrefutable. We're better off in almost every respect than people of the Middle Ages, who in turn had it easier than cavemen, who in turn were better off than apes. Just count our advantages. We enjoy the most abundant and varied foods, the best tools and material goods, some of the longest and healthiest lives, in history. Most of us are safe from starvation and predators. We get our energy from oil and machines, not from our sweat. What neo-Luddite among us would trade his life for that of a medieval peasant, a caveman, or an ape?

For most of our history we supported ourselves by hunting and gathering: we hunted wild animals and foraged for wild plants. It's a life that philosophers have traditionally regarded as nasty, brutish, and short. Since no food is grown and little is stored, there is (in this view) no respite from the struggle that starts anew each day to find wild foods and avoid starving. Our escape from this misery was facilitated only 10,000 years ago, when in different parts of the world people began to domesticate plants and animals. The agricultural revolution gradually spread until today it's nearly universal and few tribes of hunter-gatherers survive.

Diamond, Jared, "The Worst Mistake in the History of the Human Race," pp. 64–6 from *Discover*, May (1987).

From the progressivist perspective on which I was brought up, to ask "Why did almost all our hunter-gatherer ancestors adopt agriculture?" is silly. Of course they adopted it because agriculture is an efficient way to get more food for less work. Planted crops yield far more tons per acre than roots and berries. Just imagine a band of savages, exhausted from searching for nuts or chasing wild animals, suddenly gazing for the first time at a fruit-laden orchard or a pasture full of sheep. How many milliseconds do you think it would take them to appreciate the advantages of agriculture?

The progressivist party line sometimes even goes so far as to credit agriculture with the remarkable flowering of art that has taken place over the past few thousand years. Since crops can be stored, and since it takes less time to pick food from a garden than to find it in the wild, agriculture gave us free time that hunter-gatherers never had. Thus it was agriculture that enabled us to build the Parthenon and compose the B-minor Mass.

While the case for the progressivist view seems overwhelming, it's hard to prove. How do you show that the lives of people 10,000 years ago got better when they abandoned hunting and gathering for farming? Until recently, archaeologists had to resort to indirect test, whose results (surprisingly) failed to support the progressivist view. Here's one example of an indirect test: Are twentieth century hunter-gatherers really worse off than farmers? Scattered throughout the world, several dozen groups of so-called primitive people, like the Kalahari Bushmen, continue to support themselves that way. It turns out that these people have plenty of leisure time, sleep a good deal, and work less hard than their farming neighbors. For instance, the average time devoted each week to obtaining food is only 12 to 19 hours for one group of Bushmen, 14 hours or less for the Hadza nomads of Tanzania One Bushman, when asked why he hadn't emulated neighboring tribes by adopting agriculture, replied, "Why should we, when there are so many mongongo nuts in the world?"

While farmers concentrate on high-carbohydrate crops like rice and potatoes, the mix of wild plants and animals in the diets of surviving hunter-gatherers provides more protein and a better balance of other nutrients. In one study, the Bushmen's average daily food intake (during a month when food was plentiful) was 2,140 calories and 93 grams of protein, considerably greater than the recommended daily allowance for people of their size. It's almost inconceivable that Bushmen, who eat 75 or so wild plants, could die of starvation the way hundreds of thousands of Irish farmers and their families did during the potato famine of the 1840s.

So the lives of at least the surviving hunter-gatherers aren't nasty and brutish, even though farmers have pushed them into some of the world's worst real estate. But modern hunter-gatherer societies that have rubbed shoulders with farming societies for thousands of years don't tell us about conditions before the agricultural revolution. The progressivist view is really making a claim about the distant past: that the lives of primitive people improved when they switched from gathering to farming. Archaeologists can date that switch by distinguishing remains of wild plants and animals from those of domesticated ones in prehistoric garbage dumps.

How can one deduce the health of the prehistoric garbage makers, and thereby directly test the progressivist view? That question has become answerable only in recent years, in part through the newly emerging techniques of paleopathology, the study of signs of disease in the remains of ancient peoples.

In some lucky situations, the paleopathologist has almost as much material to study as a pathologist today. For example, archaeologists in the Chilean deserts found well preserved mummies whose medical conditions at time of death could be determined by autopsy. And feces of long-dead Indians who lived in dry caves in Nevada remain sufficiently well preserved to be examined for hookworm and other parasites.

Usually the only human remains available for study are skeletons, but they permit a surprising number of deductions. To begin with, a skeleton reveals its owner's sex, weight, and approximate age. In the few cases where there are many skeletons, one can construct mortality tables like the ones life insurance companies use to calculate expected life span and risk of death at any given age. Paleopathologists can also calculate growth rates by measuring bones of people of different ages, examine teeth for enamel defects (signs of childhood malnutrition), and recognize scars left on bones by anemia, tuberculosis, leprosy, and other diseases.

One straightforward example of what paleopathologists have learned from skeletons concerns historical changes in height. Skeletons from Greece and Turkey show that the average height of hunter-gatherers toward the end of the ice ages was a generous 5′ 9″ for men, 5′ 5″ for women. With the adoption of agriculture, height crashed, and by 3000 BC had reached a low of only 5′ 3″ for men, 5′ for women. By classical times heights were very slowly on the rise again, but modern Greeks and Turks have still not regained the average height of their distant ancestors.

Another example of paleopathology at work is the study of Indian skeletons from burial mounds in the Illinois and Ohio river valleys. At Dickson Mounds, located near the confluence of the Spoon and Illinois rivers, archaeologists have excavated some 800 skeletons that paint a picture of the health changes that occurred when a hunter-gatherer culture gave way to intensive maize farming around AD 1150. Studies by George Armelagos and his colleagues then at the University of Massachusetts show these early farmers paid a price for their new-found livelihood. Compared to the hunter-gatherers who preceded them, the farmers had a nearly 50 per cent increase in enamel defects indicative of malnutrition, a fourfold increase in iron-deficiency anemia (evidenced by a bone condition called porotic hyperostosis), a threefold rise in bone lesions reflecting infectious disease in general, and an increase in degenerative conditions of the spine, probably reflecting a lot of hard physical labor. "Life expectancy at birth in the pre-agricultural community was about twenty-six years," say Armelagos, "but in the post-agricultural community it was nineteen years. So these episodes of nutritional stress and infectious disease were seriously affecting their ability to survive.

The evidence suggests that the Indians at Dickson Mounds, like many other primitive peoples, took up farming not by choice but from necessity in order to feed their constantly growing numbers. "I don't think most hunter-gatherers farmed until they had to, and when they switched to farming they traded quality for quantity," says Mark Cohen of the State University of New York at Plattsburgh, co-editor, with Armelagos, of one the seminal books in the field, *Paleopathology at the Origins of Agriculture*. "When I first started making that argument ten years ago, not many people agreed with me. Now it's become a respectable, albeit controversial, side of the debate."

There are at least three sets of reasons of explain the findings that agriculture was bad for health. First, hunter-gatherers enjoyed a varied diet, while early farmers obtained most of their food from one or a few starchy crops. The farmers gained cheap calories at the cost of poor nutrition. (Today just three high-carbohydrate plants – wheat, rice, and corn – provide the bulk of the calories consumed by the human species, yet each one is deficient in certain vitamins or amino acids essential to life.) Second, because of dependence on a limited number of crops, farmers ran the risk of starvation if one crop failed. Finally, the mere fact that agriculture encouraged people to clump together in crowded societies, many of which then carried on trade with other crowded societies, led to the spread of parasites and infectious disease. (Some archaeologists think it was crowding, rather than agri-culture, that promoted disease, but this is a chicken-and-egg argument, because crowding encourages agriculture and vice versa.) Epidemics couldn't take hold when populations were scattered in small bands that constantly shifted camp. Tuberculosis and diarrheal disease had to await the rise of farming, measles and bubonic plague the appearance of large cities.

Besides malnutrition, starvation, and epidemic disease, farming helped bring another curse upon humanity: deep class divisions. Hunter-gatherers have little or no stored food, and no concentrated food sources, like an orchard or a herd of cows: they live off the wild plants and animals they obtain each day. Therefore, there can be no kings, no class of social parasites who grow fat on food seized from others. Only in a farming population could a healthy, non-producing élite set itself above the disease-ridden masses. Skeletons from Greek tombs at Mycenae ca. 1500 BC suggest that royals enjoyed a better diet than commoners, since the royal skeletons were two or three inches taller and had better teeth (on the average, one instead of six cavities or missing teeth). Among Chilean mummies from ca. AD 1000, the élite were distinguished not only by ornaments and gold hair clips but also by a fourfold lower rate of bone lesions caused by disease.

Similar contrasts in nutrition and health persist on a global scale today. To people in rich countries like the US, it sounds ridiculous to extol the virtues of hunting and gathering. But Americans are an élite, dependent on oil and minerals that must often be imported from countries with poorer health and nutrition. If one could choose between being a peasant farmer in Ethiopia or a Bushman gath-erer in the Kalahari, which do you think would be the better choice?

Farming may have encouraged inequality between the sexes, as well. Freed from the need to transport their babies during a nomadic existence, and under pressure to produce more hands to till the fields, farming women tended to have more fre-quent pregnancies than their hunter-gatherer counterparts – with consequent drains on their health. Among the Chilean mummies, for example, more women than men had bone lesions from infectious disease.

Women in agricultural societies were sometimes made beasts of burden. In New Guinea farming communities today I often see women staggering under loads of vegetables and firewood while the men walk empty-handed. Once while on a field trip there studying birds, I offered to pay some villagers to carry supplies from an airstrip to my mountain camp. The heaviest item was a 110-pound bag of rice, which I lashed to a pole and assigned to a team of four men to shoulder together. When I eventually caught up with the villagers, the men were carrying light loads, while one small woman weighing less than the bag of rice was bent under it, supporting its weight by a cord across her temples.

As for the claim that agriculture encouraged the flowering of art by providing us with leisure time, modern hunter-gatherers have at least as much free time as do farmers. The whole emphasis on leisure time as a critical factor seems to me misguided. Gorillas have had ample free time to build their own Parthenon, had they wanted to. While post-agricultural technological advances did make new art forms possible and preservation of art easier, great paintings and sculptures were already being produced by hunter-gatherers 15,000 years ago, and were still being produced as recently as the last century by such hunter-gatherers as some Eskimos and the Indians of the Pacific Northwest.

Thus with the advent of agriculture an élite became better off, but most people became worse off. Instead of swallowing the progressivist party line that we chose agriculture because it was good for us, we must ask how we got trapped by it despite its pitfalls.

One answer boils down to the adage "Might makes right." Farming could support many more people than hunting, albeit with a poorer quality of life. (Population densities of hunter-gatherers are rarely over one person per ten square miles, while farmers average 100 times that.) Partly, this is because a field planted entirely in edible crops lets one feed far more mouths than a forest with scattered edible plants. Partly, too, it's because nomadic hunter-gatherers have to keep their children spaced at four-year intervals by infanticide and other means, since a mother must carry her toddler until it's old enough to keep up with the adults. Because farm women don't have that burden, they can and often do bear a child every two years.

As population densities of hunter-gatherers slowly rose at the end of the ice ages, bands had to choose between feeding more mouths by taking the first steps toward agriculture, or else finding ways to limit growth. Some bands chose the former solution, unable to anticipate the evils of farming, and seduced by the transient abundance they enjoyed until population growth caught up with increased food production. Such bands outbred and then drove off or killed the bands that chose to remain hunter-gatherers, because a hundred malnourished farmers can still outfight one healthy hunter. It's not that hunter-gatherers abandoned their life style, but that those sensible enough not to abandon it were forced out of all areas except the ones farmers didn't want.

At this point it's instructive to recall the common complaint that archaeology is a luxury, concerned with the remote past, and offering no lessons for the present. Archaeologists studying the rise of farming have reconstructed a crucial stage at which we made the worst mistake in human history. Forced to choose between limiting population or trying to increase food production, we choose the latter and ended up with starvation, warfare, and tyranny.

Hunter-gatherers practiced the most successful and longest-lasting life style in human history. In contrast, we're still struggling with the mess into which agriculture has tumbled us, and it's unclear whether we can solve it. Suppose that an archaeologist who had visited us from outer space were trying to explain human history to his fellow spacelings. He might illustrate the results of his digs by a 24-hour clock on which one hour represents 100,000 years of real past time. If the history of the human race began at midnight, then we would now be almost at the end of our first day. We lived as hunter-gatherers for nearly the whole of that day, from midnight through dawn, noon, and sunset. Finally, at 11:54 p.m., we adopted agriculture. As our second midnight approaches, will the plight of famine-stricken peasants gradually spread to engulf us all? Or will we somehow achieve those seductive blessings that we imagine behind agriculture's glittering façade, and that have so far eluded us?

Chapter 12

The Future of Traditional Agriculture

Donald Q. Innis

Is the agricultural revolution becoming obsolete? Will what we think of as old-fashioned peasant farming be the way people farm in the future? These questions are raised by the vast changes now affecting the resources we use to grow the world's food.

The agricultural revolution began in the United States and other industrial nations about a hundred years ago and has transformed farming in those countries. Since World War II, the contents of this modern way of farming, now known as the "green revolution," have been extended to many farmers in the underdeveloped nations of the Third World.

The elements of the agricultural revolution are these: the use of fuel-powered machinery in place of human and animal labor; large-scale irrigation; the use of chemical poisons to control insects and weeds; and the additional of chemical fertilizers to supplement the organic nutrients, or plant food, of the soil. The three major fertilizers are nitrogen, phosphate and potash, familiarly known as N, P and K.

The agricultural revolution had made possible great increases in the production of food – as we repreatedly plunder the stored mineral resources of Spaceship Earth. It was also had a profound effect on the resources used for farming. Much less labor is needed for modern farming, and so many millions of people have left farming to seek work elsewhere. For example, 4 percent of Americans work in farming today, compared to 25 percent only 40 years ago. The average farm became much larger. Farmers who once were largely self-sufficient have become dependent on distant sources for the new "inputs" of modern agriculture. Most important, they have become dependent on petroleum: nitrogen fertilizer is made from natural gas, and farm machinery is powered by oil.

Innis, Donald Q. "The Future of Traditional Agriculture," pp. 1–8 from *Focus*, 30.3 (January/February, 1980).

Today the conditions under which the agricultural revolution began are changing. For a variety of reasons, including rapid population growth, many of the people now forced out of farming cannot find other work. Many parts of the world are running out of good new land to farm. And, as we are made aware every day, the era of cheap and abundant petroleum is over: fertilizer and fuel are rising rapidly in price, and may before long become scarce.

But the agricultural revolution has not taken over the entire world. Most farmers in the Third World still work the land in the traditional way. This means using a lot of labor, but few or no inputs of chemical fertilizer and fuel-powered machines. Today some people are suggesting that, when the oil and gas fields run out, traditional farming will be not just the best kind of farming – it will be the only kind.

Are the famous high yields of modern machine agriculture as compared to traditional farming based on faulty definitions of "efficiency" and "traditional"?

The best definition of efficiency in an age of food, fuel, and fertilizer scarcity should emphasize maximum crop production from each kilogram of nutrients, liter of water and kilocalorie of solar energy. Agronomists are proud that nutrient utilization in raising chickens is now so efficient that a pound of broiler can be grown for less than two pounds of feed. But agronomists are less careful in measuring food grown per pound of nutrient when they assess agriculture in the Third World. They advocate mechanized monoculture (one crop per field) with the green revolution input package of high yielding seeds, mineral fertilizers, irrigation, and sprays against insects, disease, and weeds – though it has now been shown that traditional intercropping (two or more crops in one field) with the same nutrients and no sprays often yields twice as much per hectare.

Traditional intercropping farmers don't often have access to mineral fertilizers, but where they do they make more efficient use of them than modern farms with one crop per field. The traditional farmer gets the greatest total yield for any given amount of nutrients, water, and sunlight, and has the advantage over "modern" farmers that year after he can produce a crop which will feed his family and have some crops for sale, without purchasing any inputs.

Traditional Wisdom

Many modern monocropping farmers will probably go bankrupt as costs of fuel, fertilizer and farm machinery continue to escalate. The majority of farmers in Latin America, Africa, India, China, and other parts of Asia, who are portrayed by television and in textbooks as being so poor and so poorly educated that they may never be able to benefit from modern inputs in a time of increasing food scarcity, are in fact possessed of very sophisticated methods for producing maximum amounts of food, on a permanent basis, from scarce resources.

The knowledge which traditional farmers in underdeveloped countries possess will probably also benefit developed countries in the future. In the first place, the modern machine agriculture of developed countries depends on resources which will become increasingly scarce and expensive during the next hundred years. In the second place the number of people who benefit from modern techniques is far fewer than the number who could benefit if more traditional techniques were used.

Sometimes a decision by a modern farmer will be of benefit to him but not to the community as a whole. Picking cotton by machine, for example, lowers the price of cotton by eliminating a lot of labor and increases the farmer's profits somewhat; but the rest of society has to pay higher taxes to support the newly unemployed people on welfare. The extra cost of taxes is not made up for by the lower cost of cotton. It is impossible to deny that modern cotton farmers have benefitted from modern methods, but it is also true that traditional farmers who grow vegetables between the rows of young cotton get a greater total yield from their fields.

How is it possible to sort out the problems of future agriculture in a rational and dispassionate manner? Most people are acquainted with modern agriculture with its machines, hybrids, and miracle wheat and rice with strong stems to support the heavy heads made possible by heavy doses of commercial nitrate, potash and phosphates.

Not so many people today are familiar with traditional methods of intercropping, which involves growing several crops at the same time in each field. Machines can't handle intercropping, where several crops ripen at different times, but small farmers who have never had machines have developed very sophisticated patterns of timed planting and harvesting which often give them twice the yield of a one-crop field for the same nutrients.

Two or more crops in a field can use sunlight, water, and nutrients more effectively than one crop. Several experiments have shown that leaves at different levels, where a small quick-growing crop temporarily uses the empty space between larger slow-growing plants, can make better use of the available solar energy.

Organic material enables soil to absorb water 15 to 20 times as well as non-organic soil. This reduces soil run-off and erosion and makes moisture available to crops during periods of dry weather. Intercropping reduces loss of nutrients from leaching because numerous root systems of varying depths intercept downward percolating water and retrieve dissolved nutrients which would otherwise be carried out of the root zone. Such rapid leaching is very common in the tropics, where many small farmers have declined to adopt modern methods.

If two crops in a field have their maximum periods of growth a different times, they do not make maximum demands for water and nutrients all at the same time as happens when there is only one crop in a field which all has to be ready for harvesting by machine on the same day. Traditional intercropping, where the soil is protected from erosion for long periods of time by a succession of plants, can make better use of the natural distribution of rain throughout the year and make use of organic nutrients as they are made available by the slow decay of organic material in the soil.

In addition to keeping up soil fertility by reducing erosion, losses through leaching and maintaining the organic content of the soil, traditional farmers often included legumes in their plant mixtures so that the nitrogen from the root nodules of the legume can help the other plants in the field.

What is Efficient?

One wonders why, if traditional farming with intercropping has all these benefits, it has so often been displaced by modern methods and why so little is heard about it. Lack of an objective definition of efficiency seems to be part of the problem. Examples will show what some definition problems have been.

Several experiments done a decade or more ago measured only the yield of the main crop in trying to determine whether intercropping was worthwhile. The yield of rubber or sugar when intercropped was compared with the yield when mono-cropped. It sometimes happened that the yield of the main crop was slightly reduced by the presence of the second crop. Obviously, if the value of the second crop is not considered, it is not surprising that such experiments showed that intercropping was not worthwhile.

On a big rubber plantation, a corporate owner might well not be interested in growing cowpeas in the empty spaces between the trees. Extra labor would have to be hired and the cost of the labor might exceed the value of the cowpeas. But small farmers in Malaysia grow several secondary crops with rubber and are very much interested in the value of these crops. In addition they produce more rubber per acre than commercial plantations because they plant more trees. On commercial plantations, fewer trees per acre mean larger trees, less cost in tapping them, more rubber per tree and more profit per acre, even though less rubber per acre and no intercrops are produced. Some of the problems of measuring efficiency now become apparent.

An intercropped field or garden in traditional style may produce food and other crops more or less continuously as short-term crops ripen in succession and are harvested, leaving room for larger slower-growing crops. It is difficult to measure production when some harvesting is done almost every day and where much of the production is eaten on the family farm.

Proponents of modern agriculture sincerely believe that the best thing the developed countries can do for other countries is to replace traditional farms with modern farms. But they seldom measure the inputs which are necessary to produce the enormous yields of which they are so proud. First, fossil fuels and fertilizers which accumulated in the earth's crust in the course of a billion years are being used to step up production for a couple of centuries, till the supply runs out. Second, the calories harvested from a modern field are usually much less than the calories which were used up in growing the crops. The reasons for this are that modern commercial farmers use machines which consume calories in the form of fuel and which also take a lot of fuel to manufacture. When calorie input-output is used to define efficiency, traditional methods with their healthy outdoor exercise are much more efficient than modern methods. As fuel costs increase, it will become more and more feasible for small farmers without machines, or only simple machines, to compete with the big fossil fuel farms.

Other factors which have made it difficult for scientists and the public in developed countries to understand the sophisticated accomplishments of traditional small farmers in underdeveloped contries are: the addition of commercial nitrogen fertilizer, which distorts intercropping experiments with legumes; that small farmers consume much of their production as food for their families; and that labor costs can be lower on a small farm where no supervisors, management, and stockholders have to be supplied with income.

When nitrogen fertilizer is added to the soil in intercropping experiments, which is often done routinely "so the experiment will be carried out under modern conditions," the effect is to prevent the legumes from doing their work of fixing atmospheric nitrogen (making the nitrogen available as nutrient in the soil). The legumes find that nitrogen supplies in the soil are already quite sufficient so they do not supply more. It is not surprising, then, that other crops in these experiments do not benefit from association with legumes. Traditional farmers, like the North and South American Indians, discovered long ago that beans (a legume) will help corn and squash to grow better.

One of the reasons that modern farming seems to be so productive is that each owner is getting the yield from a much larger acreage. A farmer or company manager who can harvest 1,000 acres with machines can become quite wealthy because he will have the income that used to go to several smaller farmers. Ten farmers on 1,000 acres would each make less money but the total income and the total amount produced from this 1,000 acres would be higher for the same amount of nutrients, sunshine, and water. Similarly, 100 farmers on the same amount of land would have even less income per family; but the yield of the land with the same inputs would, if they practiced intercropping as most small farmers do, be much higher than that of the big farm. Twice the rate of yield can be achieved if there are several intercrops which are carefully weeded and harvested by hand so that one crop after another is harvested from the same land.

Home Consumption

A problem often run into by extension workers trying to motivate traditional farmers to accept modern methods is that small farmers and their families eat a large proportion of their production. If they buy fertilizer, and their crops grow better, they will get more to eat, but then they won't be able to pay back the money they borrowed to buy the fertilizer. This is why modern methods have been much more valuable to big framers. Big farmers have always marketed most of what they produce, so extra yield produced with commercial fertilizer and other modern inputs can easily be sold in order to pay back the loans taken out to buy the inputs. The big farmers are so successful that they are able to buy extra land from small farmers and force them to go off to the big cities, where modern economic theory contends that they will find jobs in factories (but where many in reality remain unemployed). So small farmers who used nutrients, water, and sunlight very efficiently are displaced by less efficient big farmers – all in the name of growing more food to feed the starving.

On a big modern farm where machinery is used to increase the productivily of the few remaining workers, there is usually only one crop per field because that is all a machine can handle. There is an enormous body of evidence (a bibliography of reports on 1000 intercropping experiments has recently been published) which shows that a suitable combination of intercrops will always produce a greater total yield than only one crop in a field. But a second crop is very difficult for machines to handle, let alone a third and fourth intercrop. If the cost of producing an additional crop at the same time, in a given field, is greater than the monetary yield, then the commercial farmers will not grow it.

But a farmer who does not use machinery, or who uses animal-powered machinery, to plow the land at the beginning of the growing season, has no problem putting in several – sometimes many – additional crops. To cite two among many examples, the author found a garden with 22 crops in Jamaica and a field with fifteen crops all growing together in the Maharashtra region of India. D. W. Norman has shown by a very careful survey of work patterns among small farmers in Nigeria that the more intercrops there are in a field, the less additional work is needed in most cases for each additional crop.

Weeding and cultivating one crop automatically weeds and cultivates the other crops. The small farmer doesn't have to meet payments on his machines, or pay high-cost machine operators, or earn money for supervisors or stockholders, so the value of his marginal crop can be much lower than that on a big mechanized farm. He can use his own time to plant extra crops and can often feed his family in this way while selling the main crop for cash income.

[. . .]

Different Lifestyles

Since traditional farming with intercropping involves a lifestyle completely different from that of commercial, monocropped machine agriculture, we can best explain how this old (and perhaps future) lifestyle works by showing, one factor at a time, how commercial agriculture handles a problem and how traditional farmers handle the same problem.

A balanced diet in a country with commercialized single-crop farms is achieved only with the aid of an enormous amount of transportation. Each part of a modern country receives food from many other parts of the country and from many countries overseas. In the United States, for example, much of the food eaten on the East Coast is grown in California. As fuel prices rise, the cost of food must rise because fuel makes up a substantial part of the cost of food. By contrast, a small farmer who intercrops can grow much of his own food, which provides him with a balanced diet of much fresher and often much tastier food without involving high transportation costs.

Since locally grown food, with less fuel cost built into the price, will probably not rise in price as rapidly as food which is transported thousands of miles, it can be expected that small farms will become more economically viable. How can big farms be turned over peacefully to small farmers who can make much better use of the land?

Soil fertility is not important in modern commercial agriculture because fertilizers are added as the crop needs them. The natural organic content of the soil cannot be depended upon to provide the enormous quantities of nutrients needed to make all the plants in a field come ripe at once so they can be harvested by a machine. In fact, the addition of phosphate, nitrate, and potash quickly reduces the organic content of soil because the organic matter has to supply all the other nutrients, the so-called "trace elements," which rapidly growing hybrids need. One farmer who has tried to turn a "burned-out" former commercial field into an organic field with traditional and new types of intercropping reports that it is very difficult to get crops started on such a field.

With traditional farming, the maintenance of natural soil fertility is essential if agriculture is to continue. Natural fertilizers such as manure, compost, and mulch are used to keep up the organic content of the soil. (Eventually a new type of agriculture will have to be developed which returns sewage to the soil instead of dumping these nutrients in the ocean and then mining for new nutrients.) Organic nutrients decay gradually, making nutrients available to crops over a long period of time, during which nature also makes rain and sun available to crops. In traditional cultivation, cotton or tomatoes or other crops can be picked several times from the same plant as the plant continues to use water, sunlight and nutrients in a steady, efficient way.

Soil erosion and soil leaching seem to be much worse on commercial farms than on traditional farms. In North America when farmers used to plant clover with wheat or alfalfa with corn, the clover or alfalfa would remain on the land after the harvest of the grain and help to hold the soil. Modern spray farming which kills weeds chemically also kills all broadleaf plants, or any crop other than corn in a corn field. This makes it impossible to intercrop, so the soil is left bare after the main crop has been harvested. In some parts of Iowa, two bushels of top soil are lost for each bushel of corn harvested. Organic material stores water better than non-organic soils so the benefits of rain last longer on a traditional farm and as a result there is less run-off, less erosion and less leaching.

In tropical soils where leaching occurs very quickly a long-rooted intercrop can capture nutrients which have been leached down below the level of a short-rooted main crop. This allows a second crop to be grown which is not entirely in direct competition with the main crop. It also traps nutrients and returns them to the surface where decaying stems and leaves left after the harvest can make them available again to crops which missed them the first time around.

Weather Insurance

Variable weather conditions are a problem which all farmers have to face. Growing several crops together in a field is a form of insurance against drought, or excessive dampness, as some crops are better adapted to dry conditions and some to wet. Traditional farmers in underdeveloped countries are usually unable to defend their methods of agriculture in current scientific jargon, but they do express the idea that intercropping provides insurance against bad weather. There may never be a perfect season in which all the intercropped plants yield to their maximum since crops which develop fungus when it is too wet will suffer when moisture loving plants do very well. But since perfect weather throughout a season is very rare, it would seem that the small farmer with his traditional methods is better prepared than the commercial farmer who has to go to enormous expense to try to create laboratory conditions so his one crop will give maximum yield per acre.

Farmers who don't have access to pumped irrigation water, or chemical nutrients, or hybrids, or sprays (and these farmers will be more numerous in the future as mined resources become more expensive) are quite able to grow satisfactory crops by taking hints from traditional farmers who have managed to feed the world for millennia.

Solar energy and water are used more efficiently in an intercropped field than in one where there is only a single crop. Experiments with mixed corn and beans show that, while fewer corn plants may be put in the mixed field, it usually happens that each corn plant produces more when standing next to a bean plant than when standing next to another corn plant. This is because corn and beans have their leaves at different levels, which utilizes sunlight more effectively than if all the plants in a field are competing for sunlight with leaves at the same distance above the ground. Similarly, it has been shown that a plant with deep roots provides less competition for a shallow-rooted plant than does another shallow-rooted plant. And if the intercropped plants grow at different rates, one plant may be making its maximum demands on environmental resources while others are still getting started. This more efficient access to light, water, and nutrients by plants with different leaf and root configurations is one of the main reasons why intercropping is more productive than monocropping.

The insect problem is dealt with in entirely different ways by modern commercial farmers and by traditional small farmers. The agricultural experts who advise big farmers are convinced that the only way to deal with crop-eating insects is to spray the whole field with some insecticide. Commercial farmers then are troubled as more and more insects develop immunity to spray. New and more dangerous sprays are developed, but the process of genetic mutation seems capable after a time of developing insect species with new immunity. In fact, the natural enemies of crop-eating insects are more effectively suppressed by spray than are the target insects. Parasitic wasps, lady bugs, praying mantises, and spiders are always fewer in number than the crop-eating insects on which they prey – so their chances of developing mutations are much less than those of more numerous plant-eating insect populations.

Some advisors to commercial farmers are starting to think about intercropping. In Oklahoma, for example, rows of sorghum through the cotton fields provided a base of operations for spiders and other insect predators so that cotton rows near the sorghum produced 56 pounds per acre more cotton than rows far from the sorghum. Traditional types of intercropping in Costa Rica have proved even more effective in dealing with insect pests. The presence of squash blossoms provided food for parasitic wasps which killed corn borers. The advantages of using intercropping and predator insects to control insect pests is that the target insects never develop immunity from predators and the environment is never polluted with sprays, some of which are now quite dangerous to humans.

Diseases are controlled by intercropping because a fungus disease of one plant cannot easily reach another plant of the same species if the neighboring plant is a different species immune to the disease. In monoculture diseases spread very easily from one plant to the next because all the plants are the same. An example is the rubber plantations in Brazil which were wiped out by disease during World War II. In natural habitats, especially in the tropics, many plants grow together in the same area. One of the main reasons that this diversity has evolved is that it makes the spread of disease more difficult, and so the plants survive. Intercropping is a human re-creation of this natural diversity using plants which are useful to people.

On a modern farm weeds also are controlled by chemicals and, as we have seen, this leaves ground bare much of the time, with resulting massive soil erosion. It has been shown in an experiment with weeds, no weeds and intercropping, that weeds use about as many nutrients as a second crop. The experimenter concluded that it would seem more useful to grow a second crop than to allow weeds to grow. It would also seem wiser to grow a second crop than to poison the soil. When intercropping is practiced, hand weeding may be necessary at first, but in a few weeks the different crops soon shade all the soil and weeds for the most part are shaded out. A slow-growing large crop must be widely spaced because of the eventual size of cotton, sugar, or orchard trees. A second crop, or several other crops, chosen because they do not compete too much with the main crop, will help keep down weeds and also use sunlight and water which the large crop is not yet prepared to use.

Still another advantage of intercropping on small farms owned by the farmer is the fact that large numbers of people already understand how to practice intercropping. Many experts, and the mass media which try to convey to the public the finds of agricultural experts, are worried that so few people have enough education to understand what needs to be done if modern agriculture is to feed the world's people. It needs to be realized that most modern agricultural methods have no real future because they depend on natural resources which are in short supply and which will become increasingly more expensive. It needs to be widely understood among educated people that an excellent agricultural alternative to modern methods already exists.

Looking Backward

Learning from the traditional farmers in many parts of the world who have discovered by experimentation what crop combinations grow best in their areas is not a counsel of despair. Television keeps telling us that we can't go back – that you can't make real old-fashioned lemonade anymore, but that science has provided a pretty good substitute which is available at your nearest store. It is the same with agriculture. There are many small farmers all over the world who have an excellent grasp of the best way to grow food and other crops, for the short term and for the long term. What we need to do is start handing land over to these farmers so they can start building up soil fertility and be able to supply the world's population with food.

Intercropping cannot, of course, supply a world population which keeps growing indefinitely, but it could probably supply the present population with a good diet if people were allowed to grow their own food, and if less meat were eaten. Frances Moore Lappe begins her classic book *Food First* by giving figures for the world's total grain production and the world's total population. It is quite clear from these figures that there is enough food produced at the moment to feed everyone on the planet. The problem now is not the lack of food, but the desire of some people to feed grain to animals because they like to eat beef or pork. For every hamburger of grain-fed beef we eat, four Third-World children have to go without a meal.

Traditional agriculture is capable of growing much more from the chemical fertilizers which are now being mainly used on big monocropped farms. The reason it has been so difficult to help the poorest farmers is that any increases in their yield due to greater amounts of input mean that their families are better fed but they probably won't have enough crops for sale to pay back the loan. The rising per capita income and per capita food production of many Third World nations are usually due to increased production on middle size or large farms. The wealthy become more wealthy and buy up land from small farmers. Small farmers who lose their land often end up in the slums of big cities where hand-outs of food keep them marginally alive. If they are going to end up being given food, why not give them fertilizer? Fertilizers will not be readily available in a few decades, so perhaps the remaining amounts could be given to those who can produce the most food from them – the small farmers who intercrop and use hand labor.

When fertilizers are gone for all practical purposes, traditional farmers will be able to carry on as they have for millennia.

Chapter 13

Geography and the Global Environment

Diana M. Liverman

The study of the human relationship to the environment is one of the major traditions of geography, bridging physical and human geography, and echoing many of the major debates in the discipline. This paper offers some reflections on twenty-five years of continuity and change in the human-environment tradition of geography, and examines how geography has interacted with broader shifts in scholarship and policy on the environment. I have chosen to concentrate on geography and international environmental policy over the last twenty-five years (1972–1997), and especially on global-change research, because this period and theme allows me to provide a more personal perspective on continuities and changes. I discuss policy as well as scholarship because I am interested in how geographers have tried to change the world as well as study it, especially in the international arena.

The first part of the paper examines the development of international environmental policy from the 1972 UN Stockholm conference to the 1992 Rio Earth Summit, assessing the geographic contributions and the changing nature of geographic research over the period. The second section discusses the contemporary agenda of global-change research and policy, particularly the human dimensions, and proposes ways in which geographers might contribute to improved understanding.

Geography from Stockholm to Rio

The early 1970s were a critical period in the development of environmental research and policy. Growing concern about environmental degradation and pollution

Liverman, Diana M., "Geography and the Global Environment," pp. 107–10, 113–16 from *Annals of the Association of American Geographers*, 89.1 (1999).

catalyzed the public protest and political response now commonly termed "the environmental movement." Many students, including myself, chose to study the environment because we were influenced by books such as *Silent Spring* (Carson 1963), *Only One Earth* (Ward and Dubos 1972) and *The Limits to Growth* (Meadows et al. 1972). In countries such as Britain, Canada, the US and Mexico, this period also saw the establishment of government departments of environment, and the introduction of a wide range of environmental legislation.

I was intrigued by the Stockholm conference because of my fascination with environmental issues and because Barbara Ward, one of its architects, had been a friend of my parents in Ghana, where I was born just before Independence (producing my longstanding interest in international issues and the developing world). The 1972 Stockholm conference has often been identified as a watershed in international environmental policy because it was the first UN conference focused broadly on the environment, and it brought together government representatives from 113 countries as well as a small group of predominantly northern, environmental nongovernmental organizations (NGOs) represented at a forum adjacent to the main conference. The predominant focus of the conference was on local-level air and water pollution, the problems of urban growth, and nature conservation. There were disagreements over the risks of nuclear power and the need to protect marine mammals, and developing countries expressed concerns that the developed world was trying to slow economic growth in the south to control pollution. The most significant outcomes of the conference were the establishment of the UN Environment Program (UNEP) in Nairobi, an increase in worldwide environmental awareness, and the legitimizing of environmental policy and agencies in national governments. Geographers played a relatively minor role in the Stockholm conference and subsequent environmental policy formation, and wrote few of the popular environmental texts of the 1970s. Nevertheless, books such as Tim O'Riordan's *Environmentalism* (1976), Gilbert White's *Natural Hazards* (1974), and Ken Hewitt and Ken Hare's AAG Resource Paper on *Man and Environment* (1973) showed geographers actively engaging in the study, criticism, and development of environmental policy. Other edited books provided useful syntheses of the emerging environmental discourses and were used as texts in the growing number of environmental courses offered within geography departments or in newly created environmental studies institutes and programs. Clarence Glacken and Yi-Fu Tuan provided well-received contributions to longer term and comparative studies of human interactions with the environment.

These books were all required reading in my undergraduate courses for the BA in Geography at University College London (UCL), where I was fortunate to study from 1973 to 1976 [. . .]. Although the quantitative revolution was clearly evident in the statistics, computing, and systems framework used in many courses at UCL, we were also exposed to alternative perspectives including critiques of positivism, behavioral, marxist, and humanistic approaches, and development theory. There was also a strong tradition in applied physical geography and environmental conservation, providing a varied introduction to the discipline that heavily influences me to this day. Looking back, it is hard to remember the continuities and changes that occurred as an undergraduate, but I clearly remember reading Thomas Kuhn and discussing contemporary paradigm shifts in geography, including the move to models and the critique of positivism.

I chose to do graduate work at the University of Toronto because of the strong links between their geography and environmental-studies programs and the chance to study with geographers involved in international environmental policy, such as Ian Burton, Kenneth Hare, and Anne Whyte. While I mainly took courses in environmental law, economics, risk, ethics, and policy, I was influenced by some of the lively intellectual discussions taking place in the Toronto geography department in the late 1970s, especially concerning marxism, feminism, and phenomenology. I began to question the predominantly behavioral orientation of my research on drought and other natural hazards [. . .]. For example, I rethought my MA thesis, which analyzed response to drought on the Canadian prairies using government reports and social surveys, in terms of the politics of disaster relief and the structure of agricultural poverty.

At the same time, my interest in international environmental issues was fostered through opportunities to work with Toronto faculty on a variety of international projects and conferences, including Kenneth Hare's preparations for the 1977 UN Desertification conference and 1979 World Climate conference, as well as Anne Whyte and Ian Burton's contributions to an international comparative study of attitudes to nuclear power. A fellowship from NATO supported me to work on European responses to technological hazards and the harmonization of environmental-quality standards through UNEP's Monitoring and Assessment Research Center in London.

Within the international arena, it was becoming apparent that geography could offer useful perspectives, including: a focus on the link between the environmental and social sciences, a sensitivity to processes occurring at different scales, and the ability to provide contextualized and comparative case studies. The physical scientists still tended to dominate international environmental research, however, and geographers, including myself, were often so preoccupied with getting the "human" into the discussion that they overlooked the debates raging within the social sciences about the appropriate ways of understanding society and its relationship to nature.

By 1980, a new set of environmental concerns were emerging onto the international agenda, including ozone depletion, climate change, and biodiversity loss. Human activity appeared to be transforming the earth system through the use of chemicals that damaged the stratospheric ozone layer, the burning of fossil fuels that released greenhouse gases and caused global warming, and the conversion of ecosystems in ways that reduced biological diversity. There issues became defined as "global" environmental changes and were widely publicized by scientists, environmental groups, and some national governments.

Beginning work for my PhD at the University of California-Los Angeles in 1980, I sought continuity by returning to physical geography. I elected to study climatology because of my enduring interest in drought and the new challenges of climate change. Werner Terjung promoted a physics-based modeling approach to climatology, grounded in the systems approach I had been taught as an undergraduate at UCL. The modeling work I did with Terjung became the foundation of a dissertation on the use of global food models to forecast climate impacts on the world food system.

Yet I was drawn into developments in human geography by UCLA geographers such as Margaret FitzSimmons and Susanna Hecht, who were using political economy to study environmental aspects of US agriculture and Amazonian deforestation. As I continued to work on drought issues, our understanding of natural hazards in geography was transformed by books such as Ken Hewitt's *Interpretations of Calamity* (1984) and Michael Watts's *Silent Violence* (1983) that highlighted the importance of political economy and social vulnerability in the creation of hazard and famine. Political economy and critiques of positivism provided a second layer to my dissertation, which became both a technical and an epistemological critique of global modeling.

A dissertation fellowship at the National Center for Atmospheric Research (NCAR) in Colorado brought me back to issues of international environmental policy and to a direct engagement with the earth sciences. NCAR provided an invaluable experience of interdisciplinary climate research, including the need to defend social science and geography as valid and essential scientific approaches. NCAR scientists such as Stephen Schneider, Walter Orr Roberts, and Mickey Glantz were framing the new agenda for global change research and encouraging students to take on the challenge of understanding the global environment and participating in the policy process. Geographers associated with NCAR [. . .] provided my models for engagement with global change and international environmental policy because of their active participation in international conferences and policy debates.

As an assistant professor at Wisconsin in the late 1980s, I found myself torn between teaching, the need to publish within the discipline, and the opportunities to participate in the interdisciplinary policy debates on climate-change. Both my modeling work and critical perspectives on hazards convinced me that the developing world and the poor were disproportionately vulnerable to climate-change. I was also struck by the dominance of developed-world examples in climate-change research and concerned about my lack of Third World field experience, despite a continuing interest in developing countries.

I had resisted developing a "regional" focus because, during my years as a student, the "old" regional geography had been criticized for its descriptive nature and colonial legacy, and because global-change research seemed, initially, to demand global rather than regional approaches. But the emergence of a new regional geography, set in the context of global processes and local responses, along with the realization that global change is produced and experienced at the local level, and a request to review some work on Mexican climate and agriculture, prompted me to begin several projects on climate change and environmental issues in Mexico.

Seeking a theoretical perspective for my work in Mexico, I was, like many others, influenced by Blaikie and Brookfield's vision of political ecology, which examined how local people make decisions in the context of structural and ecological constraints. I was also interested in seeing if I could empirically examine the concept of vulnerability as developed in the critical natural-hazard literature. Using these frameworks, as well as my knowledge of climate modeling, I was able to write a series of articles describing the past and future impacts of climate change in Mexico, and documenting the ways in which technology, poverty, land tenure, and demography created vulnerability to these changes. I joined several other geographers [. . .] in contributing to various international assessments of global warming and climate impacts and arguing for attention to regional impacts and vulnerability.

The 1992 Rio conference focused on the issues of climate change, biodiversity protection, and sustainable development, and the Agenda 21 report produced for the meeting [. . .] laid out an agenda for research and action for the next century. One hundred-eleven heads of state and more than 500 NGOs attended the Rio conference. At the national level, the US Global Change Research Program [USGCRP] produced a series of reports outlining global-change research needs.

By the end of the 1990s, geographers were becoming closely identified with the interdisciplinary field of the "human dimensions of global environmental change," mainly through our work on climate impacts, but also through the study of the social causes of land-use change and through critical perspectives on international environmental policy. Geographers now chair the International Human Dimensions Program and the US National Academy of Science (NAS) Committee on the Human Dimensions of Global Environmental Change. Scientists and policy makers were calling for geographers to become more involved in the study of global change and in the development of international environmental policy, and opportunities for funding, collaborative research, and impacts on policy were apparently expanding.

There are several explanations for the inability or reticence of some geographers to engage in global-change research or policy debates. Some suggest that it can partly be explained by the small number of geographers in the influential NAS or Ivy League universities. Geography lacks the power of professions like law and economics that control the core institutions of social and political experience, and is often treated with suspicion by scientists because of our hybrid (and what they perceive as superficial) training in physical and human sciences. My own experience has been that geographers can gain the respect of earth scientists, modify the global-change research agenda, and influence public policy in ways that I outline towards the end of this paper.

But some geographers do not wish to participate in such a globalizing or environmentalist discourse. They believe that social problems are more urgent – poverty, homelessness, trade – or that local environmental issues are more important and salient. Others believe that we are being coopted to serve the agenda and maintain the funding of the earth scientists, or that it is important to remain skeptical about the metanarratives of global change and the debates over scientific "truth." There are certainly times when I have felt skeptical about global-change research. When interviewing rural farmers about climate change, it seems as though they face so many other economic and political problems that my questions are not salient. Yet, on many occasions, they have patiently explained to me how climate variability interacts with economic crisis and political disempowerment to threaten their livelihcods, and how they are concerned that pollution and deforestation have increased temperatures and delayed the rains. I have seen social-science research and the vulnerability of developing countries used to promote the agendas and funding of the earth sciences or of particular agencies, but overlooked when distributing resources or prioritizing research. The bulk of global-change funding is still targeted at physical science despite the many statements about the importance of human-dimensions research. Of the $1.8 billion budgeted for Federal global-change research in 1998, I estimate that less than five percent is for social science or human-dimensions research. More than half of the budget is for NASA's space-based observation programs using satellites.

In the remainder of this paper, I ask, [. . .] what are the continuities and disjunctures between research in geography and the demands of global-change research? [. . .] My response to the [. . .] question is based on my experiences as an advisor to several groups concerned with global change research, especially as the chair of the NAS Committee on the Human Dimensions of Global Environmental Change.

[. . .]

Geography and Global Change Research

The overarching framework for the current US Global Change Research Program is laid out each year in *Our Changing Planet*, the joint report to Congress from the agencies that contribute to global change research. For the last two years, the program has been divided into four priority areas and several crosscutting themes.

In the case of seasonal-to-interannual climate fluctuations, which has a particular focus on forecasting El Niño, geographers have already made significant contributions to both physical understanding and improved methods for climate impact assessment. For example, regional predictions have been improved through techniques that downscale from global atmospheric circulation using regional models or statistical relationships to estimate precipitation.

Geographers have played an important role in reconceptualizing climate impact assessment to take account of vulnerability, demonstrating that the impacts of climatic fluctuations and changes depend as much, if not more, on social, political, and economic conditions as they do on the magnitude of the climatic events. The lack of consensus about how climate may change at the regional level, and the recognition that changes in social systems may be more important than changes in natural systems in determining the impacts of drought and other climatic shifts, caused Working Group 2 of the second IPCC [Intergovernmental Panel on Climate Change] assessment to pay more attention to vulnerability assessment. My own research in Mexico has demonstrated that the communally owned *ejidos* are more vulnerable to drought and climate change than the larger private farms. They are more vulnerable because they were given more drought-prone land during agrarian reforms; have less irrigation; are constrained in their access to credit, subsidies, and crop insurance; and because their members are often poorer and more severely affected by economic crises.

Geographer Bill Easterling is currently chairing a National Academy of Sciences panel to define a human-dimensions research agenda relating to seasonal climate variation and prediction. One of the main concerns of this panel is to examine the socioeconomic and political implications of improved predictions of El Niño, including effects on commodity markets, the communication of uncertainty, differential ability to use the forecasts, and interaction with traditional prediction methods and livelihoods. The preliminary results of studies in Mexico and Northeast Brazil suggest that scientists have paid inadequate attention to the ways in which their forecasts are communicated and perceived, or to the vulnerabilities and adaptation options of farmers receiving predictions.

The study of longer-term climate change on decadal to centennial time scales is another area where physical geographers have been active in paleoenvironmental studies, climate-change detection, and climate modeling. This research theme, as well as atmospheric chemistry, encompasses the complex set of questions about the human causes, consequences and responses to changes in global atmospheric composition such as those caused by increasing carbon dioxide or ozone depleting chemicals. Geographers have been involved in many aspects of this research, including studies of anthropogenic greenhouse-gas emissions and mitigation of global warming. Our largest and most enduring influence has been in studies of the potential impacts of global warming and sea-level rise. Here geographers have developed methods, completed regional case studies, and coordinated major international projects. Several geographers have taken a more skeptical position on global warming, suggesting that observed warming may be explained by other factors and that climate model predictions are an uncertain basis for public policy.

I believe that geographers can make further contributions to the study of longer-term climate change and atmospheric chemistry, particularly through our understanding of regional economic restructuring, regional geographies, and consumption patterns. The increasing mobility of capital has facilitated the expansion of transnational corporations and massively restructured the geography of manufacturing, agriculture, human settlements, and all their associated environmental impacts. Further research is needed to establish the theoretical and empirical links between economic restructuring and environmental change, cultural influences on consumption, and the global and regional environmental effects of trade liberalization.

Regional geographers can provide detailed insights into critical patterns of energy consumption and materials flows, particularly in rapidly changing regions such as the former Soviet Union and Eastern Europe, China, and Southern Africa. Within the US (which produces about twenty percent of all anthropogenic greenhouse gases), the Association of American Geographers is already coordinating a study of Global Change and Local Places, which sets out to understand how local economies and land-use relate to greenhouse-gas emissions. In these studies, we need to be aware of new developments in atmospheric chemistry, which, for example, point to the significance of regional sulfur emissions and nitrogen cycling in global climatic change.

Geography lies at the heart of the new USGCRP priority on land-use change and terrestrial and marine ecosystems. Land-use and cover change are also the focus of a joint activity of the International Human Dimensions and Geosphere-Biosphere Programmes (IHDP/IGBP) – the Land-Use/Cover Change (LUCC) core project. The goal of LUCC is to link social driving forces to land-use and cover change, conduct comparative case studies, and evaluate and build land-use change models. The documentation and explanation of regional patterns of land-use and land-cover change draws on geographic skills ranging from remote sensing and GIS to census analysis, social surveys and field ethnographies. Political ecology can provide useful insights into the relative roles of structural forces, institutions, and individuals in decisions about how land is used. My own research on land-use change in Mexico has shown me how challenging it is to move across scales of analysis, to overlays different data sources, and to integrate and value the oral histories of people we talk with in our local case studies.

Of the crosscutting themes [referred to above], that of human dimensions offers many opportunities for geographic research. The human dimensions of global environmental change encompasses the analysis of the human causes of global environmental transformations, the consequences of such changes for societies and economies, and the ways in which people and institutions respond to the changes. It also involves the broader social, political, and economic processes and institutions that frame human interactions with the environment and influence human behavior and decisions. In addition to the human-dimensions questions identified in relation to the first four USGCRP priorities, the challenge of *integrated and regional assessment* is an important one for geographers.

Integrated assessment has been used to describe a variety of activities, including interdisciplinary discourse, the merger of formal socioeconomic and physical computer models, and research that links the causal chain of fossil fuel emissions and land-use to climatic changes and impacts, adaptation, and mitigation. Many integrated assessments, especially formal modeling efforts, have been used to evaluate different policy scenarios, such as carbon taxes or technology options. Perhaps the greatest insights of integrated-assessment climate-change models are that socioeconomic uncertainties dominate biophysical uncertainties, and that our ability to model regional and distributional impacts is very limited.

USGCRP has highlighted the importance of regional approaches in its most recent report to Congress by prioritizing regional-scale estimates of the timing and magnitude of global change, and by promoting regional analyses of the environmental and socioeconomic consequences of global change in the context of other stresses. During 1997 and 1998, geographers were well represented in the organization of a series of Regional Workshops around the US to discuss how climate change and variability might affect livelihoods, economic sectors, and resource management at the local level. Regional analyses provide opportunities to incorporate better understandings of local topography, climate, and ecosystems, as well as more sensitive and disaggregated analyses of human communities and their vulnerabilities.

The current research agenda of the US Global Change Research Program clearly poses many opportunities and challenges to geography. Some of the opportunities are there because geographers participated in the framing of the research agenda, but they are also, to some extent, defined for us by a broader, predominantly earth science, community. There remain important challenges and reminders that geography presents to global change research and international environmental policy. For example, many of the physical and economic studies of climate change and deforestation tend to be large-scale and aggregated, and international policy analyses tend to be state-centered. Geography can challenge global-change research to become regional and local, and to understand the role of NGOs, broader institutions involving land tenure and markets, and individual behavior in the causes and consequences of global change.

Geography also raises questions about whether global change and international environmental policy are sensitive to issues of gender, race, ethnicity and other dimensions of difference and diversity. Vulnerability is often greater among women, children, and people of color because it is often associated with marginality, powerlessness, or discrimination. Another challenge to global-change research comes from social and geographic theory that argues that quantitative modeling is inappropriate or unsuccessful when predicting social trends and human futures, or that international environmental policy and global-change research are constructed as discourses to serve particular power groups or the spread of global capitalism through economic integration. These critiques are often disturbing to colleagues in the earth sciences; they make it difficult to implement integrated quantitative models. Nevertheless, it is reasonable to question the methods and underlying objectives of global-change research, and to be aware of the interests that research and policy may serve. In that global-change research can focus on the needs and vulnerabilities of the poor, or highlight inequalities in the global system, it can also be seen to subvert powerful industrial interests, especially when research results are shared with nongovernmental and community groups.

Conclusion

In this paper, I have argued that geography has much to offer the study of international environmental and global change, and to the development of related policies. I have examined the evolution of international environmental policy and global-change research from the perspective of the role of geographers and the challenges posed to and from geography, and from my own experiences and research projects. Although I have focused on research, we also have a role to play as teachers and citizens. Faculty have already incorporated the study of global change and international environmental policy into the curriculum and are developing public education materials. Many geography faculty, students, and alumni are active with environmental, community, and political groups that attempt to influence state, federal, or international policy. Some seek continuity in the teaching of enduring texts and ideas or the protection of valued landscapes and communities. Others seek to change their students and the world through new ideas, innovative technologies, or transformed economic and political structures.

There are certain continuities in the human-environment tradition of geography and its approach to global change, including the efforts to bridge physical and human geography, and attention to scale. Changes in geographic theory, however, especially the influence of political economy in environmental and hazards research, led to an understanding of vulnerability and the role of the global economy in local environmental degradation. Meanwhile important questions arose about who was responsible for global change and who would suffer the most severe consequences. Geographers are engaging a wide range of issues in global change as defined mainly by the earth science community, including model downscaling, climate impacts, land use, regional emissions, and integrated assessment. Contemporary geographic approaches such as structure and agency, globalization, social movements, feminism, and cultural studies also have much to offer the broader study of global change and those who experience its consequences.

Chapter 14

Water Resource Conflicts in the Middle East

Christine Drake

In the Middle East, water may be more important than either oil or politics. Whereas the proven oil reserves in the area are estimated to last at least 100 years, water supplies are already insufficient throughout the region, and competition for them is inevitably going to increase in the years ahead. Already there have been a number of clashes between countries over water, and several political leaders have suggested that future conflicts may well center on access to water, both surface and sub-surface. Water is, after all, the most basic of resources, critical to sustainable development in the Middle East and to the well-being of the area's population.

The purpose of this article is to provide a background for teachers at all levels on the water situation in the Middle East. It examines the causes of the increasing pressure on water resources, considers the conditions and major sources of conflict in the three major international river basins in the Middle East, and investigates possible solutions.

Geographical and Historical Background

At the very root of the problem of limited water resources is the physical geography of the Middle East, for this region is one of the most arid in the world. Descending air (which can hold more moisture as it sinks) and prevailing northeast trade winds that blow from a continental interior region to a warmer, more southerly location explain why almost all of the Middle East is dry. Only Turkey, Iran, and Lebanon have adequate rainfall for their needs because they are located farther north and have more mountainous topography, which intercept rain- and snow-bearing westerly winds in winter. Every other country has at least part of its territory vulnerable

Drake, Christine, "Water Resource Conflicts in the Middle East," pp. 4–12 from *Journal of Geography*, 96.1 (1997).

to water shortages and/or is dependent on an exogenous source of water (a source of water originating outside its boundaries).

It has been estimated that about 35 percent of the annual renewable water resources of the Middle East is provided by exogenous rivers. Certainly, the two major river systems that bring water into the region, the Nile to the Sudan and Egypt, and the Tigris-Euphrates primarily to Syria and Iraq, have sources outside the arid zone – the Nile in the heart of East Africa (the White Nile) and especially in Ethiopia (the Blue Nile), and the Tigris and Euphrates in Turkey (and to a limited extent in Iran). Other rivers, such as the Jordan, Yarmuk, Orontes, Banias, etc., are too small to be of much significance, yet, in the case of the Jordan-Yarmuk, are large enough to quarrel over.

Droughts are common and a natural part of the climate. Yet the prolonged recent droughts suggest that even the natural aridity of the area may have been exacerbated by such human actions as the increase in greenhouse gases from burning more fossil fuels. Even without human intervention, rainfall is seasonal. The water resource problem thus concerns not only the total volume of water available but also its seasonality – the shortage of water in the dry, hot summers. In addition, most of the Middle East rainfall is very irregular, localized, and unpredictable. Furthermore, the region suffers from high evapotranspiration rates, a factor that diminishes the value of the water that is available.

In the past, people adapted to the seasonality of the rainfall and to the periodic droughts and were able to produce enough food to meet local demand. They devised a variety of ingenious ways to store water and to meet the needs of both rural and urban populations. But since the middle of the 20th century such measures have become inadequate, and a new balance must be found among competing needs for water.

Causes of Conflict

Escalation of conflict over water issues in the Middle East results from the confluence of a number of factors, especially rapidly growing populations, economic development and increasing standards of living, technological developments, political fragmentation, and poor water management. The inadequacy and relative ineffectiveness of international water laws as a means of settling and regulating freshwater issues as well as the lack of any real enforcement mechanisms compound the problem.

Population growth

Underlying and exacerbating the conflict over water resources in the Middle East is the enormous increase in population. (The Middle East is defined here as the traditional southwest Asian countries, and including Turkey, Iran, and Egypt, but excluding the former Soviet republics and the other countries of North Africa.) From somewhere around 20 million in 1750, the population tripled to around 60 million by 1950, but then almost quintupled to 286 million by 1996. It is estimated that at present rates of growth, the population will double again in less than 30 years.

Immigration has also been a significant part of the problem, particularly in the Jordan-Yarmuk watershed area, as hundreds of thousands of Jews from all over the world have moved to Israel since its establishment in 1948, and hundreds of thousands of Palestinians have relocated to Jordan from Kuwait in the wake of the Gulf War. If an independent Palestinian state comes into being, water shortages could be compounded by up to 2.2 million Palestinians currently registered world-wide as refugees who could return and settle there.

As populations grow, per capita availability of water decreases. At present, around half of the population in the Middle East depends directly on water for its livelihood. Despite efforts to attain food self-sufficiency, the region imports more than 50 percent of its food requirements now, and that proportion is expected to grow considerable over the next decades. Indeed, the Middle East now has the fastest-growing food deficit in the world, and Starr believes that food insecurity will increasingly pit nation against nation.

Rapid economic development

Rapid economic development and rising standards of living, spurred on at least in part by the oil boom, have raised the demand for water both by industry and domestic users. Urbanization also adds to the strain; over half the population of the Middle East now lives in urban areas where populations consume 10 to 12 times as much water per capita as village dwellers.

Technological developments

Technological developments now enable people to alter their environments in unprecedented ways. The balance between people and their environments and their direct dependence on the natural seasons and cyclical availability of water has been changed by people's ability to build huge dams and create vast reservoirs where increased evaporation occurs, to construct large irrigation schemes where much water is wasted through inefficient watering methods, to extract large quantities of shallow groundwater resulting in lowered water tables, and to damage or destroy rivers and aquifers by polluting them, often irrevocably.

Political fragmentation

Whereas in times past major empires covered the entire area and dampened conflict among the different peoples within them, the end of World War I saw the dissolution of the one major empire that had controlled much of the Middle East for over 500 years, the Ottoman Empire. Similarly, British colonialism and administration of most of the Nile basin reduced friction over water until the 1950s. With the creation of independent states and increasing ethnic consciousness, growing disparities and rivalries have developed within and among the very diverse populations in the region – Arabs, Turks, Iranians, Kurds, Ethiopians, and Israelis – to name just the main protagonists. All have become more competitive and nationalistic.

Overuse and pollution of rivers and shared aquifers (underground water-bearing formations) are a source of growing tension. Water was one of the underlying causes of the 1967 Arab-Israeli war and continues to be a stumbling block in the search for peace. Forty percent of Israel's water, for example, is obtained from aquifers beneath the West Bank and Gaza. Water was a major rallying cry both for the Palestinian Intifada in the Occupied Territories and for conservative parties in Israel. Whereas, in the past, the Cold War had a restraining effect on the likelihood of major conflict, that lid has now been removed.

Poor water management

Poor water management exacerbates the problem of both water quantity and quality. Great quantities of water are lost through inefficient irrigation systems such as flood irrigation of fields, unlined or uncovered canals, and evaporation from reservoirs behind dams. Pollution from agriculture, including fertilizer and pesticide runoff as well as increased salts, added to increasing amounts of industrial and toxic waters and urban pollutants, combine to lower the quality of water for countries downstream (called downstream riparians), increase their costs, and provoke dissatisfaction and frustration, again creating irritations that can lead to conflict.

International water laws

Existing international water laws are underdeveloped and inadequate and in some respects do not seem geared to the problems of arid developing countries, having been developed in the temperate and better watered areas of Europe and North America. Various legal principles exist, but there are no legally binding international obligations for countries to share water resources. Agreements must depend upon the mutual goodwill of co-riparians (the countries bordering a specific river) in any particular drainage basin. The likelihood of conflict or cooperation depends very much upon a number of geopolitical factors. These include the relative positions of the co-riparians within the drainage basin, the degree of their national interest in the problem, and the power available to them both externally and internally to pursue their policies.

Major regions of conflict

Although there are many international rivers and several important shared aquifers in the Middle East, and all have potential for water disputes, the potential for the greatest conflicts occurs in the three major international river basins: the Tigris-Euphrates, the Nile, and the Jordan-Yarmuk.

The Tigris-Euphrates Basin

In the case of the Tigris-Euphrates, there are several fundamental issues. Turkey is the source area for more than 70 percent of the united Tigris-Euphrates flow and owns large portions of the drainage basins of the two rivers (Figure 14.1). It also has the upstream position and so the opportunity to use the waters of the Tigris-Euphrates as it pleases. Indeed, the creation of Turkey's Southeast Anatolia Development Project (Turkish acronym GAP) is evidence of its felt rights. This very ambitious plan is to build 22 dams on the Euphrates in order to increase irrigation and electricity generation and to bring greater prosperity to a heretofore neglected Kurdish region of the country. Turkey argues that the GAP project will actually benefit all three riparian countries, Syria and Iraq as well as Turkey, as it will reduce damage from floods and even out the river's flow, storing excess water from the wet season and snow melt so it can be used in the dry summer season and soften the impact of droughts.

Inevitably, however, as more of the Euphrates water is withdrawn and used in Turkey, less will be available for downstream riparians. Indeed, the GAP project, if completed, is expected to reduce the flow of the Euphrates by 30 to 50 percent within the next 50 years. Furthermore, the water will be of lower quality, as increased amounts of salts, fertilizers, pesticides, and other pollutants enter the river after having been used for irrigation.

Syria depends on the Euphrates for over half its water supply and has a population growing at 3.8 percent, with almost no effort being made to reduce that extraordinarily high rate of growth. It also has plans to expand its irrigation projects. Iraq is even more dependent than Syria on the waters of the Euphrates and Tigris and claims historic rights to the water, but its position as the lowest riparian state renders it vulnerable to decreased water supply from both Turkey and Syria. A 1987 protocol in which Turkey promised 500 cubic meters per second at its border with Syria has not been solidified into a firm agreement or treaty, nor has Syria's pledge to deliver 290 cubic meters to Iraq, an amount that is only about half of what Iraq claims (570 cubic meters per second) and is clearly far below its needs. Iraq's population is expected to grow from 21 million in 1996 to around 35 million in 2010. The only ameliorating fact here is that Iraq can compensate for lack of water in the Euphrates by taking water from the Tigris, which at present is underutilized.

A related problem is the current dispute over the actual size of the annual flow of the Euphrates. Data on average discharge vary enormously. Syria's claims that Turkey is deliberately reducing the flow of the Euphrates are countered by Turkey's claim that the region suffers from periodic droughts.

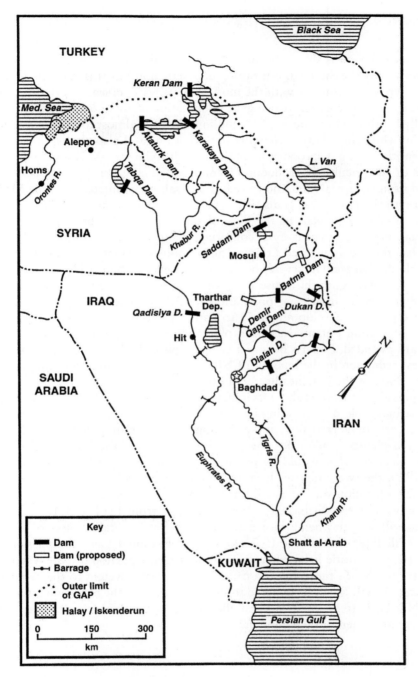

Figure 14.1 The Tigris-Euphrates basin.

The Nile Basin

The Nile catchment is shared by 10 countries, but the main disputes over water so far involve only the three largest: Ethiopia, Sudan, and Egypt (Figure 14.2). Of the three, Egypt is the country with the most obvious water crisis, and the situation is becoming more severe each year. Egypt's population of about 64 million is growing annually by almost one and one-half million. Egypt is almost totally dependent on the Nile (while contributing virtually nothing to it) and also claims that its prior usage entitles it to a disproportionate share of the Nile waters. Not only is over 95 percent of its agricultural production from irrigated land, but Egypt needs both to expand its agricultural land and to reduce the salt-water intrusion of the Mediterranean into the Nile delta, goals threatened by growing water shortages.

Since about 85 percent of the flow of the Nile into Egypt originates on the Ethiopian plateau, Egypt is most concerned about its relationship with Ethiopia. Egypt has repeatedly warned Ethiopia not to take any steps that would affect the Blue Nile discharges. On several occasions, however, Ethiopia has claimed that it reserves its sovereign right to use Blue Nile (and Sobat) river water for the benefit of its own rapidly increasing population (at 3.1 percent a year). Indeed, it has extensive plans to develop about 50 irrigation projects and to expend its hydro-electric generation potential as well, plans which are more feasible now that its civil war has ended. Experts believe it is highly possible that Egypt may experience a modest reduction in the amount of Nile water available to it as Ethiopia claims a larger share of the Nile headwaters in the future.

Egypt is also concerned about its immediate upstream neighbor, Sudan. Although Sudan is incapable of expanding its water use much at present, racked as it is by civil war, economic recession, and a shortage of foreign investment, that situation could well change. Sudan has the potential to become the bread basket of the Middle East, but that would be possible only with increased use of Nile water. Since 1929, the two countries have had an agreement allocating the Nile waters. The 1929 allocation was adjusted, however, in 1959, by an agreement which gave Sudan more water, reducing Egypt's relative share from 12:1 to 3:1.

What will happen when Ethiopia and Sudan begin demanding more of the Nile's water? Will Egypt accept the Helsinki and International Law Commission rules that irrefutably entitle Ethiopia and Sudan to a larger portion of Nile water? Will Egypt try to change those rules in order to give greater weight to the principle of prior use? Or will Egypt be tempted to use its position as the most powerful nation in the Nile basin to assure its present allocation, even if this means the use of military force and international conflict?

The Jordan-Yarmuk Waters

It is in the Jordan-Yarmuk basin that tensions have run the highest (Figure 14.3). All of the countries and territories in and around the Jordan River watershed – Israel, Syria, Jordan, and the West Bank – are currently using between 95 percent

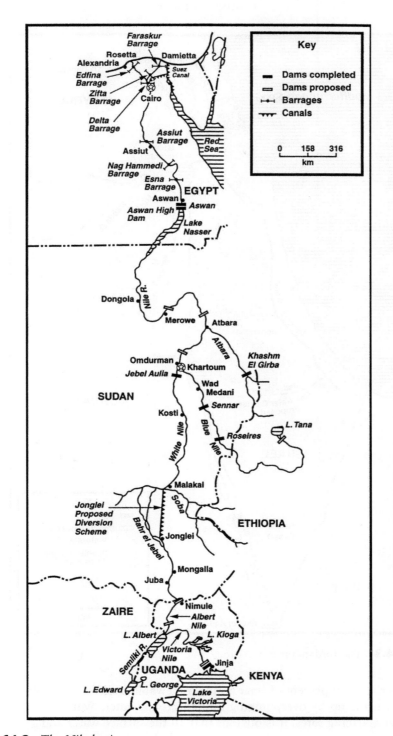

Figure 14.2 The Nile basin.
Source: Adapted from Kliot, N., *Water Resources and Conflict in the Middle East* (New York: Routledge, 1994).

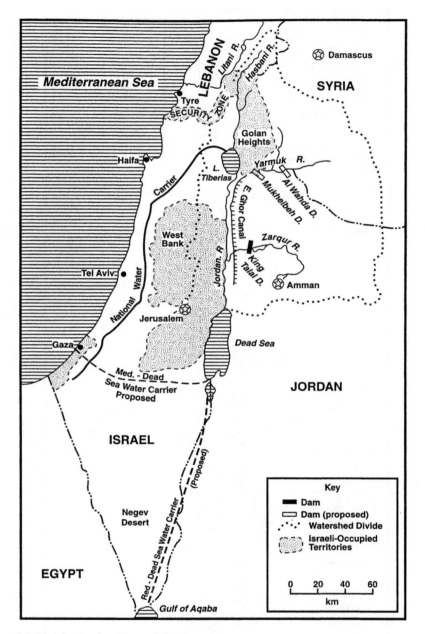

Figure 14.3 The Jordan-Yarmuk basin.

and more than 100 percent of their annual renewable freshwater supply. Shortfalls have been made up by overpumping limited groundwater. Water tables are being lowered at alarming rates. It is obvious that all the surface water and groundwater resources are over-stretched and over-utilized. Jordan's situation is perhaps the most serious. Only 5 percent of its land area receives sufficient rainfall to support cultivation and less than 10 percent of its agricultural land is irrigated at present, even though irrigation in the Jordan valley consumes about 65 percent of the country's total utilizable surface water.

Scarce water resources have either precipitated or exacerbated much of the recent political conflict in the Jordan river basin. Indeed, the Jordan basin has been described as "having witnessed more severe international conflict over water than any other river system in the Middle East . . . and . . . remains by far the most likely flashpoint for the future."

For Syria, Jordan, and Israel, the proportion of water derived from international sources is very high. Over 90 percent of Syria's water resources are shared with her neighbors, Turkey, Iraq, Israel, Lebanon, and Jordan. Jordan gets more than 36 percent of its water from sources shared with Syria, West Bank, and Israel. And more than half of Israel's water resources are shared with Syria, Lebanon Jordan, and the Palestinians. The economies and societies of the countries in the basin of the Jordan-Yarmuk are very vulnerable to any restrictions in their water supplies; hence, the situation is highly volatile.

Water conflicts among the protagonists have been longstanding, although the situation has worsened in recent years. Both overt and covert conflict has occurred over the division of the Jordan-Yarmuk waters, as both Israel and the Arab countries have tried to divert water: Israel through its National Water Carrier to expend agriculture in the Negev and the Arabs through their attempts to divert water from the Jordan basin to Lebanon, Syria, and Jordan. Disagreement over water was a major contributing cause of the 1967 Arab-Israeli war. Through its victory, Israel enhanced its water resources by capturing the Golan Heights and the West Bank aquifer. These captured sources supply as much as 25 percent of Israel's total water needs but have led to charges that Israel is stealing Arab water. On the West Bank, Israeli authorities have prevented the Palestinians from digging new wells or even finding alternative sources of water to compensate for water lost as a result of withdrawals by Jewish settlements. The disparity between the water allocations to Jewish and Arab settlements on the West Bank is enormous: the average aggregate per capita consumption for the Jewish settlements ranges between 90 and 120 cubic meters, whereas for Arab settlements the consumption is only 25–35 cubic meters per capita.

No comprehensive agreements have been reached over an equitable allocation of the Jordan-Yarmuk waters, although water was a vital and sometimes overriding factor in the peace process of the early 1990s. The October 1994 peace treaty between Israel and Jordan, which was only formalized after the last and most contentious issue – shared water resources – was agreed to, included an agreement for a Joint Water Committee to develop additional water resources, including two new dams, one each on the Yarmuk and the Jordan. Also, the creation of a Palestinian Water Authority was an important aspect of the September 1993 Declaration of Principles that allowed Israelis and Palestinians to recognize one another as legitimate political entities. Yet further agreements are urgently needed to include not only surface water but also groundwater (which desperately needs to be replenished). But given the inherent hostility in the region, it is likely that water will remain a major source of conflict and instability for the foreseeable future.

It is in the Jordan River basin, perhaps more than any other, that water has become "a highly symbolic, contagious, aggregated, intense, salient, complicated zero-sum power-and-prestige-packed crisis issue, highly prone to conflict and extremely difficult to resolve."

Possible Solutions

[. . .]

Conservation

More water can be made available through reducing waste in irrigation, municipal, and industrial uses, in transport, and in distribution. Far more can be done to encourage the more frugal use of water, through education and media campaigns, but especially by more realistic pricing for water use. However, such changes will be hard to implement and will run into enormous opposition, since water is such a politically sensitive issue; traditionally, water has been regarded as a free resource available to all who need it.

Better management

More water-efficient methods and technologies can be adopted. For example, in agriculture, it is essential to move away from inundation (flood) techniques, which currently account for about 95 percent of irrigation practices, to sprinkler techniques, trickle irrigation techniques (which take water directly to the plant roots from perforated plastic pipes), or subsurface irrigation techniques (which control the height of the water table and irrigate plants through capillary action, thus minimizing evaporation). Other management techniques include lining canals to prevent seepage losses, covering them to minimize evaporation, repairing pipes to reduce leakage, improving drainage to reduce soil salinization, minimizing evaporation by better field preparation and water application, and irrigating at night and early in the morning when evaporation rates are lower. In addition, more water can be recycled and treated sewage used at least on non-food and ornamental plants, while water quality can be preserved by preventing the contamination of water sources.

Prioritizing uses

Administrative solutions include managing the demand by reallocating water from comparatively low-value uses, such as agriculture, which currently consumes 80 to 90 percent of the region's water supplies, to essential domestic use and higher-value, industrial uses. Light industry yields about 30 times more input to GNP than does agriculture per unit of water used. However, such a strategy would lead to increased reliance upon foreign sources for food supplies, an outcome that seriously worries many policy-makers because of food security vulnerability. Such prioritizing is realistic, though, because there is enormous capacity to save water in agriculture, not only through more efficient irrigation techniques, but also by moving from water-consumptive crops such as rice and sugar cane to more water-efficient crops and increasing the use of more salt-tolerant crops, such as certain oil-seeds.

Technological solutions

There are many technological ways to help solve problems of both water quantity and water quality. The obvious and traditional response to water shortages has been to construct dams in order to retain runoff from floods, to store water for use throughout the year, and even to replenish shallow aquifers. But all dams have an impact on development downstream.

Interbasin water transfers are another technological solution, such as Turkey's proposed two "Middle East Peace Pipelines," designed to carry surplus Anatolian water from the Seyhan and Ceyhan rivers to Syria, Jordan, and Israel, and on through Iraq to Saudi Arabia and the Gulf states. Countries, however, are very reluctant to be dependent on others for their most basic need – water, which could be interrupted for political reasons. In addition, the costs for all of these projects would be enormous, probably higher than by obtaining water through desalination.

Developing cost-effective solar desalination technology is obviously a goal for the future. Already desalination of brackish water is competitive, although desalination of sea water is invariably expensive and largely influenced by petroleum prices. Another goal is to find a way to reduce evaporation on storage lakes behind dams.

Increasing cooperation among co-riparians

In order to obtain the maximum use of water, it is essential to develop each river basin in its entirety, in a fully integrated way, with comprehensive approaches to the sustainable management of water resources. Better and more detailed data need to be obtained and shared among all riparians. Such an approach is now beginning to occur with the most recent movement toward peace in the Jordan River basin.

Developing better, enforceable, international water laws

Clearly it is necessary to develop water laws that encompass all surface water and groundwater both within and outside a river basin, involve all co-riparian states, provide for sustainability of water use, prioritize water uses, and offer more incentives for water preservation and conservation. Only then will countries have their allocation assured and be able to plan their own use of water, free from threats and uncertainty. Better mechanisms to enforce water laws and solve conflicts over water resources must also be created.

Reducing population growth rates

Finally, but perhaps most significantly, it is crucial that all states in the region drastically reduce their population growth rates, for in a context of rapidly increasing population, all other efforts to ensure water availability over the long term may well be futile. Certainly population stability (and some would argue for not just reducing growth rates but also the absolute size of the population) is a long-term strategy, but it may well be the most critical strategy of all. Unfortunately, Middle Eastern traditions value large families, while in some countries with large ethnic or religious diversity promoting family planning is politically unacceptable.

Conclusion

Experts disagree on the likelihood for future conflict over water. Some argue that more water conflicts are inevitable because of the combination and synergistic effect of the causes already discussed: growing water scarcity, increasing populations, rising standards of living, and higher consumption levels. Many of the rivers and aquifers in the region are shared, and the lack of adequate treaties and international laws, added to the absence of adequate enforcement mechanisms, increases the likelihood of confrontation. There has also been a history of hostility among some of the countries and a growing nationalistic self-awareness of the differences among the varied peoples in the Middle East. One could also suggest, perhaps a bit cynically, that countries "need" enemies to deflect attention from internal divisions, political corruption, and economic hardships, and to help to unify or integrate the population. Some even contend that countries need also to justify their military forces and keep them busy!

Others argue, however, that future water conflicts are not likely for a number of substantial reasons. For one thing, cooperation is cheaper than conflict. As one person put it: "Why go to war over water, when for the price of one week's fighting you could build five desalination plants?" There is considerable international pressure to avoid war over water, partly because it could escalate into war over other, even more intractable issues. In addition, there are a number of external geopolitical forces that are indirectly exerting pressure for peaceful cooperation on water allocation issues, such as the end of the cold-war manipulation of states in the Middle East, the progress toward a peace between Israel and its neighbors, and Turkey's goal to enter the European Union. The fact that in each river basin there is one stronger military power (Turkey, Egypt, and Israel) further deters conflict. Lack of capital will probably delay and may even prohibit development of some water-using projects. Moreover, if the solutions suggested earlier are implemented, conflict will be less likely.

Furthermore, states have it in their power actually to decide to treat water use as a vehicle for cooperation. Throughout the years of hostilities in the Middle East, water issues have actually been the subject of occasional secret talks and even some negotiated agreements between the states in the region. In regional peace talks, cooperation on regional water planning or technology might actually help provide momentum toward negotiated political settlement. According to Frey and Naff,

> Precisely because it is essential to life and so highly charged, water can – perhaps even tends to – produce cooperation even in the absence of trust between concerned actors.

In any case, water is only one of many factors at work in the Middle East – certainly and important one, but only one. Israel's settlements on the West Bank and its occupation of the Golan Heights, radical groups within not only the Palestinian population and Israel, but also among the Kurds and other disadvantaged groups, irredentist pressures, economic pressures – these and many other pressures could produce bitter conflict that uses water either as a weapon or as an excuse for hostility.

Much depends on leadership in the region, including the ability of governments to control radical or conservative elements that want to exploit water issues, the ability to obtain capital for the development of industry (which will take some of the pressure off agriculture), the ability to obtain secure food sources from outside the area, the ability to reduce population growth, the ability to educate the public on water issues, develop an ethos of conservation, and change water pricing systems, and finally, the ability to promote cooperation and encourage the sharing of technology, data, and research. One has to hope that the benefits of cooperation in the development of river basins and the rule of law will be seen to outweigh the costs of conflict.

Chapter 15

Americans and Their Weather

William B. Meyer

Introduction

In the mid-1830s, the young Nathaniel Hawthorne sat reading "what once were newspapers" – a bound volume of New England gazettes ninety-odd years old. Comparing the daily life that they portrayed with his own, Hawthorne was struck by how different and how much more severe the weather appeared to have been in the past. "The cold was more piercing then, and lingered farther into the spring," he decided; "our fathers bore the brunt of more raging and pitiless elements than we"; "winter rushed upon them with fiercer storms than now – blocking up the narrow forest-paths, and overwhelming the roads."

He was not alone in thinking so. Another resident of Salem, Dr. Edward Holyoke, had been of the same opinion. In his later years, the doctor spoke as the classic authority on the weather, the Oldest Inhabitant. Born in 1728, he lived until 1829, the full span of the century that Hawthorne judged mostly at secondhand, and he had kept a daily temperature log for the better part of it. A newspaper in 1824 reported a general belief that the seasons were "more lamb-like" than in earlier times. An English visitor a few years later was frequently told that the climate was moderating. Cold and snowstorms had grown less intense and less frequent: such had been, wrote John Chipman Gray in the 1850s, "and is perhaps still a prevailing impression among the inhabitants of New-England."

All the same, that impression of the century gone by was wrong. Gray, who maintained that the winters had not changed, also tried to explain why intelligent observers could have supposed that they had. On one point, he granted, they were correct. Certainly the effects of the weather were not what they had once been. But there was no evidence that a shift in the weather was responsible. Holyoke's

Meyer, William B., "Introduction," pp. 3–15 from *Americans and Their Weather* (New York: Oxford University Press, 2000).

own records, analyzed after his death, did not bear out his belief that winter cold and storms had weakened in his lifetime. As Gray pointed out, if the impact of weather on New Englanders had changed, it was because New England society had changed.

Though the cold and snowfall had not diminished, it might well seem that they had, for winters in colonial times "were more severely felt than any winter of the same severity would now be." "Our people are better clothed," Gray observed, "our dwellings better fortified against cold," and great snowfalls interfered less with travel than they once had. Thanks to a denser population, "our roads are far more quickly rendered passable after heavy storms," the snow "beaten down in a very few days."

So in some ways New Englanders had protected themselves better from the elements. If the winter of earlier times, as a later historian would put it, was indeed "different from the modern winter," it was "because of the devices that had softened its rigours." But that, Gray continued, was not the whole story. Some other changes had had the opposite effect. They had increased the weather's importance and made it more, rather than less, of a nuisance than it had before. It was widely believed that summer droughts in New England had become more frequent. Again, the belief was an error that had a basis in fact. Dry spells had not grown more intense. Rather, Gray pointed out, "their effects have become of more consequence"; they caused more trouble thanks to changes in human activities. Waterpower from the rivers ran the spindles and looms and lathes of the factories that sprang up and multiplied in the nineteenth-century Northeast. One result of industrialization, Gray noted, had been to amplify any drop in streamflow into an economic and social crisis. Declines once too small to attract notice now commanded the attention of millowner and worker alike. The streams were watched with a new anxiety, and any dry spell was felt with a new acuteness. Even the average summer flow of the rivers was only about a tenth that of the wettest months, no small problem for mills trying to operate at a steady pace. Every year had become a drought year.

Plainly, something had changed, for the weather had not affected New Englanders in the eighteenth century in the same way it affected them in the nineteenth. It was easy to suppose that what was different was the weather itself. Just so, rooms suddenly become hotter when we become upset or excited; just so, the adult rereading a book enjoyed in childhood invariably discovers that the book has changed. That the changes occurred elsewhere is a second thought.

Hawthorne had second thoughts on one point. When he published "Old News" in the *New-England Magazine* in 1835, he added a footnote qualifying his claim that lightning had fallen "oftener and deadlier" a century before. Perhaps, he ventured, it was the spread of lightning rods that had made the difference, not a weakening of thunderstorms themselves. Even here, though, not all change was for the better. The country roads of New England were already becoming infested with a new pest, "the lightning-rod man." Recounting terrible stories of thunderbolt strikes, he frightened many farmers and householders into buying devices that were not only overpriced, but were often so badly installed that they amplified rather than reduced the dangers of lightning: "instead of proving themselves faithful sentinels and guarding in the hour of peril, they have too often turned traitors, and invited the destruction which they promised to avert."

Perhaps the metamorphoses in the weather's effects were not the reason, or the main reason, why so many New Englanders thought that their climate had grown different. Beliefs are rarely so simple to explain. But if Gray's examples do not prove the point he was making, they illustrate another and more important one: how changes in the weather's effects need not mean that the weather has changed.

Even when it has, that change is never by itself what matters. Knowing the weather's physical properties and how they have shifted is never enough to understand what they mean for those experiencing them. Any given change can have radically different results in different settings – the settings that at the same time, and to much larger net effect, determine and alter the consequences of stable and recurrent aspects of the weather.

One of the very shifts in climate that Hawthorne and Holyoke imagined had occurred in New England in the century leading up to the 1830s did take place in the century that followed: a small rise in mean temperatures. The results were not what they would have been earlier. Most revolutionary-era New Englanders lived by farming, fishing, and sailing, all highly sensitive to the weather. They generally stood to gain if the length of the growing season increased, harbors froze later and less often, and winter storms at sea became less fierce. After 1830, the relative decline of these three sectors lessened the profit that the region could expect from a warming climate. Other changes increased the losses that a warming could bring. In 1934, a New Hampshire businessman could observe how "the 'northeaster,' so dreaded by coastal shipping, is rather a blessing to the skier, since it is a father to most of our heavier snows." For winter sports, a long snowy season means a good year. A mild one interferes disastrously with business.

Even before the age of the ski resort, cold and snow had not been without their advantages. Ice cut from ponds for sale in the cities, a way of turning hard winters into hard cash, was just becoming an important article of trade in Hawthorne's New England. Throughout the progressively warmer late nineteenth century, milder winters and the "ice famines" that they could bring became a growing hazard for the booming ice business and for the urban populations that relied on it to keep food fresh in summer. In an era of horse-drawn vehicles and unpaved roads, a fall of snow, once it was beaten down, made getting about easy by sled or sleigh. Winter was the preferred time for hauling heavy loads and the season for speedy driving. A thaw or a snowless winter greatly hampered movement. First the railroad and then the automobile, the paved highway, and the airplane have changed snow from a resource into a pure hindrance for travel, and mechanical refrigeration has destroyed the natural ice trade entirely.

All of these developments and many others have determined what the effects would be of such warming as has occurred. They have also themselves transformed, in far more significant degree, the role in human life of a climate that has changed much less than the society inhabiting it has. The mid nineteenth to mid twentieth century warming is at most a footnote to New England weather history. During the same period, economic, social, and technological developments did vastly more to change the region's relations with its skies. Some other climatic shifts in other places, to be sure, have been of greater importance. Everywhere their effects have themselves depended on the evolution of society, though, and everywhere that evolution itself has repeatedly modified and transformed the meaning of weather and climate even if they have remained stable. The history of American weather to date is not principally the story of how the weather has changed, but of how Americans have changed.

Generally speaking, weather matters to people in two ways: as a help and a hindrance, as a resource and a hazard, as an opportunity and a constraints, as a source of gains and a source of losses. To what extent and in what ways it plays either role depend on the activities and wants with which it interacts.

Natural hazards, so called, are geophysical processes that threaten people or things that people value. To call the weather or anything else a "natural hazard" is misleading if to do so suggests that it is hazardous by its nature. What can make it hazardous is its relation to human affairs. It is a danger or a hindrance only if people value things that it can damage or engage in pursuits that it can disrupt. At one extreme, the damage and disruption may involve massive loss of life and property. At the other, they may involve mere discomfort, weather as disamenity.

How much discomfort the weather causes anyone depends on that person's standard of comfort, and such standards vary greatly. One person's oppressive heat can be another's cozy warmth, one's bitter chill another's bracing freshness. So, too, severer impacts of weather as hazard depend on more than simple exposure to a weather event. No two individuals, groups, or communities exposed to the same weather will ever be affected by it in precisely the same way. Some may be highly sensitive to it, others not at all. Among the former, some may be far better able than others to cope with the consequences. A drought will affect agriculture far more than it will affect most industries or services. Farmers who irrigate with groundwater will have less to fear than those who rely on rainfall, and they may gain if the loss of rain-fed crops drives prices higher. Of two nonirrigating farmers, one may have tools for coping – insurance, savings, off-farm employment, the support of an extended family – that the other lacks. All exposed to the same weather, they are vulnerable to it to different degrees; it is more of a hazard to some than to others, and to some it is no hazard at all.

Thus some recurrent weather event or some stable feature of the climate may become a hazard where it was not one before, or cease to be one, or become more or less of one with changes in society: in where people live, what they do, what they own, and how they arrange their relations to one another. The change can be as simple as a change in expectations. A higher standard of comfort makes the weather more of a disamenity than it was before. A higher standard of punctuality makes the same weather-related delays in travel more of a problem.

If weather is a hazard or a hindrance when it threatens anything people value, it is a resource when it is in any way useful. People benefit in a host of ways, often unwittingly, from sun, rain, wind, snow, heat, and cold. They may find the weather useful simply by finding it pleasant. But weather is an amenity, as it is a disamenity, not for its own qualities alone but also because of the standards by which it is judged. So too weather events and climatic patterns are – and are not – natural resources more generally in precisely the way they are – and are not – natural hazards. Just as the lives and livelihoods it affects are what make weather a hazard, they are what make it a resource. Without the defining elements of "human wants and human capabilities," the economist Erich Zimmermann pointed out, there are no resources in nature, only "neutral stuff." "The word 'resource' does not refer to a thing or a substance," Zimmermann observed, "but to a function which a thing or a substance may perform, or to an operation in which it may take part, namely, the function or operation of attaining a given end such as satisfying a want."

It follows that natural resources, like natural hazards, change as human wants and the means of satisfying them change. They can appear and disappear without any alteration in the natural environment. Two developments made the warm climate of the American South a richer resource in the late eighteenth century than it had been before. The mechanization of spinning and weaving in Great Britain increased the demand for the cotton that could be grown in the South, and the invention of the cotton gin in the United States made it possible to increase the supply. The climate had not changed, but its usefulness had. Sugarcane can be grown in parts of the South, but the climates of those areas have long owed much of their value to tariffs and import restrictions on sugar produced overseas.

Weather as a resource has one great advantage over nonweather inputs that may be used in its place. By and large, it is free where many possible substitutes are not. Yet the tools or skills or the land needed to exploit it may be costly, and so may its frequent unreliability. Weather as a resource, perhaps even more than weather as a hazard, is likely to vary tremendously in its value and importance to those exposed to it. Some may use it intensively, many others in the same place not at all.

The more one focuses on climatic shifts as the source of past change in climate-society relations, the more one may tend to think of controlling the climate as the best way to improve what remains unsatisfactory in these relations today. The more attention, on the other hand, one pays to the social factors that have made neutral weather events into hazards or resources, the more aware one will be of other ways to make those events less dangerous or more valuable. Students of natural hazards beginning with the geographer Gilbert F. White in the 1940s have developed the concept of the "range of choice" in human adjustment to the environment. Flood impacts, White stressed, can be lessened not only by controlling the water – by trying to regulate rainfall or streamflow – but by making human activities less exposed or vulnerable to it; by regulating floodplain development, for example, or by spreading losses through insurance. A similar range of choice exists where weather as a resource is concerned. Changing the weather itself is not the only or necessarily the most effective way to enhance its value.

Doubtless people would always prefer changing the weather to changing activities of theirs that conflict with it. But they cannot often hope to do so without changing other people's weather as well, yet any weather event is likely to be both hazard and resource for different people in many different ways. As ecological concern has spread, the likely subtle and unintended effects of trying to remodel something so basic to the environment have become a worrisome matter where they were not before. But even where clear and direct consequences alone are considered, there is no wind so ill that it blows no one any good. Hurricanes top all standard lists of American weather hazards. Even they provide benefits as well, though, and some provide more benefits than costs, replenishing water supplies and rejuvenating crops suffering from summer drought. Hard winters meant suffering from the cold in nineteenth-century New England, most of all among the poor, but, as Hawthorne noted, "the coal-merchants rejoice." The best winter weather for the ice-cutter too was "just the opposite of the weather sought by the poor man," and if a mild winter meant less immediate hardship, it also meant a shortage of ice and hardship in the summer. Weather optimal for some crops will not be so for others in the same area. The humorist "Max Adeler," a contemporary of Mark Twain's and at one time nearly as popular, described a country neighbor so cheerful that he saw only the good in whatever weather happened to be prevailing, but to see the good he did not have to invent it. Was heavy rain falling? "It makes the corn jump an' cleans the sewers an' keeps the springs from gittin' too dry." Drought? "Moisture breeds fevers and ague, an' ruins yer boots. If there's anything I despise, it's to carry an umbrella." In a heat wave, he would say "Splendid! Splendid! Noble weather for the poor and for the ice companies and the washerwomen! I never saw sich magnificent weather as this for drying clothes." Was it bitterly cold in winter? "It helps the coal trade an' gives us good skeetin'." The activities helped or hindered have changed greatly since Adeler's time. The larger point remains valid.

The weather can be both hazard and resource even for the same people engaging in the same activity. Sunshine has become a valuable amenity because many people enjoy basking in it, and at the same time it is a hazard to their health. The large and rapid increase in skin cancer in the modern United States is the product of social trends that inclued more, and more irregular, exposure outdoors and a shift of population to lower and sunnier latitudes. Areas with cloudless skies, a hazard now eagerly sought, find them a rich resource for attracting tourism and settlement, and at the same time annual deaths in the United States resulting from exposure to the sun now exceed those from all weather hazards, conventionally defined, put together.

A few occurrences of a few of those hazards, a handful of famous disasters, account for much more than their share of what has been written about American weather history: 1816, "The Year Without a Summer"; the Galveston, Texas, hurricane of 1900; the northeastern blizzard of 1888 and hurricane of 1938; the Dust Bowl droughts of the 1930s on the Great Plains. To make weather history solely or even mainly the history of great weather disasters would be narrowing of its scope as drastic and as unjustified as making it only the story of climate change and its effects. But these episodes are a part of the story, and their lessons hold true for weather history in a wider sense.

One of those lessons is that the category of weather disasters is itself – like those of weather hazards and resources – one to use with caution. There are disasters that do not involve the weather, but none are caused by it alone. September 8,

1900, was a day of calamity in Galveston not only because a hurricane struck but because a sizeable city had grown, force-fed by federal spending for harbor improvements but unprotected by any barriers against storm surges, on a low, flat coastal island in a climate prone to powerful storms, because most buildings were low and flimsy, because warnings of the storm were not rapidly or readily communicated, and because transportation was so slow and exposed that evacuation was hardly less risky than staying put. It was as much a land-use or a transportation disaster as it was a weather disasters. Most Galvestonians decided that it had been a disaster of political institutions. Fifteen years later they could judge themselves vindicated. The voters replaced their mayor and council after the 1900 hurricane by a novel system of government, a streamlined municipal commission. It set to work at once on a project that had long been considered but never begun: raising the city and building a protective sea wall. Another major hurricane that struck in 1915, after the work's completion, did vastly less destruction than the earlier storm had. The *Galveston Daily News* gave credit for the difference to the commission system, a "new form of government . . . a powerful instrument in the hands of the people for the management of their affairs."

At the same time, the weather is also a factor in many disasters usually classified under other headings. The Great Chicago Fire of 1871 is not generally listed as a natural or a meteorological catastrophe. Yet it happened because of a severe summer and fall drought that had left the crowded city, built of wood down to its pavements and sidewalks, parched and highly flammable and because of a strong wind that spread the flames, while the means of fire fighting were primitive. Identical weather in Chicago today would threaten no such catastrophe. On the other hand, drought and high winds in the mountains of southern California today are far more of a menace to life and property than they were a hundred years age. Forest and brush fires mattered relatively little when the land was thinly settled. Today it is occupied by affluent suburbanites who favor wood construction for their houses, the highly combustible native brush for their yards, and narrow, winding streets that are hard for fire engines to negotiate. Population and property have moved straight into harm's way, making drought and wind immensely more destructive agents than in the past.

A good way to see how a disaster involving the weather is never its doing alone is to ask, as in these cases, how the same weather's effects in the same place would have been different at some earlier or later time. Further examples would be easy to multiply. Many can be found in Blake McKelvey's *Snow and the Cities* (1995). It tells in engaging detail how the troubles and the opportunities caused by recurrent blizzards in American urban areas have endlessly metamorphosed over the past several centuries, how "the impact of similar storms . . . changed radically as the cities grew in size technological complexity." But it is not just exceptional storms or droughts that shed old meanings and take on new ones as human activities change. It is everyday weather as well, and to far greater net effect. Extreme events are involved in only a small part of weather-society interaction. As McKelvey traces the evolving impacts of urban blizzards, Bernard Mergen in *Snow in America* (1997) documents the more general transformation in the problems and possibilities of snow as a routine phenomenon, the ways in which social changes changed it "from resource to refuse to resource again" though its physical properties changed not at all. Every weather event and every feature of the climate, whether as dramatics as a hurricane or as mundane as rain, clouds, fog, or sunshine, has repeatedly shifted over time as a help and a hindrance in American life.

It has done so in two ways. Much of weather history is the story of devices that have been conceived and adopted at least in part with the goal of dealing better with weather challenges and opportunities. Physical tools of this class would fill a gigantic museum – whose own walls, windows, roofing, and heating and cooling systems would be as much exhibits as anything else on display. They range from covered bridges, street paving, and storm sewers to skis, sleds, and sleighs, to snow shovels, snowplows, snow tires, and snowblowers to umbrellas, parasols, sunscreen lotions, and sunglasses. Social coping devices include such institutions as weather forecasting, disaster relief, and insurance reimbursement for losses suffered from adverse weather or income lost from seasonal unemployment due to low demand and layoffs in certain livelihoods at certain times of the year.

Much of weather history is the development and deployment of such coping tools. Few of them, though, belong to weather history alone. A closer look reveals that weather protection has by no means been the only consideration governing their use. Even television weather forecasting is watched partly for entertainment. Roofing is a matter of taste, tradition, style, and display as well as a shelter from the elements overhead. Much seasonal unemployment is determined by the social rather than the meteorological calendar. Clothing provides protection, but fashion dictates many clothing choices that worsen rather than temper the weather's effects. It turns out too that some coping measures – certain kinds of insurance or flood protection works are good examples – end up worsening the weather's effects by rewarding risky behavior or increasing people's sense of security more than they increase security itself.

Thus even in this sphere weather history is not a simple story of progress. Moreover, changes in activities not at all motivated by concern with the weather, yet incidentally altering its role, form a second major class of factors – possibly the more important of the two. They are much less likely than the changes of the first class to improve weather-society relations, though they can happen to do so just as readily as they can happen not to. Many devices have lessened the problems that automobiles have with the weather, but the ways in which the automobile itself is used, the rising demands of mobility, speed, and punctuality, are the dominant reasons why those problems came to exist.

Few major shifts in life have failed to register incidentally on Americans' relations with their weather, and by no means always for the better. The landmark dates in weather history are less the familiar ones specific to it – 1816, 1888, 1900, 1938 – than the familiar landmark dates of American social, political, and technological history. Even 1870, the founding date of a federal weather bureau, owes much of its importance to developments in other areas: to better communications allowing forecasts and storm warnings to be more rapidly distributed. Every change in American life that has made activities less flexible and schedules more imperative has made forecasts less useful.

To say that the weather only matters because of how societies oraganize their lives is far from saying that it necessarily matters little. They are the reasons why it can matter tremendously. It is equally far from saying that dealing with the problems that weather does pose in any given situation is simple matter because solving the problem requires only a change in human wants or activities. Such things are not easily changed, and any different way of life will likely only mean different, not fewer, weather problems. Nor does it mean that those who suffer from the weather, even from foreseeable hazards, are necessarily to blame for their plight, for they may have had little choice in the face of other compelling reasons to act as they did.

Certainly, it makes little sense to condemn any change solely because it makes the weather either more of a nuisance or less of a resource. Such a change may still, overall, be for the better because the improvements that it brings in other areas more than outweigh these losses. Nor, for the same reason, is a change that improves weather-society relations necessarily an improvement overall. To assume that it must be one form of what is called *climatic determinism*, a particularly dangerous temptation to annalists and analysts of weather and society. Climatic determinism here involves treating weather or climate as something that people should have regarded as supremely important, around whose presumed imperatives they should, if sensible, have shaped their lives.

This form of climatic determinism takes the weather as the key to what should be. Another form takes weather as the key to what actually is. The second form sees the weather and climate as having shaped people's lives whether they were aware of it or not. Such reasoning asserts that trait y follows from climate X as an effect follows its cause. A classic example is the assertion that a certain building style or style of clothing prevailed in a particular location because it was dictated by the weather. Another is the assertion that civilization (or manufacturing or some personality type or outlook or aptitude) appears in one area and not in another because the climate of the former stimulates it and that of the latter depresses it.

What these two distinct forms of climatic determinism share – apart from their tendency to exaggerate the weather's importance – is the assumption that the weather's human significance is determined by its physical characteristics. Both forms are often attacked for the supposed reactionary political implications of such a stance. Each is often accused of being "part of an ideology which rationalizes and naturalizes an existing social order" and a "resistance to social change," for being "a theory which operates to justify an existing social order and the vested interests connected with that order," for necessarily being "strongly politically conservative since, like its close relative and accomplice biological determinism, it presents human behavior as 'naturally given,' plays down the responsibility of the individual and collective for political behavior, and undermines the role of human agency in changing attitudes."

If climatic determinism is true and such are its necessary implications, does it follow, as the argument suggests, that it should be ignored? But they are not its necessary implications [. . .]. Climatic determinism can be made to support any leftist, centrist, or conservative stand on any political or social issue. What is objectionable, rather, is that it is not true. One of the critics of the supposed reactionary tendencies of climatic determinism was on much stronger ground in lodging a second objection against it. "The same area and climate maintains itself through kaleidoscopic changes in economic and social life," he observed, evidence enough that there is something wrong with a thesis that would explain economic and social life as largely the climate's products. The explanation of architectural form as imposed by the environment, in the words of the folklorist Henry Glassie, "always seems to work in given situations, and it always falls apart when the architecture of different areas sharing similar environments is compared" – or when the same area is examined at two different periods. "When southern football was at the bottom of the heap, practice in the debilitating heat of the southern autumn was taken to explain the players' comparative lack of stamina," the sociologist Rupert Vance wrote in the 1930s. "Now that southerners hold their own or better in intersectional competition, such writers for the sporting press as George Trevor and Grantland Rice see reflections of the man building power of the climate."

The other form of climatic determinism – which urges that activities in an area be made to conform to the natural environment, to what nature "intended" and be changed back, as is often said, from what "nature never intended" – is no sounder. For nature has no plans or intentions, and the environment never dictates anything, even for success or failure in certain activities, for the activities and what constitutes success and failure in them are themselves matters of human definition. There are innumerable different ways to inhabit the same climate. If there seem to be few, it is less the work of the climate than of commitments to particular ways of life that make some choices unthinkable and others seem to be necessities.

A defender of the thesis that weather is at least sometimes the sole and sufficient determinant of its social consequences offers an example meant to clinch the point. "When a man crouching in a ditch in the middle of an open field gets hit by a lightning bolt, the environmental influence is strictly a one-way street, with no reasonable alternatives and no conscious response." But the example only shows that one factor can be mistaken for a sufficient cause, as the 1900 hurricane can be mistaken for that of the Galveston disaster, if the other necessary causes are taken for granted. The lightning in this case had the effects that it had only because a man was crouching unprotected in the ditch in its path. But the reasons why he was there at that moment, whatever they were, will never turn out to have been determined or imposed by the weather. The physical fact of a thunderstorm occurring never necessarily implies the presence of a victim exposed to its strike. Social changes affecting the exposure of Americans to lightning are apparent over the course of the past century. Exposed outdoor occupations, such as farming, ranching, and construction, are much less common than they were, and even they, by and large, enjoy better protection than before. At the same time, the decline in casualties would have been greater still but for the rise in outdoor recreation in the same period. Fewer deaths have occurred in fields and building sites, but a rising number on beaches, at sports events, and on pleasure boats in open water.

Lightning's impacts have changed in many ways. A consistent climatic determinist, taking the weather itself to be the chief cause of the weather's effects, could only conclude that thunderstorms have changed radically in frequency, intensity, and place of occurrence. But they have not. Instead, their effects have differed from period to period because in each, they have encountered a different way of life – and so too has every other kind of weather.

Chapter 16

The Trouble with Wilderness; or, Getting Back to the Wrong Nature

William Cronon

The Time Has Come to Rethink Wilderness

This will seem a heretical claim to many environmentalists, since the idea of wilderness has for decades been a fundamental tenet – indeed, a passion – of the environmental movement, especially in the United States. For many Americans wilderness stands as the last remaining place where civilization, that all too human disease, has not fully infected the earth. It is an island in the polluted sea of urban-industrial modernity, the one place we can turn for escape from our own too-muchness. Seen in this way, wilderness presents itself as the best antidote to our human selves, a refuge we must somehow recover if we hope to save the planet. As Henry David Thoreau once famously declared, "In Wildness is the preservation of the World."

But is it? The more one knows of its peculiar history, the more one realizes that wilderness is not quite what is seems. Far from being the one place on earth that stands apart from humanity, it is quite profoundly a human creation – indeed, the creation of very particular human cultures at very particular moments in human history. It is not a pristine sanctuary where the last remnant of an untouched, endangered, but still transcendent nature can for at least a little while longer be encountered without the contaminating taint of civilization. Instead, it is a product of that civilization, and could hardly be contaminated by the very stuff of which it is made. Wilderness hides its unnaturalness behind a mask that is all the more beguiling because it seems so natural. As we gaze into the mirror it holds up for us, we too easily imagine that what we behold is Nature when in fact we see the reflection of our own unexamined longings and desires. For this reason, we mistake

Cronon, William, "The Trouble with Wilderness; or, Getting Back to the Wrong Nature," pp. 7–9, 15–24 from William Cronon (ed.), *Uncommon Ground: Toward Reinventing Nature* (New York: W. W. Norton, 1995).

ourselves when we suppose that wilderness can be the solution to our culture's problematic relationships with the nonhuman world, for wilderness is itself no small part of the problem.

To assert the unnaturalness of so natural a place will no doubt seem absurd or even perverse to many readers, so let me hasten to add that the nonhuman world we encounter in wilderness is far from being merely our own invention. I celebrate with others who love wilderness the beauty and power of the things it contains. Each of us who has spent time there can conjure images and sensations that seem all the more hauntingly real for having engraved themselves so indelibly on our memories. Such memories may be uniquely our own, but they are also familiar enough be to be instantly recognizable to others. Remember this? The torrents of mist shoot out from the base of a great waterfall in the depths of a Sierra canyon, the tiny droplets cooling your face as you listen to the roar of the water and gaze up toward the sky through a rainbow that hovers just out of reach. Remember this too: looking out across a desert canyon in the evening air, the only sound a lone raven calling in the distance, the rock walls dropping away into a chasm so deep that its bottom all but vanishes as you squint into the amber light of the setting sun. And this: the moment beside the trail as you sit on a sandstone ledge, your boots damp with the morning dew while you take in the rich smell of the pines, and the small red fox – or maybe for you it was a raccoon or a coyote or a deer – that suddenly ambles across your path, stopping for a long moment to gaze in your direction with cautious indifference before continuing on its way. Remember the feelings of such moments, and you will know as well as I do that you were in the presence of something irreducibly nonhuman, something profoundly Other than yourself. Wilderness is made of that too.

And yet: what brought each of us to the places where such memories became possible is entirely a cultural invention. Go back 250 years in American and European history, and you do not find nearly so many people wandering around remote corners of the planet looking for what today we would call "the wilderness experience." As late as the eighteenth century, the most common usage of the word "wilderness" in the English language referred to landscapes that generally carried adjectives far different from the ones they attract today. To be a wilderness then was to be "deserted," "savage," "desolate," "barren" – in short, a "waste," the word's nearest synonym. Its connotations were anything but positive, and the emotion one was most likely to feel in its presence was "bewilderment" or terror.

Many of the word's strongest associations then were biblical, for it is used over and over again in the King James Version to refer to places on the margins of civilization where it is all too easy to lose oneself in moral confusion and despair. The wilderness was where Moses had wandered with his people for forty years, and where they had nearly abandoned their God to worship a golden idol. "For Pharaoh will say of the Children of Israel," we read in Exodus, "They are entangled in the land, the wilderness hath shut them in." The wilderness was where Christ had struggled with the devil and endured his temptations: "And immediately the Spirit driveth him into the wilderness. And he was there in the wilderness for forty days tempted of Satan; and was with the wild beasts; and the angels ministered unto him." The "delicious Paradise" of John Milton's Eden was surrounded by "a steep wilderness, whose hairy sides / Access denied" to all who sought entry. When Adam and Eve were driven from that garden, the world they entered was a wilderness that only their labor and pain could redeem. Wilderness, in short, was a place to which one came only against one's will, and always in fear and trembling. Whatever value it might have arose solely from the possibility that it might be "reclaimed" and turned toward human ends – planted as a garden, say, or a city upon a hill. In its raw state, it had little or nothing to offer civilized men and women.

But by the end of the nineteenth century, all this had changed. The wastelands that had once seemed worthless had for some people come to seem almost beyond price. That Thoreau in 1862 could declare wildness to be the preservation of the world suggests the sea change that was going on. Wilderness had once been the antithesis of all that was orderly and good – it had been the darkness, one might say, on the far side of the garden wall – and yet now it was frequently likened to Eden itself. When John Muir arrived in the Sierra Nevada in 1869, he would declare, "No description of Heaven that I have ever heard or read of seems half so fine." He was hardly alone in expressing such emotions. One by one, various corners of the American map came to be designated as sites whose wild beauty was so spectacular that a growing number of citizens had to visit and see them for themselves. Niagara Falls was the first to undergo this transformation, but it was soon followed by the Catskills, the Adirondacks, Yosemite, Yellowstone, and others. Yosemite was deeded by the US government to the state of California in 1864 as the nation's first wildland park, and Yellowstone became the first true national park in 1872.

By the first decade of the twentieth century, in the single most famous episode in American conservation history, a national debate had exploded over whether the city of San Francisco should be permitted to augment its water supply by damming the Tuolumne River in Hetch Hetchy valley, well within the boundaries of Yosemite National Park. The dam was eventually built, but what today seems no less significant is that so many people fought to prevent its completion. Even as the fight was being lost, Hetch Hetchy became the battle cry of an emerging movement to preserve wilderness. Fifty years earlier, such opposition would have been unthinkable. Few would have questioned the merits of "reclaiming" a wasteland like this in order to put it to human use. Now the defenders of Hetch Hetchy attracted widespread national attention by portraying such an act not as improvement or progress but as desecration and vandalism. Lest one doubt that the old biblical metaphors had been turned completely on their heads, listen to John Muir attack the dam's defenders. "Their arguments," he wrote, "are curiously like those of the devil, devised for the destruction of the first garden – so much of the very best Eden fruit going to waste; so much of the best Tuolumne water and Tuolumne scenery going to waste." For Muir and the growing number of Americans who shared his views, Satan's home had become God's own temple.

[. . .]

[. . .] [The] decades following the Civil War saw more and more of the nation's wealthiest citizens seeking out wilderness for themselves. The elite passion for wild land took many forms: enormous estates in the Adirondacks and elsewhere (disingenuously called "camps" despite their many servants and amenities), cattle ranches for would-be rough riders on the Great Plains, guided big-game hunting trips in the Rockies, and luxurious resort hotels wherever railroads pushed their way into sublime landscapes. Wilderness suddenly emerged as the landscape of choice for elite tourists, who brought with them strikingly urban ideas of the countryside through which they traveled. For them, wild land was not a site for productive labor and not a permanent home; rather, it was a place of recreation. One went to the wilderness not as a producer but as a consumer, hiring guides and other back-country residents who could serve as romantic surrogates for the rough riders and hunters of the frontier if one was willing to overlook their new status as employees and servants of the rich.

In just this way, wilderness came to embody the national frontier myth, standing for the wild freedom of America's past and seeming to represent a highly attractive natural alternative to the ugly artificiality of modern civilization. The irony, of course, was that in the process wilderness came to reflect the very civilization its devotees sought to escape. Ever since the nineteenth century, celebrating wilderness has been an activity mainly for well-to-do city folks. Country people generally know far too much about working the land to regard *un*worked land as their ideal. In contrast, elite urban tourists and wealthy sportsmen projected their leisure-time frontier fantasies onto the American landscape and so created wilderness in their own image.

There were other ironies as well. The movement to set aside national parks and wilderness areas followed hard on the heels of the final Indian wars, in which the prior human inhabitants of these areas were rounded up and moved onto reservations. The myth of the wilderness as "virgin," uninhabited land had always been especially cruel when seen from the perspective of the Indians who had once called that land home. Now they were forced to move elsewhere, with the result that tourists could safely enjoy the illusion that they were seeing their nation in its pristine, original state, in the new morning of God's own creation. Among the things that most marked the new national parks as reflecting a post-frontier con-sciousness was the relative absence of human violence within their boundaries. The actual frontier had often been a place of conflict, in which invaders and invaded fought for control of land and resources. Once set aside within the fixed and care-fully policed boundaries of the modern bureaucratic state, the wilderness lost its savage image and became safe: a place more of reverie than of revulsion or fear. Meanwhile, its original inhabitants were kept out by dint of force, their earlier uses of the land redefined as inappropriate or even illegal. To this day, for instance, the Blackfeet continue to be accused of "poaching" on the lands of Glacier National Park that originally belonged to them and that were coded by treaty only with the proviso that they be permitted to hunt there.

The removal of Indians to create an "uninhabited wilderness" – uninhabited as never before in the human history of the place – reminds us just how invented, just how constructed, the American wilderness really is. To return to my opening argu-ment: there is nothing natural about the concept of wilderness. It is entirely a crea-tion of the culture that holds it dear, a product of the very history it seeks to deny. Indeed, one of the most striking proofs of the cultural invention of wilderness is its thoroughgoing erasure of the history from which it sprang. In virtually all of its manifestations, wilderness represents a flight from history. Seen as the original garden, it is a place outside of time, from which human beings had to be ejected before the fallen world of history could properly being. Seen as the frontier, it is a savage world at the dawn of civilization, whose transformation represents the very beginning of the national historical epic. Seen as the bold landscape of frontier heroism, it is the place of youth and childhood, into which men escape by abandoning their pasts and entering a world of freedom where the constraints of civilization fade into memory. Seen as the sacred sublime, it is the home of a God who transcends history by standing as the One who remains untouched and unchanged by time's arrow. No matter what the angle from which we regard it, wilderness offers us the illusion that we can escape the cares and troubles of the world in which our past has ensnared us.

[. . .]

But the trouble with wilderness is that it quietly expresses and reproduces the very values its devotees seek to reject. The flight from history that is very nearly the core of wilderness represents the false hope of an escape from responsibility, the illusion that we can somehow wipe clean the state of our past and return to the tabula rasa that supposedly existed before we began to leave our marks on the world. The dream of an unworked natural landscape is very much the fantasy of people who have never themselves had to work the land to make a living – urban folk for whom food comes from a supermarket or a restaurant instead of a field, and for whom the wooden houses in which they live and work apparently have no meaningful connection to the forests in which trees grow and die. Only people whose relation to the land was already alienated could hold up wilderness as a model for human life in nature, for the romantic ideology of wilderness leaves precisely nowhere for human beings actually to make their living from the land.

This, then, is the central paradox: wilderness embodies a dualistic vision in which the human is entirely outside the natural. If we allow ourselves to believe that nature, to be true, must also be wild, then our very presence in nature represents its fall. The place where we are is the place where nature is not. If this is so – if by definition wilderness leaves no place for human beings, save perhaps as contemplative sojourners enjoying their leisurely reverie in God's natural cathedral – then also by definition it can offer no solution to the environmental and other problems that confront us. To the extent that we celebrate wilderness as the measure with which we judge civilization, we reproduce the dualism that sets humanity and nature at opposite poles. We thereby leave ourselves little hope of discovering what an ethical, sustainable, *honorable* human place in nature might actually look like.

Worse: to the extent that we live in an urban-industrial civilization but at the same time pretend to ourselves that our *real* home is in the wilderness, to just that extent we give ourselves permission to evade responsibility for the lives we actually lead. We inhabit civilization while holding some part of ourselves – what we imagine to be the most precious part – aloof from its entanglements. We work our nine-to-five jobs in its institutions, we eat its food, we drive its cars (not least to reach the wilderness), we benefit from the intricate and all too invisible networks with which it shelters us, all the while pretending that these things are not an essential part of who we are. By imaging that our true home is in the wilderness, we forgive ourselves the homes we actually inhabit. In its flight from history, in its siren song of escape, in its reproduction of the dangerous dualism that sets human beings outside of nature – in all of these ways, wilderness poses a serious threat to responsible environmentalism at the end of the twentieth century.

By now I hope it is clear that my criticism in this essay is not directed at wild nature per se, or even at efforts to set aside large tracts of wild land, but rather at the specific habits of thinking that flow from this complex cultural construction called wilderness. It is not the things we label as wilderness that are the problem – for nonhuman nature and large tracts of the natural world do deserve protection – but rather what we ourselves mean when we use the label. Lest one doubt how pervasive these habits of thought actually are in contemporary environmentalism, let me list some of the places where wilderness serves as the ideological underpinning for environmental concerns that might otherwise seem quite remote from it. Defenders of biological diversity, for instance, although sometimes appealing to more utilitarian concerns, often point to "untouched" ecosystems as the best and richest repositories of the undiscovered species we must certainly try to protect. Although at first blush an apparently more "scientific" concept than wilderness, biological diversity in fact invokes many of the same sacred values, which is why organizations like the Nature Conservancy have been so quick to employ it as an alternative to the seemingly fuzzier and more problematic concept of wilderness. There is a paradox here, of course. To the extent that biological diversity (indeed, even wilderness itself) is likely to survive in the future only by the most vigilant and self-conscious management of the ecosystems that sustain it, the ideology of wilderness is potentially in direct conflict with the very thing it encourages us to protect.

The most striking instances of this have revolved around "endangered species," which serve as vulnerable symbols of biological diversity while at the same time standing as surrogates for wilderness itself. The terms of the Endangered Species Act in the United States have often meant that those hoping to defend pristine wilderness have had to rely on a single endangered species like the spotted owl to gain legal standing for their case – thereby making the full power of the sacred land inhere in a single numinous organism whose habitat then becomes the object of intense debate about appropriate management and use. The ease with which anti-environmental forces like the wise-use movement have attacked such single-species preservation efforts suggests the vulnerability of strategies like these.

Perhaps partly because our own conflicts over such places and organisms have become so messy, the convergence of wilderness values with concerns about biological diversity and endangered species has helped produce a deep fascination for remote ecosystems, where it is easier to imagine that nature might somehow be "left alone" to flourish by its own pristine devices. The classic example is the tropical rain forest, which since the 1970s has become the most powerful modern icon of unfallen, sacred land – a veritable Garden of Eden – for many Americans and Europeans. And yet protecting the rain forest in the eyes of First World environmentalists all too often means protecting it from the people who live there. Those who seek to preserve such "wilderness" from the activities of native peoples run the risk of reproducing the same tragedy – being forceably removed from an ancient home – that befell American Indians. Third World countries face massive environmental problems and deep social conflicts, but these are not likely to be solved by a cultural myth that encourages us to "preserve" peopleless landscapes that have not existed in such places for millennia. At its worst, as environmentalists are beginning to realize, exporting American notions of wilderness in this way can become an unthinking and self-defeating form of cultural imperialism.

Perhaps the most suggestive example of the way that wilderness thinking can underpin other environmental concerns has emerged in the recent debate about "global change." In 1989 the journalist Bill McKibben published a book entitled *The End of Nature*, in which he argued that the prospect of global climate change as a result of unintentional human manipulation of the atmosphere means that nature as we once knew it no longer exists. Whereas earlier generations inhabited a natural world that remained more or less unaffected by their actions, our own generation is uniquely different. We and our children will henceforth live in a biosphere completely altered by our own activity, a planet in which the human and the natural can no longer be distinguished, because the one has overwhelmed the other. In McKibben's view, nature has died, and we are responsible for killing it. "The planet," he declares, "is utterly different now."

But such a perspective is possible only if we accept the wilderness promise that nature, to be natural, must also be pristine – remote from humanity and untouched by our common past. In fact, everything we know about environmental history suggests that people have been manipulating the natural world on various scales for as long as we have a record of their passing. Moreover, we have unassailable evidence that many of the environmental changes we now face also occurred quite apart from human intervention at one time or another in the earth's past. The point is not that our current problems are trivial, or that our devastating effects on the earth's ecosystems should be accepted as inevitable or "natural." It is rather that we seem unlikely to make much progress in solving these problems if we hold up to ourselves as the mirror of nature a wilderness we ourselves cannot inhabit.

To do so is merely to take to a logical extreme the paradox that was built into wilderness from the beginning if nature dies because we enter it, then the only way to save nature is to kill ourselves. The absurdity of this proposition flows from the underlying dualism it expresses. Not only does it ascribe greater power to humanity that we in fact possess – physical and biological nature will surely survive in some form or another long after we ourselves have gone the way of all flesh – but in the end it offers us little more than a self-defeating counsel of despair. The tautology gives us no way out: if wild nature is the only thing worth saving, and if our mere presence destroys it, then the sole solution to our own unnaturalness, the only way to protect sacred wilderness from profane humanity, would seem to be suicide. It is not a proposition that seems likely to produce very positive or practical results.

And yet radical environmentalists and deep ecologists all too frequently come close to accepting this premise as a first principle. When they express, for instance, the popular notion that our environmental problems began with the invention of agriculture, they push the human fall from natural grace so far back into the past that all of civilized history becomes a tale of ecological declension. Earth First! founder Dave Foreman captures the familiar parable succinctly when he writes,

> Before agriculture was midwifed in the Middle East, humans were in the wilderness. We had no concept of "wilderness" because everything was wilderness and *we were a part of it*. But with irrigation ditches, crop surpluses, and permanent villages, we became *apart from* the natural world. . . . Between the wilderness that created us and the civilization created by us grew an ever-widening rift.

In this view the farm becomes the first and most important battlefield in the long war against wild nature, and all else follows in its wake. From such a starting place, it is hard not to reach the conclusion that the only way human beings can hope to live naturally on earth is to follow the hunter-gatherers back into a wilderness Eden and abandon virtually everything that civilization has given us. It may indeed turn out that civilization will end in ecological collapse or unclear disaster, whereupon one might expect to find any human survivors returning to a way of life closer to that celebrated by Foreman and his followers. For most of us, though, such a debacle would be cause for regret, a sign that humanity had failed to fulfill its own promise and failed to honor its own highest values – including those of the deep ecologists.

In offering wilderness as the ultimate hunter-gatherer alternative to civilization. Foreman reproduces an extreme but still easily recognizable version of the myth of frontier primitivism. When he writes of his fellow Earth Firsters that "we believe we must return to being animal, to glorying in our sweat, hormones, tears, and blood" and that "we struggle against the modern compulsion to become dull, passionless androids," he is following in the footsteps of Owen Wister. Although his arguments give primacy to defending biodiversity and the autonomy of wild nature, his prose becomes most passionate when he speaks of preserving "the wilderness experience." His own ideal "Big Outside" bears an uncanny resemblance to that of the frontier myth: wide open spaces and virgin land with no trails, no signs, no facilities, no maps, no guides, no rescues, no modern equipment. Tellingly, it is a land where hardy travelers can support themselves by hunting with "primitive weapons (bow and arrow, atlatl, knife, sharp rock)." Foreman claims that "the primary value of wilderness is not as a proving ground for young Huck Finns and Annie Oakleys," but his heart is with Huck and Annie all the same. He admits that "preserving a quality wilderness experience for the human visitor, letting her or him flex Paleolithic muscles or seek visions, remains a tremendously important secondary purpose." Just so does Teddy Roosevelt's rough rider live on in the greener garb of a new age.

However much one may be attracted to such a vision, it entails problematic consequences. For one, it makes wilderness the focus for an epic struggle between malign civilization and benign nature, compared with which all other social, political, and moral concerns seem trivial. Foreman writes, "The preservation of wilderness and native diversity is *the* most important issue. Issues directly affecting only humans pale in comparison." Presumably so do any environmental problems whose victims are mainly people, for such problems usually surface in landscapes that have already "fallen" and are no longer wild. This would seem to exclude from the radical environmentalist agenda problems of occupational health and safety in industrial settings, problems of toxic waste exposure on "unnatural" urban and agricultural sites, problems of poor children poisoned by lead exposure in the inner city, problems of famine and poverty and human suffering in the "overpopulated" places of the earth – problems, in short, of environmental justice. If we set too high a stock on wilderness, too many other corners of the earth become less than natural and too many other people become less than human, thereby giving us permission not to care much about their suffering or their fate.

It is no accident that these supposedly inconsequential environmental problems affect mainly poor people, for the long affiliation between wilderness and wealth means that the only poor people who count when wilderness is *the* issue are hunter-gatherers, who presumably do not consider themselves to be poor in the first place. The dualism at the heart of wilderness encourages its advocates to conceive of its protection as a crude conflict between the "human" and the "nonhuman" – or, more often, between those who value the nonhuman and those who do not. This in turn tempts one to ignore crucial differences *among* humans and the complex cultural and historical reasons why different peoples may feel very differently about the meaning of wilderness.

Why, for instance, is the "wilderness experience" so often conceived as a form of recreation best enjoyed by those whose class privileges give them the time and resources to leave their jobs behind and "get away from it all"? Why does the protection of wilderness so often seem to pit urban recreationists against rural people who actually earn their living from the land (excepting those who sell goods and services to the tourists themselves)? Why in the debates about pristine natural areas are "primitive" peoples idealized, even sentimentalized, until the moment they do something unprimitive, modern, and unnatural, and thereby fall from environmental grace? What are the consequences of a wilderness ideology that devalues productive labor and the very concrete knowledge that comes from working the land with one's own hands? All of these questions imply conflicts among different groups of people, conflicts that are obscured behind the deceptive clarity of "human" vs. "nonhuman." If in answering these knotty questions we resort to so simplistic an opposition, we are almost certain to ignore the very subtleties and complexities we need to understand.

But the most troubling cultural baggage that accompanies the celebration of wilderness has less to do with remote rain forests and peoples than with the ways we think about ourselves – we American environmentalists who quite rightly worry about the future of the earth and the threats we pose to the natural world. Idealizing a distant wilderness too often means not idealizing the environment in which we actually live, the landscape that for better or worse we call home. Most of our most serious environmental problems start right here, at home, and if we are to solve those problems, we need an environmental ethic that will tell us as much about *using* nature as about *not* using it. The wilderness dualism tends to cast any use as *ab*-use, and thereby denies us a middle ground in which responsible use and non-use might attain some kind of balanced, sustainable relationship. My own belief is that only by exploring this middle ground will we learn ways of imagining a better world for all of us: humans and nonhumans, rich people and poor, women and men, First Worlders *and* Third Worlders, white folks and people of color, consumers and producers – a world better for humanity in all of its diversity and for all the rest of nature too. The middle ground is where we actually live. It is where we – all of us, in our different places and ways – make our homes.

That is why, when I think of the times I myself have come closest to experiencing what I might call the sacred in nature, I often find myself remembering wild places much closer to home. I think, for instance, of a small pond near my house where water bubbles up from limestone springs to feed a series of pools that rarely freeze in winter and so play home to waterfowl that stay here for the protective warmth even on the coldest of winter days, gliding silently through streaming mists as the snow falls from gray February skies. I think of a November evening long ago when I found myself on a Wisconsin hilltop in rain an dense fog, only to have the setting sun break through the clouds to east an otherworldly golden light on the misty farms and woodlands below, a scene so unexpected and joyous that I lingered past dusk so as not to miss any part of the gift that had come my way. And I think perhaps most especially of the blown-out, bankrupt farm in the sand country of central Wisconsin where Aldo Leopold and his family tried one of the first American experiments in ecological restoration, turning ravaged and infertile soil into carefully tended ground where the human and the nonhuman could exist side by side in relative harmony. What I celebrate about such places is not *just* their wildness, though that certainly is among their most important qualities; what I celebrate even more is that they remind us of the wildness in our own backyards, of the nature that is all around us if only we have eyes to see it.

Indeed, my principal objection to wilderness is that it may teach us to be dismissive or even contemptuous of such humble places and experiences. Without our quite realizing it, wilderness tends to privilege some parts of nature at the expense of others. Most of us, I suspect, still follow the conventions of the romantic sublime in finding the mountaintop more glorious than the plains, the ancient forest nobler than the grasslands, the mighty canyon more inspiring than the humble marsh. Even John Muir, in arguing against those who sought to dam his beloved Hetch Hetchy valley in the Sierra Nevada, argued for alternative dam sites in the gentler valleys of the foothills — a preference that had nothing to do with nature and everything with the cultural traditions of the sublime. Just as problematically, our frontier traditions have encouraged Americans to define "true" wilderness as requiring very large tracts of roadless land – what Dave Foreman calls "The Big Outside." Leaving aside the legitimate empirical question in conservation biology of how large a tract of land must be before a given species can reproduce on it, the emphasis on big wilderness reflects a romantic frontier belief that one hasn't really gotten away from civilization unless one can go for days at a time without encountering another human being. By teaching us to fetishize sublime places and wide open country, these peculiarly American ways of thinking about wilderness encourage us to adopt too high a standard for what counts as "natural." If it isn't hundreds of square miles big, if it doesn't give us God's-eye views or grand vistas, if it doesn't permit us the illusion that we are alone on the planet, then it really isn't natural. It's too small, too plain, or too crowded to be *authentically* wild.

In critiquing wilderness as I have done in this essay, I'm forced to confront my own deep ambivalence about its meaning for modern environmentalism. On the one hand, one of my own most important environmental ethics is that people should always be conscious that they are part of the natural world, inextricably tied to the ecological systems that sustain their lives. Any way of looking at nature that encourages us to believe we are separate from nature – as wilderness tends to do – is likely to reinforce environmentally irresponsible behavior. On the other hand, I also think it no less crucial for us to recognize and honor nonhuman nature as a world we did not create, a world with its own independent, nonhuman reasons for being as it is. The autonomy of nonhuman nature seems to me an indispensable corrective to human arrogance. Any way of looking at nature that helps us remember – as wilderness also tends to do – that the interests of people are not necessarily identical to those of every other creature or of the earth itself is likely to foster *responsible* behavior. To the extent that wilderness has served as an important vehicle for articulating deep moral values regarding our obligations and responsibilities to the nonhuman world, I would not want to jettison the contributions it has made to our culture's ways of thinking about nature.

If the care problem of wilderness is that it distances us too much from the very things it teaches us to value, then the question we must ask is what it can tell us about *home*, the place where we actually live. How can we take the positive values we associate with wilderness and bring them closer to home? I think the answer to this question will come by broadening our sense of the otherness that wilderness seeks to define and protect. In reminding us of the world we did not make, wilderness can teach profound feelings of humility and respect as we confront our fellow beings and the earth itself. Feelings like these argue for the importance of self-awareness and self-criticism as we exercise our own ability to transform the world around us, helping us set responsible limits to human mastery – which without such limits too easily becomes human hubris. Wilderness is the place where, symbolically at least, we try to withhold our power to dominate.

[. . .]

The myth of wilderness [. . .] is that we can somehow leave nature untouched by our passage. By now it should be clear that this for the most part is an illusion. [. . .] If living in history means that we cannot help leaving marks on a fallen world, then the dilemma we face is to decide what kinds of marks we wish to leave. It is just here that our cultural traditions of wilderness remain so important. In the broadest sense, wilderness teaches us to ask whether the Other must always bend to our will, and, if not, under what circumstances it should be allowed to flourish without our intervention. This is surely a question worth asking about everything we do, and not just about the natural world.

When we visit a wilderness area, we find ourselves surrounded by plants and animals and physical landscapes whose otherness compels our attention. In forcing us to acknowledge that they are not of our making, that they have little or no need of our continued existence, they recall for us a creation far greater than our own. In the wilderness, we need no reminder that a tree has its own reasons for being, quite apart from us. The same is less true in the gardens we plant and lend ourselves: there it is far easier to forget the otherness of the tree. Indeed, one could almost measure wilderness by the extent to which our recognition of its otherness requires a conscious, willed act on our part. The romantic legacy means that wilderness is more a state of mind than a fact of nature, and the state of mind that today most defines wilderness is *wonder*. The striking power of the wild is that wonder in the face of it requires no act of will, but forces itself upon us – as an expression of the nonhuman world experienced through the lens of our cultural history – as proof that ours is not the only presence in the universe.

Wilderness gets us into trouble only if we imagine that this experience of wonder and otherness is limited to the remote corners of the planet, or that it somehow depends on pristine landscapes we ourselves do not inhabit. Nothing could be more misleading. The tree in the garden is in reality no less other, no less worthy of our wonder and respect, than the tree in an ancient forest that has never known an ax or a saw – even though the tree in the forest reflects a more intricate web of ecological relationships. The tree in the garden could easily have sprung from the same seed as the tree in the forest, and we can claim only its location and perhaps its form as our own. Both trees stand apart from us; both share our common world. The special power of the tree in the wilderness is to remind us of this fact. It can teach us to recognize the wilderness we did not see in the tree we planted in our own backyard. By seeing the otherness in that which is most unfamiliar, we can learn to see it too in that which at first seemed merely ordinary. If wilderness can do this – if it can help us perceive and respect a nature we had forgotten to recognize as natural – then it will become part of the solution to our environmental dilemmas rather than part of the problem.

Part IV

Cultural Geography and Place

Introduction

David A. Lanegran

The few articles contained in this section cannot convey the depth and scope of research and writing on cultural geography. Indeed, some writers assert that the recent developments in cultural geography imply that it will soon encompass all of human geography. Rather than use a handful of research projects to define cultural geography, we have chosen to provide a glimpse of the range of research topics within the subfield. More specifically, we have selected articles that attempt to explain the spatial pattern of cultural traits and those that illustrate how humans, through their culture, create places. We use the word "place" in this context to refer to parts of the earth's surface that have been given particular meaning by various groups of people. For decades, geographers have written about the ways people can perceive the same location in different ways. In this sense, a specific location or environment can have several different meanings, although its physical characteristics do not change. This concept is complementary to the notion of cultural landscape or the study of how humans have modified the surface of the earth to meet special economic and cultural needs. Cultural geographers write about places – locations with meaning – and placelessness – locations empty of meaning. They also write about people who are rootless, or have no place, and are relegated to spots the powerful have no interest in occupying.

Because cultural geography can be studied at a variety of scales around the world, we have selected research and theoretical pieces about places that will be familiar to most, if not all, readers. The first essay invites the reader to consider how recreation or playing can be used to define places. It also stresses how the physical environment can stimulate or hinder certain uses of the landscape. It further illustrates how values about place can vary according to social class and geographic location. Through it we will enter discussions about the geography of consumption. Humans have long used symbols to convey status and define themselves as individuals and members of groups. Today people increasingly define themselves not by their work or what they produce but by how they play and what they consume. Our lifestyles demand either specialized places like golf courses and hunting grounds or generic spaces like fairgrounds or arenas that can be converted or repurposed to accommodate a series of special events ranging from muscle car shows to art exhibitions. In some cases, competition for places such as remote forest lands generates heated political struggles. All readers of this article should be able to rewrite this essay about their province, county, or state. Try it! The background research for the essay is great fun.

Some of you reading this book may be inclined (and legally able) to do some fieldwork on the relationship between beer drinking and the sense of locale as described in Wes Flack's essay on microbreweries. In a sense he has expanded the old maxim "you are what you eat" to include "you are where you drink." This essay provides an excellent example of how the culture of consumption has affected the geography of production. People want to have a sense of the local so they support very small-scale breweries. Other drinks, such as wine, whisky, and vodka, have been identified with special places or regions, but that practice is different from the use of microbreweries and brewpubs to assert a sense of localness. Having made his point about the cultural role of these small breweries, Flack goes on to raise another geographical question, but at a different scale. Why, he asks, is there a "microbrewery desert" in the middle of the continent? Do residents of that area have no feelings of the locale? What do people in your community feel about their place, and do they drink to show their feelings for it?

Carolyn Prorok opens our eyes to the fascinating process of how new sacred places have been created by immigrants from Europe and Asia to the Americas. Sanctity of places is the most complex concept within the general notion of environmental perception. These are places where the divine and profane worlds intersect. They are not to be explained by concepts of style, fashion, recreation, or landscape tastes. The article raises questions about our needs for sacred places, the rituals with which we set them, and our buildings of worship apart from the rest of the landscape. After reading it, discuss what sort of places you might consider sacred and what you might select as a destination for a pilgrimage.

Maria Elisa Christie adroitly explains some of the differences between the old and new forms of cultural geography while she transports us into the interior spaces of homes in central Mexico. There we find a variety of places defined by function and special ceremonial activities. We encounter the importance of gender in establishing the meaning of places. We also see how traditional cultural practices are challenged with rural to urban movement and the consequent changes in roles within families and between neighbors. Fiestas play a vital role in the maintenance of culture, and they not only define spaces but are in turn defended by them. How are spaces used in your residence? Are there special ceremonial places set aside by gender rules?

DISCUSSION READINGS

Lanegran, David A. (2000). "Minnesota: Nature's Playground." *Daedalus*, 129(3): 81–100.
Flack, Wes. (1997). "American Microbreweries and Neolocalism: 'Ale-ing' for a Sense of Place." *Journal of Cultural Geography*, 16(2): 37–54.

Prorok, Carolyn V. (2003) "Transplanting Pilgrimage Traditions in the Americas." *Geographical Review*, 93(3): 283–307.

Christie, Maria Elisa. (2004). "Kitchenspace, Fiestas, and Cultural Reproduction in Mexican House-Lot Gardens." *Geographical Review*, 94(3): 368–90.

Chapter 17

Minnesota: Nature's Playground

David A. Lanegran

Minnesotans have fun. We see our state as a place filled with opportunities for adventure, relaxation, and "edutainment." Frequently referred to as "the theater of seasons," the state's changing weather multiplies the varied landscapes by four. Each lake, valley, hilltop, forest, bog, and field has four distinct personalities created by the weather. In the winter, Minnesota gets very cold and normally has considerable snowfall. By contrast, the summers are hot with sudden storms. The change from summer to winter produces a fantastically colorful landscape through which pass hundreds of thousands of migratory birds. The spring, although not as colorful as fall, is characterized by racing streams, a northerly migration of birds, and vegetation bursting with life. Minnesotans have developed special ways to play on all landscapes in all seasons. An army of hunters, several thousand strong, fills the forests and fields every fall. In the subzero dead of winter perfectly normal people sit on overturned pails, staring at holes they have bored in the ice, waiting for a fish to swim by and take their bait. In the summer, a huge fleet of pleasure boats is launched to carry people in circles around the lakes. Special vehicles are purchased to carry us off the roads into the depths of swamps so we can get away from it all. Are we different from other Americans? "You betcha" – we have learned to enjoy our time in Minnesota.

Walking on the Water

In Minnesota we all can walk on water. In fact, we drive trucks on it. For at least three months, and in most years five months, the 10,000-plus lakes, the rivers, and the ponds of Minnesota are covered with a layer of ice strong enough to

Lanegran, David A., "Minnesota: Nature's Playground," pp. 81–100 from *Daedalus*, 129.3 (2000).

support mini-settlements of ice-fishing houses. Minnesotans have fished through the ice for decades. It is possible that the first people to develop the technology were commercial fishermen who strung their nets under the ice. Perhaps the first ice-fishermen were dairy farmers with time on their hands during the winter. However it began, ice fishing is a signature event in Minnesota. Each winter there are ice-fishing contests attracting thousands of entrants. One wonders what the fish think when one morning the lake is suddenly full of dangling hooks and the noise of happy people and thousands of footsteps crunching on the ice. It is not too surprising that the contestants usually catch very young and small fish.

For several years various entrepreneurs have tried to promote stock-car races on the frozen lakes, but have met with limited success. Parka-clad spectators peering through clouds of their condensed breath and cars spinning around on ice lack the appeal of NASCAR racing on sun-drenched raceways in the South. Perhaps racing on frozen lakes is too similar to the normal winter commute on icy, snow-filled streets to be amusing.

Why Don't We Stay Inside and Curl Up by the Fire?

This is not the place to trace the development of recreation and sport in modern American culture, but a few generalizations about that process may help explain some of our behavior. During the last half of the twentieth century Minnesota has gradually evolved from a landscape of work toward a landscape of play. During those five decades the average income and amount of leisure time available to individuals and families gradually expanded. With increased time and money, Minnesotans, like all Americans, followed the admonishments of advertisers and began to develop ways to fill their leisure time and spend their money. In this regard Minnesotans are like all citizens of wealthy countries. However, there are a few pieces of conventional wisdom and some scholarly observations that may be useful in understanding why the special recreational landscape of Minnesota has been developed.

Most Minnesotans will tell visitors that the best way to survive in Minnesota is to be active. Do not fight the environment; find a way to enjoy it. If days are cold and snowy, take up winter camping, cross-country skiing, skating, or any one of innumerable winter sports. If the weather is hot and humid, go swimming, enjoy the breeze on a golf course, or get the wind blowing through your hair on a power-boat racing around in circles on a lake. This attitude may spring from the early agriculturalists' bouts with cabin fever, a specific form of madness associated with being confined to a small room during the harshest times of winter.

Not everyone believes that intense activity is the best way to deal with the changes in the weather. Indoor recreation enthusiasts, those who curl up with a good book in front of a roaring fire as winter descends, balance outdoor aficionados. These "couch potatoes" prefer drinking a cold beer or iced tea in a shady spot to playing a round of golf or game of tennis during the heat of summer. In fact, the nonactive may outnumber the outdoors enthusiasts in the state, if we consider the fact that, along with other Americans whose lifestyles have become sedentary, a large fraction of adult Minnesotans are overweight.

Conventional wisdom aside, scholars have recognized special aspects of Minnesota culture. John Rooney and Richard Pillsbury have placed Minnesota in the "sports for sports' sake" region. In this portion of the United States, schools and recreation programs offer almost everyone a chance to participate in the sport of their choice. High-school athletics are supported as recreational outlets for participants and spectators. Although most towns support basketball for high-school boys and girls, very few elite basketball players are produced in the region. In addition, Rooney and Richardson describe this region as a "bastion of girls' high school athletics." The "sports for sports' sake" region is vast. Its eastern border begins west of Green Bay and runs south through central Wisconsin to the Mississippi River and follows the Mississippi south to southern Missouri, but excludes St. Louis. The southern border runs west from Memphis through Arkansas along the northern Oklahoma border to the Rocky Mountains is southern Colorado. There it runs northward along the Rocky Mountain front through eastern Colorado, Wyoming, and Montana and along the Rocky Mountains to the Canadian border (it also includes Alaska). The region contains only three cities that support major-league teams in baseball, basketball, football, or hockey.

Just as in other states, recreation and sports have been embedded into the school culture of Minnesota for many reasons. Participation in sports teaches leadership and aids personal development. It also promotes community spirit, both within the schools and in the larger community that supports the schools. Minnesotans expect their children to participate in sports; therefore schools offer a variety of activities that runs the seasonal gamut and appeals to all.

While everyone is encouraged to participate, recreation in Minnesota is undoubtedly gendered. Males dominate the popular images of hunting. In fact, the most frequent justification for hunting is the camaraderie of the hunting camp. Fishing is harder to categorize. Males are most frequently portrayed, but advertising images also depict happy families in fishing boats. Increased gender equality is also apparent in other landscapes. Ladies' days at golf courses have essentially disappeared, and young men and women are seen on ski slopes in approximately equal numbers. There seems to be a trend toward more equal participation in tennis, jogging, and biking. While Minnesota shares many attributes with the other parts of the "sports for sports' sake" cultural region, there are several special recreational landscapes that warrant further investigation.

Classification of Landscapes

The meaning of places is determined by complex interactions between the physical environment, buildings and other modifications humans have added to the landscape, and interpretations made by individuals of the landscape. Children are experts at transforming humdrum landscapes into enchanted places. In Minnesota nature helps children by changing golf courses into snowy slopes perfect for skiing or sliding. Snowplows create great banks of snow that are perfect for playing "King of the Hill." This works for adults as well. A high retaining wall can become a perfect face for rock climbers, harvested cornfields become hunting grounds, and cutover timberlands become spiritual retreats.

Writers such as Leo Marx, Yi-Fu Tuan, and Roderick Nash have described a gradient in landscape values that ranges from urban through rural and pastoral to wilderness. The values attached to these landscapes have varied over time. Tuan argues that in the late eighteenth century the "Jeffersonian ideas categorized the city as profane, the pastoral or middle landscape as Edenic and the wilderness as also profane." But by the late twentieth century, values had shifted. The center of large urban areas and the landscapes of urban sprawl were still profane, while the middle landscape and threatened wilderness became Edenic. Wilderness has become an ecological ideal and no longer thought of as a profane place to be conquered and transformed into a cultivated area. The pastoral areas between the city and the wilderness consist of a variety of places. Some are agricultural; others are locations where mining or lumbering occurs. And others may be resorts and small towns. These diverse places have distinctive landscapes that are the physical expression of the environmental processes and human activities found within those areas. The landscapes can be thought of as the cultural footprint on the land. According to the above-mentioned authors, Americans have differing opinions about these landscapes. Some places are thought to be beautiful or romantic and are highly valued. Others are considered ugly and dangerous and are to be avoided. As will be discussed later in this essay, the values about landscapes held by Minnesota residents vary by social class and geographic location.

It is possible to classify recreational landscapes according to a set of gradients that, while separate, have strong relationships. At one end we have the landscape of home, which is comfortable and predictable, but affords few opportunities for recreation and physical activity. At the other end are the dangerous landscapes that are filled with risk and demand mental and physical preparation. The wilderness is both dangerous for the average or unskilled individual and safe for those who are well prepared. It can be a place for personal testing or quiet communion with nature.

Another gradient of landscapes is the degree to which they are modified by human activity. Frequently called the cultural landscape, the built environment reflects the values, needs, and desires of humans. Built recreational environments range from backyard swing sets and jungle gyms, to ball courts, gymnasiums, and swimming pools, to area stadiums and golf courses. The reservoirs constructed behind dams are probably the largest recreational landscapes that have been created by direct human activity.

In addition to built recreational landscapes are those places that, while not actually built or cultivated by humans, are heavily managed. Minnesota's lakes, marshes, streams, rivers, and forests are all controlled areas. Water bodies are regularly stocked with fish, streams are managed for trout habitat, forests are harvested for timber, and marshes are drained or sometimes flooded for waterfowl. At the extreme are landscapes that are protected from human activity. What we call wilderness in Minnesota exists because as a community we have decided to limit the depredations of human economic activity. Thus we can see at least two gradients in the landscape: one based on the degree to which humans have altered the place and the other based on the degree of danger or amount of special knowledge needed to survive in the place.

Rituals of Place in the Recreational Landscapes

Rooney points out that Minnesotans would rather participate in sports than watch them. High-school sports and amateur leagues are used to define communities to a remarkable degree. Towns of all sizes boast baseball and softball fields, basketball courts, football fields, hockey arenas, and ice rinks. Brilliant lights on high poles pierce the dark humid nights each summer as the "town ball" leagues pit the local townsmen and farmers against those down the road. Agriculturists take pride in maintaining immaculate turf playing fields. The crowds are small but enthusiastic. In the fall, town ball yields to football leagues tailored to the size of the school. Some schools field teams with only nine players, and there are four levels of regular eleven-man teams. All through the harvest seasons the teams compete for the right to play in Minneapolis's Hubert H. Humphrey Dome for the state championship. Although not as football-crazed as Texans, Minnesotans still promote the sport.

We all work together while we play against each other. Both boys' and girls' athletics are used to enact ritually the regional struggles between various parts of the state. The title "state champion," whether for volleyball, swimming, dance teams, football, or wrestling, is an ardently pursued prize. Each year it is suburbs against the city, the north battling the south, and the metropolitan area versus the rest of Minnesota. Hockey teams from Baudette and International Falls, wrestling teams from Caledonia and Blue Earth, basketball teams from Lychfield and Minneapolis North, cross-country and track teams from Moundsview and Still-water struggle before hometown and community fans for statewide bragging rights. The images and myths spun around the adolescent athletics hark back to older times when parents and other relatives competed. Regional images are also honed through sports. Hockey players from the north are reputed to have skated to school in bitterly cold temperatures on frozen rivers with the howling of wolves ringing in their ears. Wrestlers from the south are said to possess iron grips and bulging arm and shoulder muscles earned by hand-milking herds of Holsteins before catching the school bus. Football players with a blue-collar work ethic are extolled along with prized basketball players who learned their moves on the tough playgrounds of the inner city. When all the state tournaments are over, the round of play practice and competition begins again with a new cohort to replace the graduates.

Once upon a time young people played games and sports without the interference of adults. Today, in order to produce athletes, parents and communities have combined to create landscapes and lifestyles organized around recreational activities. Communities have built athletic fields and ice arenas to provide spaces for children to learn, practice, and compete. Elaborate systems of leagues have been created to ensure that children get the proper training and competition. Baseball, soccer, and hockey are probably the most extreme examples of this phenomenon. Modeled after baseball's "Little League," other sports established similar layers of competition. In some cases the parents have actually defied the weather and now both hockey and soccer players compete year-round. Because "ice time" in the indoor arenas is limited, games are scheduled at all times of the day. Hockey parents (usually moms) ferry the boys and girls to various venues in vans filled with the paraphernalia of pads, sticks, skates, and uniforms. Minnesota even hosts an international soccer tournament each summer.

Along with the leagues, games, and practices have come a host of specialized camps for budding athletes. There are goalie camps, power-skating camps, and "big-men" basketball camps, among others. The specialized athletic camps compete with the more traditional summer camps of the YWCA, YMCA, Scouts, and churches.

The Lake Cabin Up North

In Minnesota there is a generic place called "up north" or "at the cabin." Approximately 5.6 percent of the households in Minnesota own about 132,000 seasonally occupied properties in the state. The actual location of the family's lake place may or may not be north of its primary residence. It may be a very simple structure without indoor plumbing, or it may be a five-bedroom, three-bath house. No matter; it is still "the cabin." Having a "summer home" is too pretentious for Minnesotans. That is what the bosses of the railroads and the mill owners had. Real Minnesotans have cabins. This fascination with a cabin on a lake may be traceable back to the Scandinavian culture of many of the immigrants; today many of the families in Sweden and Norway own second homes, although many are farmhouses rather than lakeshore properties. Whatever the reason, twentieth-century Minnesotans love lake cabins.

At first the cabins were built on lakes close to towns or on lakes that could be reached from the Twin Cities by trains. The glacial moraine region of central Minnesota is pocked with hundreds of ideal lakes. They have sandy bottoms with a sharp slope down to the lakeside. The best lakes have good populations of fish. The mixed forests of the transition zone between the prairies of the south and west and the pine forests of the north are perfect places for cabins. They were not all log cabins in the pines, but the first cabins were primitive. Water had to be pumped by hand, and outdoor privies were standard. Baths were taken in the lake, and all the cooking was done on wood stoves. But working while everyone else played made homemakers unhappy, and whenever possible the cabin was improved. Electricity for lights and appliances, propane for stoves or furnaces, and indoor plumbing were added over the years. In fact, shortly after the midpoint of the century, the suburban lawn was introduced to the vernacular cabin landscape design.

The Minnesota Fleet

Unlike other navies, the Minnesota fleet has more captains than crew. The crafts are generally small and carry arms only during the waterfowl hunting season. The fleet is large and consists of 793,107 bottoms not including canoes, duckboats, riceboats, or seaplanes. The fleet grows about 1 percent a year. At first, fishing boats designed by local Scandinavian builders, such as Lund or Larson, were rowed or pushed by small outboard motors made by other Scandinavian firms such as Evinrude and Johnson. Neither the boats nor motors had to be big, because families were not in a hurry and most lakes were not large. However, once waterskiing was invented in Lake City, Minnesota, life at the cabin was altered forever.

The peaceful mornings and evenings that had been spent in quiet conversation and contemplation of the ways of nature (especially fish) were shattered by the roaring ski boats pulling a new form of athlete, the water-skier. After a short time, lakeshore owner organizations and townships adopted rules to confine waterskiing – and, more recently, jet skis (sort of a motorcycle for use on water) – to certain hours of the day and to certain lakes. New water sports have made lake cabins even more popular with the young and athletic. Fishing has not disappeared, but the concept of a primitive fishing cabin has.

With the prosperity of the last three decades of the twentieth century, the number of developed lakeshore properties has skyrocketed. The wealthy new-comers have changed the culture of the north. There is now a huge market for a wide range of consumer goods, higher quality roads, entertainment facilities such as golf courses and restaurants, and services needed by the summer population to maintain its suburban lifestyle.

Canoeing

The many lakes of Minneapolis are great places for romantic canoe rides. On warm Wednesday nights a small flotilla assembles off the shore near the Lake Harriet Band Shell to languish in the sounds of pop tunes wafting out over the water. The state's rivers have become popular places for downstream travel in rented canoes, usually in the spring when the water is high. More recently the kayak has become popular for those who like to skim over the water without a partner.

For most Minnesotans, canoeing and the Boundary Waters Canoe Area Wilderness are inseparable. The BWCAW is located in northeastern Minnesota. Established as a special management area within the Superior National Forest, the area is managed by the Department of the Interior for three primary purposes: wilderness and recreational activities, watershed management, and the protection of threatened and endangered species. The BWCAW is not a huge area (about one million acres) but it has over 1,200 miles of convoluted canoe routes. The two hundred thousand people who get permits to canoe it each year are spaced out in what amounts to long lines with significant intervals. Thus, even though it is regarded as the most heavily used wilderness area in the United States, canoe parties can still feel alone and refresh their souls. Although we canoe in all sorts of water bodies, the archetypal trip is one to the Boundary Waters where cold lakes, granite outcrops, islands, and dense forests define the wilderness experience.

Hunting

In 1999, slightly over 8 percent of the state's population – 359,690 Minnesotans – bought licenses to hunt white-tailed deer and took to the woods. They hunted in all sections of the state, from the cornfields of the south to the bogs and aspen forests of the north. It is not possible to know how many were afield at any one time, but it is safe to assume that the vast majority were out on the opening day of the season. In the forested sections of the state all outdoor activities are limited during "The Season." Hunters are required to wear blaze-orange clothing, and bikers, walkers, dogs, and horses are advised to wear bright clothes as well. While not frequent, accidental shooting deaths occur each season.

Rituals are important in hunting. Hunting companions are selected with great care. While solitary hunters are common, hunting is most often done in intergenerational groups. Boys and a growing number of girls are apprenticed into the sport after passing firearms safety classes. Hunting shacks, like lake cabins, come in all styles and sizes. Most are spartan and decorated with antlers, old furniture ample larders, and tables for playing cards. The hunting camps are egalitarian places where all are expected to contribute to the success of the hunt. However, expertise is respected, as some butcher, some cook, and others tell "Sven and Ole" jokes.

During the fall in northern Minnesota most men are not expected to be available on weekends for several weeks before the hunting season begins because they are preparing their camp and deer stands. During the season they are in the woods, and after the season they are talking about the activities of the earlier weekends. There are actually several different deer seasons. Hunters using bows get the first chance at the deer herd; those using firearms, mostly rifles but some shotguns, follow them. Finally the traditionalists who use old-fashioned "black powder," percussion rifles, try their hand. Those interested in hunting moose need a special permit and follow greater restrictions. Fat and sleepy bears on their way to hibernation are also hunted. When the season finally draws to close in late November or early December, the annual population of deer, moose, and bears has been reduced, but the populations of all three animals continue to expand in response to favorable environmental conditions.

Big game hunting with firearms for deer, moose, and bear is only one form of this popular sport. In the agricultural landscapes of the southern part of the state, the pheasant hunters take the fields. Some take up positions on the edges of fields of corn, soybeans, or prairie, and others in the party walk through the fields driving the wary birds toward them. Heavy birds, the pheasants are reluctant flyers and prefer to elude their pursuers by running through the vegetation or remaining concealed. Thus, good bird dogs are invaluable companions to the hunters. The dogs flush the birds, then locate and retrieve them after they have been shot. Pheasant hunting can be an idyllic walk through the sunny autumn landscape in the company of friends and loyal canine companions. Small-town social organizations hold special hunters' pancake breakfasts to raise money, but there is usually no expectation that hunters will pay for permission to hunt private land. Similar to the pheasant hunters in the fields, hunters in the forests pursue woodcock, partridge, and grouse.

Duck and goose hunting, on the other hand, is best on cold rainy days when the birds fly low and stay close to the marshes. Although some try to sneak up on ducks resting on small bodies of water – called "jump-shooting" – most hunters conceal themselves and their dogs in blinds or camouflaged boats behind strings of decoys. The take to their stations well before dawn, and when the sun rises they attempt to call the birds into shooting range. Their quiet solitary pastime is generally cold and uncomfortable. But when the fast-flying waterfowl come into range, pumping adrenaline raises the temperature of hunters, both human and canine. The dogs, whether Chesapeakes or Labradors, are born to swim and joyfully plunge into the icy water after downed birds.

The most solitary of the bird hunters are the approximately forty thousand who seek wild turkeys. This is a relatively new sport, growing rapidly in response to the population explosion of the once nearly extinct birds. The Department of Natural Resources, in cooperation within sportsmen's clubs, has restocked wild birds in woodlots and farm fields in the southern and central parts of the state. Turkey hunters dress like trees, cover their faces with camouflage paint, and, in the wee hours of the morning while the birds are roosting, take up their hiding places. When the sun finally rises they attempt to call tom turkeys to them by imitating the seductive calls of lonesome hens.

Turkeys are not the only wild birds that are increasing as a result of landscape management by humans. The population of Giant Canada geese is exploding. These birds were thought extinct until a small flock was discovered living permanently on a reservoir in Rochester that was kept ice-free year-round by warm water discharged from a local power plant. These birds were local favorites and fed by the townsfolk. Once the DNR realized the birds were living in Rochester, conservation agents captured young birds and relocated them to new breeding grounds each summer for several years. The relocation program was a stunning success. It turns out that geese love parks, and they especially love the suburbs. They like the warm water of urban parks and thrive on the lush grass of golf courses and cemeteries. Now the bird has become something of a problem. Although not quite as numerous as pigeons, the birds soil the jogging trails and golf links. Guardian ganders frequently challenge golf carts and slow-moving cars. The burgeoning numbers of offspring of the urban geese created the need for yet another relocation program. Each year city park rangers rounded up the goslings before they could fly and shipped them off to game reserves in other states. Minnesota has exported so many geese there are no more places willing to take surplus birds. The large number of resident geese has made a special hunting season necessary.

Fishing

There is nothing in Minnesota quite like "the opener," or the opening weekend of fishing. While all sorts of fish are popular with anglers, the state's premier fish is the walleyed pike. This native fish can grow very large, but most of those caught are less than five pounds. The fish are said to have soft lips, and one must be careful when they nibble bait. If one is overly eager the fish will get away. In most years the governor participates in a media event during the opener. The Friday night before opening weekend the northward-bound lanes of all the roads are jammed with pickup trucks and sport utility vehicles pulling boat trailers.

This sort of fishing is very social. There are no solitary fishermen on the opener. Even though it is seldom a warm weekend, it is considered the beginning of summer. For several years the weekend coincided with Mother's Day. This presents a dilemma that some have attempted to solve with the "take a mother fishing weekend." While it is a time for bonding and relaxation, the fishing opener is occasionally marred by drownings and traffic accidents.

Trout fishing has several openers, but unlike the walleye opener there are no traffic jams, drownings, or accidents. Trout streams are found in southeastern Minnesota along the limestone bluffs of the Mississippi and also along the north shore of Lake Superior. These two beautiful but sharply contrasting landscapes attract fly fishermen, who prefer to work the streams by themselves. Because there are no "stream cabins," trout fishermen stay in motels or, even better, pitch tents in the parks or public land close to the streams. The spring nights are cool and so they pack themselves in layers of sleeping bags and blankets. Shortly after sunrise the crisp smell of campfires made with dry oak fills the misty valleys. After a few cups of scalding coffee the men and women don their thigh-high boots and wade into the cold water. It only seems that they are lashing the water with their fly rods when, in fact, they are carefully positioning their flies so the wily trout strike without thinking. Most trout fishermen do not keep all they catch. Many use barbless hooks and prefer to return their catch to the streams.

Minnesota landscapes are managed for trout. Although a sizable natural or native population exists, trout are also stocked in some streams. The DNR has several programs designed to maintain the fast-flowing clear streams of the limestone bluffs. The banks of streams are stabilized and logs or low barriers of rocks are installed so that they jut out into the stream. These structures, called wing dams, force the stream into narrow channels where the water picks up speed. The faster flowing water is able to scour the streambed and create holes, which provide an environment more conductive to trout.

Family Feuds – Private Recreation on Public Land

The public owns much of the land in Minnesota. The state and federal governments own approximately 23.5 percent of the entire state. The vast majority of public land is in the northern forest zone, where the US Department of Agriculture Forest Service, the US Fish and Wildlife Service, and the National Park Service combined hold 6.5 percent. Another 5.5 percent came to the countries as tax-forfeited lands. The Minnesota DNR owns 10.31 percent, and various other state departments own 0.06 percent. The vast majority of the land is northwest of Duluth.

The presence of so much public land in northern Minnesota has created a major controversy over the proper use of the land and the denizens of the forest. It is a clash between those who want to use the land for a variety of recreational purposes and those who view it as a commercial resource. The population living in the rest of the state has two sometimes conflicting views of the region. There are those who believe the land should be managed for sports such as hunting, snowmobiling, and fishing. Others view it as a preserve for wild animals such as moose, deer, and otter, or a place for contemplative individuals to interact with the wilderness and thereby find a deeper meaning in life. To provide for their needs is the BWCAW as well as a large section of the area designated the Voyageurs National Park, both located along the Canadian border. The most persistent controversy involves the use of the forest outside the special protected areas. Pulp and paper companies' desire to harvest timber clashes with the views of environmentalists such as the Minnesota Center for Environmental Advocacy, who believe that too much timber is being cut too quickly to maintain the necessary habitats for animal life and water quality.

The Singing Wilderness: BWCAW

Superior National Forest was established in northern Minnesota through several administrative processes between 1905 and the present. Shortly after World War I, when the highway system was developed in this part of the state, camping and outdoor recreation in the national forest began to become popular. By 1919, about 12,750 people had visited the forest. Competition between the new outdoor enthusiasts and the timber companies working in the forest soon developed. The two decades between 1920 and 1940 were filled with controversy between those interested in developing hydropower and those interested in recreation. In the late 1920s the secretary of agriculture, William M. Jardine, issued a proclamation creating a "primitive area." In 1958 the present name was established. Although we call it a wilderness, it is not a virgin forest. It has been largely cut over and experienced various forms of sparse settlements. Today the BWCAW is a roadless area, and air travel below 4,000 feet is forbidden. The use of motors in the area is severely restricted, but those who want to use motorized fishing boats and snowmobiles in the area believe the landscape should be made available to a wider fraction of the population and not just limited to the canoeist.

For many canoeists the BWCAW is already too crowded. Some feel that the wilderness experience begins only after they have paddled a full day without seeing another human. The YMCA and Scout camps using the area have developed special traditions and cultures based on the wilderness experience; for example, some camps use only handcrafted wooden canoes that reflect the fragility of the wilderness. But no matter what material is used for canoes, all the camps extol the virtues of the simple life and teach campers to care for the environment.

Infernal Machines

While canoeists are quiet and fishers and hunters – whether after waterfowl, deer, wild turkeys, or small game – are expected to be silent while in pursuit, during the past few years a new machine has posed problems for the landscape. A class of motorized vehicles with four or six wheels designed to travel off roads has become increasingly popular in the rural regions of the state – the All-Terrain Vehicle, or ATV. While some hunters use these to get to and from their "stands," recreational-use ATVs have caused a major conflict on public land.

In Minnesota, ATV registrations have exploded 803 percent since 1984, going from 12,235 to today's 110,449. Hunters are angry because the ATV riders break trails through the forest, disturbing their hunt. It is legal to drive an ATV off a state trail, but ATV opponents contend the machines are tearing up public lands, creating noise problems, and frustrating those who are looking for solitude in the woods. ATV advocates argue they have an equal right to use public lands. They further contend that their license fees should be used to make more trails for them on the public land. In response, the DNR attempted to classify state forest lands into three groups for the purpose of managing off-road vehicle use: managed, limited, and closed. In the managed forest (90 percent of the total), all roads and trails would be open to ATVs. They also suggested that off-trail riding should be banned in the remaining 10 percent. Legislators rejected their proposal. The debate between the riders and the environmentalists is not over, but it appears that new a form of recreational landscape will be created in the forest.

Right to Hunt

Tension over the use of the publicly owned forest also generated an intense debate in the late 1990s over the right to hunt. As a result, the Minnesota legislature passed a law guaranteeing residents of Minnesota the right to hunt and fish, despite the protests of various groups of animal rights advocates. In addition, Minnesota's residents and political leaders have been engaged in a lengthy debate on the management of the wolf and deer populations in the northern part of the state. Deer hunters encourage the Division of Forestry and other sections of the DNR to create a landscape that will support a large number of deer so the hunters may harvest them.

The Great State Get-Together

Lovers of solitude avoid one of the state's most famous recreation landscapes: the 360-acre Minnesota State Fair grounds. The twelve-day-long fair is one of the nation's largest and best-attended agricultural, educational, and entertainment events, in recent years attracting over 1.6 million people annually. The fair's agricultural and creative competitions draw over 35,000 entries each year. Livestock, fine arts, crafts, school projects, baked goods, fruit, vegetables, bee and honey products, flowers, butter, and cheese are all brought to the fair. But that is not all. In addition to the exciting carnival rides, six stages provide over 500 free performances during the exposition. The grandstand, originally built to showcase horse races, now features pop, rock, and country music artists as well as comedians. It is also a great place to shop, browse, or learn. Over four million square feet of exhibit space contain booths housing manufacturers, retailers, educational institutions, artisans, politicians, news media, and a wide variety of government agencies.

Best of all, the fair is a great place to eat! It boasts the Midwest's largest collection of food vendors, with more than three hundred culinary concessionaires. Everything from ethnic foods to traditional favorites like mini donuts, fried cheese curds, and frosty malts, along with twenty-five different foods-on-a-stick, all can be found at the fair. There are so many cauldrons and vats of hot grease bubbling that some say that the air of the fair grounds gets saturated with fat molecules after a couple of days, allowing a person to gain weight by just walking around at the fair and inhaling the ambient atmospheric calories.

The fair is the last great ritual of summer. It ends with Labor Day and the start of school. For the rest of the year the fair grounds are essentially idle, although a few buildings are used for special events. The hippodrome hosts horse shows and sporting events. In June the many streets of the grounds are converted into parking lots for the fancy cars entered in the "Back to the Fifties" car show. Brilliantly painted hot rods and dream machines create one of the most festive landscapes imaginable.

Historic and Cultural Landscapes

There is another sort of recreational landscape developing in Minnesota and the rest of the United States. These are the historic sites and places that have been determined to have some message for the present and future generations. In recent years, people have flocked to places like Historic Fort Snelling, where reenactors show visitors what fort life was like in 1828. The State Historical Society manages several rebuilt trading posts, such as Grand Portage, where the great rendezvous between the traders who worked in the boreal forests north of the Arctic Ocean met with the factors from Montreal who came west across the Great Lakes in huge cargo canoes. There are also living history farms and lumber camps, which employ reenactors to illustrate working and living conditions in the nineteenth century.

In Minneapolis, the milling district at the Falls of St. Anthony has been declared a historic district. Here visitors can go on a walking tour or engage a guide for a lively interpretation of the ruins and rebuilt structures. Forestville Park in southeastern Minnesota contains a fully stocked country store from the 1930s, but little is for sale there. There are few sites associated with the pre-European populations that are open for viewing. Access to most of them is restricted to protect the pictoglyphs and mounds. One of the most interesting of these sites is the Pipestone National Monument in southwestern Minnesota. There visitors can visit not only outcrops of the sacred calumet stone, but also see the traditional quarries and watch Native Americans produce artwork with the freshly cut stone. These places provide opportunities for "edutainment" – a mixture of education and entertainment attracting cultural tourists.

Theater of Seasons

The bounds of this essay prohibit a view of all the landscapes and activities developed by Minnesotans over the years to keep themselves amused. The ever-changing landscape constantly calls to us. In the long summer days, golf courses, lakes, forests, and trails pull us out of the air-conditioned comfort of our apartments and homes. Every town in the state takes a weekend to transform itself into a playground. There are Polka Days, Corn Days, Pumpkin Festivals, and a variety of celebrations named after some local claim to fame. The streets are converted to shopping and socializing spaces, and for a day the town is the recreational center of the area. The brilliant change in colors of fall draw even the most obstinate "couch potato" out for a walk. During the short winter days the crystal fields of winter have a more limited appeal. The sidewalks are treacherous for the elderly and the cold can kill. But nonetheless, bike paths are brushed free of snow for joggers and walkers. The parks are crisscrossed with ski trails. Most families have a few snowbirds who head for Arizona or Florida each winter, frequently reminded of the fun they are missing back home. With the coming of spring the snowbirds return, and the cycle of preparation for the intense summer begins again.

Conclusion

Are we different? More adventurous? More willing to come to terms with the environment? The Minnesota navy plies the lakes and rivers; the woods and fields are full of hunters. Temporary villages appear on the lakes each winter, and St. Paulites insist on celebrating the Winter Carnival during January's coldest weeks. We try our hand at every conceivable sport, even if we are not particularly good at any of them. We probably are not all that unusual. We have just learned to have fun in the landscape and enjoy our time in Minnesota.

Chapter 18

American Microbreweries and Neolocalism: "Ale-ing" for a Sense of Place

Wes Flack

A University of Kansas student recently had a visit from her father. He stayed in town for a few days, and on the day of his departure she took him to the Free State Brewery for lunch. This brewpub is located in a celebrated area of downtown Lawrence. Inside, historical pictures hang on the walls. Each table has a display with bits of Kansas history. Behind the bar is a full-size Kansas State flag with the motto Ad Astra per Aspera (to the stars through difficulties). After lunch, while sipping his Ad Astra Ale, the father said, "I finally feel like I'm in Kansas." The feeling is shared by many patrons. The Free State Brewery operators have made deliberate attempts to associate the establishment with its setting, attaching it to a sense of place. This microbrewery is but one example of hundreds that have recently opened.

The American brewing industry is markedly different today from 10 years ago. This is evident to anyone who has studied beer labels in the last decade. Industry sales are still dominated by the old Germanic giants such as Anheuser Busch, Miller, and Coors, while smaller regional brands continue to cling to the edges of the market. What is striking is the phoenix-like ascent of small, local breweries.

This microbrewery success may also be a key to understanding something deeper within the American psyche. Perhaps Yi-Fu Tuan most aptly characterizes the rootlessness of many Americans when he suggests that the frequent and massive migrations to and from places with a desideratum of distinctiveness [have] brought about a disdain for much of national culture. Nowadays, Americans are more likely to long for and seek out unique places. Some may argue that Tuan's vague and esoteric theory has little empirical basis, but microbrewery proliferation provides a basis. America's rootless angst has spawned a cultural countercurrent "neolocalism." Microreweries are one example of this self-conscious reassertion of the

Flack, Wes, "American Microbreweries and Neolocalism: 'Ale-ing' for a Sense of Place," pp. 37–54 from *Journal of Cultural Geography*, 16.2 (Spring/Summer, 1997).

distinctively local. Other examples of neolocalism are the growth of farmer's markets, the seemingly growing popularity of local festivals, and even the defensive battles that towns are waging to keep Wal-Marts from opening. While other social forces are at work, microbrewery success cannot be grasped without recognizing this neolocal component.

This article is an attempt to explain the recent changes in the United States brewing industry, most specifically the rise of the microbrewery. After a brief historical review, it will discuss the origin and diffusion of microbreweries in the United States. It will then focus on how microbrewery success relates to sense of place. The closing of the Pabst Brewery in Milwaukee demonstrates the significance of the changes that are occurring in the industry; these changes can be seen as related to postmodern shifts away from the mass production of high modernism.

Beer in History

Beer has been brewed since the beginning of seed agriculture. Physical evidence has been found among ancient Sumerian and Egyptian societies, as well as most every other culture classified as civilized. The ingredients, grain and water, were plentiful in early agricultural societies. Allowing grain to soak in water for a few days or a week produced beer; yeast from the atmosphere would begin to grow in the mixture and fermentation would take place. Improvements and variations in methods abounded and spread quickly. For example, Sauer speculated that the practice of chewing grains to start fermentation began in southern Asia and diffused as far as South America. Beer was not the sole fermented beverage of ancient human beings, but others such as wine and mead required fruits, honey, and other ingredients more exotic than the grain and water easily obtained by any farmer. The common working man adopted Budweiser's ancestor almost as soon as he settled into a sedentary lifestyle.

In American history the primary position of beer is demonstrated by its presence as part of the limited cargo allowed aboard the ships of the first settlers. A Mayflower document suggests the actual reason for the landing at Plymouth: "For we could not now take time for further search or consideration; our victuals being much spent, especially our beer." Lack of beer was a common hardship endured by early colonists, but not for long; homebrewing was soon ubiquitous, and the priority placed on the drink helped make brewing one of the first American industries. Many commercial breweries and taverns were established in New Amsterdam as early as the 1630s.

Until the mid-1800s, American beer was made exclusively with a top-fermenting yeast that produced English-style ales, porters, and stouts. In the 1840s, Germans brought over a bottom-fermenting yeast that required months of cold storage and produced a lagerstyle beer. The popularity of lager spread quickly. Schlitz, Blatz, Anheuser, Liebmann, Miller, and Busch all established breweries in the 1850s, and German immigrants opened beer gardens and breweries nearly everywhere they settled.

Two types of lager beer, Munich and Pilsener, initially vied for preeminence, but even before the Civil War it was evident that the pale, effervescent, low-alcohol Pilsener beer was going to dominate the rapidly expanding industry. The result is that when Americans think of beer they think of Pilsener, or its descendent, the American lager.

With the development of new transportation networks, Milwaukee became the dominant beer-producing city. The first large-scale refrigeration systems were built to chill beer, but before this century large quantities of ice were necessary for the cold-fermenting lager process, and Wisconsin's numerous small lakes provided a ready source. What is more important, the agglomeration of beer-drinking Germans in the region furnished the brewers with a large market.

The opening of the western frontier provided opportunities for brewers in every town; early migrants were heavy drinkers. In 1852 San Francisco had a legal saloon for every 100 residents. By 1873, the number of legal breweries in America peaked at 4,131. This number would decline for the next 100 years.

Consolidation and centralization then became the dominant trends in the industry. Larger companies often undercut the prices of local breweries, while taverns were enticed to become "tied-houses," pubs that were owned by, or had exclusive contracts with, a single brewer. Because little drinking was done at home, when small breweries could not sell their product in local taverns, they were soon out of business. Tied-houses were effectively outlawed in America with the passing of the Federal Alcohol Administration Act of 1935, but actually, the effects of Prohibition on industry structure were only temporary, though it hastened the demise of many smaller breweries that could not handle the suspension of cash flow.

Economies of Scale

Today three types of breweries can be distinguished based on production capacity and distribution patterns. Large breweries are almost all part of multiplant operations with national distributions. Midsize breweries tend to have regional distribution. Microbreweries usually have local distribution, although the increasing use of niche marketing among the two smaller classes confuses the distribution distinctions. Granting that this threefold division is a sound means of distinguishing among breweries, it becomes a problem for the researcher to draw a definitive boundary between two of the classes.

The author chose to input the brewery production capacity data provided by the Brewer's Digest Annual Guide into a Jencks Classification Program to come up with the breaks among the three classes. The boundary between the large and midsize breweries was then adjusted so that all the breweries that were part of national distributions in multiplant operations were included in the large brewery class. Thus, all large breweries were defined as having production capacities from 2.8 to 22 million barrels per year, midsize breweries from 150,000 to 2 million barrels per year, and microbreweries from 70 to 90,000 barrels per year. The Institute for Brewing Studies is one entity that draws the divisions among these three classes at different points, but qualitative anomalies seem to be minimized with this article's classification system. Furthermore, the use of the Jencks program provides a sound quantitative rationale for the results.

In the three decades after World War II a handful of Germanic giants became multiplant operations. With large advertising budgets, economies of scale, and lethal competitive tactics that included taking localized short-term losses to undercut the prices of smaller breweries, they drove hundreds of smaller breweries out of business. The number of breweries of all sizes shrank significantly until the recent microbrewery explosion. Studies of brewery distributions have dwelled upon this consolidation trend, calling the industry "market-based" or "market-oriented," but such descriptions hold true only for the national breweries. The smaller breweries have a more culturally complex distribution in which there is little correspondence to population numbers.

The 1972 location of midsize breweries shows a strong correspondence to ethnicity. The breweries are concentrated in areas that Zelinsky identifies as having a strong Germanic influence: Pennsylvania, Cincinnati, and a belt across the southern Great Lakes area. In the early 1970s the brewing landscape in these areas was much like that of Germany, where local and regional brands flourished. By 1982 over half of these breweries were victimized by consolidation, but their spatial arrangement remained much the same. A decade later the West Coast had lost its midsize breweries and the rest of America showed a serious decline. Pennsylvanians, though, remained loyal to their breweries. On a humanistic level, it is not difficult to find an example like the displaced Pittsburghian that the author met in suburban Atlanta. He keeps his refrigerator stocked with Iron City and Rolling Rock beers. Even though neither beer is readily available nearby, it is worth the extra effort and expense to have his hometown Pittsburgh beer on hand.

Microbrewery distributions over the same 20-year period are more problematic. The pattern in 1972 could almost be mistaken for that of midsize breweries with very similar German concentrations, but with the accent on Wisconsin. The only anomalies were the Spoetzl Brewery in Shiner, Texas, and the Anchor Brewing Company, in San Francisco, both of which survive today. By 1982 Wisconsin's microbrewery tradition had withered, but new ones were just appearing in California.

Rebirth of the Microbrewery

The resurgence of the American microbrewery in the early 1980s had a familiar hearth – California. To speak of the California culture hearth has become a cliche, and while the state's lead role in American foodways is well documented, little scholarly attention has focused on the origins of Californian innovations. Researchers have rarely looked outside American borders for the source of a popular culture innovation. In the case of microbreweries, the impetus may be traced to Britain. The Campaign for More Real Ale (CAMRA) was a grassroots drinkers' revolt inspired by the closing of 40% of Britain's breweries in the 1960s. According to Glover, small brewers began to reappear in the early 70s, and by the early 80s the trickle had become a flood with 36 new breweries opening 1981 alone. Thus, the rebirth of microbreweries in Britain clearly predates the phenomenon in California, and the timing of microbrewery proliferation strongly suggests that the international hearth may be found in Britain.

The form of the new American microbreweries also suggests a British link. It is obvious at first sip that microbrewed beers are different from typical national brands. Most are English-style ales, fuller in taste than the crisp American lagers. Most of the new breweries also have taken a form that was borrowed from Britain – the brewpub. Brewpubs, which brew and serve beer on the same premises, were made illegal in the United States along with the tied-house in 1935, but almost every state has now legalized them.

Washington, Oregon, California, and Colorado were the early leaders of the microbrewery revolution. Spurred by the success of Anchor Brewing Company, Yakima, Washington, became home to North America's first brewpub, Grant's Brewpub, in June 1982. San Francisco, Portland, and Seattle remain leading microbrewing centers, and the idea of a fresh local brew seems to fit very nicely into Ecotopia. The strong environmental sentiment of the region breeds a powerful local pride and commitment to community, but other areas also use beer for local boosterism.

When microbreweries are considered on a per capita basis, Vermont emerges as the leader. This distinction seems to be related to tourism. Wisconsin is also an important center. It represents a revival of the art form with more emphasis on the German style lagers than is found elsewhere.

Perhaps most fascinating is the conspicuous L-shaped "microbrewery desert" that extended through the Midwestern and Southern states of North Dakota, South Dakota, Nebraska, Kansas, Oklahoma, Arkansas, Mississippi, Alabama, Georgia, and South Carolina in 1992. Only three anomalies existed then, two in the college towns of Lincoln, Nebraska, and Lawrence, Kansas, and one in Atlanta. People from this belt will be quick to inform you that this map is no longer accurate. Numerous microbreweries have recently opened in these states, but the 1992 snapshot of the diffusion process reveals an interesting cultural lag. Though the southern lag may be attributed to legal restrictions stemming from Bible Belt religious taboos, it may also indicate a generally conservative attitude toward any trend of popular culture. This is a theme that warrants further research.

Until recently, the large brewers shrugged off microbreweries as minuscule and insignificant, but they are now legitimately concerned over the loss of shelf space. Though microbreweries presently capture only 1 or 2% of the national beer market, they have moved into the most lucrative segment. Their success has forced large breweries to become more diverse with non-Pilsener brands like Augsburger Rot, Elk Mountain, and Killian's Red. The industry giants are also buying microbreweries to cash in on the trend by providing small brewers with capital for expansion and growth. The author wonders how buyers would be affected if they knew their favorite little brewery was part of a corporate conglomerate. The introduction of "dry" beers and "ice" beers is yet another creative answer to capturing the upscale market, but none of these tactics is slowing microbrewery growth.

Microbrewery success is also reviving midsize brewers. Midsize breweries are reformulating and repositioning their products to adapt to the changing landscape of American brewing. Brand names like Pig's Eye Lager and Blackened Voodoo appear to be microbrewery products, and capitalize on the same antiestablishment sentiments. The increase in contract brewing has also helped midsize brewers. Contract brewing companies handle the marketing of their beer, but rely on midsize breweries to brew and package the product. Midsize breweries also augment production of microbreweries that cannot keep up with demand. The whole industry is being shaken up as Americans demand more variety and quality in their beer selection.

Looking for Flavor

A subculture of beer connoisseurs has emerged in tandem with the rise of microbrewers. These people are sophisticated beer drinkers who are familiar with terms like hallertauer, lambic, and doppelbock. They know how to pronounce wort, and scoff at the insipid Pilsener. Perhaps in response to growing anti-alcohol sentiment, and groups such as Mothers Against Drunk Driving (MADD), many beer drinkers have changed the nature of their consumption from beer swilling to beer tasting. As with almost everything in this society of conspicuous consumption, the beer that a person drinks has become a sociological marker or symbol of self-definition.

Boutique wineries might be said to have paved the way for microbreweries, but the haughty oenophile is a clearly different creature. For one thing, beer connoisseurs swallow what they taste. They must, to get the full flavor of the product. While a wine taster uses only the taste buds on the front of the tongue, a beer taster must also engage the buds on the very back. One could even argue that the beer taster must therefore have a more sophisticated palate, because while the wine taster uses only his salt, sweet, and sour buds, beer appreciation also requires use of the bitter buds.

National serials such as American Brewer, Zymurgy, The New Brewer, and Beer educate the new connoisseurs. There are also local publications such as Ale Street News in New York, Celebrators in Hayward, California, and The Midwest Beer Notes from Wisconsin. Beer-of-the-month clubs, such as Chicago's Beer Across America, will deliver a different microbrew six-pack to your door once a month. Many of the connoisseurs are homebrewers belonging to clubs such as The Unfermentables of Arvada, Colorado; The Dead Yeast Society of Lafayette, Louisiana; or The Sultans of Swig in Buffalo, New York. These people ponder and discuss beer; the drink is no longer just a part of the backdrop in social situations. A beer drinker of the 1990s is more likely to appreciate the foamy head of an ale, to dwell on the bouquet, and to savor the hoppy carbonation as the drink slides down her or his throat.

"Ale-ing" for a Sense of Place

While America's beer drinkers are becoming more sophisticated and passionate, their demands do not require microbreweries. There is a wide array of fine beers available from importers and larger breweries. These beers may satisfy the palate, they do not satisfy the neolocal craving. "Is a Beer Local If It's Produced Not So Locally" is the title of an article that appeared in The Wall Street Journal. The concern of this article seems to be at the curx of understanding the microbrewing phenomenon, and numerous conversations with brewpub patrons confirmed a strong attachment between breweries and localities. In answer to why he drank the local brew, one brewpub patron put it succinctly, "It's a matter of city pride."

Setting is an important part of beer consumption. While visiting St. Louis, a trip to the Anheuser Busch brewery is enlightening. After a tour of the fermentation coolers, the bottling plant, the granary, and the Clydesdale stables, the visitor is served a complementary glass of history. Sipping on a Budweiser in this setting becomes a sublime experience. In Moline, Illinois, it's just not the same.

Michael Jackson is a person who has made a life out of traveling to taste the beers of the world. As others now follow in his footsteps, there are numerous books aimed at the beer tourist and armchair traveler. Tourists have been noted for their frequent and immense consumption, and visiting a brewery is a part of itineraries more and more. Many brewpubs are dependent upon business from outsiders trying to find the local flavor.

Most of America's microbreweries are young, and have not yet had time to burrow into the heart of the symbolic place-consciousness of their localities, but there are notable exceptions. The Spoetzl Brewery in Shiner, Texas, has survived for over three-quarters of a century. The brewery is ingrained in the character of the town. Legend says that Kosmos Spoetzl used to give away more beer than he sold, but he did not care. He told his disgruntled bookkeeper, "[T]hese are my people, I want to help them." The people of the town and the brewery are still inextricably linked. Many of the employees have worked in the brewery for over 20 years. Picture cheerleaders leading their classmates in the singing of The Shiner High School Anthem: "When we founded the brewery the sun was shining . . . we had a good time eating and drinking." High school anthems like this could not exist in mainstream suburban America. Therein lies a beauty that most microbreweries will never achieve.

Much of the appeal of a microbrewed beer is that it is a rejection of national, or even regional, culture in favor of something more local. Nevertheless, the widespread success of microbreweries may endanger their existence. The cookie-cutter approach is a serious threat to the uniquely local experience. The successful formula of gutting and renovating a historic building to brew five or six shades of the amber spectrum behind a Plexiglas wall has become all too common. Less than a decade ago each brewpub was a truly unique local gem. Today they are trendy and quickly becoming unremarkable. Future success may hinge on the perceived distinctiveness of the operation and its relative attachment to the local sense of place.

The Spoetzl Brewery has a history that recalls a time when microbreweries were a part of vernacular culture. The recent ascendance of microbreweries is interesting because it has been decidedly within the realm of pop culture, but unlike most pop culture phenomena, microbreweries engender a strong, self-conscious attachment to their localities.

This neolocalism of microbreweries is an intriguing attempt to create a sense of place. The Weeping Radish Brewery and Restaurant has served fine German food and lager beer since 1986 in the same place where the original settlers of the Lost Colony presumably brewed the first beer in the New World. This Eurocentric historical "imagineering" may be inaccurate, but it is a valiant attempt to further anchor the establishment in its place. At the Weeping Radish the customer finds appealing food and drink in a faux German atmosphere, but what makes the establishment so successful is the simple fact that you cannot get a Black Radish Dark Lager anywhere else in the world but Manteo, North Carolina.

Conclusion

Over the last 15 years the United States brewing industry has gone through some rather remarkable structural and spatial changes, especially the microbrewery segment. This article is an attempt to explain the origin and diffusion of microbreweries and how their success relates to a sense of place. There are geographic questions that deserve attention. These include: How is the prevalence and power of neolocalism changing in American culture? Could the "microbrewery desert" of the Midwest and South indicate a generally conservative attitude toward any trend of popular culture within these regions? With the international link to Britain established and the subsequent appearance of brewpubs in places as far flung as Moscow, Russia, would a study of the worldwide diffusion be revealing? It remains to be seen how much the microbrewery segment can continue to grow; nevertheless, geographers with an interest in American culture should stay tuned to the changes and all the inherent space and place implications.

Chapter 19

Transplanting Pilgrimage Traditions in the Americas

Carolyn V. Prorok

Transplanting a pilgrimage tradition is a precarious endeavor. In theory the possibilities are endless, but in practice many difficulties must be overcome. Notions about how the sacred shows itself are carried easily enough from one land to another, but whether one will recognize the sacred there is an entirely different matter. The myths that tie specific supernatural entities to specific places at home may not be conducive to transplantation, and the collective conscious that produces a community of potential pilgrims may be so frayed by the migration experience that its original form cannot be recovered. Moreover, the new society may be unreceptive to, or outright intolerant of, one's traditions. Under these circumstances, diasporic communities with pilgrimage traditions have had varying degrees of success in recreating a sustained, organized, and functional pilgrim circulation system.

This article is concerned with the prevailing strategies that underlie the transplantation and reinvention of an already established and deeply embedded pilgrimage tradition by migrant communities – primarily from Catholic Europe and Hindu South Asia to the Western Hemisphere. This entails the struggle to make new sacred places. Making and remaking sacred place is essential to pilgrimage circulation systems. Three metascenarios for the potential emergence of a sacred place for transplanted peoples are presented in this essay. These scenarios and their associated strategies are not necessarily progressive or interdependent, although more than one of them may have been employed at any given site. It is also important to note that these scenarios are not based on specific ethnic, cultural, religious, political, social, or economic predispositions and operant behavioral interactions. Countless empirical studies have already focused on some combination of such

Prorok, Carolyn V., "Transplanting Pilgrimage Traditions in the Americas," pp. 283–303 from *Geographical Review*, 93.3 (July, 2003).

factors in the character and development of specific pilgrimage sites, such that they are often presented as unique in time and space. Earlier typologies tend to focus on the same types of surface features of sites instead of the processes that produced them.

Here I seek to elaborate the panhuman processes that underlie, drive, and ultimately reproduce the surface features that appear as ethnic, religious, cultural, social, political, and economic in their material forms – simply because these are the means of expression that specific groups of humans at certain times and places have at their disposal. Such underlying processes are linked to the very material forms so dear to a person's or people's heart. Reconciling, yet not assimilating, the material with the spiritual, the I with the We, and the past with the present is made possible when people redeploy their sacred travails and travels in new times and places. An end result is what can be called the "collective selfhood." Transplanting pilgrimage traditions is not the only way to create collective selfhood, but it is a very successful means for doing so. Thus it remains a profoundly human endeavor that may diminish at times but never wholly disappears. Although it is impossible to capture fully the multiplicity of actions and reactions of millions of people, of varying cultural heritage, on two continents, over several centuries of migration experience, I offer my typology as an initial means for creating dialogue on this topic.

Sacred Place as the Basis of Pilgrimage Systems

In recent ruminations on traditions, or the lack thereof, V. S. Naipaul shares with us his observation that his homeland, Trinidad, has no sacred places:

> I began to feel when I was quite young that there was an incompleteness, an emptiness, about the place, and that the real world existed somewhere else. I used to feel that the climate had burnt away history and possibility. . . . We who were Indian were an immigrant people whose past stopped quite abruptly with a father or grandfather. . . . [This] agricultural colony, in effect a plantation, honored neither land nor people. But it was much later, in India, in Bombay, in a crowded industrial area – which was yet full of unexpected holy spots, a rock, a tree – that I understood that, whatever the similarities of climate and vegetation and formal belief and poverty and crowd, the people who lived so intimately with the idea of the sacredness of their earth were different from us.

In this passage Naipaul eloquently captures an important and defining difference between peoples of the Old World homelands and the descendants of migrants to that other world across the ocean. This divide also exists between the traditional and indigenous past, where the sacred infuses every nook and cranny of the lived world, and the modern, transplanted, and relatively desacralized present. Naipaul recognizes for himself the absence of that critical element of all pilgrimage traditions, sacred place, and thus by implication he is also letting us know that Trinidadians, Hindu Trinidadians in particular, do not have a developed pilgrimage circulation system as it is known in the Indian homeland. His assessment of the lack of sacred connections in his Trinidad homeland continues:

> Too late, then, I remembered with a pang a story I had heard about when I was a child. . . . Every now and then, according to this story, groups of aboriginal Indians in canoes came across the gulf from the continent (where remnants of the tribes still existed), walked to certain places in the woods in the southern hills, performed certain rites or made offerings, and then, with certain fruit they had gathered, went back home across the gulf. This was all that I heard. I wasn't of an age to want to ask more or to find out more; and the unfinished, unexplained story now is like something in a dream, an elusive echo from another kind of consciousness. Perhaps it is this absence of the sense of sacredness – which is more than the idea of the "environment" – that is the curse of the New World. . . . And perhaps it is this sense of sacredness – rather than history and the past – that we of the New World travel to the Old to rediscover.

Naipaul is onto something here. Although I would disagree that the sense of the sacred is absent among the colonizing and colonized peoples of the Western Hemisphere, it has certainly diminished. The depreciation of sacred consciousness to which he speaks did not occur overnight; it took centuries. Its roots are embedded in the rise of the modern era in Western Europe, which brought with it the impersonality of industrialism and early capitalism – neither of which has need of sacred places in the traditional sense. The grand colonial projects of several Western societies, and the Protestant Reformation – with its focus on "the word" over ritual – also had their parts to play. In the face of such sweeping changes many sacred sites were destroyed or built over by the conquering party, especially in the Western Hemisphere, and especially those of indigenous peoples whose lands were being absorbed or who were forcibly removed from favored lands. Add to this the inundation by foreign migrants who arrived by the hundreds of thousands and brought with them their own notions of what constituted a sacred place, even though transferring those ideas to their new circumstances would often prove to be difficult. Many communities willfully abandoned practices; others simply lost them. For some communities, holding on to certain aspects of their traditions became a foundation for their collective identity. Such projects are ongoing, and today they are the basis for a resurgence of the search for the holy.

One could argue that the desire to travel – to briefly break away form the routine of the everyday – is a root cause of pilgrimage and that journeying as existential quest is, in and of itself, a powerful motivation for many people to travel. Yet this desire alone is not enough reason to account for pilgrimage circulation in the traditional sense, in that one needs a sacred destination. Although there will always be those individuals who derive satisfaction from aimless wandering, such wandering is not the basis of traditional pilgrimage systems. As Rebecca Solnit notes, "To travel without arriving would be as incomplete as to arrive without having traveled."

Before the advent of agriculture and its concomitant settled lifestyles our forebears were nomadic. During the course of their journeys certain places likely took on great significance and carried special meaning for them as aggregation sites where celestial confluences were conflated with special or unusual natural features that figured prominently in the traveling memories of countless bands of humans who gathered for companionship and friendly competition. Pilgrimage by early agricultural peoples could have been an attempt to recover their nomadic heritage in an attenuated form, and it would have been directed toward specially remembered places of their nomadic pasts. J. McKim Malville, an astrophysicist, explains that Nabta Playa, an ancient site in the northern Sudan, was sacred to nomadic groups and settled people for millennia. He wrote to me:

> There was a ritual-like repetition of return, an act of synchronization between people and the cosmos, as they kept coming to that basin which would fill with water each summer solstice due to the monsoon rains. Not only were people in synchronism with the great cosmic cycle of rain and sun, but they were reenacting the deeds of the past. . . . Home was on the trail, and pilgrimage was at home; pilgrimage was not departure from home but a return to the center.

We know that many sacred places are of more recent vintage and have been invented and reinvented many times. Without these sacred places religious journeys would not exist. Where the entire breadth of a people's lands is understood to be sacred, believers may distinguish between places with particular qualities or may identify some places as more sacred than others. In either case, this relationship arises out of a traditional milieu in which a group of people has had a long, thorough, and intimate relationship with the local environment. Contemporary circumstances for ever-increasing numbers of people, especially in the lands of industrialization and colonial migration in the Western Hemisphere, have shifted this relationship from one of intimacy with the living, breathing, earthiness of Earth to a search for such intimacy. The root of this shift derives largely from the rise of the modern era and the cataclysmic ways in which millions of people were simultaneously uprooted and transplanted. At the same time, traditional systems have been "disembedded" from their specific time- and place-centered meanings. More recently, individuals born into a (re)embedded postmodern sensibility are searching for a new intimacy with certain times and places, with the earthiness of Earth, by recovering them and reshaping them via slippery, and often fragmentary, processes deriving from the existential dilemma of creating a collective selfhood. Under such circumstances, Elvis Presley can sing "You Ain't Nothing but a Hound Dog" and still become a shining beacon of hope for life after death and the desire to be close to an authentic voice.

Pilgrimage – Transplanting Scenarios

For Muslims, pilgrimage to a specific, extraordinarily sacred site is literally a commandment from the almighty, and for more than a millennium tens of millions of the faithful have turned their devoted gaze toward Mecca regardless of migratory experiences or the salience of local sacred sites. Hindus and Catholics have no such commandment that establishes the one and only sacred site for faithful observance, yet Hindu India and Catholic Europe have exceptionally well developed pilgrimage circulation systems that incorporate thousands of sites of varying degrees of sacredness and importance.

Peoples of both faith systems have migrated to the Western Hemisphere in large numbers, though Catholics more so than Hindus. Today Catholicism is the dominant faith in much of Latin America, with significant minorities in North America, whereas the Hindu presence tends to be concentrated in several of the former British and Dutch plantation colonies (Trinidad and Tobago, Guyana, Jamaica, Suriname) and is becoming more evident in contemporary North America.

Indigenous peoples of the Americas felt the full brunt of an aggressive, colonizing Christianity in the first centuries of contact. Catholic migrants to an already overwhelmingly Protestant North America over the past two centuries generally met with intolerance up to the World War II era. During the late nineteenth and early twentieth centuries hundreds of thousands of South Asian Indians, primarily Hindus, were transported to already Christianized sugar colonies and met with intolerance for their faith traditions as well. Contemporary Hindu migrants to North America also face such difficulties despite civil laws that protect them. Even under the most conducive of migrant circumstances – such as moving to similar physical and social environments as the homeland, traveling voluntarily, migrating with the larger share of one's family and community, the ability to carry one's personal effects conveniently, being welcomed with open arms – it would be difficult to transfer a pilgrimage tradition because of its typically place-bound character. Yet many migrants would have been fortunate to have even one of these facilitating factors apply. Instead, alien environments, hardship, and intolerance were more often the order of the day; thus the transfer of pilgrimage customs was indeed a precarious one. Under these circumstances in the Western Hemisphere several metascenarios emerge as primary strategies of recovery: co-opting indigenous sites, maintaining links with the homeland, and re-creating sites for transplanting a pilgrimage tradition. Some sites likely have a history of multiple scenarios, either simultaneously or serially, but none of these approaches is codependent on any other. The examples I use highlight only one of many possible strategies used by any given cohort of pilgrims.

Co-Opting Indigenous Sacred Sites

Long before the Columbian voyage indigenous peoples established sacred sites and created pilgrimage traditions in association with them. Such sites still exist; many are still important to native communities. Contemporary worshiping communities visit them as native, converted, or plural shrines where African traditions can also be incorporated into the ritual character of the site.

People, whether native themselves or not, visit native sites as native sites. The San Francisco Peaks and several other mountains in Arizona, for example, hold extraordinary meaning for the Navajo and Hopi peoples, but they are also open to the public. For nonindigenous peoples, visits to these mountains and other such sites may take on a touristic quality or may involve spiritual dimensions, such as adopting some version of a native faith system or creating a new spiritual meaning for them within the context of their traditional meaning.

Conquerors and the converted – however nominally – faithful imposed, adapted, and resisted conversion by syncretizing native sacred sites with Christian elements. Many indigenous religious sites and a great deal of material culture were purposely destroyed or invalidated through elimination and renaming by Christian conquerors. It was also common for Iberian conquerors to raze pyramids and other indigenous sites only to build cathedrals or churches on them. In addition, newly emerging native converts might have an extraordinary experience on or near an already established native site, making possible its rededication to a Catholic saint. The shrine of the Virgin of Guadeloupe in Mexico City, the patroness of all Mexicans, is one such example.

A plural shrine can be found in Trinidad, where a Catholic shrine to Our Mother La Divina Pastora was established more than two centuries ago on or near what is believed to have been a native sacred site in the town of Siparia. As more and more Hindu Indians from southern Asia settled in the area, they too offered their devotions, so much so that today the shrine is also known as Sipari Mai. Hindus honor it with a major festival and pilgrimage during the week before Easter, when the statue of the Virgin Mary is moved to another room so she can be adorned and worshiped in the Hindu manner. She is placed back on the main altar of the church on Good Friday for the Catholic services during Easter weekend. Thus, this place simultaneously has indigenous Caribbean roots and is Catholic and Hindu in its most crucial observances.

Some sites are invested with a multiplicity of meanings by groups with varying beliefs and practices that conflict. Mount Shasta in California is one such contested site: The local native community struggles to maintain a traditional relationship with a place that now attracts thousands of New Age spiritual pilgrims as well as environmental pilgrims.

Maintaining Links with the Homeland

Contemporary Catholics and Hindus, particularly in North America, continue to go on pilgrimage by returning to the homeland. The return to the homeland can act as a pilgrimage in and of itself, in which case home is distinguished as a nation-state and made sacred by its role in the diasporic imagination. But some people return home to visit remembered holy places and participate in the pilgrimage rituals of a knowable, traditional homeland with specific sacred sites to which they have access. The town of Medjugorje, Bosnia is one such place for Croatian American.

In the Caribbean, Hindus have, by and large, lost their traditional pilgrimage circulation system, although some have attempted to reconstruct a semblance of one over the years. While visiting communities in the ports of New Nickerie and Paramaraibo, Suriname, I found no specifically Hindu sacred site. Some Surinami Hindus, who are generally third- or fourth-generation descendants of late-nineteenth-century migrants, indicated that going to India, or to a specific place in India such as Varanasi, would constitute a pilgrimage for them, but most could not afford the costs involved; thus, this is not a common practice. Surinami Hindu temples are important as ritual and social centers, but none of them plays the role of pilgrimage place in a traditional sense. Trinidadian Hindus have no Hardwar (the holy Hindu city on the Ganges at the foot of the Himalayas) or Kumbha Mela (the holy Hindu festival that occurs there every twelve years). Nor has the mythical nature of Indian holy sites been easily transferred by a group of people with knowledge of and experience with such places in India. Rama did not canvas this land searching for Sita, nor did dismembered parts of Sati – consort of Shiva – fall in Trinidad. Yet Trinidadian Hindus did manage to re-create local sacred sites.

Re-Creating and Reinventing Sacred Sites

If an immigrant group derives from a land with a significant pilgrimage circulation tradition, then its notion of what constitutes a sacred destination already has meaning and coherence. As such, any sacred destination in the new land is not simply created, it is re-created. This scenario entails at least five possible strategies: replication, (re)recognition, creating movable rituals, celebrating sites of sacred embodiment, and ritual historicizing.

Replication

The first method involves the erection of a replica of an image, temple, or any other important sacred object from the homeland. Both Hindus and Catholics have deployed this strategy for establishing new sacred sites far from the homeland. In the 1970s Sri Venkateswara, an incarnation of Vishnu enshrined at Tirupati, in Andhra Pradesh, was replicated first in Pittsburgh, Pennsylvania and later at several other locations in North America with support from the homeland shrine. The Tirupati Temple supplied the artisans and priests necessary for the transferral projects, and the Pittsburgh temple depends on support from a broad base of pilgrims across North America to maintain its compound of religious structures. The Sri Venkateswara Temple in Pittsburgh hosts more than 150,000 North American pilgrims annually.

Another example is the National Shrine of Our Lady of Consolation in Carey, Ohio, about 50 miles south of the western end of Lake Erie. In the late nineteenth century a small Luxumbourgian community enshrined a replica of an image from its homeland that was subsequently associated with miraculous events. This shrine is now a center of pilgrimage for Catholics in the Great Lakes region every year for the Feast of Assumption.

(Re)Recognition

The second process involves the (re)recognition of the sacred in one's midst with a direct relationship to traditional means for understanding hierophanic experience (when the sacred shows itself to us). This entails knowing the sacred when we see it, with the use of any of our other senses, or being able to recognize it again in a new context. This process has been especially significant for the descendants of immigrants whose numbers have grown over the years.

The Hindu population in Trinidad became demographically stronger by the mid-twentieth century and comprised mainly Trinidad-born individuals when locally produced Hindu sacred sites began to emerge. Several temples in Trinidad have lingams, stones representing Lord Shiva, which Trinidadian Hindus believe have grown in size since they were discovered. Informants claim that true faith and worship cause the lingams to grow. In each case a stone was found protruding from the ground, and a temple was erected. A sacred story is associated with the lingam of two separate temples, similar in form. The more popular of the two, located in southwestern Trinidad, is known as the Patiram Trace Shiva Temple. According to my informants, a man hired to clear out undesirable jungle growth sharpened his cutlass on a stone protruding from the earth. As a result the stone chipped, and milk (some say blood) flowed from it. The stone is said to have grown more than a foot since the 1940s, according to one of my informants, Sanachariya. Now it appears that another stone is emerging out of its side. According to Sanachariya, several people visit the temple every day to perform *puja*, the basic Hindu ritual of worship, as witnessed by the numerous ceremonial symbols left by the visitors, such as *jhandi* flags. Sanachariya estimates that more than 5,000 people pay their respects to the lingam on Shiva Ratri, a Hindu holy day.

In North America, apparitions, weeping images, and other spontaneous miracle events have become more common over the last three decades. In 1989, in Ambridge, Pennsylvania, outside Pittsburgh, devotees believe that a crucifix of Christ closed its eyes during the Good Friday Mass. No one actually saw the eyes of Christ's image close on that memorable day; the young men serving the mass simply thought the eyes of the crucifix were different. In an interview for the American television program *Unsolved Mysteries*, Mr. Leo, a local artist who had recently restored the image, reported that the eyes appeared fleshy and teary and that, he added, "the left eye was closed and the right one was slightly open." Over the next year thousands of pilgrims flooded the church as more people learned of the miraculous event.

In both of these cases, as in countless others, the protagonists knew the sacred when they saw or otherwise sensed it and acted on that sensibility. Their respective communities validated the original encounter through continued, persistent visitation of the sites. If the stones in the Trinidad bush had been ignored or removed, or if the changing demeanor of the Ambridge crucifix had gone unrecognized, neither place would be so special to its community today. The ability to (re)recognize the sacred, as one's forebears recognized it in the homeland, would eventually disappear or might reappear in a new form. With the strategy of (re)recognition, a very ancient means of accessing the sacred can be maintained in new contexts and forms.

Creating movable rituals

Utilizing movable rituals as temporary sacred destinations is a third method for re-creating the sensibility of traditional pilgrimage. Devotees take advantage of already institutionalized, and otherwise ordinary, ritual events in order to travel for a religious purpose. This method emerges most clearly in the absence of opportunities to visit specially sacralized sites, although an absence of such sites is not necessary for this process to occur.

In Trinidad, Hindus have created a ritual event known locally as the *jag*. This activity is centered around the classical ritual known as the *yagna*, although in Trinidad it has been altered in form. Traditionally the yagna is a Vedic sacrifice ritual, but in Trinidad it has taken on new meaning and function. Traveling to yagnas sponsored by an extended family, a pundit, or a village temple is very popular. Bhagwat Jag usually lasts for seven days; Ramayana Jag, for nine. Handbills are prepared and distributed. Each night of the jag puja is performed, the Ramayana or Bhagavad Gita is read, and *prasad*, sweets offered at the puja, are distributed to the guests. On the final night a feast is served, and most people attend at this time. The meetings accrue merit to those who prepare them, especially by feeding the holy men and poor who flock to the event. Jags can be held any time of the year, and some people, especially older women, make their rounds to as many of them as possible. Families and pundits who sponsor such events do so only occasionally, because they are so expensive. Temple committees usually sponsor a jag every year, for donations given at this time are significant in meeting the temple's maintenance costs. Religious events like the jag, which have no special association with sacralized physical features or distance traveled, are more easily attended by a great number of worshipers than are many other religious events.

Similarly, Catholics take advantage of the sunrise mass offered by some churches at an open-air site on Easter Sunday to create a religious excursion, although this practice is not nearly as common or as important to the larger community as the Trinidadian one of attending yagnas. For some Catholics, seizing an opportunity to hear a mass conducted by the Pope is so special that such an event can draw thousands of people from great distances. One pilgrim commented to a reporter for the National Broadcasting Corporation that she was spiritually fulfilled because she attended a mass offered by the Pope himself.

Celebrating sites of sacred embodiment

An age-old practice from the homeland that transfers quite easily is the belief that a specific person embodies divine power. For Catholics, a public appearance by the Pope is reason enough to travel to see him, whether or not he performs mass. The same can be said of saints, and those who are beatified or declared blessed – or more commonly, the sites where such people are buried or where their relics are enshrined. Examples include the shrine of Santa Rosa de Lima (canonized in 1671 in Peru), the Shrine of the Holy Relics maintained by the Sisters of the Precious

Blood in west central Ohio, and the National Shrine of the North American Martyrs in Auriesville, New York, west of Albany, for the eight seventeenth-century Jesuit Martyrs who died Christianizing and colonizing northeastern North America.

Individual bodies may exhibit sacred characteristics such as stigmata or are believed to heal those who visit with full faith – such as twenty-year-old Audrey Santo in Worcester, Massachusetts, who fell into a coma after an accident when she was three years old. Lying perfectly still, she receives many visitors seeking a divine experience. Some devotees call her a "victim soul," referring to a traditional Catholic belief that some women suffer greatly to atone for the sins of the world and thus become a repository of divine power.

Hindus similarly travel long distances to visit swamis (high-level spiritual authorities) or gurus (spiritual mentors) when they appear in public. Hindus will travel to the ashrams (spiritual centers) of specific swamis or gurus to receive their blessings. Not surprisingly, swamis regularly tour the Americas, and some have established ashrams and temples in the Western Hemisphere to serve its growing Hindu population as well as recent converts. The International Society for Krishna Consciousness is probably the best known among a number of such groups to establish themselves, through Swami Bhaktivedanta Prabhupada, in the Americas and worldwide. Despite being a center of controversy for nonbelievers, the temple commune of New Vrindaban in West Virginia continues to draw Hare Krishna pilgrims, and Hindus in general, from across North America, partly because it was Swami Prabhupada's Western home and is his designee's current home.

Conferring sacrality to the personhood of specific individuals is not confined to Hindus and Catholics. This practice is so ancient and so common that it re-emerges even in populations that are theologically moving away from the material expression of the sacred to an emphasis on the word, as is the case for most Protestant Christians. In the latter half of his ministry, Billy Graham would fill whole stadiums, and today Benny Hinn draws tens of thousands to any location where he appears in public. Americans of many religious and nonreligious persuasions invest a similar sense of the sacred in specific individuals not usually thought of as religious. The greatest such example of this is the reification of Elvis Presley through his voice, his body, and his public persona. Pick up any newspaper or magazine, or watch any news broadcast from August 2002, to see that the twenty-fifth anniversary of Elvis's death was more than a media event; it was memorialized by millions. Graceland, his home and burial site near Memphis, Tennessee, receives several thousand people daily, and tens of thousands visit on his birth and death anniversaries.

Ritual historicizing

The fifth method whereby people re-create sacred destinations is an especially complex one that entails the reification of particular historic moments as epitomized in the structures, people, and locational features associated with those moments or periods of time. This is quite different from the often desacralizing act of simply explaining an important event. These structures and sites represent more than ordinary sacralized place. A church or temple encompasses ordinary sacred space where prescribed rituals are an ongoing part of its raison d'être. But churches and temples are not automatically pilgrimage destinations by virtue of their ritualized character; nor are they necessarily historically important, although all of them have a history. Instead, epitomized sites and structures are ritually invested with the emotional, political, and social moments that capture a people's recognition of their own history, their own identity. They answer the question, "Who are we?" with "We are Mormons," "We are Vietnam veterans and Americans," "We are Trinidadian Hindus," "We are Cuban Exiles," and so on.

Contributing to what Wilbur Zelinsky calls "the uniqueness of the American religious landscape" are Mormon scared sites. These sites are embedded in the formative history of Mormonism and include such important places as Kirtland, Ohio, site of the first temple; Nauvoo, Illinois, where the martyred Joseph Smith is buries and the temple was burned by anti-Mormon mobs; and Salt Lake City, Utah, with its grand temple and Brigham Young's home. Ritually historicized sacred sites conflate moments in time with points on Earth's surface to the degree that the group believes that it owns such places to the exclusion of other groups of people because of what was experience – and such a sense of ownership is crucial to group identity. Recently, Mormon pilgrims retraced Brigham Young's great trek to Utah, thus revalidating that journey as the epitome of their own historical sense of selfhood.

A site that reflects the investment of a deeply felt spiritual sensibility into what is otherwise a secular and civil site is the Vietnam Veterans Memorial on the Washington Mall, as it captures a particular period in the American collective conscious. It is a memorial that reminds us that death is real and not merely absurd or noble. Miles Richardson explains:

> On the Mall, we follow a path leading among the trees to a grassy knoll. Presently, we can discern a V of black marble extending into the knoll. At first the wall of the V is at our feet, but it rises as we go down toward the apex. At the apex, the wall rises over our heads. We are in the middle of a black mirror of names: Melvin G. Cormier, Walter L. Burroughs, Hector S. Acevedo, Michael L. Poletti, Grady E. McElroy, Mary T. Klinder. Your hand, with a will of its own, reaches out to trace the curve of letters; mine follows. In the black mirror of dark marble we see our hands touching the words, and we see the self and the other, the living and the dead, meet. As a monument, the Vietnam Veterans Memorial achieves its power through the manner in which it, a controversy itself, encapsulates the greater controversy. . . . The memorial's unique reinsertion of the past into the present permits us now, at long last, to place the past into a perspective that ameliorates our nightmares and eases the burden of our guilt.

Unlike many of the other monuments on the mall, which play their own role in American civil religion, the Vietnam Veterans Memorial is the center of much ritualizing on the part of its visitors, from leaving mementos at its base to taking home a rubbing of its surface. It is a traditional pilgrim's destination. Every day is a day to visit the site, but Memorial Day has taken on special significance known as

"Rolling Thunder," when more than 250,000 motorcyclists descend on the site in remembrance of prisoners of war and those missing in action.

In Trinidad a temple is perched on a platform in the sea. This is no ordinary Trinidadian Hindu temple: Its history captures the story of its people in an extraordinary way. In this case, a people's civil history intersects symbolically with their religious history and is exceptionally epitomized by the Temple in the Sea. Just after World War II a gentleman known simply as "Sadhu" to the local people erected a small temple on the beach near the village of Waterloo. All beaches in Trinidad and Tobago are government property, and, unlike Christian churches, Hindu temples were not tolerated on public property until recently. Caroni Limited, the government sugar company, destroyed the temple. Sadhu built it again. The government fined and jailed Sadhu and again destroyed the temple. Sadhu rebuilt the temple in the sea itself, on a platform the made of rocks. He built a rocky pathway out to the temple, such that the temple was only accessible at low tide. The temple was now safe from colonial interference, but not from the elements or neglect after Sadhu died in 1970.

Yet this place was special. Before World War II people had illegally cremated their dead nearby, and after the war, when cremation was made legal, they continued to do so and spread the ashes in the sea. This site has always been popular for the performance of puja by the sea in celebration of the full moon of the Hindu month of Kartik (around October), when the tidewaters enter the temple. Until 1994 people continued to perform puja on the temple platform even though the platform had long since begun to deteriorate and its ritual paraphernalia had disappeared. The past ten years have seen a resurgence of pride in Hindu identity in Trinidad, and 1995 saw the election of Trinidad's first Hindu prime minister. Since then a memorial statue of Sadhu has been erected, and a visitor's center now awaits the pilgrim and tourist alike. A new, contemporary, Trinidadian-style temple has been built on a platform behind the original one, and it has become the focus of the annual Indian Arrival Day ceremonies, which commemorate the first landing of South Asian Indians in 1845. Already, thousands of Trinidad's Hindus have come to this site to simultaneously honor their gods and celebrate their own survival of colonial history.

Cuban exiles in Miami have created an extraordinary shrine on Biscayne Bay, just south of the downtown. Here the patron saint of Cubans, the Virgin Mary as Señora de la Caridad del Cobre, or Our Lady of Charity from Cobre, is honored simultaneously in her Catholic role of charitable mother and as Oshun, the Yoruba goddess of fertility, beauty, love, and generosity, as well as a symbol of national pride and longing. Periodically pilgrimage picnics are held at the shrine for people from specific provinces in Cuba, and La Caridad's feast day, 8 September, is celebrated with thousands of worshipers gathered in one of Miami's stadiums or parks as the priest calls for Cuban liberation during the mass. Cubans in Miami, as Thomas Tweed noted, recognize two key changes in their religious practices here as compared with Cuba. All exiles are more religious in Miami than they are in Cuba, and a significantly higher number of men worship at the Miami shrine than at the original shrine in Cuba. While fighting for independence from Spain, Cuban soldiers wore La Caridad's image during battle, and today Cuban exiles are drawn to her in even greater numbers as a unifying and liberating force. The Miami shrine is ritually historicized repeatedly as its role of symbolizing collective selfhood achieves greater depth and significance for increasing numbers of Cuban exiles.

Unlike the holy wells of Ireland, where historicization has led to the atrophying of localized spiritual power, the temples and memorials of the post-Columbian Americas have been raised up and ritually epitomized into sturdy and sublime places that shoulder the weight of a people's burdened past while simultaneously mirroring a collective consciousness of selfhood.

Collective Selfhood as Postmodern Anchor

What this is all about is a collective selfhood within which individuals are straining to define themselves through resacralization, replicated over and over in the places we make sacred so that we can visit them and remind ourselves of ourselves. As we move from the edge of one millennium that ushered in the full-throttled transformations of modernity, impersonality, and desacrality and into another, relinking the fragments of our remembered pasts becomes a reification of an imagined heritage for posterity. At the cusp of that modernity giving way to postmodernity, we search for meaning, for relevance, for that which elevates us, by rooting around in our indigenous and migratory pasts, where co-opting native spiritual sites, maintaining ties with the homeland – or losing them – and re-creating the sacred in our midst have taken on heightened significance.

This heightened consciousness of the significance of sacred places in our lives is created over and against the pervasive desacralized, rationalized would around us. Just like the exaggerated peaks resulting from the slope-profile exercises we do in our map-reading classes, we make sacred places stand out more than ever in an exaggerated way. Their numbers are growing – not diminishing – as we become more technologically advanced and more "connected" with the world around us, a connection to ill-defined somewheres and nowheres that produces an existential dilemma that is, in part, solved by anchoring one's relationship to the divine through knowledge and experience of places with "real" meaning.

For Sartre, the world around us was like a fine-printed tablecloth with his gloves upon it. To see the gloves, or in our case the sacred places, is to not see the cloth's design, which has faded into the background of our view. To focus on the print design, or our modern desacralized milieu, is to lose sight of the gloves or sacred places, which then lose their acuity and significance. Thus contemporary re-creation of sacred place – and an active engagement with it – requires highlighting the sacred places in the geographical space that surrounds them. This perceptual process is easier than ever with new technologies; what a paradox, when we consider the role of new technologies in desacralization and spiritual disconnection through their focus on "explained" geographical space that hides the sacred places that abound within it. We must search for them, and if we are fortunate they present themselves to us. An openness to a mystical interpretation of earthly phenomena may be a requirement for some but is not necessary for all.

Over the past century a number of great minds foresaw the conundrum we are currently facing in the search for a relevant selfhood. According to Robert Mugerauer, Jacques Derrida and Michel Foucault would have us continue to "undo tradition and create whatever temporary meanings and values we can for ourselves." In light of this perspective, the search for the sacred and our ability to hold on to relevance slip-slides away in a world where meaning is increasingly plasticized and fragmentary. In the marketplace of globalized choices and localized experiences, the search for the sacred is becoming increasingly decentralized – the Catholic hierarchy, for example, rarely validates reports of miracles any more – despite the powerful role of a central authority in creating a media-oriented diocese without official parishioners. The plethora of new sacred places identified in our nightly news are as fleeting as the words used to describe them. Thus old, peeling paint on an Ohio barn became the Madonna holding her child in 1990, and in 1995 Surnami Ganesha (a Hindu God with an elephant's head) statues drank milk from teaspoons in empathy with those in India. Did the paint stop peeling? Are Ganesha idols in Suriname still drinking milk? Is the spirit of Elvis really a healer? Postmodern sceptics see devotees swimming in a soup of credulity.

Mircea Eliade – and, according to Mugerauer, Martin Heidegger too – would have none of this. Unlike Foucault and Derrida, Eliade believed that historicism (not ritual historicizing) as an explanatory model had not yet gained the upper hand and that it was still possible to rejuvenate our experience of the sacred for our time and place. I believe that Eliade would see in Elvis the healer an attempt to recover substantive meaning by those who participate in its making. Moreover, Eliade thought it possible to retrieve the sacred from cultures to which we never did, or no longer, belong.

Both perspectives have something to contribute to our understanding of how we make sacred places in new times and new lands. The salience of particular traditional meanings may be recast, (re)presented, and even temporary, but they are still drawn from that deep well of historically particular, collective consciousness; a consciousness of collective selfhood constantly renegotiated and constantly relevant.

The phrase "collective selfhood" would seem to be an oxymoron, but it is not. Instead, it reconciles without assimilating, thus obliterating one or the other state of being, collectivity or individuality, the We with the I. Remaking sacred places, and visiting them, is an intensely personal and material experience for so many individuals. Pilgrims see the sites on their own terms. They smell the smells and walk the walk on their own, all the while capturing the past and the spiritual and making it relevant to a present sensibility. When visiting a sacred site, the pilgrim can really feel that sense of belonging to a group that requires no explanation or validation of one's publically expressed, personal experience. This is not simply the communitas described by Victor and Edith Turner, though communitas may be experienced by the pilgrim (for example, liminality, antistructural belonging, rite of passage, or undifferentiation). Collective selfhood does not require the obliteration of the I; nor does the sense of belonging thus created end with the pilgrimage event. It expands and solidifies through the pilgrimage experience into the everyday existence to which the pilgrim returns. What a wonderful way to stave off the ever-threatening existential darkness of being alone in the world, sitting right there on the edge of the horizon. Giving up one's individual sense of self is one solution – a solution that is not uncommon. But why give up so much when you can have your cake and eat it too! The postmodern lifeworld of so many in the Americas seems to require an increasing frequency and intensification of experiences which produce collective selfhood that does not simultaneously threaten individuality in order to innoculate oneself against the ever-present threat of aloneness. To this end, one can recount an endless number of attempts to resacralize space, even temporarily, in the name of collective affirmation as a stopgap against personal annihilation.

Native Americans temporarily produce moveable sacred places in a series of sacred commons in the form of powwows where their collective selfhood becomes both a destination and a journey. Sri Ganapathi Sachchidananda, a guru from Mysore, India, finds Shiva in a rock 60 miles north of Pittsburgh, Pennsylvania. He tells us:

> This is a powerful rock. . . . Now it is a powerful soul. There is a good vibration here, come and touch it! It is not for testing with machines. If you touch with that kind of intention, nothing happens. If you feel there is something, if your heart, mind and soul's power make a connection with the rock's power, then the healing power is coming. This rock is the same shape as the Kedarnath lingam. . . . So I call this the American Kedarnath.

When Swami Sachchidananda visits this site, usually in August, his devotees – both Indian and Anglo Hindus – converge to honor him, God, this place, and themselves. What then of the pilgrims celebrating the Feast of the Assumption for Our Lady of Consolation in Carey, Ohio? Or the Trinidadian pilgrims honoring Shiva's growing lingam on his most holy day? And those who adamantly attest to the closing of Christ's eyes on his crucifix in their local church? What about those who were healed by Sipari Mai in Trinidad, the Virgin of Guadeloupe in Mexico, the Black Christ of Esquipulas in Guatemala, or even the spirit of Elvis himself? Then there are those who persist in building temples in the sea and those who leave a piece of themselves at the base of a black wall. What they are doing is making sacred places – sacred destinations that will capture this moment in their life's journey and give it collective meaning, at least for now. Some of these endeavors grow in significance and solidify a sense of collective selfhood through repetition; many others wither and disappear, only to be reborn in another time and place.

Chapter 20

Kitchenspace, Fiestas, and Cultural Reproduction in Mexican House-Lot Gardens

Maria Elisa Christie

[. . .]

Cultural Reproduction in House-Lot Garden Kitchenspaces

In Xochimilco and many other semiurban communities in central Mexico, the house-lot garden is a space where old and new elements are in constant engagement and where changing cultural identities are negotiated, re-created, and celebrated as "tradition" is continually redefined. No clear boundary separates the kitchen from the house-lot garden or the private space of the household from the semipublic space of the community. "Kitchenspace," as I came to call the combination of indoor and outdoor spaces where food is prepared, is a privileged site of cultural reproduction and plays a central role in family and community life. Gendered and embodied knowledge – including how to prepare traditional foods and when a particular dish is appropriate – is selectively transmitted from one generation to the next, and children are fed the tastes, traditions, and beliefs of older generations through quasi-sacramental food rites that make up the fabric of everyday life.

In this article I consider the function of kitchenspace in nature-society relations at the household and community level, its spillover into the house-lot garden, and women's participation in the community through the staging of fiestas that mark the annual cycle of culture and place. Based on a qualitative study of food-preparation spaces in three semiurban communities in central Mexico – Xochimilco, Ocotepec, and Tetecala – and working within geography's tradition of nature-society relations, I adapt a feminist political ecology framework to an exploration

Christie, Maria Elisa, "Kitchenspace, Fiestas, and Cultural Reproduction in Mexican House-Lot Gardens," pp. 370–83, 385–8 from *Geographical Review*, 94.3 (2004).

of gendered spaces, genderéd knowledge, and narratives of cultural identity in the house-lot garden. In this region, centuries of careful observation of nature and the stages of the agricultural cycle are represented in a cultural complex with Nahuatl roots. The annual fiestas of the religious calendar are a syncretic blend of the Catholic faith and a pre-Hispanic indigenous cosmovision. Ritual foods such as mole and tamales are offered to the spirits of the dead, the winds, the hills, and even the Popocatépetl volcano in an effort to appease the forces of nature.

Traditional fiestas are as much a product of *mestizaje* (the mixture of Spanish and Indian elements) as is the rich mole sauce that many consider the quintessential Mexican dish. Many types of mole exist, but common ingredients include chilies, chocolate, and tomato of Mexican origin, almonds, raisins, and garlic brought by the Spaniards but of Arabic origin, and pepper, cinnamon, and cloves from the Orient. Served with chicken or turkey, it is also the favored dish for weddings, birthdays, and community celebrations, although it is increasingly being replaced with fried pork, partly because of the rising cost of dried chili. Pigs, on the other hand, can be raised on kitchen scraps in house-lot gardens. Mole and other traditional foods reflect family heritage and regional cultural inheritances, as do ritual and beliefs surrounding their preparation. When I asked people to tell me about their community, they would inevitably begin by calling attention to their particularly tasty mole sauce. Although many cooks in Ocotepec use cacao rather than chocolate for a more bitter flavor, in Tetecala they add plantains and cookies for extra sweetness. Throughout the region the sight of a large clay pot signals similar traditions.

Building on previous relationships and fifteen years of experience in the region, I spent eleven months in 2000–2001 dividing my time between households and work parties in the study communities. I worked in half a dozen homes per site, visiting them periodically throughout the year, as often as weekly and even daily when they were involved in final fiesta preparations. Inspired by Miles Richardson's creative and multidisciplinary approach to place in his article "Being-in-the-Market versus Being-in-the-Plaza," I sought to understand the experience of "being in kitchenspace" using three qualitative methodologies: participant observation, ethnographic interviews, and participatory mapping. I borrowed the dynamic and existential concept of "embodiment" from medical anthropology to incorporate research subjects' multiple experiences of "dwelling" in particular environments into my inquiry – including their emotions, beliefs, and knowledge associated with kitchenspace. This helped me approximate a "sense of a place" rooted in the spaces of everyday living and cooking. Despite the difficulty of gaining access to the private space of the home and the semipublic space of the house-lot garden – as well as of women's hectic schedules – informants were generally pleased to have someone lend a pair of hands to help with their work and listen to what they had to say.

The principal question guiding this inquiry was what role women play in nature-society relations through kitchenspace. After four months of participant observation, dozens of unstructured interviews in each site, and coming progressively closer to the spaces and issues that seemed to matter – and with the help of local research assistants – I developed and applied a series of structured interviews to address three areas: gendered spaces in the landscape and adaptation to change; women's knowledge about the natural environment in the context of gathering and preparing food; and food narratives reflecting culture and identity. Participatory mapping proved more effective than participant observation or interviews for understanding spaces from the perspective of women living in the study communities and brought attention to the modern-traditional duality of kitchenspaces in the house-lot gardens.

Kitchenspace is vital to understanding gender, place, and culture in this region. Although food is certainly a concrete manifestation of humans' link to the earth and food preparation reflects cultural traditions and beliefs, this study was also strategic: It was intended to incorporate women's work and spaces in a social context where these are too often left unrecognized. In a preliminary research project with Mexican immigrant women in Texas I found that, even when asking them about gardens they had planted and cared for, they consistently referred me to the man of the house; changing the focus to food and kitchens provided me direct access to women even in the most gender-segregated and conservative communities in Mexico. This study was informed by feminist critiques of Western science that question the exclusion of everyday life experience and contributions of ordinary people and by the social science literature on social reproduction that specifically validates their importance. It responds to repeated calls within the discipline to pay more attention to the female "half of the human in human geography," something Latin Americanist geographers have been particularly slow to do.

Three Increasingly Urban Communities

Xochimilco, Ocotepec, and Tetecala are located along the neovolcanic axis in the Mesa Central of the Mexican Plateau and share many of the cultural traits characteristic of Mesoamerica. According to Robert West, this area "is the largest and culturally the most significant of the Middle American tropical highlands. From the archeological record it appears that since Preclassic, or Formative times (1500–200 BC) the high plateau has supported a large population. Here are found some of the largest of the ancient ceremonial and urban centers of Mesoamerica, particularly in the Valley of Mexico and environs on the eastern side of the plateau. Still today, the Mesa Central forms the core of Mexico's population and economy."

The three communities in this study are pre-Hispanic in origin. Xochimilco was settled in the twelfth century by one of the original Nahuatl groups, the Xochimilcas, who extended southward to parts of what is now the state of Morelos in the 1300s and also founded one of the original barrios of Ocotepec. Tetecala was founded in 1680 by mestizo and mulatto immigrants from what is now the state of Guerrero, south of Morelos, after an earthquake destroyed the original settlement. These place-names are derived from Nahuatl: "Xochimilco" means "where flowers are sown"; "Ocotepec" refers to the "hill of the pine tree"; and "Tetecala" describes a "place with many houses with stone vaults."

Xochimilco and Ocotepec have experienced dramatic change and growth since the early 1970s as the nearby cities of Mexico City and Cuernavaca have expanded, transforming their communities into suburbs, bedroom communities, and periurban areas. Between 1970 and 2000, Xochimilco's population (my work is focused on one of its seventeen traditional barrios) more than tripled, while Cuernavaca's population, which includes Ocotepec, more than doubled. In three decades these places each became an urban center of roughly one-third of a million citizens. In the same period, Tetecala, the study site farthest from Mexico City, grew by more than a third to nearly 7,000 inhabitants. Population increased in Tetecala with a steady trickle of migrants from the south; it remains a relatively isolated but significant regional market and agricultural center and the seat of the municipal government. The similarities between Xochimilco and Ocotepec, and the differences between them and Tetecala, are partly ethnic in origin. In Tetecala, residents refer to the neighboring indigenous community of Coatetelco, where fiesta and culinary traditions are more similar to the other sites, in disparaging tones. Xochimilco and Ocotepec still have Nahuatl speakers among its elders; all three sites have indigenous identity movements and groups offering Nahuatl or "Mexicano" language classes.

In Xochimilco, people have been producing food crops and flowers for more than 500 years, and the chinampas remain the basis for the region's intensive raised-bed agriculture and cultural identity. Morelos, on the other hand, has long been known for its plantations of rice and sugarcane and for a campesino tradition that gave rise to the agrarian hero of the Mexican Revolution, Emiliano Zapata. In Ocotepec, most of the people who once worked the land have sold it or rent it out. For the most part, small-scale farming has ceased to be viable in Tetecala, and many lease their land to foreign investors who grow produce for export or plant cane for the sugar industry that once employed many townspeople.

Common features in the region include changes in land use from one generation to the next, so that it is increasingly rare to find people under the age of sixty who still farm the land. Although some occasionally obtain fresh produce from their own fields or from neighbors and family, women purchase most of their fresh fruit and vegetables daily at local open-air markets where the produce is as often resold by vendors purchasing from the national market in Mexico City as sold by local producers. Young women increasingly question traditional gender roles as they seek more opportunities outside the home. Food preferences and traditions nonetheless persist, even when women must spend hours cooking after having worked all day or take a "vacation" from their jobs in order to spend two weeks preparing food for the community. Corn and beans remain staples, and people still use firewood for cooking, if only for tortillas and fiestas. Some families plant subsistence corn, a few women grind it, and others boil it at home and take it to the mill to grind. Though few in number, young men are involved in commercial agriculture in Tetecala and, especially, Xochimilco.

Wave after wave of indigenous, rural migrants from poorer areas, an ongoing exodus from the pollution, crime, and poor quality of life in Mexico City, and out-migration to the United States constantly redefine boundaries in the three communities. The collective identity in each place is based in part on marking differences between longtime residents and relative newcomers and between each place and nearby cities and towns. Only people whose families have worked the land for generations consider themselves and are considered by others to be "from here." Locals deny that newcomers are "from here," particularly in decisions involving land, regardless of how many years they have lived in town. In Xochimilco and Ocotepec, localities with centuries of history between their traditional barrios as well as with other communities in the region, people identify and are associated with a particular barrio more than with the town itself.

I selected the three study sites, as well as the women in the study, in part for their diversity and also because of prior relationships that would facilitate access to what many called "the most intimate space in the home": the kitchen. Sometimes I chose informants because they were hosting a special meal. I sought out working people and ordinary places, like kitchens and house-lot gardens, that are often overlooked. Despite their importance to residents and increasingly for local tourism in both Xochimilco and Ocotepec, most people in Mexico City and Cuernavaca are oblivious to the fiestas' existence. Even within Tetecala, longtime residents from one neighborhood ignored the dimensions of the annual fiesta for the Virgin of Coatetelco on the other side of town; there, women worked collectively for several days in one house-lot garden to prepare food for hundreds of guests, most of them pilgrims in procession from the neighboring indigenous community of Coatetelco who returned the religious figure to its church on the same date as the Niñopa celebration in Xochimilco.

Study participants included women of different ages and educational levels. Younger women were invariably more educated, including some who had attended a university. Few informants over the age of fifty, though, had completed primary school. The women in this study were lower or lower-middle class, and some of them were struggling to make ends meet. None was short of ingenuity, character, or ability to stretch their resources, occasionally even scavenging for food in the countryside. All of them, regardless of age, had some business experience selling food, plants, or other products in the street or in the local market. Most consider themselves humble people. The only woman I would consider "poor" was one whose location on the outskirts of town reflected her social status and lack of belonging. Susana, a squatter recently displaced from her land in nearby Yautepec, lives in a shack on the outskirts of Tetecala with no electricity or running water. Her "house-lot garden" at the edge of a field has no formal boundaries but includes the usual chilies, herbs, and chickens. The large hearth made of scrap materials – including a tractor tire filled with cement – seems to anchor her family to the earth.

One elderly widow I interviewed said she was too poor to participate in fiestas, but she had dozens of coffee mugs hanging on her adobe wall. She needed these to send off her dead, she explained, with a collective mourning ritual requiring eight days of prayer, food, and drink. Several women complained not of their material poverty but of Protestant groups who wanted to "steal their dead" by bringing an end to these and other traditions, such as setting out food offerings for the dead in November. From a Nahuatl cultural perspective, this would jeopardize the very survival of the living, given the function of the dead, who work on their behalf to guarantee a plentiful harvest.

Most of the women with whom I worked were from the three study communities; some who said they were not "from here" had married in from an adjacent barrio. Doña Eustoquia is an exception: A migrant from the state of Guerrero, she had come to Tetecala fifty years earlier, when her future husband "stole her" from her family – a relatively common occurrence for women at that time. She represents the community as much as does any other individual in my study and offers a partial perspective on the region.

Kitchenspace in Geographical Garden Studies

Since the mid-twentieth century cultural geographers have shown interest in gardens and yards, including their food-related aspects. Although a "masculinist bias" in geography – and a bias toward "field" research and toward agriculture over domestic spaces and gardens – may have discouraged consideration of spaces close to the home, geographers have increasingly remarked on their cultural and social significance. Clarissa Kimber was a pioneer in studying gardens, with her early research in the West Indies showing dooryard gardens to be "an intimate form of land use . . . particularly revealing of cultural habits and inheritances." Hinting at the emotional and social importance of gardens, Kimber pointed out that their general purpose "seems to be for consumption and exchange with neighbors and for the use and pleasure of the gardener," and she found it "a matter of status to be able to give presents from the garden." She noted that the exchange of garden products supported reciprocity networks.

More recently, Antoinette WinklerPrins stressed the importance of garden products to critical social networks in the case of rural-to-urban migrants in Brazil. In Mexico a different sort of "garden" product – food prepared in the house-lot garden – confers status (on the cook, the household, and the barrio that receives guests) and helps to sustain critical social networks. In this way, house-lot gardens play an indirect role in subsistence when their function as an extension of the kitchen for household chores and for entertainment, recreation, and display – functions Richard Westmacott identified in his study of African American gardens and yards in the rural US South – combine to strengthen social networks that provide a safety net and material support.

J. B. Jackson stated that a garden tradition "almost sacred in its general acceptance, was that the vernacular or working garden was the domain of the woman of the house." In Mexico gardens are both the domain of individual women and, at times, community space. During fiestas, the house-lot garden becomes ritual space with clear gender lines, the women clustered near the corn and the rice and the men near the meat and the alcoholic beverages. But beyond gendered space, it is women's territory. Women use it for everyday chores and have a claim to it for small-scale economic opportunities such as egg production. Just as one woman rules the kitchen and house-lot garden in any given household, the woman who hosts a community meal is the unquestioned authority: Her female helpers look to her for guidance, and the men stay out of her way.

In his feminist political ecology study of urban kitchen gardens in highland Guatemala, Eric Keys reported that Mayan women not only supplement household needs in the house-hot garden but have a primary role in educating children – transmitting knowledge and values – regarding the natural environment. Stressing that the garden is the location of "important non-material elements of Mayan lifeways," Keys emphasized that the educational role of women in this space "surpasses that of material production, gender empowerment, and horticulture architecture of the garden, those elements that have received the most attention from cultural and political ecology geographers." In her study of ethnicity and change among Yucatec immigrants in Quintana Roo, Laurie Greenberg linked the house-lot garden with the maintenance of cultural identity. She found that species native to the Yucatán or long used in typical Yucatec dishes were the most common plants in the house lots and concluded that "house lots are an important space for ethnic continuity because they offer families a site for ethnic and individual expression, autonomy in continued subsistence practices, and control over diet." Likewise, although the house-lot gardens in my study provide space for women to raise small animals on food scraps, their nonmaterial elements of culture are most significant.

Cultural inheritances in the house-lot garden go beyond the embodied knowledge or reciprocity networks required to prepare community feasts – and even beyond the recipes themselves. Women transform raw ingredients into calories sufficient to support human existence – quite a feat considering the precarious economic circumstances of many in the study region – and into culturally appropriate dishes that satisfy the palate and prejudices of those who eat them. Given the importance of food and fiestas in the house-lot garden to maintaining a sense of cultural continuity and critical social networks, changes in this intimate form of land use should become a greater priority for cultural and political ecologists, as well as for feminist and cultural geographers.

[. . .] So integrated is the house-lot garden into everyday life and so subtle the progression from "indoors" to "outdoors" that it was practically invisible to me. Not until María Teresa mapped her modern and smoke kitchens on one page was I jarred into recognizing the vital but humble existence of this outdoor kitchenspace. The "everyday" and the "smoke" kitchens – or, as other women put it, the "modern" and "traditional" kitchens – often coexist and, despite some overlap, are associated with different social functions. One is family space, the other community space, although community is largely made up of kin, just as everyday life includes a never-ending cycle of fiestas. Everyday food preparation pushes the boundaries of kitchenspace into the house-lot garden, where the sink and the hearth are located, together with traditional grinding implements such as the three-legged metate that is still used to knead tortilla dough, if no longer to grind corn. On special occasions, members of the community cook, eat, and generally make themselves at home in what can no longer be considered a private house-lot garden. Both household and community kitchenspaces spill over into the house-lot garden.

The reciprocity networks that transform the house-lot garden during these preparations involve community members of all ages: They are a traditional system of mutual support throughout the region that links individuals together within

communities, just a formal "visits" and processions at the time of annual celebrations connect one barrio or community with another. A visiting delegation from
one place may provide the candles, flowers, music, fireworks, or other essential
components for another town or barrio's fiesta. The visitors are received with a
meal by specially designated hosts, many of whom commit to this role in writing
one year in advance. The receiving community, in turn, sends delegations to towns
with which it is in a reciprocal relationship to coincide with their fiestas; they too
are inevitably received with a meal, and relations between the two communities
(or two barrios in different communities) are renewed. The woman who hosts a
special meal calls on women from her extended family network for help. "Family"
extends beyond blood relatives to include "comothers" incorporated into the family
or community based on their previous support with food for a particular celebration, their sponsorship of a child at baptism or of a girl celebrating her fif-
teenth birthday, always a formal and lavish affair that marks her transition into
womanhood. This ever-expanding extended family provides an "insurance
umbrella" of sorts.

With the support of her extended network, María Teresa hosted the traditional
"meal for all the neighborhoods" on 3 May, the Day of the Holy Cross, in the
barrio by that name. Everyone from the three other barrios on Ocotepec was
invited, and hundreds of guests sat and ate in what had been a small cornfield in
the house-lot garden just days before. The next morning María Teresa served
warmed-up leftovers to the neighborhood committee in a gathering that concluded
with a discussion of community affairs and commitments for the following year's
celebration. She wept with relief as the celebratory meal drew to an end. A returning migrant with centuries-old roots in Ocotepec, María Teresa was anxious to
prove herself a member of the community; she paid into the cash collection twice,
in her husband's and her father's names, so both would be read aloud by the committee. "The family name must be kept very clean," she explained, so that one can
count on community support in times of need, as when her mother passed away
recently: The church bells immediately announced her death and launched eight
days of mourning.

[. . .] The house-lot garden provides key cultural and social space for the performance of rituals that reaffirm participants' sense of belonging – the collective
preparation and consumption of typical foods linked to fiestas – particularly those
that mark the religious and agricultural calendar. It allows women to play a vital
role in community affairs and to feed their family even in difficult circumstances.
As in other parts of the globe, women in Mexico are rarely recognized for their
work preparing daily household meals. During collective food preparation for
religious fiestas, however, the reputation of the host family and barrio is literally
in women's hands. For women like Doña Margarita, whose daughters and granddaughters allow her little responsibility for the household, it provides a welcome
opportunity to contribute.

In this region the house-lot garden is a place many women enjoy visiting with
guests, caring for their plants, or simply resting. Women reported experiencing joy
and pleasure being in their gardens, enjoying nature in the form of potted plants,
caged birds, and the fresh food they washed and cooked there. Every house-lot

garden had the ubiquitous ornamentals selected and tended by women, potted in recycled kitchen containers in a curious integration of the kitchen and the garden.

[. . .]

The house-lot garden is a site of gendered knowledge and cultural transmission, maintained to a great extent through multigenerational households in which older women take care of young children and teach both boys and girls how to prepare food and acquire a taste for local dishes. Women are responsible for a variety of food-related activities here, from raising pigs to stirring pots and flipping tortillas, as well as tending plants and small children. Girls learn that their role is to nurture and serve others. Most women said they taught their sons to cook – eggs and beans at a minimum – in case their future wife was sick or the boy remained single; but in reality it is mothers, sisters, grandmothers, and even neighbors who fill in for an absent, sick, or "delinquent" wife. One persistent pattern is that an unmarried daughter is expected to cook for the family. Another is that the grandmother chooses one person to be the repository of her cooking knowledge and does not fully disclose her recipes until she is ready. Young women complain that their grandmothers hide kitchen secrets from them, just as men complain of not being allowed in the kitchen other than to eat. Clearly, women maintain a certain degree of control over household relations through kitchenspace.

In addition to cooking in the house-lot garden, women transmit everything from knowledge of plant names and how to raise animals for food to a love of living things. Several women told me that, along with recipes, they teach their children to respect the labor of the farmer and the bounty of nature. Joining the preparations and celebrations of a fiesta, young people learn social obligations and moral values, including service to community. Every person who comes to the table – or the house-lot garden – must be fed, if only a taco. At the same time, multitiered menus before and during fiestas reflect the social stratification that has characterized Mexico for centuries. The hostess prepares simple menus for the women who work with her, and for any children they bring along, while they prepare the main meal for the guests. A small number of honored guests may be distinguished with a different menu on the feast day or offered a basket of house mole and tamales to take home after the meal.

[. . .]

House-lot gardens in the study communities are more important in terms of cultural values and sense of place than for their contribution to the physical sustenance of the family. Although the gardens provide the household with some fruit on a seasonal basis, growing vegetables there is rare, with the exception of an occasional volunteer chayote squash. One woman explained this phenomenon with the popular saying "paws or plants," a comment on the incompatibility of animals such as chickens with plants in the ground. Women grow herbs and chilies for cooking and medicinal use in this space, and they may raise small animals for a special meal or to stretch the family budget. Not every house-lot garden has food plants and live animals, but enough do that a sense of immediate connection with nature through the food cycle is part of the collective experience and sense of place. Significantly, women's response to my query about whether they lived in the country or the city was often justified in terms of their house-lot gardens. Women with working spaces and animals or plants in the house-lot garden pointed to these as evidence that they lived in the country, even as they pointed to city services and increased crime and pollution as evidence of urbanization.

[. . .]

The house-lot garden offers opportunities to study gendered strategies of adaptation to change on the urban/rural interface, including, given its semipublic nature at times of community celebrations, changes in population. It is a place for the very young and the very old, for longtime residents and newer immigrants, for work and play, for education and celebration. The house-lot garden provides a connection with the land – a space for the symbolic reenactment of such a connection – and the past in communities, such as Ocotepec and Xochimilco, that are increasingly engulfed by cities. As one informant in Ocotepec exclaimed sadly to me, "The city is swallowing us."

Household and community easily share space in the house-lot garden, but rural and urban elements have a more antagonistic relationship. Raising, slaughtering, cooking, and eating animals there allows people to remain conscious participants in the life cycle, with full awareness of how wastes literally feed into their consumption process. Reuse and recycling are part of the landscape, with tortillas laid out to dry and slop buckets collecting food wastes a common sight, even if destined for animals somewhere else in the barrio. Used containers and materials are utilized for storage and cooking: scrap metal for a griddle, plastic bags as lids on clay pots, cans for potting plants. Pigs, in particular, represent an economic and cultural strategy that supports both household and community needs and, like traditions regarding the dead – but regardless of religious practice – that people in this culture region find extremely disturbing to lose. Yet even in Tetecala, the most rural of the study sites despite its classification as a city, new neighbors from more urbanized areas complain about the smell of pigs. Esmeralda's family faced a legal battle with neighbors who attempted to introduce a city ordinance on this issue. The ordinance did not pass, but it illustrates the tension between urban and rural lifestyles that exists in all three communities. Curiously, the same people for whom animals in the house lots are intolerable swell the ranks of the community feasts.

House-lot gardens are losing ground to overcrowding, construction, and changing values and lifestyles, although, for the most part, outdoor kitchenspaces have retained their function and significance. Throughout Ocotepec, house-lot gardens showed signs of recent construction, either as people sold off parts of their land or as younger members of the family built homes on the family plot. Yet women resist losing their fiesta or smoke kitchen: Rosalinda, for example, moved her smoke kitchen to her rooftop when she built up the edges of her house-lot garden to rent out space for extra income, and she was proud to provide the women who helped her with the mole for Easter with the best view in town of the festivities below. One woman I interviewed as she was making tortillas in her house-lot garden expressed her sadness as we listened to the hammers pounding and watched young men pour cement just a few meters away from the hearth. With her view of the countryside blocked and no more cornfield to look at, she said, more to herself than to me, "How will I live?"

Fiestas play a role in integrating population sectors in the community and forging alliances with the outside, with migrants from rural areas providing much of the energy and faith that are critical to carrying on agricultural traditions – including the religious fiestas. Kitchenspaces in house-lot gardens offer migrants opportunities for meaningful and embodied participation in their host community. Migrants who have married into the community – as in Don Miguel's case – or locals who once farmed for a living, and even children of locals who return after a period outside their hometown – as with María Teresa – may host a meal for a neighborhood fiesta to express religious devotion, build alliances, and increase their social status in the process. Those with money can give cash to help with the cost of the fiesta. Those with little money or political capital may still contribute to the preparations, which, for women, usually means working in the house-lot garden. One church official in Xochimilco remarked that new arrivals from surrounding states are the most enthusiastic participants in local celebrations.

In central Mexico, who "we" are and what "here" represents have been changing to absorb new influences since long before the Spaniards arrived 500 years ago. People in the three study sites express suspicion of all newcomers, but they are particularly resentful of city folk and, in Xochimilco and Ocotepec, the urban sprawl that is changing their landscape and way of life. They are more sympathetic to rural migrants, some of whom sought work in the city and ended up as hired hands in local agriculture. Throughout the region people believe that their way of life is threatened by an erosion of values palpable, among other things, in the disregard for peasants and what they consider the "authentic" taste of the Mexican countryside. In this context, women in kitchenspaces walk a thin line between adaptation and resistance, adjusting food recipes to availability and to cost of ingredients and cookware as they seek to provide the tastes their families and communities expect despite changes in everything from environments to lifestyles.

Food celebrations in the house-lot garden have grown even as the agricultural spaces in which they were rooted have shrunk. As people in Xochimilco and Ocotepec have become less dependent on agriculture, the resource base that sustains the fiestas has changed from an uncertain harvest to the steady accumulation of capital from a salaried job or the informal sector. At the same time, locals increasingly invite outside guests as their alliances extend into the city. One seventy-year-old woman in Ocotepec told me that today's huge fiestas are not so traditional. In the old days, she explained, when people prayed for a harvest and had a couple of chickens at most, they could not count on having enough for a feast.

House-lot gardens reflect the changing cultural values and needs of the people who inhabit them and offer unique perspectives on the relationship between society and the natural environment. Increasingly urban communities adapt to change, and their mechanisms for community participation vary from one locality to the other, much like the mole recipe. In central Mexico, gendered spaces in the house-lot garden must be part of inquiries into nature-society relations. Women's ability to feed their family on an everyday basis and to supply their community with the special foods that are at the center of religious rituals and celebrations merits more attention, such as the role that transnational links and contributions from displaced community members play in celebrations of place and whether their importance is greater than that of relative newcomers who do not "belong." Gardens offer fertile ground for further research, particularly if preconceived notions about "field" and "garden" do not restrict our ability to understand change in different cultural contexts.

Part V

———

Urban Geography

Introduction

David A. Lanegran

Urban geography's twin themes of the analysis of cities as centers of interaction in a network of places and the analysis of the arrangement and function of areas inside a city have been used to organize the readings in this section.

Cities are landscapes in a constant state of change. They are impacted by processes of the global economy and cultures as well as local conditions. In addition, they are the result of the values and attitudes of the local population that manifest themselves in the private and public plans for, and investments in, cities. Cities are extremely local and intimate places where people live and create spaces for themselves. At the same time they are the product of complex interactions with other places near and far away. In order to begin to understand a city, we must know about the details of its site on the physical earth as well as its ever-changing location in cyberspace. We need to know who lives in the city and their patterns of residence, work, and entertainment. To cap it off, we need to view their plans and dreams for the city. Ideally, when studying a city, we experience it first hand. We can listen, observe, and feel the place and its people. Since such fieldwork is not usually possible, we rely on the observations and reports of others. Our goal for this section is to provide you with a range of views of cities around the world that will both encourage you to explore your home city and provide you a framework for your observations and thoughts.

We begin in the United States with an essay on how large-scale processes of urban development were manipulated by local entrepreneurs to first develop and then reinvent Greenville, South Carolina. Kennedy used concepts of site and situation to determine the factors behind the initial growth of Greenville. Among them are the waterfalls and river, the agriculture settlements that produced crops needing to be refined, the railroad network, and a series of innovations in the manufacturing of textiles combined with the growing demand for their product. This combination of local, regional, and global connections enabled mill owners to create a thriving industrial center that attracted large numbers of workers from the region and spurred further investment in the area. Changes in the textile industry else-where in the world deprived Greenville of its special advantage and one by one the mills closed. This study illustrates how places can reinvent themselves by investing in human resources and the creation of new transportation and communication infrastructure. Today a city founded on the local site advantage of a waterfall flourishes because of connections with places all around the world. After you finish reading this essay, discuss how your city leaders are planning to deal with the technological changes that will affect the local economy and culture.

Cities have been described as the world of strangers, attracting immigrants from diverse places to join the local urban economy and culture. According to this view, residential patterns and preferences help the newcomers become a part of the local scene, and where they live is a function of both their desire to live with people like themselves and segregation pressures from the powerful groups in the local area. The process that transforms immigrants to residents and urban citizens is complex and is examined by several academic disciplines. One of the aspects of the process that is particularly interesting to geographers is where the immigrants settle in the metropolitan area and how that pattern of settlement affects their involvement in the life of the city. Allen and Turner study several metropolitan areas to determine differences and similarities in the residential pattern and degree of concentration of recent immigrants to the United States. The article discusses the two major theo-ries about the need for ethnic residential concentrations in the contemporary city. The view, based on early twentieth-century immigration, assumed newly arrived immigrants would settle in older neighborhoods close to the city center to be near a support network. This view is countered by the notion that current technologies of transportation and communication make concentrations unnecessary. This study illustrates how complex the process actually is and how each ethnic group and each city has different kinds of residential concentrations. After finishing this essay, discuss how recent immigrants to your community are finding homes and being assimilated.

"South Africa's National Housing Subsidy Program and Apartheid's Urban Legacy" examines how the planning process and policies can control the residential patterns of diverse groups in cities. The apartheid policies of the former South African government were the most extreme cases of official racial segregation in the contemporary era. These policies, combined with an unequal distribution of wealth, resulted in dire residential situations for blacks. This essay describes how the government's housing policies impact the previously established patterns of racial segregation. It highlights the necessity for governments and citizens to make difficult tradeoffs between two valued outcomes: easing the housing crisis versus achieving racial integration. After reading about the way the leadership of George, South Africa, resolved this tradeoff, discuss the difficult tradeoffs being made by your community.

The authors of "World-City Network: A New Metageography?" try to help us understand how the hierarchy of cities around the world is interconnected and how it can be a force of opposition to the system of nation-states. Most descriptions of the urban hierarchy categorize cities by the numbers and kinds of functions that occur within them. These works assume that a variety of interactions link the cities together but do not try to measure them. We know that flows of information, materials, and people among cities are enormous and critical to the function of the world economy. The authors also elaborate on the current global division of labor and the concept of cities as command and control centers. They attempt to measure the connections among the cities by examining the pattern of businesses that maintain offices in different cities around the world. The various connections among the world cities focus wealth and further differentiate them from the surrounding national territory. While this process creates huge economic and cultural divides, these same cities are places where diverse cultures can be encountered and blended. After reading this essay, discuss how cities you are familiar with fit into this hierarchy and how flows from these places will influence where you will live.

DISCUSSION READINGS

Kennedy, Eugene A. (1998). "Greenville: From Back Country to Forefront." *Focus on Geography*, Spring. Pp. 1–6.

Allen, James P. & Turner, Eugene. (2005). "Ethnic Residential Concentrations in United States Metropolitan Areas." *Geographical Review*, 95(2): 267–85.

Lanegran, Kimberly & Lanegran, David. (2001). "South Africa's National Housing Subsidy Program and Apartheid's Urban Legacy." *Urban Geography*, 22(7): 671–87.

Beaverstock, Jonathan V., Smith, Richard G., & Taylor, Peter J. (2000). "World-City Network: A New Metageography?" *Annals of the Association of American Geographers*, 90(1): 123–34.

Chapter 21

Greenville: From Back Country to Forefront

Eugene A. Kennedy

What factors are crucial in determining the success or failure of an area? This article explores the past and present and glimpses what may be the future of one area which is experiencing great success. The success story of Greenville County, SC is no longer a secret. This article seeks to find the factors which led to its success and whether they will provide a type of yardstick to measure the future.

The physical geography of this area is explored, as well as the economic factors, history, transportation, energy costs, labor costs and new incentive packages designed to lure new industries and company headquarters to the area.

Physical Geography: Advantageous

Greenville County is situated in the northwest corner of South Carolina on the upper edge of the Piedmont region. The land consists of a rolling landscape butted against the foothills of the Appalachian Mountains. Monadnocks, extremely hard rock structures which have resisted millions of years of erosion, rise above the surface in many places indicating that the surface level was once much higher than today. Rivers run across the Piedmont carving valleys between the plateaus. The cities, farms, highways and rail lines are located on the broad, flat tops of the rolling hills.

Climatologically, the area is in a transition zone between the humid coastal plains and the cooler temperatures of the mountains, resulting in a relatively mild climate with a long agricultural growing season. The average annual precipitation for Greenville County is 50.53 inches at an altitude of 1040 feet above sea level.

Kennedy, Eugene A., "Greenville: From Back Country to Forefront," pp. 1–6 from *Focus*, 45.1 (Spring, 1998).

The soil is classified as being a Uti-soil. This type of soil has a high clay base and is usually found to be a reddish color due to the thousands of years of erosion which has leached many of the minerals out of the soil, leaving a reddish residue of iron oxide. This soil will produce good crops if lime and fertilizer containing the eroded minerals are added. Without fertilizers, these soils could sustain crops on freshly cleared areas for only two to three years before the nutrients were exhausted and new fields were needed. This kept large plantations from being created in the Greenville area. The climate and land are such that nearly anything could be cultivated with the proper soil modification. Physical potential, although a limiting factor, is not the only determining factor in the success of an area. As Preston James, one of the fathers of modern geography pointed out, the culture of the population which comes to inhabit the area greatly determines the response to that particular physical environment.

From European Settlement through the Textile Era

An Englishman named Richard Pearis was the first to begin to recognize the potential of what was then known as the "Back Country." The area was off limits to white settlers through a treaty between the British and the Indians. In order to get around the law, Pearis married a native American and opened a trading post in 1768 at the falls of the Reedy River. He soon built a grist mill and used the waterfalls for power. Pearis prospered until the end of the Revolutionary War. He had remained loyal to the British, lost all his property when the new nation was established and left the country.

Others soon realized the potential of what was to become Greenville County. Isaac Green built a grist mill and became the area's most prominent citizen. In 1786, the area became a county in South Carolina and was named for Isaac Green. The Saluda, Reedy and Enoree Rivers along with several smaller streams had many waterfalls, making them excellent locations for mills during the era of water power. During the Antebellum period, Greenville County's 789 square miles was inhabited by immigrants with small farms and also served as a resort area for Low Country planters who sought to escape the intense summer heat and the disease carrying mosquitoes which flourished in the flooded rice fields and swampy low country of the coastal plains. Most of the permanent residents farmed and a few mills were built to process the grains grown in the area.

Although very little cotton was ever actually grown in Greenville County, cotton became the driving force behind its early industrialization. Beginning with William Bates in 1820, entrepreneurs saw this area's plentiful rivers and waterfalls as a potential source of energy to harness. William Bates built the first textile mill in the county sometime between 1830 and 1832 on Rocky Creek near the Enoree River. This was known as the Batesville Mill. Water power dictated the location of the early southern textile mills, patterned after the mills built in New England. Mill owners purchased the cotton from farms and hauled it to their mills, but lack of easy transportation severely limited their efforts until 1852. That year, the Columbia and Greenville Railroad finally reached Greenville County. Only the interruption of the Civil War kept the local textile industry from becoming a national force during the 1850s and 1860s.

The area missed most of the fighting of the Civil War and escaped relatively unscathed. This provided the area with an advantage over those whose mills and facilities had been destroyed during the war. The 1870 census reported a total $351,875 in textiles produced in the county. This success encouraged others to locate in Greenville. Ten years later, with numerous mills being added each year, the total reached $1,413,556.11. William Bates' son-in-law, Colonel H.P. Hammett, was owner of the Piedmont Company which was the county's largest producer. Shortly after the construction of the water powered Huguenot Mill in the downtown area of the City of Greenville County in 1882, the manufacture of cotton yarn would no longer be controlled by the geography of water power.

The development of the steam engine created a revolution in the textile industry. No longer was the location of the mill tied to a fast moving stream, to turn a wheel that moved machinery. Large amounts of water were still needed but the dependence upon the waterfalls was severed. Between 1890 and 1920, four textile plants were built in the county outside the current city limits of the City of Greenville. At least thirteen large mills were built near the city to take advantage of the rail system, as shown on the map, "Greenville County Mills." Thus, with cheaper and more efficient steam power, transportation costs became a deciding factor. These mills built large boiler rooms adjacent to their plants and dug holding ponds for water.

Another drastic change took place in the textile industry around 1900. This change would provide even greater flexibility for the mill owners. A hydroelectric dam was constructed on the Saluda River, five miles west of the city of Greenville. It was completed in 1902 and would provide cheap electricity for the county. John Woodside, a local mill owner who foresaw electricity as the next step in the evolution of the industry, built what was then the largest textile mill in the world in the city of Greenville that same year. He located it further from a water source than previously thought acceptable. However, John had done some primitive locational analysis and chose the new site well. It was located just beyond the city boundary to limit his tax liability and directly between the lines of two competing rail companies – the Piedmont Railroad and the Norfolk and Western (now known as Norfolk and Southern). John Woodside's mill proved to be a tremendous success. With water no longer a key factor of location, the owners identified transportation as the key factor of location. Others began to build near rail lines.

The textile industry made Greenville County very prosperous. The mills needed workers and shortly outstripped the area's available labor supply. Also, many did not want to work in the hot, poorly ventilated, dangerous conditions found in the mills. When most of the mills were still built of wood, the cotton fibers floating in the air made fire a very real danger. Many businesses sprang up to service the needs of the workers and the textile mill owners. Farmers, sharecroppers, former slaves and children of former slaves were recruited to work in the mills. Housing soon became scarce and the infrastructure wasn't equipped to handle the influx of new workers. To alleviate the problem, the mill owners built housing for their workers. These were very similar to the coal camps of Appalachia and other factory owned

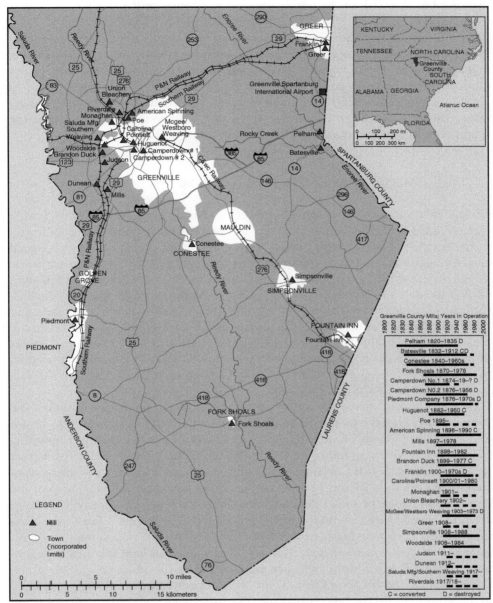

Figure 21.1   Greenville County, South Carolina.
Source: Karen Severud Cook, University of Kansas Map Associates.

housing in the north. They were very simple dwellings built close to the mill so the workers could easily walk to and from work. They also provided company owned stores, doctors and organized recreational activities for their employees, creating mill communities. Many people who worked for the mills would have told you they lived at Poe Mill or Woodside, the names of their mill communities, rather than Greenville.

In the 1960s, rail transportation of textiles was a cost the owners wished to lower. They found a cheaper, more versatile form of transportation in the trucking industry. The interstate highway system was now well developed and provided a means of keeping costs down for the operators. In the 1970s, owners began to identify wages and benefits as a major factor in their cost of operation and many firms relocated in foreign countries, which offered workers at a fraction of the wages paid in the United States and requiring few if any benefits.

Meeting the Challenge of Economic Diversification

Greenville County used its natural physical advantage to become the "Textile Capital of the World." Many of the other businesses were tied directly or indirectly to the textile industry. These ranged from engineering companies who designed and built textile machinery to companies which cleaned or repaired textile machines. Employment in the textile industry in Greenville County peaked in 1954 with 18,964 workers directly employed in the mills. As the industry began to decline, the leaders of the industry along with local and state leaders showed great foresight by combining their efforts into an aggressive move to transform Greenville County into a production and headquarters oriented economy. A state sponsored system of technical schools greatly facilitated this effort. Workers could get the training they needed to pursue almost any vocation at these centers. This system still is a factor in Greenville County's success.

The group emphasized the ability to make a profit in Greenville County. The focus of their efforts was turned to creating a sound technical education network along with the flexibility to negotiate packages of incentives to lure large employers. Incentives included negotiable tax and utility rates, plus a strong record of worker reliability due to South Carolina's non-union tradition, with very few work stop-pages. The foresight of this group has paid off handsomely. The majority of the textile mills which provided the backbone of the economy of Greenville County are no longer in business. Many of the old buildings still stand. Ten of the mills built before 1920 now are used in other capacities. American Spinning was built in 1896 and now is used as a warehouse, office space and light manufacturing all under one roof. Most of the mills are used for warehouse space or light manufac-turing such as the Brandon Duck Mills, which operated between 1899 and 1977 as a cotton mill. It now houses two small factories which assemble golf clubs and part of the mill is used as a distribution center. The low lease cost (from $1 to $15 per square foot) is an enticement for other businesses to locate in these old buildings.

The old Huguenot Mill, the last water-powered mill built in the county, was recently gutted and has been rebuilt as offices for the new 35 million dollar Peace Center entertainment complex in downtown Greenville. The Batesville Mill, the first in the county, was built of wood. It burned and was rebuilt in brick in 1881. It closed its doors in 1912 because the water-powered mill was not competitive.

The mill was purchased by a husband and wife in 1983, converted into a restaurant, and was the cornerstone and headquarters of a chain of FATZ Restaurants until it burned again in 1997. So, in considering diversification, one of the first steps was to look for other uses for the facilities which already existed.

Other efforts also met with great success. As businesses began to look south during the 1970s for relocation sites, Greenville began to use its natural advantages to gather some impressive companies into its list of residents. By 1992, the combination of these efforts made Greenville County the wealthiest county in the state of South Carolina. Twenty-five companies have their corporate headquarters in the county, as shown in Table 21.1.

Forty-nine others have divisional headquarters in the county, as shown in Table 21.2. This constitutes a sizable investment for the area, yet even this list does not include a 150 million dollar investment by G.E. Gas Turbines in 1992 for expansion of their facility. This was the largest recent investment until 1993.

Along with American companies, foreign investment was sought as well. Companies such as Lucas, Bosch, Michelin, Mita and Hitachi have made major investments in the county. Great effort has been put into reshaping the face of main Street in Greenville as well. The city is trying to make a place where people want to live and shop. Many specialty stores have opened replacing empty buildings left by such long time mainstays as Woolworths. The Plaza Bergamo was created to encourage people to spend time downtown. The Peace Center Complex provides an array of entertainment choices not usually found in a city the size of Greenville. The Memorial Auditorium, which provided everything from basketball games, to rodeo, concerts, high school graduations and truck pulls, has closed its doors and was demolished in 1997 to make way for a new 15,000-seat complex which will be named for its corporate sponsor. It will be called the Bi-Lo Center. Bi-Lo is a grocery store chain and a division of the Dutch Company, Ahold. A new parking garage is being built for this center and two other garages have recently been added to improve the infrastructure of the city. City leaders have traveled to cities such

Table 21.1 Corporate headquarters in Greenville County

1. American Leprosy Mission International	13. JPS Textile Group, Inc.
2. American Federal Bank	14. Kemet Electronics Corp.
3. Baby Superstores, Inc.	15. Leslie Advertising
4. Bowater, Inc.	16. Liberty Corp.
5. Builder Marts of America, Inc.	17. Mount Vernon Mills, Inc.
6. Carolina First Bank	18. Multimedia, Inc.
7. Delta Woodside Industries, Inc.	19. Ryan's Family Steakhouses
8. Ellcon National, Inc.	20. Span America
9. First Savings Bank	21. Steel Heddle Manufacturing Co.
10. Heckler Manufacturing and Investment Group	22. Stone Manufacturing Co.
	23. Stone International.
11. Henderson Advertising	24. TNS Mills, Inc.
12. Herbert-Yeargin, Inc.	25. Woven Electronics Corp.

Table 21.2 Divisional headquarters in Greenville County

1. Ahold, Bi-io.	24. Insignia Financial Group, Inc.
2. BB&T, BB&T of South Carolina	25. Jacobs-Sirrine Engineering
3. Bell Atlantic Mobile	26. Kaepa, Inc.
4. Canal Insurance Company	27. Kvaerner, John Brown Engineering
5. Coats and Clark, Consumer Sewing Products Division	Corp.
	28. Lawrence and Allen
6. Cryovac – Div. of W. R. Grace & Co.	29. LCI Communications
7. Dana Corp. Mobile Fluid Products Division	30. Lockheed Martin Aircraft Logistics Center, Inc.
8. DataStream Systems, Inc.	31. Manhattan Bagel Co
9. Dodge Reliance Electric	32. Mariplast North America, Inc
10. Dunlop Slazenger International Dunlop Slazenger Corp.	33. Michelin Group, Michelin North America.
11. EuroKera North America, Inc.	34. Mita South Carolina, Inc.
12. Fluor Daniel, Inc.	35. Moovies, Inc.
13. Fulfillment of America	36. Munaco Packing and Rubber Company.
14. Frank Nott Co.	37. National Electrical Carbon Corp.
15. Gates/Arrow, Inc.	38. O'Neal Engineering
16. General Nutrition, Inc, General Nutrition Products Corp.	39. Personal Communication Services
17. Gerber Products Co. Gerber Childrenswear, Inc.	40. Phillips and Goot
	41. Pierburg
18. GMAC	42. Rust Environment and Infrastructure
19. Goddard Technology Corp.	43. SC Teleco Federal Credit Union
20. Greenville Glass	44. Sodotel
21. Hitachi, Hitachi Electronic Devices (USA)	45. SouthTrust Bank
	46. Sterling Diagnostic Imaging, Inc.
22. Holzstoff Holding Fiberweb North America, Inc.	47. Umbro, Inc.
	48. United Parcel Service
23. IBANK Systems, Inc.	49. Walter Alfmeier GmbH & Co.

as Portland, Oregon to study how they have handled and managed growth and yet kept the city friendly to its inhabitants.

The largest gamble for Greenville County came in early 1989. The automaker BMW announced that it was considering building a factory in the United States. Greenville County and the state of South Carolina competed against several other sites in the midwest and southeast for nearly two years. On June 23, 1992, the German automaker chose to locate in the Greenville-Spartanburg area. Although the plant is located in Spartanburg County, the headquarters are in Greenville and both counties will profit greatly. When the announcement was made, the question was: what ultimately swayed the automaker to choose Greenville? One of the main reasons was physical location. The site is only a four hour drive from the deepwater harbor of Charleston, SC. Interstates 26 and 85 are close by for easy transportation of parts to the assembly plant. The Greenville-Spartanburg Airport is being upgraded so that BMW can send fully loaded Boeing 747 cargo planes and have them land within five miles of the factory. Plus, the airport is already designated as a US Customs Port of Entry and the flights from Germany can fly directly to Greenville without having to stop at Customs when entering the country. Other incentives in the form of tax breaks, negotiated utility rates, worker training and state purchased land helped BMW choose the 900 acre site where it will build automobiles.

The large incentive packages might appear self-defeating but BMW's initial investment was scheduled to be between 350 and 400 million dollars. The majority of the companies supplying parts for BMW also looked for sites close enough to satisfy BMW's just-in-time manufacturing needs. The fact that Michelin already made tires for their cars here, Bosch could supply brake and electrical parts from factories already here and J. P. Stevens and others could supply fabrics for automobile carpets and other needs readily from a few miles away also was a factor.

One major BMW supplier, Magna International, which makes body parts for the BMW Roadster and parts for other car manufacturers, located its stamping plant in Greenville County. Magna invested $50 million and will invest $35 million more as BMW expands. Magna needed 100 acres of flat land without any wetlands and large rock formations. This land needed to be close enough to provide delivery to BMW. After studying several sites, Magna chose South Donaldson Industrial Park, formerly an Air Force base, just south of the city of Greenville. The county and state will help prepare the location for their newest employer.

Road improvements, the addition of a rail spur and an updating of water and sewer facilities will all be provided to Magna in this agreement. Also, Magna will receive a reduced 20-year fixed tax rate along with other incentives for each worker hired. These incentive packages may seem unreasonable but they have proven to be necessary in the 1990s when large organizations are deciding where to locate.

The Future: Location, Location and Location

From the time of the earliest European settlers, the natural advantages of Greenville County helped bring it to prosperity. The cultural background of the settlers was one of industry and a propensity for changing the physical environment to maximize its industrial potential. Nature provided the swift running rivers and beautiful waterfalls. The cultural background of the settlers caused them to look at these natural resources and see economic potential.

The people worked together to create an environment which led Greenville County to be given the title of "Textile Center of the World" in the 1920s. Then, again taking advantage of transportation opportunities and economic advantages, the area retained its textile center longer than the majority of textile centers.

Today, after 30 years of diversification, economic factors now are normally the deciding factor in the location of a new business or industry. Greenville County with its availability of land, reasonable housing costs, low taxes, willingness to negotiate incentive packages, and positive history of labor relations helped make it a desirable location for business. Proximity to interstate transportation, rail and air transport availability help keep costs low. The county's physical location about half way between the mega-growth centers of Charlotte, North Carolina and Atlanta, Georgia places it in what many experts call the mega-growth center of the next two decades. Now, with BMW as a cornerstone industry for the 1990s and beyond, Greenville County looks to be one of the areas with tremendous growth potential.

Thus, a combination of physical, environmental and cultural factors greatly influence the location of businesses. Transportation costs, wage and benefit packages and technical education availability are all interconnected. The newest variable involves incentive packages of tax, utility reduction, worker training, site leasing and state and local investment into improving the infrastructure for attracting employers. The equation grows more and more complex with no one factor out-weighing another; however, economic costs of plant or office facilities, wages and benefits and transportation seem to be paramount. Greenville County is blessed with everything it needs for success. It will definitely be one the places "to be" in the coming years.

Chapter 22

Ethnic Residential Concentrations in United States Metropolitan Areas

James P. Allen and Eugene Turner

Around 1970, metropolitan areas in the United States began to receive increasing numbers of immigrants. However, little is known about the extent to which these immigrants, their US-born children and grandchildren, and others with the same ethnic identity have clustered together to form neighborhood residential concentrations. We explore the extent to which ethnic groups are concentrated residentially in metropolitan areas and how groups and places vary in their levels of concentration.

Identifying and understanding such concentrations is important for three reasons. First, both assimilation theory and recent research suggest that the proportion of an ethnic group living in a concentrated settlement is an indicator of the group's relative cultural assimilation in the United States and, perhaps, its economic status. The greater the proportion of the group that is residentially concentrated, the weaker the group's presumed assimilation. We probe this relationship by examining group differences in level of residential concentration and how they relate to the percentage of the group that is foreign-born and to the percentage that is proficient in English.

Thus, a group's settlement pattern can give a clue as to how its members are adapting to life in the United States. As phrased by other scholars studying immigrant suburbanization, "One important set of questions concerns the settlement patterns of immigrant groups within suburbia and, more specifically, the degree to which suburban settlement will result in ethnic concentrations . . . or dispersal in largely white communities."

Second, a theoretical disagreement exists as to whether ethnic residential concentrations should even be found in modern metropolitan areas. If traditional

Allen, James P. and Turner, Eugene, "Ethnic Residential Concentrations in United States Metropolitan Areas," pp. 267–73, 275–84 from *Geographical Review*, 95.2 (2005).

assimilation theory applies to recent immigrants, concentrations should be expected, at least as a stage in the process of adaptation. However, a contradictory view states that improved transportation, communication, and changes in lifestyle make ethnic concentrations unnecessary.

The third rationale for this analysis is that studies measuring ethnic residential concentrations have dealt only with the New York, Los Angeles, and San Francisco areas. Although concentrations are clearly evident in those places, the fact that these large places are among the largest receivers of immigrants clearly raises the question as to whether they are typical. To what extent are residential concentrations found in smaller metropolitan areas that have received fewer immigrants?

Why have residential concentrations – a possibly important component of the fabric of contemporary America – been so little investigated? One likely reason is that they are difficult to define. They are usually smaller than and independent of the municipal jurisdictions for which segregation indices based on census data are easily calculable. In addition, traditional theory based on the experience of the early twentieth century suggests that such concentrations should not be found in suburbs because the more assimilated immigrants should residentially disperse among the mostly white suburbanites. Assuming the theory to be correct, scholars may not even have looked for ethnic concentrations in suburbs.

Residential Concentrations, Enclaves, and Ghettos

Ethnic residential concentrations are neighborhoods in which members of ethnic groups live much closer to each other than would be the case if they were distributed randomly. The method by which such concentrations are defined is complex, and we explain it in detail below.

The concept of "enclave" can overlap with residential concentration, but we do not use that term in this research because it has multiple meanings that could make it potentially confusing. In the sense of residential concentrations, some scholars have used "enclave" for neighborhoods in which the ethnic group is found in fairly high proportions, and Peter Marcuse stresses the voluntary nature of contemporary enclaves. On the other hand, when many scholars in sociology and geography refer to an "enclave" they mean an "ethnic-enclave economy." In that sense an enclave is a spatial concentration of ethnic businesses or their employees, particularly of employees in the same ethnic group as their employer. Larger ethnic residential concentrations are sometimes located near such business enclaves or other neighborhoods in which the institutions, social services, businesses, and professional offices of the ethnic group are focused. However, this is not always the case, and some of the smaller residential concentrations covered in our research may have no associated ethnic commercial or institutional area.

A "ghetto" is a type of residential concentration, but one produced by "restriction" on residential choice, whereas the term "ethnic concentration" implies essentially "voluntary" residential choices by members of a group. In the United States, black, Mexican, Puerto Rican, Chinese, Japanese, and Filipino ghettos were formed a half century or more ago when whites prevented most members of these groups from living outside certain neighborhoods.

American society has changed significantly since those days. Some residential concentrations of Asian and Hispanic groups began as ghettos (for example, Chinatowns, Little Manilas, barrios), but the majority of their current residents settled in them after 1970, exercising voluntary choice within the limits of available financial resources. Although the locational decision is usually to some extent constrained by other factors – limited financial resources, employment locations, or perhaps steering to certain neighborhoods by realtors – members of ethnic groups can essentially choose whether to live in or outside a concentration of their group.

The voluntary nature of modern residential decisions can be illustrated by the Chinese in New York City, many of whom were interviewed by the sociologist Min Zhou. Although Chinatown in Manhattan was established as a defensive bulwark against a hostile white society, by the late 1980s that Chinatown and two others on Long Island were growing due to "voluntary segregation in order to preserve group solidarity for mutual help and for linguistic and cultural security. Today, the voluntary aspect of segregation has become more pronounced as the amount of hostility faced by immigrant groups has decreased. Also, the preference of immigrant Chinese for proximity and accessibility to the economic enclave largely determines their residential choices."

Historical Ethnic Concentrations and Spatial Assimilation

The large numbers of European immigrants who settled in America's cities between the 1860s and the 1920s represent our country's earlier period of large-scale immigration. The ethnic concentrations that developed a century ago in Chicago and other large US cities received much attention from sociologists, particularly those at the University of Chicago. Their observations and understandings of immigrant settlement processes and patterns were later formalized into what is called "Immigrant Spatial Assimilation Theory."

According to this theory, immigrants settle initially together and only assimilate spatially or disperse after they have become able to function culturally in American society and have achieved some economic success. A century ago most European immigrants arriving in large numbers came from rural areas, were poor and illiterate, and spoke little English. They could afford to live only in low-rent areas of cities. In such neighborhoods people of the same national origin often clustered together residentially for mutual support as they adjusted to urban America. These concentrations contained neighbors with whom the newcomers could easily talk, as well as familiar ethnic churches, food stores, and social organizations. They were often located near large factories or other major employers, accessible by walking or streetcar. Ethnic concentrations seemed to play a necessary role in the adaptation of most immigrants in cities at that time. But during the first half of the twentieth century, with increased economic success and acculturation to the English language and mainstream American culture, most of the children and grandchildren of immigrants dispersed into suburban areas, where the Euro-American or white population was dominant. Thus, spatial assimilation followed from cultural and economic assimilation.

Although Immigrant Spatial Assimilation Theory did not deal with ethnic proportions in the areas of concentration, historical evidence indicates that well-known ethnic neighborhoods were ethnically mixed. The leading ethnic group often comprised less than half the neighborhood's population. In 1910 Chicago, where ethnic concentrations were probably as pronounced as in any city, the majority of residents of the city's eleven Little Italys were not Italian, and only a third of the residents of Little Ireland were Irish. Less than a third of the residents of German and Czech enclaves were German or Czech. Similarly, almost half the residents of neighborhoods described as "Little Polands" were not Polish, and 40 percent of Poles did not live in those "Polish" neighborhoods.

Conflicting Theoretical Expectations

To the extent that Immigrant Spatial Assimilation Theory remains valid, modern immigrants should still need to cluster residentially as a stage in their adaptation to this country. On the other hand, major transformations in cities, suburbs, employment, immigrant acceptance, and immigrants themselves over the last several decades suggest to some scholars that residential concentrations may no longer be necessary for immigrant adaptation in the post-1970 period. We explain each of these two opposing expectations.

Reasons for not expecting residential concentrations

Since World War II urban centers have undergone substantial population growth and vast areal expansion. Manufacturing jobs in central-city industrial districts, which were once within walking distance of nearby ethnic concentrations, have generally disappeared or moved to distant suburbs. The more complex, service-based economy of today results in more varied employment opportunities for immigrants than were available a half century ago, and these are widely scattered across metropolitan areas. Automobiles, improved roads, and inexpensive and efficient means of communication diminish the advantages of residential concentration. Despite the expectation that residing in an ethnic concentration should improve employment opportunities, the opposite was demonstrated for Mexican and Vietnamese immigrant women in greater Los Angeles, presumably due to an oversupply of competitive labor in ethnic residential concentrations.

Characteristics of recent immigrants have also changed. Many people who arrived in the United States during the last three decades have some English-language skills and advanced education. Some also bring substantial wealth with them, thus facilitating the purchase of homes and the development of new businesses. The more affluent newcomers are much freer to choose from a range of residential locations than were immigrants a century ago, and many rent or buy homes in attractive neighborhoods soon after they arrive. Poorer immigrants settle in lower-cost housing. Their residential location decisions are not necessarily based on the presence of an ethnic concentration and institutions in the neighborhood. For these reasons an ethnic community can theoretically function and flourish without being geographically concentrated. Wilbur Zelinsky and Barrett Lee developed this idea most thoroughly and termed it "heterolocalism," to indicate that an ethnic community can be viable without being based on residential concentration.

Reasons for expecting residential concentrations

Although the argument that residential concentrations should not be necessary for the viability of modern ethnic communities seems reasonable, it may not be the entire story. Heterolocalism may not acknowledge sufficiently the importance of culture in some immigrants' lives, the relative comfort levels people feel in different neighborhoods, and the attractions to immigrants of an already developed concentration. Moreover, survey research from the Multi-City Study of Urban Inequality has shown that many Hispanics and Asians, as well as whites and blacks, have some preference for living near members of their own group and avoiding certain other groups. Such preferences tend to accentuate ethnic concentrations. Among Asians, the reputation of local public schools seems to be of particular importance in residential decision making, so that immigrants may concentrate residentially in preferred school districts.

Many large residential concentrations include an ethnic economy in which business-owing members of the group employ others in the group. To illustrate, 40 percent of all the Chinese working in the cities of Monterey Park and Rosemead, in suburban Los Angeles, live in one of those two cities, and 78 percent of Chinese workers in those two cities live in the larger Chinese concentration that includes the two cities. Some immigrants who do not speak English well may locate in a residential concentration to be closer to jobs that do not require English, as in Manhattan's Chinatown, which contains some higher service-sector jobs for those immigrants who are educated and skilled but do not know English. Residential proximity to ethnic shops, realtors, professional and health and social services, house of worship, private schools, and other ethnic institutions is also desired by many immigrants.

A visible clustering of ethnic businesses and services also can symbolize and help publicize the group and serve as a community marker for political purposes. Well-known ethnic concentrations can attract nonethnic customers to restaurants and other businesses located in those areas, thus helping the ethnic group economically.

People who anticipate prejudice and discrimination on the part of whites or others may see ethnic concentrations as havens from potential racist threats of all types. Among Chinese in New York, for example, "Within the enclave, racial/ ethnic tensions are minimal, but outside it immigrant workers have to overcome presumed racism. In Chinatown the culture instills pride and confidence in individuals, thus building and strengthening ethnic identity and solidarity."

The evidence so far

Regardless of theory, the size of a residential concentration or its absence is most directly explained demographically by the size and direction of net ethnic-group movement into or out of a neighborhood. Such net movement results from the cumulative effect of countless individual and family decisions. If an ethnic group contains few people who clearly prefer to live near others in the group, formation of a residential concentration is unlikely. If one has already been established and its residents and new arrivals prefer to live there rather than outside it, the concentration will expand.

Ethnic residential concentrations have been measured in three of the largest metropolitan areas in the United States. Residential concentrations were found for several large immigrant groups in greater New York and Los Angeles, and the characteristics of their residents were compared with those of members of the same group living outside concentrations. Maps also revealed numerous ethnic clusters in middle- and upper-income suburbs of Los Angeles as well as in poorer, central-city areas. Depending on the group and precisely how residential concentrations are defined, between about 25 percent and 60 percent of most group members in greater Los Angeles lived within these as of 2000. In San Francisco, contemporary residential concentrations for Mexican, Chinese, and Filipino immigrants were clearly present in 2000.

Methodological Problems in Measuring Concentrations

Measuring residential concentrations poses methodological challenges, which is a major reason for the lack of agreement as to how they should be delineated. One difficulty relates to the fact that concentrations can be viewed at various scales, each of which suggests different areal units of measurement.

Areal units and boundaries

Concentrations can be measured in city blocks, where the proportion of the ethnic group may be much higher than if the larger areal unit of the census tract is used. To illustrate, some large block-level variations in ethnic proportions occur within the tracts of large Los Angeles concentrations, such as Koreatown and the Cambodian section of Long Beach. Also, small concentrations located entirely within single apartment buildings can be identified with block-level data yet may be missed with larger areal units. However, our desire to avoid trivial concentrations with very small absolute populations suggests that a larger areal unit is better. For the present study, residential concentrations are appropriately measured in terms of census tracts, the areal unit preferred by most researchers for similar purposes.

Another measurement problem is the frequently broad and complex transition zone between the central core of a concentration and its periphery. But some studies indicate that the specific boundary definition method may be less important than it appears. In research on the characteristics of residents of ethnic concentrations in greater Los Angeles and New York, various criteria for defining residential concentrations were investigated. These included a minimum group representation of 10 percent in a neighborhood and a minimum group representation at five times the group's percentage in the metropolitan area. Differences in definition did affect the number of tracts identified as belonging to a concentration, because a few census tracts on the fringe of multitract concentrations dropped out when higher threshold definitions were used. However, findings regarding the characteristics of residents of ethnic concentrations were consistent regardless of definition.

Some scholars may think that ethnic residential concentrations must necessarily be areally extensive, perhaps composed of a minimum number of contiguous census tracts. But no theoretical reason for this exists. The method should measure only the degree to which members of the group locate in the same neighborhoods rather than in a dispersed or random pattern across the metropolitan area. A single census tract that meets the definition of a concentration should be as valid as a group of contiguous tracts. If the threshold definition is set high enough for random locational processes to seem insufficient as an explanation of the clustering, then the concentration presumably reflects the cumulative decisions of those who reside within it rather than some meaningless pattern.

[. . .]

Variables, Areas, and Groups Selected for This Research

In this research we used two different files from the 2000 census. Residential concentrations and size of ethnic populations were measured with complete-count data by a method explained below. We also explored how the demographic variables of ethnic-group size and proportion and two assimilation variables related to the level of residential concentration. To measure the level of cultural assimilation of groups in different place we used the percentage foreign-born and the percentage aged eighteen through sixty-four who spoke only English or spoke it very well. Those variables where chosen because Immigrant Spatial Assimilation Theory suggests that the percentage residentially concentrated should be directly related to the percentage foreign-born and inversely related to English-language proficiency. This is because groups with higher percentages of foreign-born may want to cluster residentially more because of less familiarity with the United States. On the other hand, groups with better knowledge of English may have less need to cluster because of their greater familiarity with this country's dominant language. To obtain these assimilation variables, it was necessary to use 16 percent sample data.

For our purposes it was important to investigate the possibility of concentrations across broadly defined metropolitan areas, in order not to overlook any concentrations in outer suburbs. Metropolitan Statistical Areas (MSAS) formed the regions in which we searched for ethnic concentrations. Where once-separate metropolitan areas coalesced, the CMSA [Consolidated Metropolitan Statistical Area] was the relevant unit.

As of 2000, five CMSAS in the United States – New York, Los Angeles, Chicago, Washington, DC, and San Francisco – had populations of more than 7 million residents; our study included all five because they are places in which ethnic concentrations may be most important. For somewhat smaller places, we randomly selected urban areas from two additional size categories. Of the seventeen MSAS with between 2 million and 7 million residents, we sampled four: Houston, Texas; Cleveland, Ohio; Denver, Colorado; and Tampa, Florida. Of the twenty-seven metropolitan areas with populations of 1–2 million, we sampled six: Cincinnati, Ohio; San Antonio, Texas; Las Vegas, Nevada; Charlotte, North Carolina; New Orleans, Louisiana; and Grand Rapids, Michigan (Table 22.1).

Within each of these fifteen CMSAS and MSAS, we measured concentrations separately for the total Hispanic and the total Asian populations and for their

Table 22.1 Residential concentrations of Hispanics and Asians in fifteen US Metropolitan Areas, 2000[a]

Metropolitan area	Total population	Hispanics in the total population (%)	Hispanics residentially concentrated (%)	Asians in the total population (%)	Asians residentially concentrated (%)
New York	21,199,865	18.2	51.2	6.8	18.5
Los Angeles	16,373,645	40.3	74.3	10.7	23.7
Chicago	9,157,540	16.4	56.3	4.3	22.3
Washington	7,608,070	6.4	18.1	5.3	5.4
San Francisco	7,039,362	19.7	36.7	19.0	36.7
Houston	4,669,571	28.9	56.1	4.9	18.2
Cleveland	2,945,831	2.7	44.8	1.4	9.8
Denver	2,581,506	18.5	42.1	2.9	1.7
Tampa	2,395,997	10.4	17.6	1.9	2.8
Cincinnati	1,979,202	1.1	9.5	1.3	18.6
San Antonio	1,592,383	51.2	78.3	1.6	0.7
Las Vegas	1,563,282	20.6	35.7	5.2	1.0
Charlotte	1,499,293	5.1	14.3	1.9	1.2
New Orleans	1,337,726	4.4	5.7	2.2	22.8
Grand Rapids	1,088,514	6.3	23.9	1.6	16.5
Mean		16.7	37.6	4.7	13.3

[a] Most metropolitan areas are CMSAS, which are identified by their largest city rather than their official name. Where groups constitute 8 percent or more of the total population, the percentage concentrated is the percentage in tracts more than 40 percent Hispanic or Asian. In all others, the percentage concentrated is calculated as the percentage living in tracts where the proportion of Hispanics of Asians is five times that of the metropolitan area as a whole. Means were not weighted by population.
Source: US Census Bureau, 2001, Census of Population and Housing, 2000. Summary File 1 (factfinder.census.gov).

leading nationality groups. Only Asians reporting a single race were included, thus keeping the analysis much simpler than if multiracial Asians had been included. It was important to identify concentrations for specific nationalities because distinctive languages and cultures have been the main basis for forming a residential concentration. Because ethnic groups varied in their relative numbers from one metropolitan area to another, we measured concentrations for the three largest Asian groups and the two largest Hispanic groups in each area.

However, measuring panethnic Hispanic and Asian concentrations was a complementary part of our method. The larger numbers in these aggregations made possible some statistical analysis, and among the US-born of these groups the tendency appears to be to self-identify more frequently as Asian or Hispanic – or Latino – than to name the specific national origin of the parents or grandparents. In addition, for Hispanics the Spanish language and national cultures of the various ethnic groups are somewhat shared, resulting in some likely overlap in social networks and residential concentrations. In order not to overemphasize the role of the largest metropolitan areas, in our calculated averages for the fifteen areas we did not weight the means by population.

Measuring Residential Concentrations

We used two methods to measure the level of concentration, because the wide range in ethnic-group proportions made any one threshold definition unrealistic. At one extreme, Hispanics constituted more than 30 percent of the population of three metropolitan areas, and Asians represented more than 10 percent of residents in two metropolitan areas. On the other hand, nationality groups in many places numbered less than 5 percent of the total metropolitan population. After some experimentation with different thresholds to determine what levels of concentration would be unrealistic to expect, we chose two definitions.

Definition 1: For lower percentage groups, five times the metropolitan-wide percentage

For groups representing less than 8 percent of the total population of a metropolitan area, the threshold for defining a residential concentration varied according to the group's percentage in the total population. A varying definition was chosen so that a residential concentration could be identified even if the group's percentage in the total tract population was quite low. Apart from differences in ethnic-group characteristics and assuming random group distributions, it would appear that the most important underlying factor behind varying ethnic percentages in tracts should be the group's percentage in the metropolitan area. The best way to control for that factor was a varying or sliding scale for defining the percentage threshold needed for a concentration.

We defined residential concentrations as including all census tracts in which the group was represented at five times its percentage in the entire metropolitan area.

The use of this value – essentially a location quotient of five – had been used successfully and seemed sufficiently high to indicate meaningful, nonrandom concentrations. Virginia Parks used the same five-times criterion in her research on the significance of residential concentration for employment.

We are convinced that tracts identified by the five-times threshold reflect real decisions by members of the ethnic group to concentrate residentially their shared locational preferences. However, the varying ethnic proportions represented in residential concentrations as defined by us suggest the need for caution in interpreting comparatively the meaning of the concentrations or the likelihood of associated ethnic institutions or businesses.

To eliminate from our analyses any groups so small that meaningful concentrations would be almost impossible to achieve, we arbitrarily established a bottom threshold of 1 percent of the total metropolitan population for a group's inclusion in our study. This threshold is the reason why our results for many metropolitan areas do not include each of the leading Hispanic or Asian nationality groups in those areas. Use of this threshold meant that each ethnic group in each metropolitan area comprised more than 14,000 persons, indication that all measures of residential concentration in our study were base on nontrivial population numbers.

Definition 2: For higher percentage groups, a 40 percent threshold

For groups that constituted 8 percent or more of their metropolitan populations, concentrations were defined differently. They were considered to include all census tracts in which the group was represented at 40 percent or more of the total tract population. Our assessment of previous research was that this threshold was sufficient and appropriate – even for groups that comprised well over 10 or 15 percent of a metropolitan population. Michael Poulsen, Ron Johnston, and James Forrest graphed the cumulative percentages for Asians and Hispanics in the New York PMSA [Primary Metropolitan Statistical Area] at different threshold values and found fairly consistent slopes, suggesting that groups would likely retain the relative importance of their concentration regardless of the threshold selected. The 40 percent threshold seemed appropriate because it minimized any break in measurements calculated by the two definitions for those groups comprising close to 8 percent of the total metropolitan populations. Thus, if an ethnic population constituted 8 percent of the total metropolitan population, application of the five-times method would result in the same 40 percent threshold used for higher percentage groups.

Overall Levels of Group Concentrations

With all metropolitan areas weighted equally, 38 percent of Hispanics and 13 percent of Asians were residentially concentrated (Table 22.2). The high proportion of Hispanics who were residentially concentrated reflects a substantial overlapping of neighborhoods among the different Hispanic ethnic groups, including some

Table 22.2 Mean levels of residential concentration and characteristics of Hispanic, Asian, and specific nationality groups in fifteen US metropolitan areas, 2000[a]

Nationality group	Residentially concentrated (%)	Foreign-born (%)	Speak English only or very well (%)
Hispanic (15)	37.6	50.0	56.3
Mexican (11)	59.4	50.5	44.5
Central American (5)	26.7	79.8	41.0
Puerto Rican (4)	32.7	44.3	71.3
Asian (15)	13.3	75.9	58.6
Asian Indian (4)	27.3	80.5	75.8
Chinese (5)	33.9	76.2	48.2
Filipino (3)	13.7	73.0	75.3
Korean (2)	33.3	81.5	40.0
Vietnamese (3)	42.5	77.0	35.7

[a] The table is based on those metropolitan areas in which the ethnic group constituted at least 1 percent of the total CMSA or MSA population. The numbers in parentheses represent the number of metropolitan areas in which the given group qualified for these calculations. Means were calculated from values in Tables 22.1, 22.4, and 22.5, not weighted by population. Puerto Rican foreign-born includes those born in Puerto Rico. English proficiency was calculated only for those aged eighteen through sixty-four. The Dominican group is not shown because it was represented by only one case.
Source: US Census Bureau, 2001 [as Table 22.1]; US Census Bureau, 2003, Census of Population and Housing, 2000. Summary File 4 (factfinder.census.gov).

national groups not identified in our research. The much lower percentage of Asians residentially concentrated is partly explainable by the fact that the many Asian ethnic groups aggregated for the Asian concentration measure resulted in high thresholds for Asians, but the distinct cultures and social networks of each Asian nationality means that each developed largely separate concentrations. Thus, it is difficult for a threshold to be reached by the total Asian population. The 13 percent figure really indicates the importance of pan-Asian settlements or multiethnic Asian concentrations. These may occur most frequently where members of different Asian groups are attracted to similar suburbs, especially those with excellent schools. Such multiethnic Asian settlements may also be geographical indicators of the growing salience of a pan-Asian identity.

On average a majority of Asians and Hispanics were living outside residential concentrations. This suggests the ability of immigrant communities to thrive while dispersed residentially, as stressed by Zelinsky and Lee. However, it is possible that a large proportion of the ethnic group living outside concentrations are the US-born children of immigrants, not immigrants themselves, together with immigrants who are well assimilated to the English language and US culture.

Average levels of concentration for specific Hispanic and Asian nationality groups varied greatly (Table 22.2), from Filipinos with less than 14 percent residentially concentrated to Mexicans, 59 percent of whom were concentrated. Means for specific Asian groups provided a better measure of concentrated settlement than did the 13 percent mean for the Asian aggregation because areas of concentration for those nationality groups typically did not overlap a great deal.

Theoretically, a higher percentage of a group living in residential concentrations should be associated with a higher percentage foreign-born, but, as Table 22.2 shows, this appears not to be the case. Although Filipinos were relatively low in both their level of concentration and their percentage foreign-born, as expected, Mexicans were much more highly concentrated than any other group but not high in percentage foreign-born. Moreover, Central Americans and Asian Indians were highest among the groups in their percentage foreign-born but relatively much lower in the percentage residentially concentrated.

We would also expect groups averaging higher levels of English-language proficiency among adults (aged eighteen through sixty-four) to be less residentially concentrated. This relationship is indeed suggested by our findings for Asian Indians, Chinese, and Puerto Ricans, compared with Vietnamese and Mexicans. The fact that Vietnamese had the highest level of concentration among Asian groups and were lowest in English proficiency is consistent with the grater adjustment difficulties many Vietnamese faced as refugees. Our findings regarding residential concentration and English-language skills are generally consistent with studies of Los Angeles, New York, and San Francisco, where residents of ethnic concentrations tended to be less assimilated to the mainstream United States culture than were members of the same groups living outside concentrations.

To better understand variations in levels of residential concentration among metropolitan areas, we calculated Pearson correlation coefficients between the percentages of Asians and Hispanics living in concentrations and possibly related variables for the fifteen areas (Table 22.3). The small number of metropolitan areas for which we measured the various nationality group concentrations precluded us from a similar analysis of those groups.

The percentages of Hispanics and Asians in concentrations correlated highly with the percentage of the group in the total population. Thus knowing the percentage of either Hispanics or Asians in the local population provides a good indication of the relative level of concentration. If the .87 and .66 values of Pearson correlation coefficient are squared and given their appropriate interpretation, 76 percent of metropolitan differences in level of Hispanic residential concentration could be explained by varying Hispanic proportions, and 44 percent of metropolitan differences in Asian residential concentration could be explained by varying Asian proportions. Similarly, the greater the size of local Asian or Hispanic populations, the greater their residential concentration. It is not unreasonable to think that absolute size and proportion can be used to predict levels of concentration of other groups in other metropolitan areas, although the smallest metropolitan areas may have too few members of ethnic groups to form concentrations even if some wished to do so.

However, metropolitan population totals were not significantly related to the level of ethnic residential concentration. Thus, one should not assume that ethnic residential concentrations are more significant in the largest metropolitan areas. The insignificant correlations between levels of concentration and percentage

Table 22.3 Levels of residential concentration in fifteen US metropolitan areas, 2000: selected correlations

Group	Pearson correlation coefficient
Percentage of Hispanics living in concentrations, correlated with:	
Total metropolitan population	.46
Total Hispanic population	.63*
Percentage of Hispanics in the total metropolitan population	.87**
Percentage of Hispanics foreign-born (outside the fifty states)	−.45
Percentage of Hispanics speaking English only or very well	.03
Percentage of Asians residentially concentrated	.08
Percentage of Asians living in concentrations, correlated with:	
Total metropolitan population	.42
Total Asian population	.61*
Percentage of Asians in the total metropolitan population	.66**
Percentage of Asians foreign-born	−.09
Percentage of Asians speaking English only or very well	−.24

*$p < .05$ **$p < .01$
Sources: US Census Bureau, 2001, 2003 [as Table 22.2].

foreign-born and percentage speaking English very well reflect differences between groups within the Asian and Hispanic aggregations, the complexity of influences affecting residential concentration, and the fact that the differences between metropolitan areas in any group's characteristics were typically very small.

The very low correlation, .08, between Asian and Hispanic concentrations indicates that one cannot assume that metropolitan areas in which one group has a high percentage of concentration will have either a similarly high or a complementarily low level of concentration for the other group. This result confirms the value of treating these two populations separately rather than combining them to examine residential concentrations in general.

Residential Concentrations in Specific Places

Hispanics and Asians

Consistent with the findings from correlation analysis, the proportionately larger Hispanic and Asian populations tended to have higher levels of residential concentration (Table 22.1). Many of these represent the growth of concentrated settlements that formed before 1960 as ghettos, but their recent expansion reflects more the voluntary processes of developing concentrations. In addition, a shortage of financial resources still limits residential choice, particularly among recent Hispanics, as it did in the earlier period.

Table 22.4 Concentrations of Hispanic nationality groups in selected US metropolitan areas, 2000

Nationality group / metropolitan area	Total ethnic population in the metropolitan area	Hispanics in the total population (%)	Hispanics residentially concentrated (%)
Mexican			
Los Angeles	4,962,046	30.3	61.4
Chicago	1,121,089	12.2	45.3
Houston	985,197	21.1	46.0
San Francisco	981,311	12.2	45.3
San Antonio	572,323	35.9	61.6
Denver	312,598	12.1	29.6
Las Vegas	232,145	14.8	29.1
Washington	75,617	1.0	17.6
Tampa	53,732	2.2	44.8
Grand Rapids	46,942	4.3	26.5
Charlotte	46,574	3.1	23.1
Central American			
Houston	886,227	1.8	10.6
Los Angeles	262,904	2.7	32.2
Washington	134,562	1.8	42.2
San Francisco	100,853	1.4	25.0
New Orleans	14,821	1.1	23.7
Puerto Rican			
New York	1,325,778	6.3	20.5
Chicago	164,509	1.8	45.0
Tampa	75,621	3.2	2.9
Cleveland	47,444	1.6	62.5
Dominican			
New York	551,538	2.6	48.2

Source: US Census Bureau, 2001 [as Table 22.1].

For groups represented in lower proportions, the proportion of groups living in ethnic residential concentrations sometimes varied substantially among metropolitan areas. Nevertheless, for most places some ethnic-group members were clearly choosing to live in the same neighborhood as others in their group.

We illustrate the use of Tables 22.1, 22.4, and 22.5 for New York and Cincinnati. In New York, Hispanics represented 18.2 percent of the total CMSA population, and 51.2 percent of Hispanics were living in census tracts that were 40 percent or more Hispanic. In Cincinnati, where Asians comprised only 1.3 percent of the metropolitan population, 18.6 percent of Asians lived in tracts that were more than 6.5 percent Asian (five times the metropolitan-wide 1.3 percent).

Because of our varying measure of residential concentration, metropolitan differences are most convincing when comparisons are made between places having

Table 22.5 Concentrations of Asian nationality groups in selected US metropolitan areas, 2000

Nationality group / metropolitan area	Total ethnic population in the metropolitan area	Asians in the total population (%)	Asians residentially concentrated (%)
Asian Indian			
New York	400,194	1.9	28.9
Chicago	116,868	1.3	37.1
Washington	88,211	1.2	13.1
Houston	51,959	1.1	29.9
Chinese			
New York	504,615	2.4	43.1
San Francisco	470,705	6.7	18.4
Los Angeles	414,582	2.5	51.7
Washington	77,513	1.0	21.6
Houston	48,537	1.0	34.8
Filipino			
Los Angeles	371,421	2.3	19.2
San Francisco	323,606	4.6	22.4
Las Vegas	33,558	2.1	0.0
Korean			
Los Angeles	252,975	1.6	42.9
Washington	74,454	1.0	23.7
Vietnamese			
San Francisco	146,613	2.1	45.8
Houston	63,924	1.4	33.0
New Orleans	14,864	1.1	48.6

Source: US Census Bureau, 2001 [as Table 22.1].

similar proportions of a group and thus similar thresholds for defining concentrations. For example, Hispanics were residentially concentrated much more in Grand Rapids than in New Orleans. Asians in Cincinnati, New Orleans, and Grand Rapids had much higher levels of residential concentration than did Asians in Tampa, San Antonio, and Charlotte. Asians in New York were much more concentrated than were Asians in Washington.

Nationality groups

Place differences are also evident for nationality groups, including cases where groups comprised fairly similar proportions in the total population. In Tampa, the contrast in residential concentration between Mexicans and Puerto Ricans is striking. Central Americans were much more residentially concentrated in Washington than in Houston. Mexicans were more concentrated in San Francisco than in

Denver or Las Vegas (Table 22.4). Asian Indians in Chicago were more concentrated residentially than were Asian Indians in Washington, despite similar proportions in their metropolitan areas (Table 22.5). Similarly, Filipinos were more concentrated in Los Angeles than in Las Vegas. The substantial place variations in percentage residentially concentrated presumably result from the characteristics of the group, the spatial patterns of housing types and prices, and the social and economic context of the group's reception in specific metropolitan areas.

The actual numbers of people residentially concentrated may be larger than expected, especially where the group proportions in the metropolitan area were very low. For example, the residentially concentrated Central Americans in Houston numbered more than 9,000. Also, more than 15,000 Asian Indians were residentially concentrated in Houston, and Koreans and Chinese in Washington each had more than 16,000 members living in ethnic residential concentrations. When one remembers that these nontrivial numbers were established by means of a stringent criterion, it seems possible that our measurement of residentially concentrated ethnic populations underestimates the actual degree of ethnic clustering as perceived by ethnic-group members.

The Varying Importance of Ethnic Residential Concentrations

This is the first systematic comparative study of ethnic residential concentrations in a large number of metropolitan areas. Concentrations were defined by two methods, depending on the ethnic group's proportion in the metropolitan area. Both the 40 percent and the five-times criteria, also used by other scholars, are sufficiently high to indicate that members of the ethnic group were residing together for conscious, nonrandom reasons. Thus, even smaller concentrations representing low proportions of the group should represent meaningful shared preferences to members of the group.

Ethnic concentrations were found for most of the larger immigrant ethnic groups in most metropolitan areas with a population of more than 1 million. This indicates that they are widespread outside the very largest metropolitan areas and are an important part of ethnic-group settlement. Such concentrations are expected, according to Immigrant Spatial Assimilation Theory.

In contrast to the situation several decades ago, when members of many groups were prohibited from living outside certain areas (often called "ghettos"), members of contemporary immigrant ethnic groups have been essentially able to choose to live in a residential concentration of their group. Clearly, many members of ethnic groups find satisfaction in living close to others of their group. Despite the argument of heterolocalism that technological and other changes have diminished or even eliminated the need for ethnic residential clustering, our measurements have demonstrated that contemporary ethnic residential concentrations are alive and well.

However, the fact that most Hispanics and Asians did not live in ethnic residential concentrations also lends support to the notion of heterolocalism, in which contemporary immigrants are thought to be able to adapt successfully without forming residential concentrations. Clearly one should not assume that the majority of ethnic populations are residentially concentrated.

Ethnic groups differed in the relative importance of residential concentrations. Groups that were less proficient in English tended to have higher percentages of the group living in residential concentrations, a finding consistent with Immigrant Spatial Assimilation Theory.

The best indicator of the likely importance of ethnic concentrations is an ethnic group's percentage within the total metropolitan population. We found that varying Hispanic proportions explained 76 percent of metropolitan differences in Hispanic residential concentration levels. Similarly, 44 percent of metropolitan differences in Asian residential concentration could be explained by the varying Asian proportions in those areas.

Although ethnic residential concentrations tended to be more important in larger metropolitan areas, the correlation between metropolitan population size and the percentage of a group residentially concentrated was not significant. Because few studies exist of residential concentrations in places other than the largest immigrant gateway centers, our finding that such concentrations frequently appear in smaller metropolitan areas – those with a population of less than 3 million – is particularly significant. To illustrate, we point to Mexican concentrations in Tampa, Charlotte, Grand Rapids, and San Antonio, to the Puerto Rican concentration in Cleveland, and to the Central American and Vietnamese concentrations in New Orleans. These findings may prompt scholars to recognize that ethnic residential concentrations not known to them might exist in their own localities.

Chapter 23

South Africa's National Housing Subsidy Program and Apartheid's Urban Legacy

Kimberly Lanegran and David Lanegran

The great transformation of South African society that accompanies the country's transition to democracy provides a fascinating field of inquiry for urban studies. Currently, government officials are devising and implementing policies explicitly intended to redress the infrastructural inequalities and inadequacies that constitute apartheid's urban legacy. The national housing subsidy policy is one such effort. As a pre-election promise in 1994, the African National Congress (ANC) announced that it would address the chronic backlog in housing for the poor by facilitating the building of one million affordable houses in its first five years in office. In this paper, we question specifically whether the resultant housing policy can overcome the race- and class-based urban spatial order established and perpetuated by apartheid.

A number of observers see the cleaved urban landscape of race-based, unequally served and balkanized neighborhoods remaining for many years to come. Residential data suggest that in the 1990s few people have moved into neighborhoods previously reserved for another race. Furthermore, the bulk of this small degree of desegregation is occurring in affordable formerly White neighborhoods into which mainly middle-class Coloreds and Indians are moving. Extremely few Whites are moving into other neighborhoods aside from the "gentrifying" racially-mixed neighborhoods in the Cape Town city bowl.

This study examines whether the South African national government's low-income housing subsidy program redresses segregation while providing housing stock for the millions whom apartheid left homeless or in informal housing (in 1994). We use a case study of the city of George on the Western Cape Province's southern coast in order to illustrate trends across the country. With a population

Lanegran, Kimberly and Lanegran, David, "South Africa's National Housing Subsidy Program and Apartheid's Urban Legacy," pp 671–86 from *Urban Geography*, 22.7 (2001).

of about 135,000, George exhibits the challenges of all urban areas in South Africa both large and small. Yet; it is an especially interesting case because of its major housing policy accomplishments.

We have followed the political transformation of George since the late 1980s when Black residents of the Lawaaikamp neighborhood resisted a forced removal order and demanded *inter alia* the upgrading of their housing. The political transformation of George in the 1990s has been remarkable. A number of local authorities, each previously exclusively for one race, have been amalgamated into modern George. This has brought a dramatic change in political leadership as the conservative White community, whose member of parliament for years was former State President P.W. Botha, has seen its political strength atrophy. With Colored and Black voters added to the local government electoral role, the ANC and its allies won the majority of seats on the local council in 1995. The first two mayors of post-apartheid George have both been members of the ANC. One, Melford Notshokovu, rose to that post from his role as a community activist who resisted local authorities' efforts to destroy his neighborhood.

Parts of George have also been physically transformed as thousands of small new cement-block houses have mushroomed across hillsides on the edges of neighborhoods. We seek to understand the patterns, impacts, and implications of this new physical landscape. Policy-makers and community elites active in formulating and implementing the local housing policies have been our main informants. During several phases of field work from 1992 through 2000, we conducted interviews with mayors, councilors, top municipal officials and the Town Clerk of George as well as business-people of all races, housing developers and Lawaaikamp activists.

This paper reviews the evolution of the South African urban political structure, discusses the formulation and results of the post-apartheid national housing subsidy policy, and highlights how the local government transformation and housing policy have altered the political and geographic landscapes of our case town. Two lessons emerge from this study. First, across the country as in George, the housing projects using the government subsidies have not fostered meaningful desegregation in urban areas. Officials' policy choices demonstrated that any desire to engineer a new social reality in urban South Africa has been superseded by the goal to quickly satisfy demands for improved services. Second, by basing its housing policy on such disparate elements as private ownership, community participation, and private sector delivery, the South African government is implementing an innovative but risky policy.

Urban Political Structure

The racial division of power and living space so noteworthy of South African cities prior to the mid-1990s has roots that extend back through the entire century. The Native Land Act of 1913 established the racial character of land-ownership as 93% of the territory was reserved for Whites' ownership. The control by Whites of other races in urban settlements, although long-standing particularly in mining areas, was further codified by the Native (Urban Areas) Act of 1923. It defined an African's legal ability to be in urban areas as contingent upon employment and empowered White authorities to control non-Whites' access to urban areas. An African not needed to work for Whites had no right to urban residency; those with permission to be in towns lived in segregated areas. Whites monopolized political rights. Thus, as Paul Maylam noted, even before the National Party leadership devised and implemented apartheid, "The whole apparatus for regulating and controlling the movement and daily lives of urban Africans had already been constructed."

Apartheid's urban project was largely implemented via the Group Areas Act (GAA) of 1950, which empowered White authorities to demarcate urban neighborhoods for specific races and to remove people living in the "wrong" areas. Coloreds and Indians living in areas reserved for Whites, such as Cape Town's lively District Six, were the bulk of the people uprooted and moved under this act. Pass Laws enabled White authorities to control Africans in urban areas, and thousands without the correct documents were arrested annually. White authorities initially administered African townships although those areas were expected to be self-funding through rent and service charges and alcohol sales. This period prior to 1960 witnessed the government's heretofore greatest investment in urban housing for Africans as townships were developed with small, poorly serviced predominantly government-owned rental houses.

In the early 1980s, the national government's urban policies changed significantly. The complete implementation of the GAA was never achieved, and in the 1970s authorities' control over the urban landscape diminished. This was due largely to Blacks' constant efforts to enter urban areas and white capital's need for that exploited labor force. Some *de facto* mixed-race areas, such as Durban's Warwick Avenue Triangle, survived apartheid's social engineering efforts. Other inner-city neighborhoods, such as Johannesbrug's Hillbrow, gradually became (illegally) desegregated due to economic considerations as landlords sought to replace existing White tenants. Consequently, the government legislated reforms. First, governance of Black townships changed as legislation made them self-governing under elected Black Local Authorities. Second, authorities accepted the inevitability of urbanization and strove to make it "orderly" through instruments such as squatting laws rather than explicitly race-based policies.

Authorities built extremely few formal houses in the townships during this period preferring to provide a small number of serviced sites to address a fraction of the housing backlog and ignore the rest. Consequently, the huge influx of urban Blacks built informal and often illegal homes (few were better than shacks) for themselves in backyards of formal houses or on any vacant land. Even cemeteries, flood plains and steep hill-sides were appropriated. Conditions were atrocious. Residents crowded into inadequate houses that, if they did not disintegrate altogether in the face of heavy rains or fires, often left inhabitants shivering in the cold months and sweltering in the hot months. Women in particular spent long days struggling to provide for their families in neighborhoods lacking adequate clean water, sewerage, electricity, telephones, and streetlights. Stress from these hardships, crime, unemployment, and in many cases political persecution was severe.

The 1990s brought dramatic change in urban policy. As part of the democratization negotiations of the 1990s, means of transforming the apartheid cities were formulated. It had become clear by the late-1980s that the existing system was untenable. Township Black Local Authorities (BLAs) in particular were incompetent, insolvent, and illegitimate in the eyes of residents who called for the formation of united non-racial municipalities. In the face of protracted protests by township residents and BLAs' consistent inability to wean themselves from financial dependence on the provinces, many government officials realized that local apartheid was a failure.

Consequently, in March 1993, representatives of government, political parties, and community organizations formed the Local Government Negotiating Forum to propose both a new system of democratic nonracial local government and the process through which to shift to that new system. Its eventual proposal was promulgated as the Local Government Transition Act of 1994 (LG Act), which laid out a three stage transformation process. During the pre-interim phase, local authorities were replaced by appointed inclusive and representative local forums that governed newly united urban areas that were "economically and historically bound." Thus White municipalities and nearby townships were first united. There was some choice concerning the exact nature of those transitional bodies, but their memberships had to be evenly divided between representatives of the existing government of the one hand (statutory) and those who had previously been denied political power (nonstatutory) on the other. These transitional bodies governed until the local government elections of 1994 and 1995, which launched the interim phase.

The LG Act was criticized for enshrining race in those first elections. Sixty percent of the council seats for any new municipality were allocated to wards, half of which were in the former White and Colored and Indian municipal areas and half of which were in the area of the former BLA. The remaining 40% of the new councils' seats were allocated via a party-based proportional representation ballot. These interim elected councils governed until the transition ended in late 2000 with local government elections under South Africa's final new Constitution promulgated in 1996.

The final new local government structures are different once again in terms of electoral formation and power. Municipal wards are no longer allocated along racial lines. Furthermore, executive functions given to local governments under the 1996 Constitution put local government on an equal footing with national and provincial authorities. South Africa's local governments have been given a new responsibility to facilitate development by giving particular attention to the basic needs of the community and are more powerful than ever before.

However, the need to quickly address the pressing demand for affordable and adequate housing has and will continue to greatly tax those new capacities. As estimated in 1994, apartheid policies left a huge backlog of 1.3 million urban houses; the total need was for three million houses if people in rural areas and residents of overcrowded hostels were also to be adequately housed. The National Housing Forum estimated that in 1994 approximately seven million South Africans lived in informal shacks on unserviced sites, another two million lived in shacks on serviced sites, at least 1.5 million households were homeless (roofless), and another 2.1 million people were crowded into hostels where often a family shared one bed. This housing shortage disproportionately hurt Black households as approximately 20% lived in informal dwellings; less than 1% of White households were thus disadvantaged.

National Housing Policy

The government's current housing subsidy scheme had its genesis in the National Housing Forum (NHF) convened in 1992, which included representatives from government, political parties, unions, lending institutions and community organizations. Just prior to the 1994 election, agreement was reached on the details of a subsidy scheme. South African households earning less than R3500/month could receive a one-time cash subsidy on a sliding scale up to R12,500 (later R15,000) ($1 = R3.66 in 1995). The ANC's chief negotiator at the NHF, Joe Slovo, brought the Forum's preferred plan with him when he became Minister of Housing in Nelson Mandela's government.

Debate surrounding the policy was contentious. An early breakthrough resulted in agreement to abandon the apartheid government's approach of offering interest rate subsidies in favor of a cash subsidy. Deciding the size of subsidies, and thus the quality of housing options to be offered, was also difficult. Eventually "breadth" won over "depth" since the scheme embodies a "progressive housing" strategy. The subsidies would be inadequate for providing both a serviced site and a four-room formal house. However, nearly 86% of South African households would be eligible for them. They could be applied to anything from a portion of the cost of a formal house, for those with additional access to financing, to a serviced site for those who could afford nothing other than building their own informal house.

Another difficult issue was determining an acceptable balance between the role of the private sector and the ANC alliance's desire to facilitate community-led development. Basing the program on home ownership rather than government-owned rental housing marked a change away from the ANC's earlier advocacy of socialist planning. But negotiators determined that building and administering rental housing stock would have been prohibitively expensive. The issues of finance and delivery were resolved by agreeing to make the private banking, mortgage, and building sectors partners in the program. Means of protecting lending institutions from defaulters would facilitate their provision of additional funding to households who wanted to supplement the subsidies. As Mary Tomlinson noted, private developers would deliver the houses "applying for subsidies on behalf of communities, identifying and servicing land, and constructing, wherever possible, a structure." However, the housing scheme also requires the active involvement of clients in all subsidy programs. A "social compact" stating the agreement of "the community," the developer, and any other party to the housing proposal is required before provincial housing boards allocate subsidies.

Some observers have asserted that the policy is seriously flawed because it is market-centered, and the social compact agreements do not empower recipients to participate in specific housing projects. Patrick Bond and Angela Tait called the housing subsidy program a "failure," arguing that market forces dominate. They state that the program *inter alia* favors families who can get additional financing, ignores conflict-ridden areas, disempowers communities, and will not result in a humane level of service provision. Mary Tomlinson conducted focus group studies of over 140 housing subsidy recipients across the country two years into the program and found evidence of very little community participation in social compacts.

The delivery of houses was initially very slow, and the one million houses took longer than five years to build. In the first year (1994–1995), only 155,000 subsidies were allocated, and only 878 houses were built. It is clear that the early period was dedicated mainly to building the administrative apparatus for the program, achieving commitment from key actors such as mortgage lenders and even ANC provincial officials who wanted more generous subsidies, and achieving means of overcoming the paradox of being both market-driven and people-centered. By March 2001, however, subsidies for a total of 1,351,260 housing options had been approved and 1,167,435 top structures were completed or under construction. In her April 2001 speech to the Free State Housing Conference, Housing Minister Sankie Mthembi-Mahanyele announced that approximately five million South Africans had been housed since 1994.

With implementation, the policy has evolved. In an effort to address inflation, the subsidy itself was increased to a top limit of R16,000 from April 1999 ($1 = R6.2 in 1999; $1 = R7.98 in 2001). A rental housing element has also been added to the program; this became one of the Ministry's priorities in 2000. That year the Ministry supported 24 pilot rental housing projects that involve 4671 housing units. In reaction to complaints by recipients, the Ministry also shifted its focus to "qualitative measure of housing delivery rather than quantitative" and to that end has set standards for the allocation of the subsidy so that the top-structure is not neglected. Finally, in response to recipients reselling their subsidized house, the Housing Minister proposed a refinement in the program that will enable the government to buy back a subsidized unit and reallocate it to another family on the waiting list.

The housing subsidy program has been criticized along a number of fronts. First, some have argued that even with the subsidy many of the South Africa's poor will either still remain inadequately housed or will not be able to afford – and consequently default on – the mortgage and/or service charges that come with their formal house. Second, since most of the new houses are being built near the former townships due to availability of cheap land, some fear the continuation of many of apartheid's urban flaws. Alan Morris, for example, has lamented the lack of encouragement of racial or class mix. Tomlinson and Kriege have worried about perpetuating economically unstable and dependent poor communities like huge Botshabelo. On a third issue, Crankshaw and Parnell have expressed fear that because the housing policy subsidizes rural houses for migrant workers, the pattern of labor migrancy will continue. Finally, even in the few cases where the housing subsidies were used for developments to serve the isolated poor in largely middle-class communities, Grant Saff has argued that desegregation is not achieved. In a situation common in many neighborhoods around the world, the poor "remained functionally segregated from the rest of the residents of these suburbs." We will return to these points in evaluating the implementation of housing programs in George.

Case Study of George

The town of George lies eight kilometers from the Indian Ocean on a plateau that descends sharply from the Outeniqua mountain range 430 kilometers east of Cape Town. Its immediate environment is dramatically varied and beautiful. The nearby Outeniqua mountain range (1000–1700 meters high) dominates the northern and western horizons. Its forestry resources have attracted people from the original Gouriqua and Attaqua Khoi-groups of 2000 years age, to the Dutch and British colonial authorities of the 18th and 19th centuries, to the foresters and tourists of today. The narrow fertile coastal plain and its Mediterranean climate continue to support a productive agriculture sector – 11% of the district's total economic output in 1994. Agricultural output is dominated by production of animal products. Yet on the other side of the Outeniqua range, the semi-desert Little Karoo stretches for 60 kilometers north to the Swartberg mountains and 300 kilometers east and west along the Outeniqua and Langeberg ranges. Rivers, wetlands, lakes, bays and estuaries punctuate the scenic coastline of the George Magisterial District. As the biggest town in the popular "Garden Route" along the Indian Ocean from Still Bay in the west to Plettenberg Bay in the east, George has served as a tourist service center. However, government and business leaders in recent years have promoted George itself as a destination for environmental and cultural tourism. Several large world-class golf courses have been built and esthetic guidelines and a historic district have been created for central George. A cable car up a nearby mountain is also planned.

Spatial History

George's urban landscape reveals apartheid's impact. Racial groups have been politically and physically separated since the establishment of the first large settlements in the early 19th century. The town of George was founded in 1811 when the British Cape Colony authorities separated the new Drostdy (or district) of George from the larger Swellendam Drostdy. Today, the central business district remains at the historical core of the town laid out in the original 77 erven (plots) between York, Courtenay, Meade and Market streets (Figure 23.1). Its extraordinarily wide main street was reportedly designed to enable six-yoke ox teams to turn around. A Colored community began in the same decades six kilometers south of George Town based at a missionary station of the London Missionary Society. Even though its residents were integrated into George's economy, Pacaltsdorp remained politically autonomous achieving in 1975 the unique status as South Africa's only municipality for Coloreds. When the apartheid era began after the

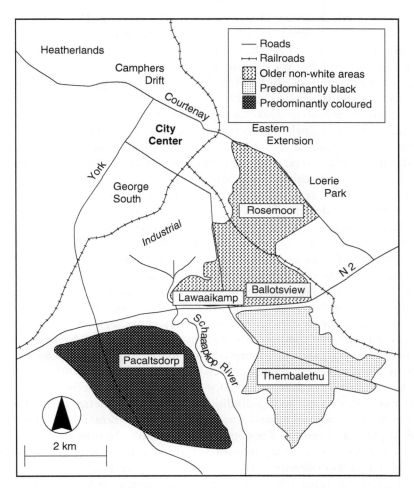

Figure 23.1 Map of built-up districts of George. As the city of George expanded from its original core near the intersection of Courtenay and York Streets, the non-White residents were settled across the railroad tracks and industrial area on the eastern fringe of the community. The newer Colored and Black settlements were distant from the center and across the Nation Highway #2, which is a major barrier between communities. The highest status white neighborhoods are to the north and west of Camphers Drift.

1948 election, the George Magisterial area (which included Pacaltsdorp) contained approximately 18,000 Colored, 15,000 White, and 1,800 Black residents.

During the height of apartheid, the area's Colored population grew dramatically, and the Black population remained small. A manufacturing boom beginning in the 1960s sparked an exceptionally rapid growth in the size of the Colored population. Because the national government's Coloured Labor Preference Policy for the Cape penalized employers who hired Blacks rather than Coloreds, George's boom did not draw a marked influx of Blacks. By the mid-1980s, Coloreds comprised over 60% of the population in the Magisterial district. Small formal houses for Colored residents were built southeast of George's industrial area. In 1987, these neighbor-hoods came to be governed by a Coloured Management Committee. The Black population grew slowly to about 5000 people in 1985. Most of those employed worked as unskilled labor for the municipality. They originally lived informally in the Colored community of Blikkiesdorp (Rosemoor). But in 1976, in order to more closely conform to apartheid regulations, the municipality moved them to a small area south of the industrial area (Lawaaikamp) where families had to build infor-mal homes. The municipality collected service charges from the 5000 residents for providing four communal taps and weekly emptying of bucket toilets; there was no electricity, paved streets, refuse removal or street lights. Meanwhile lovely, fully serviced garden neighborhoods for White residents expanded out from the core west of the industrial area and north of Courtenay Street.

The 1980s was a decade of both violence and transformation across the country in part because municipal authorities and Black residents battled over the future of the now rapidly growing urban Black community. George's officials regarded the settlement of Blacks in Lawaaikamp as a temporary step on the way toward establishing a formal autonomous township for Blacks further from town. Conse-quently, in 1982, the municipality began planning a new township at Sandkraal three kilometers farther from George. Initially, Lawaaikamp residents were open to the idea of moving because conditions were so atrocious where they were, and they believed that the municipality had promised services and brick homes at Sandkraal. However, soon the material and political rights of Blacks became the subject of often violent conflict between Lawaaikampers and White authorities. Many Lawaaikamp residents eventually refused to move further from jobs and services particularly since living conditions would be no better in Sandkraal.

However, resistance in Lawaaikamp did not keep Sandkraal (now Thembalethu) from being bult and settled. The municipality remained committed to building it for a number of reasons. First, authorities did not want a Black area within view of the new by-pass of the national road (N2). Consequently, the parts of Sandkraal behind a hill on the other side of the by-pass were developed first. Second, national reform policies, in particular the lifting of the Coloured Preference Labor Policy in 1984 and repeal of the Pass Laws soon after, prompted a dramatic influx of Blacks, largely from the Eastern Cape, into the area. George was attractive to newcomers because it was enjoying a period of sustained economic growth based on the development of its service industry. The population of Blacks more than trebled from 1985 up to 18,000 in 1991. Although many of the established families in Lawaaikamp refused to move to Sandkraal, there were plenty of new Black families who were willing to settle there. Finally, officials wanted the municipality to more completely conform to Group Areas legislation. A formal Black township should replace the anomalous Lawaaikamp settlement.

In 1987, the Western Cape province proclaimed a Black Local Authority for the Sandkraal township and thus formally absolved the George Municipality of any responsibility to provide residents with improvements. Lawaaikamp officially came under the jurisdiction of the Coloured Management Committee, and efforts to force Blacks to leave escalated. About half of the original 5000, however, stayed and resisted even in the face of bulldozers, mysterious fires, mass firings, intimidation and police violence. Lawaaikamp residents fought their forced removal with court cases and publicity. Eventually, in 1989, the municipality capitulated and agreed to use a loan from the national government to upgrade Lawaaikamp for its current residents.

Thus, in January 1995, when greater George became amalgamated, apartheid bequeathed balkanized racially exclusive and unequal neighborhoods, separated from one another by physical obstacles such as highways, industrial areas, rivers and open land. The 1996 census revealed the high degree of racial segregation in George (Table 23.1). The dominance of one race ranged from 89% to 97% in the neighborhoods. Apartheid had made standards of living highly unequal across these neighborhoods. For example, residents had unequal levels of education and employment. The 1996 census found that while only 16% of George's White residents had not received any secondary education, 58% of the Black and 51% of the Colored residents were thus undereducated. Likewise unemployment hit the races differently with 5% of the White, 18% of the Colored, and 32% of the Black residents recorded as unemployed. A study by the Development Bank of Southern Africa determined that human development across the races was also grossly unequal. In its measure of standard of living, based on access to primary healthcare and education, infant mortality rates, and average life expectancy, with 1.00 being the highest standard possible, George's White residents received a score of 0.94, while Coloreds scored 0.52 and Blacks 0.49.

Similarly apartheid bequeathed George with profoundly unequal hosing stock and pockets of squatter an informal settlements. In White areas, 95% of the homes were formal and of beauty and quality to rival those of middle-class European and American homes. In Thembalethu, in contrast, 75% of the homes were informally built of scrap materials on minimally serviced plots (Table 23.2). The informal settlements have special features that make them a unique category of urban landscapes. Although they are high-density settlements, they are not completely urban. While some have municipal services, most do not. Residents must walk some distance to water and sewage disposal. The areas are homes to litters of pigs, flocks of chickens, small herds of cows, sheep, goats and the occasional donkey and horse.

Table 23.1 Segregation of George in 1996

Neighborhood	Total population	% Black	% Colored	% White
George Central	24,001	2	5	91
Pacaltsdorp	13,221	1	97	<1
South Eastern Town (area of former George Management Committee)	32,129	9	89	<1
Thembalethu	18,413	97	2	<1

Source: George Development Consortium, 2000, Greater George: Development Profile, Table 20.

Table 23.2   Unequal housing stock in George in 1996

Neighborhood	Percent formal[a]	Percent informal
George Central	95	<1
Pacaltsdorp	82	8
South Eastern Town	71	23
Thembalethu	21	75

[a] Formal is defined as a single family house, a townhouse, a flat, or residence in a retirement village.
Source: George Development Consortium, 2000, Table 24.

These animals roam freely through the communities and onto the common lands and right of ways. The former mayor of George, a resident of Thembalethu, complained about the free ranging milk cows and goats that eat his garden. The cattle graze along the N2 highway right of way and scavenge among the community's litter. These fringe settlements are essentially residential and contain only a few small shops, bars, and barber and beauty shops. Residents must do all their major shopping in town establishments, most of which are owned by Whites.

National racial inequality left by apartheid is also bringing significant challenges to George as large numbers of Blacks are moving to George to take advantage of the town's and region's relative prosperity. The George Development Consortium (GDC) estimates that from 1996 to 1999 George's population increased approximately 6% annually. The bulk of this increase came via in-migration of Blacks largely from the Eastern Cape; George's Black population increased 16% annually during that period. People from the historically disadvantaged Eastern Cape, which had the highest poverty rate of all the provinces in 1999 at 71%, are attracted to the opportunity for jobs and better services in the richer Western Cape where the poverty rate is markedly lower at 28%. Leaders in George expect that this high in-migration of Blacks will continue for the next decade until the area's demographics more closely resemble those of the Eastern Cape. These new residents will continue to challenge the municipality's ability to deliver services.

Housing Delivery

In 1999, the Western Cape Province named the George Municipality's housing division the best of the province. The award recognized George's remarkable success in addressing residents' housing needs via projects funded by the national housing subsidy program. The municipality has been lauded for facilitating the building of nearly 7000 houses. Although many families still remain in informal housing, the greater part of the housing backlog that existed in 1996 had been eradicated by 1999. This policy's operational success has required cooperation between local and provincial officials since the provincial housing development board approves the housing development proposals and allocates the subsidies.

However, local leader's political will to make George's housing crisis a top service delivery priority is ultimately the *sine qua non* of the housing division's success. We believe this commitment and confidence of success has its roots in George's earlier experience with community upgrading. Early in the 1990s, after Lawaaikamp's reprieve, municipal officials and community leaders cooperated closely to provide residents with improved infrastructure including flush toilets, running water, and street lights. Valuable experience in cooperative development was learned by ordinary residents, their leaders who have since been elected into municipal government, and municipal officials. Therefore, when the ANC became the dominant party in the local council, it was able to form a consensus among officials, politicians, residents and the business sector to give top priority to fully utilizing the subsidy program to the benefit of George's most needy.

A number of things have gone particularly well in George. First, when residents began to complain about how small the houses were that could be bought with the subsidy once the infrastructure had been built, the housing division encouraged optional programs that allow recipients to utilize additional funding from sources such as savings clubs or loans from employers. Over 1000 homes were built this way in Thembalethu, for example. Similarly, in Lawaaikamp, some residents have joined the National Homeless Federation and are gradually building their new homes using the subsidy and other savings programs. Second, the decision by building contractors in George to make use of available local labor rather than machinery means that money is recycled back into the local community and leveraged several times over. As intended, the housing policy is helping local residents learn new occupational skills. Finally, services have been targeted at the poorest communities first. Thembalethu, where almost 73% of the population lived in informal houses in 1996, has received nearly two-thirds of the new subsidized housing. We expect, however, that attention will have to turn now to addressing the housing needs of people in the predominately Colored neighborhoods in particular.

Continuity of segregation

A close look at George's housing projects reveals, however, that with only one exception they have reinforced rather than undermined racially segregated living patterns. Rather than being integrated on vacant plots among established neighborhoods, the new houses have been built *en masse* on the fringes of former township and Pacaltsdorp. The single largest number of houses have been built just south of the N2 adjacent to Thembalethu. This means that the poorest residents remain in underserviced neighborhoods far from places of employment and shopping. Furthermore, even though many of the new houses are extending the Colored area of Pacaltsdorp and the Black area of Thembalethu toward each other in the Schaapkop River area, no roads have been built to link the two neighborhoods (Figure 23.2). Colored and Black residents of these two new housing areas may live rather close to one another, but lack of infrastructure will encumber their integration.

Local leaders admit that they decided to deliver housing before fostering integration. Speed in delivery was a political necessity for ANC councilors in particular

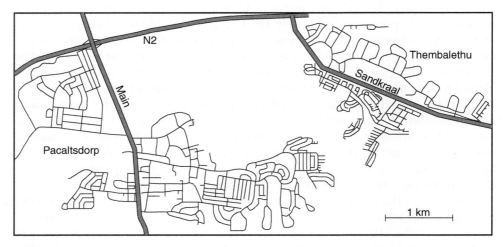

Figure 23.2 Street pattern of Pacaltsdorp and Thembalethu. The Colored and Black communities are separated from one another by the shallow, steep-sided valley of the Schaapkop River. No bridges cross the ravine. The layout of the roads provided limited access and would make the communities easy to isolate if trouble developed.

whose constituents were impatient to see tangible benefits in the new political dispensation. George's ANC leadership was certainly eager to prove itself. Extending existing Colored and Black neighborhoods was doubtless socially easier than building a consensus among residents of all races and classes for integrating low income housing throughout established neighborhoods. Furthermore, the municipality already owned a good deal of land around Thembalethu, which facilitated building there.

Only one of George's housing projects has been explicitly designed to perpetuate desegregation. In late 1999 the municipality submitted a proposal to the Western Cape Housing Board that Mayor Notschokovu billed as "the first integrated sub-economic housing project for all races in South Africa. The planned 2500 houses will be built linking Pacaltdorp with the southern edge of White neighborhoods and is intended to attract residents of all races. The Mayor particularly expects that poorer Whites, who have thus far not been served by the housing policy, will apply for and receive subsidies for this new neighborhood. He hopes it will "integrate two towns divided for many years along racial lines." This development may indeed succeed in undermining apartheid's urban legacy. As of yet, however, the delivery of housing in George has demonstrated apartheid's staying power.

Innovation and risk

As noted above, the government's housing policy is risky because its success depends on recipients being able to afford home ownership. Water, sewerage, and electricity bills and a mortgage accompany all but the most modest houses. Although there has not yet been widespread defaulting on loans in George, there are reasons to fear that this calamity may befall many of the impoverished households. Becoming home-owners and mortgage-holders will require a change in residents' attitude toward the municipality and banks. During apartheid, poor South Africans around the country were mobilized in campaigns of refusing to pay rents and service charges to protest their atrocious living conditions. Thembalethu and Pacaltsdorp municipalities brought R25 million of accumulated debt due to nonpayments when they amalgamated with George in 1995. The rates of nonpayments continued to alarm the ANC-led council later in the decade. Many residents are not only impoverished but also remain justifiably dissatisfied with their services and accommodations in George. However, lending institutions will not tolerate serious delinquency, and the government of George knows that it must become fiscally sound. Therefore, it is possible that many families may eventually become homeless again if they are unable or unwilling to pay their mortgages and service charges.

The program is also risky because in some cases it is failing to keep up with resident's expectations. Some residents of Lawaaikamp, unwilling to wait through the formal allocation process, have taken matters into their own hands. At the end of 1999, 100 people left Lawaaikamp to squat on a piece of vacant municipal land in Pacaltsdorp. The Mayor and other ANC leaders tried to persuade them to move to a different area so as to keep the social compact required for the allocation of the subsidy and eventual provision of good services. The squatters refused to move while the Colored community pressured the city government to remove them by force. It is ironic that the Mayor, who cut his teeth in politics resisting a forced removal of his "squatting" community, considered issuing removal orders himself. Tension between the groups was visible in community meetings over squatter settlements in January 2000.

Conclusion

Implementing the housing subsidy program, as experienced by the new political leadership of George, indicates that there will be no short-term solution to the apartheid landscape. Yet, it has benefited many families as the program has significantly alleviated the immediate housing shortage that disproportionately hit the Black residents. This success notwithstanding, the housing program alone will not unite racially balkanized neighborhoods. Perpetuating rather than undermining race-based living patterns via the housing program has enabled the new ANC-led local government to deliver an important tangible service to its disadvantaged constituents without extensively threatening George's wealthier White community. Thus stability has been preserved, and George has not experienced "White flight."

However, the difficult but necessary social engineering required to dismantle urban apartheid cannot be postponed indefinitely or segregation will undermine South Africa's larger nation-building efforts. Urban planning can contribute to the elimination of the existing segregated landscape. We think that local authorities can learn from George's successes and continued challenges by considering the following strategies. First, alter transportation infrastructure so as to link previously separated areas. Second, create new mixed residential communities on the suburban fringe similar to George's one integrated housing project. The mix can be encouraged by building houses of varying costs so that residents of different socioeconomic classes could live together in neighborhoods. Third, promote the development of new commercial facilities across metropolitan areas for Black entrepreneurs, especially in any new integrated neighborhoods. Finally, pursue a cultural and historical preservation strategy that recognizes the merit of the many cultures in the urban area. The Pacaltsdorp community's effort to preserve and promote its historic church is an example of this strategy at work.

A number of immediate challenges facing George and similar cities provide opportunities for further research into the post-apartheid city. Most problematic, will urban economies provide enough jobs and growth to absorb the new in-migration? The ability of George's economy and urban services to successfully address the pressures of urbanization could provide lessons for other cities.

Another issue for further research is the impact of the next round of demarcation of local authorities. Many of the original authorities of 1995 have proved too small to be viable. Consequently, a round of consolidation occurred leading up to the 2000 local elections. The redistricting of George means that two higher income ocean front communities will become part of the George municipality. This will increase the area of the municipality ten-fold, yet, since most of this area is sparsely settled, the population size will not rise dramatically. This change will, however, increase the number of wealthy Whites and middle-class Colored residents of George. Since services are rather well developed in these communities, this change is not expected to impose a significant burden on municipal services. However, the planning for new housing and suburban retailing may raise new issues. Therefore, local government structures are continuing to evolve in South Africa, and scholars should continue to engage in research into their political and economic viability.

Finally, in evaluating the housing subsidy program, researchers must continue to examine the ability of recipients to pay their mortgages and service charges. Residents in George have not been defaulting in large numbers but service charge arrears remain a major problem for the municipality and fear of mortgage defaults are real. The financial viability of South Africa's new local authorities will be seriously threatened if they cannot retrieve the costs of service provision.

Chapter 24

World-City Network:
A New Metageography?

Jonathan V. Beaverstock, Richard G. Smith, and Peter J. Taylor

[...]

Historically, cities have always existed in environments of linkages, both material flows and information transfers. They have acted as centers from where their hinterlands are serviced and connected to wider realms. This is reflected in how economic geographers have treated economic sectors: primary and secondary activities are typically mapped as formal agricultural or industrial regions, tertiary activities as functional regions, epitomized by central-place theory. Why is our concern for contemporary cities in a world of flows any different from this previous tertiary activity and its study? First, the twentieth century has witnessed a remarkable sectoral turnabout in advanced economies: originally defined by their manufacturing industry, economic growth has become increasingly dependent on service industries. Second, this trend has been massively augmented by more recent developments in information technology that has enabled service and control to operate not only more rapidly and effectively, but crucially on a global scale. Contemporary world cities are an outcome of these economic changes. [...]

This paper, which divides into six parts, reports preliminary research on the empirical groundwork required for describing the new metageography of relations between world cities. Such a modest goal is made necessary because of a critical empirical deficit within the world-city literature on intercity relations. In the first part, we show this to be a generic problem across all the different research schools within the literature. By concentrating on the attributes of world cities and neglecting their relations, we learn a lot about the nodes in the network, but relatively little about the network itself. In a brief second part, we introduce Castell's concept of network society, in which the world-city network does feature, and although

Beaverstock, Jonathan V., Smith, Richard G., and Taylor, Peter J., "World-City Network: A New Metageography?" pp. 123–32 from *Annals of the Association of American Geographers*, 90.1 (2000).

this provides a conceptual framework for our research, the empirical problematic remains. Our particular solution to this data problem is to focus on the global office-location strategies of major corporate-service firms; in the third part, we outline this data-collection exercise. Analysis of this data is presented in two ways: the first defines a network; the second deals with relations of a single city. In part four, we provide a glimpse of the world-city network by focusing on only the ten leading world cities. In part five, we present a case study of the global reach of London in a more detailed analysis, using fifty-four other world cities. We claim both of these analyses to be unique, first empirical studies of their kind. In a brief conclusion, we consider the future implications of this new metageography: are we witnessing a dystopia in the making?

Attributes without Relations: Research Clusters in World-City Studies

Studies of world cities are generally full of information that facilitates evaluations of individual cities and comparative analyses of several cities. Yet the data upon which these analyses are based has been overwhelmingly derived from measures of city attributes. Such information is useful for estimating the general importance of cities and for studying intracity processes, but it tells us nothing directly about relations between cities. Hence cities can be ranked by attributes, but a hierarchical ordering aimed at uncovering flows or networks requires a different type of data based upon measures of relations between cities. It is the dearth of relational data that is the "dirty little secret" of this research area. In other words, we know about the nodes but not the links in this new metageography. Of course, a proper understanding requires an integrated knowledge of both nodes and links. Hence, our brief reviews of the main clusters of world-city research has two purposes: first, to illustrate the pervasive nature of the Achilles heel, and second, to find world-city formation processes that can direct our search for information on world-city network-formation processes.

Early studies: From cosmopolitanism to corporate economy

Peter Hall initiated the modern study of world cities with a very comprehensive study of the attributes – politics, trade, communication facilities, finance, culture, technology, and higher education – that placed London, Paris, Randstad-Holland, Rhine-Ruhr, Moscow, New York, and Tokyo at the top of the world urban hierarchy. Stephen Hymer initiated the "economic turn" in world-city studies that has continued to dominate to the present. In an emerging global economy, he argued, corporate control mechanisms were crucial, and hence multinational corporation headquarters tend to be concentrated in the "world's major cities – New York, London, Paris, Bonn and Tokyo . . . along with Moscow and Peking." Using the distribution of headquarters to rank cities has since become commonplace, but although such attribute data can define the relative importance of cities, it cannot specify a hierarchy within a network.

Command centers and basing points: The new international division of labor and world-city hypothesis

Most studies of world urban hierarchies have drawn inspiration from John Friedmann's seminal world-city hypothesis. [. . .] [S]ubsequent research has allocated cities to hierarchies based upon their command-and-control criteria, measuring attributes of world cities and then ranking them in order of magnitude. [. . .]

World Cities in a Network Society

One author, in particular, has attempted to advance theoretical knowledge of the world-city network. Castells conceptualizes the contemporary informational economy as operating through a "space of flows" that constitute a network society. This operates at several levels, one of which is the world-city network. [. . .] Castells conceptualizes world cities as processes "by which centers of production and consumption of advanced services, and their ancillary local societies, are connected in a global network." Hence, cities accumulate and retain wealth, control, and power because of what flows through them, rather than what they statically contain, as is typically measured with attribute data.

It was not part of Castell's brief to engage in new data generation, and therefore, despite his theoretical contribution, his work reflects the prevailing use of attribute data. [. . .] Castells does not offer an empirical advance on the world-city network, but with the other theoretical studies of nodes, he provides a framework for our empirical work on world-city network formation in a space of relations. World cities are produced by relations of corporate networking activities and connectivity between cities based upon knowledge complexes and economic reflexivity. These fruitful concepts notwithstanding, the key to unlocking the "spaces of relations" of world cities is new data collection.

Global Office Location Strategies

The only published data available for studying relations between cities at a global scale are international airline-passenger statistics. Not surprisingly, therefore, empirical studies that present *networks* of world cities have focused upon this source. There are, however, serious limitations to these statistics as descriptions of relations between world cities: first, the information includes much more than trips associated with world-city processes (e.g., tourism), and second, important intercity trips within countries are not recorded in international data (e.g., New York–Toronto does feature in the data, New York–Los Angeles does not). While the latter can be overcome by augmenting the data with domestic flight statistics, the particularities of hub-and-spoke systems operated by airlines creates another important caveat to using this data to describe the world-city network.

Studying the global location strategies of advanced producer-service firms is an alternative approach for describing world-city network, one which overcomes these problems. Firms that provide business services on a global scale have to decide on the distribution of their practitioners and professionals across world cities. Setting up an office is an expensive undertaking, but a necessary investment if the firm believes that a particular city is a place where it must locate in order to fulfil its corporate goals. Hence the office geographies of advanced producer firms provide a strategic insight into world-city processes by interpreting intrafirm office networks as intercity relations. In this argument, world-city network formation consists of the aggregate of the global location strategies of major, advanced producer-service firms.

Information on the office networks of firms can be obtained by investigating a variety of sources, such as company web sites, internal directories, handbooks for customers, and trade publications. We have collected data on the distributions of offices for 74 companies (covering accountancy, advertising, banking/finance, and commercial law) in 263 cities. An initial analysis of this data identified the 143 major office centers in these cities, and 55 of these were designated world cities on the basis of the number size, and importance of their offices. No other such roster of world cities exists; it is used here as the basic framework for studying the world-city network.

An Intercity Global Network

The roster of 55 world cities is divided into three levels of service provision comprising 10 Alpha cities, 10 Beta cities, and 35 Gamma cities. Only the Alpha cities – Chicago, Frankfurt, Hong Kong, London, Los Angeles, Milan New York, Paris, Singapore, and Tokyo – are used in this section to illustrate how office geographies can define intercity relations. Note the geographical spread of these top 10 world cities they are distributed relatively evenly across three regions we have previously identified as the major "globalization arenas": the US, western Europe, and Pacific Asia. World-city network patterns are constructed for these Alpha world cities, using simple presence/absence data for the largest 46 firms in the data (all of these firms have offices in 15 or more different cities).

Shared presences are shown in Table 24.1. Each cell in this intercity matrix indicates the number of firms with offices in both cities. Thus, London and New York "share" 45 of the 46 firms; only one firm in the data does not have offices in both of these cities. Obviously these two cities are the places to be for a corporate-service firm with serious global pretensions. This finding is not, of course, at all surprising; interest comes when lower levels of intercity relations are explored. In Figure 24.1(a), the highest 20 shared presences are depicted at two levels of relation. The higher level picks out Sassen's trio of global cities – London, New York, and Tokyo – as a triangular relationship (but note that, in addition, Hong Kong has such a relationship with London and New York). Bringing in the lower level of relations, London and New York have shared presences with eight other cities in all, but note again the high Pacific Asia profile in this data: Singapore joins

Table 24.1 Relations between Alpha world cities: shared firm presences

	CH	FF	HK	LN	LA	ML	NY	PA	SG	TK
	Number of firms with offices in both cities									
Chicago										
Frankfurt	21									
Hong Kong	21	30								
London	23	32	38							
Los Angeles	21	23	29	33						
Milan	19	28	29	32	22					
New York	23	32	38	45	32	32				
Paris	21	30	32	35	27	28	34			
Singapore	20	30	34	35	26	29	35	32		
Tokyo	23	30	34	37	30	29	37	32	32	

with Tokyo and Hong Kong in showing relations with five other cities, the same level as Paris. This contrasts with the US world cities below New York; Los Angeles is in the next-to-bottom class of shared presences with Frankfurt and Milan, and Chicago stands alone, with no intercity relations at the minimum level for inclusion in the diagram. This pattern can be interpreted in terms of the different degrees of political fragmentation in the three major globalization arenas. In the most fragmented, Pacific Asia, there is no dominant world city, so that presences are needed in at least three cities to cover the region: Hong Kong for China, Singapore for southeast Asia, and Tokyo for Japan. In contrast, the US consists of a single state such that one city can suffice for a presence in that market. The result is that New York throws a shadow effect over other US cities. In between, western Europe is becoming more unified politically, but numerous national markets remain so that London does not dominate its regional hinterland to the same degree as New York.

Shared presences define a symmetric matrix that shows sizes, but not the direction, of intercity relations. By contrast, Table 24.2 is an asymmetric matrix showing probabilities of connections. Each cell contains the probability that a firm in city A will have an office in city B. Thus, Table 24.2 shows that if you do business with a Chicago-based firm, then there is a 0.91 probability that that firm will also have an office in Frankfurt. On the other hand, go to a Frankfurt-based firm, and the probability of it having an office in Chicago is only 0.66. Such asymmetry is represented by vectors in Figures 24.1(b) and (c). Primary vectors are defined by probabilities above 0.95. Note that all cities connect to London and New York at this level (Figure 24.1(b)). As in Figure 24.1(a), only Tokyo and Hong Kong reach this highest category of connection, but each with only one link. Again, it is also interesting to look at the lower level relations, and these are shown in Figure 24.1(c). This diagram reinforces the interpretation concerning the three globalization arenas presented above: Chicago and Los Angeles have no inward vectors from the other arenas in what is largely a Eurasian pattern of connections. Vectors to the Pacific

Table 24.2 Matrix of office-presence linkage indices for Alpha world cities

Linkage from	Linkage to									
	CH	FR	HK	LN	LA	ML	NY	PA	SG	TK
Chicago		89	89	100	91	79	100	89	83	100
Frankfurt	67		93	100	72	87	100	95	94	95
Hong Kong	60	82		100	80	80	100	85	92	90
London	59	77	87		78	78	98	83	83	86
Los Angeles	67	73	89	100		70	97	84	81	89
Milan	59	88	93	100	67		100	88	91	93
New York	59	77	87	98	77	77		79	83	85
Paris	64	85	90	100	80	81	97		90	90
Singapore	60	87	98	100	78	83	100	92		95
Tokyo	64	84	93	100	83	81	100	87	88	

Asian cities dominate, but Frankfurt and Paris also have a reasonable number of inward vectors.

This is the first time intercity relations on a global scale have been studied in this way. As expected of such initial research, several opportunities for further investigations are suggested, not least using more cities and more sophisticated network analysis to tease out further features of the contemporary world-city network. But the most urgent task is to go beyond this cross-sectional analysis and study changes over time in order to delineate the evolution of world-city network formation. Only in this way will we be able to make informed assessments of how the network will develop in the new millennium and how this will affect different cities. For instance, is the New York shadow effect growing or declining? We simply do not know.

Case Study: London's Global Reach

There is no published study assessing the global capacity of a world city in terms of its relations with other world cities. The producer-service-office geography dataset is particularly suited for such an exercise; here we illustrate this with a brief case study of London (Figure 24.2).

The data we employ for London differ from those used in the last section in three ways. First, it is obvious that since we will consider only London-based firms, one of the firms used previously is dropped. In addition, we add data for smaller London-based firms, creating a total of 69. Second, we consider all 55 world cities in our roster. Third, for many firms, there is richer information than simply whether they are present or absent in a city. Further information provides interval-level measurements, on the numbers of practitioners or professionals employed by a firm across all its offices, as well as ordinal-level measurements in which the

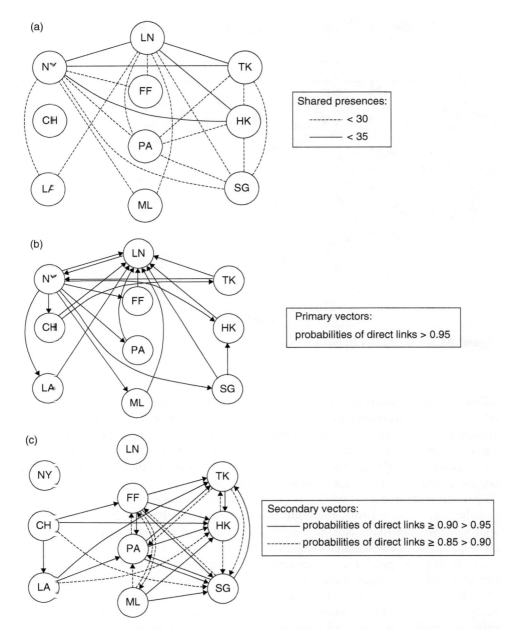

Figure 24.1 (a) Shared presences among Alpha world cities; (b) primary vectors (probabilities of links) among Alpha world cities; (c) secondary vectors (probabilities of links) among Alpha world cities.

importance of offices was allocated to ranked classes on the basis of given functions. In order to combine these data into a single, comparable set of measures, all thee levels – interval, ordinal, and nominal (presence/absence) – were combined as a single ordinal scale. For every world city, each firm is scored as one of the

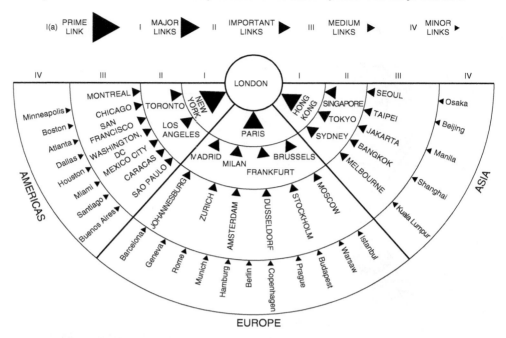

Figure 24.2 World city links to London.

following: (0) indicating absence; (1) indicating presence, or where additional information is available, indicating only minor presence; (2), when additional information indicates a medium presence in a city; and (3), when additional information indicates a major presence. In delineating these data when additional information is available, we were careful to be sensitive to the range of data; for large accountancy firms, for example, "minor presence" was defined as less than 20 practitioners in a city, while "major presences" required more than 50 professionals; yet, for law firms, the equivalent figures were 10 and 20. Through this approach, we can move beyond simple geographies of presence to geographies of the *level* of producer services available in a city.

For each of the producer-service sectors represented in our data, levels of service are summed for London-based firms in each of the other 54 world cities. This provides an estimate of the level of external service that can be expected when doing business in another world city from London. In Table 24.3, the top 10 world cities are ranked in terms of service available for each of the producer services represented in our data. As world be expected, the Alpha cities, identified in the last section, figure prominently in these rankings, with New York first or first equal in all four sectors. Yet, other world cities now make an appearance: the notable examples are the key political cities of Washington, DC and Brussels featuring prominently in law, Dusseldorf easily out-ranking Germany's Alpha world city Frankfurt in accountancy, and Britain's imperial links being represented by Sydney and Toronto in several lists. Average levels of linkage have been computed from

Table 24.3 Top ten office linkages to London by advanced producer services

Accountancy	Advertising	Finance	Law Services	Average
1. Dusseldorf, New York, Paris, Tokyo, Toronto	1. New York	1. New York	1. New York	1. New York
	2. Brussels, Madrid, Sydney, Toronto	2. Singapore	2. Washington	2. Paris
6. Chicago, Milan, Sydney, Washington		3. Hong Kong, Tokyo	3. Brussels, Hong Kong	4. Hong Kong
	6. Milan, Paris	5. Frankfurt	5. Paris	5. Tokyo
10. Atlanta, Brussels, Frankfurt, San Francisco		6. Paris, Zurich	6. Los Angeles	5. Brussels
	8. Los Angeles, Singapore, Stockholm	8. Sydney	7. Tokyo	6. Singapore
		9. Madrid	8. Singapore	7. Sydney
		10. Milan, Taipei	9. Moscow	8. Milan
			10. Frankfurt	9. Frankfurt, Los Angeles, Toronto

standardized sector scores (city totals as percentage of maximum possible; i.e., 3 [maximum score] × number of firms in a given sector), showing all the Alpha cities in London's top 10 except Chicago. Given also Los Angeles's bottom ranking in the list, this can be interpreted as the New York shadow effect operating even from London.

Average levels of linkage with London, when computed for all other world cities, provide an illustration of London's global reach within the world-city network. These average percentages range from a top score of 87 for New York, followed by Paris (68) and Hong Kong (64), to the lowest score for Minneapolis of only 15, with Osaka (21) and Munich (22) just above the bottom. Using these averages, world cities can be divided into five groups in terms of the intensity of their relations with London. Out on its own is New York, the "prime link," followed by Paris and Hong Kong as the other two "major links." Below these three and all with scores over become 9 "important links." The remainder of cities are divided between 18 "medium link" (36–50) and the remaining 24 "minor link." These links are arrayed in Figure 24.2, showing a relatively even distribution across the three globalization arenas and their adjacent regions, the New York shadow effect notwithstanding.

The big question for London, as we enter the next millennium, is whether it can retain its position as Europe's leading world city. With the European Central Bank located in Frankfurt the scene is set for some intense intercity competition. Currently, as we showed in the previous section, London is clearly preeminent in relation to all its European rivals but, as before, in order to see which way this competition is moving, we need to supplement our cross-sectional analysis with evolutionary data and analysis and repeat the exercise across several cities.

Conclusion: Metageographic Dystopia?

Riccardo Petrella, sometimes referred to as the "official futurist of the European Union," has warned of the rise of a "wealthy archipelago of city regions . . . surrounded by an impoverished *lumpenplanet*." He envisages a scenario in which the 30 most powerful city regions (the CR-30) will replace the G-7 (the seven most powerful states), presiding over a new global governance by 2025. Such a scenario is given credence by the fact that contemporary world cities are implicated in the current polarization of wealth and wages accompanying economic globalization. World-city practitioners and professionals operating in a global labor market have demanded and received "global wages" (largely in the form of bonuses) to create a new income category of the "waged rich"; with reference to London, they have been called the new "Super Class."

Petrella sets out his global apartheid dystopia as a warning about current trends so as to alert us to the dangers ahead. But cities do not have to play the bête noire role of the future. It is within cosmopolitan cities that cultural tensions can be best managed and creatively developed. Certainly modern states, in their ambition to be nation-states, have an appalling record in dealing with maters of cultural difference. But the key point is that this is not a simple matter of cities versus states.

World cities are not eliminating the power of states, they are part of a global restructuring which is "rescaling" power relations, in which states will change and adapt as they have done many times in previous restructurings. The "renegotiations" going on between London's world role and the nation's economy, between New York's world role and the US economy, and with all other world cities and their encompassing territorial "home" economies, are part of a broader change affecting the balance between networks and territories in the global space-economy. In this paper, we have illustrated how empirical analysis of city economic networks might be undertaken to complement traditional economic geography's concern for comparative advantage between states. Our one firm conclusion is that in the new millennium, we cannot afford to ignore this new metageography, the world-city network.

Part VI

Economic Geography

Introduction

William G. Moseley

Traditional economic geography has been concerned with the location, spatial distribution, and organization of economic activity. Economic geographers have often studied the location of industries and businesses, transportation networks, trade flows, and the changing value of real estate. Economic geography overlaps with other subfields of geography, particularly urban and development geography. This is also an area of geography that has been of great interest to the private sector, as understanding the spatial relationship between a business, its customers and suppliers is often critical to the success of the enterprise. However, this specialty within geography has undergone a certain amount of change in recent years as new concerns and insights (e.g., globalization, consumption, and gender) are mixed with traditional forms of analysis.

Like many of the social sciences, geography in the English-speaking world underwent a transformation in the 1950s and 1960s as a result of the quantitative revolution. This broader trend in academia emphasized the increasing use of quantitative methods, modeling, and positivism (or the classic scientific method) in the social sciences. Economic geography was especially influenced by this trend. For example, models such as Walter Christaller's central place theory gained heightened importance as geographers attempted to explain the distribution of different urban centers and the businesses located in these places. The gravity model, borrowing principles from physics, was developed in order to determine the best location for a retail business in relation to its customers. While quantitative methodologies and strict positivism have subsequently been critiqued, especially with the rise of postmodern understandings, such approaches are still common in economic geography.

Economic geographers have long been interested in the organization and spatial distribution of industries and businesses. The particular location chosen for a business or industry is often explained in terms of the relative importance of a number of factors, including: the accessibility to material inputs (raw materials, energy);

the availability of labor with certain skills; the importance of processing costs (i.e., costs of land and buildings, machinery and hardware, salaries, taxes, etc.); the importance of being near customers; and transfer costs (costs of transferring inputs to the factory and goods to the market). In "Geographies of Knowledge, Practices of Globalization: Learning from the Oil Exploration and Production Industry," Bridge and Wood extend traditional industry location analysis and organization theory to account for knowledge economies and globalization. According to the authors, certain changes in the oil exploration and production industry (reductions in exploration and production costs, the opening up of new geographical opportunities and organizational restructuring) mean that success is increasingly knowledge dependent. Andrew Herod also addresses the impacts of globalization in his article, "The Impact of Containerization on Work on the New York–New Jersey Waterfront." Herod is particularly interested in how changes in the global shipping industry have impacted longshoremen or dock workers.

The article by Grigg, entitled "Wine, Spirits, and Beer: World Patterns of Consumption," analyzes global patterns in the consumption of different alcoholic beverages. The study of consumption by economic geographers is a relatively new, but incredibly lively, phenomenon. Interest in, for example, commodity chain analysis has been especially strong. In this article, the author relates the geographies of the consumption of wine, beer, and spirits to a number of factors, including where the key ingredients may be grown, the relative cost of transporting the beverage, the ethnic origins of the producers and consumers, and religion.

In "Producing and Consuming Chemicals: The Moral Economy of the American Lawn," Paul Robbins and Julie Sharp discuss consumption of a very different sort, the consumption of lawn care chemicals by American home owners. In this article, the authors wonder why well-educated consumers continue to use potentially dangerous chemicals. They explain this paradox by relating the increasing use of lawn care chemicals to two different processes. First, economic restructuring in the lawn care industry has resulted in a more competitive industry and more aggressive advertising. Second (and perhaps most interestingly), the authors describe a moral economy at play in many suburban residential areas where neighbors feel obliged to maintain a certain lawn aesthetic. This article is particularly innovative in the way it stretches the bounds of traditional economic geography by borrowing ideas from political ecology (concerning the way broader economic changes may influence local human–environment interactions) and cultural ecology (regarding the importance of understanding local norms and community dynamics).

The final selection, by Mona Domosh and Joni Seager, "Women at Work," is representative of the increasing gender awareness in economic geography. The article demonstrates how attention to gender informs our understanding of work, labor, and globalization. Among other issues, the authors highlight how unpaid work (often performed by women) is not accounted for in national economic statistics, how the globalization of certain industries has especially impacted female laborers, and how gender influences experiences in the workplace.

DISCUSSION READINGS

Bridge, Gavin & Wood, Andrew. (2005). "Geographies of Knowledge, Practices of Globalization: Learning from the Oil Exploration and Production Industry." *Area*, 37(2): 199–208.

Herod, Andrew. (2004). "The Impact of Containerization on Work on the New York–New Jersey Waterfront." *Social Science Docket*, 4.1 (Winter/Spring): 5–7.

Grigg, David. (2004). "Wine, Spirits, and Beer: World Patterns of Consumption." *Geography*, 89(2): 99–110.

Robbins, Paul & Sharp, Julie T. (2003). "Producing and Consuming Chemicals: The Moral Economy of the American Lawn." *Economic Geography*, 79(4): 425–51.

Domosh, Mona & Seager, Joni. (2001). "Women at Work." In *Putting Women in Place: Feminist Geographers Make Sense of the World*. New York: Guilford Press. Pp. 35–66.

Chapter 25

Geographies of Knowledge, Practices of Globalization: Learning from the Oil Exploration and Production Industry

Gavin Bridge and Andrew Wood

Globalization and the Knowledge Economy

The concept of *globalization* has emerged as a central theme within geography and the social sciences over the last decade. Contemporary research by economic geographers is largely critical of orthodox accounts, which tend to portray globalization as a systemic and inevitable force. To challenge conventional representations, a number of economic geographers recently have turned attention to the *practices* that constitute globalization and, in particular, to the ways in which firms achieve global reach. These studies frame global reach as a strategic challenge – a set of practices that must be initiated, developed and maintained over time if firms are to 'go global' – and begin to map the networks of actors and institutions that enable firms to successfully operate in diverse, often unfamiliar environments. Although still emerging, such critical 'mappings' of globalization capture the contingencies and complexities of achieving global reach.

At the same time, the last decade has also seen a proliferation of popular and scholarly literature on the 'knowledge economy'. Much of this literature asserts that knowledge has become increasingly significant as an economic resource and that 'the ability of labour, firms, regions and nations to produce, circulate and apply knowledge is fundamental to economic growth and competitiveness'. Evidence for the emergence of distinctive 'knowledge economies' frequently turns on the rise of knowledge-intensive sectors, the reshuffling of the division of labour to create a class of 'knowledge-workers', and a relative shift in the significance of knowledge vis-à-vis raw materials, capital or labour, as a factor of production.

Bridge, Gavin and Wood, Andrew, "Geographies of Knowledge, Practices of Globalization: Learning from the Oil Exploration and Production Industry," pp. 199–207 from *Area*, 37.2 (2005).

Yet these two literatures and the key concepts that underpin them are rarely coupled. While work on economic globalization addresses the stretching of commodity chains and/or the integration of cities, regions and national economies into transnational networks, the role of knowledge in enabling and structuring these geographies of globalization is rarely considered. Similarly, geographical research on the knowledge economy has – until very recently – adopted the local scale as its primary entry point: in work on spatial clustering and learning regions, for example, the analytical claim that knowledge is socially embedded has tended to equate embeddedness with spatial proximity, neglecting the ways in which knowledge is acquired, developed and mobilized in the context of transnational economic networks. We argue that there is an opportunity here to critically harness these two bodies of work to (1) understand how and where different types of knowledge are produced, acquired and mobilized by firms as they seek to 'go global' and (2) to examine the ways in which these *networks of knowledge* structure emerging geographies of production, by influencing the ability of firms to integrate operations from socio-economically and geopolitically diverse environments into coherent production networks. In this paper we use the example of the oil industry – specifically oil exploration and production (E&P) – to illustrate how work on knowledge and knowledge economies might be deployed in developing a fuller understanding of the ways in which transnational firms construct and maintain global production networks.

[. . .]

The Oil Exploration and Production Industry as Empirical Context

On the face of it, the oil industry would appear to be an established, stable and mature industry with relatively little scope for radical innovation via the harnessing and mobilization of new forms of knowledge. Yet *technological change* (e.g. new subsurface imaging and visualization techniques), *organizational restructuring* (e.g. mergers, corporate downsizing, outsourcing and the emergence of niche markets for specialist firms), and the emergence of *new geographical opportunities* (e.g. exploration in non-traditional locales, such as the deepwater Gulf of Mexico, offshore China and West Africa, or in transition economies like Russia, Kazakhstan and Angola) are driving a re-evaluation of the way knowledge is produced, valued, communicated and harnessed within the industry. Anecdotal evidence suggests that in turn the ability to acquire, process and channel knowledge along the production chain is critically significant for the competitive position of oil producers. According to some observers, competitive success is now determined less by the marginal costs of extracting raw materials than by access to, and ability to use, knowledge. As one commentator recently put it, 'knowledge, not petroleum, is becoming the critical resource in the oil business'.

In addition to being knowledge-*intensive* and knowledge-driven, E&P is also the most knowledge-*extensive* phase of the commodity chain, meaning that a wide range of knowledge types must be deployed, coordinated and integrated in order to locate and develop an oil reservoir. Whether in Ecuador or California, successful development of an oil reservoir requires that knowledge relating to hydrodynamics, sedimentology and petrophysics be integrated with knowledge related to drilling targets, well planning and the estimation of completion costs, and that these in turn be integrated with knowledge associated with securing land rights, evaluating social and environmental risk, and community relations. Knowledge relating to E&P is then integrated with a set of more directly economic knowledges concerning market conditions, forecasts, logistics that also extend to the downstream phases of the production chain. The knowledge environment surrounding E&P is currently being radically reworked as a result of technological, organizational and geographical shifts in the way production is organized. Thus the structure of the exploration and production business in the 1990s was

> turned on its head ... the pigeon-holed, assembly-line approach of geoscientists studying data and generating prospects, and then handing them over to drilling engineers ... gave way to an integrated team approach, from authoring a play through enhanced recovery.

While cautious of the normative tone running through much of this management-oriented literature, we find such descriptions highly suggestive for what they say about an emergent knowledge economy (and geography) within the oil industry.

Restructuring in the Oil Industry: The Role of Knowledge in Enabling Global Reach

> *The past is not prologue. New forces are re-shaping the energy industry's structure, its organisation, and markets, driving it toward a future that will be very different from anything it has ever seen. (Oil and Gas Journal 2001, 8)*

Despite their tendency towards hyperbole, such assessments indicate that the oil industry is currently undergoing changes that are interlinked, relatively complex and potentially far-reaching. We identify three primary shifts: (1) historic reductions in production and exploration costs; (2) the opening up of new geographical opportunities, increasing the number and complexity of regulatory environments and exposing firms to new forms of investment risk; and (3) organizational restructuring, including both merger activity and an increased use of outsourcing. Table 25.1 summarizes each of the changes, and outlines working hypotheses linking them to the acquisition and mobilization of knowledge. We examine each in turn, paying particular attention to their implications for the geographies of knowledge within the industry.

Reductions in production and exploration costs

Understanding the role of knowledge in enabling global reach requires moving beyond technical knowledge to capture the full breadth and diversity of knowledge

Table 25.1 Metrics of restructuring within the oil E&P industry and a provisional assessment of the significance of different types of knowledge

Metric of change	Posited relationship between knowledge and metric of change	Posited relationship to geographies of knowledge
COSTS Decrease in production ('lifting') costs and exploration ('finding') costs	• Declining costs result from improvements in fundamental geological and petrophysical knowledge (e.g. depositional processes, reservoir mechanics, geophysics, stratigraphy and petrophysics) • Enabled via enhanced technical knowledge (e.g. computational mathematics, statistics and visualization) which have improved subsurface imaging and drilling accuracy	• Regionally based knowledge and experience (e.g. knowledge of a particular oil field, trend or play) now less valuable than knowledge of geological/petrophysical fundamentals • May indicate a shift towards de-territorialized/portable forms of knowledge • Shift in the knowledge-base may facilitate the globalization of oil exploration and production by US firms
INVESTMENT ENVIRONMENT Increase in number and complexity of regulatory environments Increase in the significance of environmental and social performance as components of investment risk	• Increased salience of non-geological knowledge in managing investment risk • Demand for new types of knowledge associated with managing mineral rights/resource access, navigating regulatory frameworks and politics, and managing the social and environmental aspects of development • Increased significance of 'soft' (i.e. social/cultural) types of knowledge (vs. 'hard' technical or geophysical knowledge)	• 'Local', place-specific knowledge increasingly important to the success of globalization strategies • Question of how best to acquire and develop these new types of knowledge: should it be 'produced' within the firm or acquired via 'contract'? To what extent can aspects of soft knowledge be globalized?
ORGANIZATIONAL STRUCTURE Increased outsourcing, changing role for smaller companies in partnerships/strategic alliances with majors and major suppliers	• Re-evaluation of strategic significance of different types of knowledge • Changes in technical knowledge requirements create opportunities for new market entrants around specialized knowledge sets • Stratification of knowledge within the industry as firms recognize which types of knowledge are core assets and which can be outsourced	• Organizational knowledge network increasingly complex: organizational decentralization of knowledge/expertise via outsourcing, occurring simultaneously with organizational and geographic centralization in majors • Organizational complexity increases the significance of certain nodes within the knowledge network at expense of others, e.g. emergence of 'super-node' in Houston vs. second and third tier oil capitals

flows within the industry. Changes in technical knowledge can, however, radically affect the value of other types of knowledge: improvements in drill rig design which enable production in greater depths of water, for example, or enhancements to seismic analysis enabling the identification of oil reservoirs below salt layers, have driven interest among oil producers in acquiring deepwater and sub-salt acreage. This, in turn, has created demand for the knowledge necessary to design optimum acreage acquisition strategies or to determine the relative risk/reward ratios of exploring traditional and non-traditional plays.

Recent innovations in the technology of oil exploration and production are best characterized as involving incremental rather than radical change. Yet because many innovations are interlocking, their cumulative effect has been a dramatic reduction in finding and producing costs. Improvements in data processing capability, for example, have made 3-D seismic imaging and analysis cost and time efficient for many applications. 3-D seismic technology enables geologists to construct three-dimensional images of the earth beneath the surface *before* drilling. Between 1985 and 1996, the percentage of wells drilled using 3-D seismic imaging in the Gulf of Mexico increased from 5 per cent to 80 per cent, while over the same period the success rate of exploratory wells increased from 36 per cent to 51 per cent. By increasing the accuracy of drilling targets, 3-D seismic imaging has in turn improved the economics of directional drilling and measurement-while-drilling, both of which have seen an increase in applications. The net result of these changes is that the costs of producing oil (known as 'lifting costs') and the costs of adding reserves (known as 'finding costs') have declined. Domestic lifting costs in the US in 1997 were 38 per cent *below* their level in 1986, when adjusted for inflation, while finding costs fell by 54 per cent over the same period. The overall effect is that the volume of oil discovered per well drilled is six times greater at the end of the 1990s than a decade earlier.

A number of commentators have argued that such dramatic changes amount to a definitive transformation in the industry:

> Finding and producing oil is still about poking holes in the ground and bottling what comes out . . . In a number of respects, however, the oil business has begun to behave more like the New Economy than the Old. It is in the midst of the sort of technological change that (former US Treasury Secretary Lawrence) Summers compared to an avalanche; and the bang that started the avalanche came not from the oil fields but from Silicon Valley.

While appealing in their breadth and simplicity, such claims tend to conflate knowledge with data or information and assume a simple linkage between technology and knowledge production. Technologies like 3-D seismic imaging, horizontal drilling and monitoring-while-drilling are clearly transforming the quantity and quality of information available to the industry. However, the extent to which increases in information imply quantitative and qualitative changes in *knowledge production* remains to be determined. It is certainly possible that a fundamental shift in the significance and value attached to specific types of knowledge may drive changes in the geographies of knowledge and knowledge production within the industry. For example, advances in data processing in the last few decades have driven a shift towards exploration based on understanding and modelling basic principles, as opposed to exploration via reference to regional analogues (i.e. by modelling existing oil reserves in the same region). In this case, technological change has tended to reduce the value of place-based, regionally specific knowledge accumulated over time, and has increased the portability (i.e. geographical mobility) of the knowledge sets necessary to develop oil reserves.

This is particularly intriguing in the context of recent work on the geographies of the knowledge economy which has commonly focused on place-based or 'territorialized' forms of knowledge and knowledge flows. Preliminary evidence suggests that in the oil sector the geographies of knowledge are considerably more complex than this position allows. While organizational restructuring may increasingly territorialize or embed the production of knowledge within specific urban nodes like Houston or Aberdeen, technological changes are simultaneously making the requisite knowledge that enables oil exploration *less* place-bound by abstracting it from the actual sites of extraction. In this particular knowledge economy, it would seem that geography matters both more *and* less.

Emergence of new regulatory environments and new forms of political risk

There are more companies than ever before seeking opportunities worldwide, and never have so many countries been open for business. (Oil and Gas Journal 1999, 16)

While the major oil producers have long had an international presence, the past decade has witnessed a diversification of global exploration following the liberalization of investment regimes in many developing countries. Over 90 countries have revised their investment and mineral exploration laws to encourage foreign investment since 1985, opening up highly promising basins that were previously inaccessible to international oil companies either because of *de jure* political restrictions (e.g. Venezuela, Russia), or because political-economic risk was sufficiently high to deter prudent investment (e.g. Sudan, Angola). Of the 40–50 countries that currently grant exploration rights each year, nearly one-third were not even 'open for business' ten years ago. Thus, in the last 15 years US oil companies have more than doubled foreign exploration and development spending, while non-US oil majors, such as BP and Shell, have engaged in similar strategies. Because the largest oil firms are now active in a diverse set of socio-political contexts – and, therefore, must negotiate access to resources across a range of different regulatory environments – specific local and regional knowledge has become increasingly important as a way of managing investment risk.

In addition, technological advances (particularly those relating to deepwater offshore and sub-salt exploration) have opened up new physiograhic environments to oil producers. Deepwater is now a major focus of worldwide exploration, particularly in the Gulf of Mexico and on either side of the South Atlantic. Because these environments traditionally have not been regarded as economically viable resource areas, the regulatory frameworks governing resource access are evolving rather than well-established, especially when compared to more conventional, land or near-shore environments. For example, the federal Minerals Management Service (MMS) – which governs access to oil resources in the offshore Gulf of Mexico by auctioning mineral leases – has experimented in the last few years with incentives to encourage deepwater leasing. The 1995 passage of the Deep Water Royalty Relief Act, for example, led to record leasing rates in subsequent years: whereas only 17 per cent of leases issued in 1994 were in deep water, 70 per cent were in deep water in 1997. The evolving nature of these regulatory environments means that both regulatory agencies and oil firms are in a learning phase, in which the relative significance of conventional and new forms of knowledge (relating, for example, to optimum bidding strategies and risk assessment) are being constantly evaluated.

Venturing into non-traditional regulatory environments can introduce significant new forms of investment risk for oil firms. The general 'retreat of the national state' from direct intervention in the economy has, in many cases, created a dynamic and at times uncertain political environment in which the relationship between the central state and its regions is renegotiated. Oil firms making investments in emerging markets, therefore, enter a political environment in which different tiers of government (national, regional, local) compete for a measure of control over investment. Oil and gas producers on the Indonesian island of Sumatra, for example, find themselves in the middle of a regional separatist struggle against the central Indonesian state, in which contracts concluded at one administrative level and/or geographical scale of authority (e.g. at the national scale) are not respected at other levels (e.g. within the Sumatran province of Aceh). As oil firms operating from Ecuador to Russia have found out, sub-national governments (i.e. local and regional authorities) have increasingly attempted to tax or otherwise control oil production in – and oil transportation through – their territories during the 1990s as part of domestic political struggles to redefine the territorial authority of the state. Entry into 'emerging markets', therefore, places a premium on types of knowledge that are able to bridge between a firm's global investment strategies and its ability to implement those strategies in particular places. This strongly suggests a renewed emphasis on 'local', place-specific forms of knowledge, particularly knowledge about the legal and political environment in which firms seek to operate, as well as 'softer' forms of knowledge about the practical, socio-cultural 'know how' of getting things done in unfamiliar places. How firms form, trap, integrate and deploy such place-specific knowledge within the organization is a strategic challenge that lies at the heart of transnational firms' efforts to be simultaneously global *and* local.

Further, by increasing the openness of a national economy, policies of economic (and political) liberalization expose firms to increased demands for – and scrutiny of – standards of social and environmental performance. Boycotts and shareholder resolutions against Shell over its involvement in Nigeria, high-profile inquiries about the environmental and cultural impacts of foreign oil operations in Ecuador, and the political activities of civil organizations like Greenpeace more generally, demonstrate how issues of environmental and social risk have largely supplanted earlier concerns about national sovereignty, working conditions or the interregional transfer of resource rents as primary challenges to the investment strategies of multinational resource firms in the developing world. Established mechanisms adopted by oil firms for accessing land, compensating landowners, and mitigating social and environmental impacts are increasingly insufficient for securing access to mineral deposits and bringing them into production. Resource firms increasingly seek advice from, and form strategic partnerships with, non-traditional sources of knowledge – including anthropologists, international development agencies, community dispute resolution specialists and experts in environmental communications – in order to successfully access, and remain active in, new environments.

Organizational restructuring

The global oil industry consists of large multinational integrated companies (the 'majors') encompassing all operating aspects of the industry, state-controlled companies in a number of oil-rich nations and a much more diverse group of firms specializing in upstream (exploration and development), midstream (processing and transportation) or downstream (refining and marketing) aspects. Over the last few years, these smaller companies have gained a larger role, especially within the US industry: for example, oil production by non-majors in the lower 48 onshore fields has exceeded that of majors since 1990. Yet the increasing role for non-majors within the US oil sector, or indeed in the UK, is taking place against a backdrop of mega-mergers among the largest firms (e.g. Exxon and Mobil in 1999; BP-Amoco and ARCO in 1999; TotalFina and Elf in 2000; Chevron and Texaco in 2001; Conoco and Phillips in 2001). This double movement suggests that the relationship between knowledge production and organizational form is a complex one. One possible explanation is that the knowledge sets associated with technological advances not only create opportunities for new market entrants, but also lead to a process of organizational sorting as firms recognize which knowledge types are key assets and which can be outsourced. This outsourcing of specialized functions and activities helps to account, at least in part, for the reduction in corporate research and development spending attributable to the majors. In terms of production, however, while smaller companies tend to drill less extensive fields and have faster depletion rates than the majors, their access to advanced technologies enables them to reduce finding costs close to those of the majors. Thus the availability of these technologies to smaller companies has

> liberat(ed) them from the need to operate only on familiar territory because they know the geology and accompanying quirks. Access to technology opened up the whole world as an exploratory arena for most any size company with astute management.

Despite the geographic spread of their interests and activities, US oil exploration and production firms are remarkably concentrated in a small number of urban nodes (e.g. Houston, TX; Tulsa, OK; LaFayette, LA). Houston, for example, has emerged as a global centre of excellence for deepwater exploration and development, and its dense networks of key institutions and individuals provide the means by which industry-specific knowledges are generated and circulated. As an industrial cluster of upstream oil producers and headquarter operations, Houston has consolidated its position as a key knowledge node: thus, companies 'locate (in Houston) so they can plug into cutting-edge activity and be part of the industry's knowledge loop'.

Recent research by economic geographers (and others) on the organization of the oil industry has tended to work within a regional development/learning region tradition: work by Chapman, Cumbers, MacKinnon and others in Scotland, and Feagin in the US, examines the regional development impacts of the oil industry in and around the key nodes of Aberdeen and Houston, respectively. While these studies provide valuable insight into the ways in which innovations are generated within key knowledge nodes or clusters, understanding the geographies of knowledge in the oil industry – an industry that is currently intensifying its global reach – requires a focus on both localized nodes and the more extensive (global) networks within which these local nodes are embedded. To focus exclusively on the region (e.g. Houston), for example, is to miss much of what makes the knowledge economy significant in an era of globalization: its ability to achieve cost reductions by centralizing certain functions (e.g. seismic analysis, 3-D imaging), while enabling the more extensive distribution of others (e.g. production).

Globalization and Geographies of Knowledge in the Oil Industry

Despite their potential analytical and commercial significance, emergent geographies of knowledge in mature industrial sectors like the oil industry have not been examined closely. Anecdotal evidence suggests that the relative significance of different knowledge types is changing within the industry. On the one hand rapid technological change in exploration is creating valuable sets of technology-specific skills that are portable and largely independent of local conditions. This holds the potential to devalorize locally specific geological knowledge while simultaneously enabling the extension of global reach by oil firms. On the other, the opening of countries to foreign investment and the proliferation of different physiographic and socio-political regulatory environments within a company's portfolio of projects create new knowledge requirements, many of which are highly locality-specific. It would appear, therefore, that the oil industry exhibits at least two contradictory trends in terms of its geographies of knowledge: technological change is increasingly de-territorializing some types of knowledge (i.e. making them less place-specific) while organizational and geographical shifts are simultaneously territorializing other forms of knowledge (Table 25.1). We argue that these trends are significant not only for what they can tell us about restructuring within the oil industry, but also because they provide an opportunity to critically evaluate, through empirical study, a number of broader assertions about the extent and significance of the knowledge economy.

Critically evaluating such claims should be a significant part of any research agenda that is designed to harness work on geographies of knowledge to that on the practices that constitute and sustain global reach. Our use of the oil industry to illustrate how such research might develop highlights two further challenges. The first is to recognize the complexity of changing geographies of knowledge within mature industrial sectors. While some changes serve to centralize certain types of knowledge and associated practices, others encourage a more distributed or dispersed network of agents and institutions through which knowledge is mobilized. Some of these changes clearly serve to territorialize economic activity, while others have the opposite effect. Moving beyond the traditional conflation of tacit knowledge with the local scale, and distinguishing between knowledge types – as exemplified in Table 25.1 – allows for a more nuanced assessment of the changing geographies associated with developing knowledge economies. The second challenge is to recognize and interrogate the embeddedness of knowledge and knowledge networks within the broader political economies that structure mature industrial sectors. Recognizing the limits of knowledge and knowledge economies – or, at a minimum, the ways in which knowledge networks are shaped by broader political and economic dynamics – provides critical leverage for understanding the dynamics of contemporary economies and, in turn, holds much promise for informing the debate over the prospects for, and limits of, economic globalization.

Chapter 26

The Impact of Containerization on Work on the New York–New Jersey Waterfront

Andrew Herod

Today you can walk along the shoreline in Hoboken or Manhattan and see rows of abandoned piers. A century ago, these piers bustled with activity as ships brought goods from across the world to New York City and the surrounding region. Thousands of longshoremen or dockers worked these piers, and generations of families made a living from them. In the early 1950s, when the movie *On the Waterfront* was made, 40,000 dockers toiled in the port. Their work has mostly been replaced by a new form of cargo handling called containerization. As a result of this change, in the year 2000, 3,000 dockers in the Port of New York handled almost 65 million tons of cargo.

Traditionally, longshoring was a labor intensive industry. Low levels of capital investment required moving most solid cargo through ports on a piece-by-piece basis. Loose export cargo would first be delivered to the pier by truck where dockers would sort and check the goods. Usually dockers worked for stevedores contracted by particular steamship companies to load and discharge their ships, although sometimes ocean carriers set up their own in-house stevedoring subsidiaries. Once the cargo had been checked, dockers would place each individual piece onto pallets which were then lifted into the hold of a waiting ship. For a ship bringing goods into port the process would operate in reverse, with dockers discharging cargo from the hold, where it would be moved piece-by-piece to the local seaport terminal. From there, truckers would either load the cargo directly into their trucks or haul it to local trucking terminals for reloading into over-the-road vehicles (a practice known as "short-stopping") for delivery to its ultimate destination.

Despite its labor intensive character, the very nature of longshoring and the industry meant that labor was required only intermittently. Longshoring employment was tied to the vagaries of cargo transportation and ship schedules. While in

Herod, Andrew, "The Impact of Containerization on Work on the New York–New Jersey Waterfront," pp. 5–7 from *Social Science Docket*, 4.1 (Winter/Spring, 2004).

other industries, the demand for labor might fluctuate with the seasons or the economy's position in the business cycle, a steamship company's need for dockers varied on a day-by-day, hour-by-hour basis. Such irregularity of work was particularly evident in New York because of the port's status as the nation's primary point of entry for goods coming from Europe. Shipping on domestic coastal routes could usually be reliably scheduled, but the larger distances covered in the deep-sea foreign trade meant that ships carrying goods from Europe often arrived late or in groups.

The lack of automation in cargo handling meant that the port's steamship companies required a reserve army of dockers constantly at hand to ensure that during times of peak labor demand ships would be loaded or unloaded as quickly as possible. This reserve army of dockers, who were not paid when they were idle, was continually replenished by the millions of immigrants who landed at the port and sought employment on the piers.

Employer control over the work process and hiring was both a symptom and a cause of the weakness of the dockers' union, the International Longshoremen's Association (ILA). The union was unable to limit the labor supply which placed organizing efforts at a great disadvantage. The large supply of labor made restrictive practices unpopular with rank and file workers. The ease of replacement dampened militancy on the job. During strikes, local employers recruited strikebreakers, relying on ethnic divisions on the waterfront to play different groups of workers off against each other.

"Shape-Up"

The organization of the hiring process came to be known as "shape-up". Whenever a ship docked, hiring bosses would call the dockers to collect or "shape" in a semicircle at the head of the pier. Hiring bosses typically controlled hiring for between six and a dozen piers. They were ostensibly representatives of the employers. However, in 1916 the ILA negotiated an agreement giving work preference to union members. To enforce this agreement, the union insisted on the right to choose the employers' hiring bosses. The New York Shipping Association (NYSA) agreed in return for the union's maintenance of an oversupply of labor and suppression of strikes.

Because of the chronic oversupply of labor, dockers commonly offered bribes, or borrowed money at high interest rates from the hiring bosses to better their chances of being chosen for work. The potential for corruption and crime in the form of kickbacks and loan-sharking was immense. The close links between the shape-up and criminal activity frequently resulted in the hiring of convicted criminals as pier bosses. Although investigators of waterfront crime usually assumed that such bosses were forced on hapless employers by corrupt union officials, this was not always the case. One industry representative admitted that many employers preferred using thugs because of the fear they instilled in the workforce and the ability they had to keep a docker in his place and maintain order.

Historically, in New York, a longshoring gang generally consisted of 21 members. Eight worked in the hold, four on deck, eight on the dock, plus a gang boss. Sometimes dockers were hired as individual workers and formed into gangs. At other times they were hired as a group. Crews that regularly worked for particular companies were given hiring preference at those companies' piers. After the regular gangs were hired, vacancies and extra labor were filled by dockers picked from the shape-up. On the odd occasion when the shape failed to produce enough gangs, a hiring boss would contact a local union office to request a traveling gang. Traveling gangs were most commonly employed on Manhattan's East Side where the geography of scattered piers hindered the dockers' ability to move quickly from piers where there were too many dockers to piers where there was a labor shortage. Although it might seem that the core group of dockers on a large steamship company's pier enjoyed some security of employment, these dockers were still subject to replacement by casual workers on the whim of the hiring boss.

The irregularity of work encouraged by the shape-up entrenched the sectionalism born of ethnic and political rivalries in the port. The lack of enough regular work meant that the right to work particular piers were fiercely guarded. The West Side Manhattan piers were almost exclusively worked by Irish-Americans, while many of the Brooklyn piers were the domain of Italian-American dockers. Dockers who fell out of favor at their regular shape-up locations often found it very diffcult to obtain work on another ethnic group's section of the waterfront. One of the consequences of shape-up was the development within the union of many small power enclaves. Local ILA leaders relied heavily on the hiring bosses' abilities to reward friends and censure opponents.

As a result of the organization of the labor market, low wages and poor working conditions were endemic to the industry. The casual-labor market which evolved on the New York waterfront condemned all but a minority of dockers to the risk of unstable employment. This instability was reflected in the distribution of hours worked and wages. Between October 1, 1949 and September 30, 1950, 12,777 of the port's 36,540 dockers employed by NYSA members worked fewer than 100 hours. This amounted to 35% of the total workforce.

Containerization on the Waterfront

The most significant technological change to have taken place in the longshoring industry was the development of an integrated system of freight transportation which made possible containerization. Containerization is essentially the putting of individual pieces of cargo into large metal boxes of standardized size that can be transferred between different forms of transportation – ships, trucks, and trains. It was first introduced into the industry in the 1950s and soon began to threaten traditional longshoring work. The first company to operate a door-to-door distribution network using containers was the Pan Atlantic Steamship Corporation (Sea-Land Services).

Containerization brought many benefits for the employers. It allowed ships to be loaded and unloaded much more quickly than in the days when every piece of cargo had to be handled by hand and drastically reduced the need for labor. For manufacturers, containerization has radically transformed the geography of product distribution. Goods shipped between Asia and the east coast of the United States that previously were sent through the Panama Canal now can be unloaded at west coast ports and travel across North America by train.

Employers introduced containerization to reduce their cost of doing business. They were also able to weaken the longshoremen's union and eliminate traditional work rules and practices. They especially targeted "feather-bedding," which forced employers to hire many more dockers than they believed were necessary for a particular task. The ILA, fearing that containerization would idle thousands of waterfront workers, sought financial security for its members. While accepting that they could not prevent the employers from adopting the new technology, ILA officials and rank and file workers fought for protective contract clauses to minimize work dislocation and its impacts on waterfront workers.

During the 1950s, containerization helped restructure employment relations on the waterfront. As ship owners and manufacturers increasingly used containers, labor productivity rates climbed. Because fewer dockers were required to load and unload the ships, it became more difficult for some dockers to find work and many left the industry. In 1952 over 44,000 dockers and cargo checkers actively worked on the waterfront. In 1970, there were still 21,600 names on the Waterfront Commission's longshoring roster. By 1980, the number had decreased to 13,177, and in 1989 there were only 8,000 registered dockers and checkers working in the port. Today, the average salary for a docker is $83,000, the result of the ILA's ability to negotiate better contracts with the employers. On the other hand, the number of dockers who work the waterfront has been dramatically reduced.

The loss has not been distributed evenly throughout the port. The longshoring work which once kept the piers of Manhattan, Hoboken, and Jersey City bustling with activity has mostly migrated to the huge container facilities at Port Newark and the Elizabeth Marine Terminal. Hoboken now has no active piers, while in New York City, only the Red Hook Terminal in Brooklyn, Piers 1 to 8 in Brooklyn, the Passenger Ship Terminal on Manhattan's West Side, and the Howland Hook Marine Terminal on Staten Island continue to function. The development of the facilities at Port Newark-Elizabeth and the Port Authority Auto Marine Terminal in Jersey City-Bayonne have shifted the focal point of the port decidedly to the New Jersey side. This focus has been further reinforced by Jersey City's privately held Global Marine Terminal and the Army's Military Ocean Terminal in Bayonne. New Jersey accounted for only 18.4% of the ports hiring in 1958. By 2000, 75% of all hiring took place on the Jersey side.

Chapter 27

Wine, Spirits, and Beer:
World Patterns of Consumption

David Grigg

Thirty years ago few geographers showed much interest in food, with the exception of agricultural geographers who discussed the *production* of food. Since then there has been a growing interest in other aspects of food, and a revival of interest in the geography of food *consumption*. There has also been some interest in the geography of the consumption of alcoholic beverages. This article aims to outline world patterns of wine, spirits and beer consumption.

Measuring Consumption

Alcoholic beverages are consumed for different reasons, and they provide for different needs. They are a kind of food, although providing 2.5% of the total world calorie supply, and even in Europe where the most alcoholic drinks are consumed, 5%. They are also a way of quenching thirst, though not as efficiently as water. However many of the sources of drinking water are polluted, and bacterial infection spreads disease in many parts of the less-economically developed world, and did so in the more-economically developed countries until the provision of clean water supplies in the late nineteenth century. The processes of fermentation and distillation usually destroy harmful bacteria and so in this sense alcoholic beverages are safer to drink than water. Until the advent of coffee and tea, the preparation of which requires the boiling of water, there were few safe alternatives. Alcoholic beverages are consumed mainly because they are intoxicants and relaxants; they have been taken as medicine and as part of religious ceremonies, but their prime purpose is for pleasure.

Grigg, David, "Wine, Spirits, and Beer: World Patterns of Consumption," pp. 99–110 from *Geography*, 89.2 (2004).

The only comprehensive international statistics on the consumption of alcoholic beverages are in the Food Balance Sheets collected by the Food and Agriculture Organization (FAO), available for most member states from 1961 to 1999. Consumption is measured in several ways: calories, grams of fat, grams of protein, all per capita per day, and also in kilograms per capita per year. In the metric system a litre of water weighs 1 kg, thus this also provides an approximate measure of the consumption of wines, beers and spirits by volume. These figures are not strictly of consumption but of available food supplies. They are calculated by deducting from production exports, alcohols not used in drinks, and beverages put in store. Imports and beverages withdrawn from store are added to production. Statistics on the consumption and production of alcohol have considerable limitations. Because they are highly taxed, illicit production is common in some countries. Smuggling, both past and present, may lead to a considerable understatement of consumption, and in many less-economically developed countries much production is unrecorded. The figures provided by the FAO are per capita of all the population, but in many countries there are numerous total abstainers. In 1988, 10% of men in the (then) European Community never drank alcohol, but this varied from 2% in Denmark to 25% in Ireland. It is not possible to allow for these variations, for estimates of the number of abstainers is available for only a few countries. It is possible, however, to correct for variations in the number of children, who drink little alcohol in any society. Those under 15 years of age vary from only 15% of the total population in parts of Europe to 50% in some African states. Hence those under 15 have been excluded and the consumption figures used here are per adult.

The FAO distinguishes four classes of alcoholic beverage: beers made from barley, the principal commercial beer; beers made from other cereals, drunk mainly in tropical Africa; wine made by the fermentation of grape juice; and distilled spirits. Some beverages do not fit into these categories; special note should be taken of the means of producing alcoholic beverages in China, Japan and Korea. Very little wine is drunk is these countries and the traditional Chinese drink is *chiu*, or *jiu*, a fermented grain beverage brewed from millet, rice or sorghum but with an alcoholic content of 10% or more and often referred to in translation as rice wine. European beers are made in two stages: in the malting of barley, starch is converted to fermentable sugar, then the addition of yeast converts the sugar to carbon dioxide and ethyl alcohol. In the preparation of *chiu* one microbial culture is used that both produces sugar and ferments. Chinese distilled spirits are also produced in a different manner from those in Europe.

Patterns of Consumption

If the consumption of alcoholic beverages is measured by volume or weight then beer is by far the most important drink. It accounts for nearly four-fifths of the world total, compared with spirits and wine which account for only slightly more than one-tenth each.

Nor is beer consumption confined to one part of the world. It is the leading drink in 126 countries, whereas wine and spirits each lead in only 10 countries.

However there are considerable variations in the alcohol content of wine, beer and spirits and where the importance of these drinks is measured in terms of their absolute alcohol content, rather than volume, a quite different pattern emerges. Half of all absolute alcohol is obtained from spirits, one-third from beer and the rest from wine.

But spirits are the leading beverage in only two of the major regions, i.e. South America and Asia.

Barley beer accounts for over half the alcohol consumed in North and Central America and Oceania, but is second in importance in Africa, South America, Asia and Europe. Wine is of little importance outside Europe and Oceania whilst non-barley beer is confined to tropical Africa where it is the most important drink. There are great differences in the amount of alcohol, from all beverages, consumed per adult; it is highest in Europe, then Oceania and North America; it is lowest in Africa and Asia.

Three-quarters of the world's wine is drunk in Europe, with levels of consumption per capita only matched in Oceania. More barley beer is drunk per person in Oceania and North America than elsewhere; consumption per capita is very low in Asia and Africa, but non-barley beer is only of any significance in Africa. Regional contrasts in the consumption of spirits are less striking, but the highest levels are in Europe and Asia, and the lowest in Africa.

Where the composition of consumption is considered at the national level then matters become highly complex. International variations are therefore simplified here by classifying countries solely by leading beverage; countries where annual consumption of absolute alcohol is less than 0.5 kg have been excluded. A relatively simple pattern emerges (Figure 27.1).

Wine is the leading beverage in southern Europe, parts of central Asia, and the southern-most three countries of the Americas. Barley beer predominates in northern Europe, North America and Australasia, while non-barley beer is the leading drink only in tropical Africa.

From Poland eastwards to Japan, spirits are the preferred beverage, as they are in parts of Central and South America. To the south is a great band of countries, running from the west coast of Africa into the Middle East, South Asia and much of South East Asia, where very little alcohol is drunk. In many of these countries, from Mauritania to Pakistan and further east to Indonesia, Muslims are a majority of the population and their religion forbids consumption. In India and much of South East Asia, Hindus and Buddhists are the most numerous; their religions do not proscribe the consumption of alcohol but discourage it. In the original constitution of independent India, alcohol was prohibited but enforcement was left to individual states. There is now a more liberal view of both consumption and production.

Wine

Wine is made by fermenting the juice of the grape of the vine *Vitis vinifera*. Although it has been made for over 7000 years, it is the least consumed of the

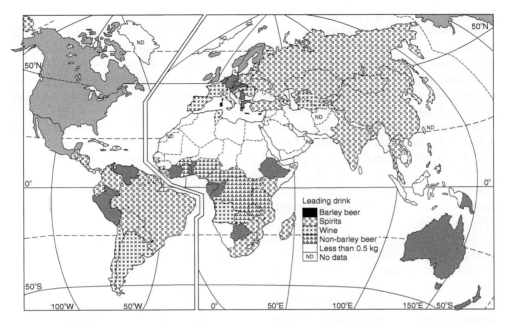

Figure 27.1   The leading alcoholic beverage, 1997–9. Countries where total consumption of absolute alcohol is less than 0.5 litres per adult per year are omitted from the classification.
Source: Food and Agriculture Organization, 2002, "Food Balance Sheets," www.fao.org.

three types of alcoholic beverage, accounting for less than one-seventh of the world's consumption of alcohol; world per capita consumption has nearly halved since the early 1960s. It is the leading drink in relatively few countries – five in Central Asia, three in South America and twelve in southern Europe. The vine is indigenous to the southern Caucasus although the first archaeological evidence is from the Zagros mountains of Iran in the sixth millennium BC. By the second millennium BC viticulture had spread to the Levant, Turkey, Egypt and Greece from whence migrants took it to the West Mediterranean. By the end of the Roman Empire, viticulture was established throughout the Mediterranean region, on the shores of the Black Sea, and had been taken to the Danube and as far north as the Moselle. Further expansion northwards was limited by the frequency of frost and cool summers: the highest yields are obtained in Mediterranean type climates. To the south, viticulture contracted with the end of the Empire. The Arab expansion from the seventh century AD and the later expansion by the Ottoman Turks brought an end to the consumption of wine in much of the Middle East, North Africa, Turkey and Central Asia, although Muslim attitudes to prohibition varied; wine continued to be made and drunk in Spain.

The expansion of viticulture began again in the sixteenth century when the Spanish took *Vitis vinifera* to Mexico; from there it was taken to California, to Peru, Chile and Argentina. But the output of these regions only began to increase substantially in the twentieth century, partly due to the emigration of wine growers from southern Europe after the *phylloxera* epidemic of the late nineteenth century. The Cape was settled by the Dutch, and French vines taken there in the seventeenth century, while in Australia and New Zealand viticulture did not begin until the nineteenth century and only started to flourish after the Second World War, possibly due in Australia to immigration from the Mediterranean and hence growing demand for wine. Viticulture was revived in the nineteenth century in some Muslim regions; French, Spanish and Italian occupation of North Africa prompted a great expansion of wine production, particularly in Algeria, although since independence and rule by Muslims output in the region has greatly diminished. Wine production had a long history in the Caucasus and Central Asia, but in the latter area declined under Muslim rule. Under the Soviet regime viticulture was encouraged until the 1980s; it remains the leading drink in spite of the predominance of Muslims in the population. However consumption per adult is low, except in Georgia (Figure 27.2).

There are many reasons for the variations in the consumption of alcoholic beverages. In the case of international variations, however, consumption patterns are often closely related to production, due, until recently, to the high cost of transporting beverages over long distances. This is true of wine; until the 1960s 90% of all wine output was consumed in the country where it was produced, although a greater proportion of the *value* of output was exported; the trade in wine between southern and northern Europe has existed for at least a millennium. There is a high correlation between the present consumption and production in spite of the increase

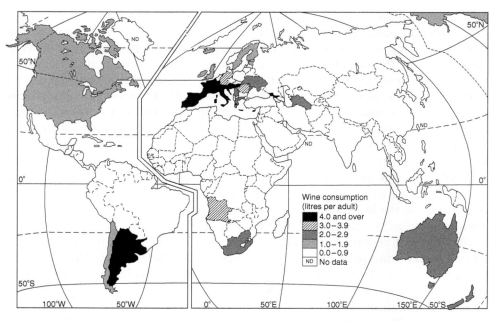

Figure 27.2 The consumption of wine, litres per adult of absolute alcohol per year, 1997–9.
Source: Food and Agriculture Organization, 2002, "Food Balance Sheets," www.fao.org.

in the proportion of production exported, which reached nearly a quarter in the late 1990s. This is partly because limited areas of the world produce high grape yields and of a suitable quality for wine-making. The early development of viticulture took place in the coastal regions of the Mediterranean and the Black Sea, where warm dry summers and mild wet winters gave good yields. When taken abroad by Europeans, viticulture initially thrived best in similar climates in California, Chile, Cape Colony and South West and South East Australia. Viticulture has since expanded into cooler climates such as New Zealand and drier but hot sunny areas where irrigation is necessary, such as Argentina. Nonetheless countries that experience Mediterranean climates still account for 78% of current wine output.

It is in these and similar climates that consumption per capita is highest (Figure 27.2): in the West Mediterranean, Argentina and Uruguay each adult drinks in a year over 4 litres of absolute alcohol derived from wine, while in Australia, South Africa and some other European countries consumption is between 2 and 4 litres. But the growth of exports since the 1960s has not spread wine drinking to many new regions; in Asia, in tropical Africa, in Central and South America (other than the south) and in the former USSR less than 1 litre is consumed per adult each year. The non-producers of wine account for little more than one-eighth of all imports. Most of the exports of wine go to other wine producers – for not all countries produce every type of wine – or, since the 1950s, to some countries of northern Europe where wine consumption has greatly increased as a result of greater travel to the Mediterranean, and higher incomes. In spite of this, beer remains the leading beverage in Northern Europe (Figure 27.1).

In many studies of international differences in food consumption, income per capita is often found to be a major cause of variation. Studies of populations within more-economically developed countries have shown a high correlation between income and the consumption of all alcoholic beverages and some have claimed a correlation over time, although recent declines in alcohol consumption seem related more to health concerns than economic factors. At first sight there is some relationship, for major regions, between income per capita and the consumption of wine: consumption is highest in Europe, Australasia, South America and North America and lowest in Africa and Asia. But an analysis of the relationship between gross domestic product (GDP) per capita and wine consumption per adult at the national rather than the regional level reveals only a moderate correlation and a very weak r^2; income apparently explains very little of the international variation in consumption.

A third factor explaining the world pattern of wine consumption, touched upon earlier, has been the migration of Europeans to non-producing areas. The Americas were settled by Spanish and Portuguese who were familiar with viticulture and accustomed to drinking wine; they made wine not only to drink with food but to use in the Eucharist. In the late-nineteenth century migrants from Iberia were joined by Italians, who both increased the market for wine in Argentina and Uruguay and provided many of the wine-makers, as they did in Brazil. Viticulture was revived in Central Asia after Russian conquest and rail lines to Moscow were built. Russian Jews revived viticulture in Palestine in the 1880s. French wine-makers went to Chile and Algeria after the *phylloxera* outbreaks of the 1870s, while in the seventeenth century French Huguenots were influential in Cape Colony in its early stages. In short, production and consumption of wine is dominated by Europeans. Europe and peoples of European origin produce 95% of the world's wine and consume 93%.

Beer

Beer consumption is much more widely distributed than wine consumption. It is the leading drink in Northern Europe, North America, Australasia and tropical Africa (Figure 27.1). It is also consumed in moderate quantities outside these regions (Figure 27.3), notably in Latin America, where beer is challenging spirits as the leading drink, in the former Soviet Union, and in Mediterranean Europe where consumption has risen since 1960. It is only in the Muslim countries and in East, South and South East Asia that the consumption of beer falls below 1 litre of alcohol a year. Beer is made by the fermentation of cereal grains, and cereals are widely grown so that the production of the raw material is not greatly limited by climate. In Europe and European settlements overseas beer is made from barley, but in Africa from sorghum, millet and maize; in Latin America *chicha* is made from maize. In China *jiv* is made by fermenting rice and other cereals and in Japan *saké* is also made by the fermentation of rice, although the much higher alcohol content of these drinks means they are not always classed as beers.

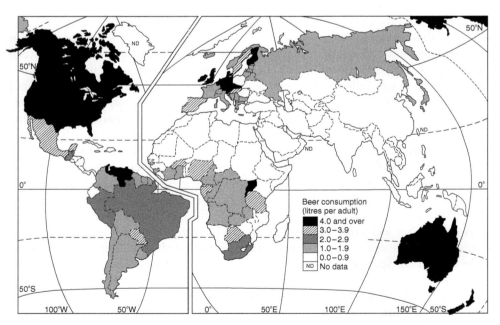

Figure 27.3 The consumption of beer, litres per adult of absolute alcohol per year, 1997–9. Includes barley and non-barley.
Source: Food and Agriculture Organization, 2002, "Food Balance Sheets," www.fao.org.

The first evidence of brewing is in the foothills of the Zagros mountains in Iran in the fourth millennium BC and it spread north west into Europe and south west into Egypt and the Sudan. By the time of the Roman Empire the distinction between wine drinking south of the Alps and beer drinking to the north was already apparent. Brewing was probably independently discovered in the Americas and East Asia. When Europeans reached West and Central Africa they found beers made from millet, sorghum and maize. Alcohol was unknown to most of the peoples of North America at the time of European contact but in South America *chicha* was widely drunk and its production was a state monopoly in the Inca Empire. The *chiu*, or *jiv*, of China and the *saké* of Japan have been known for at least two millennia.

Beer made from barley now predominates; very little *chicha* has been consumed – or at least very little recorded in the statistics – in the last 50 years, although it is certainly still made in rural parts of South America. Maize beers are still the leading drink in many countries of tropical Africa, but barley beer consumption is rising in that continent, accounting for 15% of all alcohol from beer in the 1960s, to 25% at present. Barley beer now accounts for nearly nine-tenths of the world's alcohol derived from beer. Beer is consumed almost exclusively in the countries where it is produced; only 5% of output crosses international boundaries and half a century ago this was less than 2%. In eighteenth-century England beer was rarely transported more than 6 miles from a brewery and because beer in casks deteriorates rapidly, regular deliveries in comparatively small quantities were necessary. More importantly, because water accounts for a very high proportion of the content of beer, this made transport over long distances uneconomic, hence beer production was market orientated.

The advent of the railway and the motorway has reduced the cost of transport and conveying beer in bottles, cans and kegs rather than casks has reduced the rate of deterioration. Even so there is still a very high correlation between consumption per capita and output per capita at the national level, and the location of production explains a high proportion of the international variation in consumption. Although barley was first domesticated in the Middle East, good malting barleys need a short and relatively cool growing season, and so while barley is widely grown in the subtropics, it is for food and not for malt, while in the wetter tropics it is rarely grown, except in upland areas. Thus very little is grown in tropical Africa or Latin America; the brewers of the latter region are mainly dependent upon imports of barley malt from the United States. The major producers and exporters of malting barley and of malt are mainly in the cooler temperate regions, as are the hop growers. Hops were originally used to improve the keeping qualities of beer, but are now valued for their bitter taste.

In the early twentieth century breweries were established in East and South East Asia, often by German brewers. Nevertheless, consumption remains low in Asia except in Japan and South Korea, where its increase since the 1950s is probably due to American influence. Europeans, particularly the Germans, have been influential in establishing beer production and consumption elsewhere in Asia. In North America, English barleys and yeasts were not successful in the seventeenth and eighteenth centuries and it was not until German immigrants in the 1840s brought the technology of lager making, as well as yeasts that proved successful, that beer became the leading drink in the United States. The British in Australia attempted to establish beer, but top fermentation beers were unsuccessful and it was not until the introduction of bottom fermentation – lager – in the 1880s that beer drinking boomed. Beers are usually the cheapest of the three alcoholic beverages, but international differences in income per capita have only a moderate correlation with consumption and appear to have little influence on variations in consumption. Over the last century, however, beer consumption has increased in a number of regions at the expense of other beverages, notably spirits.

Spirits

Spirits are made by distilling a fermented beverage; the beverage is heated, and because the boiling point of alcohol is lower than that of water, a vapour made up mainly of alcohol is produced. When cooled it condenses and, mixed with water, gives the spirits a content of 30–50% alcohol. In contrast to wine, and beer made from barley malt, spirits can be made from a great variety of plants; indeed almost any carbohydrate can be used for fermenting prior to distillation. Sugar-cane, sugar beet, potatoes, maize, barley, wheat, rice, the sap of oil palms, grapes and numerous other plants are used. All spirits consist of pure alcohol and water. The distinctive flavour of each comes either from the method of processing, such as rum which is matured in oak casks, from the addition of flavours, from juniper to gin, aniseed to ouzo, often at a different site from the production of the alcohol, or from the material fermented and distilled, as with whisky.

Spirits are the leading alcoholic beverage in three regions (Figure 27.1): first, much of Central and South America; second, Eastern Europe and most of the countries of the former Soviet Union; and third, East, South and parts of South East Asia. There are also high rates of consumption in some areas where spirits are not the leading drink, such as Central Europe (Figure 27.4). Distillation was unknown to the peoples of the Americas until the arrival of Europeans. The Spanish introduced *Vitis vinifera* and some brandy was distilled from wine – as it still is. But the primary source of spirits in Latin America is sugar-cane; the plant was introduced by the Spanish in the sixteenth century and was widely cultivated in the tropics and sub-tropics, usually on plantations, by African slaves. Sugar did not deteriorate on the long journey across the Atlantic and had a high price. Spirits are distilled from sugar-cane juice, with the general name of *aguardente*, with local variants such as *kachassa* in Brazil and *canazo* in Peru. But the most important product was, and is, rum, distilled from molasses, the residual in sugar-cane processing; it is stored in oak casks for several years before sale. Rum was drunk not only in Latin America, but was the leading drink in the British colonies in North America until replaced in the 1830s in the United States by whisky, which was itself overtaken by beer in the 1880s. At the beginning of the last century beer was the leading drink in North America, wine in Chile, Argentina and Uruguay, and spirits elsewhere. Since the 1960s the consumption of beer per capita has increased more rapidly than the consumption of spirits in this zone. Indeed in six countries consumption per capita has fallen, so that beer has replaced spirits as the leading

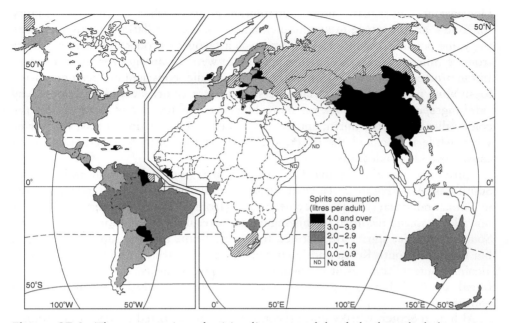

Figure 27.4 The consumption of spirits, litres per adult of absolute alcohol per year, 1997–9.
Source: Food and Agriculture Organization, 2002, "Food Balance Sheets," www.fao.org.

drink in a number of countries and seems likely to do so in several more in the near future.

Europe probably obtained the art of distillation – of perfumes, not alcohol – from the Arabs in the eleventh century. Knowledge of the distillation of spirits spread from Italy slowly through Europe, not reaching Scandinavia or Russia until the sixteenth century. Until the eighteenth century wine was the leading drink in the Mediterranean, beer in the rest of Europe and Russia; however there was then an increase in the production of spirits. Gin became the leading drink in southern England although only temporarily, but gin, schnapps and acquavit replaced beer as the leading drink in The Netherlands, northern Germany and Scandinavia, respectively, while vodka overtook beer in Russia in the nineteenth century. Thus at the beginning of the twentieth century spirits were the leading drink in Northern and Eastern Europe, wine in the Mediterranean and beer in between. Throughout the twentieth century governments attempted to reduce spirit consumption by prohibition, heavy taxation, rationing and warnings about the dangers to health of spirit drinking; by the 1970s or earlier, beer had replaced spirits as the leading drink in Scandinavia, Germany and The Netherlands. Attempts in the 1980s to reduce spirit consumption in Eastern Europe and the Soviet Union were less successful.

Although the recent decline of spirit consumption in Northern Europe is understandable, its rise to pre-eminence in the eighteenth century is less-easily explicable.

However, it is possible to use for distillation grain which is of too low a quality for food – an advantage in northern climates – while distillation greatly increased the value per unit weight of grain, and was a favoured product in regions remote from commercial markets. Furthermore there were advantages for the consumer. In the nineteenth century much of the European diet consisted of bread and pota-toes. Most men were manual labourers, and extra calories could be acquired by drinking spirits rather than yet more bland-tasting bread and potatoes. In the colder climates of the north, spirits had a warming effect, in contrast to beer or wine, while it also had the effect, still valued by some in Northern Europe, of causing rapid intoxication.

Spirits are also the leading drink in a third region: East, South and parts of South East Asia (Figure 27.1). Distillation was discovered, probably independently, in China and India; the earliest evidence dates from the sixteenth century. However not all the spirits recorded in this region are a result of distillation. In South and South East Asia, spirits are distilled from sugar-cane and the sap of palm trees, but in China, South Korea and Japan many of the fermented grain beverages have alcohol contents that result in them being classed as spirits. In addition to tradi-tional distilled beverages, Japan has high rates of whisky production and consumption.

Although Scotch whisky and French brandy are exported all over the world, a surprisingly small proportion of world spirit production is exported. The location of production is not a powerful factor in explaining the variation of consumption as it is with beer or wine, and income per capita seems to have very little influence on international variations. In contrast to wine or beer, the production and con-sumption of spirits is far less concentrated in Europe and European settled areas: indeed two-thirds of production and consumption is in Asia. However, it must be remembered that although the alcohol content of these beverages is high, many of them are the result of fermentation and not distillation (Figure 27.4).

Discussion

Although there are clear international variations in the relative importance of wine, beer and spirits, there is no simple explanation for these patterns. Perhaps the dis-cussion should be at the regional level, where differences within a country can be explained. Unfortunately there are very few countries where data on consumption are available. In the United States data at the state level are available, but have not revealed factors other than those discussed above. Of the factors discussed earlier, production is of great importance. Most discussions of food choice emphasise the wide range of products available to consumers in rich Western countries and there-fore discount the location of production as an important factor in determining consumption. Yet the greater part of agricultural production is consumed in the country where it is grown and this is true also of alcoholic beverages. People eat and drink the products most easily available, and often thus the cheapest. Beer, which consists largely of water, is exported rarely and non-barley beer hardly ever, because of the cost of transport. Wine production and consumption is limited to only a few areas. The rise of wine consumption in Northern Europe since the 1960s gives a misleading picture of *world* trends.

A second factor of great importance is the ethnic origin of the producers and consumers of alcoholic beverages. Although these beverages are consumed everywhere except in the Muslim countries, both production and consumption is dominated by people of European origin. Furthermore the diffusion of beverages around the world has been dominated by Europeans: wine production has been taken to the Americas and Australasia by Europeans; beer production and consumption was taken by the English to North America, although modern American beers are largely German in origin, while the British and Germans have played a major role in spreading beer production in Asia, mainly since the 1850s. Japan is perhaps a special case in the changing pattern of alcohol consumption in Asia. At the end of the nineteenth century traditional spirits were almost the only drink. However as part of their aim to catch up with the West, and to accept Western attitudes, the Japanese studied whisky-making methods in Scotland, and established distilleries in Japan in the 1920s. Since 1945 production and consumption of whisky in Japan has greatly increased. The American presence in Japan after 1945 led to the rise of beer production and consumption, so that the structure of Japanese consumption of alcoholic beverages is now more like Europe than the rest of Asia.

Income is a powerful factor influencing the consumption of most foods at the international level. In poor countries the cheapest source of calories and protein are cereals, but they are of much less significance in the richer countries. Animal-derived foods, which are an expensive source, are little eaten in poor places such as Africa, but are an important if declining part of the diet in more economically developed countries. It might be expected that income would also influence the relative consumption of the alcoholic beverages for beer is generally cheaper than wine or spirits, and spirits the most expensive. Yet income seems to have relatively little influence on consumption. There are two possible reasons for this. First, there are great variations in the quality and cost of different beers, wines and spirits. Thus wine produced in Europe may vary in price from less than 1ª a bottle to thousands and there are similar ranges in quality and cost between Cognac and the spirits of much of South America or Asia. Second, the price of alcohol is greatly influenced by the rate of taxation. Alcohol was, and still is – in spite of attempts by the European Union to standardise taxation – more heavily taxed in the UK and Scandinavia than in France or Italy. These two factors blur the relationship between income and consumption.

Cultural factors have been given great emphasis in human geography in the last 20 years, and one such factor – religion – is of considerable importance in accounting for world variations in both the amount and type of alcohol consumed. The consumption of alcohol is forbidden in Muslim countries and frowned upon in much of South and South East Asia. But attempts to limit the consumption of alcohol have also occurred elsewhere, notably in the United States in the 1920s. In Scandinavian countries various attempts to limit the consumption of alcohol – mainly spirits in the 1920s – have resulted in the decline of spirit consumption; beer is now the leading drink in Scandinavia. Attempts to prohibit the consumption of alcohol in the nineteenth century were prompted by the often dreadful social and economic consequences of excessive drinking, particularly on family life. More recently it is the adverse effects upon health that have been emphasised and this has influenced trends in consumption over time, if not yet international patterns. However it should not be thought that the relative preference for wine, beer and spirits in a country is unchanging. Indeed the historical geography of consumption merits further research.

The consumption of alcoholic beverages is part of the broader pattern of food consumption; indeed drinks may be chosen on the grounds that they complement particular foods. The geography of the consumption of alcoholic beverages, like that of food, reflects a variety of factors from climate to religion, and to understand the modern patterns much further research is needed.

Chapter 28

Producing and Consuming Chemicals: The Moral Economy of the American Lawn

Paul Robbins and Julie T. Sharp

In the United States, the economic boom of the late twentieth century led to an unprecedented level of spending power for the majority of middle-class Americans. The resulting changes in everyday urban practices had profound implications for urban environments, in the form of the degradation of the quality of air and water, the disposal of an ever-growing mountain of household waste, and the increases in atmospheric carbon loads through the daily commuting patterns of consumers.

One of the most profound though understudied impacts of this growth is the transformation of land cover and ecological change in the wake of urban expansion. Specifically, with a conservative estimate of 23 percent of urban cover dedicated to lawns and with 675,000 hectares per year converted to urban development in the United States, the spread of lawn cover has become a major force for ecological change, blanketing the urban landscapes of the United States. Typically, threats to the environment are blamed on agricultural and industrial enterprises. Urban construction and runoff from urban and suburban areas, however, contribute significantly to water pollution, although these sources are often overlooked in regulations. As a result, one of the most profound but overlooked impacts of changes in land cover has been the spread of the suburban lawn and the concomitant rise in high input systems of management that it demands, including the application of chemical fertilizers, herbicides, and insecticides to residential yards.

The scale of the lawn-care industry alone suggests the importance of more thorough analyses. In 1999, Americans spent $8.9 billion on lawn-care inputs and equipment. In the same year, 49.2 million households purchased lawn and garden fertilizers, and 37.4 million households purchased insect controls and chemicals.

Robbins, Paul and Sharp, Julie T., "Producing and Consuming Chemicals: The Moral Economy of the American Lawn," pp. 425–45 from *Economic Geography*, 79.4 (2003).

The purchase of these inputs, moreover, steadily increased during the past decade.

This expansion of use and purchase has occurred specifically among a section of consumers who explicitly and disproportionately acknowledge the risks associated with chemical deposition and express concern about the quality of water and human health. What drives the production of monocultural lawns in a period when environmental consciousness has encouraged "green" household action (e.g., recycling)? And why does the production of chemical externalities occur among individuals who claim to be concerned about community, family, and the environment?

To answer these questions, we take a political ecological approach to the economic geography of the lawn in the United States. Operating from the understanding that decisions about land management are constrained by "parameters of choice" that are set by larger social, political, and ecological actors and processes, political ecology has been successful in explaining the degradation of agricultural land and water in the global South even while it has demonstrated that global economic and political processes are mediated by local-level ecological realities. This approach, we suggest, can be equally effective when applied to urban and developed settings. Viewing the use of chemicals in lawn management as the structured environmental decisions of individuals that are embedded in larger social, political, and economic processes at multiple scales, our investigation yields a clearer understanding of the continual and increased use of lawn chemicals by affluent Americans despite widespread knowledge of their possible negative environmental impacts. Moreover, it provides a better picture of the emerging environmental implications of the private consumption and public production of suburban landscapes.

[. . .]

Distinctiveness of the Lawn as a Site of Production and Consumption

Intensive lawn maintenance requires the use of diverse inputs, each with specific associated risks. Pesticides pose risks to both human and nonhuman health if they are found in either surface or ground water. Excess fertilizers in water supplies lead to the eutrophication of water bodies and the contamination of drinking water. Common lawn chemicals include both fertilizers and pesticides, a category encompassing insecticides, herbicides, and fungicides. [. . .]

Although lawn chemicals do not represent an immediate and proximate risk to consumers if they are used properly, the effects of their sustained use over time are less clear. Even Scotts's [a major lawn chemical formulator and service provider] CEO admitted that "we cannot assure that our products, particularly pesticide products, will not cause injury to the environment or to people under all circumstances." As a result, lawn-care chemicals have received increasing attention as a persistent risk. Concern at the EPA [Environmental Protection Agency] has heightened in recent years, and its studies have increasingly pointed to the uncalculated risks of exposure to lawn-care chemicals. Assessments of human exposure have shown that lawn chemicals are more persistent than was previously thought, especially when they are transported into the indoor environment, where their reported laboratory half-lives become relatively meaningless.

These chemicals track into homes easily and have been shown to accumulate in house dust, especially in carpets, where they are most available for dermal contact and where young children are placed at a significant risk. Furthermore, the effects of these toxins, especially insecticide neurotoxins, on children is not well understood, but modeled impacts of children's exposure to chemicals have suggested that serious risks result from normal but persistent exposure. The deposition of common lawn chemicals on clothing during application has also been demonstrated to lead to persistent risks of exposure. Therefore, even apart from the water and energy demands of these high-input systems, intensive lawn management carries with it some dilemmas of chemical use that are serious enough to have engaged the EPA's attention.

These risks are increasingly well communicated, to the point that formulators worry about the marketability of lawn-care products. For example, William Foley, head of the consumer products division of Scotts Company, reported as early as 1990 that "we're concerned about the overall growing presence of chemophobia in the minds of both the trade and the consumer." In their forward-looking statements for fiscal 2002, Scotts officials further stated their concern that the public's perception of chemicals could adversely affect business. Even so, trends in consumers' use of chemicals show no sign of flagging.

Trends in the use of chemicals on high-input lawns

In the national survey of US lawn owners, 11 percent of the respondents reported that they had eaten dandelions (*Taraxacum officinale*) from their lawns. This revelation, however astonishing to students of consumer behavior, is not a surprise to major input producers and suppliers, who urge homeowners to treat dandelions more aggressively: "Don't Eat 'Em Defeat 'Em." The degree to which the lawn has not yet been fully colonized by intensified, high-input systems marks the extent to which aggressive chemical sales continue to have room to grow and expand to new markets. As a result, the high-input lawn is distinctive in that it represents a case of the expanding use of chemicals, even in the face of the increasing acknowledgment of negative externalities, where all other forms of chemical use are declining.

Tracking the sales in the yard chemical-formulator industry suggests the degree of recent expansion. Although they do not manufacture the active ingredients in pesticides and fertilizers, formulator firms purchase them from large chemical companies, mix the active ingredients with other solvents, and package and market the final products for retail sale. In this industry, growth is ongoing. Whereas the overall use of agricultural pesticides in the United States has decreased sharply since the late 1970s, as has the use of pesticides in the commercial and governmental sectors, the sales of residential lawn and garden chemicals are stable and increasing. Between 1994 and 1997, national use of agricultural herbicides decreased by

15 million pounds of active ingredient (3 percent of the total) while the use of household herbicides increased by 3 million pounds (or 6.5 percent of the total). Similarly, for insecticides, agricultural usage decreased by 8 million pounds of active ingredient (9 percent of the total) while household usage remained nearly unchanged. Over the same period, the total retail sales of private lawn-care products increased from $8.4 million to $8.9 million, making this segment the largest and fastest-growing one of the entire lawn and garden industry, including ornamental gardening, tree and shrub care, and vegetable gardening. In 1999, 55 percent of US households applied insect controls (some 136 million pounds of pesticides), and 74 percent applied fertilizers. Even though the total quantity of lawn chemicals applied in the United States remains lower than that applied to agricultural fields, the rate of applications per hectare is far greater. So while total deposition of chemicals applied in agriculture can be estimated to have decreased as a result of land-use conversion, these gains are increasingly offset by the greater use of chemicals on home lawns.

The environmental and popular presses have increasingly scrutinized the conventional yard as a potential environmental problem. Nevertheless, US homeowners apply chemicals to their lawns even though they understand the negative environmental impacts of doing so. Higher rates of chemical use have previously been shown to correlate with higher incomes, greater levels of education, and high degrees of environmental knowledge and concern.

In the national survey, the use of a chemical lawn-care company was associated not only with individuals with higher incomes and higher-valued houses, but disproportionately with individuals who believe that homeowners' lawn practices and lawn-care services have a deleterious impact on the quality of local water supplies. Moreover, those who use chemicals or chemical application companies are significantly *more likely* to perceive that their own or their neighbors' chemical-use practices have "a negative effect on water quality" than are those who do not use inputs. Thus, despite greater environmental knowledge and concern, high-energy lawn-care inputs are increasing among the most environmentally sensitive and aware. Therefore, the US lawnscape presents a significant problem, and the increasing production and consumption of these products demands an explanation, as do the complex moral economies that surround them.

Limits to current modes of explanation

To date, such questions have been approached largely from an economic perspective, with lawn management described and theorized as individuated, economically rational behavior that is meant to maximize the economic utility of the yard. From this perspective, the use of chemicals has remained steady in the face of widespread knowledge of its negative impacts because of (1) broad economic and demographic trends and an increase in the total area of lawns, (2) an increase in the number of people who are likely to use chemicals, and (3) the labor burden that is offset by their use.

In addition to fueling a housing boom, the protracted economic expansion of the late 1990s meant that many Americans had more discretionary income, and the low interest rates of the late 1990s fed the boom in the construction of new single-family homes. Simultaneously, there was an increase in the proportion of the lot committed to lawn as ranch-style construction gave way to multistory dwellings. This increase in gross yard space provided more opportunity for the use of chemicals.

Second, demographic shifts are increasing the number of people who are likely to take yard work seriously enough to use chemicals. Market research has suggested that Americans in their 50s are more likely to work extensively in their yards than are those of any other age. Disposable income rises dramatically for Americans in their 50s, in particular, and this extra income is often invested in home improvements, including the yard. People in this cohort are more likely than are others to own homes with yards. The first baby boomers turned 50 in 1996, bringing the largest group of Americans into their prime yard-management years. As this generation continues to age over the next two decades, the number of people who engage in yard-care activities can be expected to increase dramatically.

Finally, economists and market researchers have asserted that homeowners who engage in yard care tend to use a highly intensive style of management. The geography of new home construction contributes to this intensity, since the majority of new homes that were constructed in the last 20 years were built in metropolitan areas, where residents are more likely to use yard chemicals than people in small towns or rural areas. In addition, the majority of new homes were built in the southeastern and southern central portion of the United States, where a longer growing season and more virulent insects mean that homeowners have a greater opportunity and incentive to use yard chemicals. These factors, combined with the decreased labor requirements of chemical inputs relative to their manual alternatives, can be used to explain the persistence of the use of lawn chemicals. Thus, many scholars view the continued use of yard chemicals in the United States as being coincident with economic expansion and demographic change and use rational actor models to explain why Americans mow, clip, and spray every Saturday.

These economic explanations, we argue, are insufficient to elucidate fully the sustained and increasing sales of chemicals or to explain the specific cultural economy of the lawn. Describing market behaviors in the absence of a wider economic context, these approaches do not place lawn managers' decisions within the social and cultural processes that operate on both the local and global scales. Nor do such explanations posit why specific practices, especially the greater use of chemicals, prevail even in the face of changing public values. They cannot answer why Americans, known for their environmental awareness, continue to manage land in contradiction to their increasing environmental knowledge.

We suggest, therefore, that a robust explanation of this problem lies in understanding the social construction of the lawn aesthetic within the wider context of the restructuring of the chemical industry at the global scale, as conditioned by residential class and community identity at the local scale. By examining both locations, we find that there is an increasing imperative to produce monocultural lawns and that the demand is created both by formulators who must sell and by local consumers who must buy the monocultural aesthetic of the American lawn. Formulators are forced by declining margins to expand sales aggressively through representational techniques that sign the lawn as part of consumers' identity. Local lawn owners, in contrast, are driven to maintain the monocultural lawn with an urgency rooted in their perceived alienation from community, family, and environment. We consider each process in turn.

The Drive for Markets: Economic Imperatives to Expansion

Over the past 20 years, formulator firms – companies that purchase raw chemical inputs for lawn care, combine them, brand them, and supply them to retail outlets – have faced several new challenges that have forced them to expand and adapt. These challenges have included declines in retail outlets, difficulties in financing, the rising costs of raw materials, and regulatory and ecological limits to production.

First, as in most traditional Fordist industries, the cost of standing warehouse stock, essential in this highly seasonal industry, has become prohibitive for traditional retailers, who rarely want to stock spring merchandise the previous fall. As Scotts executive Charles Berger explained, "Nobody wants March merchandise in November." At the same time, there has been an increasing shift in retail sales toward the cheap prices of mass discount and home improvement stores, which have become the new centers of lawn and garden retailing.

As a result, hardware stores and nurseries, the traditional outlets for lawn-care products, have lost market share in chemical sales, and formulators have come to rely more heavily on a relatively smaller number of larger-scale customers: home improvement and mass market retailers. Ten North American retailers account for 70 percent of the sales of the Scotts Company, for example. Home Depot, Wal-Mart, Lowe's, and the increasingly troubled Kmart provide 60 percent of the sales, with Home Depot alone accounting for 28 percent. In addition, competition among these retailers is intense. If any of these customers falters, formulators may lose important outlets.

At the same time, many formulators are facing increasingly difficult financial situations. Scott's leveraged buyout in 1986, as a prominent example, cost $211 million, of which $190 million was financed by an investment banking firm. This debt was blamed for the 11-percent fall in Scotts's stock share price from June 1999 to June 2000.

In an attempt to increase sales through acquisition, formulator firms have assumed even more debt with the purchase of new product lines, resulting in declines in credit ratings. Other expenses in the industry, including company software, the closing of facilities that operate at a loss, severance pay for redundant employees, and costs associated with product recalls, have also driven significant debt. In fiscal year 2000, Scotts spent $94 million on interest payments alone, a figure inflated by the high interest rates of that year, requiring Scotts to increase sales to generate a sufficient cash flow.

Formulators must also deal with the increasing costs of raw materials. Scotts sold its professional golf-turf business partly because of the increased cost of raw materials, such as urea and fuel. In addition, the costs of most pesticides' active ingredients have been steadily rising since the early 1980s.

Expiration of patents and environmental regulation further threaten formulators. The patent for glyphosate, for example, the active ingredient in one of Scotts's best-selling herbicides, expired in September 2000, opening production opportunities and tight competition for market share. Neither are formulators immune from the complexities of state regulation. Active ingredients in pesticides can be removed from the market under the Food Quality Protection Act, and companies must be prepared to find new sources of raw materials for all of their pesticides, as well as be prepared for the potential costs of remediation or liability if any pesticide causes harm.

In addition, the harvesting of peat for potting soil is subject to environmental regulation in both the United States and Britain. The US Army Corps of Engineers has sued Scotts over surface water contamination from its peat-harvesting activities at a New Jersey plant and the company only recently reached an agreement with British environmental officials to close down its peat-harvesting plants at several sensitive sites in the United Kingdom. Federal, state, and local environmental regulators strictly regulate the disposal of wastes from fertilizer- and pesticide-formulating plants. Scotts has been paying fines and cleanup costs for unlicensed waste disposal and asbestos contamination at several sites in the United Kingdom and Ohio.

Moreover, the ecological cycles of the industry pose problems for formulators. The cyclical nature of grass and garden growth means that cash flow is cyclical, since early spring and summer bring the highest sales of lawn and garden products. To meet this demand, fall and winter are the highest production times at formulation plants. Yet fall is the time of the lowest cash flow because receipts from spring and summer sales have not yet been received. As a result, formulators must maintain their highest production at a time when their cash flow is the lowest. This cash-flow "crunch" has implications for financial integrity. The Scotts Company's executives are unsure of their ability to make even minimal debt-service payments in fall and winter when their cash flow is the lowest. Because debt service is so crucial, the company must boost sales enough to provide adequate capital even in the fall and winter "crunch."

Changing weather affects formulators, as well. A wet spring slows fertilizer sales but increases pesticide sales. Conversely, a dry spring increases fertilizer sales but decreases pesticide sales, while a cold spring can slow all lawn and garden sales. This is one reason why formulators seek a global market, hedging against a cold spring in the United States with sunny weather in Europe, and vice versa.

To pay off their considerable debt, to overcome the rising costs of raw materials, to deal with the possibility of losing an important retail customer, to ensure sufficient funds to acquire new active ingredients, to manage environmental liabilities, to meet winter debt-service obligations, and to compensate for fluctuations in the weather, formulators of the early twenty-first century must increase sales of lawn chemicals and do so at an increasing rate. Fortunately for firms, changes in the retailing environment have led the industry into a new era of consumer advertising, resulting in increased sales, which the industry needs. These direct ("pull") marketing systems depend, to a great degree, on carefully representing the lawn aesthetic to potential consumers.

Signification: Creatively Representing the Lawn Aesthetic

Like most formulators, the dominant firm, Scotts, sold yard chemicals prior to 1990 through a "push" strategy, in which incentives were provided to a close network of retailers – usually independent hardware stores, nurseries, and specialty garden stores – who ordered large shipments of merchandise. Products were shipped to stores in the fall and then held by retailers until spring sales, when the retailers were responsible for selling the products, relying on advertising and knowledgeable, motivated sales staffs.

But in 1986, following a leveraged buyout from its parent company ITT, Scotts proceeded with an innovative marketing tactic: "pull marketing." On the basis of direct advertising to consumers by the formulators themselves, via television, radio, and print advertising, a "pull" approach concentrates on creating demand at the customer level. Rather than rely on a retailer to sell a specific brand, the formulator presents its products by promulgating novel imagery and signifying the lawn.

The move to a pull marketing strategy now extends to new products that attempt to "turn more dirt – branded dirt – into dollars" and to branded plants, sprouted with company products. Moreover, the current marketing strategy seeks to increase applications per user. "Consider the $900 million lawns category: almost 30% of homeowners are do-nothings! The average do-it-yourselfer still makes fewer than half the recommended product applications each season. If every homeowner made just four applications a year, lawns could be a $2.8 billion market!" In addition, advice is readily available through toll-free help lines, in-store counselors, extensive web pages, and e-mail reminder services, all backed by a guarantee of satisfaction for markets in both the United States and Europe.

This emphasis on marketing is capital intensive. After purchasing a new pesticide line, Scotts spent twice as much as its former owner to advertise it. In 1998, with only about half the market share in yard-care supplies, Scotts spent 75 percent of all the advertising dollars in the sector, and in 2002, it purchased $8 million of television airtime. In the process, the lawn-care industry has reinvented itself as a directly marketed aesthetic tied to community values: family, nature, and collective good.

Traditional images generally showed manicured yards, menacing magnified pests that inhabited lawns that received poor care, and specific branded compounds that provided solutions. Recent images have followed this approach, but with many new symbols apparent. Specifically, the lawn is increasingly represented as something that transcends personal value to managers of home lawns with collective activites and pride among neighbors much more prominent, where the lawn becomes a community-activity space for parents and children.

These advertisements reinforce the lawn as a symbol both of collective consumption and of competitive social status. One typical advertisement simply shows a square of turf grass in a saturated green shade, accompanied by the caption, "Not only will your grass be this color, your neighbors will be too." As typically depicted, the monocultured lawn is pictured as an enviously ("green") coveted symbol of community status where the goal is to produce collective social value and to accrue individual merit.

Second, the lawn continues to be depicted as a way to participate in and strengthen the traditional nuclear family. [. . .] [L]awn-advertising images depict typically young, heterosexual couples working and relaxing amid a healthy sward of monoculture lawn and portray the lawn as a place where children learn to play and share and where turf grass bonds and secures the relationships between fathers and their offspring. Advertisements for lawn chemicals never depict two men or two women, a child with an elderly person, or a group of schoolchildren at play. It is always the nuclear family that enjoys the lawn.

Finally, lawn chemical companies build on and reinforce the sense of lawn management as a bridge to the biotic, nonhuman, natural world. [. . .] [T]he yard [is shown] as a place in which the suburban homeowner engages in the timeless human activity of planting growing things in the soil. By sowing and nurturing living green plants, these advertisements suggest, modern suburbanites can reconnect with the soil, sun, and water.

Thus, the formulator industry, under pressure to find new markets in an increasingly constricted sales environment, has come to produce and reproduce an aesthetic of the lawn that associates the preservation of community, family, and environment with the production of monoculture. The rising lawn-chemical purchases by consumers, in a period when other chemical uses are decreasing, coincides with a period of more aggressive and creative marketing.

But to imagine that the formulator industry, by itself, is responsible for the increasing consumption of chemicals and the specific aesthetic and social association of lawnscape production is to overlook a highly localized moral economy. Increased advertising budgets cannot explain the specific character of the emerging aesthetic and its appeal, particularly to collective values. To do so requires a reorientation to local-scale analysis and an understanding of the classed character of consumer communities.

Lawn Aesthetics: Classed Expressions of Community Desire

For the most part, yards are not managed for physical resources, such as food, fuel, or shelter, or for environmental purposes like the control of erosion. Instead, yards are managed for other qualities. Specifically, lawn managers overwhelmingly associate their lawns with the preservation of community, family, and environment.

Lawnscape as participation in community

The results of the survey indicate that lawn managers who use chemicals are more likely to know their neighbors by name than are those who do not use chemicals. Moreover, the majority of the respondents reported that their neighbors used chemicals. [. . .] While most of the respondents reported that their neighbors' practices had no impact or negative impact on the quality of water, most agreed that these practices had a positive impact on both property values, and more significantly, "neighborhood pride."

As a result, intensive lawn management tends to cluster. If one's neighbors use lawn chemicals, then one is more likely to engage in a number of intensive lawn-care practices, including hiring a lawn-care company, using do-it-yourself fertilizers and pesticides, and applying chemicals more frequently if one uses chemicals.

In addition, lawn management, in general, is associated with positive neighborhood relations. People who spend more hours each week working in their yards and report greater enjoyment of lawn work, feel more attached to their local community. Data from the interviews supported the idea that people associate yard work with a sense of neighborly attachment. One 29-year-old male informant explained: "It's nice just to have people on either side of us who are out doing things in their yard, whether they're planting flowers or whatever they're doing. . . . It's more about the neighborhood. That's kind of the reason why we like where we are."

This sense of community action was supported in follow-up interviews, in which the respondents commonly reported an "obligation" to manage their private lawns intensively, not only in defense of their neighbors' property values, but also in support of "positive neighborhood cohesion," "participation," and "holding the neighborhood together." Thus, yard management is not an individual activity; rather, it is done for social purposes: the production of community.

Lawnscape as family space

Second, lawn managers see their yard work as a way to strengthen the traditional nuclear family: family members play an important role in passing on the correct way to maintain a lawn. Among the respondents who used do-it-yourself chemicals of some sort, those who learned about lawn management from a family member were more likely to use chemical fertilizers regularly than were those who learned about lawn management from another source. Data from the interviews also revealed the importance of nuclear family relationships, and many respondents explained the importance of the lawn for family life. When asked why he maintained a lawn, the 29-year-old male respondent did not espouse the virtues of higher property values; instead, he suggested that he managed his lawn for his wife: "Jenny [his wife] loves the house and the neighborhood. She just really enjoys going out and being in the sun and pulling weeds. I guess that's why we have the lawn."

Lawnscape as environment

The third distinctive feature of the production and consumption of lawn is its strong and increasing association as a form of care for the environment. In this regard, chemical users were more likely to worry about the quality of the water and reported a greater willingness to pay for clean water than did nonusers. Lawn managers who seemed the most concerned about the quality of the water were also the most likely to contribute potential pollutants to the water supply in the form of lawn chemicals.

In addition, the respondents often considered working in their yards to be a link between people and the nonhuman world. The belief in yard work as a connection to nonhuman nature was expressed by the respondents, regardless of their lawn-management style. One 47-year-old woman told us: "I really do enjoy being outside. That's really why I do it. . . . It's fun to watch things grow. . . . I'm sure when I retire, I'll find some reason to get out there in the lawn and dig around. It just makes you feel better to be out – in the earth." Another woman in her late 50s described her yard work in glowing terms: "I see my yard as . . . my communion with our environment. It's the way I mark the seasons, the way I reaffirm who I am as a member of the community of earth. I go out and . . . benefit from the wonderful fragrance of the fresh air. . . . The birds just find our yard to be a fabulous feast. . . . I just love the capacities to ever tune in to the way the world works."

In this way, the practices and aesthetics of lawn managers who use inputs are associated with a concern for community, family, and environment. Herbicides that flow off lawns and represent a risk to the good of the community are seen as fundamental to proper community behavior. Lawn chemicals that are potentially harmful to children and collect in carpet dust are viewed as important for the family. Lawn chemicals with potentially detrimental impacts on the ambient environment are understood as taking care of the environment. Chemical users are more likely to be concerned about their neighbors' values and feelings. They are more likely to get their lawn-management information from family members. They are more likely to be concerned about the quality of water. These local actors thus closely resemble the figures who occupy the frozen advertising images of the formulator industry, whose drive for new markets has led to the direct marketing of just such practices and aesthetics. What does this coincidence tell us?

The Moral Economy of the Lawn: Production and Consumption, Public and Private

The relationship of chemical firms and suburban consumers to one another and to the environment and the apparently contradictory practices of lawn production and consumption that result suggest several conclusions both for explaining environmental behaviors and for interpreting landscapes like the lawn. First, the case exposes the difficulty in identifying and isolating sites of production and consumption, showing the mutual coercion and constitution of chemical formulators and lawn managers. Second, it suggests the porousness of public and private spaces and the degree to which their intermingling is fundamental to contemporary cultural and economic practices, characterized by a moral economy of the lawn.

Producing/consuming authentic community, family, and the environment

Materialist theory suggests that consumer desires are forged in the production sector of the economy to maintain levels of surplus. Support for such a view may be drawn from the case of the lawn. Chemical marketers are implicated in the production of desire for the monocultural lawn through unique and powerful marketing programs, essential to the survival of their economic enterprises. Their receipts depend on successfully conveying to nonusers the personal, social, and environmental importance of proper lawn care; formulators produce images that lawn managers consume.

At the same time, however, the drive for the manicured lawn is clearly a result of localized desires for conspicuous performance of class identity: the use of lawn chemicals is positively correlated with household income, level of education, and market value of the home. The creative lawn industry may therefore be seen as simply responding to patterns of locally classed conspicuous consumption whereby the ability to refrain from productive work is demonstrated through rituals that suggest freedom from labor. Agrochemicals, it may be argued, are an essential tool in such rituals, allowing homeowners to project a social landscape of laborious hours spent pulling dandelions, removing insects, and reseeding yards. Lawn managers produce the monocultural lawn in the formation of identity.

The identity derived from production of the lawn is of a specific sort, however, one that accrues status as much to community and collectivity as to individuality. Unlike many conspicuously consumed goods, such as automobiles, the lawn carries the moral weight of participating in a greater community or polity, touching on the relationship of the consumers not only to their families and neighborhoods, but to the broader natural world, over which high-input lawn managers express an explicit sense of stewardship.

These specific goals – community, family, and a "green" environment – may be viewed as a triumvirate of alienated desires. As local communities expire, families fragment, and natural environments are lost, the desire for them grows in an increasingly alienated and individuated society that "goes bowling alone." What is more critical, these desires may be seen as reconsumed fetishes, marketed back to increasingly alienated consumers in the form of "natural" products. In this view, the human need for creativity and productive work, frustrated by the contemporary system of production, makes consumption the last-resort source of personal identity; the lawn is an arena in which alienated homeowners use energy and skill in yard management to recover personal and community identity based on the creation of a specific commodified landscape: the manicured lawn.

Yet this interpretation requires that one posit an "authentic" moment from which family, community, and nature have been lost. Careful historical and ecological scrutiny do not support the existence of any such condition, yet the recapture of that moment commands the attention and capital of homeowners who establish monocultural landscapes for personal and collective gain. That urge to restore lost social-environmental relationships is also a goal of the formulators, whose narrowing margins depend on the increased demand for these moral landscapes of collective desire.

[. . .]

Privately producing public space

In much the same way that production and consumption are enmeshed in the lawn and made difficult to distinguish, the public and private spheres of producer-consumer activity are also hard to distill. By examining the porousness of this boundary, some otherwise-intuitive notions about the American consumer can be called into question.

Specifically, in surveys or interviews, lawn managers rarely emphasize issues of rights to private property, concepts usually stressed in analyses of alienated, industrial, suburban consumers. Rather, it is the public nature of the front yard that is most often championed. Lawn managers consistently speak of "obligations," "community," and "neighborhood pride," rather than "rights," in their explanation of activities and choices. Private spaces are managed as public goods.

Drawing on research in cultural and political ecology, this kind of action, with its simultaneously redistributive and disciplinary implications, recalls the actions of peasants in the "moral economy." According to Scott [*The Moral Economy of the Peasant*, 1976], the moral economy is the collective culture of redistributive obligation in which the risks of failed harvests and poverty are spread through extended villages and families by shared harvests and shared poverty. This economy transcends the neoclassical model of rational household action, demonstrating the emergence of a shared culture of collective good. Ecologics are managed with sensitivity to collective, as well as individual, needs.

Although this analysis depends on an explicitly economic rationale of collective good through shared risk, it makes a convincing bridge between private land management and shared-collective good with implications for the lawn. In their consistent, indeed emphatic, insistence on collective good, suburban peasants redistribute public value through private investment in collective monoculture. As seen from the air, the unbroken spaces of the lawn do, indeed, suggest community parkland, rather than private holdings.

In the process, the lawn inverts the traditional "tragedy of the commons" scenario. Rather than create collective externalities in pursuit of personal gain, lawn managers create personal externalities in pursuit of collective gain. The apparent contradiction (why do lawn owners who are environmentally concerned use chemicals?) is resolved if the actions are seen as resolute markers of collective responsibility.

The implications of this moral economy are several. First, they suggest the harsh and disciplinary regimes that prevent the changing of land-management practices at the local level. The reluctance to disintensify inputs or to allow more heterogeneous ecological landscapes (e.g., dandelions) to flourish is not simply a product of individual choices, time, the optimization of resources, or even individual planning and desire. Rather, it is bound up in the social obligations for the production of public space in the form of the lawn, a landscape that is under constant collective scrutiny and carries great moral weight. In this way, it is difficult to reform.

On the other hand, it opens up opportunities for reform of action, consciousness, and change, especially when we consider cases of other ecological practices in the urban system. Recycling, for example, has been criticized for moving from a rational exercise to one with moralistic overtones, an irrational crusade that brainwashes unsuspecting citizens, especially children. Yet it is the moral reversal, from an ethic of disposal by which materials disappear into the waste stream, to an ethic of recycling, by which geographic and ecological consciousness follows materials through complex life cycles, that makes radical changes in behavior possible. Therefore, the profoundly moral character of the lawn economy may yet be leveraged to produce changing consciousness and practice in the suburbs. Organic lawn-care options increasingly appear both in do-it-yourself form (organic fertilizers, how-to books, and nonpower mowers), as well as in the commercial lawn-care sector, where dozens of organic lawn-care companies have sprung to life in recent years. Thus, the blurred line between the public and the private breaks both ways, allowing both the colonization of "private" life worlds by economic imperatives traveling in the guise of community and new community visions to disturb the status quo of accumulation. An understanding of the political ecology of the lawn thus enables the critical possibility of uniting *meaningful work* with sustainable suburban landscapes.

Chapter 29

Women at Work

Mona Domosh and Joni Seager

In December 1999, in the last session – of the class, the year, the century – of my "Gender, Space, and Environment" course, I (J. S.) cajoled my students into a free-flowing discussion about the future. All of these (then twenty-something) university students recognized that for them, as for their parents, working out their marital or partner relationships would mean that they would have to come to terms with gendered expectations regarding relationships to home and work. In a sign of the times, all the women assumed they would work in the waged workforce, and all the men assumed they would have female partners who would do so. Almost all of them who imagined themselves with an opposite-sex partner also imagined an egalitarian future, in which they and their partners would be *equally* responsible for work, income, home, and children. But when I pressed them for specifics about how they thought they might achieve this parity, the mood turned surlier. Well, they proclaimed, they simply would not settle for/with a partner who didn't share this vision. (I refrained from pointing out that this rosy path had turned into a blind alley for millions who had gone before.) And then I asked the men in the class a pointed question: How many of them would feel uncomfortable with a female partner/wife who earned more – perhaps much more – than they did? Two or three men in the class openly scoffed and said that would be just fine with them, they would have no problem with a "power wife"; another two or three were brave enough to admit that the prospect was discomfiting; the remaining handful shifted uncomfortably in their seats, not committing themselves one way or another.

This discussion was probably broadly representative of how the twenty-first century opens for middle-class North Americans: with high hopes for a

Domosh, Mona and Seager, Joni, "Women at Work," pp. 35–41, 47–50, 52, 60–3 from *Putting Women in Place: Feminist Geographers Make Sense of the World* (New York: Guilford Press, 2001).

harmonious gender future, and for an egalitarianly balanced work–home relationship, yet with a limited understanding of the structures that stand in the way,
and – lingering just beneath the surface – a nagging ambivalence about women's
place (and success) at work.

Issues about "work" occupy a position at the center of gravity of cross-gender
relationships. There is relatively little controversy about *men* working – it is widely
recognized that men do, "should," and always have "worked." (Indeed, to the
extent that there is controversy about men and work today in North America, it
is about men *not* working. The stay-at-home Dad is still viewed as an odd cultural
hybrid, and men who choose this role often struggle for respect.) The relationship
between "women" and "work" is more complex and controversial, and is often a
flashpoint for personal and social conflict between women and men.

Even the most cursory historical and global surveys suggest that when men and
women "work," they do so under different conditions and constraints, they tend
to work at different jobs, and they work in different places. Such differences are
the result of a carefully constructed social calculus – but one that varies over time
and from place to place. For example, the "gendering" of particular jobs reveals
some of the complexities and contradictions about the social construction of work.
Currently, in the United States, clerical work is women's work, while in India most
office clerks are men. In Canada road building is men's work, while in Nepal it's
women's work. On Sri Lankan tea plantations, most tea pickers are women, while
almost all of the tea tasters are men. On commercial banana plantations in Costa
Rica, the banana harvesters are men, the banana washers are women. In the United
States when the telephone switchboard was first developed, the switchboard operator
corps consisted almost exclusively of young men and boys. Within fifty years,
switchboard operator had become an entirely feminized occupation; by the 1990s,
it had switched again, so that now both men and women work as telephone operators. Similarly, typewriting at first was a male job in the United States, but then
quickly became defined as women's work. Computer programming followed the
reverse course: at first it was a woman's job, now it is deeply masculinized. Cooking
in the home is women's work, but the most highly valued and highly paid restaurant
chefs everywhere in the world are men. In the late 1990s in the European Union,
women comprised more than eighty percent of all secretaries, nurses, and elementary school teachers; in the United States at the same time, women represented
ninety-eight percent of secretaries, ninety-two percent of bookkeepers, and ninety
percent of nursing aides.

How do we make sense of these seemingly capricious and chaotic gendered
identifications? Sometimes we can't. But if we look closely, we can see common
presumptions that weave throughout the differences and that paint a broad picture
of the ways in which "work" is so often different for men and for women:

- Some version of a sexual division of labor appears to be evident in virtually
  all societies throughout the historical record; the Industrial Revolution,
  however, codified "work" (and "nonwork") in distinctive and enduring ways
  that were then replicated around the world with the spread of industrial
  capitalism.

- Relatively few jobs are gender-neutral: *most* work is defined as either "men's work" or "women's work" (although the particulars of these designations can and do change).
- Only work for wages (or within the cash economy) is defined as "work."
- Much of what women do to contribute to the economy is defined as "not-work."
- Men are seen to have the primary prerogative (or "need") to undertake work for wages; and/or it is men's prerogative to control the money that comes into the household from participation in the cash economy. Women "shouldn't" earn more than men, nor "take jobs away from" men.
- Assumptions about "natural" affinities (temperamental, biological, cultural) of men and women – or of *some* men and women of a particular age, race, class – shape the definition of men's and women's work.
- Men occupy the best paying, highest prestige jobs; almost by definition if women are doing it, it's neither.

By focusing on the *spatial* conveyances or containers of ideologies about women's and men's "place," a geographical curiosity illuminates particular dimensions of the gendering of work. [. . .] *Where* work occurs has considerable influence on whether it is considered to be "work" or not and on whether it is counted as work or not. Finally, a gendered geography of work focuses our attention on the ways in which certain work*places* are defined as appropriate or inappropriate places for women to be.

What is Work?

The emergence of industrial capitalism and the ideology of "separate spheres" assigned women, at least in principle, to the private home sphere, and men to the public work sphere. The definition of "work" as an exclusively waged activity that was to be complemented by a nonwaged household support system was central to the ideological – and actual – development of industrial capitalism. The benefits of this system to capitalism are myriad, and one can see how this work/nonwork dichotomy evolved as a powerful new economic system that generated considerable profits for the capitalists. Among other things, for the payment of one wage the employer got a wage earner plus an entire unpaid support system.

But economic imperatives alone don't fully explain this work/nonwork dichotomy. Why it is *men* who came to be associated with work and workplaces and *women* who come to be associated with nonwork and the household is not explained solely by capitalism. Feminist analysis suggests that the configuration of work in this *particularly* gendered way is so universal and so enduring because it suits not just capitalism, but patriarchy. Simply put, this dualism creates an economic dependence of women on men – which enhances the power and privilege of men, even of relatively ordinary and not very powerful men.

Feminist geographers add to this analysis by drawing attention to the spatial system that makes "patriarchal capitalism" possible: the geographic separation of work from home, city from suburb, (paid) workplace production from (unpaid) household production, and the myriad zoning laws, property laws, mortgage systems, and transportation networks that facilitate these arrangements. In a key article, Ann Markusen (1980) outlined the ways in which both patriarchy *and* capitalism benefit from the spatial arrangement that separates men's work from women's nonwork. For example, she argues that defining an ideal home by the absence of waged work ensures that the economic well-being of the home depends on male wages; this positions men as the "natural" heads of households. Confining women to homes in residential locations isolated from work opportunities ensures their economic and social dependence on individual men. The ideal of a nonwaged (female) worker supporting the individual material needs and desires of each waged (male) worker is an inefficient use of the woman's labor, but it maximizes the comfort of the male in the household – that is, providing meals to order, on an individual schedule, makes life comfortable for men but squanders women's labor and time. The single-family, suburban dwelling discourages extended family or community sharing of housework, and advances the interests of capitalism by maximizing consumption and the purchase of goods for the household. (It is no coincidence that feminist and socialist utopias almost always reconfigure the spatial separation of work and home. Noncapitalist and feminist designs for reimagining urban spaces almost always feature collective living of some kind, and designs that allow for the integration of work and residential activities. They also reorder household support systems by promoting, for example, collective child-care or cooking arrangements, and shared household technology.)

However, the convergence of capitalism and patriarchy on particular configurations of work and home, while ideologically powerful, is imperfectly executed. On paper, capitalist patriarchy may look good, as it were, but in real life it's not so easy to pull off. There are gaping contradictions between the ideology (of how women and men are "supposed" to relate to work and to each other) and the reality. For example, the removal of women from waged work is, in fact, not practical; the assumption that a single household should be supported by a single (male) wage is largely unachievable given other priorities in capitalism (such as paying workers the lowest possible wages). In addition, the assumption that most people do or will live in nuclear families in individual households is erroneous. Further, the benefits to men of the patriarchal division of gendered labor, of the subordination of women to their needs, and of the banning of women from waged work are easily overstated. Many men chafe at the roles that this ideology assigns them; being the breadwinner and stoic standard bearer is wearing. The confinement of women in households dominated by men, removed from wage-earning possibilities, has social, cultural, financial, and emotional limits for *both* men and women.

Even the central prop of capitalist patriarchy, the assumption that women don't, won't, or shouldn't "work," is flawed. In fact, what women do in the home is in most instances quite "work-like." Most women need to (and want to) participate in the public sphere, and a substantial proportion of women do now and have always worked for wages. When viewed in terms of the ways that people really live their lives and what they do inside and outside the home, rather than through ideology and rhetoric, the dividing line between "work" and "home" appears more fuzzy than sharp.

However, while this "ideal" system in its purest expression may be unattainable in the real world, economic and cultural elites have invested too much in the ideology to let it go. Instead of giving up the game, they focus considerable attention on papering over the gaps. The biggest gap between rhetoric and reality is the fact that most women, like most men, do "work" most of the time. But because so much of the modern Western social order has been predicated on sustaining the myth that women don't work (or *shouldn't*) work, there has been energetic ideological maneuvering to define away or minimize women's work. The success of this effort is evident in the fact that, almost everywhere, women's work is defined either as less serious than men's or simply as nonwork. The rhetorical and ideological devices deployed to minimize or "domesticate" women's work include:

- Defining "work" only as those activities that involve cash or other wage exchange, and simultaneously defining work in the home as an act of loyalty, duty, or "love" (and thus as nonwork).
- Defining waged work as a temporary stage for women: it is fine for young women to work, but once they marry they should stop. Or, in times of crises such as "manpower" shortages during wars, women's work is acceptable, but once the crisis is over women should return the jobs to the men and themselves to the home.
- Diluting the reality of women at work by defining certain jobs as "naturally" feminized. Sewing, for example, is often defined as a natural extension of women's feminine affinities, so when they do this they remain cocooned within a realm of acceptable female activity.
- Defining some women – by race, ethnicity, or national origin – as "naturally" suited to some work, thus liberating and protecting the femininity of other women from the necessity of engaging in that work. The black mammy in 1920s America, the Jamaican nanny in 1980s Toronto, and the Filipina maid in 1990s Hong Kong are good examples of this process.
- Defining work (for wages) as defeminizing and coarsening, and/or defining women who undertake certain work as defeminized and coarse. Calling into question the femininity of women who defy social norms by actively seeking and enjoying certain work (for example, driving trucks, reporting on sports, building bridges).
- Defining the necessity to work as a misfortune, one that all women of all classes could aspire to overcome, and construing the nonworking wife as a sign of successful upward social and class mobility.
- Prohibiting *some* kinds of women (e.g., pregnant or married women) from waged "public" work.
- Prohibiting *all* women from some kinds of work (such as military combat or mining or airplane piloting).
- Keeping women in the home by bringing work for wages inside; most industrial economies depend on "homework," such as home sewing or light assembly.

- Creating cultural angst about the extent to which the psychological and physical well-being of children requires them to be raised by a full-time stay-at-home mother.
- Constructing social policy to support this angst – through tax systems, maternity leave policies, provision (or lack thereof) of publicly funded child-care.

But how is "work" really made into "nonwork"? It would not be possible to define away women's work as nonwork by ideology or rhetoric alone. Indeed, the ways in which work is made into nonwork are more tangible than that – large bureaucratic, cultural, and spatial structures are brought to bear to sustain this deceit. Among the most important of these are national and international systems of economic and demographic accounting: censuses and "national accounts" systems.

[. . .]

Footloose Factories and Nimble Fingers: The New Industrial Order

One might think that the prevailing ideologies of "appropriate" femininity would keep women out of factory work. Work in an industrial factory is often dirty, dangerous, and may involve heavy machinery. The factory is usually a place where men are found in great numbers. All of these factors "should" exclude women from such workplaces. However, industrial production brings toe to toe the competing demands of patriarchy ("Women 'should' stay at home to provide the support system for their working husbands") and capitalism ("We need workers who will do tedious work without complaint and to whom we can pay the lowest wages"). These competing impulses are reconciled by defining *some* factory work as "naturally" feminized.

Industrial production, from its start, has depended on women's labor. Women have been a significant part of the industrial labor force from the time of the very first factories in 1700s Great Britain. In the early British industrial model of textile mills, which was also adopted in the United States, whole families were hired by mill owners. Typically, families moved into mill villages and lived in tenements owned by the company; all members of the family, including children over about age six, worked in the mill. Women were the preferred workers in certain parts of these factories – for example, in the sorting, weaving, and spinning rooms of textile mills.

In the "Lowell model" of industrialization, developed in Massachusetts in the early 1800s, women – without their families – were even more central in the industrial labor force. In rural New England at this time, there was virtually no "surplus" male labor: immigrants were few, and most US-born men were engaged in agriculture or commerce. To fill their factories, Lowell and his partners instituted a system that brought in a rotating workforce of young, unmarried women from rural New England. To overcome the prejudice against women undertaking factory work, Lowell provided company-run boardinghouses, overseen by matrons who enforced the company's paternalistic policies of strict curfews, mandatory church attendance, and abstinence. The "Lowell mill girls" have become an icon of early industrialization. By the beginning of the nineteenth century women's labor was firmly in place at the core of factory production. By the late nineteenth century, mills became less dependent on female labor as a male immigrant labor force became available.

More than a century later, the new industrial economy at the end of the twentieth century seems far removed from the mills of Lowell and Manchester. But the geographies that define, contain, and shape the new economy – global production sites, homework venues, sweatshops – and the ways in which these geographies are gendered are simultaneously very old.

The geography – literally, the distribution – of industrial production has changed dramatically over the last forty years or so. Perhaps the single best defining characteristic of the new economy is that production is now scattered around the globe: industries have become "footloose," and production sites are fluid. While the brilliance of the "original" Industrial Revolution was in bringing together company headquarters, research, and production all under one roof, success in the "new" industrial revolution depends on constantly shifting production in search of the cheapest labor. The map of production and consumption is now complex and dense with labels from around the world. US car manufacturers produce cars in Brazil and Mexico; Japanese computer companies farm out chip production to factories in Malaysia; the French soccer team kicks around balls sewn in Pakistan. In the 1980s most Americans were wearing sneakers made in South Korea; by the 1990s, they are made in China. Most Europeans are wearing clothes stitched in Sri Lanka, Vietnam, or Indonesia. In the new industrial system, the headquarters and research-and-development side of business typically stays in the corporate home country in the First World, while assembly and production has been shifted to the Third World.

One of the most distinctive features on the new globalized industrial landscape is the 'export processing zone" (EPZ). EPZs are industrial zones – literal, demarcated areas, typically fenced off and gated – put aside for production by foreign companies. More than sixty countries, mostly in the Third World, have established EPZs. Host governments encourage foreign companies to locate in EPZs by offering a range of inducements, such as tax holidays, or waivers of labor laws for factories inside the zones. EPZs (and their Mexican and Central American equivalents, *maquiladoras*) are the entryways for industrial development in countries at the periphery of the global economy. EPZs are the heartlands of the global economy. As zones where the host government has an explicit commitment to and a vested interest in providing a cheap, placid labor force for foreign investors, they are also sites of considerable exploitation and labor repression.

Geographers have been prominent in mapping and describing these shifts in the global economy, although until recently little attention was paid to the gendered dimensions of the new economic realities. But a gendered division of labor is deeply embedded in the global economy. Indeed, it's hard to explain how the global economy functions without paying attention to the gendered division of labor that sustains the new world order. The EPZ and *maquiladora* heartlands are feminized places The "global assembly line" of export-oriented industry (whether in an EPZ or not) runs largely on women's labor. Most of the workers sewing Nike sneakers in China, cleaning microchips in Malaysia, or assembling blue jeans in the Philippines are women. [. . .] Recent surveys show that women constitute more than eighty percent of the industrial workforce in EPZs in Mexico, Taiwan, Sri Lanka, Malaysia, and the Philippines, and more than seventy percent of the workforce in South Korea and Guatemala. More particularly, the global assembly line runs on the labor of *young, unmarried* women.

Why women? Employment practices vary from EPZ to EPZ, within and between countries, so generalizations need to be constantly checked out on the ground, but there is a "package" of gender assumptions and stereotypes that typifies employment practices in export-oriented industries. Precisely because of all the ambivalence around women and "work," women have been construed as the ideal flexible labor force in the new industrial regime. Because work is not considered to be primary in women's lives, they can be paid less than men. In economies where formal-sector jobs are scarce, and where women are excluded from many of the nonfactory jobs that might be available, there is a vast pool of women workers eager for employment in the new factories of the Third World. Under these conditions, the female labor force can be continually renewed, such that older (and more expensive) workers are replaced with fresh, cheaper, recruits (reminiscent of the Lowell system). Young, single women are assumed to have fewer family responsibilities that would distract them from their jobs, but also will be more likely to have high rates of voluntary turnover due to the demands imposed when they get married or have children. Women are considered to be a "disposable" labor force: they can be hired or fired at will because a job is not supposed to be a permanent feature of women's lives, and employment is not supposed to be for a lifetime. Cheap, flexible, and replaceable, women have become the ideal labor pool in the new global economy.

There is also an even more distinctive rationale often touted by managers for hiring women to work the assembly lines, especially in electronics production: their "nimble fingers." Many managers claim that women have smaller fingers than men, greater dexterity, more patience and are more tolerant of tedium – and are thus naturally good at jobs requiring the delicate assembly of small parts. The "nimble fingers" explanation for global investment also clearly plays on racial stereotypes. In the 1970s, just as the global economy was poised for lift-off, an official Malaysian brochure to entice foreign investment proclaimed: "The manual dexterity of the Oriental female is famous the world over. Her hands are small and she works with extreme care. Who therefore could be better qualified by nature and inheritance to contribute to the efficiency of a production line than the Oriental girl?" The convergence of racist and sexist stereotypes is a powerful factor in explaining the particular geography of multinational footlooseness – and it may explain, in part, why assembly production first went to Asia, and not, for example, to Africa. (The representation of Asian women as bright, docile, pliable, and eager to please is a palpable cultural presence in the Western "orientalist" imagination; there is no comparable imagining of African women in which they would be constructed in the Western view as an "ideal" factory workforce.)

A close ideological relative to the "nimble fingers" explanation for why women are preferred workers on electronics assembly lines is another explanation that garment-factory managers often invoke: that sewing comes "naturally" to women, or is one of their "traditional" activities. The "natural tendencies" argument is a key rationale for labor exploitation: managers can pay workers less for a skill that is merely "natural" (as opposed to an acquired skill, one that is the result of training and learning and application, for which workers will need to be rewarded).

There is room for feminist debate about the extent to which women's work in the EPZs and factories of the global economy represents an opportunity for women, or unremitting exploitation of them. The new global economy has brought new jobs to places where none previously existed; factory work offers women opportunities to escape narrow social and economic confines, it gives women some discretionary income, and it allows women to extend their social and political networks through workplace contacts. As feminist geographers have pointed out, "Waged work spaces . . . create opportunities for gender identities to be renegotiated, perhaps even to be reconstituted, and in which new forms of femininity might emerge." In many instances, women have "found their voices" and have developed skills and confidence through organizing and collaborating with fellow workers.

[. . .]

Gender in the Work*place*

[. . .]

Geographers Susan Hanson and Gerry Pratt argue that distance helps to create a sex-differentiated job market because men and women do not have equal resources to overcome the "friction" of distance. In other words, finding jobs and getting to work is usually more difficult for women than for men. This helps explain the segregation of jobs. Hanson and Pratt also focus attention on the role of job-information networks in employment: while many economists suggest that the job search is a rational and linear purposeful activity, Hanson and Pratt find that most people find jobs through informal social contacts and "accidents of place." Job information circulates through local geographies and networks. To the extent that men's and women's daily geographies are different, so will be their job search process and access to information about jobs. In particular, Hanson and Pratt found that women who learn about jobs from other women are more likely to end up in female-dominated jobs. Concomitantly, they found that women who have broken into male-dominated jobs learned about those jobs through *male* family members. This geographical network-based analysis illuminates the ways in which sex-based occupational patterns are created and perpetuated.

Geography is important in other ways (both literally and metaphorically) in the segregation of men's and women's work. In most cultures, there are work*places* from which women are prohibited – sometimes by law, sometimes by "social policing." In the recent labor history of the United States and Great Britain, for example, women have been excluded by law from working in mines, piloting commercial airplanes, driving tanks in the army, and doing most maritime jobs. Around the world, in industrial economies, social and cultural policing has kept women out of the dock-yards, off oil rigs, out of the ranks of orchestra conductors, off the stock market trading floor, on the fringes of most industrial trades (plumbing, electrical work, printing, machine tooling), and out of most scientific and engineering professions.

It is important – and not coincidental – to note that many of these men-only (or mostly male) occupations are among the highest paying. On the flip side of the coin, most women-dominated occupations (which includes nursing, teaching in primary schools, bank telling, or clerical work [in the United States]) are neither high-prestige nor high-paying jobs. Men who breach gender barriers to take up "women's work" face real social penalties – male nurses, child-care workers, or secretaries often find their masculinity called into question, or their motives sus-pected. Women who step into men's workplaces are subjected to the same social scrutiny, but additionally face sexual harassment, violence or threats of violence, and daily on-the-job hostility – sometimes of the severest sort.

Women's presence in workplaces that are deemed to be men's is disquieting – to individual men, to a collective (heterosexual) masculine identity, and to a broader sense of social order. In her study of the exclusion of women from merchant banking in Britain, geographer Linda McDowell makes the point that the very presence of women in the banking profession forces men "to face their preconcep-tions and privileged position and to deal with issues they define as 'private.'" McDowell suggests that as we enter the twenty-first century, an *increasing* share of jobs involve the marketing of personal attributes – the smile of the airline atten-dant, for example – and that this is especially true of women's jobs. It is still the case – and perhaps increasingly so – that women have to present a particular "look" and body performance for job success. Especially when women enter men's occupa-tions and workplaces, they have to walk a fine line: between making a convincing display of their commitment to conventional feminine and heterosexual attributes on the one hand (to avoid being accused of being lesbians, man haters, or "ball-busters") and, on the other hand, suppressing feminine traits and activities that may make their male colleagues especially uncomfortable (not breastfeeding infants in the workplace, not crying or being too "emotional," adopting a masculinist version of self on the job). This often means that women have to accept a high level of "teasing" on the job; they have to fine-tune their dress code (the woman lawyer's standard scarf-tie, for example, resembling closely enough a male tie to signify professional decorum, but floppy and bow-like enough to be feminine); and they have to not stand up too often for "women's issues." If women sometimes have a difficult time constructing a stable and appropriate sexual and gender identity in the workplace it is usually because they are not "supposed" to be there.

Gender, race, and class create different spatial experiences for people in the workplace, even in the same environmental setting. For example, architect Leslie Weisman "deconstructs" a typical US office skyscraper. From top to bottom, the white-collar office workers and the blue-collar maintenance workers inhabit dis-tinct, barely touching, zones of the tower. The assignment of private space reflects hierarchy: secretaries (mostly female) typically are assigned to "open" floor-plan space, while executives (mostly male) are buffered by receptionists, doors, and locks. The assignment of space and light is similarly indexed to one's gender-based occupational status: interior, windowless, fluorescent-lit space is invariably allocated to clerical workers (predominantly women), exterior offices with natural light and views to executives (mostly men). Weisman quotes a study from the 1970s that showed that women receive the same proportion of office space as they do pay, about twenty to fifty percent less than men doing the same work in the same office. In 1999, a group of female scientists at the Massachusetts Institute of Technology forced the administration there to admit to years of discrimination against women. The discrimination took several forms, but closely twinned were the same space: pay continuum that Weisman noticed: women on the science faculties were paid less than their male counterparts and were allocated smaller laboratory space – in about the same proportions!

Because of work*place* segregation of men and women, legislation that mandates equal pay between men and women has a limited effect on closing the earnings gap. In the 1980s, feminists crafted an alternative legislative and conceptual approach to this problem, focusing on "equity" rather than "equality." Rather than simply saying, for example, that male secretaries and female secretaries must be paid equally, the "comparable worth" approach assigns equivalent value to jobs across gender-segregated categories – assigning "equal worth," for example, to secretaries (mostly women) and to painters (mostly men), or comparing the worth of librarians (mostly women) to that of sports coaches (mostly men). Comparable worth legislation exists in only a handful of countries, but in 1999 the Canadian government took a bold step forward in making comparable worth a workplace reality. "Equal pay for work of equal value" is written into Canada's Human Rights Act, but it had languished there for almost two decades until legal action by a group of women federal workers forced the hand of the government. In late 1999, the Canadian government agreed to pay back wages (in the amount of more that $2 billion) to redress the gender inequity caused by occupational segregation and by the failures of equal pay legislation to achieve gender equity.

Part VII

The Geography of Development and Underdevelopment

Introduction

William G. Moseley and Kavita Pandit

Geographers and other social scientists have long been concerned with the social and economic inequities that exist between countries and regions. Their work has contributed to our understanding of development, generally defined both as a process by which a nation improves the economic and social well-being of its citizens and as the outcome of this process. Scholars from different disciplines such as economics, sociology, anthropology, and political science have brought different perspectives to the study of development; the distinctive contribution of geographers is that they view the process in a broad and holistic framework that meshes the human and environmental attributes of a country with its unique historical legacy and its interconnections with other countries.

Although the term is widely used, the conceptualization of development as a process has changed over time and continues to be highly contentious. The idea of development became popular in the 1950s when many former colonial possessions began to gain independence. For these countries, the post-World War II success of the Marshall Plan in Europe became the model to follow. As a result, development in the 1950s and 1960s emphasized GNP per capita growth through investment in key economic sectors and infrastructure projects, expert-driven technical exchange, and reliance on open markets. This development approach or model was termed "modernization" and was associated with scholars such as Walter Rostow, who wrote a highly influential article titled "The Stages of Economic Development" in 1959.

By the 1970s it became clear that, despite several decades of effort, many Third World countries were not experiencing the type of development predicted by modernization theory. Indeed, in several of these countries, conditions of poverty and inequality had worsened. Another group of scholars began to assert that modernization simply reinforced historical colonial patterns as the only way poor countries could raise investment capital was to continue exporting crops and raw materials to the industrialized nations. Writers like Frank[1] asserted that this triggered a process of underdevelopment because the cost of poor countries' primary sector exports was driven down over time while they were forced to pay for expensive manufactured imports from the industrialized nations. Wallerstein[2] used this framework to arrive at a "world-system" comprising a core, semi-periphery, and periphery, spatially presenting a pattern of industrialized (or core) nations that were developed at the expense of Third World (or peripheral) countries that supplied them with raw materials. Semi-peripheral countries were those that shared attributes of both groups. According to Frank and Wallerstein, the nature of the world-system doomed efforts by the countries of the periphery to develop their economies.

This critique of the modernization project has been termed variously the structuralist, dependency, or world-systems approach. It suggests that instead of primary export-led growth, countries in the periphery should strive to become self-sufficient in manufactured goods by imposing high taxes or tariffs on imports of industrial goods, combined with the nationalization of key industries as a means of breaking the cycle of dependence on core countries. More broadly, though, the term structuralist is now used to refer to any approach that recognizes that development inequalities are brought about by an interconnected global system in which the development of some countries occurs at the expense of others. The first article in this section, by Grant and Nijman, titled "The Re-scaling of Uneven Development in Ghana and India," is a good example of this perspective, with the authors suggesting that contemporary globalization trends have accentuated processes of uneven development in Ghana and India.

The late 1980s and early 1990s brought about the breakup of the Soviet Union and a switch to free market approaches in many former socialist and communist countries. The state-centered model of development advocated by structuralists fell into increasing disfavor, and development policy took a neoliberal turn, with an emphasis on the reduction in the size of government, privatization of state-owned industries, elimination of price controls and subsidies, and promotion of exports through the devaluation of currency. This package of policy prescriptions, termed structural adjustment, was heavily promoted by international lending agencies like the World Bank and the International Monetary Fund (IMF) as difficult but necessary "medicine" to enable the developing countries to strengthen their economies. Now, after over twenty years of structural adjustment programs and only dubious results in most instances, the critiques of this approach have begun to multiply. The article by Cupples, entitled "Rural Development in El Hatillo, Nicaragua: Gender, Neoliberalism, and Environmental Risk," is in part a critique of structural adjustment. The article also describes how rural women are facing up to the development challenges of their region. This last point is important because one concern about the older structuralist literature on development is that it failed to recognize the ability, or agency, of local people to play a significant role in shaping the development process.

Finally, a growing number of scholars have proposed alternative approaches to development that go beyond the structuralist versus neoliberal dualism. The article by Bebbington and Bebbington, entitled "Development Alternatives: Practice, Dilemmas, and Theory," examines alternative development scholarship. The authors critique theories of alternative development and argue that development scholars must engage with real-world policy. This article also touches on the role of non-governmental organizations (NGOs) in the development process, a vaguely defined type of development actor that proliferated massively in the 1980s and 1990s. This is also the type of development work that Batterbury enthusiastically describes and endorses in his article on the West African Sahel. Some have questioned whether increasing calls for participation and development alternatives represent real change, or a simple repackaging of development without addressing fundamental structural issues of inequality and power.

Another reaction to the failure of neoliberal economic reform has been the rise of "new economic geography." The great irony is that the largest number of scholars in this rapidly emerging subfield are development economists, not geographers. Economists operating in this arena claim to have rediscovered the importance of geography and are using this to explain why, despite neoliberal economic reform, some areas of the Global South continue to experience lackluster development performance. The concern of many geographers is that this approach may essentially attribute difference in development performance to "nature." This is a problem because it obscures the power differentials within and between nations, and unfair trading relationships, that have a tremendous influence on development trajectories. These opposing arguments are nicely summarized in an opinion piece in this section, entitled "Geography, Culture, and Prosperity," by Andres Oppenheimer.

From these readings it becomes clear that no single theory can fully explain why geographical differences in development persist across the globe. However, taken together, they give us a rich picture of the many factors that contribute to development and the complex task of defining this process, provoking us to continue working in this important area.

NOTES

1. A. Frank, *Dependent Accumulation and Underdevelopment* (New York: Monthly Review Press, 1979).
2. I. M. Wallerstein, *The Capitalist World Economy: Essays* (New York: Cambridge University Press, 1979).

DISCUSSION READINGS

Grant, Richard & Nijman, Jan. (2004). "The Re-scaling of Uneven Development in Ghana and India." *Tijdschrift voor Economische en Sociale Geografie*, 95(5): 467–81.
Bebbington, A. J. & Bebbington, D. H. (2001). "Development Alternatives: Practice, Dilemmas, and Theory." *Area*, 33(1): 7–17.
Cupples Julie. (2004). "Rural Development in El Hatillo, Nicaragua: Gender, Neoliberalism, and Environmental Risk." *Singapore Journal of Tropical Geography*, 25(3): 343–57.
Batterbury, Simon. (1996). "The Sahel of West Africa: A Place for Geographers?" *Geography*, 81(353): 391–5.
Oppenheimer, Andres. (2000). "Geography, Culture, and Prosperity." *Miami Herald*. P. B-9.

Chapter 30

The Re-Scaling of Uneven Development in Ghana and India

Richard Grant and Jan Nijman

Introduction

For quite some time now, pervasive state-centric perspectives in the social sciences have been under fire by critics. Geographers have played an important role in these debates and they have led attempts to articulate and conceptualise alternative spatial scales and units of analysis. The surge in research on the theme of globalisation in more recent years has underscored the significance of the spatial dimensions of social relations 'above' and 'below' the state.

In this paper, we argue that the acceleration in trends of economic globalisation in recent decades has simultaneously exacerbated uneven development among places and led to a re-scaling of uneven development. In other words, it is not simply matter of given places becoming more uneven – rather, entirely new places or regions are created and recreated, giving way to more dynamic and volatile economic geographies. What this means, then, is that it is increasingly important to investigate trends of uneven development, theoretically and empirically, at a variety of spatial scales.

Current research has only just begun to reveal these complexities, and we are still far from reaching a consensus on the emerging patterns. In the words of Neil Smith: 'The solidity of the geography of twentieth century capitalism at various scales has melted; habitual spatial assumptions about the world have evaporated . . . Putting the jig-saw puzzle back together – in practice as well as theory – is a highly contested affair'.

We think that these unresolved questions about the spatial outcomes of globalisation explain, in part, the inconclusiveness of more general debates about the

Grant, Richard and Nijman, Jan, "The Re-scaling of Uneven Development in Ghana and India," pp. 467–78 from *Tijdschrift voor Economische en Sociale Geografie*, 95.5 (2004).

positives and negatives of globalisation. Such inconclusiveness is especially salient in debates about development in less prosperous region of the world. For example, in a recent IMF report, on one page it is stated that 'the distribution of income among countries has become more unequal' and that 'the gaps may have narrowed'. It is also stated that, despite 'unparalleled growth', 'far too many people are losing ground'.

And yet, while empirical knowledge about the spatial dimensions of economic development is scant, there appears to have been a strong policy orientation in most of the developing world in support of what has been termed 'regional push': the active government support for spatially concentrated economic growth poles or regions, based on the assumption that such regional engines of growth will drive the larger national territorial economy to higher levels of development. Such policies are part of a more general strategy that emphasises de-regulation, liberalisation, and an embrace of the free market.

Such policies are, of course, reminiscent of more dated notions of cumulative causation and growth pole theories, and more generally of neo-classical or liberal ideological persuasions. But times have changed. The increased exposure to external economic forces in the global era implies faster change, less governmental control and less certainty than ever before. Hence, the regional push phenomenon may become more spectacular in its potential, but so may its less desirable potential corollaries of inequality, territorial fragmentation and volatility.

By definition, things are not the same everywhere. We focus our attention on two specific regions in the periphery of the world economy: Ghana and India. Both countries are traditionally considered 'underdeveloped', and both have undergone substantial policies of economic liberalisation since the mid-1980s. As a consequence of these policy changes, Ghana and India represent comparable 'laboratories' in which to examine the spatial impact of globalisation. We postulate that peripheral zones of the world economy that have recently been drawn (more intensively) into the capitalist global system and are particularly prone to a dramatic restructuring of their space-economies.

In our research on Ghana and India, we have tried to mine the existing appropriate available data on economic growth and development pertaining to various geographical scales. The comparability of data over time and across spatial units is critical, but this also means that data availability to some degree has to steer the research and that it is difficult to go beyond more or less established administrative units (states, districts, etc.). Nevertheless, the findings are quite significant and point to what we believe is a hyper-differentiation of space at various geographical scales inside Ghana and India.

There are five parts to the rest of this paper. First, we present a general theoretical argument on the re-scaling of uneven development in the global. This is followed by a brief section in which we discuss the cases of Ghana and India in the context of their sweeping economic policy reversals that opened the doors to economic globalisation. Subsequently, we illustrate our argument with data at a variety of scales in both countries. Finally, we turn to some implications of our findings for regional planning and economic policies in Ghana, India and beyond.

The Re-scaling of Uneven Development

We view economic globalisation as a process that is essentially driven by a search for profits and that is first and foremost expressed in the increasing mobility of capital. The search for investment opportunities has been a constant factor since the inception of the capitalist world economy some five centuries ago. But the process of globalisation, while progressive in the long run, has not been a linear one. It has been characterised by sudden accelerations, periods of stagnation, eras of steady advancement and times of regression.

In general terms, the process has been conditioned by two additional factors aside from the ceaseless drive for capital accumulation. One relates to innovations in transport and communication technologies that enable accelerations of globalisation. Examples include steamships and the telegraph in the latter part of the nineteenth century and mass air travel and telecommunications in the latter part of the twentieth century. If capital accumulation is the primary driver of the process, technology is the primary facilitator. The third factor involves the potential mediator of the process: government policies. Governments can interfere in the market, impose regulations, impede the mobility of capital (and labour), or enable capital's free movement. Over time, state governments have altered their roles *vis-à-vis* the market: switching from spoilers to sponsors of the process of globalisation. Even though there is notable variation among different states in the world, there have been general trends across the system. For example, in the late nineteenth and early twentieth century liberalism prevailed across the advanced economies of the world. This came to an abrupt end, again across the system, with the onset of the First World War.

The acceleration in the process of globalisation since about 1980 is the combined result of these two factors: technological innovation (mass air travel, global communications and falling transport costs) and a powerful surge of transnational liberalism among an unprecedented number of countries around the world. Advances in communications technology (telephone, fax, e-mail and video conferencing) have facilitated co-ordination of capital accumulation in diverse locations around the world. Just as significant as technological developments were the changes in government policies that took place in major national economies like the United States, United Kingdom and Germany as well in some smaller countries such as the Netherlands and Sweden around and after 1980. By the latter part of the 1980s, the trend toward transnational liberalism had culminated in the 'Washington consensus'.

The introduction of liberalisation policies across the developing world ushered in the forces of globalisation. Since then, academics and policy-makers have debated the outcomes. There are two dominant views of globalisation in the social sciences that we think are erroneous. First, globalisation is generally, and incorrectly, understood as a historical process in which time increasingly prevails over space. In much thought about globalisation, space is reduced to distance and relative distance is translated in time. For instance, the hyper-mobility of capital in the age of globalisation is often thought to have diminished or even eradicated the meaning of distance.

A second strand of thought, equally fallacious, views the world as increasingly homogeneous in economic and cultural terms. Proponents of this perspective emphasise the scaling up from the national to the global scale of the idea of 'modernisation', meaning that common global norms about markets, business practices, consumptions standards and cultural practices are spreading everywhere.

We argue that globalisation is in essence a geographical concept. We acknowledge the emergence of a new global economy and its geographical structure in the recent round of globalisation. In our definition, globalisation refers to a process of re-scaling. It is the re-scaling of economic relations so that these relations are increasingly conditioned at larger scales. This is not to imply that smaller scales matter less in an absolute sense. Rather we recognise that economic processes must increasingly be understood at a variety of scales, from restricted local scales all the way to the global scale. The latter represents the end, or rather culmination, of a scale spectrum that includes international regions, territorial states, sub-state regions, cities and towns, and neighbourhoods. Once the process of globalisation is conceived as one of re-scaling, it follows that geography is as much in flux as history is. Geography is never static and, like history, its significance never expires. Thus, geography does not become less relevant, but it does become more complex.

The increased mobility of capital is in part the result of market de-regulation in many parts of the world. We think that the most dramatic accelerations of uneven development in this era of globalisation occur in peripheral regions of the world economy. These kinds of regions, we argue, have become characterised by a hyper-differentiation of economic space, which forms a logical accompaniment of the hyper-mobility of capital or of the hyper-volatility of financial markets. The reproduction of space has accelerated to unprecedented levels.

The notion of hyper-differentiation of space comprise more than conventional definitions of uneven development. To be sure, in recent times, certain regions of the global economy have become more unevenly developed, but the hyper-differentiation of space involves both quantitative change and qualitative transformations. There is increased economic divergence among certain places, but in addition there is an ongoing re-configuration and re-division of the global space-economy at a variety of scales. In other words, not only is the developmental gap increasing among existing economic spaces, there is also a rapid creation and re-creation of entirely new spaces, much along the lines of Harvey's argument of the 'spatial fix'. Increases in spatial differentiation are especially salient where the state retreats markedly from established dominance over the market, that is, where it substantially changes its policy from market interference to laissez-faire and does so at a time of high global mobility of capital. In such circumstances, spatial differentiation will be wrought at once by domestic and foreign capital. Hyper-differentiation takes shape simultaneously at various scales and is expressed in the economic fracturing and re-division of conventional spatial entities, such as national states, regions, provinces, and cities.

In the rest of this paper, we substantiate our argument with evidence from India and Ghana. The common characteristic of these countries (critical for our purpose) is the profound change in central government policies around the middle of the 1980s, away from a pronounced regulatory regime to a free market. As such, both countries exposed themselves rapidly to global market forces, and they were, differentially, swept up in the tide of economic globalisation. Ghana and India are similar, then, in their histories of the recent international political economy: moving from colonialism, to 'nationalism', to globalism. The two countries are very different in terms of size, physical geography, culture, main economic activities and regional context. It is a good pair, therefore, to examine the pervasive effects of global capitalism.

Ghana and India in Global Context

After independence (India in 1947 and Ghana in 1957), national development policies and ideological perspectives in the two countries were quite similar. Nkrumah and Nehru, respectively, articulated a nonaligned position in world affairs and promoted national economic policies of self-reliance. An elaboration of the nature of these policies and of their effects on the economic geographies of the two countries is beyond the scope of this paper, but a few general points provide some historical context to our main argument.

Ghana's and India's economic policies during their 'nationalist' phase implied severe curtailments of the free market. Concretely, this was achieved through the imposition of high trade tariffs, the nationalisation of industries, widespread subsidies for selected consumption and production, tight regulation of foreign investments, and so on. At a basic level, the purpose was to transform an unbalanced, fragmented, and dependent colonial economy into a diversified, integrated and sustainable national economy.

From a geographical point of view, these policies resulted in considerable constraints on the mobility of capital (especially foreign or global capital), and these, in turn, impeded the penchant for uneven development inherent to the free market. While there continued to be differences among various regions (particularly inside the huge and diverse areas that make up the Indian economy), it is hard to find strong evidence for increasing spatial differentiation in this historical period. Indeed, geographically even development was often an integral goal of Ghanaian and Indian development strategies.

It is quite clear that the policy environments in Ghana and India changed drastically after the mid-1980s. In both countries, reforms entailed both short-term stabilisation measures and long-term economic growth measures. The global engagement of the two economies increased, and all the indices of economic globalisation showed increasing global integration at the aggregate level.

Ghana has been acclaimed as the 'star pupil of structural adjustment' because of the government's successes in implementing liberalisation policies without back-tracking. The growth of foreign investment, trade, and foreign corporate collaborations, and the internationalisation of the stock markets have been extensive. Some liberal commentators have deplored the allegedly slow pace of reform in India, especially when compared to the more liberal policy environments in South East

Asia. But India has come a long way in dismantling one of the most densely regulated economies in the world.

While there is no question that the external sectors of the Ghanaian and Indian economies (i.e., the globalisation of these national economies) are now much more significant than before the 1980s, it remains unclear how globalisation has affected the overall economic development of these countries. In both, reform is widely believed to have resulted in significant economic growth at the aggregate national level (though some dispute the causality). Indian GDP grew by 4.1% per year during the 1990s. This compares to an average 1.8% per year from 1965 to 1988, which used to be derisively referred to as the 'Hindu rate of growth'. The growth of the Ghanaian economy accelerated at a similar pace: a consistent growth in GPD at an average of 5–6% between 1984 and 1991 and 4% since 1992, compared with negative growth rates from 1974 to 1983.

But opinions vary widely about the effects of liberalisation and globalisation for development. [. . .]

The main questions in the development debate revolve around the relationships between growth, equality and poverty. Considerable research has been done in Ghana and India, and large amounts of data have been collected. Some argue that growth has contributed to the alleviation of poverty. Others argue that growth has caused poverty to rise. And yet still others maintain that growth has led to more inequality.

Liberalisation and globalisation affect various groups in various places differentially, which makes it hard to generalise about the overall effects. It appears that reforms have often either been associated with or have been unable to prevent growing inequalities. The differential effects of liberalisation and globalisation are not confined to people according to socio-economic characteristics such as class – the effects also vary across space. It is important not only who you are but where you are.

We argue that one important reason for the inconclusiveness of these debates in Ghana and India lies in the spatial differentiation of globalisation and economic development. Nationally aggregated statistics, then, have lost much of their meaning. The question is to what extent the transition from a highly regulated, insulated and socialist-oriented regime toward a liberalised and globalised market environment has resulted in a faster differentiation of economic space.

The uneven spatial development of India and Ghana since the inception of market liberalisation is best observed at a variety of scales distinguishable in the main geographical 'theatres of accumulation'. In the following two sections, we present evidence for trends of spatial differentiation in the two countries, with particular attention for the roles of Greater Mumbai and Accra as the main regional engines of uneven development.

The Re-scaling of India

Debates in India about economic growth, equality, and development have a long history of intensity and contentiousness. But recent research findings are unequivocal about trends of economic divergence among the states in the Indian federation. The increasing regional disparity is illustrated with an increasing coefficient of variation among states' gross domestic product (NSDP) from 31.10 in 1980 to 39.98 in 1995. The GINI coefficient for incomes in all of rural India increased from 30.10 in 1983 to 30.56 in 1997 and rose further to 37.8 in 2002. For urban India, the value increased from 34.08 to 36.54 over the same time period. World Bank research also supports the argument that liberalisation made the income distribution worse in India.

Within the Indian federation, Maharashtra was already one of the most 'advanced' states of India before the mid-1980s and since liberalisation it has extended its lead. From 1980 to 1995, Maharashtra had the highest economic growth rate of all Indian states at 85% – the average was 52%. Rapid economic growth in Maharashtra coincided with substantial increases in foreign investment. For all of India, incoming foreign direct investment (FDI) increased fivefold between 1990 and 1999, with the largest share, 15.6%, going to Maharashtra. Karnataka and Tamil Nadu shared second place at 6.8%.

Maharashtra's agricultural share of the state economy is the smallest of all Indian states, and its share of the tertiary sector is the largest. Between 1990 and 1995, the state had the fastest growth of the share of the service sector and by far the steepest growth of the finance sector. Maharashtra is also unequalled in the number of per capita internet connections: it has about three times as many as Karnataka, which ranks second, and about 68 times as many as Orissa, which ranks the lowest.

Intra-regional differentiation

If India is increasingly too diverse to be represented in a meaningful way with singular development statistics, the same is true for Maharashtra. It is the most urbanised of all Indian states. In 1991, almost 40% of the population was classified as urban, as compared to an average of 25.7% for all of India. But most parts of the state are still rural, and some interior parts are very remote and isolated. The state consists of 31 districts and 41,336 towns and villages, most of which are a long way from Mumbai, in space as well as in time.

Of all approved foreign collaborations in Maharashtra in 1997, 82% of the Indian partners were headquartered in Mumbai. In 1989 and 1993, Mumbai's share was, respectively, 83% and 86%. Elsewhere in the state, foreign investments were increasingly concentrated in the so-called Mumbai-Pune corridor and in the city of Pune itself. Pune's share of foreign collaborations went from 9% (1989) to 11% (1993) to 13% (1997). Indeed, data from a variety of sources show that Pune has drawn considerable manufacturing activity from Mumbai, while the latter increasingly specialises in finance and producer services – yet another form of spatial differentiation. From 1989 to 1997, in the rest of the state of Maharashtra, taken together, there was a relative decline in foreign collaborations.

In terms of development measures, Maharashtra is an interesting case of intra-state disparities. The state enjoys a very high level of per capita income (surpassed only, slightly, by Punjab): in 1997 it was almost 60% higher than the national average. But in the same year, rural poverty there was the second highest in the country, after Bihar. A recent comparison of agro-climatic regions within India's states revealed that Maharashtra has become the most disparate of all. The difference in the incidence of poverty between Maharastra's central inlands and the Bombay region is not matched in any other state.

The contrasts have been growing since the introduction of liberalisation policies and the onset of globalisation. GINI coefficients for rural and urban areas in 1983 and 1994 show Maharashtra as the only state in India where rural inequality has increased (the coefficient rose from 28.82 to 30.65). Urban inequality in Maharashtra increased as well, from 34.25 to 36.67, and is now the highest of all states.

Intra-urban differentiation

The spatial differentiation of the impact of globalisation is evident in Greater Mumbai, even to the casual observer. Foreign companies are highly concentrated in the 'island city', the southern part of the peninsula. And within the island city, a distinct global central business district (CBD) has emerged that is separate from the traditional bazaar as well as from the former colonial centre of the city that was largely 'Indianized' after 1947.

This global CBD is centred in Nariman Point. What London's City is to the UK, Nariman Point is to India: a remarkable cluster of global linkages in finance and producer servers – banks, investment firms, consulting agencies, real estate companies, accounting firms, and so on. Yet, about eight miles to the north is Dharavi, known as 'the biggest slum on earth' and as 'Mumbai's sweatshop'. There, economic activities are of an entirely different order, ranging from tanneries (cleaning and cutting of hides and leather) to soap making and refuse picking.

Real estate values in the global CBD skyrocketed after liberalisation, in part as a result of the entry of foreign-controlled multinationals. In 1995 and 1996, this business area was the most expensive in the world. Residential real estate prices spiralled up as well, in part in response to the influx of money from non-resident Indians. In the mid-1990s, apartments in Malabar Hill changed hands for the equivalency of US$2.5 million. In Dharavi, in contrast, the going price for a lot big enough for a tent was about US$3,000 – for many the investment of a lifetime.

Charles Correa, one of India's most famous architects and noted public intellectuals, raging about Mumbai's poverty and disparity, called the city 'pathological – a terrifying morass of filth and decay. Dharavi sprawls in stinking mockery of Bombay's pretensions to sophistication and prosperity. The pavements heave with hawkers, forcing pedestrians onto crumbling streets where traffic is stuck in a gridlock that never stops. Overlooking this madness are tower-block apartments worth a million dollars; the greatest juxtaposition on earth of rich and poor'.

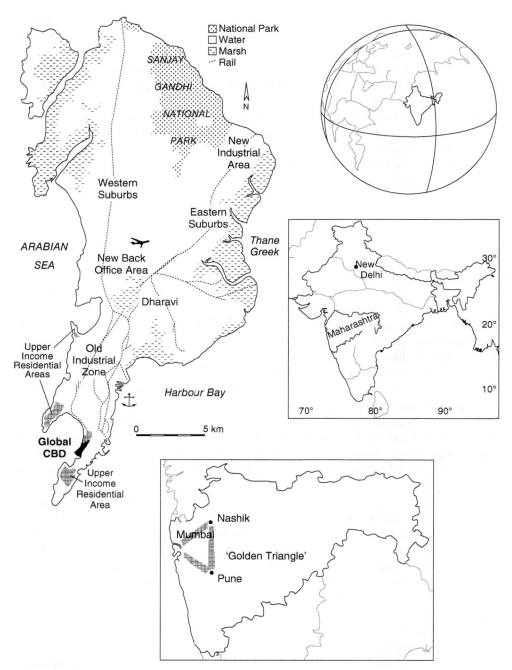

Figure 30.1 Mumbai's regional push and scales of uneven development in India.

The Re-scaling of Ghana

As in India, uneven development in Ghana since the introduction of liberalisaiton policies is also best observed at a variety of scales within 'theatres of accumulation' Figure 30.2 represents the different scales of analysis in Ghana.

Recent research findings are explicit about trends of economic divergence among the regions of Ghana. The increasing differentiation is illustrated by an increase in the GINI coefficient from 35.50 in 1960 to 39.80 in 2000 and remained at the same level in 2002. Apart from the Greater Accra Metropolitan Area (GAMA) and Kumasi, the country remains rural, and there is arguably a heavy concentration of population in just two urban economic centres. World Bank research based on household surveys also confirms that the income distribution worsened in the same period.

GAMA has emerged as the gateway and prime region in the country. It is the most diversified in the country, contributing more than 20–30% of GDP. Spatial disparities in the regional geography of FDI and the headquartering of foreign companies have accelerated since the introduction of liberalisation policies. Areas outside of GAMA account for a declining proportion of FDI. For instance, the share of FDI of Ghana's second most prosperous economic region (Ashanti Region) declined from 18% in the 1970s to 9% in 1999. The Ghana Investment Promotion Centre (GIPC) (2001) estimates that Accra accounts for 86% of Ghana's FDI. Moreover, 84% of all companies (both domestic and foreign companies) in Ghana are located in GAMA. The growth of GAMA has been in part facilitated by the availability of land for commercial development because of the deterioration of the traditional land-holding system. In contrast, land outside of the region remains outside of the free market because the traditional land-holding system is still in place and serves as a barrier to capitalist development.

There is unevenness to the geography of well-being and access to basic services in Ghana. Researchers have underscored the hardships and poverty that have emerged in the liberalisation era, particularly in rural areas. Konadu-Agyemang's research shows that while there were some modest improvements in education, health care, and access to basic services (electricity, water, etc.), inter-regional variations were essentially unchanged nationally, and that intra-regional variation may be higher now than 15 years ago. For instance, only 6% of rural residents have access to electricity compared to 81% of Accra residents. Even Ghana's Ministry of Finance acknowledges that the incidence of poverty (measured in terms of income) in the Upper West and Upper East regions now approaches a staggering 90% of the population.

The effects of globalisation on spatial development appear to lead to hyper-differentiation at the national level. Konadu-Agyemang notes that liberalisation policies 'have made matters worse, and rewidened the gaps'. There appears to be increasing differentiation between GAMA as a command, gateway and service centre and other regions in Ghana on the margins of global capitalist and national development.

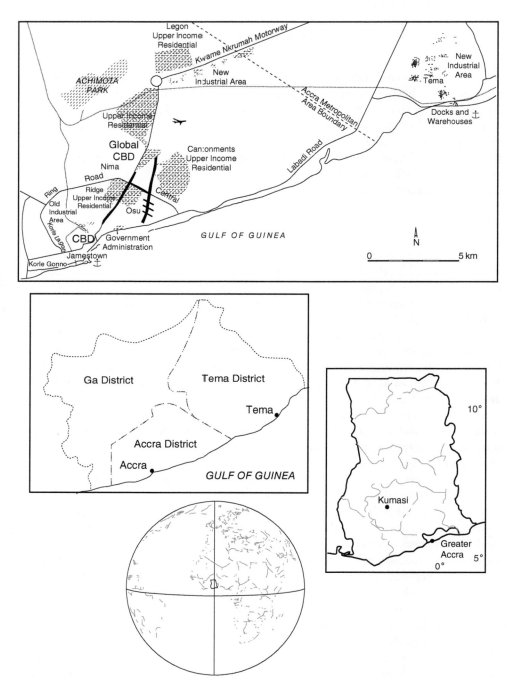

Figure 30.2 Accra's regional push and scales of uneven development in Ghana.

Intra-regional differentiation

Within GAMA we can differentiate Accra District, Tema District and Ga District. Apart from Accra District, only the Port of Tema (in Tema District but in close proximity to Accra) and its surrounding area could be considered as economically developed. Most of the remainder of Tema and Ga districts reveal peri-urban development, where informal economic activities such as home-based economic enterprises predominate.

The gaps between Accra and Tema and other peri-urban districts are apparent even to the casual observer. Economic development has been concentrated in the Accra-Tema corridor. The rise of this commercial hub has also been facilitated by the growth and expansion of Tema port, Kotoka international airport, and expenditures on developing the road network in and around the centre of Accra. Earmarking the largest portion of infrastructural expenditures for 'gateway project' in the city of Accra has widened the gap between it and the rest of the country.

Intra-urban differentiation

Within the Accra District there is a sharp contrast between the formation of a 'new global CBD' in the Osu-Cantonments area containing domestic and foreign companies and the low-income housing areas where the majority of people live and work. The global CBD is a remarkable cluster of finance and producer service companies as well as upscale retail establishments and restaurants. The upper end of the housing market is close to this area (e.g., East Legon Extension). Here private developers are building four-bedroom houses that can cost up to US$460,000. This is in sharp contrast to lower-income, overcrowed, deteriorating rental accommodations where 60% of Accra's residents live and work without basic amenities (sanitation, proper roads, drainage, water and waste disposal systems). There, economic activities are of an entirely different order, mostly micro-enterprises in production and services, particularly located in homes and along the major thoroughfares, in road reservations, and in areas reserved for other purposes within the built environment. Typically, home-based enterprises have been characteristic of residential communities on the urban fringe, but they are now representative of all low-income areas in Accra.

The World Bank notes that 'against a general trend of economic recovery and growth, the decline in living standards in Accra is a major source of concern'. Despite the globalisation of aspects of the Accra economy, poverty levels in the city may have tripled during the liberalisation era, and a noticeable poverty gap has emerged between the poor and an emerging middle class. The GINI coefficient of income distribution in Accra increased from 38.30 in 1985 to 43.00 in 1994.

The increasing number of individuals seeking refuge in the informal economy illustrates the fragmentation of the economy. The ratio of workers in the informal sector to those in the formal sector in Accra increased from 2:1 in 1980 to 5:1 by 1990. The retrenchment of 70,000 government workers since the introduction of liberalisation policies, many of whom continued to stay in Accra, makes the employment situation even more difficult. In addition, low-income residents are spending a greater share of their incomes on feeding themselves (up to 60% in some instances). Vulnerable groups are borrowing money for food and/or relying on someone outside the household for food security. Household indebtedness is also on the increase (monthly interest rates on debts can be as high as 50% in low-income areas). Increases in malnutrition among children under five years, deteriorating environmental standards, growing informalisation of jobs (especially hawking), relative deprivation, decreasing access to health care, social exclusion, and declining nutritional diets have all been documented for particular Accra groups. As a result more and more individuals rent single-room accommodation.

Residential areas like Cantonments, Airport RE, the Ridge, Legon, and most recently Osu have prospered from the liberal economy. New gated housing developments with resort amenities are being built in East Legon to cater to the elite. East Legon is so out of touch with most Ghanaians' reality, illustrated in part by private developers' offers of pre-construction house models with names like 'the Monarch', 'the King' and 'the Emperor'. This is in sharp contrast to the low-income areas where most have their 'family home' (particularly the Ga – the original setters) in overcrowed and unhealthy places, without proper roads, sanitation, and green space.

Policy Implications

We are only beginning to understand the new spatial dynamics of uneven development, particularly in the less developed world. The newly emergent economic geographies are complex, dynamic and potentially volatile. We propose the notion of a hyper-differentiation of space to connote the impact of these global economic processes at a variety of scales. The hyper-differentiation of space is a corollary of the hyper-speed of capital movements in the current global era: the unprecedented velocity of capital shifts cannot but bring about corresponding spatial reconfigurations. With the general sectoral shift from manufacturing to information-based services and the lowering of political and ideological barriers, capital and investments are increasingly less embedded and most places and regions face uncertain economic futures.

Current trends of hyper-differentiation of space are different from older notions of uneven development in that the process has become much more intense, particularly in regions such as India and Ghana since the mid-1980s. Historically, there is no precedent for a region undergoing such important policy changes towards a free market at a time of such highly mobile global capital. It is this combination of contextual factors that has been at the basis of the hyper-differentiation of space in India and Ghana.

It is, of course, not easy to *prove* that the hyper-differentiation of space in both countries is caused by globalisation per se. One of the main challenges of globalisation studies is to distinguish global dynamics from domestic (or local) processes. It is evident that the key to the changes in India and Ghana lies in the implementation of liberalisation policies. This dramatic shift toward deregulation should itself be understood as part of the globalisation of free market ideologies. Liberalisation, in turn, has caused enormous changes in the domestic economy as well as in the external economic sector. It is hard to say to what extent global capital has been exclusively responsible for the unprecedented fragmentation of Ghana and India, but it seems clear that it played a significant part, as is evident in the rapid increases in foreign direct investment, foreign corporate collaborations and foreign corporate control. Thus, if Accra and Mumbai function as the main 'theatres of accumulation' this is to a substantial degree due to global capital investments.

Governments do have the option to interfere with the market and restore stability. There are, of course, well-known cases of national governments making major adjustments after their economies proved too vulnerable to the vagaries of global capitalism (e.g., Malaysia at the time of the Asian crisis or Argentina in 2002). What makes Ghana and India rather different is that these countries have turned only relatively recently toward liberalisation and deregulation. The ideological rhetoric in policy circles in both countries is decidedly free-market oriented and appears to leave little room for alternative reflection.

The government of Ghana's 'Vision for 2020' hinges on accelerating growth and urban development in order to optimise the rate of economic development so that the country can become a middle income country within twenty years. The thrust of government policy is to build up the infrastructure of Accra as a gateway for the entire economy of Ghana. These same policies also privilege private sector investment in technology, services and basic manufacturing. President Kuffour of Ghana has lauded this as the 'Golden Age' for business in Ghana and aims to further facilitate this by his establishment of a special office of the president called the Ministry for Private Sector Development (MPSD). At the same time, the government has been forced to acknowledge the widening of inequalities among regions and within urban areas in Ghana. The greatest policy challenge is whether Greater Accra will indeed be able to serve as the regional growth engine to drive the large national territorial economy to middle income status.

India is too large to be dominated by one single 'theatre of accumulation', but the 'regional push' that emanates from Mumbai has notable effects at a range of scales. First, Mumbai is the core of a highly urbanised region that comprises cities such as Thane, Nashik and Pune. But Mumbai's presence reaches much further than that. Within the state of Maharashtra, Mumbai's dynamism is responsible for the wide gap in prosperity between the western coastal region and the districts in the interior, the greatest inequality found in any state in the Indian union. And it is thanks to Mumbai that Maharashtra leads the nation in terms of economic growth and a host of 'modernisation' measures.

The Maharashtra government at times acknowledges the seriousness of these escalating inequalities, but this clearly takes a backseat to concerns of economic growth. A recent report of the Maharashtra Economic Development Council (2002) sets a goal of average growth rates of 15% a year over the next ten years. One of the ways to realise this is the development of 'Mumbai as a major services hub and international financial centre'. The report also refers to the 'Golden Triangle' of Mumbai, Nashik and Pune: the 'industrial hotlands of Maharashtra and India'.

Nowhere in this strategic report is there any mentioning of the potential problems of uneven development.

We think that the implications of these spatial dislocations may be more significant than is currently realised. The geographical dimension of development strategies is fast becoming a very salient issue. As such, the accelerated spatial differentiation within national economies will pose severe economic and political challenges to central, regional and municipal authorities in both Ghana and India. We do not question the obvious advantages of rapid economic growth in these poor regions, but we do think there is an urgent need to re-assess matters of efficiency and equity, and to determine the economic, social and political costs of starkly uneven development. In Ghana and India, pre-occupation with growth has all but precluded attention to balanced spatial planning.

Chapter 31

Development Alternatives: Practice, Dilemmas, and Theory

A. J. Bebbington and D. H. Bebbington

Introduction

The relationship between research and practice constantly challenges development studies in general, and development geography in particular. Professional and departmental incentives do not encourage such links, and some researchers steer clear of them for fear that engaging with development practice might be to be complicitous in a project of 'mindless modernization' or cultural destruction. While, as Gregory notes, the relevance of research lies as much in its contribution to teaching and critical thinking as in any direct relationship to practice, such arguments cut little ice with critics who have declared much development research 'irrelevant' or 'negative'. These critical voices are not only from the North: they are increasingly audible among those whose livelihood struggles many geographers would study, as well as those whose efforts to 'do' development we are inclined to criticize.

Notably, many of those criticizing development research themselves share similar concerns to those of critical development theorists: they too criticize much mainstream development practice and speak of the need to build alternatives grounded in the initiatives of popular organizations. Why then the charge of irrelevance – or at least the demand for grater relevance – if the concerns and keywords are apparently similar?

Is something wrong with academic notions of 'development alternatives'; are concepts deployed too loosely;

Bebbington, A. J. and Bebbington, D. H., "Development Alternatives: Practice, Dilemmas, and Theory," pp. 7–16 from *Area*, 33.1 (2001).

in failing to ground notions of alternative in specific practices do such invocations
    elide real dilemmas;
and if so, does this imply problems with theory?

In this paper we want to suggest that to some extent this is the case. Similarly we
wish to suggest that an engagement with the day-to-day dilemmas faced by those
aiming to translate notions of development alternatives into practice would be a
constructive challenge to some of the theoretical claims made in academic work
on alternative development and would point to paths for further conceptual development. In short, beyond arguments about relevance, the case for engagement can
be made on scholarly grounds also.

In this paper we focus on those notions of alternative with a local and rural
focus that look to grassroots, popular, social and other types of movement as the
bearers of such alternatives. In particular we want to draw attention to three tendencies in this writing that are problematic, at least when considered in the light
of experiences in the Andes:

1.   overgeneralizations about popular organizations;
2.   overdrawn distinctions between popular organizations and the state; and
3.   limited attention to the technical and economic dimensions of alternatives.

We then discuss the case of highland Bolivia, focusing in particular on two organizations that worked with local social movements in an effort to pursue development alternatives. In each case, the initiatives encountered a series of difficulties
and dilemmas related to each of these three problematic tendencies in alternative
development writing. Elements of these experiences suggest further lines of empirical and theoretical enquiry that could enrich both academic and practical notions
of alternative development.

Development Alternatives and their Missing Details

Diversity in civil society

A substantial body of work in critical development geography views civil society
as the sphere from which alternatives to development will emerge. Yet, there is a
tendency to 'sing the praises of civil society's democratizing potential' and to gloss
over the divergent interests, organizational forms and relationships of power in
civil society. It is, therefore, important to distinguish among different actors. Analyzing Salvadoran civil society McIlwaine, for instance, draws the simple but
important distinction between 'informal civil society organizations' such as neighborhood groups and social movements 'that emerge from the bottom up', and more
'top-down . . . formal civil society organizations', such as non-governmental organizations (NGOs). Others have worked with similar distinctions, and this has led
to a more nuanced view of the capacities and limitations of NGOs as agents of
more inclusive forms of development. Less critical scrutiny has been directed at the

popular organizations of McIlwaine's 'informal civil society', and as Watts notes these are the organizations that are most often viewed as the source of alternative development or of 'new narratives of life and culture'. Yet, Watts continues, 'it is nonetheless difficult to generalize about these movements and what they represent'. This is a critical observation, yet one to which discussions of development alternatives pay too little attention. Indeed, many such discussions seem so disenchanted with 'the power of development . . . to generalize, homogenize, objectify', that they pay too little attention to the details of alternatives. Thus, even if some commentators have begun to note the heterogeneity among, and tensions within social and popular movements, the dominant tendency is still to look to them as vehicles of 'development alternative[s] . . . based on collective aspirations'. While these generalizing assertions about social movements may by 'strategic essentialisms' they nonetheless beg a series of critical questions.

How will 'collective aspirations' emerge from the diversity of interests and orientations that exist within and among popular organizations?

How and with who do those formal civil society (and other) organizations concerned to foster such alternatives work?

How will societies, at whatever scale, live with the conflict and tension deriving from these differences?

We suggest that these questions constitute one of the most complicated everyday dilemmas for many actors motivated to pursue alternative notions of development. Engaging with these dilemmas might enrich the ways in which critical development geography theorizes, and add nuance and detail to how it speaks of alternatives.

Alternatives and the local state

A related problem of much alternative writing lies in its treatment of the distinction between the state and civil society. While some recent work has begun to explore the ways in which 'the boundary between civil society and the state often becomes blurred in the practices of Latin American social movements', there is still a tendency to understate the importance of the state in any project of alternative development, and to counterpose 'liberating' social movements against a 'dominating' state that imposes modernizing development. While the state may indeed often play this role, such an approach diverts attention from the webs of relationships that link civil society organizations and the state and that may offer the prospect of changing forms of state action.

More has been said about the nature of these relationships for the case of NGOs, and the possibilities and risks entailed in building them; far less has been said about the relationships between popular organizations and the state. Yet these relationships are important empirically (for they often exist, especially at a local level), as well as theoretically and strategically. Theoretically, if it is accepted that there are significant relationships of difference, power and exclusion within and among popular organizations, then the question of governance – the process through which a society governs itself, its differences and its capacities, and through which it allocates resources across these differences – becomes pivotal to alternatives. This necessarily implies a concern for both civil society and state. Indeed, the two become part of the same question: namely under what forms of state-civil society embeddedness and relative autonomy are more inclusive development alternatives likely to emerge? Indeed, this is a strategic question for many popular organizations, at least in the Andes. As they pursue their alternatives, the questions of how and when to engage with the state, and even to become involved in formal political and electoral processes have become everyday dilemmas, particularly as national policies delegate responsibilities and (somewhat greater) resources to local governments.

Alternatives and markets

The technical and economic foundations of any alternative development, while critical to its viability, have received limited attention in the literature. This may reflect the profound critique (in critical development geography and elsewhere) of the ways in which markets, and particularly neo-liberal regimes and structural adjustment have excluded the popular sectors. Though important, such critique has rarely gone the next step to imagine with some specificity the ways in which the governance of markets might be changed, or existing markets be re-negotiated, so that economic processes become more inclusive and patterns of accumulation become more decentralized. The tendency is simply to assert that economic strategies grounded in criteria 'that are not strictly those of profit and the market' will be found within social movements, and that these will constitute a viable basis for local alternatives.

The lack of specificity on economic alternatives is often accompanied by similarly general assertions that a basis for alternative rural livelihoods can be found in indigenous natural resource management practices. Yet some of the most careful and sustained analytical work on indigenous technical practices in the Andes has noted that rural people base much of their choice of crops and crop varieties not on whether they are 'indigenous', 'alternative' or 'modern', but rather on how well suited they are to market conditions, to the non-agricultural dimensions of farm families' livelihood strategies, to farmers' migration calendars, etc. This suggests that any invocation of alternatives ought be based on a more nuanced and disaggregated understanding of existing livelihoods.

Much critical thinking on alternative development, therefore, steers away from reflecting on the details of the livelihoods and economic institutions that might sustain alternative projects aimed at shifting the geography and social control of accumulation. Imagining, identifying and making functional such institutions has, however, inspired significant degrees of grassroots collective action (at least in the Andes) and constitutes one of the most serious concerns of the foot soldiers who pursue alternative development in the field. This is not to say that critical development theory should dedicate itself to resolving all the details of practical challenges such as these. But if we engaged with them more, then we might indeed find that much empowerment passes through a reshaped market that resolves some of the power-based and institutional obstacles to popular participation in economic activities. If one dimension of development alternatives revolves around the reciprocal embeddedness of society and state, another therefore revolves around the reciprocal embeddedness of society and market.

From practice to theory?

The general problem at issue is, we suggest, that academic formulations of alternative development are often as universalizing as are the formulations of modernizing development that they critique so profoundly. Such 'strategic essentialisms' may help move arguments forward in the short term. Ultimately, however, they have to be able to speak to empirical variation: to the extent that they are unable to do this, there are probably deficiencies in such formulations. These deficiencies weaken the relevance and theoretical acuity of such approaches. We suggest that one means of moving forward on each of these fronts is to engage in a fuller and more nuanced way with the efforts, dilemmas, successes and failures of organizations aiming to foster development alternatives.

Seeking Alternatives in Highland Bolivia

Popular organization, NGOs and the state in highland Bolivia

To elaborate these points we draw on recent work in the Bolivian highlands, though the observations are also informed by our work elsewhere in Latin America. The highlands and *altiplano* of the departments of La Paz, Oruro and Potosí are the highest habitable parts of Bolivia, a home to families pursuing livelihood strategies at altitudes of over 4000 metres above sea level. It is a region of both Aymara and Quechua communities, as well as *mestizos*. Economically these regions are depressed and poverty levels are chronic: in the departments of La Paz and Potosí (the departments from which the two case studies are drawn), 95.5 and 94 per cent respectively of the rural populations have unsatisfied basic needs. The mining economy collapsed in the 1980s and agricultural trends suggest declining crop and livestock productivity over the last decade. In some locations, particularly those close to the Peruvian and Chilean borders, as well as those within the orbit of La Paz (the capital of Bolivia), trading economies have become more significant; elsewhere, however, opportunities remain much more limited. This has led various observers to question the viability of highland livelihoods, and increased a sense of urgency as to the need to identify economically-viable alternatives for the local population. Indeed, for several decades periodic and permanent out-migration have been increasing, and in some parts population is declining.

This geographical concentration of extreme rural poverty has attracted a wide range of development organizations to the same areas. Among government and multilateral agencies, US bilateral programmes were the earliest to arrive in the

1950s and 60s, followed in the 1970s by the World Bank and European Union who invested in large-scale, modernizing rural development programmes of the sort criticized by critical development theory. These programmes had consistently disappointing results, leading these agencies to withdraw from the highlands in the 1980s and 1990s. They were duly replaced, however, by European bilateral programmes 'impressed by the levels of poverty and the persistence of many traditional elements of Andean culture'. Meanwhile, similar factors plus state repression of rural social movements in the 1970s and early 80s attracted 'formal civil society organizations' to the region, in the shape of Bolivian and international NGOs. Today, NGOs channel some $100 million to the high Andes; in the department of La Paz, where most official Aid has withdrawn because of disappointing results, NGOs are responsible for almost all development initiatives.

The label NGO covers many types of organization: indeed, in order to distinguish themselves from what they saw as more conservative NGOs, a number of Bolivian organizations committed to more politically radical forms of development alternative began to call themselves Private Institutions for Social Development (IPDS), forming networks of their own. Most of these NGOs have attempted to pursue some form of alternative development through engaging with popular organizations. Increasingly, though, the dilemma has been *which* popular organizations to engage with. The preference of most NGOs has been to work with rural *sindicatos* on the grounds that these are the most legitimate and inclusive form of popular organization. However, this claim is not without its problems, and inevitably NGOs are confronted with a range of people's organizations as they begin working in a locality.

The *sindicato* was created in the aftermath of the Bolivian revolution of 1952. One of the fruits of that revolution was a land reform programme that redistributed property from large rural estates to indigenous populations. In order to receive property, these local populations had to create themselves as *sindicatos*. These *sindicatos* were to be the basis for administering the affairs of these newly-formed communities, and had their own elected councils to do this. The *sindicato* was, then, part civil society, part state: it was created as a mechanism to administer and represent the concerns of rural people to the state, at the same time as being the mechanism through which the state (and indeed the governing party of the time) could deal with a dispersed rural population and consolidate the new revolutionary and party order at a local level. This sense of being a parallel representative structure to the state was also reflected in the overall organization of the *sindicato* movement – its internal structure mimicked to a considerable degree the administrative structure of the state, with village level *sindicatos* grouped into provincial and departmental federations, and ultimately a national confederation.

Sindicatos were not, though, created on an organizational *tabula rasa*. In many areas, especially in parts of the altiplano and Potosí, populations were already organized in *ayllus*, a form of community governance tracing its roots to the pre-Hispanic period. Even in areas where the *ayllu* had been largely destroyed by rural estates, a range of informal organizational forms based on kinship, generation, natural resource management etc. also existed. Subsequently, in the period since the initial creation of *sindicatos*, a wide range of other organizations have also emerged further complicating this local organizational landscape. Some are gender based, others product based, others natural resource based, others activity based and so on. Just like the *sindicatos*, many of these new organizations have been partly induced by external actors and subsequently become more locally owned, though in some cases (e.g. new marketing organizations) they appear as local responses to changes in the broader political and economic environment.

Popular organizations have always had complex and often conflictive relationships with the Bolivian state. This has been especially so for the *sindicato* movement. Sometimes the state has aimed to incorporate *sindicatos* into state policies; at other times, especially during periods of repressive rule, the state persecuted *sindicato* leaders and much of the movement assumed a far more oppositional stance to government policies. This oppositional heritage, from the period of radical repression of the Bolivian left and centre left, meant that *sindicatos* became an obvious counterpart for many organizations interested in fostering alternative development and social change.

In the 1990s, government reforms changed the nature of the state-*sindicato* relationship once again. One of these reforms, the *Law of Popular Participation*, strengthened the role of municipal government in local development planning, and greatly increased the degree to which popular organizations could participate in these planning processes as well as in the periodic auditing of local government. Though initially many organizations – especially the *sindicatos* – contested the legislation, once the law recognized them as legitimate participants in local development planning, most began to support its implementation, as also did the majority of IPDS-type NGOs (including those working in Potosí and La Paz). The local state, therefore, began to assume far more prominence in the strategies and objectives of those formal and informal civil society organizations committed to alternative development. In a number of municipalities, in particular in parts of Potosí, popular organizations began to move into local government through the electoral process, blurring the boundaries between them and the state.

In general, then, the highlands are characterized by a complex and diverse landscape of formal and informal civil society organizations, an on-going reflection among many of these organizations on the possible progressive role of the local state, and serious discussions among many of them on the urgent need to develop economic alternatives for local livelihoods. The following sections discuss briefly the experiences of two external organizations concerned to foster some form of development alternative in such a context. Each organization worked primarily with *sindicatos*; each encountered tensions within *sindicatos*, and between their priorities and those of a range of other popular organizations and interests; and each was constantly challenged to rethink which local organizations they should work with and why. Each was also pulled by local processes to consider in more detail the economic dimensions of alternatives, while national policy forced them to consider some form of engagement with the local state.

The first of these organizations, ALTERNATIVO, is an NGO tracing its roots to the struggle against the dictatorships of the 1970s and early 1980s. It has long had a reputation for being particularly radical in its orientation, has been closely aligned with the *sindicato* movement and committed to the notion that any development alternative in the highlands must be pursued under the coordination of *sindicato* organizations at their different levels (local, provincial, departmental and national). It has, therefore, dedicated significant resources to strengthening the national *sindicato* organizations, and maintains only small field program-mes. These programmes, which have a strong focus on agricultural technology and local organizational strengthening, are viewed as experiments in local develop-ment whose lessons can, if successful, be scaled up through the *sindicato* movement.

The second organization, ANTIPOV, is a special poverty reduction programme linked to the United Nations system. Working in several provinces of two separate departments of Bolivia, it maintains a far larger field presence and staff than ALTERNATIVO, and has a far larger budget. During much of the 1990s it was probably the largest poverty reduction initiative in the north (or *Norte*) of the department of Potosí. In addition to sharing ALTERNATIVO's focus on agricultural technology and local organizational strengthening, the programme also works in women's literacy training, children's education and basic water and health services. In Norte Potosí (the region considered here) most of this work has been pursued in conjunction with *sindicatos* at the regional and community level.

ALTERNATIVO in La Paz

ALTERNATIVO works in 36 communities of the regions of Los Andes, Ancoraimes and Puerto Acosta in the altiplano of the department of La Paz. In essence, its alternative for these communities is one of a *sindicato* controlled agro-ecological development, revolving around the restoration of pre-Hispanic fertility and humid-ity management practices (terraces and raised fields) and the recovery and multi-plication of native varieties of potato. Activities are intended to be coordinated and supervised by *sindicatos*, with the NGO serving as advisor to the *sindicato*. In this way, ALTERNATIVO argued that the *sindicatos'* authority, legitimacy and capac-ity would be strengthened, a small step in the process of building a basis for the consolidation of regional *sindicato*-based social movements able to gain presence within processes of regional governance.

In practice, however, most of the *sindicatos* with which ALTERNATIVO works have been weakened by the combined effects of periodic migration and the influ-ence of political parties: this reduces their ability to play such coordinating roles, and while they play a role in everyday community governance, the extent to which they are the hearth of development alternatives is limited. Meanwhile, the alterna-tives proposed by the NGO have elicited very partial response. Terracing and raised-field technologies have only elicited interest in those few locations where ecological conditions are appropriate and labour availability is not constrained by migration. The potato seed has had more general appeal, but most has been lost to climatic vagaries. In only one community in Ancoraimes was there any signifi-cant appropriation of native potato varieties, and this occurred at the margin of the *sindicato*. Instead a sub-group of families within the community formed a seed-producing cooperative to multiply and sell the introduced seed to other *campesinos* in the area. In due course, this became a relatively successful local business, somewhat to the chagrin of some members of the *sindicato* who wanted profits to accrue to all members of the *sindicato*. While the Ancoraimes field staff of ALTERNATIVO were happy to work with any local organization that appropriated at least some of the NGO's technical suggestions, their support to this local seed-producing organization in turn created conflicts with the leadership of the NGO which insisted that all initiatives be pursued through the *sindicatos*.

Ironically, given ALTERNATIVO's very critical attitude to the market, the NGO's presence appeared to have most success in stimulating collective action in those cases where *sindicatos* took a more mercantilist approach to local development. In Puerto Acosta, the loose federation of eight *sindicatos* with which ALTERNATIVO collaborated decided (again to the initial vexation of ALTERNATIVO) that, rather than distribute the tools which the NGO gave them for terracing and other soil conservation measures, they would sell them, and with the income create rotating savings and credit associations (ROSCAs). These ROSCAs provided three financial services to villagers – they offered:

1. a chance to earn interest on savings;
2. a form of agricultural insurance to *campesinos* who lost crops; and
3. loans to members whom the community decided were most likely to pay them back.

The ROSCAs were managed by member committees (ALTERNATIVO had very little role in this) who studiously monitored all loans – indeed, these were all repaid, even though interest rates were above market rates (a decision of the committees themselves). While not all the *sindicato* participated in the ROSCAs, this was the most significant and sustained form of collective action elicited by the NGO's various interventions. It appeared to speak to a wider range of interests within communities than did a focus on seeds, particular technologies or even a particular view of the *sindicato's* role in alternative development.

It is important to be careful before generalizing too much from this experience. There were particular reasons why this should happen in Puerto Acosta. Its location close to the Peruvian border meant there was active (if illegal) cross-border trade in cattle and other items. This increased the demand for loans, and the possibility of paying them back. However, even if the conditions were special in Puerto Acosta, the experience of the second case study organization, ANTIPOV, suggests that there may be something more general at work here.

ANTIPOV in Norte Potosí

In much of Norte Potosí, *sindicatos* exist side-by-side with the *ayllu*. While the *ayllu* traces its roots to pre-Hispanic forms of kin-based community governance, the *sindicato* – as noted earlier – is entirely a modern artifact of the Bolivian revolution. It has, though, been appropriated in Norte Potosí by important parts of population. In particular, *sindicatos* appeal to segments of the community who under *ayllu* systems of land management and governance would have to wait a long time before acceding to land and positions of authority. In the *sindicato*, selection criteria and procedures are more inclusive and are particularly attractive to young adults, who often have the most restricted access to land, and the most ambition to assume local leadership positions. While many localities achieve relationships of understanding and a division of labour between the *sindicato* and *ayllu*, the tensions are nonetheless real. These tensions also play out at the level of the different regional federations of *ayllus* and *sindicatos*, each of which aims to represent the rural population, while having different views of the cultural foundations on which local development ought to be based, as well as of the ways in which it should be governed.

During and following the dictatorships of the 1970s and early 1980s, a number of IPDS-type NGOs working in Norte Potosí sought to strengthen *sindicatos*, given their apparently more liberal democratic principles. Many of these NGOs envisioned political alliances between *sindicatos* and parties of the radical left. In the process, partisan politics intersected with discussions of community governance, both among NGOs and *within* communities. It was in this context that ANTIPOV, when it began work in 1989, also decided to work with the *sindicato* movement, focusing in particular on support to the departmental federation. Indeed the federation became the principal local counterpart of the programme, organizing and implementing many of its activities.

This role greatly increased the visibility and capacity of the federation. Following the *Law of Popular Participation*, the federation began to launch candidates for the position of several mayorships in the region with some successes, as well as candidates for the national parliamentary elections (in many cases through the same partisan affiliations that NGOs had promoted within the *sindicato* movement). This visibility, however, led to consistent tensions between the federation of *sindicatos* and that of the *ayllus*, as well as tensions with other civil society organizations in the region who were either committed to an *ayllu*-based form of local development, or concerned about the particular intersection of party politics and the *sindicato* federation. These tensions were in part issues of power: of *who* within civil society and popular organizations should lead local development processes; but they were also differences of vision. The idea of 'local development' meant something quite different depending on whether it was seen through the *ayllu* or the *sindicato*. The implications for notions of governance, authority, leadership and democracy were not the same, though they were equally grounded in social movements – but in *different* movements.

As ANTIPOV's work unfolded it also became apparent that there was a similar diversity of popular organizations and aspirations at the village level. One of these revolved around gender differences, and particularly the limited voice of women within the *sindicatos* with which ANTIPOV worked. The programme responded by forcing a greater focus on gender inclusion. As women's concerns were sought out, aspirations for literacy training and gender-based organization were voiced. In response, a Freirian style literacy programme was launched and as it unfolded a regional women's movement emerged, existing somewhat independently of the *sindicatos*. Indeed the local literacy groups became new arenas of collective action, to some extent supplanting the *sindicatos*. Similar to the case of Puerto Acosta, the most successful initiative of these groups (aside from the literacy training) was the organization of village banks. The number of banks grew quickly, each charging interest rates considerably above the rate of inflation, but also offering interest on savings. Loans from the banks, very much in demand, were used to fund petty commerce in urban areas, livestock raising, horticultural crop production and other small-scale market oriented activities. Again, the demand to be involved in such banks appeared to reflect the fact that they helped remove obstacles to women's and men's participation in a range of markets that they knew existed – or could exist – but from which they were excluded because of limited savings and lack of access to loans.

Implications for Alternatives

While it is important to avoid generalizing from limited cases, we believe that the issues raised by these experiences have wider relevance at least for discussions of rural alternatives in the Andes. In particular, the cases demonstrate the remarkable diversity of informal (and formal) civil society organizations in the region. These organizations have differing interests, priorities and ideas about development. This suggests that there are several development alternatives being pursued at any one time, even at local levels, and that even if the different alternatives are not necessarily mutually exclusive (this is an empirical question) they certainly pull in different directions and imply different ways of allocating local and external resources.

This sits uneasily with the tendency, also noted by Simon, of many commentators to make relatively unproblematized claims regarding the immanence of alternatives in the practices of social movements and grassroots actors, and to celebrate diversity rather than follow through on its practical implications. This must surely be insufficient: discussions of alternatives must at least address how a development strategy might engage this broader range of organizations and interests, and need to reflect much more critically on the conditions under which 'development alternative[s] . . . based on collective aspirations' might in practice emerge. At least in the regions discussed here, these aspirations will not emerge from the voice of a single popular organization. Indeed, if they emerge at all, it will only be through a process that is likely to be at times conflictive, and will need mediation and arbitrage: at village and regional scales. This cautions academic statements to be far more nuanced in their discussions of social movements, civil society and alternative development.

These cases also suggest that elements of alternatives with more collective appeal might be found in spaces that have received less attention than they might in critical writing on development. The first of these spaces is the market – or more precisely the reworking of social relationships underlying market transactions. At least in these cases, the collective management of money (in the form of village banking) in order to facilitate people's access to a range of markets elicited some of the more interesting forms of sustained and broadly-based collective action. While it is important to recognize that financial services can, in certain circumstances, decapitalize poor people and themselves contribute to already existing forms of social differentiation, two interesting insights derive from these experiences. The first is simply that, to the extent that money is relevant to many more people's livelihood circumstances than are, say, terracing, raised fields or potatoes, the management of money can become a more significant and inclusive axis of collective action than technologies or practices linked to particular livelihoods. The second insight is that, to the extent that rural financial services allow people to participate in new markets, to accumulate capital (albeit in small amounts), and to profit through new economic activities, then they can help foster forms of local accumulation that constitute an important counterpoint to the leakages of capital fostered by most economic institutions in the Andes. In a context as disadvantaged as highland Bolivia, any viable alternative that will avert the pressures on people to migrate *must* address this issue of accumulation. These cases suggest that services such as village-based banking offer more hope of this than does the promotion of indigenous agricultural technology. More generally they challenge us to think more carefully and critically about the material bases that will sustain any development alternative.

The second space is the state, particularly the local state. The current context of decentralization in Bolivia challenges reflection on the potential role that a local state subject to greater degrees of popular involvement and social control might play in fostering more inclusive forms of local development. Certainly the peasant federations in the two regions do not seem likely, at this stage, to be the vehicles through which a convergence of different interests within regional civil society will occur. This raises the question as to whether the debate and grassroots planning processes around the new *Law of Popular Participation* might constitute a more likely vehicle for the emergence of 'collective aspirations' than any single popular organization. This question obviously raises a whole series of issues that go beyond the scope of this paper: but at the very least this possibility is being considered by many IPDS and some regional social movements in Bolivia who have decided to work more closely with the local state. Engaging with these experiments, and the dilemmas and opportunities that they generate, will shed further light on the conditions under which the 'new' local government in Bolivia might constitute a space for the pursuit of alternatives.

Indeed, this is the more general point. In trying to operationalize an approach to development that works primarily with popular organizations the experiences discussed here challenge generic assertions about development alternatives to be more nuanced in their treatment of civil society, state and market. This is not necessarily to say that these experiments are successful development alternatives that point a way forward, but rather that their own dilemmas in operationalizing some of the core principles of much alternative writing raise a whole series of questions that are too easily glossed over. Engaging more fully with experiences such as these offers the prospect not only of making our work slightly more relevant to practical struggles but also of improving our own conceptual frameworks.

Chapter 32

Rural Development in El Hatillo, Nicaragua: Gender, Neoliberalism, and Environmental Risk

Julie Cupples

Introduction

El Hatillo, a rural community of 350 inhabitants in the Sébaco valley in the central-northern highlands of Nicaragua (Figure 32.1), could be classed as both economically and ecologically vulnerable. It suffers from an eroding resource base, high levels of poverty and malnutrition, and a high susceptibility to hazards, especially droughts and flooding. Security on the land, as in most parts of rural Nicaragua, is precarious. Indiscriminate deforestation on the surrounding hillsides, which has led to considerable land degradation and decreasing fertility, also makes the community particularly vulnerable to landslides and flooding in heavy rains.

I first visited El Hatillo in early 1999, just a few months after Hurricane Mitch had devastated the area, destroying houses and livelihoods as well as the connecting road and bridge over the Río Grande de Matagalpa that linked El Hatillo to Sébaco, the nearest urban centre. Later that year, the Department of Matagalpa, in which El Hatillo is located, suffered heavy flooding. The rains had a major impact on El Hatillo, cutting it off from both Matagalpa and Sébaco. The barely accessible road became impassable, and for several weeks, I was unable to get there to carry out my interviews. Finally I had to do so by a much longer, alternative and fairly precarious route.

When I returned to El Hatillo in May 2001, the community was suffering the effects of a prolonged drought. The river, which had claimed lives and homes in 1998, was now completely dry. Trees and chickens were dying and the inhabitants were desperately awaiting the first rains of the season, by then long overdue, in

Cupples, Julie, "Rural Development in El Hatillo, Nicaragua: Gender, Neoliberalism, and Environmental Risk," pp. 343–57 from *Singapore Journal of Tropical Geography*, 25.3 (2004).

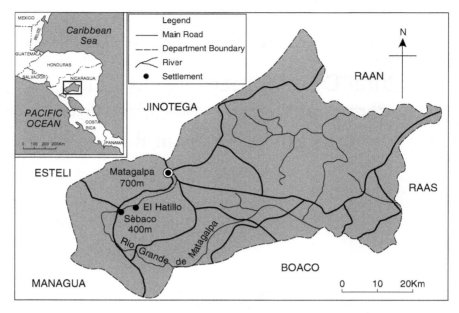

Figure 32.1   Location of El Hatillo, Department of Matagalpa, Nicaragua.

order to begin planting the basic grains and chayotes on which they depended for economic survival. In 2001, the community lost its entire harvest of beans and maize to drought. During my stay in 1999, two severely malnourished children aged below five perished and both respiratory and intestinal illnesses were common, particularly among children. In many senses, then, El Hatillo is a marginal environment, but it is a community that displays a high level of social cohesion and significant levels of community participation, particularly by women.

This paper explores initiatives to promote sustainable development in El Hatillo in the context of structural adjustment and increasing environmental degradation. Structural adjustment policies, with their emphasis on privatisation and export-oriented growth, have been devastating for small and subsistence farmers (*campesinos*), increasing social marginalisation in rural Nicaragua. The women in this community have adopted a grassroots, local empowerment approach to development, based on participation, organisation and disaster mitigation in an attempt to cope with high levels of poverty and environmental risk. These small-scale and participatory initiatives to promote more sustainable futures simultaneously contest and operate within a broader context of neoliberal development, seen by many to run counter to sustainability. However, many critical accounts of neoliberalism have failed to explore the complex ways in which people in the South engage with these processes. Just as the apparently monolithic neoliberal model in Latin America is both fractured and contested, different social actors and resource users have very different notions of what rural development should entail.

This paper draws on qualitative research, mainly participant observation and in-depth semi-structured interviews conducted in El Hatillo in 1999 and 2001 with a number of women who had been made homeless by Hurricane Mitch. It considers their role as multiply-positioned social actors and resource users who were organised to implement initiatives to mitigate environmental risk and alleviate poverty. It draws on poststructuralist theory which sees discourses and discursive practices as both constitutive of the social world and as inherently unstable. Consequently, while hegemonic discourses of gender might legitimise and reproduce structural gender inequalities, these discourses are constantly open to challenge and contestation, particularly as they intersect with other political, economic, cultural and environmental processes. Given that processes of neoliberalism therefore intersect with local place-based practices, politics, and constructions of masculinity and femininity, place-specific analyses can be disruptive to universalising discourses of neoliberalism. This approach also contributes to the growing critique of the gender and development (GAD) paradigm. GAD emerged as a critique of the prevailing women in development (WID) paradigm that focused primarily on bringing women into processes of modernisation and making them visible in development. GAD analysts insist that the power relations between women and men need to be properly considered in the development process and they have increasingly become part of the development policies of national governments and non-governmental organisations (NGOs). Both WID and GAD have been accused of ethnocentrism because of the ways in which they tend to homogenise women and treat them as victims of their own cultures.

My aims in this paper are threefold. First, I outline ways in which my participants have through resource management and poverty alleviation techniques made attempts to address the multiple facets of rural poverty and environmental risk, both of which are exacerbated by structural adjustment policies. Second, I explore the gendered environmental relationships which exist in El Hatillo, and the outcomes of these relationships for both gender and environmental vulnerability. Third, I aim to contribute to the growing literature which moves away from addressing neoliberalism solely in terms of impacts to focus on the multiple and fractured ways in which processes of neoliberalism take shape. I begin by providing some context for structural adjustment, neoliberalism and the devastation caused by Hurricane Mitch in October 1998. I then look at social mobilisation in El Hatillo and the strategies deployed by my participants to cope with economic marginalisation and environmental risk. I end by discussing the potential of the resource management strategies adopted in El Hatillo for gender equality and empowerment.

Structural Adjustment, the Environment, and Hurricane Mitch

While the Sandinista Revolution (1979–89) largely failed in its attempt to bring about development, the Sandinista government in 1979 created Nicaragua's first ever National Environmental Agency (Instituto Nicaragüense de Recursos Naturales y del Ambiente), making sustainable development a part of national policy. A process of agrarian reform, which redistributed land to small rural producers, was implemented initially in the form of state farms and cooperatives, subsequently in individual plots. In addition, the government provided credit, agricultural inputs and technical assistance to small farmers to revitalise the farming sector in the attempt to achieve self-sufficiency in basic grains. After 1990, most of these processes were reversed with the electoral defeat of the Sandinistas and the implementation of structural adjustment under the guidance of the International Monetary Fund. As elsewhere in Latin America, structural adjustment has aimed at stabilising the economy, increasing agricultural exports and raising foreign exchange to enable countries to keep up with debt service payments, by cutting public spending and promoting privatisation and export-led growth. Although the Nicaraguan economy has been growing steadily since 1995, this growth is fragile, it is skewed towards consumption rather than production and its benefits have not reached the majority poor. Furthermore, Nicaragua continues to face one of the highest per capita external debts in the world. Servicing that debt requires a continued emphasis on exports.

The globalisation of Latin American economies, which through structural adjustment is promoting continued emphasis on natural resource exploitation, poses a serious threat to local ecosystems. While the rhetoric of sustainability and sustainable development is now commonplace in Nicaragua and elsewhere in Central America, a number of commentators have stressed the disastrous environmental consequences of structural adjustment policies, in particular the ways that these are leading to the overexploitation of natural resources. It is relatively easy to identify what is not sustainable about the rural economy in Nicaragua. The emphasis on export-oriented growth, central to structural adjustment, has pushed marginal farmers to more marginal environments, on the slopes of hillsides and volcanoes or further into the rainforest, where slash and burn techniques are deployed in order to grow subsistence crops. These processes speed up deforestation, intensify processes of land degradation and soil erosion and make flooding, landslides and drought more likely. As Faber has argued, "the resource base for much of Central America's peasantry has reached the point of ecological collapse".

The end of price controls means that *campesinos* are now free to charge higher prices for their crops. However, the privatisation of the banking sector has created a scarcity of credit for small-scale agricultural producers, decreasing productivity, heightening the precariousness of land ownership and forcing many farmers into bankruptcy. Banks, which are now forced to operate according to criteria of profitability, are reluctant to lend to small farmers who are growing crops for domestic consumption. The State Development Bank (BANADES), which had provided credit to rural farmers at favourable interest rates during the 1980s, was closed. At the same time, trade liberalisation under structural adjustment brought in floods of cheap imports which are undercutting locally grown crops. These impacts on the rural sector are fuelling migration to urban areas and inflating the already saturated informal sector of the economy. A recent report by the Unión Nacional de Agricultores y Ganaderos, the National Union of Farmers and Ranchers, states that the principal challenges to small rural farmers in Nicaragua are the lack of access to credit, high production costs because of the high cost of inputs, exposure to pests, and soil erosion and infertility. While the rural development services previously provided by the state to some extent have been picked up by NGOs, there are often huge differences in terms of how rural communities insert themselves into and benefit from the development process.

The force of Hurricane Mitch in these socioeconomic conditions in October 1998 was deadly. The hurricane brought continuous torrential rain for five days over the Nicaraguan-Honduran border where it met a strong anti-cyclone that prevented it from advancing. Unprecedented levels of precipitation caused massive flooding and landslides. Mitch left 11,000 people dead in Central America: 3,000 in Nicaragua. Disease and illness spread in the days after the hurricane owing to the contamination of the water supply by pesticides and chemical waste, by the decomposition of human and animal corpses, and by the hundreds of latrines that had overflowed during flooding, a situation which caused the Ministry of Health to declare an epidemic emergency.

In total in Nicaragua, there were 865,700 *damnificados*, or people directly affected by the hurricane, which amounted to 20 per cent of the total population. The majority of these were left homeless, their houses, livestock, agricultural machinery and crops destroyed. Infrastructure losses, in particular damage to roads, bridges, power lines and sewerage systems, were considerable. The cost of reconstruction and rehabilitation was estimated by the government to be in the order of USD 1.4 billion.

A political ecology framework, which focuses on the intersections between neoliberalism, poverty and environmental degradation, has been central to critiques of structural adjustment in Nicaragua. This approach dominated understandings of Hurricane Mitch, which clearly revealed both the extent of socioeconomic vulnerabilities and environmental degradation. Analysts within the media, civil society and the academic community saw the devastation caused by the hurricane not as an extreme and inevitable natural phenomenon, but as the outcome of the cultivation of marginal land as well as deforestation without soil conservation measures and adequate watershed management, a process fuelled by the growing marginality of the Nicaraguan population. A publication by the Coordinadora Civil para la Emergencia y la Reconstrucción, a civil coalition of 320 NGOs created in the aftermath of Hurricane Mitch to coordinate and evaluate the reconstruction process, stated that the "devastating effects brought about by Mitch are closely related to the consequences of the historical model of development and the prevailing neoliberal economic model" (my translation). Poverty and marginalisation are perceived as direct consequences of transnational practices, where transnational corporations and large landowners growing export crops take up the most fertile land, while *campesinos* are forced to deforest more marginal land in order to plant and build. It is estimated that 80 per cent of all corn and 90 per cent of beans (crops produced for domestic consumption) are grown on slopes, evidence of the extent to which *campesinos* are pushed onto marginal land. This situation is compounded by other aspects of neoliberal structural adjustment policies, such as the cuts in health and education spending and the lack of access to credit schemes for small-scale agricultural producers, leading to deepening inequalities and, consequently, growing vulnerabilities to disaster. It is these economic conditions which are seen to have created such a large-scale disaster, and which make recovery so difficult.

Social Mobilisation and Disaster Response in El Hatillo

El Hatillo was particularly badly affected by Mitch: the deep valley leading to El Hatillo had filled with water, drowning people who had hung onto trees for survival, and because the bridge and the road connecting El Hatillo to Sébaco were destroyed, vehicular access was only possible by driving through the river. Many houses were destroyed, household livelihoods were undermined by the loss of agricultural production, including the chickens and rabbits kept for domestic consumption, and 35,000 seedlings recently planted by the community in a reforestation project were washed away. The community was also forced to close its *comedor infantil*, the communal dining room run for all children under 12, as food supplies were destroyed and other more immediate needs became pressing.

Disasters can provide opportunities for social mobilisation and the possibility to challenge local and national authorities on other aspects of the development process. Puente believes that the spontaneous solidarity which emerged in Mexico City after the 1985 earthquake empowered survivors to tackle the authorities on other issues. In the days following Mitch, high degrees of social mobilisation were reported across Nicaragua and the urgent needs of survivors became linked with protests over the absence of disaster relief. When the community found that neither the municipal nor the national government provided any form of disaster response, they quickly organised an emergency committee in order to bring food in and get the sick and injured out. Silvia Montiel, my key informant in El Hatillo, referred to this process as "*trabajo de hormigas*" – or like the work of ants, which continued until help came from NGOs such as CARE, Fundación Augusto César Sandino (FACS), and the Communal Movement (Movimiento Comunal). By the time I arrived in El Hatillo in 1999, there was a significant NGO presence there and both the Communal Movement and FACS were providing funds for housing, reforestation and agricultural rehabilitation.

Not all communities I worked in who had been affected by the hurricane received aid to rebuild. The resilience of a community after a disaster is often dependent on the levels of organisation within that community, both in terms of its ability to cope and its ability to attract funds from NGOs and aid agencies. It appeared that the most organised communities, with high levels of social mobilisation, were more effective at attracting aid regardless of damages suffered. The women interviewed in El Hatillo were organised into various all-women groups that were involved in a whole series of disaster mitigation and reconstruction measures. These included road clearance and gabion construction, reforestation projects, and the development of vegetable gardens (*huertos familiares*). The women's group in the community had also managed to secure Spanish funding to provide every woman in the community with her own cow (*vaca parida*) which could provide milk and curd for family consumption. In 1999, the group were documenting the ages, heights and weights of all the children in the community to produce a census on child malnutrition levels, armed with which they successfully lobbied agencies and secured funding to reopen the *comedor infantil*. They also ran workshops on reproductive health, aimed primarily at empowering young people to protect themselves from sexually transmitted diseases. The adult education programme had been particularly successful at increasing literacy levels in the community. The women of El Hatillo extended their sense of sacrifice beyond their immediate families to the whole community, carrying out vast amounts of unremunerated work on a rota basis:

> We sacrifice ourselves for the good of the community . . . We don't receive any salary, but work for the whole community, not for personal benefit, but to improve the community. The whole community has agreed to work like this, and this way there is more progress (Rosa Laviana, 13 August 1999).

Local Communal Movement branch leader, Sergio Sáenz, stressed to me that despite the high NGO presence, these groups had emerged autonomously from within the community and were not promoted by any external organisation. There were also uncharacteristically high levels of cooperation during the reconstruction period. When livelihoods are threatened by unsustainable practices, this often leads to conflict, apathy and non-cooperation. In contrast with El Hatillo, the other communities in which I worked did not show such a high degree of cooperation; in other parts of Matagalpa, conflicts were common and aid had a more divisive impact. El Hatillo, faced with extreme environmental and economic conditions, displayed a high degree of social cohesion and cooperation. People willingly helped out in the construction of other people's homes with the aim that, at the end of the project, everyone would have *"una casa bonita"*, a nice house (personal communication Sergio Sáenz, El Hatillo, 13 August 1999).

While disasters often promote social mobilisation, it is important to point out that community organisation in El Hatillo did not emerge with the hurricane but many years prior, with initiatives to improve the water situation:

> It happened like this, that we began to try and find different ways of working, and to be very organised into a women's group. . . . And so we started to appeal to agencies, based on training we had received [from NGOs], and we were learning how to make appeals, and not to focus just on one thing. And that was how the community's work began, and we started to go to Managua, to see what we could do. We couldn't sit back with our arms folded when we had people who were able to work (Silvia Montiel, 10 October 1999).

Silvia was convinced of the value of organisation and that it had helped to generate improvements and reduce the community's vulnerability to disaster. It was community organisation that was creating vegetable gardens, reforesting the hillsides, rearing livestock and protecting the river banks. While Silvia never talked to me about sustainable development as such, as the following quote illustrates, there is a strong concern for the future and posterity, one of the central tenets of the sustainable development paradigm:

> We have a very high level of organisation and I hope that it doesn't fall, but instead of falling, it is increasing – there are people who are becoming more motivated . . . I really think we are doing well. Thanks to God, and that very brave women's group as we call them. They have learnt to value their work, and it involves both young women and adult women, like women of my age, some old already, we are all working, and we have three committees, one for young women, one for middle-aged women and one for the older women, and we are the ones who guide the work . . . we are making plans, just in case we die tomorrow and there is no-one to continue our work. . . . But we know how to use our hands and feet so we will continue struggling for the wellbeing of the community (Silvia Montiel, 10 October 1999).

Although aid dependency was evident in El Hatillo (as even Silvia acknowledged), aid was also constructed as a generator of community motivation and mobilisation. Silvia often referred to the donors, who had brought much needed funding into the community, whom she called "*hermanos donantes*" (literally donor brothers/ sisters):

> because with so many traumas that we have to live through, wars, hurricanes and all that, just like when I lost everything. It was something hard. If it wasn't for the Communal Movement, if it wasn't for the *hermanos donantes* that help us, I don't know what we would have done (Silvia Montiel, 2 December 1999).

However, while acknowledging dependency, she was also careful to stress that the people of El Hatillo were not passive recipients of aid, but rather that the high level of community organisation would ensure that that aid was put to its most effective use:

> the *hermanos donantes* from other countries, they are with us, and it makes us so happy, because they are struggling for us. If it wasn't for them, we wouldn't be alive, and I think it is a very good gesture, and I ask my God for them to continue contributing that grain of sand, because we make good use of it. We are not sitting down doing nothing (Silvia Montiel, 10 October 1999).

Attempts to regenerate or protect natural resources, by planting trees or building gabions to protect riverbanks, are, however, fraught with difficulties in El Hatillo, as are strategies to improve food security and nutrition levels. After Mitch, the government announced that the structural adjustment programme would continue. Cannon has argued that governments' abilities to provide forms of social protection from disaster are limited when they are pursuing an economic policy which is itself the cause of disaster vulnerability. Amidst all the aid and reconstruction efforts, there is overwhelming evidence of a whole series of ongoing vulnerabilities. Poverty, malnutrition and illness persist despite all the organisational efforts and the massive presence of NGOs. Sonia Aguirre's two-year-old son, who repeatedly succumbed to illnesses and was the only live birth of her three pregnancies, had received neither breast milk nor formula milk as a baby and was fed fresh (unpasteurised) milk from Sonia's father's cow. Silvia Montiel told me in 1999 that they had decided not to plant basic grains at all, out of fear that they could lose their land altogether if they took out a loan and the harvest failed (as it did in the drought of 2001). At the end of 2002, the community once again was forced to accept food aid because of the partial loss of the maize harvest through drought. Lack of agricultural credit has forced a number of small ranchers in the community to abandon their land and migrate to Sébaco or Matagalpa. Many of the women in the community had adopted alternative income-earning strategies. While Silvia had managed to create a small shop at her home to sell drinks and snacks, other participants relied on taking on sewing work or jobs as domestic servants in Sébaco. I asked Rosa Laviana what she thought was the biggest difficulty facing the community:

> Poverty, especially for the children who do not have a healthy diet. There is a lot of malnutrition. And that is what causes illnesses, the coughs and colds (Rosa Laviana, 13 August 1999).

The ongoing environmental vulnerabilities of El Hatillo became clear during the heavy rains at the end of 1999. The rains severely tested the community's disaster mitigation measures, especially the gabions that they had been constructing since Mitch. Silvia described the situation to me:

> At the moment we feel sad about this heavy rain, but we have already lost the road, it has been like this for more than two months. What did the mayor of Sébaco say? That there was no problem, that we have only been cut off for six days. But that is not true, there are illnesses, there is diarrhoea, respiratory illnesses, our food has run out. How could we bring food in, even if we wanted to? It is difficult. Our gabions are already loose, which was good work we did with CARE, which involved men, women and children, and Sadie [a CARE worker] told us to look after them. But unfortunately, those in Las Pozas [a nearby rural community] have rolled over, there are several that have rolled over, and here in El Hatillo there are some that are about to roll over . . . It makes me really nervous, because if the water gets in here, we will lose our houses again (Silvia Montiel, 2 December 1999).

It is clear from the persistence of ongoing vulnerabilities in El Hatillo where aid and NGOs have been present that disaster mitigation is really about access to resources, both natural resources such as land and water, and financial resources such as access to credit. Attempts to regenerate resources by planting trees or protecting riverbanks are subject to constant setbacks. In the context of structural adjustment, it is important to focus on long-term economic and environmental vulnerabilities and not just on a major event such as a hurricane. In many ways, the maldistribution of resources is far more serious than an extreme event like a hurricane and can render both aid and organisation far less effective.

Gender Equality and Empowerment

There is very little in the way of formal or informal sector employment for women in El Hatillo and agricultural production displays a marked gender division of labour with men and women growing different crops for different purposes. Women (and children) are largely responsible for the collection of firewood and water, both time-consuming activities. After the hurricane, with NGO funding for agricultural rehabilitation, a group of 18 men, organised into a cooperative, continued to grow chayotes destined for the Managua market. There were no women members in the chayote cooperative. Women, on the other hand, ceased their own commercial agricultural production in order to concentrate on repair and reconstruction work. The year before the hurricane, the women's group had successfully produced and sold soya, but more than a year after they were still working on post-hurricane reconstruction and had not been able to replant:

> We have a plot of land but as we got involved in the business of the houses, the business of the gabions, that is all so difficult. But we have already produced too, we have experience in growing soya, we were selling it, our first experience went so well, we sold heaps of soya (Silvia Montiel, 2 December 1999).

So, although the women in El Hatillo were visibly engaged in hard physical labour usually associated with men, this was done at the expense of other productive activities. The women's group had formulated a number of plans to increase their own production and nutrition levels in the community, including the vegetable garden and milk cow schemes mentioned above. Many of these initiatives, though significant to the nutritional level of the community, also meant that women were focusing more on subsistence style agriculture while the men controlled the more lucrative commercial agriculture, as was the case with chayote production.

Disaster reconstruction work can make women more visible in male-dominated spaces, as it did in El Hatillo, but it also considerably increases their workload, and the associated stresses can delay recovery. Bradshaw has indicated that participation in the reconstruction process after Hurricane Mitch did not necessarily bring benefits to women as it may reinforce rather than challenge "traditional" gender roles. Given that the women in El Hatillo put their own productive activities on hold to focus on disaster reconstruction work, it might seem obvious to conclude therefore that women have been disadvantaged by their involvement in disaster reconstruction processes and that agricultural rehabilitation initiatives promoted by NGOs have brought greater benefits for men. Shifts in gender relations appear not to be taking place. However, by focusing not just on gender relations but also on gender identities, it became clear to me that these processes are not so straightforward and can have contradictory outcomes, as the involvement in the milk cow scheme demonstrates.

To reiterate, women in El Hatillo were engaged primarily in unremunerated work in the community or in subsistence agriculture, while the more profitable work was entirely controlled by men. Laurie has pointed out how the GAD paradigm has tended to relegate these kinds of activities carried out by women to the realm of the "feminine" and the "traditional" and to assume that they cannot be empowering. Feminists working in Nicaragua have criticised the way in which NGOs working in rural communities tend to promote such subsistence activities – known as *economía de patio*, literally patio economy – for women, rather than more large-scale and profitable agriculture such as cattle-ranching or coffee production. When I visited El Hatillo in 1999, the women were seeking funding from a Spanish aid agency for the milk cow programme primarily to cater for family consumption. When I returned to El Hatillo in 2001, the first phase of the programme was underway; 20 women had their own cows, with a revolving credit fund of C\$20,000 (about USD 1,400). I had not expected such an excited response, but Silvia Montiel told me happily how she had a cow that gave up to six litres of milk a day in winter.

In many ways, the milk cows enabled women to better fulfill their maternal roles and obligations in providing food and improving family nutrition. Such a scheme did not challenge the gender division of labour in the community and is not disruptive to gender relations: according to Silvia, the men in the community had been very supportive of the project. From a development perspective, it is easy to see the way in which traditional gender roles are being perpetuated. But, in terms of gendered subjectivities, it would be misleading to suggest that the cows were not empowering for a number of reasons. First, the successful implementation of an aid programme attests to the power of community-based struggles and leads women to believe that their problems are not insuperable. A milk cow will not end gender inequality; but the resolution of a practical need and being able to produce something that would otherwise have to be purchased can in itself be empowering. Finding a way out of poverty is empowering even if existing gender relations are barely challenged. Second, it was clear to me that such programmes were seen as part of a process, not as an end in themselves. In many ways, it seemed that the women in El Hatillo were strategically working towards greater gender equality in a way which was *seen* as less disruptive to gender relations and, therefore, less likely to bring about conflict in the community. These women could be seen as implementing what Vargas calls "an intuitive sort of political calculation". Vargas' work on Peru has highlighted what she sees as the contradictory nature of emancipation. She demonstrates how women can simultaneously occupy different subject positions and how gender awareness can in itself bring about democratic change in other subject positions. However, in some areas, traditional behaviour is maintained, and sometimes even reinforced. This can be attributed to the ambiguous and painful nature of liberation. Women often recognise the presence of discrimination, but might find comfort in it because it provides a sense of continuity and prevents the uncertainty of new positions and subjectivities from being overwhelming. As Sweetman has indicated, "women as well as men might have a vested interest in keeping up the illusion that gender ideology is being adhered to".

The women of El Hatillo, while deprived for the time being from full access to the means of production by both sociocultural norms and the aid distribution process, were nonetheless managing to negotiate considerable freedoms and respect from their menfolk, which suggests that gender relations and identities are often redefined in unexpected ways. While women in other communities expressed desperation at their situation, the women of El Hatillo expressed a sense of both liberation and happiness in how they managed to negotiate the time and space to experience themselves positively, and not only through social and political organisation, but also through music, sport and religion:

> Now I give thanks to God, that after I suffered so much, now I have a happy life, relaxed, and I have my kids . . . [my husband] has seen how much I've suffered, that I wasn't allowed to go out, to live my life. I learnt to play the guitar, I don't play well, but I have some idea and I enjoy myself. I go out, I sing songs, I dance, I'm relaxed . . . and at the moment I am 38 years old and I feel like I have the spirit of a child, I skip, I jump, and so on, and I like enjoying myself. And I tell the young girls and women of my age too, to liberate themselves, to be happy, to skip, to jump, because it is good exercise for the body (Rosa Laviana, 2 December 1999).

> I have learnt to use my manners, thanks to my parents, who brought me up this way, and thanks to the Communal Movement, who guided me, and all the other organisations that are supporting me with training and all the rest so I could change my life . . . I have learnt how to visit the communities I am responsible for. Now I go there with confidence, I eat beans with them and play with them, just like I would if I was in my own community. I like sport, I like to be shouting, I think it is what I enjoy most, and I look after my home, I love my children and I think that is something good that God has given to me (Silvia Montiel, 10 October 1999).

The struggle for gender equality, in El Hatillo as elsewhere, takes complex and contradictory forms. Single motherhood is widespread in Nicaragua and there is evidence that a number of women are adopting single motherhood as a long-term strategy in response to male irresponsibility or violence. However, it is important to acknowledge the existence of these strategies without constructing men and expressions of masculinity as monolithic, or reproducing stereotypes of irresponsible men and nurturing women. Environmental relationships are gendered, and the struggles for environmental sustainability taking place in El Hatillo cannot be separated from broader struggles for gender equality and cultural change.

What was happening in El Hatillo is illustrative of the multifaceted ways in which women negotiate gender inequality. In El Hatillo, the women I interviewed were very critical of the *machismo* in their families and their community, but were trying to find ways of resolving conflicts and working with their male partners, rather than leaving them. They also believed that tolerance of endemic gendered problems such as domestic violence, alcoholism and infidelity was decreasing in the community. Expressions of femininity also take particular forms in El Hatillo. In urban working class culture in Nicaragua, it is fashionable to dress in an overtly sexualised fashion. The women of El Hatillo told me how women in the community had begun to take pride in their appearance, which was interpreted by them as evidence of how much women had liberated themselves. Formerly, they did not comb their hair, put on make-up or dress up to avoid making their husbands jealous or suspicious. This had all changed now, they told me, and women could now make themselves look nice. They were, however, also quick to condemn the two or three women in the village who were known to have had extramarital affairs and whose behaviour was seen to represent a loss of values. This suggests that female sexuality in El Hatillo can be expressed within a context of personal hygiene, but must also be policed.

The women of El Hatillo are not straightforwardly dependent or independent, traditional or emancipated. The structural constraints in their lives, such as sexism and poverty, are enormous, but their responses to these constraints are strategic and calculated. Through their participation in autonomously defined development projects and in reconstruction work which was simultaneously unremunerated/feminised and involved hard physical labour/masculinised, they created spaces in which gender relations in the community could be reworked. These reworkings are often positive in terms of identity renegotiation. The gendered negotiations taking place in El Hatillo demonstrate the degree to which constructions of masculinity and femininity are constantly reworking themselves as they engage with processes of development and respond to both neoliberalism and environmental risk.

Conclusions

The idea that political, economic and environmental marginalisation are mutually constituted has been central to political ecology approaches for some time. Marginalisation is not, however, a straight-forward concept. In El Hatillo, marginality is simultaneously strategically deployed and resisted. Coping with environmental risk, economic disadvantage and gender inequality on this scale means that the terrains of political struggle are multifaceted and that constant tradeoffs between economic survival, natural resource management and existing cultural practices must be made. The strategies adopted in this context therefore both reproduce and challenge environmental risk and gender inequality.

The women of El Hatillo were aware of their complex positionings as natural resource managers, development actors, marginalised rural people and gendered beings. They had to negotiate a number of complex relationships of power with local NGOs, international donors, the state and the men in their lives in a geographically marginalised environment, and they did so by prioritising political and gender identities in different ways. The organisational strategies formulated in response to these relationships create what Escobar has termed "decentered autonomous spaces", in which neoliberalism, gender inequality and environmental degradation are responded to in complex ways.

As Nesmith and Radcliffe have argued, environmental feminisms articulate specific philosophies, politics and identities that may contribute to the development of a new critical geography of the environment. In a sense, the women of El Hatillo engaged in environmental feminist practices without evoking essentialism or romanticising connections to nature. To be sure, their environmental concerns can be constructed as maternal and gendered in the way that they assume (unpaid) responsibility for collective reproductive health and protecting hillsides and riverbanks. Alternative and more sustainable development models are hard to achieve when environmental and economic vulnerabilities are of this magnitude, but envisioning alternative ontologies is possible. The women in El Hatillo forged collective political identities as community managers and subjects of their own development who are visibly and decisively addressing the problems associated with land degradation, declining food security and environmental hazard. It is a gradual process; the setbacks are huge and the struggles take place within a national and global context that militates against sustainability. Natural resource management and responses to structural adjustment in El Hatillo, resulting in the active assertion of identity politics and a high level of commitment to the development process, must therefore be considered through both rural and gendered lenses. This approach enables us to see how a new critical geography of the environment which integrates disaster mitigation, poverty alleviation and gender equality is being constructed from a position of marginality.

Chapter 33

The Sahel of West Africa: A Place for Geographers?

Simon Batterbury

The term 'Sahel' is derived from the Arabic word for 'edge' or border, and describes a transitional zone forming the southern border of the Sahara desert. The West African Sahel runs for at least 4500 km from Senegal through Mauritania, Mali, Burkina Faso, Niger and Chad, and blends into the slightly less arid Sudano-Sahel belt to its southern edge (Figure 33.1). Semi-arid West Africa is a fast-changing and diverse region, containing a vast range of environments, ethnic groups, and landscapes. It was once home to powerful empires which profited from trans-Saharan trade, but with the arrival of the European colonial powers it became increasingly marginalised from world political and economic affairs. Problems of land degradation, water and food shortage cause frequent hardship and disruption for the indigenous farmers and herders. Today, droughts are frequent and many individuals lack secure access to the grazing and farming land they need. Non-agricultural income is scarce, and often requires Sahelian peoples to migrate southwards in large numbers in search of paid work or trade. These and other aspects of rural poverty are compounded by political and economic crises. Over the last few decades the Sahelian environment has been 'transformed' by social and environmental change, and its people have been forced to abandon longstanding ways of life.

The Geographer's Role

How can Western-trained geographers and social scientists find a useful role in the vast Sahel region of West Africa, given its diversity and its problems? First, linking with our African colleagues is one important task, in order to share information

Batterbury, Simon, "The Sahel of West Africa: A Place for Geographers?" pp. 391–4 from *Geography*, 81.353 (1996).

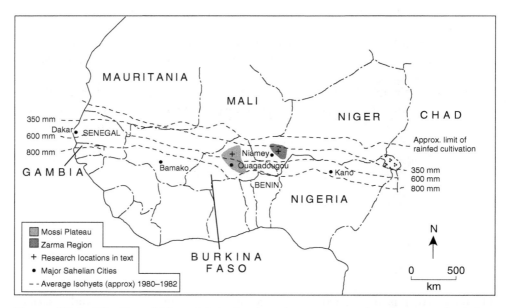

Figure 33.1 The West African Sahel, showing places mentioned in the text. The definition of the Sahel is disputed, and is best defined by its ecology and vegetation. Sahelian conditions are found where annual rainfall is between 100 mm and 800 mm, although above 500–600 mm per year the term Sudano-Sahel is often applied.

and resources, and to learn. Some of the key themes studied by geographers today include the ways in which economic, social and environmental change influence people's access to basic resources such as adequate land or animal herds, and the ways in which livelihood systems change with the region's high population growth, land pressures, new technologies, and high rates of migration. Evidence collected in recent years has shown how people cope with risk and overcome natural and human-induced hazards. These responses to environmental phenomena and to economic hardship are very diverse. For example, a poor harvest in late 1995 in one village in southwest Niger (Figure 33.1) resulted in a wide range of responses from the indigenous Zarma people over subsequent months. By the dry season in early 1996, most young men had migrated to seek paid work as petty traders in Ivory Coast, and they only returned to the village some months later to cultivate their land with their families. Other men exploited differentials in the price of cattle at local markets to buy healthy young cows and to profit from their sale close to Islamic festivals. A fortunate few sold their skills as Islamic wise men, promising good fortune to their clients. Still others went to seek work in local gold mines, worked on the fields of richer farmers or took on paid work such as feeding and watering animals. Women, not permitted by custom to sell produce at village markets and more constrained in their choices, traded from their huts in grain, wood, mats, sauce ingredients and 'fast foods', such as bean-cakes. Several took on the rearing of sheep and goats. Others found excuses to go to visit their parents in the city, where better conditions could be found for their children. These are positive efforts by people to 'diversify' their sources of income and food in bad years, and to increase their options in times of hardship. Niger, a poor francophone nation, is currently going through major political changes and economic restructuring, and the government has very few funds to support its rural communities at present.

We should remember that the types of adaptation observable in Zarma villages are not always enough to ensure a good quality of life or even survival. The same village has suffered four major famines this century, caused by drought, locusts and colonial mis-management. Under such conditions, it is hard for farmers to invest the time and capital needed to improve their agricultural systems, and in recent years wind and water erosion have stripped loose topsoil from some farmers' fields, and deposited sediment elsewhere, burying and killing the millet crop. Despite having a low population density, 62 per cent of the village lands were farmed or fallow in 1992. Crop yields vary widely, according to soil quality, moisture availability and localised damage from grazing animals and pests.

Secondly, development problems and issues of equity and justice are too pressing to ignore. An 'applied' geography of Sahelian environments should examine issues such as the 'environmental management' of land degradation, focusing on problem-solving and development initiatives and helping to translate local needs and knowledge into appropriate development strategies. We should provide opportunities for people to describe and explain their history and land use patterns, for example, by offering them air photos of their lands and creating local maps. Geographers with practical skills can also offer advice to farmers on land rehabilitation and soil and water conservation, monitor its effectiveness, and publicise indigenous methods developed by farmers themselves.

Locally based efforts to nurture and protect the resource base are a feature of many development initiatives in the Sahel today. There are literally thousands of farmer co-operatives, small scale NGO projects, internationally funded development projects and programmes involved in environmental rehabilitation, soil and water conservation, rural health, and other forms of support to rural people. All have a profound influence on rural livelihoods, but not all are beneficial. Geographers and other social scientists are urgently needed to monitor the successful and failed impacts of development projects and co-operative ventures on access to resources, social differentiation, and environmental quality. What do farmers learn from projects, and is their knowledge broadened and altered by contact with them? Practical research can permit local people to take over the management of running their *own* development initiatives, since we know that development rarely succeeds where it is imposed or where it ignores complex social and ecological realities. Work is needed within environmental programmes to help to monitor the impacts of soil and water conservation and watershed management on access to resources, livelihoods, and local ecology.

A classic case for better monitoring of the environmental impacts of development policy is the Central Plateau of Burkina Faso, occupied by the Mossi people (Figure 33.1). The Plateau, which straddles the Sahel and Sudano-Sahel zones, is a 'laboratory' for some of the most innovative techniques in soil and water conservation and agroforestry in dryland Africa. Farmers are suffering poor crop yields and pasture quality, but have proved particularly keen to embrace new ideas and methods to conserve soil and water. Some of these ideas have come from European volunteers and farmers experimenting together, and are transforming the landscape around hundreds of villages. Contour stone lines built by farmers and consisting of lines of stones and rocks placed across the land contour are cheap and popular erosion control methods and are much publicised by development projects. These are built to slow the erosive overland flow from summer rains and to encourage the deposition of sediment and nutrients up-slope, thus benefiting crops and trees.

Many projects are helping farmers to build their own stone lines. Successful examples include Oxfam's *Projet Agroforestier* in Yatenga, and PATECORE, a bilateral initiative between German Technical Co-operation (GTZ) and the Burkina Ministry of Agriculture in Bam. Both projects have hosted geographers (including the author) and other researchers, who have found project staff and local people to be highly competent at environmental rehabilitation. The Mossi are slowly being given more power in the conservation process, but these and other projects have been slower to involve women and Peul herders in their activities, and are having difficulties turning over conservation works entirely to village institutions. So although stone lines and other conservation works are now highly visible features of the contemporary rural landscape, if these techniques are to be refined and extended by village groups and volunteers, more applied research and collaboration with farmers is required.

Conclusion

The difficulties experienced by many projects are not only a function of the scale of the problem and the harshness of the Sahelian environment, but also arise from the competing viewpoints and objectives of those involved. Environmental issues in developing countries are perceived differently by diverse 'actors' and it is often a failure to communicate and understand each other that leads to a 'messy' policy 'environment', the misapplication of technology or knowledge, and the potential failure of projects. In the Sahel, we urgently need to study the important changes which development projects are setting in motion, as well as how these projects 'think' about the people and environments they are working with. Geographers are well placed to assist in this through the range of critical skills they gain in their training, especially where this involves study of 'nature-society' or 'people-environment' interactions, and long-term fieldwork. So as well as working with farmers and assessing long-term trends, we should also work with those in positions of influence and power to *improve their interventions* and to help ensure positive benefits to rural people and their livelihood systems, and to help translate the wishes of rural dwellers into 'project language'.

This is a vital aspect of geography, and of rural development, which should not be overlooked. An applied geography of environmental management must aid, assist and participate in this process, to ensure that the voices of those unable to shout loudly are heard, and to ensure communal and progressive environmental action is maintained. For, as many geographers are discovering, the Sahel is a special place indeed:

> And what a stranger feels in the Sahel, more strongly than most other places on earth, is the power of the unspoken, the impalpable. Between the lines, therefore, you must read many long silences, a lot of human warmth and laughter, a reverence for all the spirits that have been part of the world since time immemorial – and imagine above it all, from one flat horizon to the other, the great unbroken canopy of sky.

We need to challenge the thinking and actions of everybody involved in the Sahel's future, and must not overlook clashes, conflicts and failures which are often starting points for more effective action. Assisting rural people's own efforts at environmental management and problem-solving is one place where geographers can find a role in the Sahel.

Chapter 34

Geography, Culture, and Prosperity

Andres Oppenheimer

In the 1940s, a Chilean artist jokingly proposed the following idea to step up his homeland's economic prosperity: "Why don't we sell this country and buy something a little bit smaller, but closer to Paris?"

I was reminded of this line recently while reading "Culture Matters," a new book edited by Harvard University professor Samuel Huntington and a university associate, Lawrence Harrison, in which several prominent scholars argue that environmental factors such as geography, climate and religion are key reasons some nations prosper, and others don't.

Why, the authors ask, has South Korea boomed while other countries such as Honduras remained mired in poverty, when there was not much of a difference between them in the 1960s? Why is Japan a rich nation, and Peru not?

In addition to Huntington and Harrison, the book contains essays by David Landes, Francis Fukuyama, Jeffrey Sachs and Latin American writers Carlos Alberto Montaner and Mariano Grondona.

Some of its authors, such as Harvard University's Sachs, argue that geography explains much of the development puzzle. Almost all the rich countries are in temperate zones, while the vast majority of poor nations are in tropical zones, he says.

The tropics have historically suffered from poor crops because of high soil erosion and devastating pests. Infectious diseases such as malaria and the Chagas' disease spread faster in hotter climates. And landlocked countries have been handicapped by their difficulties in trading with the rest of the world, says Sachs.

Huntington, Harrison and Fukuyama, on the other hand, argue that what makes countries prosper is their cultural values. South Koreans are prospering because they value thrift, investment, hard work, education, organization and discipline.

Oppenheimer, Andres, "Geography, Culture, and Prosperity," p. B-9 from the *Miami Herald*, August 1, 2000.

In Roman Catholic societies and many former Communist countries, economic development is difficult because the poor feel justified in their poverty, and the rich feel like sinners, they argue. By comparison, in Protestant and Confucian cultures, people celebrate success as evidence of God's blessings, and the poor see their condition as God's condemnation.

"They yearn for equality in poverty," writes Landes. "As the Russian joke has it, peasant Ivan is jealous of neighbor Boris because Boris has a goat. A fairy comes along and offers Ivan a single wish. What does he wish for? That Boris' goat should drop dead!"

To their credit, the authors agree that culture can be changed, and should be. But one can't help but wonder about the exceptions.

If geography is so important, why is Costa Rica doing so much better than Guatemala, Honduras, Nicaragua and El Salvador? Why is tropical Singapore doing well, and cold Russia suffering? Or landlocked Switzerland enjoying its wealth, while Bolivia is still in poverty?

And if culture is so important, why are expatriate Cubans doing so well in the United States, while their counterparts on the island make an average wage of $10 a month, according to Cuban government figures?

There are nearly as many ways to argue that policies can turn a society around in a relatively short time. Take Chile, which has grown at phenomenal rates for the last 15 years.

"In the 1940s, it was said that Chile would never take off because it had a business class of absentee landlords that spent their time playing polo," says Andres Velasco, a Harvard University professor of international development who is somewhat critical of the book.

"Now, everybody is saying that Chile's business class is a model of entrepreneurship. What happened? Those same polo players got off their horses, and started exporting their goods as soon as there was an economic opening."

My conclusion: Yes, geography and culture do matter. But politics count more, because – to quote Sen. Daniel Patrick Moynihan – "politics can change a culture and save it from itself."

You can sell your country and buy something closer to Paris, but unless you have the right policies in place, you won't prosper.

Part VIII

Political Geography

Introduction

David A. Lanegran

Modern political geography began in the late nineteenth century as the European empires were expanding their spheres of influence in Africa and Asia and were facing rebellious "nationalities" within the boundaries of their new colonies. The field of geography that focused on the interactions among geography, military power, politics, and international relations was labeled geopolitics. This subfield began with the work of the German geographer Fredrick Ratzel, who attempted to develop a theory that would explain why certain states grew powerful and how other states might develop strategies to become powerful as well. His work led to the theory of the organic state and emphasized nationalism. Ratzel believed that control of territory was the key to the success of states and that countries needed to expand to the greatest extent possible to survive. His followers raised questions and developed theories on the nature of states: how they become organized and expand, why they decline, and what are the roles of boundaries and symbols in their functioning.

In the United States, nearly every national leader practiced "applied political geography" as they expanded the national territory and struggled to create policies to bind the country together. This work was complemented by a school of geopolitics, developed by British and American scholars, who attempted to convey insights on how geography might influence military strategies and how states interact with each other on the global scale. Sir Halford J. Mackinder and Admiral Mahan are the names most closely associated with this school of thought. The British/American school was profoundly affected by Mackinder's thinking about the relationship between land and sea power in imperial expansion and competition. Unlike his contemporaries in the British Colonial Office and the Admiralty who believed the key to maintaining the empire was to rule the seas, Mackinder argued that a land power based in Central Asia and Siberia would be invulnerable to attack by naval forces and could eventually rule the world. Mackinder restated and modified his ideas several times over the course of his life (1904, 1919, and 1943), and his theory eventually became known as the Heartland Theory. Because this theory is focused on the relationships between superpowers, it became the foundation for most international policy during the twentieth century, and its influence has continued to the present. Most of the work in this branch of geopolitics is done outside of the academic community in think tanks, government agencies, and the military.

Recently, critical geopolitics emerged in response to the notion that geopolitics is the result of dispassionate and neutral objectivity. This group of scholars argues that national leaders and others involved in diplomacy have developed ideas about the places and people that support their political agendas rather than using knowledge of places and people to develop political agendas. In his article, Nick Megoran applies critical geopolitics to the works of three scholars writing about the role of Uzbekistan and Central Asia in the emerging international political order. With these works he is able to show how some of the concepts of Mackinder have been modified to suit preconceived notions about the role of Central Asia in international relations and how differences in world cultures affect the relations of the great powers. Megoran points out that most North Americans know little about Central Asia and so the Heartland Theory is frequently accepted as fact rather than a conceptual framework.

Political geography has long focused on the nature of boundaries or limits of power and authority. Today the map most people associate with geographers is the map of countries around the world with each state neatly bounded by a line established with mathematical precision. It is interesting to note that the boundaries of the countries do not correlate with any other distribution on the surface of the earth. Some boundaries follow heights of land, some follow valleys, others are drawn straight across the landscape without regard to topography. Some cut through culture groups while others do not. Some lines, like that separating North and South Korea, are heavily fortified. Others, such as portions of the boundary between Canada and the United States, are hardly marked. Nonetheless, each line on the map resulted from some sort of struggle that established the limits of power. Recently the nature of boundaries has been changed by developments in Europe and North America. The United States has been hardening its border to control potential terrorists and limit the number of workers coming into the country without permission. On the other hand, the article by Kepka and Murphy describes how national borders separating European states have become significantly more porous, enabling transborder regions to develop.

The selection we have excerpted from the much longer article by Don Mitchell, "The End of Public Space? People's Park, Definitions of the Public, and Democracy," presents political geography at the urban scale. Using the long conflict over People's Park in Berkeley, California, Mitchell discusses the meaning of space. At this scale, concepts of ownership, citizenship, and the public replace the concepts of sovereignty, borders, and the forms of large-scale countries. Nonetheless, there are direct connections between the concepts of nationalism and the use of public space. Mitchell argues that physical public space is needed for an inclusive democratic system to function. He is careful to distinguish between public space as a physical place and the public sphere as an abstract set of institutions and values. Public spaces are needed for demonstrations, for protests, and as refuges for the subaltern population to escape from the restrictions of the dominant social group. In the case of the People's Park, the homeless are important actors because the park had become a safe haven for them. Because the homeless lack access to the institutions of political power, the use of the space was their only option for exerting public pressure. After reading this article, discuss how much open space versus public space is found on your campus. What are the public spaces? Where are the homeless in your community? How significant is public space to inclusive democracy in your communities?

DISCUSSION READINGS

Megoran, Nick. (2004). "Revisiting the 'Pivot': The Influence of Halford Mackinder on Analysis of Uzbekistan's International Relations." *Geographical Journal*, 170(4): 347–58.

Kepka, Joanna M. M. & Murphy, Alexander B. (2002). "Euroregions in Comparative Perspective: Differential Implications for Europe's Borderlands." In David H. Kaplan & Jouni Häkli (eds.), *Boundaries and Place: European Borderlands in Geographical Context*. Boulder, CO: Rowman & Littlefield. Pp. 50–69.

Mitchell, Don. (1995). "The End of Public Space? People's Park, Definitions of the Public, and Democracy." *Annals of the Association of American Geographers*, 85(1): 108–33.

Chapter 35

Revisiting the "Pivot": The Influence of Halford Mackinder on Analysis of Uzbekistan's International Relations

Nick Megoran

The editor of a recent book on security and foreign policy issues in Central Asia and the Caucasus introduced it by stating that Sir Halford Mackinder's 1904 identification of this region as the key to world geopolitics is an apt characterization of twenty-first century reality. He implied that this was reason enough to study it. Mackinder was not referred to again. What is striking is that, whereas geographers have produced much work in the past two decades exploring and critiquing Mackinder's geopolitics, Jones simply took him as a premise. This is not unusual in contemporary writing on Central Asia, and Uzbekistan in particular, which has witnessed a remarkable revival in interest in Mackinder's theory since the collapse of the Soviet Union.

This paper explores this phenomenon further and investigates the reception of Mackinder a century on, in one corner of his 'pivot'. It examines the work of an Uzbek, a Russian and an American as it seeks to demarcate their respective understandings of Mackinder as well as their conclusions regarding his application to foreign policy today. The paper pays particular attention to the strategic partnership that has emerged between the United States and Uzbekistan since the US invasion of Taliban-run Afghanistan from Uzbekistan's territory in autumn 2001.

Revisiting Central Asia with Mackinder

In January 1904 Sir Halford Mackinder delivered an elegantly crafted lecture to the Royal Geographical Society that was to become his best-known publication.

Megoran, Nick, "Revisiting the 'Pivot': The Influence of Halford Mackinder on Analysis of Uzbekistan's International Relations," pp. 347–56 from *Geographical Journal*, 170.4 (2004).

According to Mackinder, the impact on Europe of successive population move-ments over 'Euro-Asia' demonstrates that this region is the pivot on which world history turns. In the industrial age, the natural resources of this great pivot are so vast that in time the state that controls them will develop into an economic super-power and be well placed to become 'the empire of the world'. For Mackinder, who saw the powers best placed to exploit this resource (Russia, Germany, and China) as inimical to the democratic freedoms represented by Britain, this was an alarming prospect, and one that British foreign policy ought to aim to counter.

In order to assess the way in which Mackinder's ideas have influenced writing on Central Asia, it is necessary to define the region in question. The four million square kilometres bordered by the Caspian Sea in the west, Afghanistan, Iran, and Pakistan to the south, the Taklamakan desert in the east, and Siberian Russia to the north are commonly termed 'Central Asia' in recent literature, of which they have generated a great deal since the break-up of the Soviet Union in 1991. However, this has not always been the case: Lewis and Wigen observe how these lands have frequently been occluded from the gaze of Europeans, who have not consistently conceived of them as a single region. Indeed, although including them in all three iterations of his heartland thesis (1904, 1919, 1943), Mackinder himself did not single them out for particular significance. In the 1904 paper 'The geo-graphical pivot of history', presented to the Royal Geographical Society (henceforth Pivot), Mackinder projects the 'Heart-land' east of the Ural mountains as largely undifferentiated, 'unknown recesses of Europe' and 'vacant space', through which swept a 'cloud of ruthless and idealess horsemen'. Whilst the term 'Central Asia' is mentioned in passing, its geographical extent is unclear and no special signifi-cance is attached to it. His 1919 and 1943 re-workings were, understandably, pre-occupied with the core sites of the two World Wars and their aftermaths. Nonetheless, the Pivot paper has been of particular interest to Central Asianists, and has been claimed as the only major theory articulated using Central Asian source material.

In 1990 Hauner remarked that 'revisiting the heartland' and re-assessing Mackinder's theory in the light of changing realities has been a popular activity since 1945. This paper identifies three distinct periods of 'revisiting' Mackinder's relevance for Central Asia: post-World War II, the 1980s, and the period since the demise of the Soviet Union in 1991.

Unsurprisingly, in the post-World War II 'Cold War' period many attempts were made to assess the USSR in terms of Mackinder's theory, both as an academic exercise to test the theory and as a strategic evaluation of the level of threat to the capitalist world posed by the USSR. However, apart from mentioning northern Kazakhstan, these studies rarely devote much attention to Central Asia. Mineral-rich and expansive Siberia was a more alluring target of analysis and, logistically, more accessible to the gaze of Anglophone Soviet experts.

This began to change in the 1980s, as witnessed primarily by Hauner's impor-tant study of the place of Asia in Russian geopolitical imaginations, with particular reference to Mackinder. Citing the Afghan War and high birth rates in Central Asia, Hauner called for the 'heartland' debate to be revisited. But there were other reasons why foreign scholars began to conceive of Central Asia as an entity in its own right at this time. The transfer of resources meant that the region could claim higher living standards than any of its Muslim neighbours, and Central Asia became a showcase of Muslim socialist development in the midst of superpower competition, even sending hundreds of development specialists around the world. Finally, limited although rising anti-Moscow sentiment drew the attention of ideologically driven 'Sovietologists' who hoped that a resurgent Muslim Central Asia would prove the undoing of the Soviet empire. Theoretically, these developments coincided with a renewed interest in the geopolitical legacy of Halford Mackinder.

It was not until the break-up of the Soviet Union in 1991 and the emergence of independent states that Central Asia really crystallized as a concrete issue in the application of Mackinder's ideas. Geographers have, however, been relatively quiet on this topic. Blouet says of Central Asia that '[t]he geopolitical faultlines still lie around Mackinder's Heartland', but this is simply a passing observation. Geographers interested in the reception and use of Mackinder in the former Soviet Union have tended to focus on Russia rather than Central Asia. There is as yet no study of the place of Central Asia in geopolitical imaginations to even remotely match Bassin's detailed account of the Russian far east. This neglect is somewhat ironic, as Central Asia was of great significance for the institutionalization of British geography. Indeed, Watson argues that, '[t]he Royal Geographical Society established its credentials as an Orientalist authority to no small degree through the exploits of its surveys of Central Asia'. This history, with its multiple imperial entanglements and enduring legacy, is still largely waiting to be recovered and evaluated.

It cannot be said, however, that scholars of other disciplines have overlooked the geopolitical significance of Central Asia, nor been shy to consider it in the terms of Mackinder. For example, Sloan, Head of the Department of Strategic Studies and International Affairs at the Britannia Royal Navy College in Dartmouth, writes that as hydrocarbon-rich 'Central Asia is once more a key to the security of all Eurasia', Mackinder's 'understanding of the political implications of new technology with the persistence of certain geographical patterns of political history' makes him essential for the formulation of Western foreign policy in the region. In a superficial assessment of the contemporary applicability of Mackinder for Central Asia, Robbins reworks Mackinder's famous heartland dictum to read 'Who controls the Silk Pipelines controls the world'. An Internet search for 'Uzbekistan' and 'Mackinder' throws up scores of papers, newspaper articles, and teaching syllabi.

The bulk of this extensive recent literature overlooks the more in-depth geographical studies of Mackinder and his legacy over the past two decades, both sympathetic and critical. As over-simplified and mis-represented versions of Mackinder's work are used so uncritically as a premise by people who seek to influence policy-makers and practitioners, that is disturbing. Although Fettweis and Edwards have bemoaned the superficial way in which Mackinder is tacked onto analyses of Central Asia, there has not yet been an attempt to systematically and critically study how Mackinder's thought has been used in discussion of Central Asia. This paper is a modest attempt to begin that process.

Whilst this paper describes the way in which Mackinder is used to analyse Uzbekistan, it does not attempt to assess the factual accuracy or otherwise of Mackinder's ideas in the light of 'the course of events'. Rather, it is located within a different intellectual project, that of 'critical geopolitics'. This critique of the geopolitical tradition disputes the contention that geopolitics is the discovery of independent facts, but rather seeks to explore and disclose contingent political arguments concealed by apparently objective geopolitical language. In particular, this essay draws on Polelle's study of Mackinder, Haushofer and Spykman.

Polelle reads Mackinder's Pivot paper not as a morally neutral unearthing of eternal spatial verities, but as a way of depoliticizing imperialism to represent the interest of the British state in apparently scientific language, and also as the projection of an idealized image of what British identity ought to be. This paper traces this theme in the contemporary use of Mackinder. It examines the geopolitical arguments related to Uzbekistan of three of what Polelle terms 'defence intellectuals' or 'civilian militarists' – intellectuals who used their position in civil society to advocate particular foreign policy positions for their respective governments.

Uzbekistan in Central Asia

The Uzbek Soviet Socialist Republic was created in 1924 by the new Soviet authorities from territories of the abolished Khanates of Khiva and Khoqand and the Emirate of Bukhara, which had come under tsarist rule in the nineteenth century. The Soviet authorities divided Central Asia up into union republics and novel ethnicities, constructing concepts of national culture and history, and forming administrations in new capital cities within new boundaries.

It was this Soviet creation that became the independent republic of Uzbekistan (see Figure 35.1) with the termination of the Soviet Union in 1991. With no history of independent statehood to recover, the President, former Uzbek Communist Party boss Islam Karimov, legitimized the existence of Uzbekistan through the national framework created by the Soviets, a framework that had institutionalized ethnicity in Central Asia. President Karimov describes this project as the 'ideology of national independence', involving a rewriting of Uzbek history that projects putative Uzbek statehood back into the pre-Christian era. In particular, he has exalted the ruler Amir Timur (1336–1405), whose Samarkand-based empire is shown in Figure 35.1, as the paragon of patriotic Uzbek statesmanship. That Timur's dynasty was actually expelled from Central Asia by the Uzbeks is an irony that is conveniently overlooked in this narrative.

Evoking further comparisons with Timur, the authoritarian president has earned a reputation for tolerating little dissent, epitomized by his widely reported statement to parliament in May 1998 that 'Islamic extremists . . . must be shot in the head. If necessary, I'll shoot them myself'. Opponents have been silenced, imprisoned or executed: Human Rights Watch claimed in January 2003 that there were almost 7000 prisoners of conscience in Uzbek jails, and that torture is routine. Karimov is particularly hostile to any form of politicized Islam, which he identifies as having the greatest potential threat as an opposition force.

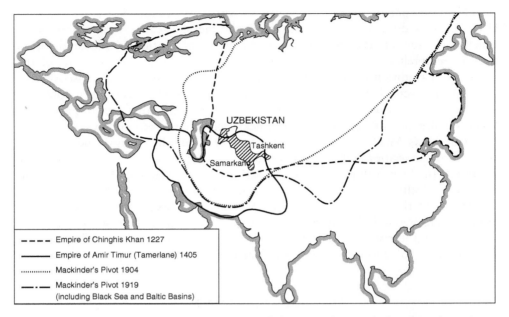

Figure 35.1 The Republic of Uzbekistan, and the 'geopolitics' of Chinghis Khan, Amir Timur, and Sir Halford Mackinder.

These fears are not unfounded: the underground non-violent Islamist group Hezb-ut Tahrir, which seeks to abolish nation states and establish a single pan-Islamic 'caliphate', has shown resilience and growth in recent years. Furthermore, the so-called Islamic Movement of Uzbekistan, claiming to be seeking to topple Karimov's secular regime, launched guerrilla raids from bases in Tajikistan in 1999 and 2000, and is blamed by Karimov for a series of devastating bomb attacks in Tashkent in February 1999. However, analysts had long warned that the government's anti-Islamic policies may themselves catalyse the politicization of Islam. They suggest that the intensity of radicalized opposition is partially a product of the absence of legitimate channels through which to express dissent, and a reaction to police brutality of those suspected of disloyalty. Karimov has, however, used the spectre of both this opposition and the civil wars in neighbouring Tajikistan and Afghanistan as sound reasons *not* to make too hasty a move towards democracy – a sentiment that many people in Uzbekistan in fact appreciate. He has used this threat to twice extend his term of office by referenda, side-stepping the constitutional provision of a maximum of two five-year presidential terms.

Western debate on how to engage with Uzbekistan has polarized between conservatives who argue that Karimov's authoritarianism is in the interests of stability and should be tolerated in the short term, and radicals who have lambasted both the human rights record of Karimov and the forms of and motives behind US support since 2001.

With 25 million people, Uzbekistan has the largest population in Central Asia. This double-landlocked state is the only one that shares contiguous borders with the four other former Soviet Central Asian republics, along with Afghanistan. In a region rich in hydrocarbon deposits, it has the most ambitious foreign policy, balancing and continually readjusting 'involvement' with pro-American (such as GUUAM – Georgia–Ukraine–Uzbekistan–Azerbaijan–Moldova), pro-Russian (the CIS – Commonwealth of Independent States), and pro-Chinese (the SCO – Shanghai Co-operation Organization) organizations, whilst all these countries compete to strengthen military ties with Uzbekistan. Indeed, as Horsman puts it, 'Uzbekistan has pursued a pragmatic and flexible but assertive and unilateralist foreign policy'. This has particularly been the case with the basing of US forces on its territory since their invasion of Afghanistan and overthrow of the Taliban regime in 2001. It boasts the largest military in the region and has not been afraid to intervene in the Tadjik and Afghan civil wars, or to engage in provocative border control policies with its neighbours. Indeed, as Cornell argues, 'Uzbekistan is the only Central Asian state to pursue a proactive and independent foreign policy, as exemplified in its relations with both its neighbours and great powers'. For these reasons, it has become the focus of a body of analytical, speculative, proscriptive and polemical literature on geopolitics and foreign policy, written by both outside and local specialists.

It is three such geopolitical works, all of which use Mackinder, which I will examine in this paper. Whilst many writers refer to Mackinder in more general geopolitical analysis of Russia or link his name in passing to a political analysis of Uzbekistan, I have chosen the authors of these three. This is because they are examples of the few who actually focus on Uzbekistan, and are civil-society based foreign policy intellectuals who take the classical geopolitical tradition seriously – or, examples of public intellectuals who engage in formal geopolitical reasoning, in Ó Tuathail and Agnew's terms. As I conclude that the first two do not engage Mackinder's writings in any depth, emphasis is placed on the work of the third, Chris Seiple.

All three experts exist in networks of other intellectuals, educational institutes and think tanks, some privately funded, others state funded. Their thoughts and pronouncements have had resonances with contemporary thinking. Whilst it is always difficult to establish the impact of any individual, they offer windows into how Mackinder's work has been appropriated and recycled. Discussion of these writers is necessarily tempered by a concern with the consequences of operating within the different paradigms of intellectual freedom that characterize Central Asian states.

Halford Mackinder and Contemporary Analysis of Uzbekistan

Russian analysis – Oleg Zotov

A growing body of scholarship has highlighted the resurgence of geopolitical thinking in 1990s Russia. In particular, it has drawn attention to a geopolitical imagination that casts recent history as that of enduring 'Atlanticist' versus 'Eurasianist' hostilities, a tradition that evinces Mackinder in support of its thesis. An example of a scholar who writes within this paradigm is Oleg Zotov, a historian at the

Oriental Studies Institute of the Russian Academy of Sciences. Although little known amongst English-language commentators, the prolific analyst of Russian foreign policy, lgor Torbakov, cites Zotov as an authority within the Russian geopolitical tradition that traces its roots back to the 1920s. For Zotov, the 'global geopolitical role' of Central Asia will be even more important than oil politics in the twenty-first century, and at the heart of Eurasia is Uzbekistan, the target for Islamic extremists and Americans alike. His English-language anti-US foreign policy polemics have been reproduced on a number of radical websites.

Zotov does not believe that the US invasion of Afghanistan and its close involvement in Uzbekistan is primarily aimed at disabling Al-Qaeda, neither is it ideological (human rights and democracy) nor economic (hydrocarbons). Rather, for Zotov, it is geopolitical. In his historical geographical imagination, there are two forces struggling for control of Eurasia: Eurasian powers that seek the good of Eurasia on the one hand, and forces of 'international terrorism' and 'Western hegemony' that seek its destruction on the other. The behaviour of any state is determined by its location. Onto this geopolitical framework he maps the characters and empires of Eurasian history, with Timur as his icon of geopolitical genius.

Zotov lauds Timur for 'eliminating chaos, establishing order, safe existence and development'. Timur turned a 'black hole' in the heart of Eurasia from a Hobbesian space of 'war of all against all' into a zone of peace, stability and development. How? Whereas contemporary works by Uzbek scholars explain Timur's 'success' as arising from his sense of justice, religion, and patriotism, for Zotov, it is simply geography. Realizing their geopolitical genius, he reconstructed the empires of Alexander and Chinghis Khan. On the one hand, he opposed 'extremism' and 'Western hegemony'. Extremism for Zotov is Timur's defeat of Sultan Bayazid at Ankara and the Golden Horde ruler Tokhtamysh. Western hegemony is the Crusaders – whose severed heads he catapulted at European warships, 'by way of persuasion', notes Zotov. The other side of his strategy was to ally with Eurasian states – Russia and China. Thus this enlightened ruler constructed Eurasia's only superpower, bringing peace and stability to Eurasia, without wanting world domination. Needless to say, the claims being made stretch the bounds of historical credibility – for example, Timur's destruction of Delhi in 1398 was shockingly savage, and he eventually died on the eve of a planned invasion of China in 1405.

For Zotov, however, this is not mere history. Rather he collapses political time into timeless geopolitical space. arguing that as 'the problems and directions of his geopolitics were the same ones that Central Asian states face today . . . the principles of his exceptional geopolitics are instructive as ever'. For Zotov, the contemporary struggle for Uzbekistan is simply the latest stage of this transcendent geopolitical struggle between timeless certitudes. Today, the international terrorists and extremists are the Islamists who have assailed Uzbekistan through direct military attack and support by US client states such as Turkey and Pakistan, and been backed by the US in the Balkans and elsewhere. The forces of Western hegemony are what he identifies as pro-US blocs such as GUUAM (which he sees as the reincarnation of the old CENTO Baghdad Pact), OSCE (Organization for Security and Co-operation in Europe) and NATO. Evincing material from the writings of

Americans such as Strobe Talbott and 'the odious' Zbigniew Brzezinski, he believes that US foreign policy is actively stirring up instability in Central Asia to excuse US interventions, and is determined to break up the CIS, block the ascendancy of China, and scupper the formation of a stable and harmonious Eurasian alliance. The USA, like Britain before it, has never been a Eurasian power, has never sought the good or stability of the region, and will never do so in the future. 'Globalization' is a strategy of US hegemony that thrives on creating instability: the antidote that he advocates is the formation of authentic Eurasian unions including the CIS and the Shanghai Co-operation Organization.

In drawing to a grand conclusion, Zotov adduces the name of Mackinder to confirm the importance of Central Asia and the veracity of his thesis. He concludes by saying that '[t]he struggle against international terrorism and hegemony of the West was quite actual in Timur's time and i[s] twice as actual today'. Mackinder is not cited nor is any evidence displayed that Zotov is familiar with his particular ideas and concerns. Mackinder is merely used to rubber-stamp the reduction of 25 centuries of history to timeless spatial truths that reinscribe Central Asia as an otherwise empty zone of great power competition, and relegate the importance of moral qualities of leadership and governance behind the ability to project geopolitical power over the 'heartland'. Whilst claiming to be adhering to objective criteria, Zotov's geopolitics reveals both post-Soviet insecurities about the relative decline of Russian power and casts Russia in the mould of benevolent Eurasian power, unlike the now-dominant Americans, who are illegitimate intruders in Central Asia.

Uzbekistani analysis – Sevara Sharapova

Just as in post-Soviet Russia, geopolitical thinking has become fashionable in contemporary Uzbekistan. In a recent example, Tolipov discusses the place of Uzbekistan in the 'Heartland' or 'Rimland', concluding that Uzbekistan's objective geopolitical destiny is probably to use the new strategic partnership with the USA to assume a 'special historic responsibility for the evolution of Central Asia'. However, whilst using classic geopolitical terminology that can be traced directly or indirectly back to Mackinder, he makes no reference to the man himself – in spite of beginning the article with mention of Hauner's study that concentrates on Mackinder! Yuldasheva begins her 1996 overview of recent Anglo-American writing on Central Asia by proclaiming, '[n]owadays, as never before, the geopolitical theory of Sir Halford Mackinder, which projected Central Asia as the core region of Eurasia, has acquired new actuality in international policy'. Sevara Sharapova, a political scientist at the Tashkent State Institute of Oriental Studies who specializes in Uzbekistani foreign policy and the place of Uzbekistan in the policies of great powers, on which she has written over 30 articles, develops this argument. In 2002 she published a paper on this theme, exploring Uzbekistan's involvement in international organizations, and making suggestions about future directions. The present study will focus on this article as she begins her theoretical analysis with Mackinder.

Her paper, entitled 'Uzbekistan's multisided diplomacy in the context of antiterrorist campaign', opens with a statement that the anti-terrorist coalition formed around the US in the wake of the September 11 attacks has 'turned Central Asia into a world political center'. However, she argues that it is necessary to dig deeper for a paradigm to explain outside, and particularly US, interest in Central Asia. She posits two possibilities. The first is geopolitics, which she explains as either the Americans trying to implement Mackinder's heartland strategy, or attempting to work towards a limited strategic partnership with Russia. The second is geo-economics, or the quest for access to the region's rich hydrocarbon deposits.

Whilst Sharapova says that it is unclear which of the paradigms will dominate, her analysis tends towards the geopolitical. She explores different possibilities, reflecting the difficulty in finding models to match the relative simplicity of 'Cold War' antagonisms. Nonetheless, she concludes by positing the existence of an old clash between the Atlantic and Eurasian worlds, with China now having replaced Russia as the leader of the Eurasian world, and the US following Brzezinski's call to prevent any single force dominating the region.

Whilst more nuanced and sophisticated, Sharapova's argument has certain parallels with Zotov's. Both employ geopolitical explanations of Uzbekistan's relations with other states, although Sharapova tempers hers with economic considerations. Both refer to Mackinder as an authority on the scientific basis of geopolitics, yet their engagement with him is superficial and there is no evidence that they have actually read him first hand – in fact, neither even cites a particular work. Indeed, in a personal communication, Sharapova explained that she heard about his ideas as a graduate but thinks that century-old notions have little place in a changed world. Both Sharapova and Zotov do, however, quote Brzezinski, whose popular 1997 book seems to be a more direct channel for their knowledge of the Anglo-American geopolitical tradition.

However, Sharapova departs from Zotov in considering Uzbekistan in its own terms, which leads her to adopt a pragmatic position that seeks to maximize Uzbekistan's advantage. She observes that, whilst relations between the US and Russia have long been based on suspicion, there is a certain overlap of interest in fighting terrorism and drugs and preventing China emerging as a dominant power. Sharapova sees in this ambiguous relationship an opportunity that Uzbekistan, with its unique position at the heart of Eurasia, must exploit:

> In this situation Uzbekistan will be free to act in the spirit of traditional geopolitics based on prolonged mutual mistrust that has existed and continues to exist between the White House and the Kremlin. This is a dignified role that leaves much space for maneuvering.

This is a classic example of 'geopolitical reasoning' as defined by Dalby, whereby the world is discursively constructed in terms of places which consign political actors to play roles dependent on their specified place in the global order. It is also a good description of the 'pragmatic' foreign policy pursued by the Karimov administration.

US analysis – Chris Seiple

The above examples drawn from Russia and Uzbekistan, whilst informed by a general body of literature on geopolitics that clearly owes a debt to Mackinder, merely mention him as a strategy to bolster authority, but make no detailed engagement with his arguments. The last example, in contrast, in Chris Seiple – an American whose work on Uzbekistan is informed by a detailed restatement of Mackinder, or, in his words, a 'rediscovery of the real Mackinder'.

Chris Seiple is the son of Bob Seiple, who served as President Clinton's Ambassador-at-Large for International Religious Freedom. A former Marine officer, he is President of the Institute for Global Engagement, which describes itself as a 'think-tank with legs', founded in 2000 by his father 'to create sustainable environments for religious freedom world-wide'. He teaches at two universities and is a member of a number of foreign policy think tanks. He has served in the Strategic Initiatives Group, a Pentagon internal think tank for the Marine Corps, where he developed new constructs regarding national and homeland security and wrote speeches and Congressional testimonies for senior Marine leaders. He helped establish a Humanitarian Operations Chair at Marine Corps University in Virginia, and his book on military/NGO relationships in humanitarian interventions is widely read among humanitarian NGOs and within the US military. He appears regularly on TV and radio and publishes frequently, addressing not only religious freedom but also US foreign policy towards Uzbekistan, and supporting recent US military interventions in Afghanistan and Iraq. A graduate of international relations at Stanford and national security affairs at the Naval Postgraduate School, he is currently completing a PhD at Tufts on US–Uzbekistan relations 1991–2003.

For this section, I will draw on material from his as-yet incomplete PhD thesis, which he has kindly allowed me to use, his publications and briefings on Uzbekistan, and email conversations and a telephone interview.

Seiple first encountered Mackinder as an officer-student in 1994, and was unimpressed at what he heard of him from his lecturers. However, it was not until 2000 that he actually read Mackinder for himself, soon after switching dissertation topic from a 'homeland security' theme to Uzbekistan, with which he had been fascinated since reading Fitzroy Maclean's *Eastern Approaches*. Seiple read Mackinder as a vision of how to create a balanced and free world, his 1919 and 1943 publications reapplying his 1904 formulation in changed strategic eras. He argues not only that the military academy version of Mackinder (as an advocate of 'land power' against Mahan's 'sea power') is a superficial caricature, but that Mackinder himself provided 'a timeless yet practical philosophy for Eurasia', combining principles of geopolitics with a concern for building global democracy. Mackinder struck Seiple as 'a profoundly philosophical and spiritual man who most of all in his writings sought balance', and 'embodied that which he sought to imbue'.

Seiple is dismissive of much of the existing scholarship on Mackinder. Seiple understands the negative characterization of Mackinder as an imperialist, but insists that the salient feature of his belief system is a staunch commitment to democracy. He admires what he sees as Mackinder's prescient grasp of the relationship between democratic civil society and geography under the closed-world conditions of what today is termed 'globalization', and his moral commitment to shape the world. He approves of Mackinder's integration of 'holistic' thought with his 'bias for action', demonstrated by developing a coherent geopolitical worldview and translating that into multiple activities such as teaching, instructing military officers, and influencing policy. In particular, Seiple respects Mackinder's geographical gaze, his 'disembodied, earth-scanning' panoptical vision of world geography, precisely that characteristic of his thinking to which Ó Tuathail objects. Thus geographical gaze mirrors and informs Seiple's vision of his own work. Speaking on 19 September 2001, he claimed that the attacks a week earlier demonstrated how critical it was for national security to develop 'intragency experts who see the whole picture all the time, *not* just a specialized field of view', and concluded by claiming that his institute was an example of an organization attempting exactly that task.

Seiple completely rejects the suggestion that Mackinder 'got it wrong' in predicting the course of events. For Seiple, this is a fundamental misunderstanding: Mackinder did not *predict*, but rather sought to *warn*, deftly re-applying timeless principles of geopolitics to the pressing issues of the day in 1904, 1919 and 1943. This being so, it follows that 'it is for the practical philosopher to figure out what the latest manifestation is'. Seiple takes this task upon himself. For Seiple, the essential geopolitical principle of the importance of the heartland in a closed system remains unchanged, but the US in 2003 has replaced Britain a century earlier as 'the primary advocate of democracy in the world and the obvious key to global balance', and Uzbekistan now plays the key balancing role that Eastern Europe did for Mackinder in 1919. Indeed, Seiple asserts that, '[a]t the center of the Heartland Hinge, that unchanging interior of the Heartland Concept across three iterations, is Uzbekistan'. He speculates that if Mackinder had lived until 1991 he 'would have foreseen Central Asia, and Uzbekistan in particular, as critical to global balance'. This being the case, Seiple believes that Mackinder's thought is the best framework within which to analyse US foreign policy towards Uzbekistan.

This reading of Mackinder informs Seiple's public-sphere engagement with US–Uzbek foreign policy. He argues that Karimov's presidency has been too easily dismissed as oppressive with superficial clichés by the left, or endorsed by security strategists on the right who overlook human rights concerns, and seeks to formulate a new mode of engagement between these positions.

For Seiple, Uzbekistan as 'the fulcrum of Asia security' and 'the backyard that everyone shares' is absolutely vital to US interest and to the future of democracy in Eurasia. Yet it is surrounded by states which include those that he terms failed, '17th century', terrorist and unstable, including one in George Bush's 'Axis of Evil', as well as by Islamic fundamentalism. Furthermore, Russia, still smarting from loss of empire, is attempting to regain control of Uzbekistan, and a resurgent China represents a new threat. It is imperative that the US is aware of and balances these threats.

In a May 2000 dissertation draft, Seiple was critical of US foreign policy towards Central Asia. He argued that, in fact, there was none – general platitudes about stability and economic and political reform could apply to 'any planet, any region'. This was confirmed by his interviews with US government officials. In considering Uzbekistan as merely a less important part of the 'former' Soviet Union and as within the Russian sphere of interest rather than a sovereign state in its own right, Seiple argues that the US is unable to think geopolitically about Uzbekistan. He cites what he describes as hopeful signs in the mid-1990s: for example, Uzbekistan's security co-operation with Israel, its desire to keep Russia at arm's length, and, in 1997, its voting alone with Israel and the US at the UN against a resolution condemning US sanctions on Cuba. However, Seiple considers that the US failed to develop this opportunity to engage more closely with Uzbekistan, and that this was a failure to think geopolitically. Seiple contrasts this with Russian President Putin's realization of Uzbekistan's importance following his rise to power in 1999. Quoting the Russophobe Lord Curzon as an authority on Russian intentions in Central Asia, Seiple casts Putin as a national leader pursuing the self interest of his state pursuing influence in Uzbekistan. Indeed, Seiple observes that almost immediately after assuming power Putin travelled to Tashkent to sign a security pact between the two states. Thus Russia grasped the strategic importance of Uzbekistan, whereas the US did not.

However, for Seiple much changed with the attacks on the US in September 2001. US forces had been based in Uzbekistan to facilitate an invasion of Afghanistan, in October 2001, a move which Seiple called for immediately following the attacks, arguing that Uzbekistan was both geographically and politically a natural ally for the US. Seiple considers that these events may prove to be a decisive break in US–Uzbekistani relations. They demonstrated to the US government what it should have known about the importance of Uzbekistan from Mackinder, and, symbolically, precipitated the first ever phone call by a US president to the Uzbekistani head of state. They clearly underlined Mackinder's contention that democracies cannot think strategically and do not appreciate the dynamics of heartland geopolitics until threatened.

Seiple was in Uzbekistan interviewing foreign policy elites as part of his doctoral research in September 2001, and was thus well placed to observe their reactions. He posits an ongoing competition amongst political elites in Uzbekistan between those who advocated pro-Russian foreign policy orientation and those who favoured closer ties with the US. He argues that prior to September 2001 the 'Russians' were ascendant and the 'Americans' dormant, but that the attacks precipitated a reversal in the fortunes of both groups. He argues that America must encourage this shift by a new policy of comprehensive engagement with Uzbekistan. He recommends in particular supporting exchanges of officials to promote the strengthening of human rights and civil society; keeping the US military in the country long term as a statement of solidarity; and providing a full Marshall Plan through the IMF and World Bank to provide employment opportunities for the burgeoning young population.

Seiple's desire to apply what he considers objective analysis of Eurasian geopolitics and the future for democracy in Eurasia ultimately leads him to advocate a position which sees Uzbekistan accepting the US as its main sponsor, and supporting a strategic alliance cemented by the controversial US invasion of Afghanistan.

Without suggesting that this is cynical, as Polelle's language might be taken to imply, this illustrates his contention that:

> The power of geopolitics was – and to some extent remains today – based on its ability to depoliticize through scientific-sounding rhetoric what are at heart deeply political and subjective choices regarding foreign and domestic policies.

Conclusion

Shortly before the demise of the Soviet Union, writing the conclusion to his important study of the place of Asia in Russian geopolitical imaginations, Hauner speculated that, 'if the empire goes, so will the heartland theory in the Mackinder mold'. This paper has shown that the emergence of independent states in Central Asia following the end of the Soviet 'empire' has occasioned a new phase in the literature on 'revisiting' Mackinder's heartland. Few other modern academic geographers have had such impact outside the discipline, and this must challenge geographers to take Mackinder more seriously than some have been wont to. Even to 100 years of age, Mackinder won't go away easily.

This paper is an exploratory essay, and points to the need for more extensive and detailed research. Further work is necessary to describe the intellectual biographies of these writers and their location in networks of foreign policy expertise, and to uncover institutional histories of how Mackinder's geopolitical ideas 'travelled' from the UK to the US and the USSR and thence independent Russia and Uzbekistan. These are important issues, but beyond the scope of this article. Nonetheless, it draws four conclusions from the case studies used.

Firstly, of all Central Asian states, Mackinder's formula has been particularly re-appropriated in analysis of contemporary Uzbekistan.

Secondly, this 'revival' has occurred largely in spite of the body of secondary geographical scholarship on Mackinder. In re-visiting his 'scope and methods of geography' paper on the centenary of its publication, Coones observed that Mackinder has frequently been lauded, but not often read carefully. Exactly the same can be said of his Pivot paper at its centenary: nor, it can be added, has subsequent work by geographers on Mackinder been much used (Seiple's extensive interaction with Mackinder is something of an exception). For the most part, Mackinder is merely taken as a premise in a strategy to bolster authority and add a false sense of profundity to writing that otherwise lacks both theoretical rigour and political and geographical nuance. This would be entirely unimportant were it to be merely a question of the wounded pride of marginalized geographers. However, this scholarship has raised serious ethical concerns about the Mackinderian tradition, accusing it of indulging great-power military imperialism, and an ambiguous relationship to democracy. That this has been largely ignored in this 'revival' is disturbing. This raises a question for further consideration: is this a failure of political geography to engage with wider policy debates?

Thirdly, whilst all three writers take Mackinder as offering timeless and objective geopolitical truths, the respective foreign policy positions at which they arrive reveal subjectivities embedded in both the time and space of the nation state. Zotov argues that it is best for Uzbekistan and the region to adopt a staunchly anti-American (and, by implication, a pro-Russian) position. Seiple, in contrast, is suspicious of the intentions and potential impact on Uzbekistan of Russia and other regional states and ideologies, and concludes that a strongly pro-US orientation is best both for Uzbekistan and Eurasia. Sharapova suggests that Uzbekistan would serve both itself and the region best by performing a pragmatic balancing act between these positions. Mackinder himself believed in universal ideals of freedom yet at the same time, as Ó Tuathail and Dalby argue, his life and work exhibited a commitment to advancing the interests of his own country in competition with other states. This contradiction, as some would see it, or paradox of necessary engagement with geopolitical reality, as others would state it, persists within what might be termed the Mackinder tradition today. It illustrates Ó Tuathail's contention that critical histories of geopolitics 'disturb the innocence of geography and politicize the writing of global space'.

Fourthly and finally, these readings of Mackinder inform comment on the foreign policy orientation of modern Uzbekistan. In the autumn of 2003, Craig Murray, the British ambassador to Uzbekistan, was at the centre of media speculation about whether he had been recalled for his controversial criticisms of Karimov's human rights record. How Uzbekistan and the West should engage with each other is thus a question of great political importance, a question for which the ideas and traditions surrounding Mackinder are of continued relevance. 'The geographical pivot of history' paper should not merely be of interest to historians of geographical ideas.

Chapter 36

Euroregions in Comparative Perspective: Differential Implications for Europe's Borderlands

Joanna M. M. Kepka and Alexander B. Murphy

During the late twentieth century, significant challenges emerged to a state-based, political-territorial order in Europe. Chief amongst these challenges was the development of increasingly numerous and significant regional structures and institutional arrangements spanning international boundaries. Although the state remains the dominant actor in the organisation and execution of political and economic activities in Europe today, other actors, including the European Union (EU), regional entities, and nongovernmental organisations, now play an important role in the organisation of society and space in the 'New Europe'.

Europe's evolving political-territorial order has attracted considerable scholarly attention among commentators concerned with European integration, the nature of sovereignty, and the changing nature of boundaries. In their studies of various types of transboundary arrangements, commentators have tried to understand not only the functions and political implications of these new structures but also what they mean for the people affected by them. A fundamental challenge to a more complete understanding of the sociocultural implications of transboundary political-territorial constructs arises from the fact that they have developed in different geographical contexts. Yet the ubiquity and novelty of this new form of governance has led some commentators, at least implicitly, to treat European transboundary governance structures as a single type of institutional development with generalisable implications for the places and peoples affected by them.

If we are to gain a more sophisticated understanding of the nature and implications of transboundary regional governance, it is important to move beyond such generalizations to consider whether there are significant differences in the function

Kepka, Joanna M. M. and Murphy, Alexander B., "Euroregions in Comparative Perspective: Differential Implications for Europe's Borderlands," pp. 50–67 from David H. Kaplan & Jouni Häkli (eds.), *Boundaries and Place: European Borderlands in Geographical Context* (Boulder, CO: Rowman & Littlefield, 2002).

and meaning of these governance structures from place to place. As a step in that direction, this chapter offers a comparative analysis of the development of so-called Euroregions in two very different geopolitical contexts: at the heart of the EU where the Dutch, German, and Belgian borders meet (the Euregio Meuse-Rhin) and at the edge of the EU where the German, Polish, and Czech borders meet (the Euroregion Nysa).

Euroregions are particular types of transboundary co-operation agreements forged not by regional actors but by associations of local authorities. Euroregions were first developed in the 1960s along the German-Dutch and German-Dutch-Belgian boundaries, but since the fall of the Iron Curtain they have become the most sought-after form of transborder co-operation in East Central Europe. Since 1990, local authorities in Poland's border regions, for example, have entered into thirteen co-operation agreements with their counterparts on the opposite side of the international boundaries. What is the significance of these developments, and how should they be understood?

To date, much of the literature on Euroregions has been largely descriptive. To the extent that evaluative claims are made, they tend to be based on extrapolations from the experiences of other places with Euroregions. Heffner, for example, simply assumes that Euroregions will work in the interests of parties on both sides of international boundaries in Eastern and Central Europe because that has been the experience of Euroregions in Western Europe. Studies of this sort perpetuate generalizations about the impacts of transboundary governance structures across geographical contexts.

This study seeks to highlight the pitfalls of generalising in this way by offering a comparative analysis of relevant social, economic, and political circumstances that are affecting transboundary co-operation in the Polish-German-Czech Euroregion Nysa and the German-Dutch-Belgian Euregio Meuse-Rhin. To provide context for the study, we begin by discussing the evolution of transboundary co-operation in the EU. This is followed by consideration of Euroregions as a class of transboundary co-operation and their role in transforming the conduct of transborder relations in Europe. We then turn to a more detailed discussion of the nature and functions of the Meuse-Rhin and Nysa Euroregions and the types of contextual differences that can render problematic broad generalizations about transboundary institutional structures.

The Evolution of Transboundary Co-operation in the EU

Since its inception in 1957, the European Economic Community (subsequently the European Community; now the EU) has gradually moved from a state-centric enterprise to one in which substate and nonstate actors have come to play an increasingly significant role in the political, economic, and social arenas. Originally, cross-boundary initiatives were of little significance. As the European integration project moved forward, however, various EU organisations became strong proponents of inter-regional contacts with a transboundary character – particularly the European Commission and the Council of Europe.

The role of the European Commission and the Council of Europe

The European Commission has supported the establishment of organisations that bring together regional and local authorities from different member states to promote regional interests at the European level. These organisations include, among others, the Association of European Border Regions (AEBR), the Assembly of European Regions, and the Council of European Municipalities and Regions – the most important European local government lobby. The Council of Europe, on the other hand, was instrumental in orchestrating several European conventions on transborder co-operation, beginning with the European Outline Convention on Transfrontier Cooperation Between Territorial Communities or Authorities, adopted in Madrid in 1980. The Council also adopted, in that same year, the European Outline Agreement on Cooperation Between Transborder Regions and, in 1981, the European Charter of Transborder Regions.

These legal enactments – along with the European Charter of Local Government signed in 1985 – paved the way for the development of transboundary contacts among and between regional and local authorities in such places as the Rhine Valley, the Saarland-Lorraine axis, and the French Upper Rhine areas. Transboundary business contacts expanded; social and cultural exchanges intensified; and people, goods, and ideas began to flow more freely across international boundaries. In the process, political boundaries lost some of their significance as social boundaries, and some transboundary areas were able to exert more political and economic clout as a consequence of their changed situation vis-à-vis the long-dominant political-territorial order represented by the map of so-called nation-states.

Transboundary co-operation had demonstrably positive economic and social ramifications for some substate regions, and certain local authorities in these regions – most notably those in Belgium and Germany – sought to capitalise on the situation in a manner that would allow them to exert more influence on the European political scene. They therefore spearheaded an effort to bring a wide range of substate political actors to Brussels and Strasbourg, where they could engage in macro-diplomacy and lobby for regional interests in the EU Commission and Parliament. Moreover, the establishment of the Committee of Regions (CoR) in 1994 allowed member regions not only to voice their demands for increased regional participation but also to lobby for EU policy approaches. For example, in 1996 the Committee set forth its Opinion on the Revision of the Treaty on European Union, in which it demanded, amongst other things, extension of the principle of subsidiarity from its current member state focus to regional and local authorities. If this demand were fully realised, the subsidiarity principle could become instrumental in fostering substate participation in EU decision making and legitimising the activities of transboundary co-operation associations.

At the moment, the majority of inter-regional organisations with a transboundary character are simple associations with no externally formalised institutional basis. The notable exception is the Euroregions, which are the products of institutionalised cross-boundary co-operation links forged by local authorities in border regions.

The Euroregion construct

Euroregions are almost as old as the European Community itself. Established in 1958 along the German-Dutch border, the pioneer 'Euregio' became the first formally organised form of cross-border co-operation in Europe. The German-Dutch Euregio was followed by the founding of similarly conceived Euroregions in 1963 (the Euregio Rhin-Waal) and in 1976 (the Euregio Meuse-Rhin). Within the plethora of transborder substate entities and structures subsumed under the umbrella of the AEBR, only fifteen can be considered Euroregions. This is due to the particular organisational structure of these Euroregions: Each of the fifteen consists of a council, a presidium, a secretariat, and several working groups. Over the past decade, however, the concepts of 'Euregio' and 'Euroregion' have become ubiquitous throughout Europe and are now frequently used to describe any substate structure with a transboundary character. Most of the fifteen Euroregions in question function along the German-Dutch and German-Dutch-Belgian borders, but since 1990 they have diffused rapidly – particularly to East Central Europe. Much of the political elite in the latter region regards Euroregions as structures that can help their countries overcome past problems (reconciliation between historically antagonistic nations) and facilitate closer relations with the EU. These goals have prompted Polish authorities to open up their borders, and those authorities have encouraged the development of formal cross-border linkages. At the time of this writing, thirteen Euroregions have been established along the country's western, southern, and eastern boundaries (so far only five are members of the AEBR).

Located on the margins of states, Euroregions are designed to enhance the economic and political significance of border areas within the larger European milieu, while undermining the arbitrary divisions among peoples that so often are the product of political boundary drawing. As Weyand explains, the objective is to create a 'we-feeling' that transcends national boundaries and to assist in the implementation of a 'Europe of Citizens'. Through the promotion of numerous exchange programs for students, families, and employees (especially civil servants), and through the organisation of various cultural and sporting events, Euroregions seek to construct subregional bridges connecting peoples; they offer the prospect of deepening the European integration processes. In fact, Euroregions are sometimes cited as the most important 'bottom-up' pressure for the deepening of European integration and as 'windows for the future evolution' of a genuine system of co-operation.

Despite growing interest in EU regional policy and the emergence of a third level of governance (i.e., regional governance) on the European political scene, until recently remarkably little attention was paid to Euroregions and related cross-border developments. At least in the Anglo-American and Polish literatures, references to Euroregions and related phenomena have been either brief or of a descriptive nature. As a result, the nature and significance of transboundary interaction is undertheorised, and we know far less than we need to know about the actual impact of cross-border co-operation.

Part of the explanation for this state of affairs lies in the continued dominance of an implicit state-based spatiality in much social scientific work. Rooted in a political-territorial system that emerged in early-modern Western Europe, the state has come to be treated as the basic spatial unit we use to make sense of the world:

> It is difficult to exaggerate the impact of the territorial assumptions that have developed in association with the . . . (modern) political order. In general terms, they have made the territorial state the privileged unit for analyzing most phenomena while discouraging consideration of the nature of the territorial state itself. In the political sphere they have directed overwhelming attention to state government and governmental leaders at the expense of extrastate or substate actors and arrangements. In the economic sphere they have prompted us to frame our most basic theories of development in state terms. In the cultural sphere they have encouraged us to collapse our understandings of diversity into state-based categories; for every reference to the Quechua, Aymara, and Guaraní peoples there are thousands to Bolivians. In the environmental sphere they have prompted us to conceptualize issues that do not correspond to state boundaries as 'transnational' (read trans-state) or 'transboundary' issues, not Upper Rhine or Southeast Asian lowland issues.

The impact of the map of so-called sovereign states on our conceptualisation of political and social processes reflects both the influence of state structures on human affairs and the role of state authorities in the collection and dissemination of information. These influences are so great that they direct attention away from the ways in which knowledge is organised in state-territorial terms, leading to the marginalisation of work on sociospatial structures such as transboundary regions that do not fit easily within the political-geograpic parameters of the modern state system.

With the rapid expansion of transboundary co-operation in recent years, forms of transboundary co-operation such as Euroregions can no longer be ignored. Yet the tendency is to see these more as novel institutional forms than as phenomena with potentially profound sociospatial significance. As a result, critical geographical dimensions of transboundary co-operation can and have been overlooked. Nowhere is this more clear than in studies of Euroregions in East Central Europe, which often start from the (at least implied) assumption that Euroregions will lead peripheral border regions in Poland, the Czech Republic, Slovakia, and Hungary down the same development path as their counterpart border regions in Germany, the Netherlands, and Belgium. Without denying that positive outcomes can result from the establishment of Euroregions in East Central Europe, a comparative analysis of the Euregio Meuse-Rhin and the Euroregion Nysa reveals the influence of geographical context on the types of economic, political, administrative, and social challenges Euroregions face. Moreover, a comparative assessment of the two Euroregions highlights critical challenges that the emerging Euroregions of East Central Europe are confronting.

The Development of the Meuse-Rhin and Nysa Euroregions

Euregio Meuse-Rhin

Established in 1976, the Euregio Meuse-Rhin is one of the pioneer Euroregions. It is centred on the confluence of the Meuse and Rhine Rivers (hence the name) and covers the areas of five regions: Limbourg (both Dutch and Belgian), Liège (Belgium), Belgium's Germanophone Community, and Aachen (Germany) (see Figure 36.1). At present, there are some 3.7 million inhabitants within the

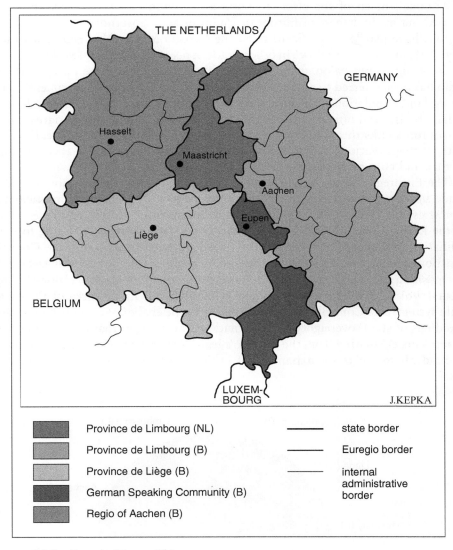

Province de Limbourg (NL) ——— state border

Province de Limbourg (B) ——— Euregio border

Province de Liège (B) ——— internal administrative border

German Speaking Community (B)

Regio of Aachen (B)

Figure 36.1 Euregio Meuse-Rhin.
Source: *Euroregio Meuse-Rhin* 1997. Brochure produced by SEGEFA (Service d'Etude en Géographie Economique Fondamentale et Appliquée de l'Université de Liège). Liège: SEGEFA.

Euro-regions, distributed across a territory of just over ten thousand square kilometers. Historically, the territory of today's Euregio Meuse-Rhin was a part of the Principality of Liège, the Duchy of Limbourg, and then the Duchy of Luxembourg – passing successively under Spanish, Austrian, French, and Dutch rule. With the rise of nationalism in the nineteenth century and subsequent delineation of political-territorial homelands, the area of today's Euregio was divided politically among the Netherlands, Belgium, and Germany. Following the Second World War, strong expressions of ethnonationalism were delegitimised in Western Europe, and six countries, led by two historical adversaries (France and Germany), embarked on the road towards economic co-operation.

Although much of the effort to build a 'common European home' has been carried out at the behest of European Union or state government officials, Euro-regions have played a significant role. The Euregio Meuse-Rhin represents European integration 'from below'; in other words, it deepens the processes of integration by fostering co-opertaion at the lowest level: the commune. The Euregio Meuse-Rhin has been referred to as 'a true laboratory for the European experiment'. Local borderland populations, speaking three languages, interact at the Euregio level on a daily basis; local officials collaborate on economic and planning initiatives; businesses form links through the Euregio Chamber of Commerce; and local inhabitants, through various sporting and cultural events, learn about their common history and cultural heritage.

The Euroregion's youngest and most promising organ, the Euregio Council, is made up of representatives from the border regions of each of the participating countries (see Figure 36.2). Significantly, in the spirit of promoting a 'we-feeling' in the Euregio, the political groups of the Council are formed according to party affiliation, not according to nationality (see Figure 36.3). Although the Council's functions and powers are consultative and its members are not directly elected, its composition challenges traditional notions of inter-regional co-operation arrangements, which have been deeply rooted in the national frameworks of the extant state system. The Council thus helps to reinforce the challenge to traditional understandings of state sovereignty and international boundaries that is associated with enactments emanating from the Euregio's legislative organs, which have the power to bind all members on a number of critical matters through simple majority votes.

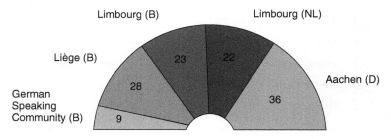

Figure 36.2 Members of the Euregio Meuse-Rhin Council by province.
Source: *Euroregio Meuse-Rhin* 1997 [as Figure 36.1].

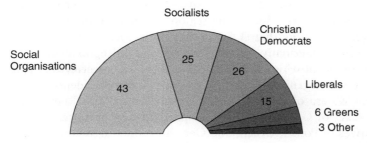

Figure 36.3 Transnational political parties in the Euregio Meuse-Rhin Council. *Source*: *Euroregio Meuse-Rhin* 1997 [as Figure 36.1].

The Meuse-Rhin's administrative program is multifaceted. In the socioeconomic realm, most efforts of the Euregio are focused on concrete everyday problems arising out of the area's border situation, including improving transportation and communication linkages, fostering and facilitating co-operation between small- and medium-sized businesses on each side of the border, and developing common regional planning and environmental conservation policies. Much emphasis is placed on economic matters, particularly the promotion of the Euregio's economic potential in the European market. The Euregio Meuse-Rhin also supports programs that help local populations understand the varying legal and social security systems of each state; it facilitates co-operation on critical health and safety issues (for example, police protection and rescue services); and it sponsors numerous exchange programs for students, families, and civil servants. In addition, cultural and sporting events are an important part of the Euregio's work. During the summer of 1998, for example, the Euregio organised a Festival of Theatres with the participation of local musical and theatrical companies, numerous programs for youth (language courses, panel discussions, excursions, rock concerts, etc.), and tennis and judo competitions. These activities are geared primarily towards promoting an intercultural dialogue, diminishing language barriers, and creating a 'Euregio identity' and a sense of place that spans national boundaries. The Euregio constitutes a model for a bottom-up approach to transborder co-operation that can serve to deepen European integration processes through participation by citizens at local levels.

Euroregion Nysa

Following the demise of the Soviet-dominated communist regime, the Polish central authorities allowed cross-border linkages to be forged along the Polish-German boundary, which simultaneously functions as an external border of the EU. The first transboundary co-operation agreement involving the former Eastern Bloc countries came out of an effort on the part of local officials on the German side of the Nysa-Neisse-Nisa River to initiate cross-border co-operation with their counterparts on the Polish and Czech sides of the border. The effort led to the signing of a formal co-operation agreement in May 1991 – bringing into being the Euroregion Nysa (Figure 36.4). The region comprises more than eleven thousand square kilometres, more than 1.6 million people, and more than twenty administrative districts in Germany, Poland, and the Czech Republic.

The conference at which the Euroregion Nysa was created took place in Zittau, Germany. It was organised under the auspices of the presidents of the three countries – Lech Walesa of Poland, Václav Havel of the Czech Republic, and Richard von Weizsäcker of Germany – with the participation of more than three hundred representatives of Polish, Czech, and German border-area communities. The presence of the heads of governments of the three countries was largely symbolic, however. Weizsäcker and Walesa were not dictating the terms of the agreement; they were simply marking the significance of the occasion. The real impetus for the initiative was local. Indeed, it was described at the time as a 'voluntary

Figure 36.4   Euroregion Neisse-Nisa-Nysa.
Source: *Euroregion Nysa* 1994. Jelenia Góra and Warsaw, Poland: Regionalny Urzad Statystyczny i Centralny Urzad Statystyczny.

community of interests of communes and districts', whose existence depends solely on the willingness of local authorities to participate. The fact that Euroregion Nysa was the first of its kind in East Central Europe rendered it of special significance; it was said to initiate an era in which relations 'East-West are shaped in new, European dimensions'.

The Euroregion Nysa was followed by similar co-operation arrangements along the Polish-German boundary: Euroregions Sprewa-Nysa-Bóbr (1993), Pro Europa Viadrina (1993), and Pomerania (1995). Thus, Euroregion Nysa seemingly initiated a 'spillover' effect whereby a growing number of local officials in border regions sought the benefits of transboundary co-operation with regions located within EU member states. Since their establishment, the Euroregions' authorities have been able to apply for funds directly to the EU. Moneys for transboundary projects have come from INTERREG II, a regional development fund for Germany's eastern *Länder*, and PHARE, an EU program designed to transfer funds to encourage further reforms and to set up democratic institutions in the countries of former Eastern Europe. In addition, the EU Commission established a special program to promote co-operation between Polish and German border regions. This program, which exists under the umbrella of PHARE, has its own annual budget of 55 million ecus and is the Polish analogue of INTERREG II. In the case of the Euroregion Nysa, for instance, the Polish communes forming part of the Euroregion received a total of 7.9 million ecus in 1995 and 9.3 million ecus in 1996 from PHARE for projects involving transport infrastructure, environmental protection, and regional infrastructure and economy.

The Euroregion Nysa provides a framework for activities that traditionally have been carried out by or within individual states. There is, for example, a Statistical Programme PL-14, which is carried out under the auspices of EUROSTAT and is co-ordinated by the Regional Statistical Office in Jelenia Góra, Poland. This program (or more precisely its principal arm, the Statistics Working Group) collects information from various parts of the Euroregion and compiles it in forms that go beyond traditional state-based approaches. In addition to statistical information on regional trade and other economic activities, the Statistics Group also provides information on matters related to demography, education, job markets, social welfare, and tourism.

The geographical location of Euroregion Nysa – along the external boundary of the EU – plays a significant role in defining the character and functions of this transboundary political-territorial construct. In contrast to the Euregio Meuse-Rhin, the Euroregion Nysa's institutional structure is much more complicated, with separate associations and working groups in the participating regions of Germany, Poland, and the Czech Republic meeting and making decisions that precede and constrain decision making on the part of the Euroregion-wide institutions. Consequently, the possibility of forming transnational political parties is curtailed in the Euroregion Nysa. Moreover, because the borders between Germany and Poland, and between Germany and the Czech Republic, are simultaneously part of the external boundary of the European Union, cross-boundary co-operation is not simply an internal EU matter. There is no single supranational political-administrative framework within which the Euroregion Nysa can develop.

Despite these obstacles to close co-operation, members of the Euroregion's various institutions meet on a daily basis to work out solutions to common problems. The working groups function within the established Euroregion framework on matters such as environmental regulation, regional planning and infrastructure, and culture, education, and youth exchanges. The Euroregion covers areas characterised by sharp differences in infrastructure and level of economic development. Consequently, the main emphasis is on developing ways to alleviate these differences. The Euroregion's programs are divided into three groups, which prioritise the projects to be addressed. The first group includes, among others, projects focused on town planning, border-crossing systems, and sewage management; the second emphasises co-operation among public security services, co-operative transportation planning, and collaborative construction projects in border towns such as Zgorzelec (Poland) and Görlitz (Germany); and the last concentrates on agricultural, energy, and environmental issues.

As is the case for the Euregio Meuse-Rhin, one of the main objectives of the Euroregion Nysa is to create a 'we-feeling' that spans the national boundaries. The residents of the local borderland communities of the Tripeland (Triangle of Three Lands) have the opportunity to participate in cross-boundary activities such as musical festivals, cross-cultural dialogues, and sporting events. There is a strong emphasis on cultural exchanges amongst pupils and students and on cross-clutural communication amongst various interest groups. Interchanges and daily contacts between local German and Polish populations, for instance, are essential parts of the Polish-German reconciliation process. In addition, EU sponsorship of various Euroregion activities ties Nysa to the wider European integration process.

The Meuse-Rhin and Nysa Euroregions in Comparative Perspective

Many of the objectives of Euroregion Nysa mirror those of Euregio Meuse-Rhin: the creation of a transborder Euro-identity, the improvement of living conditions in local communities, and the promotion of economic development in border areas. The pursuit of these objectives, however, is often hindered by circumstances prevalent along the Polish-German-Czech boundary – circumstances that are different from those along the German-Dutch-Belgian border. These differences are rooted in divergent economic and political circumstances, as well as in differing senses of identity and place.

Economic differences

The most pronounced difference between the Meuse-Rhin and Nysa Euroregions concerns the character of their respective regional economies. The Euregio Meuse-Rhin encompasses a high-technology industrial area with automobile assembly plants, electronics firms, mechanical engineering establishments, and biotechnology concerns. The presence of two scientific parks and two Business Enterprise and Innovation Centers (BICs) signals the region's high-technology emphasis, along with its focus on research and other quaternary economic activities. In contrast, border areas in the Euroregion Nysa are characterised by sunset industries – large and inefficient power plants and coal mining centres – as well as by a relatively high unemployment rate. In 1994, for example, the unemployment rate in the Polish town of Jelenia Góra and in the German town of Görlitz was 15 percent. Since 1990 there has been evidence of growth in the service sector, but considerable energy and resources are dedicated to restructuring and modernising the old industrial complexes on both the Polish and German sides of the border. This situation necessarily affects the ability of local authorities to develop and implement new initiatives and projects.

In addition to the issue of new versus old industries, there are clear transboundary economic inequalities. Whereas the five provinces of Meuse-Rhin are characterised by a relatively even, and often complementary, distribution of industries on the Belgian, Dutch, and German sides, in the Euroregion Nysa there is a striking asymmetry of economic potential and a concomitant asymmetry in the ability to finance economic initiatives. There is almost no Polish investment in German businesses, yet the Germans have supplied investment capital to more than 65 percent of the total number of firms on the Polish side of Nysa. German capital is particularly important in manufacturing (both light and heavy), retail, and construction. Moreover, while German-made products are available throughout Poland, the presence of Polish-made goods on the German market is minimal. Indeed, German enterprises and distributors have even erected barriers that discourage Polish exports to Germany.

Political differences

Beyond economic considerations, there are also differential political factors that affect the character of transboundary co-operation in the two regions. In the case of Euregio Meuse-Rhin, all provinces except Dutch Limbourg are within countries with federal systems. Consequently, the involvement of national centres in trans-border activities is minimal and, in most cases, approval from regional authorities suffices for the implementation of cross-border activities and projects. Although the same holds true for the German communities forming part of the Euroregion Nysa, Polish and Czech local authorities operate within unitary states, and they therefore must seek approval from Warsaw or Prague, respectively, for all initiatives of a cross-boundary character. In the case of Poland, the opening up of the country's borders and the emergence of Euroregions has led to a variety of legislative proposals aimed at giving local officials in border areas more autonomy. As of yet, however, these proposals have not been formally adopted because there is no legislative consensus on the degree of autonomy that local officials should have. Such obstacles to transboundary co-operation are not present in the Meuse-Rhin case.

Beyond administrative matters, the Euroregion Nysa differs from its western counterpart because many living within Nysa do not see the participants as political equals. The choice of Zittau, Germany, as the administrative centre is itself of symbolic importance. Zittau has been the prime instigator of transboundary co-operation from the beginning, and it is Zittau, not Liberec (in the Czech Republic) or Bogatynia (in Poland), that is in a position to support the day-to-day activities of the Council. The stream of administrative decisions emanating from Zittau regularly serves to reinforce the notion that the German part of Nysa is 'in the driver's seat'.

The Euroregion Nysa is also characterised by a comparatively low level of consensus on what the Euroregion means. A recent survey conducted among the Polish communes forming part of the Euroregion Nysa showed that there are two opposing views of the Euroregion construct. The first treats the Euroregion as a *framework* within which local initiatives can be realised through co-operation with other partners within and without national territories; the second is based on a perception of the Euroregion as an *institution* that develops and organises all transborder initiatives and projects. The tension between these two positions presents a clear challenge for the success of the Euroregion Nysa initiative.

Differences in sense of identity and place

Behind differing understandings of the nature of the Euroregion Nysa construct are suspicions about the transboundary co-operation process that are rooted in particular senses of identity and place that have developed along the German-Polish boundary. The survey discussed above highlights a critical potential barrier to increased cross-border contact in the Nysa region: the 'different, and not always positive, perceptions of crossboundary cooperation amongst the local borderland population'. Such views are arguably much more entrenched in the Euroregion Nysa than in the Euroregio Meuse-Rhin because of different historical-geographical influences on nationalism and national identity in the two regions.

As previously mentioned, in the aftermath of World War II, overt expressions of ethnonationalism were delegitimised in Western Europe. Economic co-operation instigated by the Treaty of Rome allowed for, among other things, an increase in mobility and transborder interaction. In contrast, transnational mobility and contacts were virtually absent in the countries of the Eastern Bloc. In the case of the Polish-German boundary, for example, the communist elite not only closed the border but also promoted anti-German sentiment in its effort to foster closer associations among Slavic peoples. Consequently, the already strong anti-German views that were rooted in the horrors of Nazism persisted unchallenged throughout the succeeding decades.

The restriction of free cross-boundary contacts created divisions that are difficult to overcome. For example, prior to 1945, when the Nysa River became the boundary between East Germany and Poland, Görlitz was a unified city with a six-hundred-year history. After 1945, the city was divided into German Görlitz and Polish Zgorzelec, and contacts across the river were severely limited. This situation persisted until the 1970s, when a treaty was signed that allowed a limited number of daily border crossings. Since 1989, the possibilities for crossboundary interaction have been unlimited, and many of the residents of Görlitz and Zgorzelec have come to question former national prejudices and stereotypes.

Yet the effects of a recent history of separation and division are not easy to overcome.

Emblematic of these effects, in the early 1990s over half of Poland's population considered the Ordra-Nysa boundary 'insecure' – believing that Germany's failure (at the time) to formally recognise the Polish-German boundary created after World War II could lead to a German effort to revise the boundary. On a local scale, in the mid-1990s close to 30 percent of the residents of the Jelenia Góra voivodship (the Polish side of the Euroregion Nysa) considered the idea of the Euroregion an attempt by Germany to subjugate Poland. The historical and contemporary dynamics of the Odra-Nysa boundary make it difficult for the Poles to come to terms with the complex history of Germany's involvement in the three partitions of Poland, as well as with the more recent tragedy of Hitler's invasion and occupation. This leads to fears and suspicions on the part of Poles in the face of Germany's growing cultural, economic, and political presence in Poland, and it presents a challenge for inter-regional co-operation in the Euroregion Nysa that is of an entirely different magnitude from the attitudinal challenges to inter-regional co-operation that are present in Euregio Meuse-Rhin.

Further complicating the picture is the fact that the border between Poland and Germany continues to play a role that is very different from the boundaries within the EU. The fall of the communist regimes in Poland and East Germany allowed for a substantial increase in transboundary contact. However, the process of German unification that followed introduced a further complexity to Polish-German relations, for the Oder and Neisse Rivers became not only a boundary between states but an external boundary of the EU. This meant that the Euroregion Nysa was in a very different geopolitical situation from the Euroregio Meuse-Rhin.

The significance of this point is evident in mobility issues. Following the signing of the Schengen Agreement (which lifted border controls and ensured free and unlimited passage for citizens of all signatory states), the borders between Germany, Holland, and Belgium began to function more as administrative divisions than as clear-cut demarcations of state-territorial control. Consequently, inhabitants of Liège, Belgium, can make weekend trips to Maastricht, Holland, just as easily as they can travel to Eupen or Hasselt, both Belgian towns. Although Germans living along the Polish-German boundary can also make daily trips to Poland, and vice versa, their experience would be different from that of the inhabitants of the Euregio Meuse-Rhin. The latter would hardly notice at which precise point they crossed into a territory of an adjacent state, whereas the former (whether Polish or German) would spend an hour or so on either side of the border dealing with passport formalities.

Clearly, being within or at the edge of the EU affects people's perceptions of state boundaries and, by extension, their views of the relationship of the places where they live to places across the border. The Euregio Meuse-Rhin is an initiative brought about by local business interests and environmental concerns. Co-operation among the five provinces within the Meuse-Rhin's framework has proven successful in the areas of environmental conservation and economy. More important, it has contributed to the deepening of the European integration process. By contrast, the Euroregion Nysa is as much a creation from above (by central authorities in Warsaw or Prague) as from below (by local authorities along the border). In the context of the EU's external borders, the Euroregions contribute to the widening, rather than the deepening, of European integration. As such, Euroregions in East Central Europe have a more pragmatic and strategic character than do their analogues in the EU. Needless to say, such differences in goals have implications for the development of 'we-feelings' across international boundaries, as well as for the ways in which individuals see their places in geopolitical context.

Conclusion

The comparative perspective adopted in this study highlights the importance of focusing on contextual influences on transboundary co-operation in Europe. In the cases of the Meuse-Rhin and the Nysa Euroregions, fundamental contextual differences call into question the assumption that the Euroregion Nysa will necessarily follow the same pattern of development as its West European analogue. Indeed, the Euroregion Nysa faces distinct challenges ranging from sharp internal differences in levels of economic development to historically rooted intraregional socio-cultural differences that cannot be easily overcome. This does not mean that the Nysa is doomed to failure. What is does suggest, however, is that a simple transference of institutional arrangements and goals from the Euroregions of Western Europe to those of East Central Europe is problematic.

The significance of this point is heightened by the more general importance of developments in border areas for the changing European scene. [. . .] [B]orderlands are often barometers of political change, and this is certainly true of border areas where active Euroregions have come into being. Many of these Euroregions are confronting (sometimes in microcosm) a set of issues that are likely to be of enduring importance in Europe's effort to forge a new political-territorial order. Our ability to understand and appreciate these developments is tied to our capacity to see them not simply as interesting institutional arrangements but as spatial structures that are deeply embedded in, and influenced by, the social, political, economic, and cultural context in which they are situated.

Chapter 37

The End of Public Space? People's Park, Definitions of the Public, and Democracy

Don Mitchell

The Importance of Public Space in Democratic Societies

Public space occupies and important ideological position in democratic societies. The notion of urban public space can be traced back at least to the Greek *agora* and its function as: "the place of citizenship, an open space where public affairs and legal disputes were conducted . . . it was also a marketplace, a place of pleasurable jostling, where citizen's bodies, words, actions, and produce were all literally on mutual display, and where judgements, decisions, and bargains were made." Politics, commerce, and spectacle were juxtaposed and intermingled in the public space of the agora. It provided a meeting place for strangers, whether citizens, buyers, or sellers, and the ideal of public space in the agora encouraged nearly unmediated interaction – the first vision of public space noted above. In such "open and accessible public spaces and forums," as Young has put it, "one should expect to encounter and hear from those who are different, whose social perspectives, experience and affiliations are different."

Young's definition represents more nearly a normative ideal for public space than an empirical description of the ways that public spaces have functioned in "actually existing democracies." This normative public space reflects Habermas' discussion of the aspatial and normative public *sphere* in which the public sphere is best imagined as the suite of institutions and activities that mediate the relations between society and the state. In this normative sense, the public sphere is where "the public" is organized and represented (or imagined). The ideal of a public sphere is normative, Habermas theorizes, because it is in this sphere that all manner of social formations *should* find access to the structures of power within a society. As part

Mitchell, Don, "The End of Public Space? People's Park, Definitions of the Public, and Democracy," pp. 108, 116–22, 123–5, 127 from *Annals of the Association of American Geographers*, 85.1 (1995).

of the public sphere, according to many theorists, public space represents the material location where the social interactions and political activities of all members of "the public" occur.

Greek agora, Roman forums, and eventually American parks, commons, marketplaces, and squares were never simply places of free, unmediated interaction, however; they were just as often places of exclusion. The public that met in these spaces was carefully selected and homogenous in composition. It consisted of those with power, standing, and respectability. Here then are the roots of the second vision of public space. In Greek democracy, for example, citizenship was a right that was awarded to free, non-foreign men and denied to slaves, women, and foreigners. The latter had no standing in the public spaces of Greek cities; they were not included in "the public." Although women, slaves, and foreigners may have worked in the agora, they were formally excluded from the political activities of this public space.

Nor has "the public" always been defined expansively in American history. Inclusion of more and varied groups of people into the public sphere has only been won through constant social struggle. Notions of "the public" and public democracy played off and developed dialectically with notions of private property and private spheres. The ability for citizens to move between private property and public space determined the nature of public interaction in the developing democracy of the United States. In modern capitalist democracies like the United States, "owners of private property freely join together to create a public, which forms the critical functional element of the political realm." To be public implies access to the sphere of private property.

Each of these spheres, of course, has been constrained by, *inter alia*, gender, class, and race. By the end of the eighteenth century:

> The line drawn between public and private was essentially one on which the claims of civility – epitomized by cosmopolitan, public behavior – were balanced against the claims of nature – epitomized by the family. . . . [W]hile man *made* himself in public, he *realized* his nature in the private realm, above all in his experiences within the family.

The private sphere was the home and refuge, the place from which white propertied men ventured out into the democratic arena of public space. The public sphere of American (and other capitalist) democracies is thus understood as a voluntary community of private (and usually propertied) citizens. By "nature" (as also by custom, franchise, and economics), women, non-white men, and the propertyless were denied access to the public sphere in everyday life. Built on exclusions, the public sphere was thus a "profoundly problematic construction."

For the historian Edmund Morgan, the popular sovereignty that arose from this split between publicity and privacy was a fiction in which citizens "*willingly* suspended disbelief" as to the improbability of a total public sphere. The normative ideal of the public sphere holds out hope that a *representative* public can meet, that all can claim representation within "the public." The reality of public space and the public sphere is that Morgan's "fiction" is less an agreeable acquiescence to representation and more "an exercise in ideological construction with respect to who belongs to the national community and the relationship of 'the people' to formal governance."

As ideological constructions, however, ideals like "the public," public space, and the public sphere take on double importance. Their very articulation implies a notion of inclusiveness that becomes a rallying point for successive waves of political activity. Over time, such political activity has broadened definitions of "the public" to include, at least formally, women, people of color, and the propertyless (but not yet foreigners). In turn, redefinitions of citizenship accomplished through struggles for inclusion have reinforced the normative ideals incorporated in notions of public spheres and public spaces. By calling on the rhetoric of inclusion and interaction that the public sphere and public space are meant to represent, excluded groups have been able to argue for their *rights* as part of the active public. And each (partially) successful struggle for inclusion in "the public" conveys to other marginalized groups the importance of the ideal as a point of political struggle.

In these struggles for inclusion, the distinctions between the public sphere and public space assume considerable importance. The public sphere in Habermas' sense is a universal, abstract realm in which democracy occurs. The materiality of this sphere is, so to speak, immaterial to its functioning. Public space, meanwhile, is material. It constitutes an actual site, a place, a ground within and from which political activity flows. This distinction is crucial, for it is "in the context of real public spaces" that alternative movements may arise and contest issues of citizenship and democracy.

If contemporary trends signal a progressive erosion of the first vision of public space as the second becomes more prominent, then public spaces like People's Park become, in Arendt's words, "small hidden islands of freedom," islands of opposition surrounded by "Foucault's carceral archipelago." In these hidden islands, space is *taken* by marginalized groups in order to press claims for their rights. And that was precisely the argument made by many of the People's Park activists and homeless residents. As the *East Bay Express* observed: "Ultimately, they claim, this is still a fight over territory. It is not just two volleyball courts; it's the whole issue of who has rightful claim to the land." Michael Delacour argued that People's Park was still about free speech, and homeless activist Curtis Bray claimed: "they are trying to take the power away from the people." For these activists, People's Park was a place where the rights of citizenship could be expanded to the most disenfranchised segment of contemporary American democracy: the homeless. People's Park provided the space for representing the legitimacy of homeless people within "the public."

The Position of the Homeless in Public Space and as Part of "The Public"

People's Park has been recognized as a refuge for homeless people since its founding, even as elsewhere in Berkeley, the City has actively removed squatters and homeless people from the streets (sometimes rehousing them in a disused city landfill). Consequently, the Park had become a relatively safe place for the homeless to congregate – one of the few such spots in an increasingly hostile Bay Area. Around the Bay, the homeless had been cleaned out of San Francisco's United Nations' Plaza near City Hall and Golden Gate Park; in Oakland, loitering was actively discouraged in most parks.

In part, the desire to sweep the homeless from visibility responds to the central contradiction of homelessness in a democracy composed of private individuals. The contradiction turns on publicity: the homeless are all too visible. Although homeless people are nearly always in public, they are rarely counted as part of *the* public. Homeless people are in a double bind. For them, socially legitimated private space does not exist, and they are denied access to public space and public activity by capitalist society which is anchored in private property and privacy. For those who are *always* in the public, private activities must necessarily be carried out publicly. When public space thus becomes a place of seemingly illegitimate behavior, our notions about what public space is supposed to be are thrown into doubt. Now less a location for the "pleasurable jostling of bodies" and the political discourse imagined as the appropriate activities of public space in a democracy, public parks and streets begin to take on aspects of the home; they become places to go to the bathroom, sleep, drink, or make love – all socially legitimate activities when done in private, but seemingly illegitimate when carried out in public. As importantly, since citizenship in modern democracy (at least ideologically) rests on a foundation of *voluntary* association, and since homeless people are *involuntarily* public, homeless people cannot be, by definition, legitimate citizens. Consequently, "[h]omeless people prove threatening to the free exercise of rights"; they threaten the existence of a "legitimate" – i.e., a voluntary – public.

The existence of homeless people in public thus undermines the ideological order of modern societies. George Will speaks for many when he argues that: "Society needs order, and hence has a right to minimally civilized ambience in public spaces. Regarding the homeless, this is not merely for aesthetic reasons because the aesthetic is not merely unappealing. It presents a spectacle of disorder and decay that becomes contagion." For reasons of order, then, the homeless have been eliminated from most definitions of "the public." They have instead become something of an "indicator species" to much of society, diagnostic of the presumed ill-health of public space, and of the need to gain control, to privatize, and to rationalize public spaces in urban places. Whether in New York City, Berkeley, or Columbus, Ohio, the presence of homeless people in public spaces suggests in the popular mind an irrational and uncontrolled society in which the distinctions between appropriate public and private behavior are muddled. Hence, those who are intent on rationalizing "public" space in the postindustrial city have *necessarily* sought to remove the homeless – to banish them to the interstices and margins of civic space – in order to make room for legitimate public activities.

When, as in Berkeley's People's Park or New York's Tompkins Square, actions are taken against park users by closing public space or exercising greater social control over park space, the press explains these actions by saying that "the park is currently a haven for drug users and the homeless." Such statements pointedly ignore any "public" standing that homeless people may have, just as they ignore the possibility that homeless people's usage of a park for political, social, economic, and residential purposes may constitute for them legitimate and necessary uses of public space. When UC officials claimed that the homeless residents of People's Park were not "representative of the community," they in essence denied social legitimacy to homeless people and their (perhaps necessary) behaviors. By transforming the Park, UC hoped that illegitimate activity would be discouraged. That is to say that the homeless could stay as long as they behaved appropriately – and as long as the historical, normative, ideological boundary between public and private was well patrolled.

Public Space in the Contemporary City

[. . .]

As a secular space, the public space of the modern city has always been a hybrid of politics and commerce. Ideally, the anarchy of the market meets the anarchy of politics in public space to create an interactive, democratic public. In the twentieth century, however, markets have been increasingly severed from politics: The once expansive notion of public space that guided early American democratic ideology and the extension, however partial, of public rights to women, people of color, and the propertyless have been jeopardized by countervailing social, political, and economic trends, trends that have caused many to recoil against any exercise of democratic social power that poses a threat to dominant social and economic interests.

These trends have led to the constriction of public space. Interactive, discursive politics have been effectively banned from the gathering points of the city. Corporate and state planners have created environments that are based on desires for security rather than interaction, for entertainment rather than (perhaps divisive) politics. One of the results of planning has been the growth of what Sennett calls "dead public spaces" – the barren plazas that surround so many modern office towers. A second result has been the development of festive spaces that encourage consumption – downtown redevelopment areas, malls, and festival marketplaces. Though seemingly so different, both "dead" and "festive" spaces are premised on a perceived need for order, surveillance, and control over the behavior of the public. As Goss reminds us, we are often complicit in the severing of market and political functions. He points to the case of the pseudo-public space of the contemporary shopping mall:

> Some of us are . . . disquieted by the constant reminders of surveillance in the sweep of cameras and the patrols of security personnel [in malls]. Yet those of us for whom it is designed are willing to suspend the privileges of public urban space to its relative benevolent authority, for our desire is such that we will readily accept nostalgia as a substitute for experience, absence for presence, and representation for authenticity.

This nostalgic desire for the market Goss calls "agoraphilia" – a yearning for "an immediate relationship between producer and consumer."

Such nostalgia is rarely "innocent," however. It is rather a highly constructed, corporatized image of a market quite unlike the idealization of the agora as a place of commerce *and* politics. In the name of comfort, safety, and profit, political activity is replaced in these spaces by a highly commodified spectacle designed to sell. Planners of pseudo-public spaces like malls and corporate plazas have found that controlled diversity is more profitable than unconstrained social differences. Hence even as new groups are claiming greater access to the rights of society, homogenization of "the public" continues apace.

This homogenization typically has advanced by "disneyfying" space and place – creating landscapes in which every interaction is carefully planned. Market and design considerations thus displace the idiosyncratic and extemporaneous interactions of engaged peoples in the determination of the shape of urban space in the contemporary world. Designed-and-contrived diversity creates marketable landscapes, as opposed to uncontrolled social interaction which creates places that may threaten exchange value. The "disneyfication" of space consequently implies increasing alienation of people from the possibilities of unmediated social interaction and increasing control by powerful economic and social actors over the production and use of space.

Imposing limits and controls on spatial interaction has been one of the principal aims of urban and corporate planners during this century. The territorial segregation created through the expression of social *difference* has increasingly been replaced by a celebration of constrained *diversity*. The diversity represented in shopping centers, "megastructures," corporate plazas, and (increasingly) in public parks is carefully constructed. Moreover, the expansion of a planning and marketing ethos into all manner of public gathering places has created a "space of social practice" that sorts and divides social groups according to the dictates of comfort and order rather than to those of political struggle. But as Lefebvre suggests, this in no accident. The strategies of urban and corporate planners, he claims, classify and "distribute various social strata and classes (other than the one that exercises hegemony) across the available territory, keeping them separate and prohibiting all contacts – these being replaced by *signs* (or images) of contact."

This reliance on images and signs – or representations – entails the recognition that a "public" that cannot exist as such is continually *made* to exist in the pictures of democracy we carry in our heads: "The public in its entirety has never met at all . . ."; yet "the public [is] still to be found, large as life, in the media." Hence: "Contemporary politics is *representative* in both senses of the term; citizens are represented by a chosen few, and politics is represented to the public via the various media of communication. Representative political space is literally made of pictures – they *constitute* the public domain." I will return to this theme of symbolic politics and resistance to it in the material spaces of the city; for now, it is sufficient to note that the politics of symbolism, imaging, and representation increasingly stand in the stead of a democratic *ideal* of direct, less-mediated, social interaction in public spaces. In other words, contemporary designers of urban "public" space increasingly accept signs and images of contact as more natural and desirable than contact itself.

Public and pseudo-public spaces assume new functions in a political and social system in which controlled representation is regarded as natural and desirable. The overriding purpose of public space becomes the creation of a "public realm deliberately shaped as theater." "Significantly, it is theater in which a pacified public basks in the grandeur of a carefully orchestrated corporate spectacle." That is the purpose of the carefully controlled "public" spaces such as the corporate plazas, library grounds, and suburban streets critiqued by Davis and the festive marketplaces, underground pedestrian districts, and theme parks analyzed by the contributors to Sorkin. It is certainly the goal of mall builders.

These spaces of controlled spectacle narrow the list of eligibles for "the public." Public spaces of spectacle, theater, and consumption create images that define the public, and these images exclude as "undesirable" the homeless and the political activist. Thus excluded from these public and pseudo-public spaces, their legitimacy as members of the public is put in doubt. And thus *unrepresented* in our images of "the public," they are banished to a realm outside politics because they are banished from the gathering places of the city.

How "the public" is defined and imaged (as a space, as a social entity, and as an ideal) is a matter of some importance. As Crilley shows, corporate producers of space tend to define the public as passive, receptive, and "refined." They foster the "illusion of a homogenized public" by filtering out "the social heterogeneity of the urban crowd, [and] substituting in its place a flawless fabric of white middle class work, play, and consumption . . . with minimal exposure to the horrifying level of homelessness and racialized poverty that characterizes [the] street environment." And, by blurring distinctions between private property and public space, they create a public that is narrowly prescribed. The elision of carefully controlled spaces (such as Disneyland, Boston's Fanueil Hall, or New York's World Financial Center) with notions of public space "conspires to hide from us the widespread privatization of the public realm and its reduction to the status of commodity." The irony is, of course, that this privatization of public space is lauded by all levels of government (e.g., through public-private redevelopment partnerships) at the same time as the privatization of public space by homeless people (their use of public space for what we consider to be private activities) is excoriated by urban planners, politicians, and social critics alike.

The End of Public Space?

Have we reached, then, the "end of public space"? Has the dual (though so different) privatization of public space by capital and by homeless people created a world in which designed diversity has so thoroughly replaced the free interaction of strangers that the ideal of an unmediated *political* public space is wholly unrealistic? Have we created a society that expects and desires only private interactions, private communications, and private politics, that reserves public spaces solely for commodified recreation and spectacle? Many cultural critics on the left believe so, as do mainstream commentators such as Garreau and conservatives like Glazer. Public spaces are, for these writers, an artifact of a past age, an age with different sensibilities and different ideas about public order and safety, when public spaces were stable, well-defined, and accessible to all. But these images of past public spaces and past public spheres are highly idealized; as we have seen, the public sphere in the American past was anything but inclusive – and public space was always a site for and a source of conflict. Definitions of public space and "the public" are not universal and enduring; they are produced rather through constant struggle in the past and in the present. And, in People's Park as in so many other places, that struggle continues.

But these kinds of spaces are dwindling, despite the fact that many cities are increasing their stocks of parks, bicycle and hiking corridors, natural areas, and similar places that are owned or operated in the name of the public. That is certainly the case in Boulder, Colorado, where the preservation of open spaces in and around urbanized areas is one of the most strongly supported city and county initiatives. Mountain parks, prairielands, small city blocks, farmlands, and wetlands have all been set aside. But are these public spaces in the political sense?

During the period of rapid suburbanization and urban renewal in the decades after World War II, North American cities: "vastly increased 'open' space, but its primary purpose was different [than public spaces with civic functions], i.e., to separate functions, open up distance between buildings, allow for the penetration of sunlight and greenery, not to provide places for extensive social contact." There are many reasons for the growth of open space – preserving ecologically sensitive areas; maintaining property values by establishing an undevelopable greenbelt; providing places for recreation; removing flood plains from development; and so on. But in each case open space serves functional and ideological roles that differ from political public spaces. It is rare that open spaces such as these are designed or appropriated to fulfill the market and civic functions that mark the public space of the city. More typically, these open spaces share certain characteristics with pseudo-public spaces. Restrictions on behavior and activities are taken-for-granted; prominent signs designate appropriate uses and outline rules concerning where one may walk, ride, or gather. These are highly regulated spaces.

In Berkeley, UC officials recognized this distinction between open space and public space. During various People's Park debates, speakers for the University never referred to the Park as public space, though they frequently reiterated their commitment to maintaining the Park as open space. Berkeley City Council member Alan Goldfarb, an occasional critic of University plans, also traded on the differences between public and open space. Speaking of People's Park, he celebrated the virtues of public space and then undermined them:

> It's a symbol for the police versus the homeless, the have-nots versus the haves, progress versus turmoil, development versus nondevelopment, all of the undercurrents most troubling in the city. You've got pan-handling going on, the business community nearby, the town-gown tensions. You have anarchists and traditionalists. People's Park becomes a live stage for all these actors. For many people around the world, Berkeley *is* People's Park.

But if "[t]hese things are real and important," he continued, it is more important to make People's Park "a viable open space" that would provide a bit of green in a highly urbanized neighborhood.

New Public Spaces?

There is an even stronger argument for the end of public space than the one that is based on the growth of open space. Many analysts suggest that the very nature of space has been transformed by developments in communications technology. They maintain that the electronic space of the media and computer networks has opened a new frontier of public space in which material public spaces in the city are superseded by the fora of television, radio talk shows, and computer bulletin boards. For many scholars (not to mention entrepreneurs), modern communications technology now provides the primary site for discursive public activity in general and politics in particular. Defining electronic bulletin boards and networks, fax machines, talk radio, and television as public space stretches our traditional assumptions about the materiality of space and replaces them with celebrations of television as a global village and disquisitions on "the creation of the first cyberspace nation." With these technologies, citizenship no longer requires the dichotomy between public and private *geographies*; access to a television set, radio, or computer with a modem is sufficient.

[. . .]

The Necessity of Material Public Spaces

[. . .]

This vision of an electronic future – and of its meanings for public space – has not gone uncontested. Opponents maintain that social movements must, and do, occupy and reconfigure material public space in the city. Indeed, these movements are premised on the notion that democratic (and certainly revolutionary) politics are impossible without the simultaneous creation and control of *material* space. The collective protest in Tiananmen Square in May 1989 offers a case in point. Although Tiananmen underlines the importance of television and other electronic media for revolutionary movements, it was above all else an occupation of material public space. Electronic communication played an important role in organizing the protest, but the uprising truly began with the transformation of the Square itself from a monumental and official space "into a genuine place of political discourse." Students and other activists "met in small groups of friends for discussion, large audiences for speeches and even more or less representative council for debating their collective strategy and carrying out self-government." The public appropriation of Tiananmen Square is incisive "evidence of the extraordinary power of apparently 'placeless' movements to create and transform space in new and authentically revolutionary ways." This place-centered struggle was *then* captured by the media. The Square became a place *for* representation – in this case the representation of a powerful popular movement opposed to the state. Spaces such as Tiananmen Square, or People's Park, enable opposition to be extended to wider scales. *After* space is taken, oppositional representations expand beyond the confines of the local struggle. Without occupation of material space, however, the kinds of protest that came to a point at Tiananmen or People's Park would have remained invisible.

For this reason, reliance on the media as the entée into the public sphere is dangerous. Media in the "bourgeois public sphere" (that is, the public sphere as described by Habermas and developed during the great bourgeois upheavals of the eighteenth and nineteenth centuries) "are privately owned and operated for profit. Consequently, subordinated social groups lack equal access to the material means of equal participation." To overcome the problem of access, "subaltern counter publics" create "parallel discursive arenas where members of subordinated groups invent and circulate counterdiscourses, which in turn permit them to formulate oppositional interpretations of their identities, interests and needs." In these arenas and spaces, counterpublics can be seen by other factions of the public. Without these spaces, "the public" is balkanized. Occupation of public space, then, "militates in the long run against separatism because it assumes an orientation that is *publicist*. Insofar as these arenas are *publics* they are by definition not enclaves – which is not to say that they are not often involuntarily enclaved."

While television has an important role to play in political movements and revolution, there has never been a revolution conducted exclusively in electronic space. Revolutions entail a taking to the streets and a taking of public space. They require the creation of disorder in places formerly marked by order (for revolution is also a pictorial event – it must be represented). Political movements must create the space in which they can be represented. While Lefebvre may theorize the continual production of representations of space and representational spaces, public social movements understand that they must create spaces *for* representation. Consider the "mothers' movements" in the Southern Cone states of South America. Mothers of the "disappeared" publicly proclaimed their cause by appropriating public squares and monuments. Their occupations of public space forced their cause to be "aired." In the absence of these spaces, the mothers' cause could not have been conveyed to the rest of the city, the region, the nation, or, through the eye of television, the world.

This pattern has been repeated elsewhere: in Eastern Europe and China in 1989 and in the Soviet Union soon thereafter. Similar strategic occupations of public space were effected by the Industrial Workers of the World in its struggles for Free Speech around 1910, and by the Civil Rights, Farm Workers', and anti-war movements of the 1960s. The pattern also held true for the fascist movements in Italy and Germany in the 1930s – a reminder that when social movements liberate space, the results are not always "progressive." The creation and maintenance of public space thus entails risks to democracy itself, which makes public space an inherently dangerous thing.

The opponents of public, unmediated, and thoroughly politicized spaces have responded to this danger with an "enclosure" of public space. Fearful of disorder and violence in public space, some developers, planners, and city officials advocate taming space by circumscribing activities within it. Powerful processes of exclusion are thus arrayed against the play of assertive, uncontrolled difference within and necessary to public spaces. As Lefebvre has argued, difference threatens social order the hence must be absorbed by hegemonic powers:

Differences arise on the margins of the homogenized realm, either in the form of resistances or in the form of externalities. . . . What is different is, to begin with, what is *excluded*: the edges of the city, shanty towns, the spaces of forbidden games, of guerrilla war, of war. Sooner or later, however, the existing centre and the forces of homogenization must seek to absorb all such differences, and they will succeed if these retain a defensive posture and no counterattack is mounted from their side. In the latter event, centrality and normality will be tested to the limits of their power to integrate, to recuperate, or to destroy whatever has transgressed.

Whether challenged from the left or the right, the established power of the state and capital are threatened by the exercise of public rights within public spaces.

The conflicting desires for order and for rights and representation structured the 1991 riots at People's Park. Activists in Berkeley fought on behalf of expansion and opposition: the power of the state and corporate capitalism, they felt, had to be opposed by (re)taking space. *Only* by taking and maintaining control over People's Park could oppositional political activity be represented and advanced. For activists such as David Nadle, the precedent was clear. The struggle in People's Park was another "Tiananmen Square" in which Park activists and homeless people together would halt the expansion of the corporate state.

Conclusion: The End of People's Park as Public Space?

[. . .] The long-simmering, and sometimes white-hot, controversies over People's Park in Berkeley are paradigmatic of the struggles that define the nature of "the public" and public space. Activists see places like the Park as spaces *for* representation. By *taking* public space, social movements represent themselves to larger audiences. Conversely, representatives of mainstream institutions argue that public spaces must be orderly and safe in order to function properly. These fundamentally opposed visions of public space clashed in the riots over People's Park, in August 1991. Though the "public" status of People's Park remains ambiguous (given UC's legal title to the land), the political importance of the Park as public space rests on its status as a *taken* space. By wresting control of People's Park from the state, Park activists held at bay issues of control, order, and state power. But for many others, the Park's parallel history as a refuge for the homeless suggested that People's Park had become unmanageable, that large segments of the public felt threatened by the Park's relatively large resident population, and that the City and University needed to exercise more control over the Park. For more than two decades, these visions of the Park as a public space collided as UC sought to reclaim the Park and to define the Park's appropriate public and what counted as appropriate behavior there.

As the history of People's Park has unfolded, the homeless have become rather iconographic. One of the issues raised by the struggles over People's Park (and one that I have not completely answered), is the degree to which "safe havens" like People's Park address the needs of homeless people themselves. Certainly the provision of "free spaces" for the homeless in cities does nothing to address the structural production of homelessness in capitalist societies. Nor do these "havens" necessarily provide safety for homeless people. But, as I have argued, spaces like People's park are also political spaces. For homeless people, these spaces are more than just "homes." They serve as sites within which homeless people can be seen and represented, as places within which activism on homelessness can arise and expand outward. On the stages of these spaces, homeless people and others may insist upon public representation and recognition in ways that are not possible in the vacuous spaces of the electronic frontier or the highly controlled pseudo-public spaces of the mall and the festival marketplace.

People's Park represents therefore an important instance in the on-going struggles over the nature of public space in America (and elsewhere). The riots that occurred there invite us to focus attention on appropriate uses of public space, the definitions of legitimate publics, and the nature of democratic discourse and political action. By listening to various actors as they assessed their motives in People's Park, we have seen that struggles over public space are struggles over opposing ideologies, over the ways in which members of society conceptualize public space. These public utterances reflect divergent ideological positions, adhering more or less to one of two poles in discourse about public space: public space as a place of unmediated political interaction, and public space as a place of order, controlled recreation, and spectacle. Arguments in behalf of the thesis of "the end of public space" suggest that an orderly, controlled vision of public space in the city is squeezing out other ways of imagining public space. The recent history of People's Park suggests that these arguments are, if profoundly important, too simple. Oppositional movements continually strive to assure the currency of more expansive visions of public space. Still, to the degree that the "disneyfication" of public space advances and political movements are shut out of public space, oppositional movements lose the spaces where they may be represented (or may represent themselves) as legitimate parts of "the public." As the words and actions of the protagonists in Berkeley suggest, the stakes are high and the struggles over them might very well be bloody. But that is at once the promise and the danger of public space.

Index

afforestation, 75
Afghanistan, 39, 409
  US invasion, 408, 414, 419
Africa
  alcohol consumption, 311, 312, 315,
    316, 317
  fertility transition, 90, 91
  global change research, 138
  HIV/AIDS, 87, 88, 89; age dependency
    ratios and, 87; behavioral dimension,
    86, 88–9; diffusionist approach,
    92–4; gender differences, 87; impact
    of, 83; infantile AIDS, 87, 90; life
    expectancy and, 87, 91; North
    Africa, 82; prevalence rates, 82,
    84–6, 87, 89; statistics, 81, 82,
    85–6; Sub-Saharan Africa, 81, 82, 85,
    93; transmission, 81, 87, 88, 89;
    Uganda, 83, 89, 93–4; under-
    reporting, 84, 85
  Mali, 40
  Nigeria, 127
  the Sahel of West Africa, 395–9
  soil erosion, 67, 68
  viticulture, 314
  see also Ghana; Kenya; South Africa
African Americans, 7
African Land Development Board
    (ALDEV), 69, 71, 78
Agnew, J., 413

agriculture, 114, 116–17
  agricultural revolution, 122–3
  archaeological studies, 116–21
  beans, 67, 126, 129
  Bolivia, 376–7
  chemical fertilizers, 122, 126, 128, 131
  droughts, 157, 159
  efficiency, 125–6
  energy consumption, 114, 122, 123,
    124, 125, 129
  farm acreage, 126
  "green revolution," 114, 122, 123
  health and, 117–18, 119
  home consumption, 126–7
  hunting and gathering compared, 114,
    116–21
  India, 127
  insect pests, 129–30
  insecticides, 129
  intercropping, 123, 124–5, 127, 129–30,
    131
  irrigation, 122, 159
  Jamaica, 127
  Kenya, *see* Kenya
  legumes, 125, 126, 129
  leisure and, 117, 120
  lifestyles, 127–8
  machinery, 122, 124, 127
  maize/corn, 4–5, 6, 67, 73, 126, 129
  manure, 74, 76

agriculture (*cont.*)
  Mexico, 224, 231
  monocropping, 123, 125, 127, 129
  paleopathological evidence, 118–19
  petroleum and, 122, 123
  plant disease, 130
  plows, 73–4
  population growth and: Kenya, 52,
    65–80; Malthus on, 52, 57–60, 63
  progressivist perspective, 117
  rice production, 7
  sexual inequality and, 116, 119–20
  soil conservation, 68–71, 124, 376,
    377
  soil erosion, 7, 67, 68
  soil fertility, 128
  soil leaching, 124, 128
  soils, 67
  solar energy, 124, 129
  terracing, 68–70, 376
  traditional agriculture, 122–31
  transport costs, 127–8
  tree farming, 75–6
  unemployment, 123
  United States, 122, 127, 128, 129
  viticulture, 312–16
  water conservation, 70, 129
  weather and, 128–9, 159, 160
  weeding, 127, 130
  wilderness and, 174
  women in: Kenya, 65, 68, 73, 74, 75,
    76, 77–8; in the Sahel of West
    Africa, 396; sexual inequality, 116,
    119–20
agronomists, 4–5
Ahlberg, B. M., 94
AIDS, *see* HIV/AIDS
Akamba people, 65–80
  see also Kenya
alcohol consumption, 294, 310, 320–2
  attempts to prohibit, 321–2
  Food Balance Sheets, 311
  measuring, 310–11
  patterns of, 311–12, 314–16, 317,
    318–19
  reasons for, 310
  see also beer; spirits; wine
Algeria, 40
alternative development, *see* development
anti-retroviral drugs (ARVs), 86, 95

archaeology, 116–21
area studies tradition, 18–19, 20
  spatial tradition and, 18
Arendt, Hannah, 439
Aristotle, 21
Armelagos, George, 118, 119
Asia
  alcohol consumption, 312, 315, 316,
    317, 318, 320, 321
  fertility, 90
  HIV/AIDS, 82, 86, 89
  population change, 90
  see also China; India; Japan; Korea
Association of American Geographers
  (AAG), 16, 17
Association of European Border Regions
  (AEBR), 424, 425
Australia
  alcohol consumption, 318
  geography in schools, 8
  HIV/AIDS, 82
  viticulture, 314

Barnett, Tony, 82–3
beer, 316–18, 320
  alcohol content, 312
  barley beer, 312, 317
  connoisseurs, 203
  history, 199–200, 317–18
  lager, 318
  measuring consumption, 310–11
  patterns of consumption, 311, 312,
    317
  types, 311
  see also alcohol consumption; brewing;
    microbreweries
Belgium
  Euroregio Meuse-Rhin, 427–9, 432–6
biogeography, 28
biological diversity, 172
Blaikie, Piers, 5, 7, 82–3, 114, 135
blizzards, 162–3
BMW, 244–5
Bolivia
  agriculture, 376–7
  ayllu, 374, 377–8
  La Paz, 373, 374, 375, 376–7
  non-governmental organizations
    (NGOs), 370, 371, 374, 375;
    ALTERNATIVO, 375, 376–7;

ANTIPOV, 376, 377–9; Private
Institutions for Social Development
(IPDS), 374, 375, 378, 380
Norte Potosí, 373, 374, 375, 377–9
rotating savings and credit associations
(ROSCAs), 377
sindicatos, 374–9
soil conservation, 376, 377
women in, 378
see also Latin America
Bond, Patrick, 269
Borchert, John, 5, 7
borders, *see* international boundaries
Boserup, Ester, 52, 79
Botha, P. W., 265
Botswana
fertility decline, 91
HIV/AIDS, 85
boundaries, *see* international boundaries
Bray, Curtis, 439
brewing
beer connoisseurs, 203
in Britain, 201–2
CAMRA, 201
economies of scale, 200–1
history, 199–200, 317–18
place and, 204–5
see also beer; microbreweries
Brookfield, Harold, 135
Brzezinski, Zbigniew, 415, 416
Burkina Faso, 397–8
Burton, Ian, 134
Bush, George W., 37, 418
Bushmen, 117

Caldwell, Jack and Pat, 90, 92–3, 94
Cambodia, 86
Canada, 8
Carney, Judith, 5, 7
carrying capacity, 51, 68
cartography, 15, 42–3, 44
see also maps
cartophobia, 43–4
Castells, Manuel, 279–80, 281
Catholics
pilgrimage traditions, 206, 209–10, 211,
212, 214
central place theory, 7, 18, 293
chemical fertilizers, 122, 126, 128, 131
see also lawn-care chemicals

children
global change and, 140
human-tracking and, 46, 47
infantile AIDS, 87, 90
Chile, 401
China, 38, 418
alcohol consumption, 311, 316, 317,
320
censuses, 99–101
geography in schools, 8
global change research, 138
HIV/AIDS, 86
industrialization, 98–9
migration, 53, 96–7; censuses, 99–101;
data, 99–101; defining, 99–101;
floating population, 99; permanent
migrants, 99; population
redistribution and, 102; rates, 96–7;
regional development and, 102,
104–8; in socialist China, 98, 108;
temporary migrants, 99; theories,
97–8; in transitional China, 98–9, 108
socialist market economy, 98
Tiananmen Square, 445–6
chorographic tradition, 18–19
Christaller, Walter, 293
cities, 5, 7, 31, 235–7
central place theory, 7
ethnic residential concentrations, 236,
247–63; characteristics of recent
immigrants, 250–1; Chinatowns, 249,
252; conflicting theoretical
expectations, 250–2; enclaves, 248;
ethnic economies, 251; evidence, 252;
ghettos, 248–9; historic ethnic
concentrations, 249–50; Immigrant
Spatial Assimilation Theory, 249–50,
253; measurement, 252–6; nationality
groups, 261–2; overall levels of group
concentrations, 256–9; problems of
measurement, 252–5; reasons for
expecting, 251–2; reasons for not
expecting, 250–1; varying importance
of, 262–3; voluntary residential
decisions, 249
Greenville, South Carolina, 235–6,
238–46; BMW, 244–5; economic
diversification, 242–5; European
settlement, 239; foreign investment,
243–5; housing, 240–1;

cities (*cont.*)
  hydroelectricity, 240; physical
    geography, 238–9; railroads, 240,
    242; textile industry, 239–42
  housing subsidy program, South Africa,
    236, 264–78
  Middle East, 144
  public space, 441–3, 444
  United States, 7; ethnic residential
    concentration, 236, 247–63;
    Greenville, South Carolina,
    235–6, 238–46; immigrants, 236,
    247–63
  World Cities, 236–7, 279–80; global
    office location strategies, 281–2;
    intercity global network, 282–4;
    London, case study, 284–8; in a
    network society, 281; research
    clusters, 280–1; shared firm presences,
    282–4, 285
classical antiquity
  geography in, 2, 17, 18, 19, 21, 113
climate
  climatic determinism, 164–6
  environmental determinism, 113
  see also climate change; climatology;
    droughts; weather
climate change
  El Niño, 137
  global warming, 134, 136
  global-change research, 132, 135, 136,
    137–41
  greenhouse gases, 134, 138
  interdisciplinary research, 135
  Mexico, 135–6, 137
  United States, 156–66
climatology, 28–9, 134–5
Coale, A. J., 92
coffee growing, 67, 69, 71–3
cognitive representation, 34
Cohen, Mark, 119
collective selfhood
  pilgrimage traditions and, 207, 218–20
colonialism, 114, 135
  environmental determinism and, 113
  Kenya, 65–6, 68–9
  water resource conflicts, 144
  White Highlands policy, 65
conservation, *see* soil conservation; water
    conservation

containerization
  impact of, 306, 308–9
  see also longshoring
Coones, Paul, 420
corn/maize, 4–5, 6, 73, 126, 129
Cornell, Svante E., 413
Correa, Charles, 361
cotton growing, 71–3
countermodernist geography, 36
Craddock, Susan, 83
Crankshaw, O., 269
cultural ecology, 113–14
cultural geography, 21, 181–2
  see also microbreweries; place;
    recreation
culture historians, 20
Czech Republic
  Euroregion Nysa, 426, 429–36

Dalby, Simon, 416, 421
Davis, William Morris, 16, 17
deep ecology, 173–4
Delacour, Michael, 439
Democratic Republic of Congo
  HIV/AIDS, 85
Demographic Transition Model (DTM),
    89–91
Derrida, Jacques, 219
development, 351–3
  alternative development, 353, 369–70,
    379–80; Bolivia, case study, *see*
    Bolivia; diversity in civil society,
    370–1; local state and, 371–2; markets
    and, 372–3; non-governmental
    organizations (NGOs), 370, 371,
    374–80
  climate and, 400
  critical development theory, 374
  culture and, 401
  environmental impacts, 397–8
  gender and development (GAD), 383
  modernization and, 351–2, 357, 369,
    383
  Nicaragua, *see* Nicaragua
  non-governmental organizations
    (NGOs), role of, 353
  re-scaling of uneven development, 352,
    355, 357; Ghana, 355, 363, 365–6;
    government policies and, 356, 358,
    359; India, 355, 359–61

religion and, 401
the Sahel of West Africa, 397–9
spatial dimensions of, 354–5
women in development (WID), 383
diffusionism
HIV/AIDS and, 91–4
digital representation, 34–5
droughts, 134, 135
Dust Bowl, 68, 161
Kenya, 67, 70, 77
Middle East, 143
Nicaragua, 381–2, 389
United States, 68, 157, 159, 161, 162
see also water conservation; water
resource conflicts
Dual Independent Map Encoding system,
34

earth science tradition, 20–1
Easterling, Bill, 138
Eastern Europe
alcohol consumption, 318
global change research, 138
HIV/AIDS, 82, 86
see also Poland; Russia
ecology
biogeography and, 28
see also cultural ecology; political
ecology
economic geography, 293–4
Ecuador, 98
Edwards, M., 410
Egypt, 113
migration, 98
water resources, 143, 148
see also Middle East; water resource
conflicts
El Niño, 137
Eliade, Mircea, 219
energy consumption, 39, 41, 138
agriculture, 114, 122, 123, 124, 125,
129
Engels, Friedrich, 51–2
environment
environmental impacts on humankind,
26–7
global-change research, 132, 136,
137–41
human impacts, 26, 134
human use, 26

international environmental policy,
132–7
land-use and land-cover change, 138–9
perceptions of/responses to change in,
27
UNEP, 133
wilderness, 167–78
see also climate change
environmental determinism, 113
environmental dynamics, 27–9
biogeography, 28
climatology, 28–9
environmental possibilism, 113
environmental–societal dynamics, 26–7
environmentalism, 19, 114, 132–3, 172
radical environmentalists, 173–4
epistemologies, see geographic
epistemologies
Ethiopia
water resources, 143, 148
see also Middle East; water resource
conflicts
ethnic residential concentrations, see cities
Europe
alcohol consumption, 316, 317, 318, 319,
320
climate, influence of, 113
fertility decline, 92
geography in schools, 7
HIV/AIDS, 82
see also Eastern Europe; European
Union
European Union, 374, 422
alcohol consumption, 311
transboundary cooperation, 422–3;
Association of European Border
Regions (AEBR), 424, 425; Committee
of the Regions, 424; Council of
Europe and, 424–5; European
Commission and, 424–5; Euroregio
Council, 428; Euroregio Meuse-Rhin,
427–9, 432–6; the Euroregion
construct, 425–6; Euroregion Nysa,
429–36; Euroregions, 423, 424–6;
evolution, 423–32; Meuse-Rhin and
Nysa Euroregions compared, 432–6;
organizations of regional and local
authorities, 424
Turkey and, 154
export processing zones (EPZs), 343–4

farming, *see* agriculture
feminist geography, 36
feminist political ecology, 221–2
fertility transition, 89–91
fertilizers
    chemical fertilizers, 122, 126, 128, 131
    manure, 74, 76
Fettweis, C. J., 410
Findlay, A., 95
Finland
    human-tracking, 46
Fisher, Peter F., 47
fishing
    ice fishing, 184, 185
    recreational fishing, 184, 185, 186, 190,
        192–3
FitzSimmons, Margaret, 135
flooding, 114, 160
Foley, William, 325
Food and Agriculture Organization (FAO),
    311
foreign policy, 14, 37–8
    oil and, 39–40
    United States, 37–8, 418–19
    Uzbekistan, 413
Foreman, Dave, 174, 176
fossil fuels, 125, 134
    see also oil; petroleum
Foucault, Michel, 219, 439
France, 7
Frank, A., 351–2
Friedmann, John, 281
Fukuyama, Francis, 400

Gannett, Henry, 17
garden studies
    Mexican house-lot gardens, 221, 222,
        225, 226–32
Garreau, Joel, 443
gender
    gender and development (GAD), 383
    global change and, 140
    place and, 182, 221, 222–3, 224,
        226–32
    recreation and, 186
    see also women
geographic climatology, 28–9
geographic epistemologies, 35–6
    feminist approaches, 36
    interpretive approaches, 36

postmodernist/countermodernist
    approaches, 36
geographic information systems (GISs), 4,
    13, 34, 38
geographic perspective, 4–7
geography
    as academic discipline, 2, 7–8, 113
    area studies tradition, 18–19, 20
    biogeography, 28
    in classical antiquity, 2, 17, 18, 19, 21,
        113
    cultural geography, 21, 181–2
    defining, 1–2, 16
    domains of synthesis, 22, 25;
        environmental dynamics, 27–9;
        environmental–societal dynamics,
        26–7; human–societal dynamics,
        29–32
    earth science tradition, 20–1
    economic geography, 293–4
    feminist approaches, 36
    foreign policy and, 37–8
    geographic climatology, 28–9
    geographic epistemologies, 35–6
    geomorphology, 29
    hazards geography, 114, 135–6, 159–66
    human geography, 3–4, 21
    interdependencies among scales, 25
    interpretive approaches, 36
    man-land tradition, 19–20
    nature–society geography, 3, 4
    perspectives, 22–36
    physical geography, 3, 4, 21, 27–8
    postmodern/countermodernist
        approaches, 36
    radical development geography, 114–15
    realist approaches, 35
    scale of observation, 25
    in schools, 7–8, 37–8
    spatial representation, 23, 32–5, 37–8;
        cognitive, 34; digital, 34–5;
        mathematical, 33; verbal, 33; visual,
        33
    spatial tradition, 17–18, 19, 20
    ways of looking at the world, 22, 23–4;
        integration in place, 24;
        interdependencies between places,
        24–5
geology, 21
geomorphology, 28, 29

Germany, 37
  alcohol consumption, 317, 319
  Euroregio Meuse-Rhin, 427–9, 432–6
  Euroregion Nysa, 429–36
  geography in schools, 7
  public space, 446
Ghana
  economic growth and development, 355,
    358–9
  government policies, 358–9
  HIV/AIDS, 83
  liberalization and globalization, effects
    of, 358–9, 363, 365–6
  re-scaling of uneven development, 355,
    363; intra-regional differentiation,
    365; intra-urban differentiation,
    365–6
  see also Africa
Glacken, Clarence, 133
Glantz, Mickey, 135
Glazer, N., 443
Global Demography Project, 33
global positioning systems (GPSs), 15,
  46–7
global warming, 134, 136
  see also climate change
global-change research, 132, 135, 136,
  137–41
globalization, 40, 294, 296, 297
  acceleration in process of, 356
  capital mobility and, 356, 357
  communications technology and, 256
  containerization, impact of, 306,
    308–9
  export processing zones (EPZs), 343–4
  government policies and, 356, 358, 359
  of Latin America, 384
  liberalization policies, 356, 358, 363,
    384
  new industrial order, 343
  oil industry, see oil industry
  practices, 296
  re-scaling of uneven development, 352,
    355, 357; Ghana, 355, 363, 365–6;
    government policies and, 356, 358,
    359; India, 355, 359–61
  spatial outcomes, 354–5
  technological innovation and, 356
  women workers and, 294, 343–5
  see also World Cities

Goldfarb, Alan, 444
Goss, J., 441
Gould, Peter, 83, 92, 93
Graham, Billy, 215
Graham, E., 95
Gray, John Chipman, 156, 157, 158
Great Chicago Fire 1971, 162
"green revolution," 114, 122, 123
Greenberg, Laurie, 227
Greenhalgh, Susan, 94
greenhouse gases, 134, 138
Greenville, South Carolina, 235–6,
    238–46
  BMW, 244–5
  economic diversification, 242–5
  European settlement, 239
  foreign investment, 243–5
  housing, 240–1
  hydroelectricity, 240
  physical geography, 238–9
  railroads, 240, 242
  textile industry, 239–42

Habermas, Jürgen, 437, 439, 446
Hägerstrand, Torsten, 24
Hall, Peter, 280
Hall, S., 33
Hanson, Susan, 345
Hare, Kenneth, 133, 134
Harrison, Lawrence, 400
Hartshorne, Richard, 18
Harvey, David, 357
Hauner, Milan, 409–10, 415, 420
Haushofer, Karl, 411
Havel, Václav, 430
Hawthorne, Nathaniel, 156, 157–8,
    161
hazards geography, 114, 135–6, 159–66
Hazda Nomads, 117
Heartland Theory, see Mackinder, Sir
    Halford
Hecht, Susanna, 114, 135
Heidegger, Martin, 219
Hewitt, Ken, 133, 135
Hindus
  alcohol consumption, 312
  pilgrimage traditions, 206, 209–10,
    211–12, 213, 214
Hinn, Benny, 215
Hippocrates, 19, 20

HIV/AIDS, 52, 81–3
  Africa, *see* Africa
  age dependency ratios and, 87
  anti-retroviral drugs (ARVs), 86, 95
  Asia, 82, 86, 89
  behavioral dimension, 86, 88–9, 93,
    94–5
  data collection, 84
  deaths, 81, 84
  demographic effects, 86–8, 89–91
  Demographic Transition Model (DTM),
    89–91
  denial of treatment, 95
  diffusionism and, 91–4
  Eastern Europe, 82, 86
  epidemiological characteristics, 86
  exceptional nature of, 81, 83–9
  fertility analysis, 89–91, 94
  fertility transition and, 89–91
  gender differences, 87, 90
  infantile AIDS, 87, 90
  Latin America, 81, 82
  life expectancy and, 87, 91
  medical dimension, 84–6
  Middle East, 82, 86
  migrant workers, 98
  modeling the spread, 83
  nature of the disease, 84, 86
  public education campaigns, 93–4
  South Africa, 85, 87, 88, 91, 94
  statistics, 81, 82
  testing for, 84
  transmission, 84, 86, 88–9, 93; blood
    transfusion, 86; heterosexual, 81, 83,
    86, 87, 88, 89; intravenous drug use,
    82, 83, 86, 89; male homosexual,
    81–2, 83, 86, 87, 89
  Uganda, 83, 89, 93–4
  UNAIDS, 81, 83, 84, 93
  United States, 81–2, 83
  Western Europe, 81–2
  women and, 87, 90
Holyoke, Edward, 156–7, 158
homeless people
  in public spaces, 439–41, 447–8
Horsman, Stuart, 413
human dimensions of global change, 114,
  136
human geography, 3–4, 21
human population, *see* population growth

human–societal dynamics, 29–32
  societal synthesis in place, 30
  space and scale and, 30–2
human-tracking, 15, 46–7
  cell-phone tracking, 46
  children, 46, 47
  global positioning systems (GPSs), 15,
    46–7
hunting
  recreational hunting, 184, 186, 189–90,
    191–2
hunting and gathering, 114, 116, 174
  agriculture compared, 114, 116–21
  health and, 117–18
  leisure and, 117, 120
  sexual equality and, 119–20
Huntington, Samuel, 400
hurricanes, 162, 165
  Hurricane Mitch, 381, 383, 385, 386
Hymer, Stephen, 280

ice fishing, 184, 185
Immigrant Spatial Assimilation Theory,
  249–50, 253
immigrants, *see* cities; migration
India
  agriculture, 127
  alcohol consumption, 312
  economic growth and development, 355,
    358–9
  geography in schools, 8
  government policies, 358–9
  HIV/AIDS, 86
  liberalization and globalization, effects
    of, 358–9, 360–1
  re-scaling of uneven development, 355,
    359–60; intra-regional differentiation,
    360–1; intra-urban differentiation,
    361
  soil conservation, 69
Industrial Workers of the World, 446
Institute for Global Engagement, 417
intercropping, 123, 124–5, 127, 129–30,
  131
international boundaries, 406, 422
  transboundary cooperation in the EU,
    see European Union
International Human Dimensions and
  Geosphere–Biosphere Programs
  (IHDP/IGBP), 139

International Longshoremen's Association (ILA), 307, 308, 309
International Monetary Fund (IMF), 352, 384, 419
International Society for Krishna Consciousness, 215
interpretive approaches, 36
Iran
  water resources, 142, 143
  see also Middle East; water resource conflicts
Iraq
  water resources, 143, 146
  see also Middle East; water resource conflicts
Islam
  alcohol consumption, 312, 321
  conservative, 39
  fundamentalism, 39, 40, 411–12, 418
  Israel and, 39–40
  Koranic schools, 39
  in Mali, 40
  pilgrimage traditions, 209
  Saudi Arabia, 39–40
Israel
  immigration, 144
  Muslims and, 39–40
  viticulture, 315
  water resources, 145, 148, 151, 155
  see also Middle East; water resource conflicts

Jackson, J. B., 226
Jackson, Michael, 204
Jamaica
  agriculture, 127
James, Preston, 239
Japan, 37
  abortion, 90
  alcohol consumption, 311, 316, 317, 320, 321
  geography in schools, 7
  human-tracking, 46
  migration, 97
Jardine, William M., 194
Johnson, Emory R., 17
Jones, Huw, 81
Jordan
  immigration, 144
  water resources, 148, 150–1

see also Middle East; water resource conflicts
Jordan-Yarmuk waters, 148, 150–2
  see also water resource conflicts

Kalahari Bushmen, 117
Kant, Immanuel, 17
Karimov, Islam, 411, 421
Kenya
  afforestation, 75
  African Land Development Board (ALDEV), 69, 71, 78
  agriculture: agroecological zones (AEZs), 67; animal fodder, 74–5; beans, 67; coffee, 67, 69, 71–3; cotton growing, 71–3; Crown Lands, 75; farm output, 77; fertilizers, 74, 76; gender roles, 65, 67, 73, 74, 75, 76, 77–8; intensification, 76–7; investment capital, 76; livestock feeding, 74–5; maize, 67, 73; manure, 74, 76; new production technologies, 71–6; plows, 73–4; population growth and, 52, 65–80; tree farming, 75–6; women, 65, 67, 73, 74, 75, 76, 77–8
  the Akamba, 65–80
  colonialism, 65–6, 68–9
  droughts, 67, 70, 77
  education, 78
  fertility decline, 91
  HIV/AIDS, 90
  land ownership, 76
  Machakos District, 65–80
  Machakos Integrated Development Program (MIDP), 78
  polygyny, 77
  population growth and the environment, 52, 65–80
  soil conservation, 68–71, 78; terracing, 68–70
  soil erosion, 67, 68
  soils, 67
  water conservation, 70, 78
  White Highlands policy, 65
  see also Africa
Keys, Eric, 227
Kimber, Clarissa, 226
knowledge economy, 294, 296–7
  networks of knowledge, 297
  oil industry, see oil industry

Konadu-Agyemang, K., 363
Korea
    alcohol consumption, 311, 317, 320
    geography in schools, 7
    South Korea, 317, 400
Kuhn, Thomas, 133–4

land-use and land-cover change, 138–9
Land-Use/Cover Change (LUCC), 139
Landes, David, 401
Lappe, Frances Moore, 131
Latin America, 113
    alcohol consumption, 312, 315, 316,
        317, 318, 321
    Bolivia, see Bolivia
    globalization, 384
    HIV/AIDS, 81, 82
    migration, 98
    viticulture, 315, 316
lawn-care chemicals, 294, 323–36
    children and, 325
    demographic shifts and, 327
    economic explanations of use, 327
    economic imperatives to industry
        expansion, 328–30
    formulator industry, 328–31
    human exposure risks, 324–5
    lawn aesthetics, 330–3
    lawn as community participation, 332,
        334, 335
    lawn as environment, 333, 334–5
    lawn as family space, 332, 334
    lawn symbolism, 330–1
    lawns as distinctive sites of production
        and consumption, 324–8
    marketing, 330–1
    moral economy of the lawn, 333–6
    new home construction and, 327
    persistence, 325
    privately producing public space, 335–6
    scale of the industry, 323–4
    trends in use on high-input lawns,
        325–6
    weather and, 329
Lebanon
    water resources, 142, 151
    see also Middle East; water resource
        conflicts
Lee, Barrett, 251
Lefebvre, Henri, 446–7

leisure
    agriculture and hunter-gathering
        compared, 117, 120
    see also recreation
Leopold, Aldo, 176
Lesotho
    HIV/AIDS, 85
    soil erosion, 68
lightning, 157–8, 165–6
location analysis, 2
location control, see human-tracking
location theories, 31
London
    global reach, 284–8
longshoring, 294, 306–7
    containerization, impact of, 306, 308–9
    corruption, 307
    labor market, 307–8
    "shape-up," 307–8
    trade union, 307, 308, 309

McDowell, Linda, 346
Machakos, see Kenya
McIlwaine, Cathy, 371
McKelvey, Blake, 162
McKibben, Bill, 173
Mackinder, Sir Halford, 7, 405–6, 408–9
    Heartland Theory, 405–6; application to
        Central Asia, 409, 410–11, 413–21;
        Seiple and, 413, 417–20, 421;
        Sharapova and, 415–16, 421; Zotov
        and, 413–15, 416, 421
    see also Uzbekistan
Maclean, Fitzroy, 417
McNamara, Robert, 37
Mahan, Admiral Alfred Thayer, 405
maize/corn, 4–5, 6, 73, 126, 129
    beer, 317
Malawi
    HIV/AIDS, 83
Malaysia, 7
Mali, 40
Malthus, Thomas, 51, 54–64
    critiques, 51–2
Malville, J. McKim, 209
man-land tradition, 19–20
maps, 14–15, 17, 33, 38
    cartography, 15, 42–3, 44
    cartophobia, 43–4
    computer-generated, 15

digital mapping, 34
dual roles, 44–5
lying with, 42–5
see also spatial representation
Marcuse, Peter, 248
Markusen, Ann, 340
Marshall Plan, 351
Marx, Karl, 51
Marx, Leo, 187
mathematical representation, 33
Mayan people, 227
Mbeki, Thabo, 94
Mergen, Bernard, 162–3
Meuse-Rhin Euroregio, 427–9, 432–6
Mexico
  agriculture, 224, 231
  barrios, 225
  climate change, 135–6, 137, 139
  the dead, 222, 225, 230
  extended family, 228
  fiestas, 182, 222, 224, 226–32;
    reciprocity networks, 227–8
  food preparation, 222, 224, 226, 227,
    228
  gender roles, 221, 222–3, 224; fiestas,
    182, 221, 222, 224, 226–32
  house-lot gardens, 221, 222, 225,
    226–32
  human-tracking, 46
  kitchenspace, 182; definition, 221; as
    gendered space, 182, 222–3, 229; in
    geographical garden studies, 226–32;
    migrants and, 231
  livestock, 229, 230
  migration, 224–5
  mole sauce, 222, 229, 230
  sacred places, 211, 220
  smoke kitchens, 227, 230
  urban expansion, 224, 230, 231
microbreweries, 182, 198–205
  beer connoisseurs, 203
  in Britain, 201–2
  economies of scale, 200–1
  "microbrewery desert," 202, 205
  midsize brewers and, 202–3
  neolocalism and, 198–9, 205
  rebirth, 201–3
  see also beer; brewing
Middle East, 37
  alcohol consumption, 312, 313

barley, 317
  food deficit, 144
  HIV/AIDS, 82, 86
  immigration, 144
  political fragmentation, 144–5
  population growth, 143–4
  rapid economic development, 144
  technological developments, 144
  urbanization, 144
  water resource conflicts, *see* water
    resource conflicts
migration, 31, 52–3
  China, *see* China
  cities, *see* cities
  developed countries, 97
  developing countries, 97–8
  economic development and, 97
  ethnic residential concentrations, *see*
    cities
  HIV/AIDS and migrant workers, 98
  Israel, 144
  Japan, 97
  Mexico, 224–5
  neo-classical theory, 97
  Ravenstein's laws of migration, 97
  Russia, 98
  socialist and transitional economies, 98
  structural approach, 97
  theories, 97–8
  United States, 99
Milton, John, 168–9
Minnesota, 184–97
  see also recreational landscapes
modeling, 134–5
modernization
  development and, 351–2, 357, 369, 383
monocropping, 123, 125, 127, 129
Morgan, Edmund, 438–9
Morrill, Richard, 31
Morris, Alan, 269
Moses, 168
Mossi people, 397–8
Moynihan, Daniel Patrick, 401
Mthembi-Mahanyele, Sankie, 269
Mugerauer, Robert, 219
Muir, John, 169, 176
Murphy, Alec, 8
Murray, Craig, 421
Museveni, Yoweri, 93–4
Muslims, *see* Islam

Nabta Playa, 209
Nadle, David, 447
Naipaul, V. S., 207–8
Nash, Roderick, 187
National Center for Atmospheric Research (NCAR), Colorado, 135
National Council for Geographic Education (NCGE), 20
national parks, 115, 169, 170–1, 194
Native Americans, 56, 173
  sacred places, 210, 220
natural hazards, 114, 135–6, 159–66
nature–society geography, 3, 4
neo-Marxists, 52
neocolonialism
  microbreweries and, 198–9, 205
Netherlands
  alcohol consumption, 319
  Euroregio Meuse-Rhin, 427–9, 432–6
new economic geography, 353
New York Shipping Association (NYSA), 307
New Zealand
  geography in schools, 8
  HIV/AIDS, 82
  viticulture, 314, 315
Nicaragua
  deforestation, 385
  El Hatillo: aid dependency, 388; drought, 381–2, 389; flooding, 381; gender equality and empowerment, 390–3; social mobilization and disaster response, 386–9; sustainable development, 387–8
  end of price controls, 384
  globalization and, 384
  Hurricane Mitch, 381, 383, 385, 386; social mobilization and disaster response, 386–9
  non-governmental organizations (NGOs), 385, 386, 387, 388, 389, 390
  Sandinista Revolution, 383–4
  State Development Bank (BANADES), 384
  structural adjustment policies, 384, 385
  trade liberalization, 384
Nigeria
  agriculture, 127
  soil erosion, 68
Nile Basin, 143, 148, 149
  see also water resource conflicts

nomadic peoples
  pilgrimage traditions and, 208–9
non-governmental organizations (NGOs)
  alternative development and, 370, 371, 374–80
  Bolivia, 370, 371, 374, 375, 376–9, 380
  environmental, 133
  Nicaragua, 385, 386, 387, 388, 389, 390
Norman, D. W., 127
nuclear power, 134
Nysa Euroregion, 429–36

oil
  foreign policy and, 39–40
  see also fossil fuels; petroleum
oil industry, 294, 297–8
  globalization and geographies of knowledge, 304–5
  knowledge environment, 297–8
  new geographical opportunities, 301–3
  organizational restructuring, 297, 303–4
  political risks, 302–3
  reductions in production and exploration costs, 298, 300–1
  regulatory frameworks, 302
  technological change, 297, 298, 300–1
O'Riordan, Tim, 133
Orwell, George, 46, 47
Ó Tuathail, Gearoid, 413, 418, 421

Pakistan, 39, 312
paleopathology, 118–19
Parnell, S., 269
People's Park, Berkeley, California, 406–7, 444
  homeless people in, 439–41, 447–8
  riots, 447, 448
  see also public space
Petrella, Riccardo, 288
petroleum
  agriculture and, 122, 123
  see also fossil fuels; oil
Philippines
  migration, 98
physical geography, 3, 4, 21, 27–8
pilgrimage traditions
  Catholics, 206, 209–10, 211, 212, 214
  collective selfhood and, 207, 218–20
  Hindus, 206, 209–10, 211–12, 213, 214

migrants and, 210
movable rituals, 214
Muslims, 209
nomadic peoples and, 208–9
return to the homeland, 211–12
sacred place as basis of pilgrimage
    systems, 207–9
transplanting, 182, 206–7, 209–10
see also sacred places
Pillsbury, Richard, 186
place, 181
    beer consumption and, 204–5
    consumption and, 182
    gender and, 182, 221, 222–3, 224,
        226–32
    human–societal dynamics, 30
    interdependencies between places, 24–5
    see also pilgrimage traditions;
        recreational landscapes; sacred places
Poland
    Euroregion Nysa, 426, 429–36
    see also Eastern Europe
Polelle, Mark, 411, 420
political ecology, 7, 114–15, 135, 385
    feminist, 221–2
    see also lawn-care industry
political geography, 405–7
political redistricting, 31
polygyny, 77
population growth
    agriculture and: Kenya, 52, 65–80;
        Malthus on, 52, 57–60, 63
    carrying capacity, 51, 68
    Demographic Transition Model (DTM),
        89–91
    fertility transition, 89–91
    Kenya, *see* Kenya
    Malthus on, 51–2, 54–64
    resources and, 51–2, 57–60
    sustainable environment and, 65–80
    see also HIV/AIDS; migration
positivism, 35, 293
postmodernist geography, 36
Pratt, Gerry, 345
Presley, Elvis, 209, 215, 219, 220
Ptolemy, Claudius, 17, 18, 19
public space, 406–7
    communications technology and, 445
    contemporary cities, 441–3, 444
    definitions, 437–8, 444

"disneyfication" of, 442, 448
electronic space, 445
enclosure of, 446–7
end of, 443–4
exercise of public rights in, 446–7
importance in democratic societies,
    437–9
the media and, 445, 446
People's Park, Berkeley, California,
    406–7, 444; homeless people in,
    439–41, 447–8; riots, 447, 448
privatization of, 443
shopping malls, 441
"the public," 437–9, 443, 444, 446, 447
Tiananmen Square, 445–6

radical development geography, 114–15
Ratzel, Fredrick, 405
Ravenstein, E. G., 97
Reagan, Ronald, 37
recreation
    boats, 189–90
    canoeing, 190, 194
    fishing, 184, 185, 186, 190, 192–3
    gender and, 186
    hunting, 184, 186, 189–90, 191–2
    ice fishing, 184, 185
    landscapes, *see* recreational landscapes
    leagues, 188–9
    private recreation on public land, 193–4
    right to hunt and fish, 195
    sports, 186, 188–9
    State Fair, 195–6
    stock-car races, 185
    winter pursuits, 184–5, 186–7
    see also leisure
recreational landscapes
    All-Terrain Vehicles (ATVs), 195
    Boundary Waters Canoe Area
        Wilderness (BWCAW), 190, 194
    built recreational landscapes, 187
    cabins, 189
    classification, 186–8
    cultural landscapes, 187
    historic and cultural landscapes, 196
    managed landscapes, 187–8, 192, 193,
        195
    Minnesota, 184–97
    national parks, 115, 170–1, 194
    pastoral landscape, 187

recreational landscapes (*cont.*)
   rituals of place in, 188–9
   seasonal occupation, 189
   sports arenas, 188–9
   wilderness, 175, 187, 190, 194
regionalization problem, 25
re-scaling of uneven development, *see*
   Ghana; globalization; India
resource geography, *see* water resource
   conflicts
Richardson, Miles, 216, 222
Rio Earth Summit 1992, 136
Roberts, Walter Orr, 135
Rooney, John, 186
Rostow, Walter, 351
Russia
   alcohol consumption, 315, 316, 318
   geography in schools, 7
   global change research, 138
   HIV/AIDS, 86
   Mackinder's Heartland Theory and,
      409–10
   migration, 98
   Uzbekistan and, 413–15, 416, 418,
      419
   see also Eastern Europe

Sachchidananda, Sri Ganapathi, 220
Sachs, Jeffrey, 400
sacred places
   as basis of pilgrimage systems, 207–9
   co-opting indigenous sacred sites,
      210–11
   collective selfhood and, 207, 218–20
   contested sites, 210–11
   Cuban exiles, 217–18
   holy wells, 218
   migrants and, 182, 206–7, 210
   Mormon sites, 216
   movable rituals, 214
   Nabta Playa, 209
   Native Americans, 210, 220
   nomadic peoples and, 208–9
   plural shrines, 211
   re-creating and reinventing, 206, 211,
      212–18
   replication, 212
   (re)recognition, 212–13
   ritual historicizing, 215–18
   sites of sacred embodiment, 214–15

Vietnam Veterans Memorial, 216–17
   see also pilgrimage traditions
Saff, Grant, 269–70
Sahel of West Africa, 395–9
Santo, Audrey, 215
Sartre, Jean-Paul, 218
Sassen, Saskia, 282
Saudi Arabia, 39–40
Sauer, Carl O., 18
scale of observation, 25
Scandinavia
   alcohol consumption, 319, 321
Schaefer, Joseph, 17
Schneider, Stephen, 135
Seiple, Charles, 413, 417–20, 421
Sennett, Richard, 441
September 11, 2001, 39, 41, 418, 419
Sharapova, Sevara, 415–16, 421
Simon, Julian, 79
Singapore, 7
skin cancer, 161
Slovo, Joe, 268
Smallman-Raynor, Matthew R., 82
Smith, Neil, 354
social Darwinism, 19
soil, 5, 67, 239
soil conservation, 68–71, 124
   Bolivia, 376, 377
   India, 69
   Kenya, 68–71, 78
   terracing, 68–70, 376; bench terraces,
      68–9, 70; narrow-based terraces, 69,
      70
   water conservation and, 70
soil erosion, 7, 67, 68
soil fertility, 128
soil leaching, 124, 128
Solnit, Rebecca, 208
South Africa
   African National Congress (ANC), 264,
      265, 268, 269, 275, 276
   African townships, 266
   apartheid, 236, 264, 265–6, 270–4
   desegregation, 264, 266, 267, 276
   fertility decline, 91
   geography in schools, 8
   Group Areas Act (GAA), 266
   HIV/AIDS, 85, 87, 88, 91, 94
   housing subsidy program, 236, 264,
      265, 268–70; cash subsidy, 268;

George, case study, 264–5, 270–7;
housing delivery, 269, 274–7
land ownership, 265–6
life expectancy, 87
local government, 267, 272, 274–5,
277
national housing policy, 268–70
soil erosion, 68
urban political structure, 265–8
South America, *see* Latin America
South Korea, *see* Korea
Soviet Union, *see* Russia
Spate, O. H. K., 19
spatial representation, 32–5
cognitive, 34
digital, 34–5
mathematical, 33
verbal, 33
visual, 33
see also maps
spatial tradition, 17–18, 19, 20, 37–8
area studies tradition and, 18
spirits, 318–20
measuring consumption, 310–11
patterns of consumption, 311–12,
318–19
see also alcohol consumption
Spoetzl, Kosmos, 204
sports, 186, 188–9
leagues, 188–9
see also recreation
Spykman, Nicholas J., 411
Stockholm conference 1972, 132–3
Strabo, 18, 19
Sudan
water resources, 143, 148
see also Middle East; water resource
conflicts
Swaziland
HIV/AIDS, 85
Swedish International Development
Agency, 71
Switzerland, 7
Syria
water resources, 143, 146, 148, 151
see also Middle East; water resource
conflicts

Tait, Angela, 269
Taiwan, 7

Talbott, Strobe, 415
Tanzania
HIV/AIDS, 83
Terjung, Werner, 134–5
terrorism, 38, 40–1, 417
textile industry, 239–42
Thailand
HIV/AIDS, 86, 89
Thoreau, Henry David, 167, 169
Tiananmen Square, 445–6
Tigris-Euphrates basin, 143, 146–7
see also water resource conflicts
Timur, Amir, 411, 414
Tolipov, F., 415
Tomlinson, Mary, 268, 269
Topologically Integrated Geographical
Encoding and Referencing (TIGER),
34
Torbakov, Igor, 414
transboundary cooperation in the EU, *see*
European Union
tree farming, 75–6
Trinidad
Catholic population, 211, 214
Hindu population, 207–8, 210, 211,
212, 213, 214, 217
plural shrine, 211
Tuan, Yi-Fu, 133, 187, 198
Turkey
European Union membership, 154
water resources, 142, 143, 146
see also Middle East; water resource
conflicts
Turner, Victor and Edith, 219
Tweed, Thomas, 217

Uganda
HIV/AIDS, 83, 89, 93–4
Ullman, Edward L., 17
UN Desertification conference 1977, 134
UN Environment Program (UNEP), 133
UN Stockholm conference 1972, 132–3
UNAIDS (Joint United Nations Program
on AIDS), 81, 83, 84, 93
UNICEF, 84
United Kingdom
alcohol consumption, 317, 319, 321
geography in schools, 8
London's global reach, 284–8
notifiable diseases, 84

United States
African Americans, 7
agricultural revolution, 122
agriculture, 122, 127, 128, 129
alcohol consumption, 312, 317, 318, 321
area studies tradition, 18–19, 20
Association of American Geographers
(AAG), 16, 17
cities, 7; ethnic residential concentration,
236, 247–63; Greenville, South
Carolina, 235–6, 238–46;
immigrants, 236, 247–63;
climate change, 156–66
containerization, impact of, 306, 308–9
droughts, 68, 157, 159, 161, 162
Dust Bowl, 68, 161
earth science tradition, 20–1
foreign policy, 37–8, 418–19
geography in schools, 8, 21, 22, 37, 38
Global Change Research Program
(USGCRP), 136, 137–40
HIV/AIDS, 81–2, 83
human-tracking, 46–7
intercropping, 129
lawn-care chemicals, 294, 323–36
longshoring, 306–8
man-land tradition, 19–20
migration, 99
Minnesota, 184–97
National Center for Atmospheric
Research (NCAR), Colorado, 135
national parks, 169, 170–1
Native Americans, 56, 173; sacred
places, 210, 220
Nature Conservancy, 172
oil consumption, 39–40
People's Park, Berkeley, California, 406–
7, 444; homeless people in, 439–41,
447–8; riots, 447, 448
population census, 99
recreation, see recreation
rice production, 7
sacred places, 210–11, 212, 213, 215,
216–17, 220
September 11, 2001, 39, 41, 418, 419
slavery, 7
soil erosion, 68
spatial tradition, 17–18, 19, 20
Vietnam Veterans Memorial, 216–17

viticulture, 315
weather, 156–66
wilderness, 167–78
University Consortium for Geographic
Information Science (UCGIS), 35
urban geography, 235–7
US Geological Survey (USGS), 34
Uzbekistan, 411–13
contemporary analysis: Russian analysis,
413–15; US analysis, 417–20;
Uzbekistani analysis, 415–16
creation of, 411
foreign policy, 413
independence, 411
Islamic groups, 411–12
Mackinder's Heartland Theory, 405–6,
409, 410–11; Seiple and, 413, 417–20,
421; Sharapova and, 415–16, 421;
Zotov and, 413–15, 416, 421
Russia and, 413–15, 416, 418, 419
size, 412

Vance, Rupert, 165
Varenius, 21
Velasco, Andres, 401
verbal representation, 33
Vietnam Veterans Memorial, 216–17
visual representation, 33

Walesa, Lech, 430
Wallerstein, I. M., 352
Ward, Barbara, 133
water conservation, 129
Kenya, 70, 78
Middle East, 152
soil conservation and, 70
see also droughts
water resource conflicts
causes, 143–6
colonialism, 144
future conflicts, 154–5
history, 143
international water laws and, 145, 153
Jordan-Yarmuk waters, 148, 150–2
Middle East, 114, 142–55
Nile Basin, 143, 148, 149
physical geography and, 142–3
political fragmentation and, 144–5
poor water management and, 145

population growth and, 143–4, 154
rapid economic development and, 144
solutions, 152–4
technological developments and, 144, 153
Tigris-Euphrates basin, 143, 146–7
Watkins, S. C., 92
Watts, Michael, 114, 135, 371
weather
  agriculture and, 128–9, 159
  blizzards, 162–3
  climatic determinism, 164–5
  coping tools, 163
  flooding, 114, 160
  hazards geography, 114, 135, 159–66
  hurricanes, 162, 165; Hurricane Mitch, 381, 383, 385, 386
  lawn-care chemicals and, 329
  lightning, 157–8, 165–6
  United States, 156–66
  see also climate change; climatology; droughts
Webb, Douglas, 83
Weisman, Leslie, 346–7
Weizsäcker, Richard von, 430
West, Robert, 223
Westmacott, Richard, 226
White, Gilbert F., 27, 114, 133, 160
White Highlands policy, 65
Whyte, Anne, 134
wilderness, 115, 167–78, 187
  agriculture and, 174
  endangered species, 172
  Garden of Eden, 168–9, 172
  national parks, 115, 170–1, 194
  recreation, see recreation; recreational landscapes
  recreational landscapes, 175, 187, 190, 194
Will, George, 440
wine, 312–16, 320–1
  measuring consumption, 310–11
  patterns of consumption, 311–12, 314–16
  viticulture, 312–16
  see also alcohol consumption
WinklerPrins, Antoinette, 226
Wister, Owen, 174

women
  Africa, 87, 90
  in agriculture: Kenya, 65, 68, 73, 74, 75, 76, 77–8; in the Sahel of West Africa, 396; sexual inequality, 116, 119–20
  Bolivia, 378
  development and, 383
  global change and, 140
  HIV/AIDS, 87, 90
  hunting and gathering, 119–20
  Kenya, 65, 68, 73, 74, 75, 76, 77–8
  Mexico: fiestas, 182, 221, 222, 224, 226–32; gendering of space, 182, 222–3, 229
  Nicaragua, 383; gender equality and empowerment, 390–3; social mobilization and disaster response, 386–8
women in development (WID), 383
at work, 294, 337–47; disaster reconstruction work, 386–8, 390; equal pay legislation, 347; export processing zones (EPZs), 343–4; gendering of work, 338–9, 341–2, 390–1; geographic separation of work and home, 339–40; globalization, 294, 343–5; industrialization, 342–3; "natural tendencies" argument, 345; Nicaragua, 390–3; "nimble fingers" explanation, 344; patriarchal capitalism, 339–40; in the Sahel of West Africa, 396; work/non-work dichotomy, 339–42; the workplace, 345–7
  see also gender
World Bank, 92, 352, 365, 374, 419
World Climate conference 1979, 134
World Health Organization (WHO), 84
World Cities, 236–7, 279–80
  global office location strategies, 281–2
  intercity global network, 282–4
  London, case study, 284–8
  in a network society, 281
  research clusters, 280–1
  shared firm presences, 282–4, 285
  see also cities

Zambia
  HIV/AIDS, 83

Zapata, Emiliano, 224
Zarma people, 396–7
Zelinsky, Wilbur, 216, 251
Zhou, Min, 249
Zimbabwe, 113

fertility decline, 91
HIV/AIDS, 85
Zimmerman, Erich, 160
Zotov, Oleg, 413–15, 416, 421